DRAMA *for Students*

National Advisory Board

Susan Allison: Head Librarian, Lewiston High School, Lewiston, Maine. Standards Committee Chairperson for Maine School Library (MASL) Programs. Board member, Julia Adams Morse Memorial Library, Greene, Maine. Advisor to Lewiston Public Library Planning Process.

Jennifer Hood: Young Adult/Reference Librarian, Cumberland Public Library, Cumberland, Rhode Island. Certified teacher, Rhode Island. Member of the New England Library Association, Rhode Island Library Association, and the Rhode Island Educational Media Association.

Ann Kearney: Head Librarian and Media Specialist, Christopher Columbus High School, Miami, Florida, 1982–2002. Thirty-two years as Librarian in various educational institutions ranging from grade schools through graduate programs. Library positions at Miami-Dade Community College, the University of Miami's Medical School Library, and Carrollton School in Coconut Grove, Florida. B.A. from University of Detroit, 1967 (magna cum laude); M.L.S., University of Missouri–Columbia, 1974. Volunteer Project Leader for a school in rural Jamaica; volunteer with Adult Literacy programs.

Laurie St. Laurent: Head of Adult and Children's Services, East Lansing Public Library, East Lansing, Michigan, 1994–. M.L.S. from Western Michigan University. Chair of Michigan Library Association's 1998 Michigan Summer Reading Program; Chair of the Children's Services Division in 2000–2001; and Vice-President of the Association in 2002–2003. Board member of several regional early childhood literacy organizations and member of the Library of Michigan Youth Services Advisory Committee.

Heidi Stohs: Instructor in Language Arts, grades 10–12, Solomon High School, Solomon, Kansas. Received B.S. from Kansas State University; M.A. from Fort Hays State University.

DRAMA *for Students*

Presenting Analysis, Context, and Criticism on Commonly Studied Dramas

Volume 23

Sara Constantakis,
Project Editor

Foreword by Carole L. Hamilton

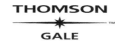

THOMSON
GALE

Detroit • New York • San Francisco • San Diego • New Haven, Conn. • Waterville, Maine • London • Munich

THOMSON
GALE

Drama for Students, Volume 23

Project Editor
Sara Constantakis

Editorial
Anne Marie Hacht, Ira Mark Milne

Rights Acquisition and Management
Lisa Kincade, Timothy Sisler

Manufacturing
Drew Kalasky

Imaging
Lezlie Light, Mike Logusz, Kelly A. Quin

Product Design
Pamela A. E. Galbreath

Product Manager
Meggin Condino

For more information, contact
Thomson Gale
27500 Drake Rd.
Farmington Hills, MI 48331-3535
Or you can visit our Internet site at
http://www.gale.com

ISBN 0-7876-8119-9
ISSN 1094-9232

Printed in the United States of America
10 9 8 7 6 5 4 3 2 1

Table of Contents

The Study of Drama

We study drama in order to learn what meaning others have made of life, to comprehend what it takes to produce a work of art, and to glean some understanding of ourselves. Drama produces in a separate, aesthetic world, a moment of being for the audience to experience, while maintaining the detachment of a reflective observer.

Drama is a representational art, a visible and audible narrative presenting virtual, fictional characters within a virtual, fictional universe. Dramatic realizations may pretend to approximate reality or else stubbornly defy, distort, and deform reality into an artistic statement. From this separate universe that is obviously not "real life" we expect a valid reflection upon reality, yet drama never is mistaken for reality—the methods of theater are integral to its form and meaning. Theater is art, and art's appeal lies in its ability both to approximate life and to depart from it. For in intruding its distorted version of life into our consciousness, art gives us a new perspective and appreciation of life and reality. Although all aesthetic experiences perform this service, theater does it most effectively by creating a separate, cohesive universe that freely acknowledges its status as an art form.

And what is the purpose of the aesthetic universe of drama? The potential answers to such a question are nearly as many and varied as there are plays written, performed, and enjoyed. Dramatic texts can be problems posed, answers asserted, or moments portrayed. Dramas (tragedies as well as comedies) may serve strictly "to ease the anguish of a torturing hour" (as stated in William Shakespeare's *A Midsummer Night's Dream*)—to divert and entertain—or aspire to move the viewer to action with social issues. Whether to entertain or to instruct, affirm or influence, pacify or shock, dramatic art wraps us in the spell of its imaginary world for the length of the work and then dispenses us back to the real world, entertained, purged, as Aristotle said, of pity and fear, and edified—or at least weary enough to sleep peacefully.

It is commonly thought that theater, being an art of performance, must be experienced—seen—in order to be appreciated fully. However, to view a production of a dramatic text is to be limited to a single interpretation of that text—all other interpretations are for the moment closed off, inaccessible. In the process of producing a play, the director, stage designer, and performers interpret and transform the script into a work of art that always departs in some measure from the author's original conception. Novelist and critic Umberto Eco, in his *The Role of the Reader: Explorations in the Semiotics of Texts* (Indiana University Press, 1979), explained, "In short, we can say that every performance offers us a complete and satisfying version of the work, but at the same time makes it incomplete for us, because it cannot simultaneously give all the other artistic solutions which the work may admit."

Thus Laurence Olivier's coldly formal and neurotic film presentation of Shakespeare's *Hamlet* (in which he played the title character as well as directed) shows marked differences from subsequent adaptations. While Olivier's Hamlet is clearly entangled in a Freudian relationship with his mother Gertrude, he would be incapable of shushing her with the impassioned kiss that Mel Gibson's mercurial Hamlet (in director Franco Zeffirelli's 1990 film) does. Although each of the performances rings true to Shakespeare's text, each is also a mutually exclusive work of art. Also important to consider are the time periods in which each of these films were produced: Olivier made his film in 1948, a time in which overt references to sexuality (especially incest) were frowned upon. Gibson and Zeffirelli made their film in a culture more relaxed and comfortable with these issues. Just as actors and directors can influence the presentation of drama, so too can the time period of the production affect what the audience will see.

A play script is an open text from which an infinity of specific realizations may be derived. Dramatic scripts that are more open to interpretive creativity (such as those of Ntozake Shange and Tomson Highway) actually require the creative improvisation of the production troupe in order to complete the text. Even the most prescriptive scripts (those of Neil Simon, Lillian Hellman, and Robert Bolt, for example), can never fully control the actualization of live performance, and circumstantial events, including the attitude and receptivity of the audience, make every performance a unique event. Thus, while it is important to view a production of a dramatic piece, if one wants to understand a drama fully it is equally important to read the original dramatic text.

The reader of a dramatic text or script is not limited by either the specific interpretation of a given production or by the unstoppable action of a moving spectacle. The reader of a dramatic text may discover the nuances of the play's language, structure, and events at their own pace. Yet studied alone, the author's blueprint for artistic production does not tell the whole story of a play's life and significance. One also needs to assess the play's critical reviews to discover how it resonated to cultural themes at the time of its debut and how the shifting tides of cultural interest have revised its interpretation and impact on audiences. And to do this, one needs to know a little about the culture of the times which produced the play as well as the author who penned it.

Drama for Students supplies this material in a useful compendium for the student of dramatic theater. Covering a range of dramatic works that span from 442 BC to the present, this book focuses on significant theatrical works whose themes and form transcend the uncertainty of dramatic fads. These are plays that have proven to be both memorable and teachable. *Drama for Students* seeks to enhance appreciation of these dramatic texts by providing scholarly materials written with the secondary and college/university student in mind. It provides for each play a concise summary of the plot and characters as well as a detailed explanation of its themes. In addition, background material on the historical context of the play, its critical reception, and the author's life help the student to understand the work's position in the chronicle of dramatic history. For each play entry a new work of scholarly criticism is also included, as well as segments of other significant critical works for handy reference. A thorough bibliography provides a starting point for further research.

This series offers comprehensive educational resources for students of drama. *Drama for Students* is a vital book for dramatic interpretation and a valuable addition to any reference library.

Source: Eco, Umberto, *The Role of the Reader: Explorations in the Semiotics of Texts,* Indiana University Press, 1979.

Carole L. Hamilton
Author and Instructor of English at
Cary Academy, Cary, North Carolina

Introduction

Purpose of the Book

The purpose of *Drama for Students* (*DfS*) is to provide readers with a guide to understanding, enjoying, and studying dramas by giving them easy access to information about the work. Part of Gale's "For Students" literature line, *DfS* is specifically designed to meet the curricular needs of high school and undergraduate college students and their teachers, as well as the interests of general readers and researchers considering specific plays. While each volume contains entries on "classic" dramas frequently studied in classrooms, there are also entries containing hard-to-find information on contemporary plays, including works by multicultural, international, and women playwrights.

The information covered in each entry includes an introduction to the play and the work's author; a plot summary, to help readers unravel and understand the events in a drama; descriptions of important characters, including explanation of a given character's role in the drama as well as discussion about that character's relationship to other characters in the play; analysis of important themes in the drama; and an explanation of important literary techniques and movements as they are demonstrated in the play.

In addition to this material, which helps the readers analyze the play itself, students are also provided with important information on the literary and historical background informing each work. This includes a historical context essay, a box comparing the time or place the drama was written to modern Western culture, a critical essay, and excerpts from critical essays on the play. A unique feature of *DfS* is a specially commissioned critical essay on each drama, targeted toward the student reader.

To further aid the student in studying and enjoying each play, information on media adaptations is provided (if available), as well as reading suggestions for works of fiction and nonfiction on similar themes and topics. Classroom aids include ideas for research papers and lists of critical sources that provide additional material on each drama.

Selection Criteria

The titles for each volume of *DfS* were selected by surveying numerous sources on teaching literature and analyzing course curricula for various school districts. Some of the sources surveyed included: literature anthologies; *Reading Lists for College-Bound Students: The Books Most Recommended by America's Top Colleges*; textbooks on teaching dramas; a College Board survey of plays commonly studied in high schools; a National Council of Teachers of English (NCTE) survey of plays commonly studied in high schools; St. James Press's *International Dictionary of Theatre*; and Arthur Applebee's 1993 study *Literature in the Secondary School: Studies of Curriculum and Instruction in the United States*.

Input was also solicited from our advisory board, as well as from educators from various areas. From these discussions, it was determined that each volume should have a mix of "classic" dramas (those works commonly taught in literature classes) and contemporary dramas for which information is often hard to find. Because of the interest in expanding the canon of literature, an emphasis was also placed on including works by international, multicultural, and women playwrights. Our advisory board members—educational professionals—helped pare down the list for each volume. If a work was not selected for the present volume, it was often noted as a possibility for a future volume. As always, the editor welcomes suggestions for titles to be included in future volumes.

How Each Entry Is Organized

Each entry, or chapter, in *DfS* focuses on one play. Each entry heading lists the full name of the play, the author's name, and the date of the play's publication. The following elements are contained in each entry:

- **Introduction:** a brief overview of the drama which provides information about its first appearance, its literary standing, any controversies surrounding the work, and major conflicts or themes within the work.
- **Author Biography:** this section includes basic facts about the author's life, and focuses on events and times in the author's life that inspired the drama in question.
- **Plot Summary:** a description of the major events in the play. Subheads demarcate the play's various acts or scenes.
- **Characters:** an alphabetical listing of major characters in the play. Each character name is followed by a brief to an extensive description of the character's role in the play, as well as discussion of the character's actions, relationships, and possible motivation.

  Characters are listed alphabetically by last name. If a character is unnamed—for instance, the Stage Manager in *Our Town*—the character is listed as "The Stage Manager" and alphabetized as "Stage Manager." If a character's first name is the only one given, it will appear alphabetically by that name. Variant names are also included for each character. Thus, the nickname "Babe" would head the listing for a character in *Crimes of the Heart,* but below that listing would be her less-mentioned married name "Rebecca Botrelle."
- **Themes:** a thorough overview of how the major topics, themes, and issues are addressed within the play. Each theme discussed appears in a separate subhead, and is easily accessed through the boldface entries in the Subject/Theme Index.
- **Style:** this section addresses important style elements of the drama, such as setting, point of view, and narration; important literary devices used, such as imagery, foreshadowing, symbolism; and, if applicable, genres to which the work might have belonged, such as Gothicism or Romanticism. Literary terms are explained within the entry, but can also be found in the Glossary.
- **Historical Context:** this section outlines the social, political, and cultural climate *in which the author lived and the play was created.* This section may include descriptions of related historical events, pertinent aspects of daily life in the culture, and the artistic and literary sensibilities of the time in which the work was written. If the play is a historical work, information regarding the time in which the play is set is also included. Each section is broken down with helpful subheads.
- **Critical Overview:** this section provides background on the critical reputation of the play, including bannings or any other public controversies surrounding the work. For older plays, this section includes a history of how the drama was first received and how perceptions of it may have changed over the years; for more recent plays, direct quotes from early reviews may also be included.
- **Criticism:** an essay commissioned by *DfS* which specifically deals with the play and is written specifically for the student audience, as well as excerpts from previously published criticism on the work (if available).
- **Sources:** an alphabetical list of critical material used in compiling the entry, with full bibliographical information.
- **Further Reading:** an alphabetical list of other critical sources which may prove useful for the student. It includes full bibliographical information and a brief annotation.

In addition, each entry contains the following highlighted sections, set apart from the main text as sidebars:

- **Media Adaptations:** if available, a list of important film and television adaptations of the play, including source information. The list may also include such variations on the work as audio recordings, musical adaptations, and other stage interpretations.
- **Topics for Further Study:** a list of potential study questions or research topics dealing with

the play. This section includes questions related to other disciplines the student may be studying, such as American history, world history, science, math, government, business, geography, economics, psychology, etc.

- **Compare and Contrast:** an "at-a-glance" comparison of the cultural and historical differences between the author's time and culture and late twentieth century or early twenty-first century Western culture. This box includes pertinent parallels between the major scientific, political, and cultural movements of the time or place the drama was written, the time or place the play was set (if a historical work), and modern Western culture. Works written after 1990 may not have this box.
- **What Do I Read Next?:** a list of works that might complement the featured play or serve as a contrast to it. This includes works by the same author and others, works of fiction and nonfiction, and works from various genres, cultures, and eras.

Other Features

DfS includes "The Study of Drama," a foreword by Carole Hamilton, an educator and author who specializes in dramatic works. This essay examines the basis for drama in societies and what drives people to study such work. The essay also discusses how *Drama for Students* can help teachers show students how to enrich their own reading/viewing experiences.

A Cumulative Author/Title Index lists the authors and titles covered in each volume of the *DfS* series.

A Cumulative Nationality/Ethnicity Index breaks down the authors and titles covered in each volume of the *DfS* series by nationality and ethnicity.

A Subject/Theme Index, specific to each volume, provides easy reference for users who may be studying a particular subject or theme rather than a single work. Significant subjects from events to broad themes are included, and the entries pointing to the specific theme discussions in each entry are indicated in **boldface**.

Each entry may include illustrations, including a photo of the author, stills from stage productions, and stills from film adaptations, if available.

Citing Drama for Students

When writing papers, students who quote directly from any volume of *Drama for Students* may use the following general forms. These examples are based on MLA style; teachers may request that students adhere to a different style, so the following examples may be adapted as needed.

When citing text from *DfS* that is not attributed to a particular author (i.e., the Themes, Style, Historical Context sections, etc.), the following format should be used in the bibliography section:

"*Our Town.*" *Drama for Students.* Eds. David Galens and Lynn Spampinato. Vol. 1. Detroit: Gale, 1998. 227–30.

When quoting the specially commissioned essay from *DfS* (usually the first piece under the "Criticism" subhead), the following format should be used:

Fiero, John. Critical Essay on *Twilight: Los Angeles, 1992. Drama for Students.* Eds. David Galens and Lynn Spampinato. Vol. 2. Detroit: Gale, 1998. 247–49.

When quoting a journal or newspaper essay that is reprinted in a volume of *DfS*, the following form may be used:

Rich, Frank. "Theatre: A Mamet Play, *Glengarry Glen Ross.*" *New York Theatre Critics' Review* Vol. 45, No. 4 (March 5, 1984), 5–7; excerpted and reprinted in *Drama for Students*, Vol. 2, eds. David Galens and Lynn Spampinato (Detroit: Gale, 1998), pp. 51–53.

When quoting material reprinted from a book that appears in a volume of *DfS*, the following form may be used:

Kerr, Walter. "*The Miracle Worker,*" in *The Theatre in Spite of Itself.* Simon & Schuster, 1963. 255–57; excerpted and reprinted in *Drama for Students*, Vol. 2, eds. David Galens and Lynn Spampinato (Detroit: Gale, 1998), pp. 123–24.

We Welcome Your Suggestions

The editor of *Drama for Students* welcomes your comments and ideas. Readers who wish to suggest dramas to appear in future volumes, or who have other suggestions, are cordially invited to contact the editor. You may contact the editor via E-mail at: **ForStudentsEditors@thomson.com.** Or write to the editor at:

Editor, *Drama for Students*
Thomson Gale
27500 Drake Rd.
Farmington Hills, MI 48331-3535

Literary Chronology

1600: Pedro Calderón de la Barca is born on January 17, 1600 in Madrid, Spain.

1635: Pedro Calderón de la Barca's *Life Is a Dream* is published.

1681: Pedro Calderón de la Barca dies on May 25, 1681 in Madrid, Spain.

1920: Reginald Rose is born on December 10, 1920, in New York, New York.

1926: Dario Fo is born on March 24, 1926 in San Giano, Italy.

1938: D. L. Coburn is born on August 4, 1938 in East Baltimore, Maryland.

1943: Dolores Prida is born on September 5, 1943 in Caibarién, Cuba.

1949: Lee Blessing is born on October 4, 1949 in Minneapolis, Minnesota.

1949: Ernest Thompson is born on November 6, 1949 in Bellows Falls, Vermont.

1950: John Patrick Shanley is born in 1950 in New York, New York.

1953: Eve Ensler is born on May 25, 1953 in New York, New York.

1954: Reginald Rose's *Twelve Angry Men* is published.

1956: Ann-Marie MacDonald is born in 1956 on an army base in West Germany.

1960: Jonathan Larson is born on February 4, 1960 in Mount Vernon, New York.

1963: Kenneth Lonergan is born in 1963 in New York, New York.

1965: Rebecca Gilman is born in 1965 in Trussville, Alabama.

1970: Dario Fo's *Accidental Death of an Anarchist* is published.

1976: D. L. Coburn's *The Gin Game* is published.

1977: Dolores Prida's *Beautiful Señoritas* is published.

1978: Ernest Thompson's *On Golden Pond* is published.

1978: D. L. Coburn is awarded the Pulitzer Prize in Drama for *The Gin Game.*

1985: Lee Blessing's *Eleemosynary* is published.

1988: Ann-Marie MacDonald's *Goodnight Desdemona (Good Morning Juliet)* is published.

1996: Eve Ensler's *Necessary Targets* is published.

1996: Jonathan Larson's *Rent* is published.

1996: Jonathan Larson dies of an undiagnosed aortic aneurysm on January 25, 1996.

1996: Jonathan Larson is posthumously awarded the Pulitzer Prize in Drama for *Rent.*

1997: Dario Fo is awarded the Nobel Prize in Literature.

1998: Kenneth Lonergan's *This Is Our Youth* is published.

2001: Rebecca Gilman's *Blue Surge* is published.

2002: Reginald Rose dies on April 19, 2002 in Norwalk, Connecticut.

2003: Doug Wright's *I Am My Own Wife* is published.

2004: John Patrick Shanley's *Doubt* is published.

2004: Doug Wright is awarded the Pulitzer Prize in Drama for *I Am My Own Wife.*

2005: John Patrick Shanley is awarded the Pulitzer Prize in Drama for *Doubt.*

Acknowledgments

The editors wish to thank the copyright holders of the excerpted criticism included in this volume and the permissions managers of many book and magazine publishing companies for assisting us in securing reproduction rights. We are also grateful to the staffs of the Detroit Public Library, the Library of Congress, the University of Detroit Mercy Library, Wayne State University Purdy/Kresge Library Complex, and the University of Michigan Libraries for making their resources available to us. Following is a list of the copyright holders who have granted us permission to reproduce material in this volume of ***Drama for Students (DfS)***. Every effort has been made to trace copyright, but if omissions have been made, please let us know.

COPYRIGHTED MATERIALS IN *DfS*, VOLUME 23, WERE REPRODUCED FROM THE FOLLOWING PERIODICALS:

— ***America,*** v. 174, May 11, 1996. Copyright 1996 www.americamagazine.org. All rights reserved. Reproduced by permission of America Press. For subscription information, visit www.americamagazine.com.—***American Theatre,*** v. 13, July-August, 1996; v. 13, July-August, 1996; v. 17, April, 2000; November, 2004. Copyright © 1996, 2000, 2004, Theatre Communications Group. All reproduced by permission.—***Australian,*** September 23, 2004 for "From Bard to Worse," by Murray Bramwell. Copyright © 2004 *Australian.* Reproduced by permission of the author.—***Boston Globe,*** April 11, 1982. © Copyright 1982 Globe Newspaper Company. Republished with permission of Boston Globe, conveyed through Copyright Clearance Center, Inc.—***Business World (Philippines),*** February 26, 2002. Copyright 2002 Financial Times Information, Ltd. Reproduced by permission.—***Commonweal,*** v. 132, April 22, 2005. Copyright © 2005 Commonweal Publishing Co., Inc. Reproduced by permission of Commonweal Foundation.—***Gay & Lesbian Review Worldwide,*** v. 10, September–October, 2003. Copyright 2003 Gay & Lesbian Review, Inc. Reproduced by permission.—***Library Journal,*** April 1, 1979. Copyright © 1979 by Reed Elsevier, USA. Reprinted by permission of the publisher.—***Los Angeles Times,*** August 13, 1990 for "Lee Blessing Takes 3 Women on Trip," by Nancy Churnin./April 23, 1999 for "A Clear View of Family Negotiation," by T.H. McCulloh. Copyright © Tribune Media Services, Inc. Both reproduced by permission of the author.—***Modern Drama,*** v. 38, fall, 1995; v. 41, spring, 1998; v. 32, December, 1998. Copyright © 1995, 1998 by the University of Toronto, Graduate Centre for Study of Drama. All reproduced by permission.—***Mosaic,*** v. 28, June, 1995. Copyright © Mosaic 1995. Acknowledgment of previous publication is herewith made.—***Nation,*** v. 265, November 10, 1997. Copyright © 1997 by The Nation Magazine/The Nation Company, Inc. Reproduced by permission.—***National Review,*** v. 48, June 3, 1996. Copyright © 1996 by National Review, Inc., 215 Lexington Avenue, New York, NY 10016. Reproduced by permission.—***New England***

Review, v. 23, spring, 2002. Copyright New England Review Spring 2002. Reproduced by permission.—***New Leader,*** v. 81, November 30, 1998. Copyright © 1998 by The American Labor Conference on International Affairs, Inc. All rights reserved. Reproduced by permission.—***New Republic,*** April 22, 1996; June 28, 1999. Copyright © 1996, 1999 by The New Republic, Inc. Both reproduced by permission of *The New Republic.*—***New York,*** v. 37, November 8, 2004. Copyright © 2004 PRIMEDIA Magazine Corporation. All rights reserved. Reproduced with the permission of *New York* Magazine.—***New York Amsterdam News,*** v. 96, April 14, 2005. Reproduced by permission.—***Salon.com,*** April 19, 2000 for "Down the Vagina Trail," by Pamela Grossman. Copyright 2000 Salon.com. Reproduced by permission of the author.—***Saturday Review,*** April 20, 1957. Reproduced by permission.—***Theatre Journal,*** v. 54, December, 2002. Copyright © 2002, University and College Theatre Association of the American Theatre Association. Reproduced by permission of The Johns Hopkins University Press.—***Times Educational Supplement,*** May 20, 2005. Copyright © The Times Supplements Limited 2005. Reproduced from *The Times Educational Supplement* by permission.—***Toronto Star,*** March 17, 2001; March 25, 2001. Copyright © 2001 Toronto Star. Both reproduced by permission of Torstar Syndication Services.—***Wall Street Journal,*** May 23, 1989. Copyright © 1989 Dow Jones & Company, Inc. All rights reserved. Reprinted with permission of *The Wall Street Journal.*—***World Literature Today,*** v. 72, winter, 1998. Copyright © 1998 by *World Literature Today.* Reproduced by permission of the publisher.

COPYRIGHTED MATERIALS IN *DfS*, VOLUME 23, WERE REPRODUCED FROM THE FOLLOWING BOOKS:

Harris, Thomas J. From ***Courtroom's Finest Hour in American Cinema.*** Scarecrow Press, 1987. Copyright © 1987 by University Press of America, Inc. All rights reserved. Reproduced by permission.—Honig, Edwin. From ***Calderon and the Seizures of Honor.*** Harvard University Press, 1972. Copyright © 1972 by the President and Fellows of Harvard College. All rights reserved. Reproduced by permission of the author.—Prida, Dolores. From "The Show Does Go On (Testimonio)," in ***Breaking Boundaries: Latina Writing and Critical Readings.*** Edited by Asuncion Horno-Delgado, Eliana Ortega, Nina M. Scott, and Nancy Saporta Sternbach. University of Massachusetts Press, 1989. Copyright © 1989 by The University of Massachusettes Press. All rights reserved. Reproduced by permission.—Rivero, Eliana. From "From Immigrants to Ethnics: Cuban Women Writers in the U.S.," in ***Breaking Boundaries: Latina Writing and Critical Readings.*** Edited by Asuncion Horno-Delgado, Eliana Ortega, Nina M. Scott, and Nancy Saporta Sternbach. University of Massachusetts Press, 1989. Copyright © by The University of Massachusettes Press. All rights reserved. Reproduced by permission.

Contributors

Bryan Aubrey: Aubrey holds a Ph.D. in English and has published many articles on twentieth-century literature. Entry on *Twelve Angry Men.* Original essay on *On Golden Pond.*

Jennifer Bussey: Bussey holds a master's degree in interdisciplinary studies and a bachelor's degree in English literature and is an independent writer specializing in literature. Entry on *On Golden Pond.* Original essay on *Eleemosynary.*

Carol Dell'Amico: Dell'Amico is a lecturer in the English Department of California State University, Bakersfield. Entries on *Accidental Death of an Anarchist* and *Beautiful Señoritas.*

Joyce Hart: Hart is a freelance writer and published author with degrees in English and creative writing. Entries on *Blue Surge, I Am My Own Wife,* and *Necessary Targets.*

Neil Heims: Heims is a writer and teacher living in Paris. Entry on *Life Is a Dream.* Original essays on *Blue Surge, Eleemosynary, The Gin Game,* and *On Golden Pond.*

David Kelly: Kelly is an instructor of creative writing and literature. Entry on *Doubt.*

Lois Kerschen: Kerschen is a school district administrator and freelance writer. Entry on *The Gin Game.*

Wendy Perkins: Perkins is a professor of American and English literature and film. Entries on *Eleemosynary, Rent,* and *This Is Our Youth*

Scott Trudell: Trudell is a doctoral student of English literature at Rutgers University. Entry on *Goodnight Desdemona (Good Morning Juliet).* Original essay on *The Gin Game.*

Accidental Death of an Anarchist

DARIO FO

1970

Dario Fo's *Accidental Death of an Anarchist* (1970) responds to events unfolding in Italy in the late 1960s and early 1970s. Generally, it looks at police corruption and suspicions regarding the government's collusion in this corruption. More specifically, it addresses the actual death of an anarchist who was being held in police custody following the bombing of a Milan bank that killed sixteen people and wounded about ninety. The police asserted that the anarchist's death was a suicide, that the man threw himself from a fourth-floor window in despair at being found out for his crime. At the subsequent inquest, the presiding judge declared the death not a suicide but an accident. Most Italians believed that the death was the result of overly harsh interrogation techniques, if not a case of outright murder on the part of the interrogators.

Accidental Death of an Anarchist is mainly about police corruption, underscored by the play's focus on impersonation, infiltration, and double-talk. A fast-talking major character, the Maniac, infiltrates a police headquarters. Posing as an investigating judge, he tricks the policemen into contradicting themselves and admitting that they are part of a cover-up involving the death of an anarchist. In infiltrating police headquarters by misrepresenting himself (impersonation), the Maniac reminds audiences of how most political groups in Italy, particularly left-wing groups, were infiltrated by police agents who acted as informers. The Maniac's flip-flop of point of view and statement achieves much the same effect as

Dario Fo © Jerry Bauer. Reproduced by permission

his impersonations do. His confusing speechifying leads to the police contradicting themselves, so that the Maniac, in all of his deceptions and distortions, is a precise reflection of what the play is designed to expose.

Accidental Death of an Anarchist is one of Fo's most popular plays both within and outside Italy. It has played around the world over the years to millions of people, a popular choice of directors who want to point to corruption in their midst. Pluto Press (London) put out the first English version, translated by Gavin Richards. In 1992, Methuen published a fine set of volumes of Fo's plays, which included *Accidental Death of an Anarchist.*

AUTHOR BIOGRAPHY

Dario Fo is one of Italy's most important and well-known literary figures, along with his partner and longtime collaborator, Franca Rame. He was born in San Giano, Italy, on March 24, 1926, the son of Felice (a railroad stationmaster) and Pina (Rota) Fo. Initially, Fo considered a career in architecture, but before he had quite finished this course of study, he discovered that he was far happier working in theatrical circles. By 1950, Fo had decided definitely on a career on the stage and began to compose plays prolifically. In June of 1954, Fo and Rame married; they have three children.

Running throughout Fo's career are certain constants. His plays are usually farcical with a satirical bite, and they tend to employ popular elements, such as slapstick. This said, there are also discernible stages in Fo's career. At first, he concentrated on creating comical farces and revues, some of which were broadcast on radio. Then, Fo's plays began to resemble more typical dramas, at least in the sense that they became less episodic and less strictly comical in effect. Later, Fo's greater engagement with Italian politics in his plays became evident. Indeed, by the time of *Morte accidentale di un anarchico* (*Accidental Death of an Anarchist*), Fo was so deep into Italian politics that he began gearing his plays toward working-class audiences instead of more typical theatergoers. He continued to attract people of all social strata to his plays, yet he began to reflect, theatrically, his sense that his life as an artist is best led in the service of those holding the least amount of social and political power in Italian society. *Accidental Death of an Anarchist* was first produced in Milan in December of 1970; it was staged on Broadway at the Belasco Theater in November 1984.

Fo is a highly influential figure in theatrical circles in and outside Italy. He has written hundreds of pieces across genres (songs, screenplays, plays) and media (stage, radio, film). His plays, which number more than forty, include *I sani da legare* ("A Madhouse for the Sane," 1954), which characterizes certain government officials as fascist sympathizers, and *Mistero buffo* (1969), a controversial improvisational play, based on the Gospels, that disparages both church and state. *L'Anomal bicefalo* ("Two-Headed Anomaly"), produced in Milan in 2003 but not published or translated into English, is a scathing satire of Italy's prime minister, Silvio Berlusconi. Fo has always been an actor in his own work; indeed, he is as well known an actor as he is a writer. He is as beloved and respected by some as he is detested and feared by others, such as those who disagree with him politically. He has even been arrested and put on trial for subversion, and he has been beaten up by rogue political foes, a fate also suffered by his collaborator, Franca Rame. Fo is, in short, a presence to contend with, an artist whose influence and genius are reflected in his having been awarded the Nobel Prize in Literature in 1997.

PLOT SUMMARY

Act 1, Scene 1

Accidental Death of an Anarchist opens in a room in a police station, where Inspector Bertozzo is interviewing the Maniac, reviewing his arrest record. He notes that the Maniac has been arrested many times for impersonation, the same reason for his arrest this time. The Maniac points out that although he has been arrested, he has never been convicted of a crime. He tells the inspector that he is insane, that he cannot be charged because he is mad. The inspector, incredulous, continues posing questions to the Maniac. The Maniac evades the inspector's questions and denies any real wrongdoing. For example, in response to the inspector's accusation that the Maniac has not only been impersonating a psychiatrist but also actually seeing patients and charging them substantial sums, the Maniac points out that all psychiatrists charge too much. The inspector replies that the specific charges are not the real issue; rather it is the question of impersonation. He points to a visiting card the Maniac has been distributing, which states that the Maniac is a psychiatrist. The Maniac quibbles over a point of punctuation, telling the inspector that, given the placement of a particular comma on the card, he cannot be said to be misrepresenting himself at all. Utterly frustrated, Inspector Bertozzo tells the Maniac that he can go.

The Maniac leaves the room, as does the inspector, for the latter is late to a meeting. The Maniac then pokes his head back into the room and, seeing that it is empty, enters and begins rifling through papers he sees on the inspector's desk. They are arrest sheets. He destroys whatever arrest sheets he feels deserve to be destroyed, leaving intact those he believes describe truly heinous crimes.

Next, the Maniac moves to the inspector's file cabinets. He is about to set fire to the whole lot of them, when he notices a dossier whose name he begins to read out loud, as follows: "Judge's Report on the Death of the . . ."; "Judge's Decision to Adjourn the Inquest of . . . ." The Maniac's words would alert the audience to the play's major topic, the death of a suspected anarchist whom most persons in Italy believed was innocent of the crimes for which he was being interrogated when he fell to his death from a window at a police headquarters. The phone rings, and the Maniac answers. It is another police inspector, calling from the fourth floor. The Maniac's words make it clear that the audience is to recall the inspector who conducted the interview with the (real) anarchist who fell or was pushed from a fourth-floor window.

The Maniac's words also make it clear that this second inspector wishes to speak to Bertozzo because he has heard that a judge is coming to the station to ask questions about the anarchist's death. The Maniac pretends that Bertozzo is in the room and making rude comments about the fourth-floor inspector. He tells the inspector that Bertozzo is saying that he might as well accept the fact that his career is over. From the Maniac's side of the conversation, it is clear that the inspector is becoming incensed, highly insulted by what he believes is Inspector Bertozzo's rude and flippant reaction to his concerns. When the Maniac hangs up, it occurs to him that he might impersonate the expected judge. He begins to practice characterizations of a judge.

At this point, Bertozzo reenters the room. He tells the Maniac to get out of the station and is surprised when the Maniac informs him that someone is looking for him to punch him in the face. Sure enough, the fourth-floor inspector arrives outside Bertozzo's door, and the audience sees an arm stretch out to punch Bertozzo in the face.

Act 1, Scene 2

The Maniac, a Constable, and the fourth-floor inspector, who is referred to as Sports Jacket, are in a room at the police station. The Maniac's behavior is mercurial. At one moment, he questions the inspector and Constable severely, as if he knows they are somehow responsible for the anarchist's death. This makes them very nervous. At other moments, however, he appears to be on their side, suggesting that while they might not have told the entire truth about the event, they are right to present themselves as innocent of any wrongdoing. Although they are somewhat befuddled, the two police officers trust in the judge's good intentions.

Then the Maniac, still acting as a judge, asks for the Superintendent to be called into the room. The Superintendent arrives, angry at the peremptory way in which he was summoned. Once he sees that a judge is present, he calms down. The Maniac begins questioning the Superintendent. He asks him to review the item of evidence that says that the anarchist fell from the window because he was seized by a raptus, a state of suicidal anxiety pursuant to extreme desperation. Sports Jacket and the Superintendent begin explaining the events that took place immediately before the anarchist's death, saying that while their line of interrogation and methods might have caused the anarchist's raptus, these methods had not been unreasonable. As the Maniac continues questioning the men, they begin to contradict themselves on many details, such as the precise time of the anarchist's raptus. The Maniac is finally able to declare that the men lied to the media, their superiors, and the original inquest judge. Completely flustered, the two men become even more helpless in the face of the Maniac's mad patter and questions. The act ends with the two policemen completely perplexed, singing an anarchist song in concert with the Maniac.

Act 2, Scene 1

The action begins with the same assembled characters. The Maniac is questioning the policemen about the anarchist's fall from the window. Was the anarchist leaning out for air? Considering the weather, why was the window open at all? Once again, there are discrepancies in what the policemen said at the inquest—that is, what is on record—and what they say to the Maniac. The Maniac is able to get them to begin changing their stories and contradicting themselves. Throughout, real facts and statements from the historical inquest and actual newspaper interviews are used.

A journalist, Maria Feletti, arrives at the station to interview the Superintendent about the anarchist's death. The policemen want to send her away, but the Maniac encourages them to allow her to ask questions. The men say that the Maniac must then leave, as his presence will only give her confidence; she must not know that a judge is interested in questioning them, too. The Maniac persuades them to let him stay, saying that he will impersonate a forensics expert. He wants to stay, he says, to help them manage the Journalist's questions. The Journalist's questions, like those of the Maniac, are peppered with facts and reports from the actual historical inquest and the real interviews with the Milan officials involved in the case. She focuses on discrepancies in the policemen's stories. First, she asks about the nature of the anarchist's fall. There were no broken bones in the body, she says. One expects broken arms and hands in a person who has fallen from a window, because the person would try to break his or her fall. The lack of broken bones suggests that the anarchist was already dead before he fell. The Maniac agrees with her, to the consternation of the assembled policemen.

Next, the Journalist asks the policemen about the mark that was discovered on the anarchist's neck. It was not consistent with the fall. Is this evidence of a blow to the back of the neck that killed the anarchist? She believes this might be so, because an ambulance had been called for the anarchist before he is said to have fallen. Was the ambulance summoned because he had been given a terrible blow? If he died from the punch, perhaps he was then thrown out the window to make his death look like an accident, she conjectures. At this point, the Maniac begins speaking of the flimsiness of the anarchist's alibi, as if to aid the policemen, yet his intention is instead to discourse on the plight of the working class. According to the Maniac, the anarchist's friends, who vouched for his presence at the time of the bombing, could not possibly remember accurately because they are old, used up from too much work, even malnourished and senile.

Bertozzo enters the room. He has with him a copy of the bomb that was set off in the bank in question. When Bertozzo catches sight of the Maniac, he is about to blurt out that the Maniac is not who he says he is, but the Superintendent and Sports Jacket prevent him from speaking. They believe he is going to say that the Maniac is a judge, which would be disastrous, given what they have told the Journalist. In fact, all Bertozzo knows is that the Maniac cannot be the forensics expert he is claiming to be, because Bertozzo is acquainted with the expert.

The Journalist begins talking about the bomb. Why was a second bomb found at the site of the bombing destroyed? Why was it not saved as evidence? If it had been saved, they would have a "signature" of the bombers, she says. This suggests a cover-up on the part of the police. As she puts it, the anarchist and his group were a ragtag band of dreamers, incapable of planning any such event and certainly not equipped to make such sophisticated bombs. Bertozzo, to the dismay of the Superintendent, agrees. He says that the bomb most likely was made by paramilitary professionals. This idea leads the Journalist to present a common theory, namely, that the bombing was organized by fascists with police support, in order to discredit left-wing organizations and frighten the people into voting for the type of government that is highly supportive of police controls. The idea is that a frightened populace submits to strong, controlling leadership, willingly giving up freedoms in return for perceived safety. As before, the Maniac pretends to be helping the policemen but instead leads them to contradict themselves.

The play ends both comically and seriously. Comically, the Maniac runs through a number of impersonations in the last moments of the play. Less comically, the Maniac speaks of scandal. He says that scandal does not necessarily bring about justice, that it does not inevitably end the careers of those involved in it. Rather, he says, it provides a brief outlet for public anger that then dissipates quickly, so that the status quo is reestablished. The play ends with the Maniac's announcement that he has recorded everything that has transpired and will send copies of his recordings to all media outlets and higher authorities.

CHARACTERS

Inspector Bertozzo

Of the three upper-echelon police characters appearing in *Accidental Death of an Anarchist*, Inspector Bertozzo spends the least amount of time on stage. He has a role at the play's beginning, as the policeman interviewing the Maniac for impersonating a psychiatrist. He sees that the Maniac has been arrested many times for impersonation and does not believe the Maniac's claim that he is mad and therefore not responsible for his actions. He seems intent on finding a way to make a charge against the Maniac stick. However, after enduring enough of the Maniac's double-talk, he becomes utterly exasperated and tells him to leave the station.

In act 2, Inspector Bertozzo returns as an important element in the play's closing farce. He knows that the Maniac is not the forensics expert that he is pretending to be and wants to expose him to the Superintendent and Sports Jacket. They forestall any revelation on the part of Bertozzo, as they believe that he is going to reveal the Maniac to be a judge, which would be disastrous, given that they have told the journalist that he is a forensics expert. Bertozzo must put up with a great number of kicks—every time he opens his mouth to protest the Maniac's deception, the Superintendent and Sports Jacket must prevent him from doing so. These farcical kicks are more than just slapstick, however; they are designed to remind the audience of the physical abuses the anarchist endured during his interrogation. Like the other police officers, Bertozzo is wary of the journalist's questions, yet they, more so than he, are targets of her questioning.

Constable

The Constable is present in most of the play but has a fairly small role, speaking only occasionally. When ordered to do something by a superior, he follows orders immediately. However, he is not above a certain self-preserving caution, in that when he is questioned pointedly by the Maniac he is unwilling to commit himself by speaking plainly and also unwilling to show clear support of any superior whom the Maniac, as judge, appears to suspect of wrongdoing.

Maria Feletti

Known as the Journalist in Fo's play, the Feletti character arrives at the police station to ask questions about the growing scandal concerning the death of an anarchist suspect in police custody. At first, Sports Jacket wants to send her away, but the Maniac convinces him that he can use her to his benefit.

The Feletti character is a faithful representation of an experienced journalist: polite, cool, and hard-hitting in her questions. As Italians following the Pinelli case would have realized, this character is based on a real journalist, Camilla Cederna, who was then a reporter for the Italian weekly *L'espresso*. Cederna, like Feletti of *Accidental Death of an Anarchist*, uncovered real evidence of police corruption, not only with respect to the Pinelli case but also more broadly, in terms of Italian law enforcement and governmental establishments. Contrary to the Maniac, the Feletti character believes that scandal is beneficial, leading to real change and having the potential to deliver justice through the exposure of lawbreakers.

Maniac

The Maniac is the pivotal character in *Accidental Death of an Anarchist*. The part was acted by Fo himself in the original staging of the play. The character of the Maniac eclipses all other characters in every sense. He has by far the majority of lines, and he is by far the most interesting element of Fo's drama. Indeed, that it is difficult to distinguish between the police figures as personalities does not matter much, as the Maniac is the play's heart and soul. Onstage from the play's beginning to its end, the Maniac uses speech and actions to directly reflect the manipulations that the play is designed to expose.

At the beginning of *Accidental Death of an Anarchist*, the Maniac is in a Milan police station—the setting of the play—because he has been arrested for impersonating a psychiatrist. The inspector questioning him (Bertozzo) decides to let him go, however, because the Maniac's fast talking is just too much to bear. But the Maniac does not leave the police station; instead, he decides to continue with his impersonations. Specifically, he decides to impersonate a judge who is scheduled to arrive soon. In this guise, he questions several policemen and station officials about the death of a suspect, a case that has attracted much attention. In the course of his impersonation, the Maniac tricks the policemen and officials into revealing that they are part of a cover-up concerning the details of the suspect's death. (Before the play's end, the Maniac will impersonate two others, a forensics expert by the name of Captain Marcantonio Banzi Piccinni and a Vatican *chargé d'affaires* called Father Augusto Bernier.)

The Maniac is such a strong character in *Accidental Death of an Anarchist* because he embodies what he brings to light in his role as judge. First, as one who impersonates another, he reminds Fo's audiences that a common practice of the time was to send out police spies to infiltrate political groups. Second, as a character whose fast talking tricks the corrupt policemen, he is a trickster who gives them a dose of their own medicine. Even more specifically, the Maniac represents a dishonest interrogator, a policeman whose questioning amounts to coercion, entrapment, and abuse. Last, in the way that he consistently contradicts himself, he reminds audiences of the discrepant testimony of the police at the inquest and hearings that followed the real-life anarchist Giuseppe Pinelli's death. He is a reflection, in other words, of the distortion of facts for which the policemen involved in the actual case became known. For example, as quoted in Tom Behan's *Dario Fo*, a real-life Milan police officer is on record as speaking as follows at a hearing about whether or not he heard another officer say something when Pinelli was being interrogated:

> I'm not able to rectify or be precise about whether I heard that phrase because it was repeated, or because it was mentioned to me. As I believe I've already testified to having heard it, to having heard it directly; then, drawing things together, I don't believe that I heard it. However I'm not in a position to exclude that it may have been mentioned to me.

The Maniac is a manifestation of the madness surrounding him and all Italians during a time of corruption, unrest, and strife in Italian life. Still, as a farcical figure, he attests to Fo's belief that political theater with a serious intent need not be dry.

Sports Jacket

Sports Jacket is the policeman who, early in the play, calls Inspector Bertozzo's office and ends up having a conversation with the Maniac. In this conversation, the Maniac learns that a judge is being sent to ask questions about an anarchist suspect who died while being interrogated. Once he is impersonating the judge, the Maniac spends a great deal of time questioning Sports Jacket, with the result that the officer is exposed as being involved in an elaborate cover-up regarding the suspect.

Fo's audiences would have understood that Sports Jacket is a representation of a real officer involved in the real-life event on which the play is based. Specifically, Sports Jacket represents Luigi Calabresi, an officer who had been in the fourth-floor room of the Milan police station when the anarchist Giuseppe Pinelli plunged from the window. Calabresi sued a Milan publication for libel when the publication intimated that he had been wrongfully involved in the anarchist's death. Fo's costume for Sports Jacket refers to this trial, as Calabresi wore rolled-neck sweaters and sports jackets throughout. Calabresi also frequently rubbed his right hand during the trial, an action that many people believe indicated that this hand delivered the brutal blow to the back of Pinelli's neck. Fo's Sports Jacket delivers a punch to Inspector Bertozzo, and thereafter he often rubs the punching hand.

Because Sports Jacket believes that the Maniac is a judge who has been sent to investigate the death of the anarchist, he is by turns wary, nervous, belligerent, pleased, or relieved, depending on the nature of the Maniac's questions and moods. Apart from this, Sports Jacket tends to display brutal behavior, at least as far he can within the context of the play's amusing farce. Clearly, Fo wants to suggest that there was indeed a police officer at Milan headquarters who went too far in manhandling Pinelli, dealing the anarchist the terrible blow on the back of the neck that left the mark the pathologists found on his corpse.

Superintendent

The Superintendent of the play is much like Sports Jacket. He reacts defensively when the Maniac, as judge, poses questions that appear to suggest a suspicion of wrongdoing on his part; he is pleased when the Maniac seems to be supporting what he did when he interrogated the anarchist; he is nervous when he cannot quite figure out what the Maniac is up to in his questioning. As in the case of Sports Jacket, the Maniac succeeds in tricking the Superintendent into incriminating himself.

THEMES

Reform versus Revolution

Those who wish to change society may think that instituting reforms is the way to go about it. Reformers have faith in existing structures and

TOPICS FOR FURTHER STUDY

- *Accidental Death of an Anarchist* employs many elements typical of farce. Research the characteristics of farce and write an essay on Fo's play as a farce.
- Research trickster literatures and write an essay comparing and contrasting figures from two different traditions, such as a Native American tradition and the African American Uncle Remus tradition.
- Research one of the American terrorist groups of the 1960s or 1970s, such as the Weather Underground or the Symbionese Liberation Army. What were their political beliefs and goals? Did they consider people acceptable terrorist targets? Who were the leaders of these organizations? What happened to them? Compile your findings into a report with appropriate subheadings.
- What were the political beliefs of anarchists such as Giuseppe Pinelli? Where did anarchist theories first develop? What are the basic tenets of anarchist politics? Present a report to your class that dispels misconceptions about anarchists and explains their core political ideals.
- At the time of writing *Accidental Death of an Anarchist*, Fo was running a drama group called La Comune. Research La Comune within the context of contemporary events in Italian social and political life. In an essay, explain how the group's ethos and goals are responses to what was happening in Italy at the time.

believe that these structures need only be perfected—or corrupt elements within them be rooted out—for desired changes to come about. Others who wish to change society for the better believe that what is called for is revolution, a radical restructuring of society and its institutions. Revolutionaries tend to think that reforms are mere bandages on never-healing sores, leading to temporary alleviation of a persistent problem, such as poverty, but never eliminating it. They believe, in short, that existing structures must be dismantled and that entirely new ones must take their place.

Fo's *Accidental Death of an Anarchist* is infused with revolutionary zeal, as is evident at the play's end, when the Maniac discourses on scandal. To the Maniac, scandals such as exposés of police corruption do little to bring about real change. Rather, scandal allows people to let off steam, with the result that the powers that be are in a stronger position than before. The implication is that scandal might lead to some reforms but never to true revolutionary change. In the following excerpt, the Maniac pretends to be translating the words of a pope who knew very well how scandal could be used to strengthen his position:

> MANIAC: Did you know that when Saint Gregory was elected Pope, he discovered that his subordinates were up to all kinds of skullduggery in an attempt to cover up various outrageous scandals? He was furious, and it was then that he uttered his famous phrase: *Nolimus aut velimus, omnibus gentibus, justitiam et veritatem.*
>
> JOURNALIST: I'm sorry, your Eminence . . . I failed Latin three times. . . .
>
> MANIAC: It means: 'Whether they want it or not, I shall impose truth and justice. I shall do what I can to make sure that these scandals explode in the most public way possible; and you need not fear that, in among the rot, the power of government will be undermined. Let the scandal come, because on the basis of that scandal a more durable power of the state will be founded!'

A bit later in the play, the Maniac speaks of scandal again:

> MANIAC: They've never tried to hush up these scandals. And they're right not to. That way, people can let off steam, get angry, shudder at the thought of it . . . 'Who do these politicians think they are?' 'Scumbag generals!' 'Murderers!' And they get more and more

angry, and then, burp! A little liberatory burp to relieve their social indigestion.

Fear and Submission

During periods of social unrest or general crisis, the political scene in a nation becomes tense. Different groups believe they have the answer to the nation's ills or a way to deal with the crisis and threat, and each group attempts to wrest control from those in power. The coalition in power naturally wishes to retain control and will often go to great lengths to do so. During the time period in which Fo wrote *Accidental Death of an Anarchist*, Italy was undergoing just such a period of extreme social unrest, when those in power wondered if they would be able to maintain authority and control.

Particularly disturbing to the authorities was the growing influence of certain groups whose politics were "far" left, calling for a radical restructuring of society, not simply reform. In an effort to discredit such groups in the eyes of the general public, members of the Italian police force—some say with the support of the government—began sanctioning the activities of agents posing as far leftists and committing terrorist acts in their name. Bomb after bomb exploded in Italian cities, and the general public began to believe that order was escaping them. This fear on the part of the general public was precisely what was sought, as a fearful and uncertain public is a public unlikely to commit to major change at the governmental level for fear of yet more chaos. Fomenting chaos and encouraging fear are standard tactics of the corrupt and manipulative. Entirely dishonest, this is nevertheless a sure way to influence voters' behavior.

At many points in the play, in which information is cited from actual documents, Fo's characters convey these various ideas. In the following excerpt, for example, the Maniac speaks of a plot to discredit "the Left":

> MANIAC: At the start you served a useful function: something had to be done to stop all the strikes . . . So they decided to start a witch-hunt against the Left. But now things have gone a bit too far.

In the following excerpt, somewhat later in the play, Fo's fictional journalist cites actual facts concerning the makeup of the activist group to which the (real) anarchist belonged. Of the ten members of the group, four were infiltrators, as the Journalist points out:

> JOURNALIST: OK. So let's take a look behind that façade. What do we find? Out of the ten members of the [anarchist's] group, two of them were your own people, two informers, or rather, spies and provocateurs. One was a Rome fascist, well-known to everyone except the aforementioned pathetic group of anarchists, and the other was one of your own officers, disguised as an anarchist.

The Journalist speaks again along similar lines still later in the play:

> JOURNALIST: *(Taking some papers from a folder)* . . . And I suppose nobody's told you either that out of a total of 173 bomb attacks that have happened in the past year and a bit, at a rate of twelve a month, one every three days—out of 173 attacks, as I was saying *(She reads from a report)* at least 102 have been proved to have been organised by fascist [rightist] organisations, aided or abetted by the police, with the explicit intention of putting the blame on Left-wing political groups.

STYLE

The Trickster

The Maniac is a variant of a trickster figure, a character who acts mad or simple but who is actually invested with more sense than anybody around him. Tricksters fool those who are vain or who believe themselves cleverer than everybody else. Tricksters are quite often lesser societal figures tricked by those more elevated. They belong to the ranks of the common people, appearing in stories as an assertion of their worthiness in the face of an elite group's disdain and ignorance. Every nation has literary traditions employing trickster figures. One very well-known trickster series in the American literary canon uses animals as characters (as do so many trickster traditions). This series is Joel Chandler Harris's Uncle Remus stories of Brer Rabbit and Brer Fox. Harris compiled these stories from those of African American storytellers, building on original African traditions. In the American context, these African American stories of seemingly weak characters winning out over stronger figures reveal the slave's or newly freed slave's assertion of his own wisdom against an elite that usually refused to see it.

Fo employs the trickster Maniac in *Accidental Death of an Anarchist* most probably in order to foster a sense of empowerment in his audiences. After all, the play addresses an event pointing to covert police criminality and likely governmental support of such wrongdoing. To know that one is being fooled by one's leaders or to believe that they are corrupt is to feel helpless, powerless, confused. Why vote if one is voting for crooks? If one's leaders are dishonest, why should anyone be honest? The clever trickster figure in Fo's play effectively exposes the lies and collusions of the corrupt police officers, conveying a sense that the truth can indeed be known and justice can indeed be served.

The Bawdy and Slapstick

Fo's employment of bawdy humor and slapstick action is, like his use of the trickster Maniac, a populist component of his play—an element designed to appeal to all audiences and not simply to elite ones. Bawdy humor focuses on bodily functions, such as the fun Fo derives from the lustily farting Maniac: "Yes, you can tell him that too: Anghiari and Bertozzo couldn't give a [sh——t]! *(He lets out a tremendous raspberry [fart])* Prrruttt. Yes, it was Bertozzo who did the raspberry. Alright, no need to get hysterical . . . !" Slapstick humor is similarly body oriented, as it involves characters tripping or falling—somehow being made ridiculous (without any lasting harm coming to them). An example of slapstick in *Accidental Death of an Anarchist* is when Bertozzo receives a big punch in the face from the inspector, who believes Bertozzo has sent the raspberry his way. Bawdy and slapstick humor is considered populist because it is humor that anyone can appreciate—such as a derisive fart.

Alienation Effects

Playwrights with strong political convictions such as Fo tend to employ and develop dramatic techniques that distance the audience from the work. These techniques might be called alienation effects, after the language of the playwright who pioneered many distancing methods, the German Bertolt Brecht. Brecht thought it important to alienate the audience from the play being performed so that they would think critically about what they were watching. For example, he would present characters performing more or less typical, everyday actions in his plays, but he would make sure that the acting was just stilted enough so that the audience would see these actions in a new light. What is strange about things so many of us do? he wanted his audiences to ask. What if things were done differently? How might the world change for the better? Two of Brecht's most famous plays are *Mother Courage and Her Children* and *The Good Woman of Setzuan*.

Other distancing effects besides acting techniques that are not quite realistic are, for example, self-reflexive strategies. This means that a playwright includes moments when the play refers to itself as a play. For example, the actors might refer to themselves as actors, or the actors might speak directly to the audience, destroying the illusion of "reality on stage" and reminding the audience that a play, something made up, is taking place. Moments such as these disturb the audience's identification with the actors and story, encouraging viewers to evaluate what is transpiring. Here is a self-reflexive moment from *Accidental Death of an Anarchist*:

> JOURNALIST: And I suppose you have plenty more of these very well-trained operatives scattered around the Left groups?
>
> SUPERINTENDENT: I see no reason to deny it, Miss. Yes we do.
>
> JOURNALIST: I think you're just calling my bluff, there, Superintendent!
>
> SUPERINTENDENT: Not at all . . . In fact you may be interested to know that we have one or two right here in the audience tonight, as usual . . . Watch this.
>
> *He claps his hands. We hear a number of voices from different parts of the auditorium.*
>
> VOICES: Sir . . . ? Yessir . . . ! Sir . . . !
>
> *The* MANIAC *laughs, and turns to the audience.*
>
> MANIAC: Don't worry—they're all actors. The real ones sit tight and don't say a word.

As this excerpt demonstrates, Fo has his actors speak directly about and to the audience.

HISTORICAL CONTEXT

Social Unrest and the "Hot Autumn" of 1969 in Italy

Politicians who were voted into Italy's parliament in the 1960s and 1970s had much to answer for. Italy's working class was fed up—with dangerous working conditions, long hours, low pay, expensive and uninhabitable housing, poor benefit packages, and more. Mobilizing, the working classes began to march and strike. Left-wing organizations, furthermore, were flourishing and gaining power, including those on the Far Left, favoring revolution over reform. The autumn of 1969 in Italy is known as the "Hot Autumn" of working class and student protest, as unrest had reached a height. On October 15, fifty thousand workers demonstrated in Milan, and on November 28, one hundred thousand engineers demonstrated in Rome. Other disturbances and changes were afoot as well. This was the time, for example, of feminist agitation, so that in November a law legalizing divorce in Italy was passed.

Contributing to the political and social heat of the time was the fact that, as in the United States

COMPARE & CONTRAST

- **Late 1960s to early 1970s:** Italians are mobilized by radical political philosophies calling for drastic changes to cure such ills as low wages and poor working conditions in factories.

  Today: Italian workers wonder whether the considerable gains won following the protests of the 1960s are threatened by the developments of a globalizing world economy. They worry that greater competition among nations will lead companies to cut worker salaries and benefits in order to remain competitive.

- **Late 1960s to early 1970s:** Countercultural youths, like the hippies, protest against what they perceive as repressive elements within Italian life, such as the premium placed on sexual abstinence before marriage. Italian feminists also stage protests.

  Today: While the most extreme positions held by counterculture enthusiasts are rejected, Italian society is radically different. For example, women are now integral in the professional workforce, and contraception is widely practiced.

- **Late 1960s to early 1970s:** The Roman Catholic Church begins losing some of its power within Italy, as is seen in the Italian government's legalization of divorce in 1969.

  Today: While most Italians identify themselves as Roman Catholics and thousands of mourners poured into the streets following the death of Pope John Paul II (1920–2005), less than half the population attends church regularly.

- **Late 1960s to early 1970s:** The business tycoon Silvio Berlusconi builds a massive complex of apartments just outside Milan, called Milano 2. Some say that he won this project with secret help and backing from a powerful anti-Communist organization known as Propaganda 2.

  Today: Berlusconi, elected twice as Italy's prime minister, is subject to charges of bribery, and a new term, *Berlusconismo*, begins circulating in Italy. The term refers to a way of life in which an Italian lives in a house built by Berlusconi, shops at markets owned by Berlusconi, eats at restaurants owned by Berlusconi, watches television stations controlled by Berlusconi, and so on.

and elsewhere, radical political organizations on both the left and the right of the political spectrum were turning to terrorism. As the Communist-inclined Weather Underground was blowing up buildings in the United States, similar underground organizations were doing the same in Italy. Indeed, as the Journalist says in *Accidental Death of an Anarchist*, 173 bomb attacks occurred in Italy in the space of little more than a year during this time. The anarchist who died at Milan police headquarters and whose death is the subject of Fo's play had been arrested on suspicion of carrying out a Hot Autumn bombing at the National Agricultural Bank in Piazza Fontana in Milan on November 12, 1969.

Giuseppe Pinelli and Pietro Valpreda

Giuseppe Pinelli and Pietro Valpreda were two anarchists arrested in the aftermath of the Hot Autumn Piazza Fontana bombing of November 12, 1969. Pinelli, a forty-one-year-old railway worker, was married with two daughters. Valpreda was a ballet dancer. Within seventy-two hours of his arrest, Pinelli was dead under suspicious circumstances. According to police statements, he had thrown himself from a window while being interrogated. However, there were discrepancies in the policemen's stories and in the evidence. At an inquest, suicide was not concluded; the death was deemed an accident. Neither Pinelli (posthumously) nor Valpreda was ever convicted of the bombing, nor were any other suspected persons, all of whom were members of neofascist organizations. Working against those trying to convict Pinelli was the sense that he was not the type of activist to carry out such an attack. This idea, that the bombing was carried out not by amateurs but by paramilitary agents, is expressed in *Accidental Death of an Anarchist*, when the Journalist characterizes the group to which the anarchist of Fo's play belongs:

> JOURNALIST: So what did you do? Even though you were well aware that to construct—let alone plant—a bomb of such complexity, would take the skills and experience of professionals—probably military people—you decided to go chasing after this fairly pathetic group of anarchists and completely dropped all other lines of inquiry among certain parties who shall remain nameless but you know who I mean.

A plaque dedicated to Pinelli can still be seen in Piazza Fontana, as most Italians believe he was a victim of police brutality.

Cornelius Booth, Paul Ritter, Rhys Ifans, and Adrian Scarborough in a 2003 production of Accidental Death of an Anarchist © Donald Cooper/Photostage. Reproduced by permission

CRITICAL OVERVIEW

Fo was already a major cultural figure in Italy when *Accidental Death of an Anarchist* was staged. Indeed, his credibility and influence were such that he was provided with copies of actual inquest and police documents as he was composing his play. *Accidental Death of an Anarchist* opened approximately one year after Giuseppe Pinelli's death, in December 1970, and it was a major hit all over Italy as it toured and played to thousands. Italian support of the play suggests the degree to which Italians were critical of authorities at the time.

Although another of Fo's plays, *Mistero buffo*, is considered his most popular in Italy, *Accidental Death of an Anarchist* is said to be his second most popular. Outside Italy, it is Fo's most-performed play, partly owing to its searing indictment of police corruption and strong suggestion that a similarly corrupt government body is underwriting this corruption. As Tom Behan indicates in *Dario Fo: Revolutionary Theatre*, directors around the world who want to respond to corruption in their own midst have turned to *Accidental Death of an Anarchist* to galvanize their audiences to political action, despite the great risks involved in doing so:

> Fo claims that *Accidental Death of an Anarchist* has been the most performed play in the world over the last 40 years. Its pedigree certainly is impressive: productions in at least 41 countries in very testing circumstances: fascist Chile, Ceausescu's Romania and apartheid South Africa. In Argentina and Greece the cast of early productions were all arrested.

Because Fo allows changes to be made to his script, foreign directors can include material that makes the play relevant to their particular local situation. Of course, if *Accidental Death of an Anarchist* were not as well written and entertaining as it is, it would not be such a favorite choice of the world's directors and drama groups. What has made Fo's and this play's reputation, finally, is his great skill as a dramatist and theatrical innovator. However, many of Fo's innovations are, paradoxically, adaptations from past theatrical traditions. Joseph Farrell discusses this paradox in "Dario Fo: *Zanni* and *Giullare*," from the essay collection *The Commedia Dell'Arte: From the Renaissance to Dario Fo*:

> The affection for, and identification with, figures from Italian theatrical tradition, be it *Arlecchino* [Harlequin] or the *giullare* [a performer who would travel from village to village], are perfect illustrations of one of the most striking and paradoxical features of the work of Dario Fo—his relentless search for models from the past with whom he can identify. If on the one hand Fo is customarily seen, and indeed goes out of his way to present himself, as the subversive, the iconoclastic revolutionary, . . . at the

same time his theatrical style is based not on any avant-garde, but on the approaches and techniques practiced by performers of centuries past.

As Farrell writes, the "figure of the *giullare*," which "provides Fo with a focus and a model" for much of his work, "is a quintessentially medieval figure, who flourished approximately from the Tenth to the Fifteenth centuries, in other words in the period before the blossoming of *Commedia dell'arte*." Still, the tradition of the *commedia dell'arte*—from which the figure of the Harlequin derives—is also an important source of inspiration for Fo. Troupes of professional actors made up the *commedia* groups. They would perform for common people in village squares as soon as they would for aristocrats on polished stages, improvising dialogue within the set limits of stock plots.

In the essay collection *Studies in the Commedia Dell'Arte*, Christopher Cairns explores Fo's relationship to *commedia* tradition in his essay "Dario Fo and the *Commedia Dell'Arte*." He points out that Fo's interest in this tradition's figures and techniques developed only after he had immersed himself in the tradition of the *giullare* for many years. Fo's newfound interest, however, resulted in the curious discovery that he had been implementing *commedia* techniques all along:

> In London in 1988, Fo admitted that he had come late to the formal study of the *commedia dell'arte*, but had found with some surprise that he had been involved in similar theatrical practice (with different roots, in variety, the circus, the silent film) already for many years.

In a comment on the *commedia* aspects of Fo's play *Harlequin* (1985), Cairns describes the relationship between tradition and innovation so characteristic of Fo's work in general:

> The extraordinary vogue for the *commedia dell'arte* as a performance language in the contemporary theatre has given rise to two distinct conventions. First [there is] the 'archaeological' reconstruction of the working methods, costumes, masks and relationships between the well-known stereotype characters, refined and polished to a high degree of professional performance. . . . Secondly, we have the adaptation or 'selection' of styles from past traditions of *commedia* for modern uses: a bringing face to face with contemporary social and political causes of a deep-rooted European theatrical tradition, particularly since the 1960s. It is to this second *modern* convention that Dario Fo's *Harlequin* belongs.

Thus, many critics do not hesitate to argue that there are *commedia* elements in those of Fo's plays written even before his formal study of the tradition.

CRITICISM

Carol Dell'Amico

Dell'Amico is a lecturer in the English Department of California State University, Bakersfield. In this essay, she explores Fo's play as a work of political theater.

The Italian actor and playwright Fo is known as a practitioner of political theater. Political theater, it is important to note, is not theater that lectures an audience on a particular political belief system (or at least it is not supposed to do that). Political theater is theater that attempts to heighten the critical consciousness of its audience. In other words, dramatists with a political bent are interested in furthering audience members' ability to sort through the complexities of modern life so as to make informed decisions about weighty issues; they are not interested only in entertaining their audiences. Thus, despite the entertaining farce of Fo's *Accidental Death of an Anarchist*, watching the play is more than just an enjoyable event. It is also a political event, as the play encourages its audience to think critically about events that were unfolding at the time in Italy.

Particularly important to playwrights interested in heightening the critical faculties of their audience members are dramatic methods that enable such effects. Some of the most commonly employed of such methods are associated with major theorists of political theater, the German playwright Bertolt Brecht foremost among them. Certainly, Fo is influenced by Brechtian theory and practice. One cornerstone of Brechtian practice is the distancing of viewers from the dramatic events unfolding onstage. To distance viewers means to employ methods that impede their ability to lose themselves in the drama, thus encouraging them to step back and think about the issues being raised by the play. The political playwright interested in distance will destroy the so-called invisible fourth wall of theater, so as to encourage a critical and evaluating mindset. The invisible fourth wall of theater is the one between audience and stage. It cannot be seen as can the other three walls of the stage (the two side walls and one back wall), but it is still there. It is there in the sense that most actors and playwrights conceive of drama as something that unfolds in front of an audience, strictly without its participation. The goal of most playwrights and theatrical directors is to create an airtight illusion: the lights go down, the curtain rises, action begins, and viewers lose all sense of themselves as thinkers as they identify with the characters and become absorbed in the story.

Playwrights who wish to destroy this fourth wall between the stage and the audience do so in numerous ways. One way is to have actors address the audience directly, occasionally or often. This direct address bridges the fourth wall, reminding viewers that a play calling for their evaluation is being performed. One scene in *Accidental Death of an Anarchist* suggests precisely such a strategy, although each individual director of the play decides, ultimately, if and when such effects will occur. At this point in the play, the Maniac has hit on the idea of impersonating a judge. To this end, he begins to try out various personas. Should the judge have a limp? Should he wear glasses? Experimenting with one persona, he says, "Well, look at that! Brilliant! Just what I was looking for!" This "look at that" is a ripe moment for the actor to address the audience—to look at the audience while speaking and break the illusion erected by the fourth wall.

In reminding the audience members that that is what they are—an audience at a play—the actor achieves a self-reflexive moment. That is, any time a work of art calls attention to itself *as a work of art*—reflects on itself as artifice—a self-reflexive moment occurs. Self-reflexivity is another major way to distance an audience. Every time the play comments on itself as a play, illusion is broken, the fourth wall is dissolved, and the audience is alerted that something that someone has created—and could have done differently—is being presented.

Self-reflexive strategies are very important to most practitioners of political theater, on principle. After all, these dramatists are always interested in reminding their viewers of the way they are often led to make political choices against their own interests: they are duped by those in power to vote in ways that further the interests of those in power, not their own interests. In other words, thanks to the way the powerful can use language and manipulate emotions, people believe that they are helping themselves when they are actually serving the interests of those who have fooled them. In this way, they have been divested of true understanding, of accurate critical insight into the nature of the world, the political process, economics, and so forth. They are in the grip, in short, of an illusion; master illusionists have fooled them. Political playwrights employ self-reflexive strategies because they are against real-world political illusion. They do not want to present important ideas to the audience obliquely, without their knowing that this is taking place. They do not want to abuse their power to influence and mold thoughts, as some politicians and political parties do. Political playwrights keep their audiences alert and distanced from characters and events so that audiences understand that this is the way to approach all important things in life: critically and skeptically.

"POLITICAL PLAYWRIGHTS EMPLOY SELF-REFLEXIVE STRATEGIES BECAUSE THEY ARE AGAINST REAL-WORLD POLITICAL ILLUSION."

Fo employs self-reflexive moments throughout *Accidental Death of an Anarchist*. For example, from the very first moments of the play, when the major character, the Maniac, is introduced, the play makes reference to itself. This is due to the nature of this character. The Maniac is a master illusionist, an impersonator of anybody he wishes to impersonate. He has been arrested for pretending to be a psychiatrist, and this transgression is but the latest in a long line of masquerades. The Maniac, in short, is very much like an *actor*. The play's self-reflexivity in this regard can be clearly felt in the following words from the Maniac's first major speech in the play: "I have a thing about dreaming up characters and then acting them out. It's called 'histrionomania'—comes from the Latin *histriones*, meaning 'actor.' I'm a sort of amateur performance artist." In commenting on himself as an actor, this character is being self-reflexive. He is reminding audience members that a play is taking place, preventing them from losing themselves unthinkingly in the action.

Moments such as these are not the only reason why there are few opportunities to identify with the Maniac and so lose sight of the fact that he is an actor going through his paces. Also ensuring that moments of identification are few, or that identification is at least shallow, is the way in which Fo casts the character as a mercurial figure. That is, the Maniac changes from one persona to another throughout the play. The Maniac's character is also

WHAT DO I READ NEXT?

- Fo's most popular play is *Mistero buffo*, which means "The Comedic Mystery." It features the comedic antics of a jester in the medieval tradition of the "jongleurs," traveling entertainers whose performances flouted the authority of church and state. It has been seen by millions of Italians and shows Fo's grounding in popular storytelling traditions. This one-man show satirizing landowners, the Roman Catholic Church, and the Italian government was first performed by Fo in 1969.
- The *Complete Plays of Vladimir Mayakovsky*, translated by Guy Daniels, contains Mayakovsky's *Mystery-Bouffe* (1918), an inspiration for Fo's own *Mistero buffo*. Mayakovsky, a Russian writer who engaged in subversive socialist political activities, was one of Fo's many influences, thanks to his revolutionary zeal on the part of Russia's then-disenfranchised peasants and lower classes.
- The *Uncle Remus* tales first published by Joel Chandler Harris in book form in 1880 were told to him by African American storytellers. These are tales employing trickster figures like the Maniac.
- The four plays of *Female Parts: One Woman Plays* (1981) were written by Fo in collaboration with his longtime partner, Franca Rame. Rame acted in these plays when they were first produced.

hyperactive, speaking continuously and quickly and jumping from thought to thought. The effect of such acting is jarring, uncomfortable, which is to say, again, that no audience member is likely to sit back in his or her chair and be absorbed into the world of the play.

Also characteristic of much political theater, including *Accidental Death of an Anarchist*, is its populist dimension. That is, playwrights such as Fo actively work against the notion that plays with serious intent are written for an educated elite and are beyond the understanding and enjoyment of the average person. This accounts for the plain, idiomatic language of *Accidental Death of an Anarchist* and its slang. Above all, Fo wants to write plays that will appeal to the very people he believes can most benefit from his work—the nonelite. (Interestingly, Fo encourages translators of his works to use local slang in place of his own, so that all audiences of his plays will have a worthwhile experience. Despite the play's having been written in language directed at Italians conversant in 1960s and 1970s Italian slang, an American translator in the twenty-first century is welcome to tinker with the script as she or he thinks fit. To allow such freedom with one's script is, of course, a populist gesture as well. Fo is not so taken with his genius and power as an artist as to not let anyone change what he has written.)

Closely related to political theater's populism is its desire to educate and empower. This desire is evident in *Accidental Death of an Anarchist* in various ways. For example, the Maniac recites laws in his speeches, imparting legal savvy to the audience. The Maniac's mad methods also highlight the illusionist methods of those of the political elite who are dishonest. That is, he is always mincing words, squabbling over the meaning of sentences, focusing upon a minute item of punctuation, encouraging other characters to revise statements so as to obfuscate the true nature of what they are saying, and so on. The Maniac, in other words, is a character who demonstrates how the truth can amount to a lie in the mouths of those who know how to manipulate language.

The comic slapstick and bawdiness of *Accidental Death of an Anarchist* do not obscure its serious intentions. Of great concern to Fo were various covert activities being carried out by the Italian police at the time, probably in concert with the Italian

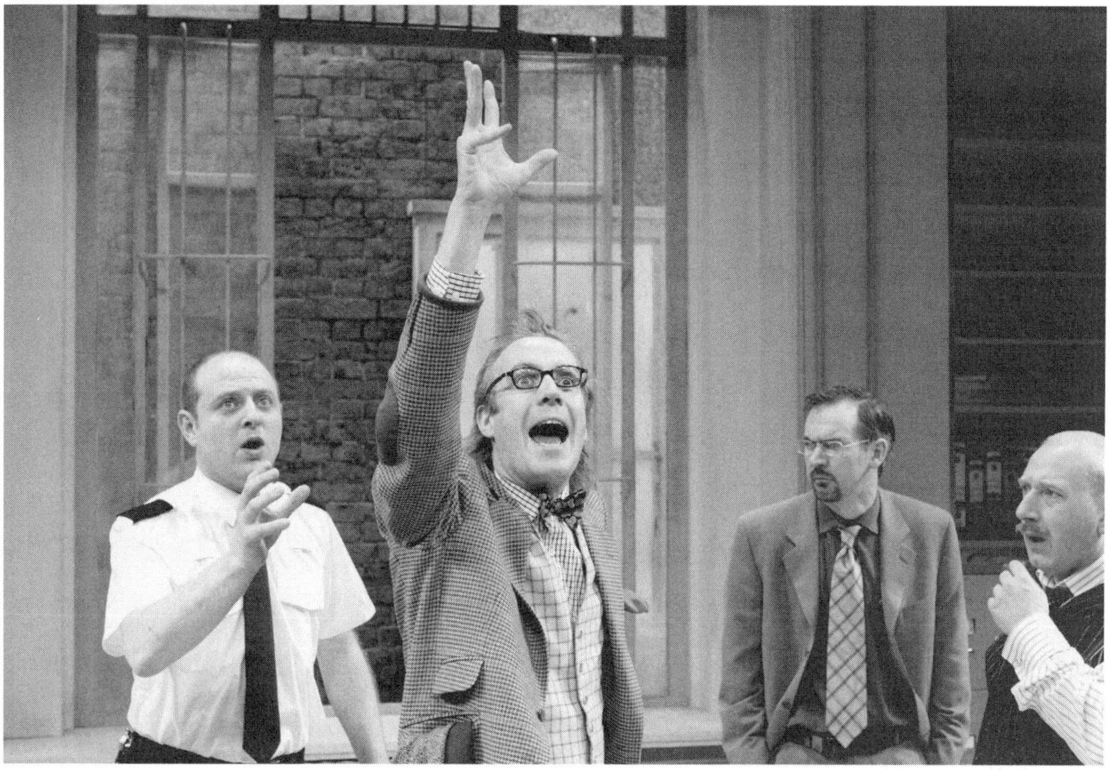

Cornelius Booth, Rhys Ifans, Paul Ritter, and Adrian Scarborough in a 2003 production of Accidental Death of an Anarchist © Donald Cooper/Photostage. Reproduced by permission

government (in the late 1960s and early 1970s). Specifically, left-wing groups were being blamed for bombings orchestrated by neofascist organizations. The Italian police would then arrest prominent left-wing agitators so as to discredit these groups in the eyes of the Italian public. The impetus behind such wrongdoing was that leftist ideologies, and not rightist (neofascist, for example) ideologies, constituted a real threat to the continued existence of the government, as Italy was experiencing a period of widespread and deep-seated discontent. This is not to say that extremist leftist groups did not set off any bombs; they did. Nonetheless, agents whose goal was to alarm the public committed a number of these acts so that voters would hesitate to enact any real political change in the fear that too much change at the governmental level would only further destabilize the country. The event of the anarchist who fell from a police headquarters window is a historical one—and one that most Italians now believe is incontrovertible proof of police and governmental wrongdoing of the time.

Source: Carol Dell'Amico, Critical Essay on *Accidental Death of an Anarchist*, in *Drama for Students*, Thomson Gale, 2006.

Domenico Maceri

In the following essay, Maceri explores the reasons why Fo won the Nobel Prize, and analyzes themes in Accidental Death of an Anarchist *and* Mistero buffo.

> Dio esiste e anche lui e un giullare. (God exists and he too is a jester.)
>
> —Dario Fo

Although the proceedings for the selection of the Nobel Prizes are secret, intriguing information inevitably leaks. Apparently it was Italy's year to win the prize for literature. Dario Fo, however, was not considered a leading candidate, in part because of the paucity of support for Italy within the Academy. One of the few Italianists there in recent memory was the late Anders Osterling, the Swedish poet and editor of a well-known anthology of Italian

"ALTHOUGH FO CERTAINLY POKES FUN AT THE POLICE OFFICIALS, HE DOES NOT PRESENT THEM MERELY AS COMIC FIGURES BUT RATHER AS DEVIOUS ABUSERS OF POWER. NEITHER DOES HE SHOW GREAT SYMPATHY FOR THE ANARCHIST."

verse covering the period between 1959 and 1975, years in which two Italian poets won the Nobel Prize in Literature (Salvatore Quasimodo in 1959, Eugenio Montale in 1975). The only other major Italian literature supporter of late is Lars Forssell, the Swedish poet and songwriter and well-known Italophile. Thus, if an Italian were to be considered a serious contender, it would quite likely be a poet, and the name that everyone expected was Mario Luzi, who in fact did entertain hopes of winning the award. It is conceivable that the Academicians wanted to give the prize to Italy but that, since the last two Italian winners had been poets, they felt it needed to go a different route.

Ultimately, the Academy members may have wanted to stress content over form and bring attention to the struggle between the weak and the powerful, as they indicated in their press release. They praised Fo as an emulator of "the jesters of the Middle Ages in upholding the dignity of the downtrodden," a writer who "opens our eyes to the abuses and injustices in society." The Academy also stressed Fo's literary qualities, adding that "his works are open for creative additions, dislocations, continually encouraging the actors to improvise, which means the audience is activated in a remarkable way."

The reaction in Italy, from the world of "traditional" literature, was predictable. One critic called awarding the prize to Fo a slap in the face to all that Italian literature has accomplished in the second half of the century. Another said it was a choice having to do more with sociology than with literature. Another critic argued that Fo might have merited the prize if it had been awarded just for theater, but for literature another name was to be expected.

Of course, the most renowned Italian winner of the Nobel Prize in Literature was a man of the theater. But in Luigi Pirandello's case (1934) no questions were raised as to his legitimate literary credentials, because, as the author of novels and short stories in addition to plays and his work as a director, he was obviously a man of letters. Fo's selection pushes the definition of literature into a broader context, for he is not strictly and only a man of letters. He is an actor, playwright, director, stage designer, popular songwriter, mime, TV personality, and political campaigner, a figure whose ideas have managed to antagonize such diverse groups as the Catholic Church and the Italian Communist Party. In fact, to understand all of Fo's "literary" qualities from written texts alone is not possible, for no written page contains what he is or what he does in his works. However, an examination of *Mistero buffo* (1973; the title would literally translate as "Comic Mystery," but Ed Emery's English edition was published under the original Italian title) and *Morte accidentale di un anarchico* (1974; Eng. *Accidental Death of an Anarchist*) can give a good idea.

In his now classic study of Italian literature, Giuseppe Petronio argues that today's theater presents directors' interpretations of plays, rather than authors' or actors', and that even when the play is from the past, the emphasis is on today's problems (961). This is certainly true in Fo's case, although in *Mistero buffo* the roles of playwright, director, actor, stage designer, and mime blend, making it impossible to see where one role begins and the other ends. As the writer and sole performer of *Mistero buffo,* Fo manages to fulfill Pirandello's view that authors and actors should "immedesimarsi" (become the characters) with the work they are composing or performing (215). Fo becomes the characters every time he stages the play, each performance presenting a different and new work because of his improvisations, which show the audiences his creative powers in action.

Although the play is therefore never totally "finished," the working texts of *Mistero buffo* and *Morte accidentale di un anarchico* contain the fundamental elements of Fo's opus, and particularly his concern for the poor and their struggle against the political establishment, elements which to a certain extent reflect the author's working-class roots (his mother was a peasant, his father a railway worker). In addition, these two works attempt to "recover" the people's language and culture going back to the Middle Ages, his role as giullare (jester), and his ideas about theater as an art form.

Fo borrows both the title and the concept of *Mistero buffo* from *Mistera-buff* (1918) by the Russian poet and playwright Vladimir Mayakovsky, who sought to rewrite sacred issues of history through parody and farce and to present the proletariat's struggle against the forces of tyranny. Fo's *Mistero buffo* returns his spectators to the Middle Ages, although he repeatedly makes pointed, often startling connections with the present. Echoing Gramsci's ideas, Fo believes in the importance of knowing oneself, which allows the self's authenticity and thus enables one to be the master of one's destiny. To accomplish this, one must know the past; thus in the 1950s Fo began a study of medieval culture, the beginnings of theater and of his Padan language, a blend of Northern Italian dialects, which he uses in *Mistero buffo.* Fo believes that the dominant Italian class has robbed poor people of their culture and their language (Hirst, 110).

His return to the Middle Ages is also an attempt to recover the vital sources of theater in a precapitalistic society before the mass media turned culture into merchandise in the hands of the rich and powerful to control the working class (lelo). Applying the knowledge he gained as a result of his study, Fo creates a number of vignettes on topics with an ecclesiastical background to show not only the corruption and repressiveness of the Church but also the political implications of its power. Stressing popular, comic, and irreverent elements of medieval mystery plays and religious cycles, Fo attacks the repressiveness of the Catholic Church and the land-owning classes, using the language of the Italian peasants, whom he sees as representatives of peasants all over the world.

At the root of Fo's world view is the idea that poor people's lives are controlled by the rich and powerful, who have stolen the downtrodden's culture. *Mistero buffo* will thus be the "giornale parlato e drammatizzato del popolo" (the people's spoken and dramatized newspaper). People must retake possession of what their masters have stolen and made their own.

In the first of the vignettes of *Mistero buffo* Fo tries to do just that. He reinterprets the classical Italian poem "Rosa fresca aulentissima" ("Sweet-Smelling, Fresh Rose") with its famous contrast between a tax collector and a woman who initially rejects his advances, a poem familiar to every student of Italian literature. Critics believe the poem was written by an aristocratic author who used refined language to turn the trivial theme of physical love into elevated poetry. Traditionally, it is seen as the first example of Italian courtly love. Fo reveals the poem's popular origins. He asserts that the poem might have been sung as a ballad in public squares. By turning the piece into a theatrical text, Fo stresses the brutal sexual oppression the tax collector imposes upon the woman, a servant girl, when he says he may even be willing to pay the "difensa" of "dumili' agostari" or 2,000 gold coins ("Rosa fresca," 91)—an allusion to what noblemen used to pay the families of raped girls in order to avoid prosecution. Fo concludes that the verses were probably composed by a social critic who wanted to draw attention to abuses of the poor.

In "Nascita del villano" (Birth of the Peasant), another of *Mistero buffo's* vignettes, Fo shows how the powerful control the poor with literature, defining the lower classes by the stories they tell about them. In Fo's version of Creation, Adam refuses to lend his rib for the creation of the peasant who is to do the master's unpleasant work; God therefore creates him from an ass's fart. Under the guise of religious instruction, the master teaches the peasant that his lot on earth is to be vulgar and repellent, though he has a soul, through which he can transcend his misery. However, an angel tells the peasant he has no soul, thus revealing the master's blackmail. The pungent satire and exaggerated low condition of the peasant's birth were designed to show the factory workers watching Fo how they lose control of their lives by accepting their bosses' stories, their oppressors' view of the world. In Fo's opinion, the powerful classes also use religion to control the poor, and he makes the Catholic Church the subject of a vicious invective in the vignette titled "Bonifacio VIII," the most celebrated single episode of *Mistero buffo.* Beginning this section with a lecture on medieval history exalting the utopian movements of the period, Fo pits this idealized background against a portrayal of the infamous pope. As Bonifacio is preparing for a ceremony, Christ appears, turning the rite into an interrogation, as the Son of God questions the pontiff about an orgy of 1301 involving bishops, prostitutes, and cardinals which Bonifacio had organized. Fo does not act out Christ's role on stage; spectators "see" him only through Bonifacio's physical reactions and words. Eventually Christ kicks Bonifacio for his pretense of not having committed any sins. Christ thus becomes a judge who punishes the pope and, by implication, the entire Church hierarchy.

This condemnation of the Church is extended to the present pontiff, as Fo embodies Pope John Paul II and mocks his right-wing ideas. Spectators see John Paul II jetting around the world like some superman endeavoring to "help" the needy. Ultimately, through a pretended slip of the tongue, Fo confuses Bonifacio and John Paul II, then returns to the person of Bonifacio, who, despite the dressing down he has received from Jesus himself, continues his blasphemies. Even divine intervention, Fo suggests, cannot end the oppression. If there is going to be a solution, it must take place outside the theater, as the audience, having been made aware of the problem, takes action in real life.

Although Fo sympathizes with the lives of poor people, he does not present them idealistically. In "Moralita del cieco e dello zoppo" (Morality of the Blind and the Lame), for example, neither the Blind nor the Lame wants to run into Christ, for fear that He might perform miracles on them and remove their income-producing afflictions. If that were to happen, they would have to get jobs with masters. As in the Bonifacio vignette, Christ does not actually appear but is instead "seen" as a presence which both the Blind and the Lame try to avoid. Through their actions and words he is also "seen" by the audience.

Poor people are also presented realistically in "Nozze di Canaan" (The Marriage at Cana), wherein a Drunkard and an Archangel vie for the right to tell the story, reminding us once again that there is more than one way to tell any tale, even one we have heard all our lives. Eventually the Archangel is driven off stage as the Drunkard plucks away at his plumes. When the Drunkard tells the familiar tale, his emphasis is on the delight of the feast, the food and drink, and other physical needs, and on the "tragedy" when the wine eventually turns into vinegar. For the Drunkard, wine solves everything and would have even prevented the fall of mankind. If Adam had had a glass of wine in his hand, he would not have fallen from grace.

In "Lazzaro" (Lazarus) a similar emphasis on the common people's world is shown. Here Fo plays the roles of mercenary, gatekeeper, sardine seller, and a man renting chairs, as well as many members of the crowd, including one who screams he has been robbed, as they all witness the miracle of Lazarus' revivification. Fo stresses again the secular qualities of the piece and of the crowd observing the miracle, as spectators see even at the end when someone comments on Lazarus' rotting and offensive-smelling body.

Although Fo presents the world of the poor in a realistic manner, stressing in part the positive aspects, he nevertheless does not allow the spectator to forget the injustices. To create a just world, the poor need help, specifically a Christ-like figure. For Fo, the giullare or jester must fill this role. In "La nascita del giullare" (The Birth of the Jester) Fo paints an exaggerated view of the poor person's adversary. A peasant who has found a mountain and cultivated its land is robbed of all his efforts' rewards by a landowner, who also rapes his wife in front of him and his children. Seeking revenge, the peasant is stopped by his wife, who soon leaves him, and his children also die. Alone, with nothing to live for, he decides to hang himself, but a passerby, who turns out to be Christ, asks him for water. Eventually Christ kisses the peasant and saves him, giving him a gift: a language which will cut like a knife and which he will be able to use against the masters to crush them. Christ turns the peasant into a giullare and instructs him to spread the message of his oppression. Thus the mission is not religious but political, and Christ brings not a message of peace but a sword. However, the hero does not know how to act and does not have to, for Fo, as always, expects his audience to act, on the outside, in real life. His lack of convention is always a political technique, never a literary flaw.

Fo's giullare serves the people, entertains them, but especially uses satire to show them their condition and spur them to action. As Sogliuzzo asserts, Fo's giullare is not based on the commedia dell'arte (72). Fo sees the comics of the commedia as having become part of the establishment. From the point of view of content, the comics of the commedia dell'arte were reactionary, because they had cleaned up their acts to please the court and the bourgeoisie. Yet there was another tradition of comics within the commedia dell'arte which is not part of the official history; these comedians performed not at court but rather in public taverns, in town squares and in even lowlier locales. Binni asserts that it is this unofficial repertory of the giullari that Fo attempts to recover (52). It is in this tradition that Fo sees himself as a giullare, someone who "nasceva dal popolo e dal popolo prendeva la rabbia per ridarla ancora al popolo perche prendesse coscienza della propria condizione" (was born from the people and from the people he would seize their rage to give it back to the people so that they could become aware of their own condition; *Mistero buffo*).

Ironically, early in his career Fo worked in the more well-known tradition of the commedia dell'arte—as jester of the powerful. He has described on many occasions his failed experience with being a giullare of the bourgeoisie. He and his wife

Franca Rame, with their Fo-Rame Theater Company, enjoyed great popular success both on stage and on television, but their audience consisted of people who were part of the establishment, unable to comprehend or accept their radical ideas. Thus, in 1959, with Italy's left-center government opening national Italian television to artists from the Left, Fo was invited to be part of the extremely popular musical review Canzonissima, which boasted a viewership of up to fifteen million across Italy. Fo's sketches included satires on real-estate speculation and on the dehumanizing working conditions in factories, but the government found his subject matter unacceptable. After the eighth program, his sketches were censored, and soon he was fired for refusing to obey the censors and banished from Italian national television for fourteen years.

Fo, as giullare, needed an audience that allowed him creative independence and at the same time accepted his revolutionary messages. In 1968, after considerable success in commercial theater, he began looking for this audience. The year 1968 was, of course, a turbulent one, politically and culturally. The demonstrations in Berkeley spread to Paris and eventually to Italy. This political activism also affected theater. Supported in part by ARCI, the cultural wing of the Italian Communist Party, Fo and Rame created a new company, Nuova Scena, and began staging their plays in such public venues as soccer stadiums, gyms, circus tents, and case del popolo (communist cultural centers) to audiences that may have never previously attended the theater. Fo now sees himself as Lungo, the protagonist in his first play, *Gli arcangeli non giocano al flipper* (1959; Eng. Archangels Don't Play Pinball), when he says to Antonia, his girlfriend, that since noblemen don't exist any more, he himself makes his low-class buddies laugh; he is their jester. Although this worked for a while, even the limitations imposed on Fo by the communists were too restrictive, and he eventually set up his own theater company, La Comune, in an abandoned building in Milan. But now, to be able to create, Fo needed not only the right audience but the right text as well. *Mistero buffo* was that text.

Although a written version of the play exists, Fo re-creates the work every time he stages it, based on what he perceives to be the audience's needs. For Fo, a theatrical text is like a musical score, with its rhythms, silences, and pauses. Little is gained from reading a score, because the work comes to life only in performance. *Mistero buffo* gives Fo the freedom to create on stage, without any political strings attached, whether from the Left or the Right. He is alone on a bare stage, wearing a black sweater, with no lighting effects, continually changing characters, going in and out of roles, the spareness of the stage setting reflecting the poverty of his audience. The effects are all created by allusions and gestures. The audience must be active and involved. In the initial performances of *Mistero buffo*, Fo would start with a lecture on the Middle Ages and would show slides of paintings and drawings of the period to give an aura of authenticity to his material. Eventually, he dropped this artifice and introduced what have become "interventi"—discussions with the audience about the different vignettes and how they relate to current events.

Unlike television, where viewers see everything laid out in front of them, Fo's audiences must participate actively with their imagination and especially with their discussions once the performance is over. He expects them to continue thinking even the day after, when they go back to work in their factories. The performance never entirely ends. Television viewers, on the other hand, have everything set before their eyes, yet go back to work with nothing in their heads, ready to be exploited again, becoming merely means of production.

Ironically, *Mistero buffo* did end up on Italian television. It was broadcast in 1977, the same year Franco Zeffirelli directed his celebrated *Jesus of Nazareth,* creating an inevitable comparison between the two artists' vision of Jesus. Zeffirelli criticized Fo's vision of Christ because of its overtly political qualities. Fo's Christ is human and tells people to have fun, not to wait for paradise, but also to take an active role in the struggle on this earth. Fo replied that Zeffirelli's pious and meek Christ made as clear a political statement as his own: by bolstering the power of the church and the state, Zeffirelli had simply created a right-wing Jesus.

The *Osservatore Vatican,* the Vatican newspaper, called *Mistero buffo* the most blasphemous show in history and accused Fo of ideological violence targeting the religious values of Italians but aiming really at the disintegration of the Italian state (quoted in *Avvenire*). But if the Vatican believed that Fo had gone as far as he could in attacking Italian institutions and the political system, they were wrong. One year after *Mistero buffo,* in *Morte accidentale di un anarchico,* Fo struck directly at the system's heart. *Morte accidentale di un anarchico* is structurally a more "traditional" play than is *Mistero buffo,* in that there are many characters, requiring a number of actors. The play is based on the death of Giuseppe Pinelli, a railway worker accused of having set off a bomb at Milan's Banca Nazionale dell'Agricoltura on 12 December 1969. The explosion killed sixteen people and wounded an additional eighty-four. After three days of interrogation, Pinelli "flew" out of a fifth-floor window at Milan's police headquarters. The government explained his death as a suicide provoked by his "guilt."

In the play Fo presents a grotesque farce which reveals the contradictions between the police officers' statements and their actions. Assuming the role of a Matto or Maniac, loose in police headquarters, Fo conducts an investigation into what might have really happened. By pretending to be, in turn, various figures of authority—psychiatrist, professor, magistrate, bishop, forensics expert—the Maniac forces officials to re-create the events with the purpose of showing the inconsistencies in the official reports of Pinellli's "leap" and to confess their responsibility in the anarchist's death.

At the very beginning of the play the Superintendent interrogates the Matto, who confesses his mental illness and explains it as "istrionamania . . . mania dei personaggi" (histrionic mania . . . mania of impersonating characters). He acknowledges having received his training in a number of mental institutions. Kicked out of the office, the Maniac eventually sneaks back in and continues to impersonate different officials. After stealing a magistrate's coat and briefcase, he questions the police as if he were reopening an inquiry into the death of the anarchist. As the Magistrate, the Maniac corrects the police versions of the events. The "Magistrate" puts the police into the position in which the anarchist had found himself—having to explain what happened. In essence, he interrogates them. He even forces them to the window and tells them to jump, as they had probably done to the anarchist.

Eventually Fo pulls back when it becomes evident that the police were guilty of the anarchist's death and suggests that the police are really being used as scapegoats by the government. Here Fo attacks further by pointing a finger at the government as a whole. In essence, he uses one part of the establishment against another (*Morte accidentale,* epilogue). Thus the Maniac-Magistrate will help the police extricate themselves by aiding them in the invention of acts of humanity toward the anarchist, such as offering him chewing-gum.

It is very easy to see through the Maniac's and the police officers' farce, but such lighter aspects of the play help balance the serious and tragic tones. For example, the Constable and the Matto try to concoct a story to explain how the police attempted to keep the anarchist from jumping: they held his foot, and the fact that they have the shoe that came off when he jumped bears witness to their efforts to save him. Unfortunately, the body was discovered on the ground with both shoes still on. But no matter, the "Magistrate" says; the anarchist must have been wearing three shoes. The system is quite reasonable, Fo suggests, if your standard is a madman's logic.

And the system is more than willing to accept insane logic when this suits its purpose. By the time a Giornalista (Reporter) enters and begins asking questions, the police have already been made aware that the Maniac is not the forensics expert he claims to be. However, his explanations support their case—his madness is useful—and so they not only allow him to continue acting out his farce for the media's benefit, but they also urge the real forensics expert to play along with him, to back up his crazy stories. Still, Fo knows that the one who tells the story has the power, and handing control of the story over to a madman is not a wise choice—as the police discover when the Maniac begins to support the reporter's suggestion that there are obvious contradictions in the police report on the anarchist's death. In the end, the system's willingness to go along with any lie, any insane story, as long as it allows them to keep their power, defeats the system.

Although Fo certainly pokes fun at the police officials, he does not present them merely as comic figures but rather as devious abusers of power. Neither does he show great sympathy for the anarchist, whom he views as inept. On stage there are no clear heroes or villains, for Fo's primary interest is not in assigning blame but rather in opening a political dialogue. The Maniac, at the play's end, reveals that he has been recording the entire proceeding and threatens to send copies to the media, the political parties, and the government. He threatens, in essence, to do what Fo has just done: to put the insanity, injustice, and hypocrisy of the system before the people; to show the absurdity of the powerful to the powerless in his audience and let them decide what to do about it.

In the first two years after its premiere *Morte accidentale* was staged approximately two hundred times and more than 300,000 people saw the play. With each staging, Fo created a new and original work. However, his most original single performance was a staging of *Mistero buffo* in Vicenza. When the production was interrupted by rain one

Thousands of striking metal and rubber workers join in a demonstration for higher wages, Italy, 1969

evening, Fo started talking with the thunder, addressing it as the voice of God and asking for lightning. Lightning in fact came, after a particularly provocative question to God. The spectators remained riveted to their seats, mesmerized, as Fo took a chance that nature or God would cooperate with him to create the desired effect. That night God himself was a jester, awarding the risk-taking Dario Fo a dramatic and most unexpected prize.

Source: Domenico Maceri, "Dario Fo: Jester of the Working Class," in *World Literature Today*, Vol. 72, No. 1, Winter 1998, pp. 9–14.

Joseph Farrell

In the following essay excerpt, Farrell examines issues associated with translating Fo's works. Accidental Death of an Anarchist, *in particular, presents a challenge because of its roots in contemporary social criticism, but it nonetheless has been Fo's most successfully translated play.*

A translator is conventionally expected to content himself with a condition of self-effacing invisibility, which surpasses anything even Victorian parents once imposed on their offspring. The good

"THE WAY DARIO FO'S TRANSLATORS HAVE COME TO BE VIEWED CONFIRMS THIS RULE. THEIR SIN IS TO HAVE MADE THEMSELVES NOTICED."

translator should be neither seen nor heard. He should fade into the background, and should expect that if his presence is noted, it is as a prelude to some censure or reproach. A translator will receive attention only when responsible for some gaffe, transgression or solecism which will require discussion and correction at a later date, once the guests have withdrawn.

The way Dario Fo's translators have come to be viewed confirms this rule. Their sin is to have made themselves noticed. Fo, as is endlessly repeated, is the most frequently performed living playwright in the world today, which is another way of saying that he has more translators than any other playwright in the world today. The nature of the performed versions of Fo's work has aroused a high level of controversy, and it appears that there has been greater interest in the process of transposing a Fo text from its original Italian into other languages than has been accorded the same process with any other writer. The nature of the translated text employed for production, principally the perceived confusion of roles between translator and adapter, has puzzled and enraged critics. Fo himself has contributed to the general air of disapproval. As he told an interviewer, in reply to a question about the productions he had seen:

> I have seen few good works. Some were respectable, others appalling, either on account of the actors, the director or the text itself, which had been supposedly corrected but often cheapened.

Fo has himself protested vociferously about specific productions, and specific published versions of his work. Although neither Dario Fo nor Franca Rame speak English, they subject translations identified as suspect to rigid, if idiosyncratic, scrutiny by having the debated translation re-translated into Italian. This process creates difficulties of its own, as the resemblance between an original text and a retranslation is comparable to that between a bullet in the barrel of a gun and a bullet which has ricocheted off a steel plate. A further level of difficulty is added by the nature of Fo's scripts. When they deal with contemporary political topics, as was the case with *Accidental Death of an Anarchist,* they are subject to regular rewrites in the light of changing circumstances and new developments. And in all cases, his plays are subject to reshaping in the light of audience response or of reconsideration by Fo or Rame. On at least one occasion, a translator was censured because his translation was based on a fifth draft, but once re-translated, the comparison was made to the fourth draft. Various cuts and additions which were put down to the translator's intrusive, slapdash or high-handed disregard for the original were actually the result of rewrites undertaken by the author.

Obscenity or vulgarity are especially delicate areas. Personal relations scarcely ever feature in Fo's work. Both Fo and Rame are scrupulous about the language they employ on stage, and in none of Fo's works is there any material which could, in the linguistic register employed, offend the most demanding Calvinist or Carmelite conscience. Even the recent *Zen and the Art of Screwing* conforms to this rule. It was written not by Dario Fo but by his son Jacopo, and Franca Rame performed it because she viewed it as a work which would further the sexual education of the young. On the other hand, in his own play *An Ordinary Day,* Fo features the case of a woman who receives phone calls from other women who believe they are calling some outre analyst. One of the callers is a prostitute who reports that, in an excess of professional pruderie, she has bitten off the testicles and related attachment of one of her clients. For the attachment in question, Fo employed the term coso, an imprecise, colloquial term which translates as "thingummy." In my translation I set aside such nicety and opted for the candid form "prick." This was retranslated in Milan as cazzo and did not pass inspection. It was excised at Franca Rame's insistence with the same ruthlessness the fictional prostitute had demonstrated towards the original offending member. . . .

The central problem with translating and staging Fo is to find a means of expressing and conveying the political fire while respecting the framework of farce. Fo has in various occasions defined his own theatre as combining "riso con rabbia" (laughter with anger) and both elements are of importance. The balancing act requires sensitivity, but the failure even to aim for it has meant that there sometimes seems to be an Italian Fo who walks on lines parallel to, but never quite coinciding with, the tracks on which British Fo, German Fo and French Fo walk.

The need to find such a synthesis of the laughter and the anger in the target language will often require a transcending of the limits normally allowed to translation. It is here that one collides with Fo's supposed supporters. No one has been so crass as to propose outright literalism, but the objection to the standard renderings of his work outside Italy takes the form of bewilderment over the (omni) presence of the adapter. One could note, in parenthesis, the curious fact that none of the exponents of translation studies have been able to incorporate the adapter into any theoretical framework. "It hardly seems useful to debate whether or not adaptation is still translation," write Basil Hatim and Ian Mason in their useful work on translation. It may not be useful in general, but it is indispensable in the case of Dario Fo.

There can be no dispute over the facts. However they have been presented in programme notes or in published editions, few of the works that have been staged, most especially in English, have been translations. The problem is to establish whether an adaptation is as welcome as a virus infecting a healthy organism, or whether it can function as a tonic restoring a waning life. Some definitions are in order. A translation is a process of reproduction, replication or transference in which the changes are purely linguistic and do not involve wider redirection of the plot or switches of setting, epoch or culture. To be such, a translation must eschew alterations to structure and characterisation, and must respect the more intangible system of values underlying the source text. This does not involve literalism but it does involve a rehabilitation of the much-maligned concept of fidelity, in the sense given to that term by George Steiner in what remains the most profound analysis of the nature and aims of translation:

> The translator, the exegetist, the reader is faithful to his text, makes his response responsible, only when he endeavours to restore the balance of forces, of integral presence, which his appropriative comprehension has disrupted. Fidelity is ethical, but also, in the full sense, economic. By virtue of tact, and tact intensified is moral vision, the translator-interpreter creates a condition of significant exchange.

The distorting presence of the translator cannot be avoided, but of itself that does not negate the validity of an aspiration to fidelity founded on an awareness of, and an attempt to maintain or restore, a previously existing balance. The nature of that balance in Fo will be discussed later.

An adaptation, on the other hand, is free of the restraints of fidelity, however it is defined. The adapter may aspire to be a co-creater, and perhaps it is helpful to view his work as the equivalent of the musical variation on a theme rather than as an operation of finding linguistic equivalences. There may be, for instance, parallels between various cults in the society described by Petronius in his *Satyricon* and the "New Age" beliefs held by certain sections of society as the Millennium approaches, but any writer who published a modern *Satyricon* updated to focus on such sects in New York or London would not be considered, and would not consider himself, to be producing a translation, any more than did James Joyce when he wrote *Ulysses.* At times, this process may have gone so far that the adaptation is a new work, in direct conflict with the original. The playwright David Hare expressed his distaste for Arthur Miller's adaptation of Ibsen's *An Enemy of the People* on the grounds that Miller had been so shocked by the anti-democratic stance adopted by the protagonist that he had in consequence arrogated to himself the right to soften that position. Miller could reply that his operation had been transparent.

The suggestion has been made that Fo has suffered from similar distortions without the benefit of transparency. "The problem in Fo's case," writes David L. Hirst, for whom it is indeed a problem, "is that the translations made in Britain have—with one exception—been effected by a combination of translator and adapter." Tony Mitchell similarly entitles his consideration of English language versions "Adapting Fo," and while he and Hirst agree that only one work escapes general censorship, they disagree over which work that is. For Mitchell that play is *We Can't Pay? We Won't Pay!,* a view Hirst dismisses with a polemical spleen others would find appropriate only when describing the activities of neo-fascist pederasts. Hirst puts forward the case in favour of *Accidental Death of an Anarchist,* which he regards as being "a playing script of immense vitality which exploits to the full the potential of both farce and of witty comedy of manners," even if he is compelled to add that "the adaptation is obliged to follow the implications of its inexorable movement away from its source to a radically different target."

In both intellectual and practical terms, the problems are complex. Certain recent critics have gone so far as to view "subversive intent" as a quality to be prized in a translator and to extol translation as "production" rather than "reproduction," but this is hardly satisfactory. The majority of readers expect to make contact with Dostoevsky and not with his translator when they pick up *Crime and Punishment*. But if fidelity is a goal, fidelity to what? Vladimir Nabokov was forthright. "When the translator sets out to render the 'spirit' and not the mere sense of the text, . . . he begins to traduce his author." Nabokov's views appeared as a foreword to his translation of Pushkin, but the situation of a playwright is more difficult. Fo himself makes a distinction between "theatre" and "dramatic literature." He consigned Pier Paolo Pasolini to the domain of "dramatic literature" on the grounds that he had no feeling for the rhythms of theatre, no sense of dramatic tension, no understanding of the primacy of the actor, no grasp of the demands of immediate communication with an audience in real time. If all theatrical texts occupy an indeterminate, intermediate space between literature and performance, not all lie on the same meridian between those two poles. Fo's preference is for those plays that incline towards performance and away from literature, as his own do. Put differently, Fo's scripts have much in common with the canovaccio of commedia dell'arte: they are, of course, more than outline plots intended as a prompt for improvisation, but they are less than the finished, polished scripts produced by such other Nobel Prize–winning dramatists as Bernard Shaw or Eugene O'Neill. The "mere sense" Nabokov referred to could not be, for Fo, something that can find expression solely on the printed page. Their "interpretation" requires a subsequent act of enhancement. Where Shaw insisted that his printed plays be furnished by the full apparatus of stage directions to assist readers who would, he wrote, be always more numerous than spectators, Fo tended towards a view he attributed to Brecht:

> Brecht once said, rightly, of Shakespeare: "A pity it reads so beautifully. It is its only defect, but a great one." And he was right. However paradoxical it may seem, a genuine work of theatre should not at all appear a pleasure when read: its worth should only become apparent on the stage.

The achievement of that pleasure requires the collaboration of those equipped to detect and convey it in its fullness. Neither a translator nor a director can claim to be faithful to Fo if they limit themselves to the beauty of the words on the page. Works so deeply theatrical by nature as are Fo's only reach ripeness when they are "interpreted," or "translated" into production by other hands. Those involved in bringing a play to stage are, as has been often remarked, involved in a work of translation, or adaptation, in the prime sense. Theatre is essentially ensemble creativity, with the writer primus inter pares, and perhaps not even primus. As was noted by George Steiner, the Italian and French word interprete can be used to denote either an actor or an interpreter. The poet or novelist has to contend with no comparable intermediaries. The ensemble creative process, with its concomitant legitimisation of intervention by other minds into the communication between writer and audience, has been a source of some resentment to certain Italian dramatists, even of the highest stature. Leonardo Sciascia wrote three plays and claimed he would have continued writing plays had he not "clashed with the figure of the director." The director was an obstacle. . . .

Pirandello considered theatre a bastard genre, which dethroned the writer's text. No one could say anything comparable about Dario Fo, who if not a figlio d'arte by birth, is the all-round man of theatre, for whom the script occupies no royal position. He belongs to the quintessentially Italian tradition of the actor-author, and part of the reason that the conferring of the Nobel Prize aroused so much controversy in Italy may be that in his own country Fo is considered primarily an actor, whereas abroad he is viewed primarily as an author. In principle he accepts a view which makes the script the written equivalent of a stage prop, to be reworked as needed—or at least when another writer is involved. If it is granted that theatre requires a variety of acts of translation, from a number of sources, there remains the fundamental question of whose act of interpretation can be accorded legitimacy. . . .

In 1981, an English-language version of Fo's own *Accidental Death of an Anarchist* had its premiere at Wyndham's Theatre in London's West End. The company was a left-wing fringe company, Belt and Braces, and although the translation was done by Gillian Hanna, the main influence was that of Gavin Richards, who was adapter, director and lead actor. Fo was present on the opening night and was enraged at what he regarded as a misinterpretation of his work. Several people tried to explain to him the differences between British and Italian traditions of comic writing and performance, attempting to placate him—for he needed placating—by talking of the vibrancy of a music hall tradition which had provided the inspiration of the British production. Was Fo, of all authors, entitled to his annoyance?

In the same year, 1981, the Teatro stabile in Turin put on a work by Dario Fo entitled *L'opera dello sghignazzo* (The Raucous Opera). In the programme and in the subsequent published version, it was described as being based on "John Gay's *Beggar's Opera,* and on some ideas from my son Jacopo." Acknowledgement was also made of the contribution of poets and rock singers including Allen Ginsberg, Patti Smith, Frank Zappa and Donovan. There was no reference to Bertolt Brecht or to his work, known in English as *The Threepenny Opera.*

In reality, the Berliner Ensemble, who invited Fo to direct a new production of Brecht's *Threepenny Opera,* initiated the project. When they saw what Fo intended doing, and the modification he intended introducing into Brecht's text, they withdrew in horror and refused him permission to make any use of Brechtian material for any production anywhere. Fo professed himself mystified and outraged by this elevation of Brecht's play into an untouchable sacred text. He devised a strategy to circumvent the legal veto imposed by Brecht's heirs. As is well known, Brecht's play was itself a reworking of John Gay's original, but John Gay is dead and gone and has no heirs to threaten recourse to law. When he was invited by the theatre directors in Turin to stage his work there, Dario Fo did what Brecht had done: he went back to Gay's *The Beggar's Opera* and recast it in his own way. Or so he said, and no one could challenge him.

In his introduction to the published version of *L'opera dello sghignazzo,* Fo justified his original script by reference to Brecht's own theories and went on to provide what appears a manifesto for translators, at least translators of Fo. . . .

Of course Fo is a creative genius who operates within a tradition and reshapes the tradition by virtue of his intervention. He plunders the work of his predecessors, as artists have always done. "Immature poets imitate; mature poets steal," was T. S. Eliot's formulation. Manet reshaped, or stole from, Poussin, as did Picasso with Velazquez, Dante with Virgil, Eliot with Dante and Fo with everyone. Nevertheless, as regards the views he has expressed on responsibilities towards authors, it is hard to avoid the conclusion that there is some form of inconsistency involved. As director or interpreter, Fo takes to himself the role of inspired and liberating contributor to the creative process, but wants his own directors and translators to be artisans, to be hewers of his wood and drawers of his water. It is not just a question of the superior claims of "genius." The paradox is that it is anything but clear that his translators would be doing his theatre justice by assuming the workaday role he confers on them. Fo the actor is the best translator of Fo the author, but in his absence the job has to be done by someone else. Translation of Fo requires audience-centred techniques, which do not necessarily coincide with the author-centred translation he himself prefers. . . .

To say that some modification or enrichment of the sort which Fo himself routinely brings to his own work by his on-stage presence is not to say that all existing translations or adaptations can be sanctioned. If it is agreed that the adaptation of Fo's *Il ratto della Francesca* into *Abducting Diana* was a work of unredeemed crassness, that the attribution of those moronic names to the Cardinals in *The Pope and the Witch* was a symptom of a profound misunderstanding which was made manifest in the resultant production, it has also to be conceded that the "faithful" translation of *An Ordinary Day* did Fo's theatre no favours. One of the problems with the latter was that it provided no guidance to directors who have now a stereotyped image of Fo and his theatre, and who, being unwilling to respect the darker tone which emerged in that play, insisted on presenting it in the style of the slapstick of his earlier years.

No matter whether the starting point is the farce or the politics, there is the same need with Fo as with other, more obviously "serious" playwrights, to identify the inner vision and to respect that vision as well as the quirks, oddities, idiosyncrasies and comic predilections of the surface. However paradoxical it may appear, this has been best done by such works as the translation-adaptation that is *Accidental Death of an Anarchist,* now become the all-purpose protest play from Tokyo to London. In that work, the cultural references have been altered to allow it to refer to the plight of airport protesters in Japan or spy-scandals in Britain, but this has prevented it suffering the fate of *Uncle Tom's Cabin* or *Gulliver's Travels,* both works that began life as political satires. The international success of that play is a testimony to the theatrical mastery of Fo, to his skill in imagining original theatrical situations and to his expertise in devising structures marrying the extra-theatrical passion to appropriate theatrical techniques, but also to the value of a process which, combining translation and adaptation, conveys all these qualities to other cultures. The result might be, for purists, a variation on a theme, but the music is Fo's.

Source: Joseph Farrell, "Variations on a Theme: Respecting Dario Fo," in *Modern Drama*, Vol. 41, No. 1, Spring 1998, pp. 19–29.

Christopher Hitchens

In the following essay written after the announcement of Fo's winning the Nobel Prize, Hitchens reviews the events that inspired Accidental Death of an Anarchist.

A half-dark stage. Sound of breaking glass. Enter burglar. His flashlight shows a living room filled with expensive things. Phone rings. Pause. Rings again. Burglar picks up phone. Very long pause. Burglar, into phone: "How many times have I told you not to call me at work?"

Thus the opening of Dario Fo's *Some Burglars Have Good Intentions,* as summarized by Ben Sonnenberg in his pithy and prescient 1993 Washington Post recommendation of Fo for the Nobel Prize in Literature. *Some Burglars* forms the first part of a quartet of one-act farces collectively titled *Thieves, Dummies and Naked Women.* With his wife, the dauntless Franca Rame, Fo has written more than sixty plays for stage and small screen and has acquired all the right enemies, from the Vatican to the State Department (which excluded him from this country for many years on the grounds of his undeniably subversive associations).

I met him in London in 1980, when he was attending the West End opening of his political masterpiece, *Accidental Death of an Anarchist.* Many of the tributes to Fo last month were of that vaguely condescending type with which the establishment often signals its broad-mindedness in recognizing a "rebel" or "gadfly" or "maverick." The Nobel committee, indeed, spoke of the irreverence of the "jesters of the Middle Ages" ("irreverent" is another contented pat-on-the-back dismissal, not unlike "provocative"). But the fact about Fo is that he is a ruthlessly realistic and practical fellow as well. You would not know, from the patronizing plaudits that he has garnered, that the entire plot of *Accidental Death of an Anarchist* has just been vindicated in real time. But so it has.

On December 12, 1969, a huge bomb exploded in the Piazza Fontana in Milan, killing sixteen people and opening the "strategy of tension" by which Italy's extreme right sought to combat the "hot autumn" of rebellion that began that year. Three days later, an anarchist militant named Giuseppe Pinelli fell to his death from an upper story of the Milan police headquarters. He was being vigorously interrogated, on suspicion of involvement in the Piazza Fontana outrage, by agents of Chief Superintendent Luigi Calabresi. Superintendent Calabresi, in his turn, was a member of the Italian

> "MANY OF THE TRIBUTES TO FO LAST MONTH WERE OF THAT VAGUELY CONDESCENDING TYPE WITH WHICH THE ESTABLISHMENT OFTEN SIGNALS ITS BROAD-MINDEDNESS IN RECOGNIZING A 'REBEL' OR 'GADFLY' OR 'MAVERICK.'"

"pare-state," linked to putschist elements in the army and the intelligence services and also to open and covert supporters of Italy's fascist movement. If you are old enough to recall the climate of the time you will remember that anything—including a strong blackshirt element in state power—was considered preferable to the apertura sinistra, or "opening to the left." Thus the "suicide" of Pinelli was just one of the many things that had to be swallowed in order to keep Italy safe for the cold war. Dario Fo concluded that Pinelli had not killed himself but had rather been suicidato—"suicided"—as part of a cover-up.

The play, it is true, does draw somewhat on the tactics of medieval revelry, in that the main protagonist is a fool or "maniac" who is so naive that he doubts the official story, and so rash and stupid that he says so out loud. Others on the Italian left made the same point in more investigative and forensic ways. The newspaper *Lotta Continua* ("The Struggle Continues"), under the brilliant editorship of Adriano Sofri, printed a number of damning exposes and nailed Superintendent Calabresi as the murderer and fascist and perjurer that he undoubtedly was. On the morning of May 17, 1972, some person or persons shot the loathsome Calabresi dead. There were those who said that *Lotta Continua,* by its incendiary talk of people's courts and street justice, had encouraged the attack. But no connection was ever shown.

Since that time, a series of trials and exposes has established that the Piazza Fontana bomb, the 1980 bomb at the Bologna railway station and a series of other gruesome atrocities were the work of the extreme right and its Mafia and Vatican and police allies. (If some burglars have good intentions, in Fo's world and in the real world, some guardians of the peace emphatically do not.) *Lotta Continua,* both as an organization and a newspaper, has disbanded. But a plea-bargain-seeking former militant has accused Adriano Sofri, now 54 and a respected writer and lecturer, of having "ordered" Calabresi's murder. In January last, just four months before the statute of limitations would have applied to the crime, the ramshackle Italian courts found him guilty of it. Sentenced to twenty-two years, he will probably die in prison if the verdict is upheld.

All the evidence in the case—the bullets, the getaway car—has long since been destroyed. The self-interest of the sole and uncorroborated witness is self-evident. More than 150,000 Italians have signed a petition, drawn up by a former president of the Constitutional Court, calling for a pardon. (Sofri, characteristically, says he wants a new trial and not a pardon because you can only be pardoned for something you actually did.) And Dario Fo, who once described himself as a member of the "unofficial left," has put his Nobel Prize purse at the service of the campaign.

So the long, long run of *Accidental Death of an Anarchist* continues. It has now surpassed the success of *Mistero Buffo* ("Comic Mystery"), which the Roman Catholic hierarchy invigoratingly described as "the most blasphemous show in the history of television." It is outperforming the great Dario Fo censorship marathon, which kept him off the airwaves of his native land between 1962 and 1977. Taken up by the strolling players of the class struggle and the democracy movement, it has acquired a life of its own as street theater and popular psychodrama. Its next act, entirely unscripted, is a fast unto death proposed by Adriano Sofri. The variations are plentiful, but the theme of power, and those who have it and those who do not, is consistent. Some subjects are so serious that they have to be left in the safekeeping of satirists and comedians.

Source: Christopher Hitchens, "Lotta continua," in *Nation,* Vol. 265, No. 15, November 10, 1997, p. 8.

Mimi D'Aponte

In the following essay excerpt, D'Aponte provides an overview of Fo's career and works, including his reception in the United States.

> Clowns are grotesque blashpemers against all our pieties. That's why we need them. They're our alter egos.
>
> —Dario Fo, Cambridge, May 1987

" IN *ACCIDENTAL DEATH OF AN ANARCHIST* THE FRIGHTENING SPECTER OF INSTITUTIONAL 'JUSTICE' APPLIED TO AN INNOCENT VICTIM IS RAISED TO THE HIGH ART OF GRISLY GROTESQUE AS AN ACTUAL CASE BECOMES THE FOCUS OF FARCE."

Americans writing about theatre have been pronouncing Dario Fo's work extraordinary, whether for performance or political reasons, or for both. "For the past decade," claimed Joel Schechter in 1985, "Dario Fo has been Europe's most popular political satirist." "So many theatres have included Fo in their recent seasons," wrote Ron Jenkins in 1986, "that he has become the most-produced contemporary Italian playwright in the U.S." American producers interested in social satire seem to have become less leery of this zany Italian genius who publicly thanked his "fellow actor," Ronald Reagan, for the marvelous promotion afforded his work when the State Department denied him an American visa for several years. . . .

To give a full account of Dario Fo's theatrical career would really be tantamount to writing a history of postwar Italy, because his work can only be understood as a continuous, uniquely creative response to the major social and political developments of the past thirty years.

Like Eduardo before him, Fo has been greeted with instant popularity in many countries while being given, initially at least, a somewhat cooler reception in the U.S. The failure, for example, of Eduardo's *Saturday, Sunday and Monday* in 1974 Broadway production despite its huge British success in 1973 seems to have been a virtual blueprint for Fo's British-American experience with *Accidental Death of an Anarchist.* This "grotesque" farce about a "tragic farce" achieved tremendous success in London during 1979–81, only to open and close rapidly on Broadway in Fall of 1984.

What seems clear, however, is that Fo's work has created an ongoing interest in American university and repertory theatres which Eduardo's did not. This is due in part to an increased American awareness of international theatre trends fostered by the academy's more frequent conference and exchange programs, and also perhaps by more frequent mass-media culture coverage. Continued American interest in Fo's work springs also from our desire to stay abreast of such trends: Tony Mitchell, in the first English-language book devoted to Fo, states flatly that by 1978, "Fo was already the most widely performed playwright in world theatre." But it is the fact that Fo and Rame have finally been able to practise their crafts of acting and directing in this country that has led to acclaim in the American theatre about this extraordinary team. . . .

In reviewing *Mistero buffo* for *The New York Times,* Mel Gussow introduced Fo as "an outrageous gadfly" and mentioned Richard Pryor, Father Guido Sarducci and Monty Python by way of comparison. Mr. Gussow concluded with mention of other names:

> With his mobile face and body, he is a cartoon in motion, loping across the stage with the antelopean grace of Jacques Tati, doing a Jackie Gleason away-we-go to demonstrate the Italian perfection of the art of women-watching.

Both sets of references are on target. Fo's performance was unforgettable because it conjured up a complex battery of historical and cultural perspectives, while simultaneously satirizing their contingent political realities. Clad in black work-day jersey and slacks and sharing a bare stage with only his translator, Fo created in the mind's eye of his audience chaotic crowds, lavish costumes, and dramatic conflicts resolved by the machinations of a laughing clown-narrator in favor of those without power.

Fo's formidable powers of persuasion through laughter illuminate his on-stage persona. These same powers are seen from another perspective in his work as teacher and director. Most immediately obvious is the appeal of the comradeship and community which Fo creates about him, beginning with that strong emotional, intellectual, and artistic partnership which he and Franca Rame, his wife, have shared for thirty-four years. This partnership extends not only to their own acting company, currently La Comune of Milan, but also to the manner in which Fo and Rame interact with any company. While Western theatre is by definition an art form organized in hierarchical fashion, Fo's concept of how to work in the theatre appears consistently egalitarian. This philosophy ultimately translates into a specific reality: everything which appears on stage and/or takes place on stage is in some fashion touched by Fo. Whatever the form of this nurturing, its manner is one of co-authorship, of "we" rather than of "I" and "you."

Along with this comradeship comes a powerful charisma which Dario Fo possesses and uses automatically, effortlessly in his quest for the ideal performance of his troupe. He is a director whose every syllable and step on stage are noted by everyone, near and far. Members of the American Repertory Theatre, a young, vital professional company with excellent credentials, spoke glowingly of their learning under Fo's tutelage during rehearsals for *Archangels Don't Play Pinball* in Spring 1987. "Dario exerts an amazing influence—he has a way of working with actors. No one at ART has ever attained this popularity." "I want to get a grant to follow Dario Fo around. This is the guy I've been waiting to learn from all my life." A visiting university director added, "I'm on leave this year. I'd be in Milan if Dario were in Milan. I'm in Cambridge became he's here." Such remarks take on additional weight when one realizes that they represent English-speaking theatre folk describing their Italian-speaking theatre mentor. Dario's ability to communicate goes beyond the limitation of language.

Then there is the power of example. Fo the performer is able to illustrate what Fo the director has to say. Fo and Rame conducted five theatre workshops in London in late spring 1983 the transcripts of which were subsequently published and translated. The student/teacher exchanges during these sessions underscore the credibility in the theatre of a director who practices in his own performances what he preaches to his students. For example:

> [*QUESTION*] *When you did the three situations exercise earlier, the only way that we spectators could laugh at the comedy of it was because we already understood the situation, because you had explained it to us. But how, then, if you are the actor, creating the situation, how do you express it without using even more obvious methods of expression?*
>
> [DARIO FO] Theatre has always had *prologues,* even when they are not declared as such. There is an old tradition of theatre in Italy, which had prologues which were really masterpieces. In fact, the rest of the plays has often been lost, and the prologues have remained in their own right. There is, for example, the famous prologue: . . . "Ah, if I could only become invisible." The situation is already presented in it . . . in that one sentence it already gives you the situation. The actor comes on and explains the things he could do if he was invisible. (*He acts out the prologue*)

The enjoyment of watching the persuasive power of Fo's directing and teaching is enhanced by the knowledge that what he offers his actors and students alike is empowerment—empowerment as actors and empowerment as authors. The answer to two questions posed to him demonstrate something of the private Dario Fo's modest character and a sense of the public Fo's ability to teach effortlessly, with "*souplesse.*"

> [*QUESTION*] *What influence do you want your work to have on American theatre?*
>
> [DARIO FO] I don't know.
>
> *What is the connection between political theatre and improvisation?*
>
> The choice of an improvisational form of theatre is already a political one—because improvisational theatre is never finished, never a closed case, always open-ended.
>
> Improvisational theatre is open on a space level. If we are performing in a large theatre, a stadium which seats 5000 in one night and in a factory which accommodates 300 the next, we must improvise, by necessity, and without a dozen rehearsals. Out of necessity we signal to one another and stretch out what we do to fill the stadium or contract it to fit into the factory.
>
> Improvisational theatre is open on an emotional level. Audiences are not the same every evening. Different things have happened to them on a political level. Someone may have been shot, someone may have died: an audience is an emotionally different entity every night. The actor in an improvisational theatre is open to audience mood and builds upon it, using it as a springboard for what he is going to do.
>
> Improvisational theatre is open on an intellectual level. New events happen every day. These events can't be ignored, but must be included, and the old ones, if they are no longer useful, put aside. The commedia dell'arte troupes were often the chroniclers of their times, bringing to their often ill-informed audiences up-dates of what was going on in the country of the audience that evening and of what was going on in outlying countries. Improvisational theatre must be a theatre of ideas, not merely of technique.

Fo's last statement holds the heart of the matter. It is clear that his concept of theatre is both improvisational and political, and it is also clear that he demands a body of knowledge, a challenge to the intellect, from a theatrical event. So do many theatre artists. What is unique about Fo is that, rather than coveting that creative act known as "playwriting" as is traditional, he asks of his actors that they become his co-writers. "After I leave [the actors] must read newspapers every day and listen to and watch news broadcasts every day, and include pertinent material into the *Archangel* performances." When an actor had suggested that perhaps one person be put in charge of updating the text, this was Fo's reply: "No, no, no one has to be in charge—you all do it! Every actor must practice self-discipline, trying out material and judging its effectiveness carefully, eliminating it if audience reaction is not favorable." It is in this manner that Fo empowers his actors to grow, to stretch, to develop, for he invites them not simply to interpret someone else's ideas, but also to initiate their own.

Which brings us to Dario Fo, playwright, produced in translation in the United States. How, given Fo's convictions concerning improvisation about current political events, does this work? A quick production/publication profile offers several revealing statistics. To date there have been American, English-language productions mounted of six full-length works by Fo (*We Won't Pay! We Won't Pay!, Accidental Death of an Anarchist, Almost By Chance A Woman: Elizabeth, Archangels Don't Play Pinball, About Face* and *A Day Like Any Other*) and two full-length works by Fo and Rame (*Orgasmo Adulto Escapes from the Zoo* and *Open Couple*). Since 1979 there have been at least one, but as many as three American productions of these works annually. Fo's plays have been mounted by regional theatres, touring groups, university theatres, Off-Broadway and Broadway producers. In addition to numerous texts imported from Great Britain, there are currently available American publications of five of the works produced here. Plans are in progress for an American translation of Fo's four-hundred-page theoretical work on theatre, *Manuale minimo dell'autore.* Finally, both American journalists and scholars have begun writing about Fo to the extent that their major contribution to an already impressive European bibliography of secondary sources about his work appears imminent.

Each published introduction or preface to a Fo work contains some reference to the need to update or adapt material, while at the same time preserving the playwright's intention. Such directives suggest the problems inherent in revision. "A Note on the Text," which introduces Samuel French's edition of *Accidental Death of an Anarchist,* for example, reads in part:

> For the Arena Stage production and the subsequent Broadway production . . . Nelson [the adaptor] revised the dialogue for the American stage, and added some references to current politics . . . Subsequently, Fo asked for further changes . . . Future productions may require further alteration of political references, unless our President is elected for a life term, and outlives the century.

. . . A perusal of American reaction to Fo's work indicates frequent critical reference, both positive and negative, to the current American politics alluded to during the course of a Fo play. Three writers had three different reactions to this question when they reviewed the Broadway production of *Accidental Death* in 1984:

> The play may have deserved to be successful in Italy, where its dealing with an actual case of police defenestration was doubtless audacious and salutary. But it has far less resonance here, and the manner in which Nelson has dragged in American references is obvious and safe.

> Although it's ostensibly an Italian subject, the play has been given emphatic contemporary American application by adaptor Richard Nelson, whose version includes some hilarious speeches for the masquerading hero about current U.S. politics.

> There are references to the Great Communicator's belief that trees pollute the air and to his habit of sleeping in cabinet meetings. . . . Not all of these jokes take wing, but it is somewhat refreshing on Broadway to hear political subjects mentioned at all.

Despite the ongoing need for relevant revision, *We Won't Pay, Accidental Death,* and *About Face* are, thanks to multiple American productions, "here to stay." These three plays appear to have graduated from the stage of "experimental" or "alternative" theatre and will, I believe, be accepted as an integral part of contemporary international repertory desirable in American theatre schedules. Fo has in essence, during the period 1979–1988, established a base, a modest body of dramatic literature which is recognized by the collective American theatre mind.

This base of three dramatic works realistically represents Fo's social and political concerns while at the same time appropriately casting him as a writer of comedy and satire. In *We Won't Pay,* the richness of which as a drama has been competently described in this journal, the grave social question of economic ineptitude on a national scale is lampooned by the madcap manner in which Mr. everyman worker and Mrs. everywoman wife deal with insufficient salaries and inflationary prices. The hilarity of the piece is caught in the unforgettable image of women leaving the supermarket with goods they have refused to pay for and which they eventually transport as unborn "babies" beneath their coats.

In *Accidental Death of an Anarchist* the frightening specter of institutional "justice" applied to an innocent victim is raised to the high art of grisly grotesque as an actual case becomes the focus of farce. Real-life anarchist Giuseppe Pinelli was arrested in late 1969, erroneously accused of having planted a bomb which killed sixteen people in a Milan bank, and "fell" to his death from a window of the Milan police station. The Fool of Fo's play portrays a mad graduate of many an asylum who arrives to interrogate police hierarchy about this scandal, who stays to re-enact Pinelli's "fall," and who seems to re-appear once again before the horrified police personnel.

In *About Face* the limitations of both management and underdog perspectives on life and love are broadly satirized by a series of fabulous switches of fate. Caricatured Fiat magnate, Gianni Agnelli, becomes, thanks to an auto accident, amnesia, and the wrong plastic surgery, a factory worker in his own plant. He is eventually "exchanged" out of this humdrum existence by both the return of his memory and the co-operation of government officials to whom he writes threatening letters.

In the first two plays the principal key, both to socio-political bite and to hilarity, is the mistaken identity of the protagonist. In *Accidental Death* police officials on stage labor under the delusion that a bureau inspector is creating havoc in their midst, while we in the audience know that a mad, self-styled investigator come from a paradise where real justice reigns is loose on the boards. In *About Face* some characters work to improve the health of someone they take for an injured factory worker, while others discover and then protect the Agnelli identity behind the surgically applied incognito. In *We Won't Pay* series of chaotic misunderstandings pave a double-edged path to social criticism and to side-splitting laughter. In an amazing scene from Act II, the police lieutenant casing the protagonist's flat searches the "pregnant" women he finds there; he is rewarded by imagined blindness when they tell him about a pregnant saint's husband who lost his sight and when, coincidentally, the long-unpaid-for electric lights suddenly dim.

When each play's ruse has been stretched to the most insane absurdity imaginable, Fo snaps us back to epic disengagement, usually through a long-winded speech delivered by a leading character which jars us into remembering a current political problem. In *About Face,* for example, Antonio/Agnelli offers a final diatribe about the power of the state equaling the power of money and caps it with, "So Aldo Moro gets 15 bullets in his gut to protect me." And from the seemingly safe shores of such "reality," we laugh madly at the horrific foibles of human society. . . .

In considering Fo's impact on theatre in the United States, it seems that two developments are taking place, the direction of which, attributable to a variety of forces, is surely Foian. The first is a new awareness, for us, that the actor need not necessarily put his own ideas aside or neglect to have ideas of his own. During his and Franca's London workshop of May 1983, Fo asserted:

> In my opinion it is more important for actors to learn to invent roles for themselves . . . to learn to be authors . . . *all* actors should do this. In my opinion, the most important criterion for any school of drama is that it should teach its actors to be authors. They must learn how to develop situations.

A *New York Times* issue chosen at random in January 1988 describes the Actors Studio search for a new direction which will include "a mandate to revive the Actors Studio's Playwright-Director's Unit and integrate its work with that of the actors." After more than fifty years of proclaiming the primacy of the actor's individual self-expression, the American citadel of "the method" has come to recognize, for instructional purposes at least, the natural relationship between acting and playwriting. The same issue of the *Times* includes Mel Gussow's enthusiastic review of the American Place Theatre's *Roy Blount's Happy Hour and a Half:* "For 90 minutes we are, figuratively, at a bar with the author and raconteur as he expounds wittily on his shaggy life and his and our hard times."

American actors who author and American authors who act have been aided and abetted by a rich backdrop of vaudeville history and its subsequent chapters in television and radio shows. More recent sources of inspiration have been our own inventive brand of improvisational group theatre (beginning with Chicago's original Second City company in the early sixties and for two decades receiving multiple resurrections around the country) and our new brand of solo, mimetic clowning (the work of the West Coast's "New Vandevillians" in the eighties). It is fascinating, in this latter connection, to note a clear example of Fo's direct influence. The actor Geoff Hoyle, who played the lead in the 1984 San Francisco Eureka Theatre production of *Accidental Death,* was subsequently invited to play the lead in the 1987 ART production of *Archangels Don't Play Pinball* directed by Fo. During my interviewing in Cambridge, two actors made mention of Fo's considerable influence on Hoyle. Later the same summer, *New York Times* reviewer Jennifer Dunning offered accolades to Hoyle for his part in the "New Vaudevillian" *Serious Fun!* Festival at Lincoln Center.

The second development in contemporary American theatre which reflects a Foian flavor is our renewed awareness of a need for theatre which speaks frequently to social and political concerns. The Eureka Theatre Company mentioned above has produced four of Fo's plays to date and has recently been awarded a substantial federal grant specifically earmarked to develop new American plays dedicated to social concerns. The recent outpouring of powerful political theatre from South Africa, the growing awareness of the impact of the AIDS epidemic around the world, the fear of nuclear holocaust shared by all nations have brought to the American theatre a new sense of urgency about the subject matter of our plays. Examining our own psyches is no longer enough.

On the broad canvas of world theatre, Dario Fo's mark is visible. He has chosen to place his enormous talents at the service of everyman and everywoman, making it plain that those who have no power are his concern. He supports the have-nots by using the theatre as a forum for paring the powerful down to size. His arms are those available to the economically and politically powerless: physical agility and intellectual wit. In Fo's version of stage reality, presidents and popes are adroitly relieved of prestige and power as ordinary people become aware of their own potential. Fo synthesizes past, present, and future concerns of society as he weds an appreciative sense of tradition with satirical but hilarious situations in which bureaucratic bunglings of immense proportions victimize the common people.

To a student in London who asked him if theatre could change the world, Fo responded: "I believe that neither theatre, nor any form of art, can, in itself, change anything . . . Not even great art." But Dario Fo is a performance artist and a playwright whose comically costumed message, *beware institutional power,* has been heard around the world. Both his comedy and his message are nourishing our theatre today.

Source: Mimi D'Aponte, "From Italian Roots to American Relevance: The Remarkable Theatre of Dario Fo," in *Modern Drama*, Vol. 32, No. 4, December 1989, pp. 532–44.

SOURCES

Behan, Tom, *Dario Fo: Revolutionary Theatre*, Pluto Press, 2000, p. 67.

Cairns, Christopher, "Dario Fo and the *Commedia Dell'-Arte*," in *Studies in the Commedia Dell'Arte*, edited by David J. George and Christopher J. Gossip, University of Wales Press, 1993, p. 1.

Farrell, Joseph, "Dario Fo: *Zanni* and *Giullare*," in *The Commedia Dell'Arte: From the Renaissance to Dario Fo*, edited by Christopher Cairns, Edwin Mellon Press, 1989, pp. 1–2.

Fo, Dario, *Accidental Death of an Anarchist*, translated by Ed Emery, in *Dario Fo: Plays 1*, Methuen, 1992, pp. 127, 136, 137, 152, 176, 190, 191, 193, 198, 200, 202.

FURTHER READING

Brecht, Bertolt, *Brecht on Theatre: The Development of an Aesthetic*, edited and translated by John Willett, Eyre Methuen, 1964.

Willett's compilation of Brecht's writings on theater is a thorough introduction to the dramatist's evolving concerns in his influential career as a writer and director of political theater.

Cardullo, Bert, and Robert Knopf, eds., *Theater of the Avant-Garde, 1890–1950: A Critical Anthology*, Yale University Press, 2001.

This anthology assembles the statements, manifestoes, and opinions of major drama theorists and practitioners, some of whom, like Bertolt Brecht, influenced Fo.

Hirst, David L., *Dario Fo and Franca Rame*, St. Martin's Press, 1989.

Hirst's book is a comprehensive general introduction to the works and collaboration of Dario Fo and Franca Rame.

Mitchell, Tony, *Dario Fo: People's Court Jester*, Methuen, 1986.

A well-known Fo scholar, Mitchell provides insight into how Fo's political convictions inform his works. Photographs that capture the farcical and daring nature of Fo's theater are included.

———, ed. *File on Fo*, Methuen Drama, 1989.

Mitchell has compiled excerpts from writings by critics on Fo and Rame and by Fo and Rame themselves. Mitchell's choice of excerpts is useful and fair, as he includes evaluations both critical and admiring.

Beautiful Señoritas

DOLORES PRIDA

1977

Dolores Prida saw and heard much to impress her in 1976 in Caracas, Venezuela, where she was reporting on an international theater festival for *Visión*, a Latin American newsmagazine. However, she was surprised to note that not a single one of the plays she viewed took up issues then being aired by the feminist movement. At the time, Prida was actively involved with feminism on her home turf of the United States, and she knew that the same issues preoccupying women there were also preoccupying women in Latin America and elsewhere around the world. When Prida discovered that plays addressing women's issues within Latin American contexts were scarce, she was determined to write a play that would help remedy that scarcity. *Beautiful Señoritas* is that play. It was staged in New York City in 1977 at the DUO Theatre.

In the essay "The Show Does Go On," published in *Breaking the Boundaries*, Prida's description of *Beautiful Señoritas* reveals its particular feminist focus. That focus is on female gender roles and stereotypes, particularly as they pertain to Latin women. *Beautiful Señoritas*, she says, is "a modest one-act musical play that poke[s] fun at long-standing Latin women stereotypes—from Carmen Miranda to Cuchi Cuchi Charo to suffering black-shrouded women crying and praying over their tortillas to modern-day young Latinas trying to re-define their images." Although it was published in 1991 in two acts, Prida would nevertheless call the work a one-act play owing to its brevity.

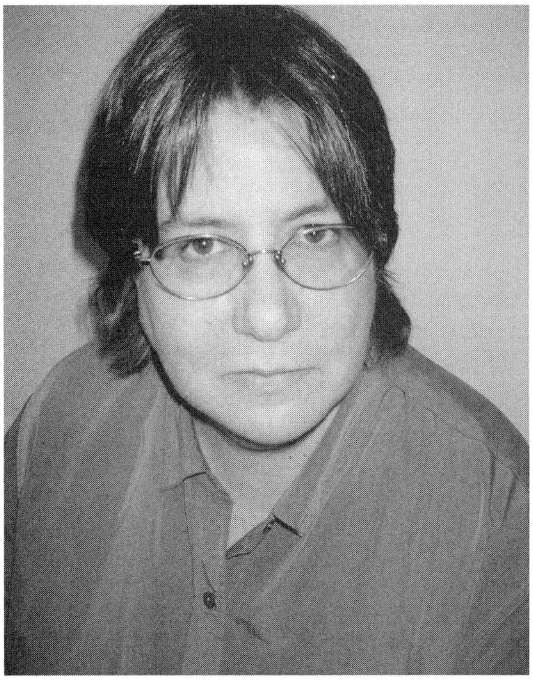

Dolores Prida Photo by Helena You. Courtesy of Dolores Prida

Like most of Prida's subsequent plays, *Beautiful Señoritas* is both comic and serious and has been staged many times. Prida is, indeed, a well-established American dramatist, and most large libraries hold volumes of at least some of her plays. *Beautiful Señoritas* can be found in the volume titled *Beautiful Señoritas & Other Plays*, published by Arte Publico Press (1991).

AUTHOR BIOGRAPHY

Dolores Prida was born on September 5, 1943, in Caibarién, Cuba. In 1959, following Fidel Castro's takeover of Cuba, Prida's father fled the country for the United States, and his family soon followed. Established with her family in New York City in 1961, Prida made Manhattan her base. In New York City, Prida began working in a bakery and attending night classes at Hunter College. Soon, she was writing for various Spanish-language publications, such as *El tiempo* and *Nuestro*. She was also writing and publishing poetry at this time.

Eventually, Prida developed an interest in the theater, forming a connection with the Latino collective group Teatro Popular on Manhattan's Lower East Side. Her first play, *Beautiful Señoritas*, was performed at DUO, an experimental theater where Prida would go on to stage more of her plays. Although Prida is best known as a playwright and has devoted most of her creative energies to writing drama, as opposed to other forms of fiction, she has written nonfiction as well. For example, in 2005 she was a senior editor at *Latina Magazine*.

A number of concerns characterize Prida's plays. Women's issues are the focus of *Beautiful Señoritas*. Prida also explores the themes of biculturalism, in *Coser y cantar* (1981), and the plight of the poor, in *The Beggars Soap Opera* (1979). Prida is very much a modern playwright, whose plays evidence the instincts of an avid experimentalist and dedicated entertainer. Prida experiments in the sense that she does not hesitate to mix and match dramatic forms and moods in a single play. Thus, *Beautiful Señoritas* is both comic and tragic and borrows from Broadway musicals. Besides borrowing from Broadway, Prida also draws on popular cultural forms, such as soap operas (as in the 1986 play *Pantallas*), in her effort to entertain her audience. While Prida might parody elements of the popular forms from which she borrows, she understands what is powerful about them and utilizes those strengths to her own purposes.

A vital figure in American drama and letters, Prida is a highly respected member of the many communities and organizations in which she is so active. She was honored with the Cintas Fellowship for literature in 1976 and the Creative Artistic Public Service Award for Playwriting in 1976, and she received an honorary doctorate from Mount Holyoke College in 1989.

PLOT SUMMARY

Act 1

Beautiful Señoritas opens with the character Don José pacing nervously and smoking a cigar. From what he says, the audience learns that he is awaiting the birth of a child, whom he expects to be a boy. On receiving the news that the child is a girl, he expresses disappointment and disgust. The man's masculine self-regard and disdain for things female set the tone for Prida's play about women's second-class status in traditional Latino and Latin American cultures.

Four Beautiful Señoritas take the place of Don José on stage. They speak nonsensically, sprinkling their speech with Spanish words. While dancing, they sing a song that, despite its nonsensical portions, still conveys coherent ideas: namely, that in the eyes of non-Latinos, Latino culture in the United States is a clichéd group of notions, among which is the female stereotype that Latin women are "always ready for Amor [Love]."

The four Señoritas exit the stage, and two different female characters, María la O and the Beauty Queen, appear. They are in a dressing room at a venue hosting a beauty pageant. They converse about their chances of making money by banking on their good looks. They exit, and the Midwife and Girl enter. As the Midwife speaks of the worries of women who rely on their beauty, the Girl sits at the dressing table at which María la O was seated earlier. She applies makeup, her back to the audience. Once the Midwife stops speaking, the Girl turns to face the audience. Her face is painted like a clown's.

A Master of Ceremonies (MC) takes the stage. He is presiding over a beauty pageant somewhere in the United States. The contestants are Miss Little Havana, Miss Chili Tamale, Miss Conchita Banana, and Miss Commonwealth. All of them, save Miss Commonwealth, sing a short song when they are introduced. They play up to the MC, who asks them ridiculous questions. They also all take the roles of different Women characters immediately after they appear as contestants. As Women characters, they express their inner thoughts and dreams.

A Man enters with a chair, places it in the center of the stage, and sits on it. The Girl enters and sits at the edge of the stage with her back to the audience. She is followed onstage by four Catch Women, who sit around the Man. As they speak, it is as if they are instructing the girl. They talk of how to tantalize and confuse men. When they have finished, the Man sings a song about how the women "do it all" for him: "They do it all for me / What they learn in a magazine / They do it all for me."

Then the Nun enters, grasps the Girl, and commands the Girl to pray. The Priest and four Señoritas enter. The Señoritas begin confessing to the priest their transgressions involving boyfriends and men. The scene ends with all except the Girl overcome by sexual hysteria.

Act 2

As the act opens, the MC is making a "welcome back" speech. A Woman sits on a swing, swinging and singing. She sings about men who promise love and say sweet things but really have only seduction and betrayal on their minds. The stage, which has been dimly lit, now is lit fully. A group of Señoritas sits together and speaks at a dance. The Girl is also present with a Chaperone. A man, a seducer, dances with various of the Señoritas. He leaves with one of the Señoritas as the others relate tales of seduction, betrayal, and reputations ruined.

The action changes as the female characters sing a wedding song. The song explains that when women marry, they give up all their dreams and devote their energies to their husbands and children and their houses. The Martyr female figures are on stage, wearing wigs with rollers. They mime typical household duties, such as ironing and sweeping. They speak of the drudgery and boredom they endure and of being physically abused by their husbands, as if this were inevitable and part of what it is to be a wife.

The Guerrillera (meaning "female guerrilla fighter") arrives in the midst of the Martyrs. She rouses them with stirring words about how women must liberate themselves and create richer and freer lives for themselves. She says that there will be a fund-raiser for the cause of women's advancement, and everybody sings a song about the fund-raising event, which will only mean more work for the women, while the guerrilla men talk about change. Afterward, the female characters remember that there are chores awaiting them, chores they are neglecting. The Martyr characters leave the stage, and a Man enters dressed as a campesino, a farm laborer. A Social Researcher questions him, and a picture of his and his wife's life emerges. The point of the scene is to show that the campesino's wife endures far more hardship than he. She has had sixteen children and works so long all day that she is still doing chores once her husband has gone to bed.

The setting shifts to a family scene. The family depicted is a traditional, poor one. The Daughter wants to go out to play but is not allowed because of her gender. The Son, on the other hand, is indulged. The Wife is submissive to her Husband, and the Mother and Father train the children in traditional gender roles. The Daughter announces that she is pregnant. The Son, as Brother to Sister/Daughter, announces that he will exact revenge for her shame. The Son says that he has made his own girlfriend pregnant, that she has nowhere to go, and that he cannot support her. The Mother tells her son not to worry, to bring the girl into their home. The play ends with Women characters speaking of what women endure: beating, rape, disrespect, lack of equal opportunity. They tell of their dream of a better future. The Girl joins in, talking about the better future that awaits women as they develop a sense of what they want from life and from the societies in which they live.

CHARACTERS

Miss Conchita Banana

The MC introduces the beauty pageant contestant Miss Conchita Banana as an invention of Madison Avenue for the United Fruit Company. In other words, this character represents a figure created by advertisers to sell bananas. Like Carmen Miranda, this figure is a tropical stereotype. As Woman 3, this character expresses her wish to one day become a real person, as if to suggest that stereotypes deny the humanity of those who are stereotyped.

Beautiful Señorita 1

No character in Prida's *Beautiful Señoritas* has a proper name, the Beautiful Señoritas of the title not excluded. Rather, four actors portray four different Beautiful Señoritas, who, as their generic naming suggests, cannot be distinguished from each other in any appreciable way other than through their costuming, which points to Latin female stereotypes propagated by Latinos themselves. These four characters appear very briefly in the play, as a group, at the play's beginning. According to the stage directions, they are to appear on stage dancing, accompanied by rumba music, and they sing a song. Quite nonsensical, the song nevertheless conveys two major ideas. One is that most people have come to think of South American Latin culture largely in terms of clichés. One typical line of the song, for example, is "Guacamole Latin Lover." The second major idea is that Latin women are "always ready for amor," "amor" meaning "love." In other words, a stereotype of Latin women is that they are sexually precocious—"hot-blooded," "hot Latin," and so forth. Of course, since the Beautiful Señoritas resemble famous Latina women in popular culture, Prida points out that Latinos themselves reinforce these stereotypes. Eager to cash in, Latinos caricature their own culture.

One señorita—perhaps Beautiful Señorita 1—is to be dressed as Carmen Miranda. Miranda is most well known in the United States as a singer and movie star who made her fortune portraying the stereotype of the heavily accented, happy-singing-and-dancing tropical woman. Her most notorious items of costuming are a dress that leaves her midriff bare and an immense headdress made of tropical fruits.

Beautiful Señorita 2

Judging from Prida's stage directions, Beautiful Señorita 2 is to act and be costumed so as to bring to mind the Latina entertainer Charo. Charo's famous suggestive trademark line "cuchi, cuchi" underscores her image as a sex symbol projecting the hot Latin stereotype.

Beautiful Señorita 3

Beautiful Señorita 3 appears as Iris Chacón, a Puerto Rican entertainer of the same stamp as Charo. Chacón hosted a widely popular television variety and talk show for many years.

Beautiful Señorita 4

According to Prida's stage directions, Beautiful Señorita 4 is to call to mind María la O, a stereotypical Latin female character in the style of Beautiful Señoritas 1, 2, and 3. María la O appears in a zarzuela (light opera) of the same name written by a Latin composer. A bit later in the play, this character is referred to quite simply as "María la O." In this second appearance, she is in conversation with the Beauty Queen. The women compare notes on how they can parlay their good looks into money.

Beauty Queen

Despite the large number of characters appearing in Prida's play, only a small number of actors are required. Actors simply exit as one character, make a quick costume adjustment, and then return to the stage as a different character. Thus, one of the Beautiful Señoritas next appears as the Beauty Queen.

The Beauty Queen converses with a character named María la O, explaining how she is tired of her life of competition and smiles. Hoping eventually to be discovered by a movie producer, in the meantime she appreciates whatever money she makes when she places in a beauty pageant.

Brother

This character appears in a scene designed to display gender roles within less educated Latino and Latin American families. In response to the news that his sister is pregnant by a friend, the Brother declares he will make his friend pay in blood ("con sangre"). Appearing as the Son, this character enjoys pride of place in relation to his sister (the Daughter figure).

Catch Women

There are three Catch Women in Prida's play, Catch Woman 1, 2, and 3. There is little difference between them. The only reason there are three and not just one is that they carry on a conversation. Their conversation is about how to please men so as to keep ("catch") them. They are manipulative and cynical characters; partnership with men brings them no joy.

Miss Commonwealth

Miss Commonwealth is the last contestant, a figure apparently representing a Caribbean hybrid culture, as her name is Lucy Wisteria Rivera. This suggests that she comes from an island that was once a part of the Spanish Empire (Rivera) before becoming part of the British Empire and Commonwealth (Lucy Wisteria). As Woman 4, she thinks of how an idyllic seaside childhood has given way to her present life in a large, unpleasant city.

Daughter

The Daughter is a somewhat tragic and pathetic figure in the play. In her guise as a tragic character, she dreams of freedoms her Mother and Father do not allow because she is a girl and not a boy. In her guise as a pathetic figure, she appears as a young woman who has been fooled by the promises of a faithless young man and who has failed to protect herself sexually. Thus she finds herself pregnant and without the means to support herself and her baby.

Father

The Father character appears as a man who enforces traditional gender roles in his children. For example, he speaks as follows to the Daughter, who has just asked permission to go out and play: "No. Stay at home with your mother. Girls belong at home. . . . Why don't you learn to cook, to sew, to mend my socks. . . ." As the Husband character, he exerts control over his deferential Wife.

Girl

The Girl is the most important character in Prida's play. Unlike most of the other characters, she appears throughout. Most often, she is in a scene observing the actions of one or a group of the women characters. Then, she mimics their actions. For example, she watches María la O and the Beauty Queen converse in a scene that takes place in a dressing room where the two women are busy with cosmetics and the like. At the end of this scene, the little girl begins to apply makeup herself. By the time she has finished, she has made herself up like a clown. In this way, Prida conveys the ideas that girls learn by example and that women's obsession with beauty amounts to a disfigurement of their humanity. The Girl's presence in Prida's play communicates in no uncertain terms that each successive generation of women will continue to struggle with the same limitations and inequalities until notions of what is gender appropriate change and these new ideas are taught to little boys and girls.

Guerrillera

The Spanish word *guerrillera* means "female guerrilla fighter." (The Spanish term for nontraditional, small-scale warfare, guerrilla warfare, has been adopted in English; *guerra* means "war," and *guerrilla* means "small war.") Male and female guerrilla fighters are recognizable figures within Central and South American cultures, as so many small-scale insurgencies have been fought in so many of these nations. Quite often, guerrilla fighters represent an indigenous peasantry or a lower class that is fighting to wrest power from a corrupt or European ex-imperial elite. The Guerrillera in Prida's play is thus a revolutionary figure, a figure wishing to liberate others from an injustice or servitude. She tells a group of female characters named Martyr 1, 2, and 3 the following: "We can change the world and then our [women's] lot will improve!" In a humorous, if sad, denouement to this scene, the roused Martyrs and the energetic Guerrillera find they must put their plans to change the world on hold, as their husbands will be home any minute wanting their dinners.

Don José

Don José is the first character to speak in Prida's play. He is pacing, waiting to hear news of his wife, who is delivering a baby. He is dreaming of what he will do together with his son, as he is certain his wife is having a boy. When he learns that she has given birth to a girl, he is disgusted.

Don José's actions and words make clear that he is a Latin macho male. He is so certain of his godlike power and superiority over women that he believes he has controlled biology to guarantee himself a male heir. That he is the first character to speak in the play is telling. This conveys the masculine character of traditional Latin culture, the way that men always come first. The birthing scene also communicates the idea that young Latins are groomed in their gender roles from the day they are born.

Miss Little Havana

Miss Little Havana is one of the play's beauty contestants. The song she sings tells the story of one class of Cuban (now Cuban American) women, those upper-class women who fled Cuba with their families and as much of their wealth as they could gather in the aftermath of Fidel Castro's takeover of Cuba in the name of the country's impoverished masses. Castro confiscated the land and monies of the wealthy, redistributing the land and reapportioning the monies. As Woman 1, this contestant's inner thoughts are divulged. She thinks of how invisible she is in the United States, how her accent renders her a nonentity, how her social status has thus changed dramatically.

Man

The Man speaks to the Social Researcher character, who is an educated outsider in his village, studying the village's ways. Answering questions about his wife, he declares that she does not work because she stays at home. Then, quite ironically, he tells the Social Researcher what his wife does all day at home: cooking, cleaning, tending the animals, and so forth. His inability to see the contradiction reinforces Prida's point that men are deluded in their belief in their superiority.

Martyr

Three martyr figures named Martyr 1, 2, and 3 appear in Prida's play. They are presented as typical Latina women of the less-educated or less-privileged classes who are bound to the house and housework. Their lives amount to endless drudgery, and they accept as natural and inevitable the physical abuse their husbands dole out.

MC

MC stands for "Master of Ceremonies." The MC appears throughout the play, as he is orchestrating the beauty pageant that, in fits and starts, unfolds as the play does. He is a stock comedic MC, always upbeat and treating the most trivial of matters with perfect seriousness, by turns smarmy and vulgar.

Midwife

The Midwife appears periodically in the play. She is an ambiguous figure, sometimes directing pernicious gender clichés in the direction of the Girl, sometimes commenting poignantly on the action. The following words illustrate this doubleness:

> Yes. You have to smile to win. A girl with a serious face has no future. But what can you do when a butterfly is trapped in your insides and you cannot smile? How can you smile with a butterfly condemned to beat its ever-changing wings in the pit of your stomach?

Mother

In her brief appearance, this character exemplifies a typical, traditional Latin mother. She grooms the play's Daughter to be meek and indulges the Son as the more important child. As the Wife, this character defers to the Husband of the play in all things, training the Daughter to follow in her footsteps.

Nun

A stock figure, the Nun interacts with the Girl, encouraging the Girl to forget the profane concerns of beauty and to embrace the piety of Catholicism.

Priest

The Priest hears a confession in Prida's play in a scene that suggests that the Christian/Catholic policing of sex amounts to an unhealthy repression that breeds sexual hysteria.

Señoritas

The Señoritas (1, 2, 3, and 4) appear in the confession scene as confessors, admitting to a priest to having kissed their boyfriends. The combination of sexual matters and the confessional proves to be a heady mixture, eliciting sexual hysteria in the Señoritas, the Priest, and the Nun.

Social Researcher

A Social Researcher appears briefly, interviewing a peasant in a Latin American village. The opposition of Researcher and Man emphasizes the outdated nature of the Man's views.

Miss Chili Tamale

The beauty contestant Miss Chili Tamale hails from Mexico. She seems meek, and she tells the MC that her dream is to marry an American man so as to become a U.S. citizen. As Woman 2, she expresses the resentment some Mexicans and Mexican Americans who live in the American

Southwest feel: they remember how the land was once part of Mexico until it was lost in land war with the United States.

Women

Four Women—Woman 1, 2, 3, and 4—have a prominent part in the ending of Prida's play. They voice the concerns, longings, and dreams of all of the women of *Beautiful Señoritas*. They mourn how women the world over are treated as second-class citizens. They lament that women are raped, abused, and beaten and often have little or no recourse to justice. They long for a new day when women will be given all the opportunities and respect that men enjoy.

THEMES

Stereotypes

A stereotype of a particular group of people, a nation, or a culture might be entirely without foundation, a caricature of an existing characteristic, or a complex combination of the two. For example, an old stereotype of women was that they were not intellectual. As more and more women attend university at advanced levels, this stereotype has lost ground. Women have entered various professions and are now successful doctors, stockbrokers, academics, and lawyers. Still, since women were excluded from education for so long, it appeared as if they lacked the ability to perform in the professions that men did. Thus, although it was without empirical foundation, this stereotype seemed true, owing to the way in which society had been organized. Prida's play attempts to expose stereotypes of Latin women. In her depiction of the group of Martyr characters, for example, she is not saying that such women do not exist. She is saying, rather, that such women do not need to exist, that this is not a natural state of affairs. If Latin society were organized differently, then Latin women would not behave like long-suffering martyrs.

Nature versus Nurture

Prida's play emphasizes the crucial role that education plays in constructions of gender. In showing how the Girl character mimics the behavior of the Women characters, Prida argues that gender-appropriate behavior is, in large part, a matter of that which is taught (nurture) as opposed to that which is biologically determined (nature). This opposition of nurture to nature is a basic feminist argument. For example, if women are nurtured to believe that they are delicate by nature or that to be delicate is to be truly feminine, they will hesitate to take up those sports that would seem to belie delicacy. For centuries, only men took part in vigorous sports. Education for Prida is not simply a matter of the formal curriculum one learns at school; it is also a matter of everyday informal training within the family, within one's community, and through pop culture via television and film. The importance of popular culture in forming people's behavior and values, particularly in the realm of gender, is seen when Prida's various female characters appear as famous celebrities and fictional characters—as the entertainer Charo, for example. Prida's point in parading Charo's image is that if women who act like so-called bimbos (attractive but stupid) succeed financially and receive a great deal of attention, then little girls will emulate them.

Masculinism

In a society where women are considered less than men, masculinism reigns. Masculinism assumes that men are the more valuable gender in the world: more intelligent, better problem solvers, harder workers, and so on. It also assumes that women, owing to their lesser capabilities, are best led by men: men should call the shots politically, culturally, and in the family; women should be followers and obey their husbands. While the feminist movement has loosened, and even shattered, many of the cornerstone beliefs of masculinism, there is evidence that a degree of masculinism persists in even the most feminist of societies. In *Beautiful Señoritas*, masculinism remains strong. No matter that Prida's play was written in 1977, the fact remains that in certain parts of the Latin world there are still men invested in macho views, those extremes of male superiority that are seen in the characters of Don José and the campesino.

Complicity

The mid-twentieth-century singer and actor Carmen Miranda was a Brazilian who spent her lucrative days in Hollywood exploiting a Latin stereotype. She appeared in films wearing outrageous costumes that conveyed the idea that Brazilians lived in a tropical paradise where everyone was happy, lusty, and wily (but just a little bit simple, too). Of course, Miranda managed to poke fun at herself while she performed in this way; she was silly and excessive enough to convey the idea that what she was doing was indeed caricaturing a

TOPICS FOR FURTHER STUDY

- Research and write a report on the Cuban Revolution, which resulted in Fidel Castro's takeover of the country in 1959. What motivated Castro and those who supported him? What were their grievances against the government? How did they succeed militarily in their takeover? What was the role of guerrilla fighting in the conflict?
- The cold war, which is now over, was the battle of beliefs between Western-style capitalism on the one side and Russian-style Communism on the other. Since Fidel Castro's revolution in Cuba was Communist in nature, Cuba became the enemy of the United States in 1959. The two most serious moments in this long-standing enmity were the events known as the Bay of Pigs and the Cuban missile crisis. Research these events and prepare a Microsoft PowerPoint presentation describing them and explaining how and why they were moments of crisis for the U.S. government.
- Form a group and watch, each person on his or her own, a few episodes of any U.S. primetime television show with a Latino character in the cast or depicting a Latin American family. Take notes on the show, with the goal of being able to argue whether the show reinforces stereotypical views of Latinos or some particular Latin group. Next, meet with your group and discuss your impressions. Present your findings to the class in the form of an oral report.
- Gloria Steinem is a major figure of 1970s American feminism. Research her career as an activist and writer. What did she try to accomplish for women in the United States? What were her and other feminists' core beliefs? Present your findings in a report.
- Many contemporary feminists say that feminists are poorly portrayed in the media. They say that instead of being presented as persons committed to the democratic ideal of ensuring equal opportunity for all, including women, feminists are portrayed as man haters. What is your opinion? Are feminists in the media portrayed as persons working toward equal opportunity for women or as persons who dislike men? State where you have encountered depictions of feminists, describe how they are portrayed, and explain why you think they are represented the way they are. Work with a group or on your own, presenting your findings to the class.

culture. Nonetheless, her career in the United States reinforced this Latin stereotype.

That Prida's play features Latins who reinforce Latin stereotypes points to Prida's conviction that Latins are complicit in their own plight. It is a plight in which they lack true visibility, since many Americans evince little interest in learning about the complexities and subtleties of Latin cultures and, instead, are content to hold on to stereotypical notions. The reality, however, is that there is not a single Latin culture; there are many. There are differences between Salvadorans, Chileans, and Mexicans, and their nations have unique histories. These peoples emigrated to the United States for a variety of reasons. As long as Latins propagate stereotypes in conjunction with non-Latins, the true nature of their cultures, and of themselves as individuals, will remain invisible to outsiders.

STYLE

New Directions in Characterization

There is not a single character in Prida's play who is given a proper name. All the characters have generic names, such as Girl, Brother, and Daughter. On the one hand, this serves the very specific purpose of *Beautiful Señoritas*, which is to point out to the audience that standard, set gender roles are doled out to men and women alike: in some senses, all girls are the same girl, all wives are the same wife. On the other hand, Prida's use of character points to new directions in characterization in contemporary drama. Playwrights no longer feel compelled to present characters who act like people in real life. This is not to say that Prida's characters act unusually all of the time. Still, the fact that the audience is not introduced to a character with a proper name who is a part of a story with other such characters suggests the degree to which Prida feels free to experiment widely.

Beyond Narrative

In reading a novel or in seeing a play, most people expect a chronological narrative (story). In this kind of narrative, a number of characters are introduced and proceed to interact in ways that produce or reveal various problems or complexities. At the end of the story, the narrative resolves—whether for good or for ill. There is no narrative in *Beautiful Señoritas*, not even in the way that the play (very loosely) takes place in the form of a beauty pageant. Indeed, this pageant is only barely felt as an ongoing, unfolding event, so that on the whole the play takes place as a series of completely unconnected events. At any given moment in *Beautiful Señoritas*, two characters will converse; at the next moment, two or three entirely different characters will interact—new characters, to whom the audience has not been introduced and whom they will never see again. Prida, in short, feels no need to present a story to her audience. Like many contemporary playwrights, Prida believes that narrative belongs to the realm of the novel and short story on the printed page and that drama, in its aural and visual—that is, live—dimensions, can and should be something entirely different.

HISTORICAL CONTEXT

The Cuban Revolution

Prida and her family are members of a particular group of Spanish-speaking immigrants and their descendants in the United States—Cuban Americans. Many of these Cubans came to the United States when Prida's family did, in the late 1950s and early 1960s. They came in the wake of Fidel Castro's takeover of Cuba in 1959. In 2005, Castro was still Cuba's leader, but he was ailing and not expected to rule for very much longer.

The situation that led to Castro's success in Cuba in the late 1950s was one that plagued not only many Central and South American nations, but also parts of the United States as well as other countries around the world. A small group of people controlled most of the nation's wealth, with a vast impoverished underclass wondering when its turn to earn would arrive. When would leaders create the conditions for the sort of industry that would improve the nation's economy and so enhance people's lives? When would the impoverished gain access to education? In the mid-twentieth century, with the existence of a Communist Soviet Union that believed in spreading its message and influence, conditions such as these were ripe for Communist revolution. Soviet Communist belief centered on the idea that workers should own the businesses in which they worked, so that profits could be equally distributed among all. Soviet Communism entailed the further belief that no one, no matter the nature of his or her job, should earn appreciably less or more than anybody else. All the wealth generated in a nation must be equally distributed.

Alarmed at Castro's success in taking over the government, many wealthy Cubans fled Cuba with whatever wealth they could take with them. Of course, not all who left were rich. Some left simply because they understood that Castro was unlikely to achieve his goals without establishing a political dictatorship. These Cubans understood that such a major restructuring of society would lead to massive governmental control and intervention in all aspects of life.

The Feminist Movement

The twentieth century was one that saw major gains for women's rights in the Western world. In the early decades of the century, feminist activists won the right for women to vote in national elections. In the later part of the century—most particularly in the 1970s, when Prida was writing *Beautiful Señoritas*—feminists were engaged in making society understand that attitudes about men and women had to change before laws that allowed the vote and other rights could be meaningful. For example, it was not considered feminine to have opinions or to be widely informed in matters outside the home. Women who challenged this status quo were labeled masculine—unnatural—and shunned. It was often the case that although women could vote, many left that job to their husbands, since not voting confirmed their femininity in the eyes of the world. Thus, societal disapproval frightened some women into conforming, because humans, above all, are social creatures, craving acceptance. Still, feminists worked hard so that in the United States

COMPARE & CONTRAST

- **1970s:** The women's movement and ethnic minority Civil Rights movements that emerged during the 1960s refine their goals and strategies for change, with women of color participating in academic feminist efforts to correct a white, middle-class bias.

  Today: Feminism is a complex set of competing and overlapping theories and practices that take race, class, gender, and sexuality into consideration.

- **1970s:** Feminists begin campaigning for social welfare bills that will allow women equal success in the workforce. For example, they advocate for preschool programs for children and parental leave from work for the first few months after childbirth.

  Today: A law requiring employers of fifty or more workers to allow twelve weeks of unpaid leave to employees with a newborn child or an ill family member is in effect.

- **1970s:** César Chávez, a Latino activist for farmworkers' rights, is at the height of his influence, organizing strikes and boycotts. The grape boycott of the 1970s initiated by Chávez is hugely successful.

  Today: Thanks to the efforts of unionists like Chávez, American farmworkers have the right to strike and demonstrate without fear of losing their jobs.

- **1970s:** The landmark Supreme Court decision of *Roe v. Wade* in 1973 establishes women's right to an abortion, without restrictions, during the first three months of pregnancy.

  Today: Numerous Supreme Court decisions have revised the terms of *Roe v. Wade*, limiting women's access to abortion. For example, individual states may now disallow abortions in public hospitals.

- **1970s:** The Title IX amendment to the Higher Education Act of 1972 had a major impact on girls' and women's participation in sports. Because the act prohibits discrimination on the basis of sex by schools and colleges receiving federal funds, schools had to begin spending as much money on girls' and women's sports programs as they did on boys' and men's.

  Today: The development of women in sports is seen, for example, in the international success of the American women's soccer team, and companies begin to recognize the profits to be made by advertising at events such as women's professional golf tournaments.

- **1970s:** Affirmative action programs—designed to ensure equal opportunity for ethnic minorities in education and the workplace, initiated in the 1960s following the Civil Rights movement—begin to encounter opposition.

  Today: Legislation limiting the scope of affirmative action programs is in effect, with states such as California voting for the end of university admission policies that take race into account.

in the twenty-first century, most women feel confident that they can pursue whatever career interests them without being accused of being unnatural. Indeed, as the cost of living rises, forcing people to spend more on such basic necessities as housing, food, medical care, gasoline, and heating fuel, a household with two good earners is a must.

CRITICAL OVERVIEW

A playwright's first staged effort, such as *Beautiful Señoritas* in the case of Prida, is lucky to receive any attention at all from critics. Yet as Prida herself has said in "The Show Does Go On," in *Breaking Boundaries*, "the play was exceptionally

Tanya Sandolval Russell, Yomi, Ingrid Wang, James Victor, Lorraine Barkley, Roseanna Campos, Gabrielle Gazon, and Frieda Woody in a 1979 production of Beautiful Señoritas Courtesy of Dolores Prida

well received—it went on to have many productions throughout the country, including a special performance at the National Organization for Women's national convention in San Antonio, Texas, in 1980." Prida's unusual good fortune is largely owing to her skill and originality as a dramatist and partly owing to the content of *Beautiful Señoritas.* Its feminist and Latino themes were perfectly attuned to a time when women and minorities were asserting themselves as voices needing to be acknowledged and heard in American culture and politics. That Prida's play was staged at the National Organization for Women's convention in San Antonio attests to this. What could make more sense as a learning tool and as entertainment than a production of the play at a meeting of a major feminist organization held in the Latino Southwest?

Among Prida's plays, *Beautiful Señoritas*, in particular, will always be remembered not only in feminist but also in Cuban American circles. The play's place in Cuban American letters is defined by Eliana Rivero in her essay "From Immigrants to Ethnics: Cuban Women Writers in the U.S.," also from the volume *Breaking Boundaries.* As Rivero says, Prida's *Beautiful Señoritas* is important as one of the first U.S. bilingual plays, a bilingualism making concrete a very particular fact of many Latinos' lives, namely, their double identity. They are both Latin and American: "this phenomenon was first registered for Cuban women authors with the presentation in 1977 of the play *Beautiful Señoritas* by Dolores Prida, a writer/journalist who has distinguished herself as a playwright (*Coser y cantar*) and as a poet."

As Rivero's comments indicate, Prida has written plays, *Coser y cantar* among them, that are more highly regarded than *Beautiful Señoritas.* As is the case with most authors, Prida's writing and concerns have gained subtlety over time. Prida has composed works entirely in Spanish, such as *Coser y cantar*, even while she continues to write bilingual works like Beautiful Señoritas.

CRITICISM

Carol Dell'Amico

Dell'Amico is lecturer in the English Department of California State University, Bakersfield. In this essay, she discusses the feminism of Prida's play.

In 1976, Prida was in Caracas, Venezuela, to report on a theater festival for a magazine. She was struck by the fact that none of the plays she saw addressed a current major area of concern, women's issues, and she decided to write such a play herself on her return to New York City. This play is *Beautiful Señoritas.*

Beautiful Señoritas explores gender roles and stereotypes as they manifest themselves in Latin American and U.S. Latino cultures. Like so many feminists of the time, Prida is driven to question notions of what women are and how they should behave. In this play, she also looks at ideas about men, masculinity, and the stereotypical concepts of Latins held by non-Latins.

Although *Beautiful Señoritas* is humorous, the play conveys serious ideas and insights. The most obvious of these insights is communicated through Prida's clever decision to present the play in the form of a beauty pageant. In this way, Prida explores the idea that women are supposed to be beautiful, that they are even encouraged to compete with other women in this regard. Feminists find this use of beauty, and its implications, disturbing, and question the beauty standard for women. For example, if a woman is concerned with being beautiful to ensnare a man, it means that she does not work directly toward her own security by pursuing an education and creating a career. Rather, such a woman ensnares a man and then expects him to take care of her. One problem with this is that people divorce. What does the divorced woman do without an education or marketable skills? As feminists point out, before alimony laws were instituted, many women remained in unhappy, even abusive marriages because they realized that if they divorced, their standard of living would be dramatically reduced.

Another disturbing implication of the beauty standard is that brainwork is left largely to men:

> "IN THE RANGE FROM THE 'TINSEL,' WHICH POINTS TO HOW WOMEN MUST PUT THEIR BEAUTY ON DISPLAY, TO THE 'MANTILLA,' WHICH IS THE VEIL LATIN WOMEN USED TO BE REQUIRED TO WEAR IN CHURCH, PRIDA'S AUDIENCE SEES IN THE GIRL THE CONTRADICTIONS OF GENDER ROLE IDEOLOGY, ESPECIALLY AS THEY PERTAIN TO LATIN WOMEN."

women are important for their bodies, men for their minds. This view not only encourages women to forgo a career but also underwrites the idea that women are not as intelligent as men. This pernicious notion has kept many a worthy (working) woman from receiving the promotion she deserves, as many companies buy into this belief about lesser intelligence and simply cannot see how a woman worker could be as competent as a male worker.

Of course, the idea that women are not as capable at work as men is a fallacy, a misleading belief with complex foundations and one of the most profound contradictions of traditional gender ideology. Prida addresses this contradiction with great skill in her play. At one point, she presents a researcher who is studying the culture of a traditional Latin American community. The researcher asks a man, a fieldworker, about his wife. The man says that his wife does not work, that she stays at home. He is the worker of the family, the man asserts, the one who earns money by working in the fields. When asked what his wife does all day at home, the man replies:

> Well, she gets up at four in the morning, fetches water and wood, makes the fire and cooks breakfast. Then she goes to the river and washes the clothes. After that she goes to town to get the corn ground and buy what we need in the market. Then she cooks the midday meal.

When the researcher asks what she does after that, the husband says that she walks the few miles

WHAT DO I READ NEXT?

- Prida's *Beggars Soap Opera* (1979) is a musical comedy like *Beautiful Señoritas* that draws on the popular form of soap operas.
- Prida's 1986 play *Pantallas* contemplates the end of the world, borrowing from soap operas much as *Beautiful Señoritas* borrows from Broadway musicals.
- *Before Night Falls*, translated from the Spanish by Dolores M. Koch in 1993, is a highly acclaimed autobiographical work by Reinaldo Arenas, a Cuban writer who immigrated to the United States, as Prida did. The book was made into a film of the same name in 2000, directed by the American artist Julian Schnabel. Both book and film address Arenas's flight from Cuba and the nature of Cuban life under the reign of Fidel Castro.
- *How the Garcia Girls Lost Their Accents* (1991) is but one work of fiction by Julia Alvarez, who came to the United States from the Dominican Republic. Like many of Prida's plays, this novel deals with the difficulties of belonging to two cultures simultaneously.

---

to the fields to bring him his lunch and then returns home to take "care of the hens and pigs," along with many other things. In short, the wife is still performing laborious household chores when her husband, following a good dinner cooked by her, of course, is tucked up snugly in bed.

This interlude seeks to dramatize the feminist argument that being a homemaker does not mean that a woman does not work. Rather, women who choose to stay home perform duties crucial to the upkeep of the family and hence vital to the well-being of the nation. Women, in other words, must be respected and acknowledged for whatever work they choose to do, no matter that this work does not take place in public. To put it another way, since women's work traditionally has taken place in the private sphere as opposed to the public one, it has not always been recognized as work. Thanks to this insight about women's work, alimony laws have been instituted in the realm of divorce legislation. Lawyers can finally argue that homemakers perform unpaid work. They can present figures for what it would cost a family to employ full-time nannies, cooks, chauffeurs, and household accountants and managers. Alimony payments are a way for society to acknowledge that women's traditional work is valuable and real. These payments also give divorced women time to train for professions that could support them when the payments might stop. (Now, of course, divorced men can and do also receive alimony payments if they took on the role of the homemaker or lesser earner in the partnership.)

Contradictions more pronounced in Latin cultures, in particular, are also addressed in Prida's play. For example, at the same time that women are encouraged to be seductive and attractive to men in these cultures, they are also supposed to emulate the Christian Virgin Mary and display innocence of mind and meek manners. Thus, Prida's preening Beautiful Señorita characters morph into the seductively teasing Catch Women, who, in turn, morph into the modest Señoritas who pray devotedly at church. Another, related contradiction is dramatized in the way in which Prida's Latin male characters expect their wives to be faithful while they themselves feel free to visit prostitutes, prostitutes whom they feel they can also despise. While such extreme and contradictory notions of gender are not limited to Latin cultures, they are more pronounced in them owing to the influence of the Catholic form of Christianity, as it is practiced by the people, which tends to encourage a dichotomous virgin/whore mentality: the Virgin Mary versus Mary Magdalene, as it were. Prida dramatizes these contradictions vividly in the confusions, costumes, and makeup of the Girl in *Beautiful Señoritas*:

> The GIRL enters followed by Mamá. The GIRL is wearing all the items she has picked from previous scenes: the tinsel crown, the flowers, a mantilla, etc.

Carmen Miranda The Kobal Collection. Reproduced by permission

Her face is still made up as a clown. . . . The GIRL looks upset, restless with all the manipulation she has endured.

In the range from the "tinsel," which points to how women must put their beauty on display, to the "mantilla," which is the veil Latin women used to be required to wear in church, Prida's audience sees in the Girl the contradictions of gender role ideology, especially as they pertain to Latin women. Further, the clownlike face of the girl suggests that women who spend a great deal of time manipulating their looks turn themselves into caricatures of humans—clowns. The clownlike face also points to the way that women who are overly concerned with men's opinion of their looks are always self-conscious, always on display, always feeling as if they are objects being looked at by an audience.

Another important component of Prida's play is its treatment of stereotypes. This is seen in the way that the Beautiful Señorita characters at the beginning of the play resemble famous female Latin icons, Charo and Carmen Miranda among them. Where the Brazilian Miranda made her money performing a tropical stereotype, Charo made hers taking advantage of the myth that Latin women are always ready for sex—the "hot Latin" myth, as it were. It is significant that Prida features Latins conforming to stereotypes. Her point is that some Latinos in American culture are quite willing to exploit stereotypes if it means making money. In other words, these stereotypes are not promulgated only by unthinking non-Latins. Likewise, she shows how women are complicit in their own objectification in the figures of the calculating Catch Women. These women pass on advice about how to keep men in sexual thrall to females. By doing so, they knowingly further the women's body-sex equation.

The world has changed radically for women in those countries that experienced the feminist agitations of the 1960s and 1970s. Before those decades, the majority of middle-class women believed that serious careers were for men only. In the twenty-first century, more women than men are graduating from medical schools in the United States. Nonetheless, at the same time, many of the social structures that feminists find contradictory persist. One has only to peruse the supermarket magazine racks packed full of fashion magazines aimed at a female audience to see that the beauty industry is booming. Indeed, its profits are in the billions of dollars worldwide, with surgeries for breast enhancements and liposuction in demand as never before. Of course, it is also true that makeup for men is now a fast-growing industry.

Has women's success in the public arena changed the meaning and effect of women's being better groomed than most men? Does the fact that men are becoming more conscious of their bodies suggest that beauty is now a way to advertise one's health and fitness? Are people who are interested in fitness expecting to have partners of like mind? Perhaps the surest test of women's definitive equality to men in U.S. society is the presidential one. When will political parties determine that running a woman for president is not a risk? When will it be true that the average American will be just as likely to vote for a woman as a man?

Source: Carol Dell'Amico, Critical Essay on *Beautiful Señoritas*, in *Drama for Students*, Thomson Gale, 2006.

Dolores Prida

In the following essay, Prida provides background information on her evolution as a playwright and comments on the growing Hispanic theater movement.

Over ten years ago, when my first play was produced in New York City, I dragged my whole family down to a dank basement in the Lower East Side to see it. My mother, who never really understood what I did in the theatre, said to me after the show was over: "Todo estuvo muy bonito, m'ija, pero, en todo eso que yo vi, ¿qué fue exactamente lo que tú hiciste?" I explained to her that I had written the play, that I was the *dramaturga.* She just said, "ahhh," and shook her head.

I fantasized about her, next morning, telling her coworkers at that factory in Brooklyn where she used to sew sleeves onto raincoats all day long, "¿Oye, Rosalía, tú sabes que mi hija, la mayor, es dramaturga?" And Rosalía answering, "¿Dramaturga? ¡Ay pobrecita! Y eso, ¿tiene cura?"

My mother passed away three years ago, and I regret I never took the time to explain to her what being a *dramaturga* meant to me, and why it can't be "cured," that once bitten by the love of the theatre, you are infected with it for the rest of your life.

Now it is too late to share with her why I put up with the long hours, the lack of money, the unheated basements: the thrill of opening night, the goose pimples when an audience laughs at the right lines, or when you can hear a pin drop at the right moment.

It is not too late to share some of it with you.

I didn't start off as a playwright. As a teenager, I wrote poems and short stories that nobody read. In fact, nobody knew I wrote them because I didn't tell anyone. Writing poetry wasn't the "in" thing among my peers. I am from a small town where there was one single bookstore and one single library, which was closed most of the time—I don't know why, maybe because it was right next door to the police station.

We had two movie houses, one that showed Mexican and Argentinian films, mostly three-hanky tearjerkers. In the other one—*el cine América*—you could watch the latest Hollywood films, with subtitles or dubbed into Spanish. I actually grew up believing that John Wayne was really from Madrid by watching movies in which he would speak perfect Castilian: "Alzad laz manoz, matonez."

One thing we didn't have in Caibarién, Cuba, was a theatre. I didn't get to see a live play until I came to New York. That was in 1961. It was a musical, and I became fascinated forever with the idea of people bursting into song and dance at the least provocation.

The first play I wrote—*Beautiful Señoritas*—was a play with music. And I wrote it in English.

In 1976, I went to Caracas, Venezuela, to cover an International Theatre Festival for *Visión,* the Latin American news magazine. It was my first festival and I enjoyed every minute of it. I saw plays from over thirty different countries, many in languages I did not understand. But one peculiar thing caught my attention: not one of those plays dealt with "the women's issue." At the time, I was quite involved in the women's movement in New York and knew that *la liberación femenina* was also being hotly debated in Latin America and Europe. Yet, the stages of an international theatre festival didn't reflect it. I decided, then and there, that when I got back to New York I would write a play about women. And I did.

"IT WAS A MODEST ONE-ACT MUSICAL PLAY THAT POKED FUN AT LONG-STANDING LATIN WOMEN STEREOTYPES."

Beautiful Señoritas was produced by DUO Theatre in 1977. It was a modest one-act musical play that poked fun at long-standing Latin women stereotypes—from Carmen Miranda to Cuchi Cuchi Charo to suffering, black-shrouded women crying and praying over the tortillas to modern-day young Latinas trying to re-define their images. The play was extremely well received—it went on to have many productions throughout the country, including a special performance at the National Organization for Women's national convention in San Antonio, Texas, in 1980.

From then on, most of my plays have been about the experience of being a Hispanic in the United States, about people trying to reconcile two cultures and two languages and two visions of the world into a particular whole: plays that aim to be a reflection of a particular time and space, of a here and now.

Of course, not all of my plays are women-oriented or totally Hispanic. Being a woman and being a Hispanic is neither an asset nor a handicap but a fact. And, as an artist, I do not wish to be categorized just as a "Hispanic Playwright" or a "Woman Hispanic Playwright," but rather as a person, a playwright who happens to be a woman and a Hispanic and who feels committed to writing on those subjects because they are part of the universe.

I find it particularly rewarding being able to write non-Hispanic characters, male or female, who are believable and authentic. And writing believable and authentic characters is what theatre is all about. Of course, good theatre also springs from writing about subjects and situations one knows best. And what I know best are the ups and down of being a Hispanic woman playwright living in New York City. And I am not contradicting myself.

THEATREWORKS

I consider myself a "theatre worker" rather than a "theatre literata." Theatre is not literature; theatre is to be "done," not read, seen, not imagined. Theatre is people. Theatre is team work. We need each other: playwright, director, designers, actors, choregraphers, technicians, carpenters, composers, ticket takers, audience. We don't exist without each other. And I have tremendous respect and admiration for the skills and talent of everyone involved in bringing a production to the stage. I love actors. I adore choreographers. I am awed by composers and musicians. Directors? Putting your play in the hands of a good director who has vision and understands your work—well, that's icing on the cake. Good directors, however, are few and far between.

The first thing I did at Teatro the Orilla, a collective theatre group in New York's Lower East Side, was to sweep the floor and collect tickets at the door. Then I ran the sound equipment, made lights from empty tomato juice cans and supermarket light bulbs, went shopping for costumes and props, filled out endless forms for grant money, and then, only then, I began to think I could write a play that would appeal to that particular audience: people who had never been to a theatre before.

My theatre life came into being soon after various Hispanic theatre groups began to get established, thanks to newly available public funds in the late sixties and early seventies. It was all part of a process, a side effect of the ethnic and racial reaffirmation that followed the black civil rights movement, the women's liberation movement, the anti-war demonstrations.

I did not get into the theatre for the "let's-put-on-a-show" fun of it, but because I felt I had things to say about immediate and relevant issues and I wanted to say them with comedy, with music, with songs. Live.

Besides those already mentioned, I have also written about gentrification (*Savings*), about anti-poverty agencies (*The Beggars' Soap Opera*), about Hispanic theatre itself (*La Era Latina*), about Latin soap operas and nuclear war (*Pantallas*), about cultural assimilation (*Botánica*). Waiting their turn are plays about AIDS (so many of my friends are gone) and teenage pregnancy (What happened to women's liberation? Have we failed the younger generation of women?).

Also, I've had plays canceled for the alleged "insidiousness" of my politics. "Maligned in Miami" is the Hispanic community's equivalent of "Banned in Boston."

The need to use the theatre as a medium to discuss relevant and immediate issues and experiences is not new, except in one sense; today, many Hispanic playwrights are writing about these experiences in English, whereas the earliest examples were in Spanish (of all my plays, only two, *Pantallas* and *Botánica,* are in Spanish).

There are two stories I always like to mention when speaking of the origins of Hispanic theatre in the New World. One is fact, and one is fiction.

The fictitious event I like best, because it concerns the earliest example of Hispanic American musical theatre. It comes from a passage of *El arpa y la sombra,* by the Cuban novelist Alejo Carpentier. One of the sections of the book, "La mano," is written as the travel diary of Christopher Columbus. Let me share it with you in its original splendor:

> Más adelante—fue durante mi tercer viaje—al ver que los indios de una isla se mostraban recelosos en acercarse a nosotros, improvisé un escenario en el catillo de popa, haciendo que unos españoles danzaran bulliciosamente al son de tamboril y tejoletas, para que se viese que éramos gente alegre y de un natural apacible. (Pero mal nos fue en esa ocasión, para decir la verdad, puesto que los caníbales, nada divertidos por moriscas y zapateados, nos dispararon tantas flechas como tenían en sus canoas. . . .)

So here we see that one of the first, although fictional, Hispanic theatre performers in the Americas (Christopher Columbus, producer) was a musical comedy, and that it was panned by the audience.

The second—and much-quoted—story is fact, according to researchers. It documents the actual first performance of what could be called a play, in what is today U.S. territory. In 1598, a group of conquistadores, led by Juan de Oñate, crossed the Río Grande from Mexico to take formal possession of all the kingdoms and provinces of New Mexico in the name of King Philip of Spain. They struck camp on a spot near the present-day city of El Paso, Texas.

Among the group was a captain of the guard named Marcos Farfán de los Godos (how's that for a stage name!), who, besides being a soldier, dabbled in the art of "dramaturgy." That evening, he prepared *un espectáculo* to entertain his fellow conquistadores. The theme of this presentation is reported to have dealt with the question of how the church would be received in the newly "discovered" lands of New Mexico.

This presentation is considered to be the first theatrical piece ever performed in what is today the United States of America. It predates, by sixty-seven years, the first recorded English play produced in the New World. It predates, by eight years, the French masque perfomed in Acadia, Canada, in 1606.

Both these theatrical events, whether fact or fiction, also sprung from the immediate reality of those first "Hispanics," and their experiences as conquistadores in a new land. Had they not come here, they would not have written those particular plays. Therefore, they are "American" plays.

Today's Hispanic American playwrights, arriving at, or being born on, these shores more like *conquistados* than conquistadores, continue that tradition.

From a Miguel Piñero, who writes *Short Eyes* from the inside the nightmare of a prison, to Eddie Gallardo's family in the South Bronx's *Simpson Street,* to Eduardo Machado's upper-class Cuban families arriving in Miami with suitcases chock-full of jewels, to Manuel Martín's working-class Cubans celebrating Thanksgiving in Union City, to Gloria González' *Café con leche,* to my own *Coser y cantar,* which deals with how to be a bilingual, bicultural woman in Manhattan and keep your sanity, to a host of as-yet-unproduced new plays by young Hispanics developing in the wings, Hispanic American theatre is slowly becoming a hall of mirrors in which our society and ourselves are reflected, sometimes documenting the intangibles of being a minority in the United States with more subtlety and depth than many an expensive sociological research paper.

However, much of this work is unknown or ignored, both by the Hispanic and the general community. For Hispanics, going to the theatre is a tradition that generally we do not bring along from our countries of origin. There the theatre is, in most cases, for the social and intellectual elites. In coming here, we find that the arts are not necessarily considered a luxury but perceived as being somewhat irrelevant, something for which one usually does not have time.

The need for many immigrants to struggle, survive, and adapt does not allow them the luxury of attending the theatre. Going out means going dancing or to the movies—what they think is accessible and "fun." Regular escapist entertainment is found nightly in the never-ending *telenovelas* and in the weekly convulsions of Iris Chacón's hips. Only a minority within our community goes regularly to the theatre. Many of our 99-seat houses are half-empty many a night.

Although non-Hispanics come to see our plays, it is more like a novelty, or a duty—as in the case of the classics. I mean, you have to see a García Lorca or a Lope de Vega play at least once in your lifetime, and, of course, the latest effort by novelist Mario Vargas Llosa.

In the Hispanic theatre community, we are aware of the need to further develop our audiences. I believe the type of plays we are now writing, in which Hispanic American audiences can identify with the characters and situations they see on stage, is contributing to that development (in 1986, *Bodega,* Federico Fraguada's first play, broke all box office records at the 20-year-old Puerto Rican Traveling Theatre in New York City. Nearly every New York City *bodeguero* and his family went to see the play. It was presented again in the 1987 season). Musicals and comedies are attracting younger audiences who used to think that going to the theatre meant they were in for a boring evening and opted to stay home and watch music videos.

Adding to the problem of lack of visibility and audience growth, we face the sad fact that in the Hispanic community we don't have a responsible media with responsible, knowledgeable writers who can discuss art and culture intelligently. American critics are, in most instances, either patronizing or insensitive to the work produced by Hispanics, even if it is English.

THE UNIVERSITY'S UNIVERSE

I feel the academic community has a large role to play in bringing Hispanic American theatre and literature into the mainstream of this country's cultural life. Fortunately, today there are many college professors who have a deep interest in our work, are studying it, writing papers, and struggling to include it in their curricula. This is a must. Because they are not only trying to enrich the lives of their students by exposing them to the art and culture of the soon-to-be largest ethnic minority in this nation, but also building theatre audiences for the future.

Unfortunately, these few pioneers face many obstacles from within and without the walls of academia. From the outside, there is the problem of not enough published literary and theatrical works by U.S. Hispanics. From inside the walls, opposition, confusion, misunderstanding, and—why not say it?—plain, ugly racism from faculty and administrators.

Because, they ask, what is "Hispanic literature"? What is "Hispanic drama"? Is there such a thing? And if so, where is it? Where does it belong in the curriculum? They don't know, or don't want to know, what to do with the whole darned big enchilada.

This metaphorical enchilada, like the small real ones, is meant to be eaten, and enjoyed! You can't worry about heartburn a priori! I say, what's wrong with bringing U.S. Hispanic literature and drama into the American Drama Department, along with black and Asian-American works? It also belongs as an interdisciplinary subject in Latin American departments. ¿Por qué no?

My increasing theatre contacts with Latin America and Spain reveal that there is a tremendous interest in what is happening in Hispanic theatre in the United States. One of my plays, *La Era Latina,* a bilingual comedy I cowrote with Víctor Fragoso, won an award in Venezuela. Right now I am busy preparing an enormous amount of information on Hispanic theatre in the U.S. for a book on Latin American theatre, to be published next year by Spain's Ministry of Culture.

YES, BUT WHAT IS IT?

I define Hispanic American theatre, or literature, as that written by Hispanics living and working in the United States whose subject matter, whether written in Spanish or English or both, reflects their expressions in this country in the same manner that, before us, the Jews, the Irish, the Italians documented their experiences and their histories that came to be part of *the* history of this nation.

Hispanics are here for many different reasons. Many have been born here. Many were here before parts of this land came to be called the United States of America. Some came a lifetime ago. Some came yesterday. Some are arriving this very minute. Some dream of returning to where they came from. Some will. Some have made this place their home for good and are here to stay.

Millions of Americans live next door to a Rodríguez or a Fernández. They go down to the corner bodega and buy Café Bustelo and Goya Beans. They eat tacos and enchiladas (big and small) as if there were no tomorrow. They work shoulder to shoulder with millions of Hispanics at every level, every day.

However, in the schools, in the universities, these same Americans learn nothing about those strangers they ride the elevator with. They are not taught who they are, what they think, why they came here.

This is the place, and this is the time. And theatre, and painting, and dance, and poetry can help bridge that gap.

In the theatre, we have that saying—you know the one: "The show must go on." As I said before, soon Hispanics will be the largest ethnic minority in the U.S. Our presence here promises to be a long-running engagement—despite the bad reviews we get most of the time, despite the problems we may have with the lights, and the curtain and the costumes, and the enter and exit cues. Despite all that, this show will go on, and you might as well get your tickets now.

Source: Dolores Prida, "The Show Does Go On (Testimonio)," in *Breaking Boundaries: Latina Writing and Critical Readings*, edited by Asuncion Horno-Delgado, Eliana Ortega, Nina M. Scott, and Nancy Saporta Sternbach, University of Massachusetts Press, 1989, pp. 181–88.

Eliana Rivero

In the following essay, Rivero surveys the history and evolution of Cuban women writers in the United States, mentioning Prida as a pioneer of linguistic dualism.

For those readers who are not in touch with the wide diversity of literary traditions present in American society, many of the artistic works produced in the last two decades are hidden behind mirrors. Texts that reflect the readers' own selves and ideas are very visible, but others, beyond the silvery white surfaces, simply do not exist. Minority writers are routinely ignored, even when they are published by mainstream presses. And if this happens regularly with male ethnic writers, it occurs even more often with the large numbers of female writers of varied nationalities that populate the literary landscapes of this country; women of all colors are even "more invisible" than men. The appearance of publications such as *The Third Woman: Minority Women Writers of the United States* in 1980 was a landmark, with a message that is yet to be recognized in its entirety within canonical circles.

More recent books, such as the widely distributed reference compilation, *American Women*

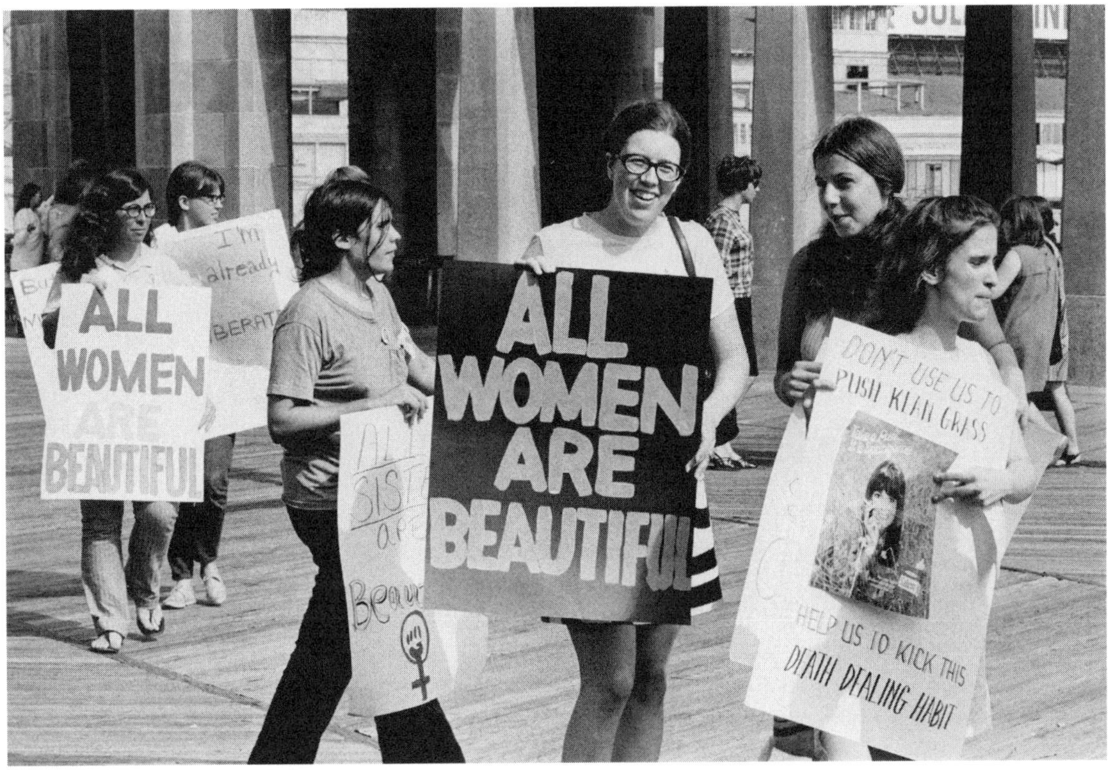

Women's Liberation Movement demonstrators protest against the Miss America Pageant in Atlantic City, 1969 © JP Laffont/Sygma/Corbis

Writers, the much-touted *Norton Anthology of Literature by Women: The Tradition in English,* and the "comprehensive" *Stealing the Language: The Emergence of Women's Poetry in America,* either totally ignore the notable contributions of U.S. Hispanic female authors who had already appeared in the *Third Woman* anthology (while at the same time recognizing the ever-growing production of African-American, Native American, and Asian American women), or severely misrepresent the numbers and importance of Hispanic women writers in our midst. Ostriker, in *Stealing the Language,* makes only a brief mention of two poems by Cherríe Moraga. And yet Ostriker's book appeared five years after the prestigious Pitt Poetry Series (University of Pittsburgh Press) had published Lorna Dee Cervantes' *Emplumada,* the first important book in English by a Chicana poet. Important fiction by Hispanic women, such as Sandra Cisneros' *The House on Mango Street* (Arte Público Press, 1983, recipient of a recent American Book Award), remains on the fringes of the canon—even the revised Anglo canon—despite the increasing attention given to it by feminist critics.

The work of Hispanic women writers in the United States has been ignored, in quite a few instances, due to an uninformed linguistic argument; the bilingualism barrier is deemed insurmountable. This, of course, does not address the prevalent absence of research about such women in departments of Spanish and Latin American studies. In many cases, the subject of U.S. Hispanic women writers is referred to its "natural habitat," i. e., women's and ethnic studies departments. But after reading works by many Hispanic female authors, especially Chicana and Puerto Rican women writing in the continental U.S., one realizes that any efforts to sustain the "linguistic handicap" criterion can only be proven ludicrous. More and more Hispanic women are writing in English, their works appearing in monolingual publications, and translations of poetry and prose are increasing by women who prefer to speak with a Spanish literary voice. Ultimately, the most powerful argument for inclusion of Hispanic minority women within the parameters of what passes for "American literature" might be the latter's characteristic pluralism. Some critics argue that since the so-called American mainstream is basically multiethnic and pluralistic, it, in fact,

"THE WORK OF HISPANIC WOMEN WRITERS IN THE UNITED STATES HAS BEEN IGNORED, IN QUITE A FEW INSTANCES, DUE TO AN UNINFORMED LINGUISTIC ARGUMENT; THE BILINGUALISM BARRIER IS DEEMED INSURMOUNTABLE."

constitutes the "macro context" for all ethnic minority literary manifestations within the U.S. border; Jewish, Afro-American, and Chicano writings, for instance, have been called the American "counter literatures." For years, this has also been the contention of MELUS (Society for the Study of Multi-Ethnic Literature in the United States). One of the underlying assumptions for this article is, then, that women writers of Hispanic ethnicity are as much an integral part of the North American literary scene as Alice Walker or Isaac Bashevis Singer.

And yet the generating conditions and surface features of literary texts produced by Hispanic women writing in the U.S. differ greatly from those that appear in the traditional mainstream publishing houses of this country. Further, particular idiosyncracies can be noted for each subgroup of Hispanic women writers: from those who write in standard Spanish and speak from an experience of immigration and middle-class origins, to those who write in standard English and speak from the conditions of a working-class background. In between, there appears a wide spectrum of bilingual and/or bicultural writers who, although with diverse origins and in very different literary modalities, seem to unfailingly address themselves to what it means to be female *and* Hispanic in this pluralistic society.

In discussing the subject of Hispanic subgroups in the United States, I make a distinction between the "native Hispanic" and "the migrated Hispanic." The first category comprises Mexican-Americans or Chicanos, as well as Puerto Ricans who live on the mainland (Neorricans); the second reflects the waves of migration that, for political or economic reasons, have deposited on these shores a vast contingent of Cubans, Central Americans, and South Americans. Most writers who are in the latter category have been born (and often raised) outside the borders of the United States; however, some among them, especially younger individuals, are in the midst of effecting the transition from emigré, exile, or immigrant/refugee categories to that of ethnic minority members. In a special sense, this transition entails coming into a personal awareness of biculturalism, and takes for granted the reality of permanence in a society other than the one existing in the country of birth. For some Hispanic women writers, a link with the native country and its literature can be maintained if return to the homeland, however short or temporary, is possible: such is the case of a few Argentine, Central American and, lately, Chilean writers who reside in the United States. They, as a rule, consider themselves as Latin American "emigré" or transplanted writers and have a niche in their own national literatures, whether these are written inside or outside the homeland. Among Cuban women who migrated to the U.S. after the Revolution in 1959, the only one that fits adequately in this category is a writer who has been considered a significant figure in the island's literary tradition since the fifties: the Afro-Cuban folktale researcher/writer Lydia Cabrera, best known for her celebrated work, *El monte* (1956).

Some other Cuban women who were writers before being immigrants are squarely situated in the "exile" modality; in their works, they mostly re-create inner and outer landscapes of their native land: social, political, and personal. Their work is tinged with nostalgia for the homeland, as in the case of the poet Ana Rosa Núñez, or their texts live within a space populated with the inner demons of individual and social analysis; the novelist Hilda Perera and the poet Belkis Cuza Malé are good illustrations. Other Cuban women who belong in that same generation are Rita Geada, Pura del Prado, Martha Padilla, and Amelia del Castillo; a younger group of often published poets also includes Juana Rosa Pita and Gladys Zaldívar. Yet none of these names exemplify the transition from exile to ethnic minority member. Their texts often bespeak an existential alienation that denotes an inner struggle with roles and identities; nevertheless, they "neither treat nor engage the U.S. experience."

A few Cuban women writers who were born around 1940 and migrated to the United States in the late fifties or early sixties began, in the mid- and late-seventies, showing in their work a consciousness of change: this was frequently a feminist awareness that at times clashed with their middle-class values and conservative ideology. Sometimes a detail as subtle as a North American geographical name or an English song title would appear in their descriptions of daily happenings; or perhaps it was a flat statement about a house in the suburbs gladly given up to return to Cuba. These authors included the poet Maya Islas (*Sola . . . desnuda . . . sin nombre,* 1974; *Sombras papel,* 1978); the poet, novelist, and short story writer Mireya Robles (*Tiempo artesano,* 1973; *En esta aurora,* 1978; *Hagiografía de Narcisa la Bella,* 1985); and the poet and short story teller Uva Clavijo (*Versos de exilio,* 1974; *Ni verdad ni mentira y otros cuentos,* 1977). *Sombras . . . , En esta aurora, Versos de exilio,* and *Ni verdad ni mentira* are among the first works published by Cuban women in the U.S. that document American society through the authors' literary *personae,* bearing witness to the cultural impact of a very different lifestyle.

It was in 1976, nevertheless, that the fully conscious recognition of a "double identity" was registered in the works of Cuban women writing in the United States. Lourdes Casal, poet, short story writer, essayist, scholar, and political activist, who died in Havana in 1981 after a prolonged illness, is exemplary in marking the transition from a consciousness of immigration to a certainty of permanent dualism, existential as well as sociocultural. After living twelve years in the United States, Casal returned to Cuba in 1973 for the first of several visits; she remained there during her last one, being hospitalized and in serious condition until her final days. Her published works are many, but most important to this study are the literary texts collected in *Los fundadores: Alfonso y otros cuentos* (1973) and in the posthumous book of poetry, *Palabras juntan revolución* (1981).

Casal's experience of living alternately in two cultures, in two radically different sociopolitical systems, profoundly affected her view of reality. Her poem, "Para Ana Veltfort" (first published in 1976), best portrays the dichotomy experienced by a Cuban outside her primary cultural milieu; her poetic *persona* functions in two different environments but fits completely in neither. The text, full of recollections and nostalgic remembrances, tells about her sense of double identity:

> . . . Nueva York es mi casa.
> Soy ferozmente leal a esta adquirida patria chica.
> Por Nueva York soy extranjera ya en cualquier
> parte.
> . . .
> Pero Nueva York no fue la ciudad de mi infancia,
> no fue aquí que adquirí las primeras certidumbres,
> no está aquí el rincón de mi primera caída
> ni el silbido lacerante que marcaba las noches.
> Por eso siempre permaneceré al margen,
> una extraña entre estas piedras,
> aun bajo el sol amable de este día de verano,
> como ya para siempre permaneceré extranjera
> aun cuando regrese a la ciudad de mi infancia.
> Cargo esta marginalidad inmune a todos los
> retornos,
> demasiado habanera para ser neoyorkina,
> demasiado neoyorkina para ser,
> -aun volver a ser-
> cualquier otra cosa.

Havana is the "mother city" of identity but New York—cultural megalopolis—is an experience that will forever define the writer's sense of marginality. The poet feels somehow alien, a stranger and a foreigner in either place, the native and the adopted space of life, yet both sites are familiar and very much a part of her being.

Such a marked self-awareness of "hybridism" appears explicitly in the fabric of such poetic texts as the one quoted above; but it was also beginning to be interwoven by Casal in her fiction writings as early as 1973. In "Love Story según Cyrano Prufrock," a double discourse of recreation about Havana and New York, a male narrator goes in search of love and identity, and is evidently much influenced, in his speech and perceptions, by Casal's own studies of Cabrera Infante's *Tres tristes tigres.* The reader finds allusions to a complex quilt of readings, noticing an American cultural presence in which, nevertheless, Cuban/Hispanic elements are basic to an understanding of the totality of the text:

> Ay poetisa, los tigres no eran tres sino miles . . . hacíamos la revolución y el amor y todo en medio de la interminable noche habanera . . .
>
> Y me senté a tu lado a declamarte discursos impresionantes sobre el destino de la década, lo que se nos habían vuelto los sesenta, el sueño de la razón engendra monstruos (fíjate, piba, terminamos con Nixon de presidente), los gallardos caballeros que se fizieron (te regalé un poster de Malcolm X), la sociedad de consumo lo deglute todo (te regalé un disco autografiado por Marcuse que se estaban liquidando en Marboro), Peter Paul and Mary se separaron y los Beatles ya no existen. . . . ("Capítulo 1. Beatriz encontrada with a little help from my friends, from Johnny Weissmuller to Jean Luc Godard")

Allusions to French film directors, Hollywood movies, Goya's "black" paintings, American radical leaders, New York stores, and legendary musical figures are interspersed with memories of the native city, speech imitations of medieval literary language, references to night life, song lyrics popular both in the U.S. and Cuba, not to mention the not-so-subtle intertextual signs pointing to T. S. Eliot, Edmond de Rostand, Erich Segal, Dante (J. Alfred Prufrock, Cyrano de Bergerac, *Love Story,* Beatriz), and Cortázar's *Rayuela* (the two-city motif, "piba"). English appears still as a point of contact, as a reference; the second language is a cultural tool that has not yet become part of the author's "natural" literary voices and rhythms. Casal wrote mainly in Spanish, but her texts—whether essays, film reviews, poems, short stories, or editorial articles—are thoroughly permeated, during the last five years of her life, with the double vision of biculturalism. There is a sense of irony when one reads, today, her young words of 1957, written while still in the native country:

> Todos los pueblos de Hispanoamérica están de acuerdo en una actitud defensiva y hasta agresiva frente a la potencia del Norte; pero el influjo del triunfo aparente de *ese estilo de vida, que nos es ajeno,* ha determinado, sin embargo, la duda y *la acceptación de costumbres importadas con etiquetas de "Made in U.S.A."* que se han ido infiltrando en nuestra América. . . .

Finally, that "alien lifestyle" also became her own, although her basic *Cubanness* was unmarred with the acquisition of cultural dualism.

To the end of her life, Casal's painful awareness of an insurmountable dual reality—one that had to be lived out daily—was still best expressed in her reiteration of motifs belonging to Havana and New York. Her own tale of two cities reflects her ultimate fear: the erosion of time, that inexorable leveler that makes contours disappear under the dust, that erases all known things:

> Que se me amarillea y se me gasta,
> perfil de mi ciudad, siempre agitándose
> en la memoria
> y sin embargo
> siempre perdiendo bordes y letreros . . .
> ("La Habana 1968," *Palabras juntan revolución,* p. 49)

The same fear of not capturing reality, of losing all memories, assaults the poet, who yearns to "name" the features of her adopted city, her second identity source:

> Recorro las calles de este New York vestido de verano,
> con sus guirnaldas de latas de cerveza
> . . .
> obsedida por la pasión de nombrar,
> azotada por la furia de fijarlo
> y recrearlo todo en la palabra,
> esta batalla irremisiblemente perdida
> contra la caducidad de todo,
> esta batalla incesante y dolorosa
> contra la erosión,
> el tiempo,
> y el olvido,
> que lo devoran todo.
> ("Domingo," *Palabras . . . ,* p. 58)

It is with Lourdes Casal that Cuban women writers in the United States can fully claim their cultural dualism as immigrants. But, more importantly, her life and works give witness to the first full-fledged step in the direction of becoming Cuban-Americans, in the best sense of that term. Ethnic name hyphenation implies a recognition of existential and sociocultural hybridism, and Cuban women in the U.S. are, at present, involved in the process of recognizing themselves as such "others," not only because of the gender imperative, but, more crucially, because of their irrevocable historical situation.

In the works of other U.S. Hispanic writers, it is usually the emergence of bilingual texts that signals, for them, an established conscientization ("self-awareness") of minority status; in other words, the political consciousness of being "dual," or "other," is clearly best expressed at the linguistic level. This phenomenon was first registered for Cuban women authors with the presentation in 1977 of the play *Beautiful Señoritas* by Dolores Prida, a writer/journalist who has distinguished herself as a playwright (*Coser y cantar*) and as a poet. She was also one of the first editorial members of the Latino publication *Nuestro,* and her work for the stage in the 1970s is pioneering among Cuban women.

But the establishment of ethnic awareness/affirmation as a permanent literary presence for Cuban-American women comes in the mid-eighties with the young poet, short story writer, and playwright from Chicago, Achy Obejas. At this writing, she has not published a book yet, but her promising works have appeared in *Woman of Her Word* (1983), *Third Woman* (1984; 1986), and *Nosotras: Latina Literature Today* (1986); a 1983 play she cowrote, "Carnicería," was highly acclaimed and is considered the most successful play in the history of Spanish-language theatre in Chicago. Her texts, whether in English, Spanish, or a language-alternation mode, are highly polished, well-crafted, and evidence the bilingual/bicultural world vision that distinguishes other well-known "native" Hispanic women poets, such as the Chicana Lorna Dee Cervantes and the Nuyorrican Sandra María Esteves. Obejas synthesizes the process of searching for roots and the consciousness of "hybridism" in texts such as "Sugarcane":

> can't cut
> cut the cane

azuca' in chicago
. . .
you can't can't cut
cut the blood
lines from this island
train one by one throwing off
the chains siguaraya
no no
no se pue'e cortar
pan con ajo quisqueya
cuba y borinquen no
se pue'en parar

In this code-switching discourse, the island motif of sugarcane, with all its implied meanings for Cuban culture, draws on an intertextual past of Afro-Caribbean poetry, on song lyrics that portray the speaker's acquaintance with popular cultural icons, and with the experience of Hispanos in the barrios of midwestern and northeastern America. The words of a fifties' Afro song by Celia Cruz—noted Cuban singer, reborn as an entertainer in the heights of *salsa* fever—constitute a takeoff point for the refrain, "no se pue'e cortar." The lyrics of the song, "Siguaraya" (tree especially revered for its magic properties in the Yoruba religious belief system), repeated the refrain: "Siguaraya, yo va tumbá, con permiso de Yemayá." Obejas changes the positive affirmation of the slave chant—"I am going to cut the tree down with permission from [the goddess] Yemayá"—into a "negatively" phrased reaffirmation of radical cultural pride ("you can't can't cut/cut the blood/lines from this island"), marked at the verse level by the imitated staccato patterns of the song. Siguaraya and sugarcane, two native, life-giving plants of the Caribbean, are intimately tied to the economic, social, and cultural life of the Great Antilles. The three islands, recognized in the text by their Taíno names (Cuba, Borinquen, Quisqueya), are equated for what they share in the "magic," the life rhythms, and the social awareness that the poet sees as vital to her bicultural life in the United States.

Obejas also publishes in standard Spanish, as with her poem, "El bote" (*Third Woman* 2, no. 1 [1984]: 33): "no nos acabamos de ir del país/tú y yo, siempre con el mapa abierto." This composition treats, in a symbolic manner, a recurrent motif for Cuban-American women: leaving the native country. The same theme forms the background for "The Escape," a sober portrayal of cultural, as well as real, death, a short story that brings into play all the elements of the Cuban experience of political flight to, and exile in, a foreign country. A seven-year-old girl looks around her and sees strange, pale, lifeless North Americans with blond eyelashes that seem "fuzzy and alien" (*Nosotras,* p. 46). She kills one of them, only to fall prey to the ocean waves, drowning herself while rafting for pleasure, at fourteen, amid the fearful, stormy Atlantic currents off the coast of Florida.

Basic distinctions between a *Cuban* woman writer in the United States and a Cuban-*American* woman writer are, thus, the full consciousness of dualism, the sense of belonging to a minority, and the use of English that appear in the works illustrated above. Cuban-born women writers in the U.S. who belong to the older generations still identify, for the most part, with a "writer-in-exile" definition. That situates them squarely within the realm of a Latin American *status quo* vision, whereas minority writers in the U.S. usually speak from an experience of marginality and discrimination due to race, class, and/or sex. More to the point, Cuban "writers in exile"—women *and* men—tend to identify with the establishment and reject the Third World stance of many native Hispanic writers, and thus do not feel part of an underprivileged ethnic minority.

In general, Cuban women who were writers before they migrated preserve the literary notions and standards they learned in their intellectual and artistic formation, often considering themselves as part of the literature of their native country and/or of Latin America. Still, some of the writings done by Cuban women in the United States present a modified vision of cultural reality due to the prevalence of a feminist ideology in their texts, and to the naked, critical portrayal of sociocultural myths, such as the submissive, petit-bourgeois wife and her pathetic Don Juanesque husband. An excellent illustration is *Hagiografía de Narcisa la Bella,* by Mireya Robles (now residing in South Africa, after almost thirty years in this country). This 1985 novel is a well-crafted, avant-garde work with similarities to some of the best productions of Latin American prose fiction in the last decades (Puig, Donoso, Lynch, Vargas Llosa). Its locale is a provincial town of Cuba in the fifties, and its plot ends with the terrible ritual death of the ugly, sensitive, clairvoyant Narcisa, victimized at the hands of her family. Jean Franco has praised the novel, saying of Robles that she has:

> el don genuino de la sátira y lo cómico, algo relativamente escaso en las letras hispanoamericanas.

Robles represents, in the characterization of Cuban women offered in these pages, the immigrant writer who associates her craft with Latin American or Hispanic/universal canonical forms, while Achy Obejas symbolizes the other end of the spectrum: the Cuban-American in her dually grounded vision of culture and society. To put it in general terms, the most distinguishable feature that separates older immigrant generations of Cuban women from their younger compatriots in the U.S., beyond their choice of language, is the problem of their cultural/political identity and affiliations. These vital connections, with their own inner and outer selves, constitute on artistic mother lode of inquiry, rejection, and affirmation.

For Cuban-American women writers, then, the process of establishing themselves in the multicultural U.S. literary scene has just begun. They are already partakers of what Lourdes Casal defined more than a decade ago as a "marginality immune to all returns"; but the road ahead promises to give them a place behind the one-mirror surfaces of the American mainstream as well. Theirs is, nevertheless, an exciting location at the margins: on the cutting edge of Latina cultural ethnicity and gender awareness.

Source: Eliana Rivero, "From Immigrants to Ethnics: Cuban Women Writers in the U.S.," in *Breaking Boundaries: Latina Writing and Critical Readings*, edited by Asuncion Horno-Delgado, Eliana Ortega, Nina M. Scott, and Nancy Saporta Sternbach, University of Massachusetts Press, 1989, pp. 189–200.

SOURCES

Prida, Dolores, *Beautiful Señoritas*, in *Beautiful Señoritas & Other Plays*, Arte Publico Press, 1991, pp. 21, 24, 30, 36, 39, 40, 41, 42.

———, "The Show Does Go On," in *Breaking Boundaries: Latina Writing and Critical Readings*, edited by Asunción Horno-Delgado et al., University of Massachusetts Press, 1989, p. 182.

Rivero, Eliana, "From Immigrants to Ethnics: Cuban Women Writers in the U.S.," in *Breaking Boundaries: Latina Writing and Critical Readings*, edited by Asunción Horno-Delgado et al., University of Massachusetts Press, 1989, p. 195.

FURTHER READING

Aston, Elaine, *An Introduction to Feminism and Theatre*, Routledge, 1995.

As the title of this work suggests, Aston's book introduces readers to the works and theories of feminist dramatists.

Kevane, Bridget, and Juanita Heredia, eds., *Latina Self-Portraits: Interviews with Contemporary Women Writers*, University of New Mexico Press, 2000.

This collection of interviews provides insights into the goals and concerns of Latina women currently writing in the United States.

Pérez-Stable, Marifeli, *The Cuban Revolution: Origins, Course, and Legacy*, Oxford University Press, 1999.

This is an accessible and thorough look at Fidel Castro's Cuba from its inception to 1999.

Sandoval-Sánchez, Alberto, and Nancy Saporta Sternbach, eds., *Puro Teatro: A Latina Anthology*, University of Arizona Press, 2000.

This anthology is a wonderful collection of plays by American Latina playwrights, Prida included.

Blue Surge

REBECCA GILMAN

2001

Rebecca Gilman's *Blue Surge*, first produced in 2001 (and published by Faber and Faber in the same year), was a bit shocking when it first opened to enthusiastic audiences at Chicago's Goodman Theatre. It is, after all, a play about prostitutes, and it utilizes full frontal male nudity in the first scene. However, audience interest in the play stemmed more from the fact that Gilman is a local Chicago playwright, and her plays are known for their cutting-edge social commentary. *Blue Surge* is no exception.

The overall theme of this play is the wide gap between the people of upper-class society, with their wealth and seemingly easy lives of opportunities, and the people of the lower, working classes, with their economic and educational limits (at least in Gilman's portrayal). This gap is dramatized through the interactions of a vice-squad policeman and his interest in two women. His live-in girlfriend comes from the privileged class. She is an art student and lives off a trust fund inherited from her grandfather. The young woman with whom the policeman would like to begin a new relationship is a massage-parlor prostitute, whose only ambition is to make enough money to retire by the time she is thirty.

The title *Blue Surge* reflects a mixture of sadness, poverty, desire, and misunderstanding, other motifs that run through the play. There is mention in the play of a piece by the jazz master Duke Ellington called "Blue Serge." The protagonist, Curt, hears the title and thinks it is "Blue Surge,"

because he finds the music rather dark and melancholic. When Curt tells his prostitute friend, Sandy, about this misunderstanding, relating that blue serge is really a type of material used to make men's suits, Sandy imagines that perhaps the songwriter felt sad because he could not afford a suit. Thus, Gilman uses the misunderstood title of the jazz piece to pinpoint one of the messages of the play, a play in which her characters have particular longings that are difficult for them to fulfill. As Gilman portrays it, the main hindrance for those who are left wanting in their desires is poverty, and the creators of that poverty are the rich.

AUTHOR BIOGRAPHY

Rebecca Gilman was born in Trussville, Alabama, in 1965 and studied at Middlebury College in Vermont. Later, she returned to her home state and gained her undergraduate degree from Birmingham Southern College. Then she attended the University of Virginia, majoring in English, because she thought she might be interested in teaching. However, she soon discovered that her real passion was writing. After receiving her master's degree at Virginia, she fought hard and eventually made it into the prestigious writers' program at the University of Iowa, where she earned an MFA in playwriting.

Her writing began with a play she wrote when she was only eighteen years old, about a group of disgruntled employees in a doughnut shop who suffocate their boss in a vat of dough. Many of her early plays were never produced. To support her writing in those early years, Gilman took on various clerical positions, never believing that she could make a living at playwriting.

Gilman wrote several plays before her first successful play, *Spinning into Butter* (1999), which probes the nature of the racism that lurks behind the mask of liberalism worn by her characters. The play received a Joseph Jefferson Award for best new play and the Roger L. Stevens Award from the Kennedy Center Fund for new American plays. *Time* magazine included this play on its list of best new plays for 1999.

The Glory of Living (1996) was Gilman's next big hit, earning another Joseph Jefferson Award as well as the *Evening Standard* (London) award for most promising playwright and the British George Devine Award. Gilman was the first American ever to receive either of these honors. The play is based on a true incident in which a young bride becomes an accomplice in her husband's serial killing. *The Glory of Living*, which was first staged in 1996 in Chicago, gained more attention and acclaim in 1999 when it traveled to London. In 2002, it was named one of *Time* magazine's best plays and was a finalist for the Pulitzer Prize.

Gilman's *Boy Gets Girl*, about a man who stalks a woman, was produced in 2001. Then came *Blue Surge*. It was followed by *The Sweetest Swing in Baseball*, which premiered in London in 2004. The play deals with a young female artist who must confront debilitating fears and eventually admits herself to psychiatric care. The young woman ends up feigning schizophrenia in an effort to convince her doctors that she is the famed baseball player Darryl Strawberry.

Gilman has been referred to as one of the most sought-after playwrights in the United States. Her plays have been called provocative and edgy. She is one of the few playwrights in America who do not shy away from taking on social issues in order to make their audiences think. Gilman once said that at the beginning of her writing career, she was afraid of voicing her opinions through her works. With repeated success, however, that has all changed.

PLOT SUMMARY

Act 1

Scene 1 of the first act opens in a massage parlor located in a midsize city in the Midwest. Sandy, the masseuse, enters with Curt. Sandy tells Curt to get undressed and then leaves the room. Curt acts nervous while he takes off everything but his underpants. When Sandy returns, Curt tries to make conversation with her, but he is awkward at best. Curt is a policeman, and he thinks that Sandy has no idea of his occupation. He tries to persuade Sandy to admit that her main purpose is not to give massages but to have sex with her patrons. Through their conversation, Curt learns that Sandy actually has no training in massage therapy, but he cannot get her to say anything that he can use in a police case against her as a prostitute. Once Sandy begins to massage Curt's back, Curt decides he cannot go through with the sting operation. He insists on getting dressed. "I don't know what I'm doing," Sandy says, as she watches Curt. Curt responds: "It's okay. Neither do I."

A week has passed when scene 2 opens. The location is the same massage parlor, but the characters are new. Doug, who is Curt's police partner, walks into the room with Heather, another prostitute. When Heather asks Doug to strip, he does so without any signs of self-consciousness. In contrast to Curt, he takes everything off and stands on the stage stark naked. Doug proceeds to ask Heather various questions about sexual acts and about whether she will perform them. While Heather does not admit to anything, she does insinuate that she would be willing to do them. Doug then reaches for his badge and tells Heather she is under arrest. Heather cries out that he has entrapped her.

Scene 3 takes place in a room at the police station. Sandy has been taken to the police station but is not charged with a crime. She is merely warned that the police suspect her of prostitution. Curt is telling Sandy that she is free to go. He warns her, though, that the next time she might not be so lucky. Before Sandy leaves, Curt asks her if she knew that he was a cop when he visited the massage parlor. Sandy admits that she did. When Curt asks how, Sandy says it was because he refused to take off his underpants.

Doug enters the room and is angry because his case has fallen through. Heather's accusation that Doug entrapped her has been upheld. Once Sandy is excused, Doug and Curt discuss how they fouled up the bust. Curt points out Doug's mistakes, and Doug emphasizes Curt's lack of experience. Then Doug talks about his sexual fascination with Heather.

In scene 4, Curt's girlfriend, Beth, is introduced. Curt and Beth are having an edgy conversation. Neither seems pleased with the other. Beth makes fun of Curt's partner, Doug. Then she demeans a restaurant that Curt mentions. Curt calls her on both points. When Curt tries to explain what he has gone through that day, Beth sticks up for the prostitutes and says the police should leave them alone. Curt counters by telling Beth that she does not know the first thing about the hazards of prostitution. When Curt offers further details about his day, Beth becomes jealous that Curt was somewhat intimate with another woman and that he seems to have been drawn to one woman in particular.

As Beth is about to leave Curt's apartment, she suggests that he find a new job. Curt mentions the limited possibilities that are open to him, since he has only a high school education. He also throws out the fact that Beth lives off a trust fund. He does so to suggest that her life is easy, especially compared with his own life. Their arguing intensifies, until Beth admits that she is really angry that Curt chose a particular masseuse at the parlor. Curt denies that he had any interest in the woman, saying at the end of the scene: "I can't even remember what she looked like."

Scene 5 takes place in a bar. Heather has lost her job at the massage parlor and is working as a bartender. Curt is listening to Heather complain, when Sandy walks in. Curt has asked Sandy to meet him there. Heather continues to talk about how Doug has cost her the massage parlor job. Sandy informs Heather that Curt knows all about the story because he, too, is a cop. Heather walks away in a huff.

Sandy and Curt make small talk. Curt tells Sandy that he wants to help her. Sandy tells him that she does not need any help. She likes what she does. The only part of her job that she does not like is turning over half the money she earns to the owner of the massage parlor. The single thing she would change about her life would be to own her own place. She could then continue as a prostitute but would not have to share the money she made with anyone else. Curt and Sandy then share personal information. They discover that their childhoods were somewhat similar. They were both raised poor. Sandy's mom has been married five times. Curt tells Sandy that his father was a grave robber. Curt encourages Sandy to get out of the prostitution business. He suggests that she take classes at a community college. Sandy believes that community colleges are only for losers. She explains how easy it is for her to earn a lot of money doing what she does. The scene ends with Curt asking whether Sandy will do him a favor, something that his girlfriend will not do. This is sexually suggestive, but the audience later finds out his favor has nothing to do with sex. He wants help memorizing the names of trees.

As scene 6 opens, Sandy and Curt are in Curt's apartment. Sandy is holding up plastic-encased leaves, which Curt is naming. Curt talks about his aspirations to one day work at a nature center. After flipping through several of the leaves, Sandy grows tired and is about to go. Before she does, she says that she would like to meet again. They set a date for the following Friday.

In scene 7, Curt and Doug are at the police station. Continuing demonstrations outside the massage parlor by citizens who want the place shut down have put pressure on Curt's supervisor. In retaliation, Curt has been demoted and transferred from the vice squad to the burglary unit, which he hates. Doug admits he has been seeing Heather, who has moved in with Sandy. Doug has talked with Sandy and insinuates to Curt that the discussion they had was about sex. When Doug suggests that he might pay Sandy to do him a sexual favor, Curt punches Doug in the mouth. Curt says that Doug is ruining his life; nevertheless, Curt apologizes for hitting Doug, and the scene ends.

In the next scene, Curt hears someone knocking on his door at home. When he answers, he finds Sandy standing there in her bare feet. She is crying. Sandy tells Curt that Heather is having a party at Sandy's apartment and that the people are getting carried away. Curt invites Sandy to stay at his place for the night. Sandy's stepfather has died, and this has made her feel miserable. Curt believes that he is part of the reason why Sandy is sad. He fears that he has put too much pressure on her to find another job and to do something more constructive with her life. Sandy does not agree with Curt, but she consents to spending the night.

Act 2

Scene 1 is set in Curt's apartment two days later. Sandy is wearing some of Curt's clothes. She seems to have remained at Curt's apartment, but no explanation is given as to why she has done so. Curt talks about Duke Ellington's "Blue Serge." Curt and Sandy agree that it is a sad song. Curt explains how he had misinterpreted the title of the piece, believing it was "Blue Surge," or a surge of sadness. This leads Sandy and Curt to discuss their sad memories of growing up. Curt tells a funny story, and as the two of them continue talking and laughing, Beth walks in on them.

Sandy wants to leave, but Curt does not want her to. Beth wants to know why Sandy is there. The conflicting needs of the three people produce much confusion. Sandy wants to get out of the way, to avoid causing a scene. Curt is torn between Beth and Sandy but leans toward wanting to make sure that Sandy is all right. After she leaves, Curt wants to go after her. He tells Beth that he wants to help Sandy, confessing that Sandy is the woman from the massage parlor. Beth calls Sandy a whore. When Beth threatens to leave, Curt does not stop her.

In scene 2, set in the bar in which Heather now works, Heather and Doug are planning a date. Curt enters and asks whether they have seen Sandy. No one has. Curt tells them that he had gone by Sandy's apartment looking for her. Instead, he found an eviction notice and a large padlock on her apartment door. Heather and Doug mention the wild party that had taken place in Sandy's apartment. They tell Curt that they, too, left Sandy's apartment while the party was still going on.

Sandy enters. She is angry because she has had to pay her landlord five hundred dollars for the damage done to the apartment. Sandy admits that she went back to the massage parlor to make the money. This angers Curt, who thought Sandy might give up prostitution. Curt tells her that he spent the whole day looking for her. The only place he did not go was the parlor, saying, "I did not once think you would be stupid enough to go back there!" Sandy leaves after Curt yells at her. In the meantime, Heather, realizing that she has to find a new place to live, asks Doug if she can move in with him.

Beth and Curt confront each other in scene 3. Curt tells Beth that he likes Sandy because he is able to talk to her. With Beth, he confesses, he only seems to argue. Curt explains that there is too much of a gap between the two of them, since Beth does not understand what it is to be poor. He tells Beth that the only reason she stays with him is that she pities him. He goes on to say that she has agreed to marry him because she wants to shock her parents. This leads Curt to explain why he hates working in the burglary unit. He goes to rich people's huge homes and must make reports of stolen items that they do not even remember they own, because they have so many things. Curt says he sweats when he is in the presence of rich people, including Beth. Rich people make him feel as though he stinks. The difference in their social status makes Curt feel less than human around Beth. The scene ends with Beth insulting Sandy and Curt defending her—or at least explaining how he and Sandy are the same.

In scene 4, Doug and Curt are back in the police station, where Doug tells Curt that the police are going to bust the massage parlor. Curt wants to know whether Heather has heard from Sandy. Doug says the two women are not talking to each other. Then Doug describes how trashed Sandy's apartment was. When Doug mentions that the police raid on the massage parlor was planned for the end of the week, Curt realizes that it is the end of the week, and he disappears.

Curt has gone to the massage parlor in scene 5 to warn Sandy that there is about to be a raid and to give her an envelope filled with money. She is to take the money and never come back to the parlor again. Sandy refuses to accept the money; by the time Curt talks her into it, the cops have arrived. Sandy notices that the money has a paper band with an evidence number around it. Curt has stolen the money from the police department, and Sandy cannot believe it. Curt takes the money back from her. The scene ends with Sandy asking: "You wanted us to live together on stolen money. What sort of stupid fantasy is that?" Curt replies: "Mine, okay?"

In scene 6, Curt is still at the massage parlor, sitting in the same room, alone. Doug walks in and tells him that half of the police department is in the lobby. They discuss what Curt should do now that the police have arrived to find him there with stolen money. Doug tells Curt to get a good lawyer and says that none of the women has been arrested. The police, however, are seizing the massage parlor. Curt is despondent; he does not care what happens to him. Doug tries to turn Curt's perspective around. "It's your life," Doug tells Curt, "and it matters." Then Doug adds: "You got to believe that you deserve the best in this world. Do you believe that?" When Curt responds in the affirmative, Doug presses on, telling Curt that he really has to believe it in his heart.

Scene 7 takes place a year later at the bar. Doug and Heather are there together, and Heather is pregnant. Curt soon enters with a takeout dinner for the three of them. They fight over who is going to pay for the food. Sandy walks in, very smartly dressed. She has brought a present for the expected baby. Curt tells Sandy she is looking good, and Sandy returns the compliment, noticing Curt's uniform. Curt explains that he is working as a security guard. His lawyer cut a deal for him, but he had to resign from the police force. Sandy tells Curt that she is still a hooker, but now she is her own boss. She keeps all the money and is doing fairly well. Curt says his new job is boring, but it gives him time to attend classes. He has not been able to take the courses he wanted, but at least he is studying.

Sandy confesses that she stole one of Curt's plastic-encased leaves from his apartment and hung it in her house. Curt tells Sandy that he probably will never get a job at a nature center now, but he is touched that Sandy took one of the leaves. The play ends with Sandy and Curt sitting on the bar stools, holding hands. As they sit there, they "look toward something outside themselves that they can't quite see."

CHARACTERS

Beth

Beth is Curt's rich girlfriend. She is the least developed of the characters, representing not much more than the privileges of her class. She does not have to work, as all the other characters in the play do. She is attending art school. The other characters cannot afford to do this, or else they do not have those kinds of aspirations. It is not clear from what Beth says whether she truly loves Curt, though she does seem to want to try, at least a little. She just does not try very hard.

Beth's big scene occurs about halfway through the play. She arrives at Curt's apartment to try to straighten out their relationship. Although she argues her case, she appears resigned to the differences between them. She is not arrogant, but she does jump to conclusions about people, often casting people unlike her into stereotypes. But she is torn. At one point, for instance, she stands up for prostitutes, telling Curt that their profession should be legalized so that they can come together and demand benefits. However, after she suspects that Curt has fallen for a prostitute, Beth refers to Sandy as a whore. Beth leaves the play quietly. Her presence is barely missed.

Curt

Curt, a policeman, is the protagonist of the drama. It is around him that all the dialogue and action take place. The play opens with Curt inside a massage parlor as an undercover cop, trying to catch one of the masseuses in the act of soliciting sex. Because of his sensitivity or his sheer innocence and lack of experience, he fails. He is portrayed as being too honest to lie about his position. He cannot go through with entrapping the young woman. It later becomes apparent that part of the reason is that he is attracted to Sandy, the young prostitute.

At heart, Curt is a romantic. He wants to help people, and Sandy appears to need his help. At least, that is what Curt believes or wants to believe. Curt seems more motivated to sacrifice most of his life doing something that he does not like (being a policeman) and waiting until he retires to do what he really wants (working as a nature guide). In Sandy, he falls for a woman who is much younger than he is and who, in Curt's view, is the victim of poverty and lack of education. Curt has seen prostitutes who are hooked on drugs and who, in many circumstances, are treated like slaves by those who make money off prostitution.

Still, Curt's ethics are not fully defined. In the end, he steals evidence, in the form of money, from the police station to help Sandy find a better way of life. In some ways, he is trying to buy Sandy, much like other men try to buy her. Even though

Curt may want Sandy for more than just sex, he uses money as a lure to get her. By the end of the play, Curt has changed, but not for the better. He has lost his girlfriend, Beth, and his job, and he has forsaken his dreams. He has been humbled by his experiences, but it is not certain that this is an improvement in his life. His humbling is more like a complete dissolution.

Doug

Doug is Curt's partner on the police force. At times, he seems to be more experienced or more tuned in to life than Curt, although his mind is often distracted by sex. Doug offers comic relief through his fascination with sex. Doug falls for Heather, although, in the beginning, it seems that he wants her only for sex. However, as the play evolves, Doug appears to be developing true feelings for Heather. His sensitivity also extends to his partner. Doug is the only character in the play who encourages Curt to stop feeling sorry for himself and to respect all the good things he has in life. In the beginning, Doug acts like a bit of a bumbling fool, but by the end he acts stronger than Curt. He has taken on the responsibilities of fatherhood and seems to be a caring spouse.

Heather

Heather is something of a bimbo at the beginning of the play. She does not pick up on clues that Doug might be a cop when he comes to the massage parlor intent on arresting her. Neither does she recognize that Curt is a policeman when he comes to the bar where Heather now works. Heather, in a drunken stupor, takes advantage of a missing bar owner by serving free drinks from behind the bar. Later, a group of people follow her to Sandy's apartment. While those people are trashing Sandy's place, Heather leaves. She does not accept any responsibility. Instead, she becomes angry when Sandy suggests that she should help pay for the damages.

However, at the end of the play, Heather speaks of how she cannot button her coat because she has grown so big with her pregnancy. She does not offer much in terms of resolving any of the issues of the play, but rather she appears to feature in the play as a statement that prostitutes are real people too.

Sandy

Sandy is the prostitute whom Curt befriends and tries to help. Of all the characters, she seems to be the only one with her head on her shoulders, despite her profession. She does not know at the start of the play exactly what she wants. She has only a vague idea, and yet she is the one whose dream comes true. She is also a very strong character. She does not fall for Curt's weak promises of a better life when she could easily have done so. She enjoys being treated well by him. Even though she finds herself in fairly dire straits throughout the play, she stands up on her own two feet.

At one point in the play, Curt tells Beth that he and Sandy are alike, and on some level this is true. Sandy and Curt have had difficult childhoods. They both come from families who have no wealth, and they would like to rise above their station in life. But it is Sandy who is able to do this, at least financially. She does it by not taking Curt's advice and instead following her own dream.

THEMES

Working Class versus Leisure Class

Four of the five characters in Gilman's play come from the working class. These are the most developed characters and the ones who are more often present on stage. Gilman's focus is on the working class, but she uses the character of Beth, Curt's girlfriend, to show contrast and to make her point about the differences between the two classes.

Beth does not have to work. She is going to school not to become a dental assistant or a data processor or take up some other practical vocation but rather to develop her creativity. She is in art school. To some people, who must struggle every day to earn minimum wage, painting might appear frivolous and a waste of time. Beth has the luxury of time, however. Her days are not spent in a meaningless job or in worrying about her next meal and how she will pay the rent. She is a shallow character, probably because Gilman did not want to portray the leisure class in a favorable light.

While Curt must work at a job that he does not like, Beth can pursue a profession in which she is fully engaged and through which she can expand her talents and nurture her soul. Beth has the potential to become an artist. She is inspired. She believes that everyone can and should follow her example. She pushes Curt to improve himself by seeking a better job. Curt, however, feels that being of the working class, he has few options. There is a ceiling over his head, and it is very low. He did not have the opportunity to go to a good college

TOPICS FOR FURTHER STUDY

- Read a history of prostitution, such as Nils Johan Ringdal's *Love for Sale* (2005) or William Sanger's *History of Prostitution: Its Extent, Causes, and Effects Throughout the World* (1986). Write a synopsis of that history, including such details as times or countries in which prostitution was looked upon differently. Have attitudes toward prostitution changed in the United States over time? Was prostitution ever legal in America, such as during the development of the West? Are there signs of changing attitudes in the twenty-first century?
- The last stage directions of this play mention that Curt and Sandy are sitting at a bar, holding hands and looking into the distance at something they cannot see. What do you think Gilman is referring to by this statement? What could Sandy be trying to see? What about Curt? Use your knowledge of the play but also use your imagination to write up an account of what both characters might be searching for.
- Listen to Duke Ellington's song "Blue Serge" and describe the way the music affects you. Research the way in which music theorists have described this piece. Go to the musical director at your school and ask her or his opinion of what this music is all about. Find out what elements within the song impart a feeling of sadness. Bring the music to class and describe what you have discovered.
- Doug often comes across in this play as a figure of comic relief, providing humor to ease some of the tension. Still, by the end of the play, Doug seems more grounded and philosophical than Curt. Compare these two characters throughout the play. Where do their characters stand in relationship to each other at the beginning of the play? When does their relationship begin to change? Which one of them, by the end of the play, appears to have changed the most? What are those changes? Write a paper describing your findings.

full time after graduating from high school. He had to find a job and provide for his mother.

Sandy also belongs to the working class, but she differs from Curt in many ways. She does not believe that education is her ticket out. She knows she can afford to attend only a community college, which she sees as not much more than a technical school, from which students emerge with minimal skills needed to perform boring jobs. She does not see community college as a stepping-stone to a bachelor's degree and a broader education. But she does have aspirations, unlike Curt, who has accepted his fate and goes through life in a sort of zombie-like sleepwalking state—not totally depressed but definitely not happy. Curt's only aspiration is to find something he might like to do after he retires.

Sandy and Beth are somewhat similar. They know what they want, and they go after it. They are independent thinkers. But while Beth uses her mind, Sandy uses her body. In society's terms Beth is legitimate, whereas Sandy must live on the outer edges of legitimacy. Through them, Gilman portrays another aspect of the differences between social classes.

Poverty

Curt wears his poverty as he wears his police badge. In some ways, his poverty gives him a weird sense of authority. He also has a poor concept of himself and does not give himself much credit for knowing anything, but he claims to know all about poverty. He knows what it is to be hungry and to struggle. He understands poverty and can relate to it. When he finds comfort in being with Sandy, it is not her personality or skills or even her appearance that attracts him. It is her poor background that puts Curt at ease. Through their similar childhood struggles Curt relates to Sandy in a way he could never relate to Beth.

Gilman seems to be saying that it is lack of money that keeps people down. Without money, the dreams of people are small. Poor people are permanently handicapped in life. They will never get ahead unless they do something that is illegal, such as prostituting themselves or stealing money. It is their poverty that leads them to break the law.

Excessive Materialism

In one long monologue, Curt tells Beth of his feelings about people who have a lot of money. He is angry that he must return to the burglary unit. He has worked in it before, and it makes him feel bad. He must go into people's houses and take reports about stolen property. He claims that often these people cannot even identify what has been stolen, because they have so many objects filling up their big houses. This excessive materialism makes him feel that he physically stinks. He sweats profusely around rich people, because they make him nervous. They make him feel worthless.

The excessive materialism reminds him of how little he had as a child and how little he still has. It makes him realize that his chances of ever catching up to the rich are nonexistent. He thinks that if everyone were poor, there would be no disparity, no jealousy, no belittlement. But when some people have so much—when their wealth in material objects is excessive—he feels that they have taken something from him. This could be one of the reasons why Curt has no second thoughts about stealing money from the police station. His attitude appears to imply that since he needs it to help someone else (as well as himself), it is his right to take it. It makes sense to him, at least while he is doing it.

Choices and Consequences

Gilman's play progresses through a series of choices and their consequences. At the beginning of the play, Beth chooses not to spend the night with Curt. This leaves him open to invite Sandy to stay at his apartment. When Beth returns to Curt's and finds Sandy there, Curt decides not to stay and explain everything to Beth but to go after Sandy instead. He has obviously chosen Sandy over Beth. Curt gives up the high-society woman he was going to marry but with whom he did not feel comfortable because he would be marrying someone beyond his social class. Curt chooses to pursue Sandy.

Sandy, however, does not choose Curt. Sandy does not seem to need a man in her life, at least outside of her business. She also chooses not to go to school. She is comfortable in her life, except for having to work for someone. She wants to become more independent, and she leaves the massage parlor and takes a chance on setting up her own private business. She is successful, enjoys what she does, and is making a fairly good amount of money—which was most important to her.

Doug chooses to allow Heather to move in with him, and the couple is going to have a baby. There is very little dialogue about Heather and Doug, but the overall sense at the end of the play is that they are both happy with the outcome.

Beth disappears about halfway through the play, so the audience does not know how she fares with respect to the consequences of her choices. Curt, however, seems to be the least affected by his choices. He has lost the woman he was going to marry. He also lost Sandy, although it is unclear if he ever had her. And he lost his job and all hope of the one dream that he had—becoming a volunteer at a nature center upon his retirement. All of the consequences Curt experiences, however, do not seem to have changed him very much. He did not seem happy at the beginning of the play, before he made all these choices, and he does not seem happy at the end. Curt seems to be neither happy nor sad. He remains somewhat numb throughout the play.

STYLE

Opposition

To add tension to her play, Gilman uses oppositions. There are oppositional characters and themes. For example, there is the aloof and somewhat sophisticated Beth, who works with children to expand their artistic talents. She is well educated, well off financially, and, during the play, quite sexless. In opposition to her is Heather, who appears a bit light in the brain department, and who is represented as sex-personified through her profession, her conversation, and her ultimate pregnancy. While Heather teeters on the verge of disaster, seemingly following a path of least resistance, Beth has a definite plan of what she wants to do and how she intends to accomplish it.

Other obvious oppositions include poverty versus wealth; the difference between money inherited, money earned, and money stolen; cop versus prostitute; and legitimate women versus illegitimate women. Opposition not only creates tension, it also provides a means for Gilman to point out some of her beliefs or some of the ideas that she wants her audience to go home and think about. By showing opposites, Gilman gives her audience a choice: she seems to be asking her audience to choose which side they are on.

Conflict: Internal and External

Conflict is the meat of most plays. It can provide action and provoke thought. Conflict can be both external and internal; Gilman's play has both.

The external conflict in the play exists in the disagreements between Curt and Beth, Curt and Doug, Curt and Sandy, and Sandy and Heather. Personal values, dreams, and intentions clash. Implied external conflict in Gilman's play is represented by the demonstrators outside the massage parlor as well as the conflict between the police department and the prostitutes. Gilman's characters are challenged by the conflict that the playwright creates for them. They must find some way to come to grips with it, and that need drives much of the action of the play.

There is also internal conflict, which heightens the effect of the external conflicts. The audience does not see the internal conflict but can infer it from the dialogue of the characters and the characters' emotional outbursts. Such internal conflict is exemplified by Curt, who is constantly questioning whether he is good enough. His conflict derives from not fitting into his society. He feels poor and criticizes the rich, but inside he wants to be part of the rich class. He has a wealthy girlfriend, for instance, but this is not enough. He is not happy with her. He criticizes the wealthy, who he claims are hoarders and extravagant materialists; still, something about them gets under his skin. The rich would not bother him if he did not have any inclinations to be like them.

Gilman's audiences stay tuned in to the drama because they want to see how these internal conflicts will play out. Audiences are interested for another reason as well. They can relate to internal conflict. Who does not experience it? Internal conflict makes Gilman's character real.

Offstage Characters

There are many offstage characters in the play, characters who are never seen. There are the other policemen and policewomen at the station. The police force is also present in the lobby at the massage parlor toward the end of the play. Then, too, there are the people who hold the party at Sandy's apartment and trash her place. And there is Sandy's landlord, who fines her. Sandy's mother and her lover play an absent role in this play, as do Sandy's stepfather and Curt's grave-robbing father. There are the groups who protest in front of the massage parlor and Curt's boss, who demotes him.

These invisible characters add to the depth and breadth of the play. Although the play has only five characters, the audience perceives the cast to be much larger. The police station and the massage parlor, for instance, are full of people, even though the audience sees only two at a time. The offstage characters provide the audience with a sense of the world around the play, rather than a world focused only on the five onstage characters. They are not isolated and unaffected by society, and this is one of Gilman's points.

Passage of Time

The first act of Gilman's play takes place over the course of two weeks. It begins with the meeting of Curt and Sandy and ends with Sandy's spending the night at Curt's place. By having everything happen so quickly, Gilman focuses her audience's attention on a brief encounter between two people—one that will eventually change their lives. They meet, become friends, share thoughts, and try to work out a relationship but fail.

Most of the action of the second act is contained in one day. In that day, a climax is reached. Until the second act, there was still a slight hope that Sandy and Curt might work things out between them, but Curt blows it. He tries to do the right thing, but he does it the wrong way. The tables are turned, and Sandy, who is supposed to represent the illegitimate one, exposes Curt's illegitimacy. This happens very quickly; after this point, there is not much more to say, so Gilman makes the biggest leap in time in the whole play. In scene 7 of the second act, a year has passed. This is the epilogue of the play, summing up what has happened to the characters and bringing the audience to the place where the consequences of the characters' individual actions have brought them.

HISTORICAL CONTEXT

Social Realism

Gilman's plays are often said to reflect the characteristics of social realism. Her concentration on certain aspects of society that are not always easily discussed in general conversation places her dramas on the edge of American theater, away from mainstream productions, such as Broadway musicals. She did not, however, create this form. Social realism has been around since the nineteenth century, a time when artists and writers turned to a more realistic approach, in defiance of the romantic movement that was, at that time, predominant. A definition commonly used for social realism refers to the influence of everyday conditions on a creative work. Whether it is a painting or a play, the artist or writer attempts to present the world as it is, not as some people might wish it be. Social realists place an emphasis on the working classes and the poor, and the work is often critical of the environment that has produced these less-than-satisfactory conditions.

Works of social realism became prevalent in the United States during the Great Depression of the 1930s and early 1940s. These works depicted the awful conditions of poverty, the hardships of bad employment environments, and the cruelty of racial discrimination. This was when Richard Wright's *Native Son* (1940) was staged. This play (and novel of the same title) is about the oppression felt by a black man living in Chicago and his subsequent violent reactions. Another popular work, John Steinbeck's novel *The Grapes of Wrath* (1940), focuses on the plight of a poor family struggling to make a living after having lost their home. No matter how hard they try, their lives keep getting worse. At this time, too, Diego Rivera, the famed Mexican muralist and avowed Communist, came to the United States and influenced the direction of American art with his realistic paintings dwelling on such themes as modern industrialization and Mexican history and peoples.

By the end of the twentieth century and into the twenty-first century, American theater was turning more toward the difficult topics of the social realists, at least off Broadway and in small regional theaters. Plays that dealt with homosexuality, AIDS, sex, and racial issues not only were produced but also won awards. Productions that dealt with socially realistic themes included Moisés Kaufman's *Laramie Project* (2000), about the brutal murder of a young, homosexual college student; Anna Deavere Smith's *Fires in the Mirror: Crown Heights, Brooklyn, and Other Identities* (1993), about race riots in New York City; Paula Vogel's *How I Learned to Drive* (1999), about incest; and Eve Ensler's Obie-winning hit, *The Vagina Monologues* (1996), about women's body parts.

Prostitution in Chicago

Massage parlors that doubled as sites for prostitution still existed in Chicago in 2005. Various websites on the Internet even featured reviews of these parlors. However, the Chicago police department was trying hard to make prostitution, if not a thing of the past, at least a matter of embarrassment. In 2004, it was reported that the police department recorded more than three thousand arrests for prostitution. According to one newspaper article, Richard Daley, who was mayor of Chicago when Gilman's play was produced there, gave the city's police department permission to engage in website postings of its own. Pictures of women arrested for soliciting sex, as well as of the johns who patronized them, were made available for viewing on special pages. Their names and addresses were also provided in an attempt to embarrass these people into quitting. Apparently, traditional arrests, fines, and impoundments of vehicles just were not working.

Community Colleges

The first public community college in the United States, Joliet Junior College, in Joliet, Illinois, was founded in 1901. Like other two-year colleges that would follow, it focused on liberal arts education. That focus changed during the years of the Great Depression, when community colleges began offering job-training programs to help ease the problems of unemployment.

By the 1960s, there were more than four hundred community colleges in the United States. Students attended these schools for a variety of reasons. Some people used them as stepping-stones to entering four-year colleges. Others went to gain associate degrees in specific trades. As of 2005, there were more than fifteen hundred community colleges, which educated more than half of the nation's undergraduates, and more than one hundred million people had taken classes at community colleges since the Joliet school was established.

CRITICAL OVERVIEW

Blue Surge premiered at the Goodman Theatre in Chicago on July 9, 2001. Chris Jones, referring to this production and writing for *Variety*, calls Gilman's play "a racy, smart piece of gritty social realism that's alternately funny and politically provocative." Although Jones finds moments in the play that seem to be forced, a plot that appears at times to be contrived, and some language that might be "more suited to cable television" than to a small theater, he also says that "Gilman's writing is heartfelt and the narrative crackles along with plenty of surprises." Jones concludes his review by calling Gilman's work "a lively, flashy, gripping and typically smart piece of theater."

Joel Henning, a critic for the *Wall Street Journal*, also writes a mixed review for Gilman's play. There are moments that Henning finds exceedingly well done and others that he considers boring. At one end, Henning states that Gilman "controls her plots to a fault." For this reason, Henning concludes that, in some ways, *Blue Surge* is "too predictable, more like pallid television than edgy theater." At the other end, however, Henning compliments Gilman's concepts. "Some of her ideas," says Henning, "and much of her dialogue—though occasionally loony—are often dazzling." Henning finds the least believable character in the play to be Beth. If this play is about stripping "away Beth's veneer of social and economic altruism," it did not work, in Henning's opinion. The dialogue that this character is provided is some of Gilman's most contrived, Henning states. It is through this character that Gilman supposedly tries to make a point about "the motives of the rich," but this attempt does not come off well. Instead, the character of Beth "never seems to be much more than a cardboard poster." In conclusion, Henning holds out hope for Gilman as a playwright. "Ms. Gilman is young," he writes. "We can hope that her future plays will remain funny and accessible, full of meaning, yes, but meaning delivered other than with a cudgel."

In an article written for *Crain's Chicago Business*, Brian McCormick comments on the audience response to Gilman's work. "Much of that response," McCormick writes, "results from the writer's intense subject matter, an in-your-face ethos that is decidedly at odds with her soft-spoken, gentle demeanor." McCormick goes on to remark on Gilman's choice of subject matter for her plays. He states that Gilman's credo seems to be that the "more incendiary the topic, the better." McCormick reports that theater critics seem to be divided in their reviews of Gilman's plays. Some critics praise her for her intelligence, while others "complain of an emptiness behind her provocations."

One year after *Blue Surge* premiered in Chicago, it moved on to a stage off Broadway in New York. Simi Horwitz, a writer for *Back Stage*, interviewed the play's director, Robert Falls. In this interview, the director says that he found the play to be "uncommonly beautiful, exquisitely written, and ultimately uplifting." Horwitz offers his own comments about the play, stating that it is "an unexpectedly touching

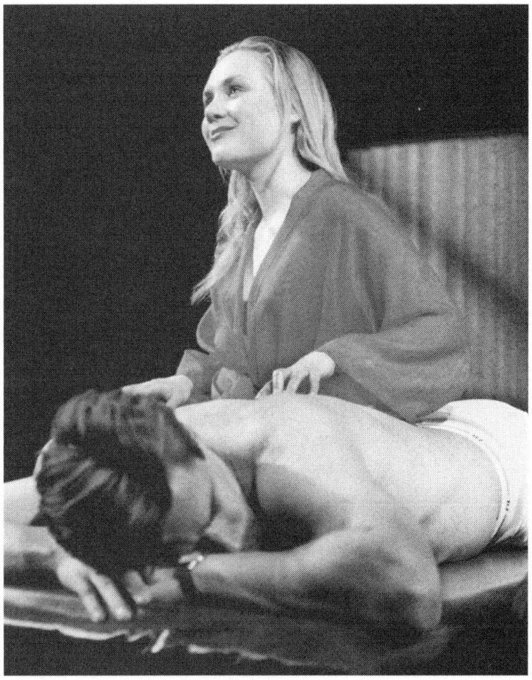

Rachel Miner and Joe Murphy in a 2002 production of Blue Surge Photo by Michal Daniel

play." Horwitz also writes that the subject matter of the play "may be a little alien, if not off-putting, to some audiences."

Another writer for *Back Stage*, Victor Gluck, refers to it as possibly Gilman's best play yet. This play, says Gluck, "is that rare play about unsympathetic people that claims your sympathy. Extremely moving and beautifully written, it dramatizes its themes of social class and poverty without preaching." Gluck goes on to praise the director and some of the specific actors of the New York City production. He then remarks on Gilman's ability, saying that she creates "character by building up specific and unusual details that fill in a complete portrait."

The reviewer Ben Brantley, writing for the *New York Times*, states that Gilman's play, despite the fact that it was written and set in the early part of the twenty-first century, makes him feel as if he were watching a "grainy black-and-white film" from the Depression era—which Brantley attributes to the subject matter of the play. Gilman's characters, Brantley finds, are similar to the "young idealists" of those early movies, who "realize they are trapped, trapped in a society that will never give them an even break." Brantley praises Gilman for her work, which often presents "impeccably detailed, clear-eyed and sometimes overly schematic works." However, he points out some weaknesses. "While the appealing young cast members all occasionally hit emotional notes that resonate," Brantley writes, "there's an air of self-consciousness abroad that teeters on the brink of melodrama." Brantley ends his review, however, on an upbeat note. "Ms. Gilman," he says, "has the undeniable virtue of focusing with lucidity and evenhandedness on subjects that are more often sensationalized in the popular arts."

> "BETH'S SUPERIORITY IS NOT ESTABLISHED FROM HAVING ELEVATED HERSELF, BUT RATHER FROM HAVING PUSHED OTHER PEOPLE DOWN TO A POSITION BELOW HER."

CRITICISM

Joyce Hart

Hart is a freelance writer and published author with degrees in English and creative writing. In this essay, she examines the function of Beth in Gilman's play and the elements that make Beth such a flat character.

Gilman's play *Blue Surge* is about class and economic structure in the United States. The playwright portrays her ideas on these topics through the various characters of her play, with four characters representing the poorer side of society and only one of them the moneyed class. The single character who is rich is Beth, the girlfriend of Curt. Beth has few lines and is seldom seen onstage, and yet hers is a pivotal role, at least in an abstract way. Despite the fact that she is a minor character, she carries the weight of the oppositional point of the argument—the argument of the working class versus the privileged.

Critics have complained about Beth, calling Gilman's creation a flat character, one that has little depth. If Beth is the only representative of the rich, does not this also mean that Gilman's reflection of the upper class is flat? To push this question a little further, has Gilman's play provided a legitimate example of the rich versus the poor, or has she merely presented a one-sided view? To see whether Gilman has, in fact, done this, one needs to look closely at the role of Beth. What lines is she given? How does she represent her class? Does she ever defend herself?

The first lines out of Beth's mouth are not very flattering to her character. They demonstrate Beth's sense of superiority and lack of compassion. She starts off with a criticism of Curt's friend and police partner, Doug. Once she finishes with Doug, Beth moves on to disparage a local restaurant that caters to people who do not have much money to spend when they go out to eat. She insinuates that this particular restaurant is no better than a McDonald's. She also implies that the people who go to this restaurant do not have good taste. They do not, in Beth's opinion, know the difference between a salad made with iceberg lettuce and one made with gourmet mixed greens, typically served in better-class restaurants.

As the dialogue continues, Beth carries on with her assessments, changing from the people Curt must deal with in his life and his job to Curt himself. As she persists in pointing her judgmental finger, she also maintains her lofty position. Through her words, Beth puts Curt in a lower position. She gives him credit, when he insists upon it, for knowing more about prostitutes than she does. But her statement is loaded, insinuating that she knows more than he does of matters that are more significant. "Okay," she says. "You know more about hookers than I do. Okay? Fine. Congratulations."

Beth's tone does not improve. After Curt explains how he bungled the arrest of the suspected prostitute at the massage parlor, Beth turns from being judgmental to being sweet, nauseatingly so. "Honey, you shouldn't feel bad that you didn't know how to go to a hooker. That's a good thing." Here Beth sounds as if she is a schoolteacher talking condescendingly to a kindergarten child who has just complained of not being able to make a spitball.

In this introduction to Beth, the audience has been given very little upon which to make a positive assessment of the play's solitary character from the wealthier class. There is not much to like about

WHAT DO I READ NEXT?

- Gilman's play *Spinning into Butter*, published by Faber and Faber in 2000, takes place at a liberal Vermont college, where political correctness prevails. Unfortunately, racial prejudice also thrives on the campus, despite many of the faculty members' denials. Gilman exposes how racism can exist in the deep recesses of anyone's mind, even so-called liberals.
- *Boy Gets Girl*, another of Gilman's plays, premiered in 2000 in Chicago. It tells the story of a blind date gone wrong. After the protagonist rejects the young man, he begins to terrorize her by stalking her.
- In 1999, Gilman's award-winning play *The Glory of Living* premiered in London, capturing the awe and fascination of Gilman's British audiences. This play takes place in the rural South and focuses on a young teenage prostitute who runs away with a no-good car thief. The couple marry, and the husband forces the protagonist to lure other young runaway girls to their house, where both husband and wife become involved in their murders.
- Neil Labute is another playwright who, like Gilman, focuses on social issues in his work. Labute is a prolific writer, and one of his best-appraised works is a collection of three one-acts called *Bash: Three Plays*, published in 2000. It includes *Medea Redux*, the tale of a woman who relates a story about a relationship with her English teacher; *Iphigenia in Orem*, about a Utah businessman who confesses to a stranger a crime he has committed; and *A Gaggle of Saints*, about a young Mormon couple who relate a violent crime in which they were involved.
- For another take on prostitution, the journalist Lael Morgan's *Good Time Girls of the Alaska–Yukon Gold Rush* (1999) can be recommended. This story chronicles the lives of some of the women who went to Alaska in search of wealth.

Beth, and the dialogue between Beth and Curt is not indicative of a healthy and loving relationship. Curt, on the other hand, has already become endearing to the audience. He has bungled his attempts to arrest a prostitute. He has admitted to Sandy that he does not know what he is doing. He is, in other words, human and thus easy to relate to. He shows humility and sticks up for his friends as well as the so-called common people. He is easy to empathize with.

Beth also exposes some of her weaknesses, but they are not nearly so appealing as Curt's. The next flaw that she demonstrates is her tendency to contradict herself. When Curt first brings up the topic of the prostitutes, Beth thinks the police should leave the women alone. She stands up for them; for a brief moment, some members of the audience might applaud her. Not only has she taken a humanitarian approach to prostitution, she has also put a positive spin on her argument. Prostitution should be legalized, she suggests, but Beth's stance turns out to be an abstract one, not all that well grounded in reality. Shortly after Curt reveals that he had to choose one of the women in particular, Beth becomes jealous. She forgets her original support for the prostitutes and now refers to them as "scuzzy girls," a description of prostitutes not meant to be flattering.

This is how the second scene of the play ends. Beth has made her appearance, and it is not a very attractive picture. She has shown herself to be wishy-washy and critical. She demonstrates when she becomes jealous of the prostitute that she is not totally secure in herself; for most of her time on stage, however, she takes a superior stance. Beth's superiority is not established from having elevated herself, but rather from having pushed other people down to a position below her.

Beth represents the privileged side of Gilman's opposition of class and money. Beth has been described as living on a trust fund left her by a wealthy grandfather. The other characters belong to the working class. They struggle through life, working at jobs they do not necessarily like. They were raised poor and had parents who were less than ideal, to say the least. They seem to trip through life, falling into one pit after another and picking themselves up and trying again. They are, as Gilman portrays them, the underdogs of life. In contrast, Gilman portrays the rich as having easy lives, with opportunities handed to them without much effort on their part (other than being born); worries are erased from their lives because they have money. In addition, the rich, as Gilman expresses it through Curt, may have it easy, but they are not very good. Rich people make poor people feel bad about themselves. They make Curt feel as if he stinks when he is in their presence.

Beth's appearance on stage reinforces Curt's description of the rich. Beth makes Curt nervous. He sweats when he is around her and has to take many showers so that he does not become smelly. Beth hears these comments from Curt, but she does not defend herself. She does not try to bridge the gap. She just stands there in front of him and takes it. It is as if she cannot speak, although she is not tongue-tied when it comes to making herself look like an arrogant fool. It seems as though Beth has been set up to be the scapegoat.

Beth does not return until act 2, and her return is not graceful. She confronts Curt when she finds him with Sandy and, before leaving the stage, quickly sums Sandy up as a whore. Beth resorts to judging people again, and she does so through unflattering and hurtful stereotyping. Calling Sandy a prostitute would be one thing, but in using the word *whore*, Beth is further denigrating her. Admittedly, Beth is angry and hurt at that moment. But her actions further alienate her from the audience, who has seen the more human side of Sandy and is beginning to relate to and empathize with her. Beth remains on the outside, and Gilman does not give Beth a chance to state her case.

Although Gilman provides details of Curt's and Sandy's lives and of their personal philosophies and opinions of life, there is little or no such exposition given on Beth's behalf. She makes quick entrances and just as quick exits. Her dialogue consists mainly of questions directed at Curt, or else she is flinging out sharp retorts meant to inflict some degree of pain. She does not try to understand Curt. Neither does she defend herself and the class of people she is supposed to represent. She is, however, given one final chance to do so. It is in scene 3 of act 2. Unfortunately, Beth blows it again. She tries to defend herself from Curt's description of how she looks at poor people, including Curt, but she never makes a statement that might turn a better light onto the wealthy class—one that might make rich people look more lovable, or even likeable.

There is nothing said in this play that is complimentary of the rich. The upper class, represented by Beth, is never developed. From beginning to end, the rich remain stick figures, while the poor characters are fully fleshed out. A more rounded play might have tried a little harder to present the other side.

Source: Joyce Hart, Critical Essay on *Blue Surge*, in *Drama for Students*, Thomson Gale, 2006.

Neil Heims

Heims is a writer and teacher living in Paris. In this essay, he argues that Gilman considers that how people are valued is more important than what values they hold.

Whatever other factors may contribute to the quality of human relationships and to the cohesiveness of society, whether people share the same values or are in conflict over their values fundamentally influences the strength and the nature of all human association. In *Blue Surge*, Rebecca Gilman explores how social and moral values and how social and moral valuation influence the way individuals react to and interact with each other and, especially, how they value themselves and each other. Against the background of an effort by a group of fundamentalist Christians to shut down a massage parlor, which is really a front for a house of prostitution, Gilman presents the story of four people—two police officers and two prostitutes—who are transformed by their contact with each other as they function inside of and respond to the larger social issue and find their own values and identities challenged and, to a greater or lesser degree, changed.

In act 1, scene 4, of *Blue Surge*, Gilman shows the antagonism that defines and seems to fuel the relationship between Curt and Beth. Curt is a police officer on the vice squad. He was raised in poverty—"a big dinner at my house was deviled ham and crackers"—by his mother after his father, a gravedigger, was sent to prison for robbing the corpses he was burying. Beth, his girlfriend, is an art teacher who is able to be unconcerned that she does not make much money, since she lives on the interest generated by stocks that her grandfather placed in her name when she was born. The disparity in their backgrounds is the cause of a constant clash between them. They argue about their values. Curt feels that Beth does not value him because of his class background, and he resents her because of hers.

"He wastes everybody's time, he totally blew it, and it's like there are no repercussions with him. He's oblivious." This is what Curt says to Beth about his partner, Doug, who, because of his clumsiness, has botched the arrest of a prostitute and, in consequence, the attempt to close the massage parlor. Beth seems to be in sync with Curt when she responds, "I don't see why you're still friends with him." Curt's answer seems straightforward, "We're not friends, really. We're just partners." Given this response, Beth's comment "He's such a jerk" appears to be inoffensive, merely an echo, in fact, of what Curt has been griping about. Curt, however, does take offense. "Could you not rag on my friends for once?" he snaps at her. The man who Curt has just said is not his friend suddenly becomes his friend, and Beth is accused of "ragging on" him when it was Curt himself who has been doing the ragging.

Rather than argue and point out the contradiction, Beth ducks. She attempts to change the subject. "So what's with this massage parlor?" she asks. But no topic of conversation is safe for them. As Curt explains, "It's right next to the Ground Round. These Christian Coalition people take their kids there. . . . They're freaking out." Flippantly, perhaps appreciating the double meaning suggested by the name of the restaurant, Beth responds, "That's what they get for going to the Ground Round." Curt does not find her quip funny. For him, rather, it is an indication of elitism. He takes it as a put-down of ordinary people and responds defensively. Another squabble begins. Again Beth retreats and says, "You know, you shouldn't close down this massage parlor, you should legalize it. These women aren't victims. They made a choice to be sex workers. If it was legal, they could unionize and get health benefits. And safe working conditions."

Curt answers her with sarcasm, saying, "Sounds good." Now it is Beth who feels demeaned by Curt. "If you think I'm full of [sh——t], tell me," she says. "Okay," he says and continues:

> You don't know the first . . . thing about it. Drive over to Malton Road some night and see if these women look like they're in charge of anything. . . . They get the [sh——t] beat out of them on a regular basis and every single one of them is hooked on something because it's just about the most demeaning thing you could possibly do.

> "RATHER THAN CONCENTRATING ON SOCIAL CONFLICTS, GILMAN FOCUSES ON THE RESULTING FRUSTRATED LONGING OF BRUISED HEARTS AND ON THE STRUGGLES HER CHARACTERS MUST ENDURE AS THEY REALIZE THE HEART'S PAIN."

Beth becomes petulant rather than explaining to Curt that his description of the situation, if it is accurate (and Gilman's portrayal of both the prostitutes, Sandy and Heather, indicates that it is not), reflects exactly what she was saying. She claims that the oppressive nature of prostitution is not the consequence of prostitution itself but of the working conditions spawned by making prostitution illegal. "Of course," she says, "you know more about this than I do." Curt responds, "On this particular subject, I do. Yes. . . . It's one very small area. But when I'm actually an authority, I wish you'd just let me be the authority."

The way in which Curt insists on his authority reveals the depth of his insecurity. This exchange between Curt and Beth, moreover, is but one example of their constant state of discord. Their discord is the result of that insecurity and of the crippling sense of inferiority that haunts him and that he fights against by blaming her for his feeling it. The source of his misery is not Beth, however, but his own self-pity and self-contempt, which he uses her to experience and which he blames on her. "No matter how hard I try," he tells her in act 2, scene 3, after they have broken up, "I am never going to be as good as you." Even though she tells him that this is not so, he dismisses what she says:

> I was so surprised when you said you'd go out with me. . . And for four years I've been . . . trying not to

> say the wrong thing. . . . I get this nervous sweat. Around you. And it smells bad. That's why I shower so much. . . . I've walked around for four years afraid that you think I stink.

It is not surprising, given how Curt feels about himself, that he is comfortable around Sandy, the nineteen-year-old prostitute whom he first tries to arrest and then makes it his mission to help. With her, he does not feel self-disdain, because he is able to think of himself as morally superior to her. His relationship to her, throughout most of the play, is defined and fueled by his attempts to raise her up from what he considers her fallen state. But the attempt to "save" her proves fatal to him, for the more deeply involved with Sandy he becomes, the more evident it becomes that his need for help is greater than hers.

When Sandy and Curt meet after she has been released, Sandy tells Curt that she does not want to stop being a prostitute, that what she really wants is not to have to hand over half her earnings to "the house." She wants to be her own boss and keep everything for herself. Ironically, this is exactly what Beth had been saying when she spoke about legalizing prostitution. But Curt does not snap at Sandy as he snapped at Beth. In fact, after she makes it clear to Curt that she does not want his help, he replies, "Well, if I can't help you maybe you could help me." He means that he wants her to help him study, by testing him to see whether he can correctly identify tree leaves by name. By the end of the play, however, it will be clear to both of them that he needs a far deeper kind of help. The scene that begins with his offering help ends with his asking for help. Even if that is only a ploy that allows him to keep seeing her, it signals the start of a painful but humanly essential transformation for him. Rather than guarding himself, as he does with Beth, Curt exposes his wounds to Sandy.

To her, he reveals a layer of himself that is hidden below the person he appears to be on the surface. Rather than a policeman, Curt really wants to be a nature guide. That is why he is learning to identify leaves. But he is incapable even of guiding himself. This becomes clear as he and Sandy grow closer. She yields to his encouragement and attempts to find work other than prostitution. When she is pressed for money, however, she returns to the massage parlor. This enrages Curt. He sees it as betrayal. His confused relationship with Beth, however, has made it impossible for him to attend to the difficulties that have forced Sandy back to prostitution. Curt's incompetence as a guide is further revealed in his final attempt to save Sandy. Instead of saving her, he endangers himself.

When he learns that there will be another raid on the massage parlor, Curt goes there to warn Sandy and brings her evidence money that he has stolen from the police station to enable her to flee and look for other kinds of work. Of course, he is caught. Through the efforts of his lawyer and the union, he escapes imprisonment but is dismissed from the police force. He becomes a security guard and begins to take biology courses at a local community college. Sandy leaves the massage parlor and establishes herself as an independent sex worker, able to pocket the full amount of her receipts.

When next they meet, it is a year later. Theirs are not the only lives that have changed. Heather has left the massage parlor, works as a bartender, and is having a baby with Doug. Because of Heather, Doug has lost some of the righteous moralizing that characterized his earlier opinions and has admitted and gratified some of his own, perhaps less socially acceptable, sexual desires. As Curt and Sandy open up to each other again, he shows a clarity of insight about himself that he had not had before. "All those years," he tells her, "and all that work. I didn't throw it away on you. . . . I got so mad and I threw it away on feeling sorry for myself. . . . All I can figure is, I just got tired." He does not say what made him tired or what he got tired of. Nonetheless, it seems clear that Curt grew tired of his own resentments and self-pity, of using them to resist his own grief and sense of need. He got tired of bearing the burden of his past, of trying to deny who he was, and of trying to meet an expectation of himself that he projected onto others, especially Beth. He got tired of trying to give help when he so much needed it.

Sandy responds to his vulnerability, and he is able to allow her to do so. She says, simply, "If you want, I could sit here for just a little while, and I could hold your hand. If you want." After a slight hesitation, which indicates his ongoing struggle with himself in order to bring himself to accept the help he so deeply wants, he gives her his hand.

Thus, *Blue Surge*, which appears to be a play about a social conflict regarding prostitution and the clash of moral and class values, does not really attempt to resolve those issues. It shifts away from them and focuses on individual experience without judging the individuals. Rather than concentrating on social conflicts, Gilman focuses on the resulting frustrated longing of bruised hearts and on the struggles her characters must endure as they realize the heart's pain. When they do—and if they can

Joe Murphy, Steve Key, and Coleen Werthmann in a 2002 production of Blue Surge Photo by Michal Daniel

surrender to that pain—Gilman suggests, they may transcend it; only then will they be able to accept the tender help of an offered hand that such surrender might make possible. In *Blue Surge*, Gilman seems to be showing that the values people hold are of less importance than how each person values himself or herself and how each person is valued.

Source: Neil Heims, Critical Essay on *Blue Surge*, in *Drama for Students*, Thomson Gale, 2006.

Robert Hurwitt

In the following review, Hurwitt calls Blue Surge *"more socially and psychologically complex" than Gilman's previous plays and compliments the "grappling with what's right" for making the play "so moving and unsettlingly familiar."*

Helping others is not only hard but also unpredictable and likely to backfire for the Midwestern characters in Rebecca Gilman's cops-and-hookers drama *Blue Surge* at the Magic Theatre. Helping oneself, however, can be immeasurably harder. More than the difficulty of doing the right thing, it's the grappling with what's right and on whose terms that makes the play so moving and unsettlingly familiar.

What starts as a routine vice raid on a thinly disguised small-town brothel—the Naughty But Nice massage parlor—turns into a life-changing situation for all involved. Cops get involved with hookers. A career and an engagement get derailed. Questions of sexual morality take a backseat to economic exigencies, lingering childhood traumas and class hatred. In a sterling West Coast premiere directed by Amy Glazer, the drama surges with sympathy for its understandably lost souls.

The *Surge* that opened Friday at the Magic has been considerably revised—tightened and honed to good effect—since its premiere at Chicago's Goodman Theatre two years ago (the published version). Though written with Gilman's usual facility for a page-turner plot and disturbing moral shadings, it's something of a departure from the issue-driven dramas that established her as one of the hot young

"Nothing terribly dramatic happens to these people in the end. But in that nothing, *Surge* offers a deeply affecting wrestle with the drama of ordinary life."

playwrights of recent years: *Boy Gets Girl* (about a stalker), *The Glory of Living* (serial killers and child abuse), *Spinning into Butter* (racism in liberal academia).

As in her less well-developed *The American in Me,* which premiered at the Magic two years ago, Gilman's scope is broader here, less headline-driven and consequently more socially and psychologically complex. Glazer, who gave *American* a dynamic staging (and directed *Butter* at TheatreWorks the same year), has responded with a production as beautifully flowing and shaded as the script.

The primary settings—a seedy massage parlor, a police station, a lonely low-budget kitchen, a small-town bar—slip easily into place on Eric Sinkkonen's open, versatile set, filling the space defined by a square blue outline on the floor and a blue-pipe square above (the blues gleaming electrically in Jim Cave's subtle use of black light). Glazer keeps her scene changes swift and smooth, establishing a cinematic flow that enhances a psychological realism within a patently artificial space.

She mirrors that effect in the performances, playing the emotional tension of Gilman's primary romantic entanglement against the slightly exaggerated comedy of the supporting couple. The vividly rendered characterizations of the cast fulfill her vision.

John Flanagan is an engagingly conflicted vice cop—displaying his nervousness and cleanliness obsession in the simple act of undressing for his undercover massage parlor bust (and carefully folding his T-shirt and jeans)—who grows compellingly more complicated in the course of *Surge.* His Curt is a man wrestling with his aspirations and class-based resentments, trying to balance the demands of his job against his desire to help others find their way out of the poverty he feels has robbed him of options in life.

Flanagan is brilliant in his confrontations with his upper-class fiancee, Beth (a smart, classy Cofie Henninger, exuding unconscious entitlement), as he tries to explain his discomfort with her class and even her ability to choose to be an underpaid artist. He's appealing, irritating and deeply moving as he tries to help the young hooker Sandy (Kirsten Roeters) and confronts his own class condescension in the process.

Roeters is a delightful Sandy, from the cold snap of distrust she registers when she realizes that her client is probably a cop, through her slow softening to Curt's appeal. She and Flanagan generate a sensual tension that enriches their interplay of trust and distrust, sympathy and disappointment. The still empathy of her watchful attention to Curt's final realization—that he has to learn to help himself before he can help anyone else—compounds and amplifies the emotional power of Flanagan's resonant performance.

Meanwhile, in the alternative reality of the less self-conscious, Curt's partner, Doug (Darren Bridgett), and Sandy's co-worker Heather (Jibz Cameron) provide comically affecting relief. Bridgett enlivens the proceedings with a boyishly breezy, unconflicted hedonism and absence of introspection—failing to notice anything ridiculous in his stark-naked badge-flashing pose as he busts Heather. Cameron is as comical in her all-business lingerie (the apt costumes are by Kira Kristensen) as in her drunken attempts at bartending.

Nothing terribly dramatic happens to these people in the end. But in that nothing, *Surge* offers a deeply affecting wrestle with the drama of ordinary life.

Source: Robert Hurwitt, "Comfort, Discomfort of *Surge*'s Strangers," in *San Francisco Chronicle*, April 7, 2003, Section D, p. 3.

Chris Jones

In the following essay, Jones uses quotes from Gilman in providing background on Gilman's art and career.

Don't let the gentle demeanor fool you. Her plays are rife with murder and mayhem.

The aging, hemmed-in Chicago suburb of Forest Park, just 15 traffic-clogged minutes west of the Loop, with its grand old Italian restaurants and hedge-rimmed lawns, is not the kind of place you'd expect to find a progressive storefront theatre premiering Rebecca Gilman's *The Glory of Living,* a dark and intensely violent play about a Texan teenage murderess who picks up vagrant girls for her boyfriend's sexual kicks.

What's even more unlikely, perhaps, considering the power pyramid that favors major theatre institutions, is that a tiny company like Forest Park's ensemble-based Circle Theatre would be sharing the prestige of a Rebecca Gilman premiere with the lofty likes of the Goodman Theatre, New York's Lincoln Center Theater Company and London's Royal Court Theatre. But then, few playwrights find success as suddenly or as prolifically as Gilman has—and few either care or can afford to be as loyal as she is to the theatre that gave her a start.

Within the last year or so, Gilman has been transformed from a struggling Chicago scribe, who did temp work by day and wrote by night, into one of America's most talked-about and sought-after playwrights. Theatres are fighting for the rights to do her plays, and the Goodman has put up two of her works in a space of no more than nine months.

Les Waters' mounting of *Spinning into Butter,* Gilman's controversial play about racial issues on a college campus, was an unequivocal hit with Chicago critics and audiences last summer (the Goodman run was extended three times), and Dan Sullivan will direct the second production of the play in July at Lincoln Center. Even before the New York critics check in, there is so much interest from regional theatres that the play is likely to show up on this magazine's next annual list of the most-produced plays of the season.

Boy Gets Girl, Gilman's new thriller about a blind date turned terribly wrong, opened on the Goodman main stage in March and appears likely to follow *Spinning into Butter's* route to New York in short order. Between those commitments, Gilman somehow found time to write another play (also about murder) for the Circle—*The Crime of the Century,* her moving portrait of the eight Chicago nurses brutally killed by Richard Speck in 1966, opened in Forest Park last December.

In London, Gilman became the first American ever to win the Evening Standard Award for most promising playwright after *The Glory of Living* was produced at the Royal Court Theatre in January 1999. The play had already notched the American Theatre Critics Association's 1998 Osborne Award for the best new work by an emerging playwright.

Commissions are nosy mounting up. In February, the Prince Charitable Trusts announced that

"'I WAS WRITING,' GILMAN SAYS, 'BECAUSE IT WAS CHEAPER THAN THERAPY. I NEVER THOUGHT I WOULD EVER MAKE ANY MONEY OFF THESE THINGS—THAT NEVER SEEMED EVEN A POSSIBILITY FOR ME.'"

Gilman and the Goodman Theatre will receive the $75,000 Prince Prize for commissioning original work—it will be used to produce Gilman's next play, provisionally titled *The Great Baseball Strike of 1994,* during the Goodman's 2000–01 season in its new building. Kent Thompson, artistic director of the Alabama Shakespeare Festival, say's he is musing over which Gilman play to produce in Montgomery—and he's also planning on commissioning an entirely new work from the 36-year-old author, who's rapidly becoming overwhelmed by offers.

A little more than two years ago, though, Gilman was clerking out a living in the Chicago accounting office of Peat/Marwick. And in most professional theatrical circles, her name meant nothing.

December 1996 was a busy month in the Chicago theatre. With a host of shows opening downtown, most of the city's leading theatre critics had bigger fish to fry than schlepping out to Forest Park for a low-profile Circle Theatre opening, especially since almost no one had heard of the playwright.

Who was she? A slight, unassuming woman with dark hair and a soft Alabama accent, whose gentle demeanor provided no clue whatsoever, then or now, to the intense content of her plays. Gilman was one of a large and varied group of resident writers at Chicago Dramatists, one of the city's most loyal incubators of young playwrights, but the primary harvest of her career to date had been a stack of some 150 rejection letters from resident theatres, including the Goodman.

"I was writing," Gilman says, because it was cheaper than therapy. I never thought I would ever make any money off these things—that never seemed even a possibility for me." Certainly, her body of work was small and perceived as rather eccentric. *Always Open,* for instance—penned when Gilman was just 18—is about a disgruntled group of Krispy Kreme Doughnuts employees who decide to suffocate their manager in a big vat of dough.

A native of Trussville, Ala., Gilman had arrived in the Midwest by a circuitous route. She studied at Middlebury College in Vermont before graduating from Birmingham Central College in Alabama and, after various digressions, finally fought her way into the University of Iowa's M.F.A. program in playwriting. Upon moving to Chicago, she supported her writing habit with a variety of clerical jobs. Aside from a small production in Houston of one of her early efforts, none of her plays had been produced professionally.

That included *The Glory of Living.* No theatre in town had been willing to touch this dark, unflinching and explicit exploration of child abuse, sexual deviance and serial murder. The piece was all the more disturbing because it was drawn from truth. "The springboard for the play," Gilman says, "came from a real Alabama murder during my senior year of college. The criminal was a young girl who had nor been taught to value her own life, so she could not be expected to value anyone else's." In Gilman's semi-fictional account, the 15-year-old protagonist, Lisa, was a child bride turned into a multiple murderer by her sick husband.

Gilman had a staunch defender in Robin Stanton, artistic director of Chicago Dramatists, who believed passionately in *The Glory of Living* and shopped it furiously around Chicago, with no success. "I was certain this was a very important piece of writing," Stanton recalls. "Rebecca is a playwright with real courage." Circle finally agreed to house the show, in part to get Stanton off its back.

It was the best decision the theatre ever made. Those few folks lucky enough to see Stanton's premiere call it a revelatory night of theatre, the kind of event that makes a critic want to shout the playwright's name from the rooftops. As would prove typical in her later works, Gilman laid out her story's lurid events with almost clinical dispatch, never shrinking from physical depictions of abuse but constantly confounding her audience's expectations. Instead of sensationalizing the killing spree or indulging in Southern stereotypes, Gilman made the case that we all bear responsibility for young people whose childhoods have been stolen by a society that no longer nurtures its young.

The reviews, phone calls and general buzz quickly reached the new-play offices of the Goodman and Steppenwolf companies. The Goodman moved fast, offering Gilman its McPherson Award, a commission named in honor of late playwright Scott McPherson. Artistic director Robert Falls read *Glory of Living* and a draft of her next play. He quickly joined the fan club. "Rebecca is both subversive and exciting," Falls says. "She uses a simple and sparse language with characters that remain unsentimental and truthful. And there's a real ferocious comic voice behind her writing."

That ferocity can also be seen in Gilman's refusal to shy away from the trickiest of themes. In the case of *Spinning into Butter,* her status as a white woman gave Gilman no qualms about exploring (sometimes in a comic mode) the effects of racism on an East Coast college campus. The play's protagonist, a youngish, liberal dean of students named Sarah, hears that someone is pinning anonymous racist notes on the dorm room door of one of her college's few black students (a character that never appears in the play) and is forced to confront her own latent culpability in the misdeed. This seemingly kind and sympathetic character confesses her own veiled racism in a searing second-act monologue that shocked the audience at the Goodman Studio into a silence so complete it seemed born of personal agony.

Gilman's point, of course, is that liberal intellectuals often talk a good game about diversity, but so fail to have the requisite experience or true understanding of minority experiences, that they end up as part of the problem.

"While the concept of political correctness has made us more sensitive to how we perceive each other;" Gilman says, "there's also a danger that the rhetoric will be allowed to mask some of our really angry feelings. People are now often afraid to articulate what they actually feel about each other."

The battleground may be gender rather than race, but objectification and fear are also the main themes of *Boy Gets Girl,* a gripping page-turner of a play with a thriller-style narrative that at first seems to recall such Hollywood attempts to exploit urban insecurities as *Single White Female.* The action starts when a single, thirty-something journalist named Theresa is set up by a friend on a blind date. At first the guy seems harmless, even pleasant. But over the course of time he reveals himself to be a dangerous stalker who threatens to unravel every thread of the now-paranoid Theresa's life.

"The pitfall is the expectations of the genre," Gilman allows. "You expect someone to get shot and that there will be a neat conclusion in some way or other. I wanted to take the subject seriously and write about it more realistically."

So the play differs from its Hollywood counterparts in several important ways. Through a host of semi-complicit minor characters (not all of whom are male), Gilman makes the point that the date from hell is not just an isolated jerk, but an inevitable product of a society that relentlessly objectifies women. One of Theresa's ongoing interview subjects is a filmmaker named Les Kennkat, a character based on Russ Meyer of Supervixens fame, who has an open obsession with women's breasts. But even as she paints Kennkat guilty as sin, Gilman also makes him into a likeable eccentric.

"I think this play is the flip side to *Spinning into Butter,*" Gilman says. "It's not about what it is to objectify but to be objectified. As a society we tend to dehumanize each other, whether through prejudice, sexism, economics or the Internet. At some point we need to stop identifying so much with the things people are trying to sell us and try to think of each other on a more human level."

That perspective seems to confirm the opinion of Michael Maggio, dean of the theatre school at DePaul University and the Goodman's associate artistic director, as to what qualities most clearly define Gilman as a playwright. "She seems to have a remarkable capacity to put her finger on the pulse of the zeitgeist," Maggio posits. "She understands how to write plays that are premised in something that seems immediate and recognizable to her audience, but she finds a way to dig very deeply into the characters and the milieu. And she has a remarkable capacity to hook you into a story."

In other words, Gilman writes accessible plays with such intriguing plots that the audience finds itself hungry for what is going to happen next—and once she has the viewer under that narrative spell, she does not shirk from exposing complex themes with a strongly feminist sensibility, dispensed with just the right quirky touch of nouveau Southern gothic.

As you read the burgeoning Gilman oeuvre, other common themes emerge. She's fascinated by crime but is determined that her perpetrators' actions are never seen as isolated from societal forces. She fights objectification but seems to understand its hold on modern consciousness. She's never crudely polemical; there's always a sense of life's ironies and ambiguities.

But perhaps the most striking (and currently unfashionable) aspect of Gilman's stance is a warm and sympathetic attitude towards the victims in her plays, especially when their humanity is negated by tensions between society's liberal and conservative factions. In *Crime of the Century* (based on the book of the same name by Dennis L. Breo and William Martin), Gilman largely ignored Speck's criminal motivations and focused instead on the lives of the nurses, lives he stole with such brutality.

"I did not find Richard Speck to be at all interesting," Gilman says. "He was a jerk, a misogynist and a petty criminal. I did not want to give him stage time." But the nurses, rendered anonymous by history, were another story.

"The dramatic version so forcibly brought through to me the sorrow and tragedy of all these lives being snuffed out," says author and Speck prosecutor William Martin, who showed up on Circle's opening night and was deeply moved by the play. "I had tears in my eyes. The play is a tribute to the nurses, their families and the tragic loss that society suffered by their lives being extinguished."

Since the original idea to write about Speck had come from a Circle ensemble member, Gilman had no qualms about putting aside more lucrative offers and debuting the work in the suburb that starred her rush to fame. "Circle took a risk on me," she reasons, "when no other theatre was interested."

Source: Chris Jones, "A Beginner's Guide to Rebecca Gilman," in *American Theatre*, Vol. 17, No. 4, April 2000, p. 26.

SOURCES

Brantley, Ben, "A Play Luxuriates in Its Own Sense of Doom," in the *New York Times*, April 23, 2002, Section E, p. 1.

Gluck, Victor, "Review of *Blue Surge*," in *Back Stage*, Vol. 43, No. 18, May 3, 2002, p. 36.

Henning, Joel, "Theater: Spinning Vice into Virtue—In Rebecca Gilman's 'Blue Surge,' Sex and Class Intermingle, but the Sermons Last Too Long," in the *Wall Street Journal*, July 31, 2001, Section A, p. 16.

Horwitz, Simi, "An American Realist," in *Back Stage*, Vol. 43, No. 17, April 26, 2002, pp. 7–8.

Jones, Chris, "Review of *Blue Surge*," in *Variety*, Vol. 383, No. 9, July 23, 2001, p. 23.

McCormick, Brian, "Rebecca Gilman 36; Playwright Provacateur," in *Crain's Chicago Business*, Vol. 23, November 6, 2000, Section E, p. 8.

FURTHER READING

Iwasaki, Mineko, *Geisha, a Life*, Washington Square Press, 2003.

Although a geisha would never call herself a prostitute, there are a few similarities in the two professions. In this book, Iwasaki exposes some of the elements of her profession, for which she began training at the tender age of five.

Partnow, Elaine T., and Lesley Anne Hyatt, *The Female Dramatist: Profiles of Women Playwrights from Around the World from the Middle Ages to the Present Day*, Facts on File, 1998.

This rare collection of historical data focuses on dramatists who happen to be women. More than two hundred female playwrights are included, with information on the plays they produced as well as the critical response that the plays received. This is a good book about the evolution of plays written by women.

Pizer, Donald, ed., *The Cambridge Companion to American Realism and Naturalism: From Howells to London*, Cambridge University Press, 1995.

The beginnings of American realism are explored in American novels written by such authors as Theodore Dreiser, Edith Wharton, and Mark Twain.

Rank, Mark Robert, *One Nation Underprivileged: Why American Poverty Affects Us All*, Oxford University Press, 2005.

Professor Rank argues that people who are poor are not totally responsible for their condition. Rank makes a powerful case that poverty is a condition imposed by the failures of U.S. economic structure and politics. He also provides a workable solution.

Sutton, Randy, *True Blue: Police Stories by Those Who Have Lived Them*, St. Martin's Press, 2004.

Sutton invited police officers from all over the United States to write stories about their lives and their line of work. This book is a collection of those stories. While some of them are naturally very sad, especially those that deal with the terrorist attacks in New York City, other stories are surprisingly funny.

Willis, Clint, *NYPD: Stories of Survival from the World's Toughest Beat*, Thunder's Mouth, 2002.

A person who has never been to New York City might never have guessed the circumstances that are captured in this book of police stories. Someone who has lived in New York City will probably still be surprised and shocked at what goes on in the city.

Doubt

JOHN PATRICK SHANLEY

2004

John Patrick Shanley's drama *Doubt* premiered at the Manhattan Theatre Club on November 23, 2004, before moving to Broadway, at the Walter Kerr Theatre, in March of the following year. It instantly became the most celebrated play of the season, taking the 2005 Pulitzer Prize for Drama; best new play awards from the New York Drama Critics' Circle, the Lucille Lortel Foundation, the Drama League, the Outer Critics Circle, and the Drama Desk; the Obie; and four Tony Awards (best play, best actress in a play, best featured actress in a play, and best director). The play was published by Theatre Communications Group in 2005.

Set at a Catholic school in the Bronx in 1964, *Doubt* concerns an older nun, Sister Aloysius, who does not approve of teachers' offering friendship and compassion over the discipline she feels students need in order to face the harsh world. When she suspects a new priest of sexually abusing a student, she is faced with the prospect of charging him with unproven allegations and possibly destroying his career as well as her own. To help build her case, she asks for help from an idealistic young nun, who finds her faith in compassion challenged, and the mother of the accused boy, who is protective of her son, the first black student ever admitted to St. Nicholas.

Beginning in early 2002, the Catholic Church in the United States was embroiled in a high-profile scandal about priests who had had sexual relations with young students and parishioners, some incidents dating as far back as the time in which Shanley's

John Patrick Shanley Evan Agostini/Getty Images

play is set. Hundreds of victims came forward, and the Church, as of 2005, was facing lawsuits and undergoing reorganization, but the shock of the abuse of trust and the Catholic Church's attempts to cover up these crimes have left a scar on the public conscience. *Doubt* faces the unthinkable aspects of this situation with knowledge and restraint.

AUTHOR BIOGRAPHY

John Patrick Shanley was born in New York City in 1950. His father, who grew up on a farm in Ireland, was a meatpacker and his mother a telephone operator. He attended Catholic schools, but with a very unstable record: he was thrown out of kindergarten at St. Helena's, and he was banned for life from the hot-lunch program at St. Anthony's. After he was expelled from Cardinal Spellman High School, a priest who knew him and believed in his intellectual ability arranged for Shanley to attend Thomas More Prep School, a private school in Harrisville, New Hampshire. It was there that he started thinking seriously of a career as a writer. After graduating, he attended New York University, left for a stint in the U.S. Marine Corps, and returned to continue his studies under the GI Bill, graduating in 1977 as valedictorian.

Since then, Shanley has had a prolific career writing for the stage and screen. By 2005, he had written twenty-three plays. In 1987, he became internationally famous for his acclaimed script for the movie *Moonstruck*, for which he won an Academy Award and the Writer's Guild Award and was nominated for a Golden Globe. On that basis, Stephen Spielberg offered Shanley the opportunity to direct a movie from his own original script for *Joe versus the Volcano*, which came out in 1990. The film met with mixed reviews, and Shanley, as of 2005, had yet to direct another movie. He has adapted novels to screenplays, and several of his plays have been adapted for the movies, but his primary focus has always been theater. Despite his decades as a successful playwright and his immediate success in writing for the screen (*Moonstruck* was his very first screenplay), Shanley never won any major theatrical awards for his works before *Doubt*.

PLOT SUMMARY

Act 1

The first act of *Doubt* consists of a sermon by Father Flynn. His theme is uncertainty, which he relates to the disorientation felt by most of the country the year before, when President John F. Kennedy was assassinated. He points out how people came together spiritually and concludes that despair does not have to be an experience that isolates people, if they have faith. To make his point, Father Flynn tells a story about a sailor, lost at sea, who uses his memory of the stars to guide his navigation, even when the stars are covered by clouds for more than twenty nights. The sailor's faith in the truth he once knew is likened to the despairing person's faith in God.

Act 2

Sister Aloysius, the principal of St. Nicholas School, meets in her office with Sister James, who teaches eighth grade. She asks about a boy who has been sent home with a bleeding nose and warns that children sometimes inflict their own injuries as a way to leave school. During the conversation, Sister Aloysius reveals her dislike of teachers who act kind in order to hide their own weakness or laziness.

The talk turns to whether Sister James stays in the room when the "specialty" instructors—those in charge of teaching art, music, physical education, and similar subjects—come in. In particular,

Sister Aloysius is interested in whether Sister James leaves the boys alone when Father Flynn teaches religion and physical education. She asks Sister James to be alert, but she cannot find it in herself to be more specific about what she suspects.

Act 3

Act 3 comprises another monologue by Father Flynn, addressing the boys during basketball. He tells them that they will be able to shoot better if they relax and quit thinking about how they might look. On the subject of personal hygiene, he tells an apocryphal story about a boy with whom he grew up, named Timmy Mathisson, who had dirty fingernails that he put in his nose and in his mouth, which resulted in his death from spinal meningitis.

Act 4

Sister Aloysius and Sister James meet in the garden. Sister James explains that the boys in her class are at a lecture, given by Father Flynn, on the subject of being a man. Sister James explains that the new African American boy in her class, Donald Muller, does not have to worry much about bullying from the other students, because Father Flynn has taken on a role as his special protector. Immediately, Sister Aloysius says that she thinks Father Flynn is planning inappropriate behavior with the vulnerable boy. Sister James recalls that Father Flynn took Donald for a private talk to the rectory and that, when he came back, Donald had alcohol on his breath.

Sister Aloysius explains that it would be difficult to have a priest removed, even if there was evidence that he had had sex with a student. Father Flynn would certainly deny any such allegation, and Monsignor Benedict would believe whatever Father Flynn said. The rules of the Church prohibit a nun from taking suspicions to any higher authority. The boy would not talk, intimidated by shame. Sister Aloysius tells Sister James that she is going to confront Father Flynn and will need Sister James there as a witness.

Act 5

Father Flynn arrives at the door of Sister Aloysius's office, but the rules forbid a priest and a nun to be in a room alone. When Sister James arrives, Sister Aloysius serves tea. Father Flynn thinks that the meeting is about the Christmas pageant. Sister Aloysius mentions Donald Muller, saying that she knows that he has given the boy "special attention" and that Donald behaved strangely when he returned to class. Father Flynn, feeling accused, starts to walk out when Sister Aloysius mentions the smell of alcohol on the boy's breath. He explains that Donald had been caught by the caretaker drinking altar wine and that he was trying to spare the boy exposure.

After Father Flynn leaves, Sister Aloysius explains to Sister James that she thinks he was lying. Sister James vigorously defends him, accusing Sister Aloysius of simply disliking him, but Sister Aloysius dismisses her defense as being grounded in youthful naïveté. Sister Aloysius phones the boy's parents and asks them to come to the school for a meeting.

Act 6

Father Flynn gives a sermon about intolerance. He tells the story of a woman who, while gossiping with a friend, sees a hand over her head. She goes to her priest, and he tells her that it is a sign of God's displeasure. He instructs her to go home, take a pillow onto the roof, slash it with a knife, and empty it out. When she returns, the priest tells her to go and gather up all of the feathers that came from the pillow. She explains that she cannot, that they scattered to the winds. The priest in Father Flynn's story explains that gossip, once it is out, cannot be recalled either.

Act 7

Father Flynn meets Sister James while she is praying in the same garden that was the setting of act 4. She has had trouble sleeping, feeling guilty about being a gossip, like the woman in Father Flynn's sermon. Father Flynn speaks comfortingly, telling her that she is free to make up her own mind about him and is not obliged to follow whatever Sister Aloysius thinks. When she asks, he tells her directly that Sister Aloysius's allegations are not true. Father Flynn contrasts his own philosophy, which emphasizes love and concern, with Sister Aloysius's philosophy of strictness and discipline. Before she leaves, Sister James tells him that she does not believe that he is guilty.

Act 8

Sister Aloysius has a conference with Donald's mother. Mrs. Muller explains that she and her husband expected Donald to have trouble at St. Nicholas, being the first black student there, and they were glad that Father Flynn was looking out for him. Mrs. Muller is focused on Donald's staying through the end of the school year, which will give him a chance at being accepted into a good high school. When Sister Aloysius expresses concern about Father Flynn, Mrs. Muller takes a defensive posture: she knows that, in the event of a public inquiry, Donald, not the priest, would be blamed. She decides that it would be better for the boy, even if Father Flynn is using him sexually, to stay at St. Nicholas until graduation.

When she leaves, Father Flynn comes in, furious. He ignores the rule that states that a priest and nun cannot be alone in a room and slams the door behind him, demanding to know why Donald Muller's mother was there. He goes through the evidence of his misbehavior and discredits each charge, until Sister Aloysius says that she has talked to a nun at his last parish. Father Flynn raises objections—that she should have gone through the parish pastor, that there is no evidence in his official record of inappropriate behavior, and so forth—but Sister Aloysius insists that she knows he has taken advantage of boys. When she starts to leave to report him to higher authorities, he stops her and listens to her demands to leave St. Nicholas. When she does leave, he phones the bishop to ask to be reassigned.

Act 9

Sister Aloysius and Sister James meet and talk in the garden. Father Flynn has been moved to another parish, but with a promotion to pastor. Sister Aloysius was unable to convince Monsignor Benedict of Father Flynn's inappropriate behavior, but she is sure of his guilt. She feels guilty herself, because, to get him to leave, she lied about having contacted someone at his previous parish, a bluff that evidently frightened him away.

CHARACTERS

Sister Aloysius Beauvier

Sister Aloysius is the principal of the St. Nicholas school. She is stern, suspicious, and cynical, making a point of showing the students no weakness and discouraging signs of weakness in the nuns under her. When she is first introduced, her suspicious nature seems excessive: she suspects a boy who went home with a nosebleed of having intentionally inflicted it himself, and she feels that ballpoint pens, as opposed to fountain pens, offer students the easy way out. Her dour attitude makes her unsympathetic, and audiences are left to wonder whether, as Father Flynn and Sister James speculate at different times, she is suspicious of Father Flynn only because she personally dislikes his compassionate demeanor.

Sister Aloysius was not always a nun: she was once married, but her husband died in World War II, nearly twenty years before this play takes place. At a previous assignment, at St. Boniface, she was involved in having a pedophile priest "stopped," but currently, at St. Nicholas, she feels frustrated, certain that the Church hierarchy will not stand behind her should her suspicions about Father Flynn prove to be true.

Throughout the play, Sister Aloysius does not waver in her certainty that Father Flynn has had improper relations with boys. In the last act, however, after the priest's resignation confirms her suspicions, she tells Sister James that she had to lie in order to trap him, referring to lying as a step away from God and the price that one must pay in pursuing wrongdoing. The last line of the play has Sister Aloysius telling Sister James, "I have doubts! I have such doubts!" Her doubts reflect her awareness that persecuting Father Flynn has had bad as well as good effects.

Father Brendan Flynn

Up until the end, *Doubt* does not make clear whether Father Flynn is a just a concerned man or an actual child molester. Throughout the play, he makes a convincing case that he is being persecuted by Sister Aloysius because she disagrees with his progressive ideas. In their final confrontation, though, when he is faced with the nun's claim that she broke the prescribed order and has spoken to a nun from Father Flynn's previous parish, he gives in and leaves St. Nicholas before she can expose him.

Father Flynn comes from a working-class background, and he is comfortable with the boys of his parish. He teaches religion and physical education. His manner with the boys, shown in act 3, is tough yet caring: he offers advice; criticizes; pokes fun; and, in the end, invites them back to the rectory with him for Kool-Aid and cookies. When he is accused of giving Donald Muller wine as a way to approach him for sexual favors, he explains that he was really protecting Donald from being thrown out of school after he found out the boy had drunk some of the altar wine. Father Flynn tells Sister James that he believes in being open and caring, that he follows the Bible's teachings of love.

In act 1, Father Flynn gives a sermon that includes a story about a man in a boat, lost at sea and with no stars to guide him; Sister Aloysius later implies that this is a sign that he himself has some secret that would prompt a feeling of despair. When he is addressing his basketball class, he tells them a story about a boy with whom he went to school, a boy who did not wash his hands properly and caught spinal meningitis and died. Later, after being confronted by Sister Aloysius and Sister James, he gives a sermon about a woman who learns that gossiping can have uncontrollable and ruinous results. Father Flynn's style is to turn events and situations from his own life, and from the world around him, into parables.

One particularly telling moment comes when, called to a meeting in Sister Aloysius's office, he walks over and sits behind her desk: rather than seeing the kindly priest fighting against a rigid and humorless traditionalist, audiences see him being cocky, proud, and a bit arrogant. He still seems defensive later in the play, when he tells Sister Aloysius that she will not be able to prosecute him, until his fear that she might actually have heard the truth about his history—he has been at three parishes in five years—forces him to ask for reassignment, indicating his guilt.

Sister James

Sister James is an earnest young nun in her twenties, who starts out eager to teach her students and pique their interest in history. She believes the best of her students and approaches their problems with compassion and sympathy. These are qualities that Sister Aloysius warns her against. For instance, Sister Aloysius explains that teachers who try to make their subjects interesting to students are really just performing and being clever. She tells Sister James that students who have to go home with physical problems might have inflicted the problems on themselves, precisely to get out of school. She makes Sister James doubt her basic assumptions about her role as a nun: as Sister James explains to Father Flynn when they are confiding in each other about Sister Aloysius, "She's taken away my joy of teaching. And I loved teaching more than anything." At the end of the play, when it is revealed that Father Flynn has been reassigned, Sister James returns after a visit to her brother, who had previously been identified as being ill.

Donald Muller

Donald Muller, the boy who is presumed to be the victim of sexual abuse, does not appear onstage, but his role is important. He is the first black student at St. Nicholas, putting him immediately in a dangerous position: the nuns accept it as a matter of course that he will be in fights with the other boys. Sister Aloysius views his difficult situation as making him an ideal candidate for the tactics of a sexual predator. This suspicion grows when Sister James tells her that Donald was taken to the rectory by Father Flynn and that he returned behaving strangely and smelling of liquor. Father Flynn explains that he was trying to protect Donald from punishment after the boy stole some of the altar wine and drank it. After the priest says this publicly, Donald is punished by being dismissed as one of the altar boys.

Donald's mother later reveals to Sister Aloysius that Donald was in fights at his previous school and that his father abuses him at home. When told that Donald might be a victim of a sexual predator, she says that she believes that he may have encouraged the relationship and that she and his father think the problems at the old school were a result of his homosexual tendencies.

Mrs. Muller

Mrs. Muller is the mother of Donald Muller, the first black child to attend St. Nicholas. She has been afraid that he would meet with hostility in the predominantly Irish and Italian neighborhood and was comforted to know that Father Flynn formed a close bond with the boy. When she is called down to talk to the principal of the school, Mrs. Muller fears that her son's school career might be in trouble: she has been counting on his being a St. Nicholas graduate in order to assure his placement in a good high school. She is aware that he has been expelled from the altar boys for drinking wine, but she thinks of that as a minor infraction that is behind them. She reveals that Donald's father beat him when he found out about the altar wine.

When she finds out that her son may be the victim of a sexual predator, Mrs. Muller does not react with outrage. She is afraid that her boy will be blamed for the crime by a community that is already inclined to be hostile to blacks. When Sister Aloysius tells her that she thinks Father Flynn has given Donald wine as a way to have sex with him, Mrs. Muller points out how, in that episode, it was her son, and not the priest, who was punished. She reveals that her son may already be a homosexual, which would make him a willing participant in Father Flynn's abuse. Overall, she is willing to accept a relationship between the boy and the priest for a few months until Donald graduates, preferring to concentrate on the good influence that Father Flynn offers to a boy who is trying to fit in to a hostile environment and to escape an abusive father.

THEMES

Certainty

One of the key elements of *Doubt* is the issue of certainty and how difficult it is to be certain, even in an environment of faith. The two main characters, Sister Aloysius and Father Flynn, each hold staunchly to their views of the world and are unwilling to see things as others do: this unwillingness to yield is both a strength and a weakness and leads to the final tragic conclusion. The other two onstage characters, Sister James and Mrs. Muller, are racked with doubt, able to see both sides of their dilemma.

Sister Aloysius is certain that there is sexual abuse going on at St. Nicholas, even before she has any substantial proof of it. She says late in the play that her certainty grew from one small gesture: the way in which one of the students recoiled from Father Flynn's touch. The evidence that she compiles as a result is flimsy and easily explained away. She takes such minor issues as the length of Father Flynn's fingernails and the fact that he lectures the boys on being men to be support of her suspicion. When Father Flynn offers reasonable explanations for his behavior, she persists. He believes that her personal dislike for his teaching style may be strengthening her sense of certainty. She is even willing to threaten trouble for the boy, who presumably is the victim in this case. She shows no sense of uncertainty until the play's last line, when she admits to having doubts.

Father Flynn is just as certain that he himself is a force for good and that, with his emphasis on love and compassion, he is better for the boys than Sister Aloysius is. In the end, his retreat from St. Nicholas seems to be an admission of guilt, but he never verbally acknowledges having done wrong.

Mrs. Muller, on the other hand, is pragmatic enough to admit that allowing a bad relationship may lead to a greater good. She suspects that her son and Father Flynn might be involved in a relationship, but she also knows that exposing their relationship would do much more damage to her son's future prospects than anything the priest could do. She weighs up the factors—the months until graduation, her husband's rage, the benefit of graduating from a good school—and decides that there are no easy answers about right or wrong.

The weight of the question of certainty makes Sister James a very important figure in this play. She starts out feeling that the best way to teach is with compassion, but Sister Aloysius convinces her that strict discipline is more important than compassion. When he needs her support, though, Father Flynn talks with her about how Sister Aloysius's stern, disciplinary approach is a violation of the Bible's focus on love. Sister James is divided between logic and emotion, reason and compassion: her certainty shaken, she is troubled, which is the effect that *Doubt* strives to evoke in its audience.

Gender Roles in the Church and the World

In general, Sister Aloysius feels frustrated in her attempts to remove Father Flynn because of the Church hierarchy. At one point, though, she recognizes that the structure of the Church is arranged to keep men in power, so that, even as the school's principal, she will be incapable of taking the actions she feels she needs to take to protect her students. In act 4, she recalls to Sister James a time at a previous parish when a sexually predatory priest had to be removed from contact with children. "But I had Monsignor Scully then . . . who I could rely on. Here, there's no man I can go to, and men run everything."

Outside the Church, society at large experiences a similar division of male and female roles. Mrs. Muller comes to meet with the principal alone because her husband has to work, enforcing the traditions of men being breadwinners and women being focused on child rearing. When their boy, Donald, is in trouble at school, however, his father becomes involved in his life by taking on the role of disciplinarian, which he approaches with a violence that is so extreme that his wife thinks it is a threat to the boy's life.

Vulnerability

There are two characters in *Doubt* who are used to represent vulnerability. The first and most obvious is Donald Muller, the student who is suspected of having been sexually abused. Donald has recently transferred from another school and is the first black student to attend St. Nicholas. When she hears that Father Flynn has established himself as a "protector" to Donald, Sister Aloysius immediately assumes that his motive is to take advantage of him. "He's isolated," she explains to Sister James. "The little sheep lagging behind is the one the wolf goes for." While the teachers who advocate compassion—Sister James and Father Flynn—see Donald's vulnerability as a responsibility, Sister Aloysius has no doubt that an unscrupulous predator will take advantage of any weakness.

TOPICS FOR FURTHER STUDY

- In the twenty-first century, the number of nuns continues to diminish, and the average age of active nuns is getting older. Interview a nun (either in person or via the Internet) and find out what factors induced her to take her vows. Have another person read the interviewee's part as you present your conversation to your class.
- Critics have tried to compare Sister Aloysius's willingness to take action, even without much evidence, to America's preemptive strike against Iraq in 2003. Research the arguments and lead a class discussion on the similarities and the differences between the two positions.
- Sister Aloysius says that she entered the convent after her husband died during World War II. Research the ways in which important social upheavals, such as wars, famines, and the overthrow of governments, affect the enrollment numbers for religious orders and create a chart that shows the correlations.
- In what ways do you think this story would have been different if St. Nicholas had been a racially integrated school? Find footage of news reports about school integration and put together a video montage of people talking about what it was like. Present it to the class, along with your views on the ways in which racial integration might have changed the story.

At the same time, Sister Aloysius is concerned with keeping Sister Veronica's weakness hidden from the Church hierarchy. Sister Veronica's eyesight is failing with age, and Sister Aloysius fears that, if her condition were commonly known, the Church would move her out of the parish. To some extent, her concern for Sister Veronica is protective, putting Sister Aloysius in the strange position of having to shield a weakened nun from the Church that she serves. But while she is telling Sister James to watch over Sister Veronica, she says, "I cannot afford to lose her." Her concern about Sister Veronica's vulnerability is based, at least in part, on her own consolidation of power. To some extent, Sister Aloysius is taking advantage of Sister Veronica's vulnerability in the same way that she assumes Father Flynn is taking advantage of Donald's.

Sexual Abuse

Any sexual relationship between an adult and a minor is technically considered sexual abuse, because the minor is presumed to lack the worldliness and experience to knowingly consent to a relationship. It is particularly immoral for someone in a position of authority, such as a teacher or work superior, to enter into such a relationship with someone who might feel intimidated by their power.

As with most moral issues, however, *Doubt* blurs the distinctions that might otherwise seem clear-cut. For one thing, it presents the relationship between Father Flynn and Donald Muller as one of emotional depth, whether it has a physical element or not. Father Flynn believes that he is a good man, that it is he, not Sister Aloysius, who is concerned with the boy's welfare. Donald's mother also seems to believe this to be true: she sees the dangers that threaten her son, both in the hostile school environment and from his abusive father at home, and she is thankful that he has a protector. She is willing to accept the idea that a sexual relationship might exist between the boy and the priest, because she fears that the threat of their having no relationship at all would be worse. "My son needs some man to care about him and see him through to where he wants to go," she explains. "And thank God, this educated man with some kindness in him wants to do just that."

Mrs. Muller also raises the prospect that Donald may have encouraged such a relationship because he is, as she puts it, "that way." While this might remove some of the stigma of it being a homosexual relationship, it does not make it any less abusive. Even if the boy is a willing participant, not forced into having sex, the adult is still guilty of abuse of power.

STYLE

Priestly Monologues

Acts 1, 3, and 6 of *Doubt* consist of monologues delivered by Father Flynn, who is onstage by himself. These monologues function as speeches in the play. Two of them are meant to represent sermons from the pulpit, addressed to parishioners during a mass, and the other one is given as a lecture to a group of boys playing basketball. In the last one, Father Flynn interacts with particular boys, responding to them as if they were there, though no actors are present.

Dramatists often use monologues to allow a character to express her or his own ideas without other characters who are involved in the story knowing what those ideas are. In such cases, characters might walk away from the action, often toward the audience, and say out loud what is going on in their minds. In this case, though, Father Flynn's words are meant to be heard by an audience. In the cases of the sermons, it would make no sense to provide an audience on the stage, since Father Flynn is just talking, and their reactions are not necessary. It would be quite possible for another playwright to have written in parts for Jimmy, Ralph, Conroy, and the other boys that Father Flynn directly addresses in act 3, but there really is no need for that, since audiences can imagine their actions from what the priest says.

Multiset Stage

Three of the play's nine acts take place in the small garden that separates the convent where the nuns live from the rectory where the priests live, and three acts take place in Sister Aloysius's office. The scenes are so short that changing sets frequently would put a disproportionate drag on the action. To keep the action moving, the script allows the different sets to be on one stage, changing from one to another by having the lights cross-fade—dim on one set as they come up on the other.

The garden is an important location for symbolic reasons. As Sister Aloysius points out, it is a small patch of land, but "we might as well be separated by the Atlantic Ocean." Sister Aloysius says that she stopped visiting the garden because Monsignor Benedict used to go there: though they live in proximity, the nuns and priests are not allowed to meet with each other one on one. This rule is presumably in place to keep nuns and priests from developing romantic relationships, though in reality it creates a sense of alienation that prohibits them from addressing problems when they arise. The garden, which could be a peaceful, spiritual setting, becomes, ironically, a place that breeds mystery and suspicion among the people it separates.

It is also important, in establishing the social dynamic of St. Nicholas parish, for the play to be based in Sister Aloysius's office. As the school's mother superior, she has authority over the nuns, and in her office she can rule, rattling off theories of education and voicing suspicions and innuendoes that she would not be able to discuss out in the open. When Father Flynn comes to a meeting there, he usurps her power by sitting down at her desk, showing that even a low-level priest is more powerful in the Church hierarchy than the highest nun. Later, when he finds out that Sister Aloysius has been talking with Donald Muller's mother, Father Flynn ignores the rule that forbids a nun and a priest to be together without supervision, and he slams the door behind himself at the start of their climactic confrontation in act 8.

Compassion as a Tragic Flaw

Father Flynn is a caring man who tries to break down the social barriers that separate him from the boys in his class. His compassion is conscious, a trait that he actively pursues, believing that it is more important for the boys to feel loved than it is for them to be pressured by rules. In particular, he makes a point of giving extra attention to Donald Muller because he feels that the boy can use a friend, given his circumstances. His extraordinary friendship with the boy is suspicious, if not inappropriate. Even if he is not, as Sister Aloysius assumes, sexually involved with the boy, Father Flynn's desire to ignore common social boundaries puts him in a position that threatens his career. By traditional dramatic standards, his need for acceptance can be seen as a tragic flaw in that it is a character trait that leads to his downfall.

While compassion is not generally viewed as a flaw, Shanley does establish a framework for seeing it as one. In act 2, discussing the teaching style of Sister James, Sister Aloysius characterizes innocence in teachers as self-indulgent and lazy. To her, a teacher who tries to befriend a student is doing so for selfish reasons. As much as Father Flynn is adamant in his insistence that children should be treated with compassion, Sister Aloysius is adamant that such ideas are a sign of impure intentions. Whether or not he is a sexual predator, Father Flynn draws attention to himself with his insistence on behaving as the boys' friend.

Parable

Although Shanley clearly takes as his subject the sexual abuse scandal that has plagued the Catholic Church for years, he has said that he did not set out to write a play about that situation. The true subject of *Doubt* is, as its title indicates, uncertainty. The play's subtitle is "A Parable," indicating that it is not meant to be any sort of analysis of the events described in the newspapers. Although the play takes place at a Catholic school, it does not explicitly address intricate matters of Catholicism; instead, it uses its setting to examine a human predicament that can occur in any religion or profession.

Traditionally, a parable is a rhetorical device used to illustrate an abstract concept. In this case, Shanley is interested in exploring the idea of doubt, which, as he illustrates in the play, is much more complex than it seems at first. The main characters behave with certainty, but the structure of the play shows audiences that they experience doubt and also why they do. The use of the word *parable* in describing this play is particularly significant because of that word's association with Christianity: many of the lessons Christ relates to his followers are told through parables. The parables of the New Testament are generally associated with universal themes that apply to all cultures and times, whereas Shanley applies the word to a story that is unfolding in the headlines of the present day.

HISTORICAL CONTEXT

Catholic Church Scandal

The history of sexual abuse in the Catholic Church is, by its very nature, shadowed, concealed over the course of decades by threats and bribes that number into the millions of dollars. The wave of public disclosures dates back to 1984, when rumors of sexual impropriety led to the guilty plea of the Reverend Gilbert Gauthe of the diocese of Lafayette, Louisiana, in molesting eleven boys. The ensuing investigation implicated nineteen other priests, and the diocese negotiated out-of-court settlements with the victims for undisclosed financial amounts. Over the next eight years, several other scandals made headlines, including at least one case involving a Chicago cardinal in which the accuser later testified that his original claim was a lie. By 1992, protestors picketing outside the conference of U.S. bishops in Washington, D.C., infuriated by the Church's position of trying to hide abuse cases at all costs, influenced the bishops to issue the first set of written principles regarding how to handle allegations. Still, accusations continued to pop up, with notable cases in Dallas, Honolulu, and New York City.

The scandal hit with full force in Boston in 2002. In January of that year, the defrocked priest John Geoghan was accused of having abused more than 130 children while serving as a priest in the Boston archdiocese over a period dating back to the 1970s. The subsequent investigation revealed that his superior, Bernard Cardinal Law, frequently hid Geoghan's crimes by reassigning him and authorizing payoff money to his accusers. Among the revelations that came out in the press was that Law had known about Geoghan's behavior since 1984; that Geoghan's victims, all boys, included one who was just four years old; and that the Catholic Church had already paid out about forty million dollars to Geoghan's victims. The shock of the Boston case spread: by the end of 2002, twelve hundred priests had been accused of sexual abuse nationwide, and five U.S. prelates (bishops or archbishops) had been forced to resign. By 2005, similar cases had sprung up in a number of other countries.

A study conducted by the John Jay College has determined that between 1950 and 2002 an estimated 4 percent of Catholic priests engaged in sexual relations with a minor, almost exclusively boys. Sex-abuse-related costs totaled $573 million, with $219 million covered by insurance companies; these numbers are lower than actual amounts paid, because some dioceses, most notably Boston, did not participate in the survey and because payments made after 2002 were not included. Most of the incidents of abuse, a full 75 percent, were found to have taken place between 1960 and 1984, but researchers are not certain of what this statistic might mean. Although the hope is that sexual abuse by priests has tapered off as time has progressed, the figure might indicate that people who are abused as children are hesitant to report it until they have grown up and that another wave of allegations will

Brian F. O'Byrne in a 2005 production of Doubt

come up in the future. In all, the John Jay study found that sexual abuse had occurred in 95 percent of the dioceses in the United States. Since 2004, another seven hundred priests have been removed from their positions in connection with this scandal.

School Integration

For a hundred years after the end of the Civil War, states were allowed to legally force black students and white students to attend different schools. The legal principle, upheld in the Supreme Court's ruling in the *Plessy v. Ferguson* case of 1896, was that different races would be provided accommodations that were "separate but equal." In practice, however, the facilities provided for white students were almost always superior. This led to the Civil Rights movement of the 1950s and 1960s, during which segregation, or separation, of the races was challenged throughout the country. *Plessy* was overturned in 1954, in the case of *Brown v. the Board of Education of Topeka, Kansas*, which ruled it illegal to refuse students admission to schools on the basis of race.

Although the law was clear, traditionalists who had grown up in a world where races did not interact with each other fought change. One of the most famous cases occurred in Little Rock, Arkansas, in 1957: black students were stopped from entering Central High School by a crowd of violent whites led by the state's own governor, Orval Faubus, and President Eisenhower had to order federal troops to the site to protect the students. Similar tensions occurred in 1963, when a black student, James Meredith, enrolled at the University of Mississippi, considered a bastion of southern segregationist tradition: riots and threats of lynching forced Meredith to live under the protection of National Guard troops for several months.

Segregation problems were most frequently associated with the South, but the struggle to integrate northern schools was just as difficult, and problems sometimes lingered longer. The schools of Washington, D.C., for instance, had been segregated for decades, with white families moving to the affluent suburbs, leaving schools in the city where blacks lived in overcrowded conditions and infrastructure was poorly maintained. After the *Brown* ruling, when the courts ordered that students from each area be transported by bus to the other areas in order to achieve more racial balance, violence became an almost daily occurrence, culminating in 1964 in a particularly bloody struggle between a predominantly white parochial school, St. John's, and the predominantly black school, Eastern.

The most notable holdout to integration in the North, however, was in Boston, where, as in Washington, whites and blacks lived in separate districts. Attempts to integrate Boston schools relied on complex busing systems, moving students of both races, often against their wills, for hours each morning to take them to learn in hostile environments. Although there were unfair aspects to busing, the alternative, which proved to be districts that were consciously arranged by the Boston School Board to keep races separate, were deemed by the courts to be even worse. The Boston plan, begun in 1974, led to years of violence and racial tension. While not always as legally complex or emotionally inflamed, similar integration struggles took place in cities throughout the North in the 1960s and 1970s.

CRITICAL OVERVIEW

There is no question that *Doubt* was a breakthrough critical and popular success for Shanley. Although Shanley had seen his plays produced in

WHAT DO I READ NEXT?

- Shanley's best-known work is his screenplay for the movie *Moonstruck.* His 1994 two-person play *Danny and the Deep Blue Sea* (2000) has a similar romantic appeal. It is available in *Thirteen by Shanley.*
- At the same time that *Doubt* was being performed on Broadway, Martin McDonagh's play *The Pillowman* (2004) was also running. The play is a hypnotic, Kafkaesque story of a writer who is interrogated by authorities in a fictitious authoritarian state for the similarities between incidents in his stories and a recent spree of child murders.
- Cheryl L. Reed's 2004 study *Unveiled: The Hidden Lives of Nuns* is not, as its title might suggest, an exposé about the women who serve the Church but is instead the honest account of a wide variety of nuns from a selection of different orders throughout North America.
- Christopher Durang's 1981 play *Sister Mary Ignatius Explains It All for You* is a comedy lampooning the stereotypical nuns that people remember from their childhood and, as such, can be seen as the temperamental opposite of *Doubt.* It is available in *Christopher Durang Explains It All for You: Six Plays.*
- For a better sense of what life was like in the neighborhood of the play's St. Nicholas, read the wonderful history *The Bronx: It Was Only Yesterday, 1935–1965* (1992). The authors Lloyd Ultan and Gary Hermalyn provide background for a wealth of photos showing a life gone by.

New York City for more than twenty years, this was the first work to make the general public aware of him as a playwright. Previously, his claim to fame had been an Oscar for his first movie script, *Moonstruck* (1987), and as writer and director of the cult favorite *Joe versus the Volcano* (1990). Within months of its Broadway debut, the play had already taken the Pulitzer Prize for Drama, the Obie for its previous off-Broadway run, and several Tony Awards.

What captured the attention of the critics, garnering *Doubt* more serious consideration than other plays about serious, topical issues, is Shanley's finely tuned balance of the moral complexity of the issues he raises. As Charles Isherwood puts it in the *New York Times*, the play "is no hand-wringing tract about the abuse of power and religious hypocrisy." He goes on to see its larger implications: "The play is a quiet indictment of the reverence for righteousness that has become a hallmark of American culture in recent years." Robert Brustein, writing in the *New Republic*, dubs it "the strongest play about the Catholic clergy since Christopher Durang's *Sister Mary Ignatius Explains It All to You*, which also featured a splendid characterization . . . of a less-than-charitable nun." Brustein mentions in passing that the play might be a little too direct and unambiguous, but he generally finds it a "significant advance" for Shanley. As Richard Zoglin puts it in a *Time* magazine article about must-see shows on Broadway, "Shanley's work packs more complexity, humanity—doubt—than plays twice its length."

CRITICISM

David Kelly

Kelly is an instructor of creative writing and literature. In this essay, he examines the relationships that the characters in this play have with the world outside the Church.

Shanley's drama *Doubt* centers on a nun in a Catholic parish in the Bronx in 1964. She starts the play with suspicions that a priest in the affiliated church is a sexual predator, and she makes it her mission to have him removed, regardless of the cost to herself, his presumed victim, or anyone else. The play is carefully crafted to raise important

"SISTER JAMES AVOIDS ENDING UP BEING A JUNIOR VERSION OF EITHER SIDE OR A COMBINATION OF TRAITS LEARNED FROM SISTER ALOYSIUS AND FATHER JAMES, BECAUSE SHE HAS A LIFE OUTSIDE THE WALLS OF ST. NICHOLAS SCHOOL AND PARISH HOUSE."

issues—from faith to cynicism, compassion to discipline, and righteousness to obedience—but it recognizes the complexity of all these ideas and avoids taking sides. For all the attention *Doubt* has gained in the media because of its timely subject matter, Shanley's real interest is in the interplay between certainty and uncertainty and how too much of either can be destructive. As such, the play's main character is neither the accuser, Sister Aloysius, nor the accused, Father Flynn; it is rather the young nun, Sister James, who can see the merits of being both steadfast and tolerant. Sister James could be considered a surrogate for the audience: a reasonable, neutral party who is willing to listen to what each side has to say. It is strange, then, that Shanley has her disappear from the play at the climactic moment. It is strange, but it works, because the absence of reason is the whole point.

Shanley uses the word "doubt" in two specific, deliberate places, defining the extremism of the two main characters. Early on, before audiences have even been made aware of Sister Aloysius's suspicions of Father Flynn, the subject of his possibly having a shameful secret is raised when Sister Aloysius and Sister James are discussing his latest sermon, on the topic of Doubt. (Shanley uses the capital "D" in the published script, even though theater audiences would not be aware of it.) Sister Aloysius wonders in a provocative way, "Is Father Flynn in Doubt, is he concerned that someone else is in Doubt?" Much later, when her allegations of sexual abuse become apparent, this question makes sense; outside the context of his crime, however, it seems that Sister Aloysius, who is stringent in her ways, looks down on the priest only because he lacks absolute certainty. At the end of the play, though, having won a battle of wills over Father Flynn, Sister Aloysius suffers from her own uncertainty. "I have doubts!" she exclaims to Sister James. "I have such doubts!" If certainty is what allows Father Flynn to continue as a child molester without crumbling under a guilty conscience and what allows Sister Aloysius to doggedly pursue a possibly innocent man, then uncertainty in the play is not presented as being any more attractive.

This is not a play about the relative merits of child molesting or kindness but about that terrible feeling that one does not know the right course. The two main characters are each insulated, wrapped so deeply in their own self-assurance that they cannot relate to the world outside of themselves. They each feed off the self-righteousness of the other to nourish the righteousness of their own causes, unable, owing largely to surrounding circumstances, to see things in a larger context. Shanley uses the self-contained world of the parish to parallel the self-assured worlds of his characters' minds.

This is why Sister James is such a potentially important figure. Sister James agrees with many of the views of Father Flynn in regard to education and Christian behavior, approaching her job as a teaching nun with the attitude that love, not discipline, is the most important thing to offer her students. She is also in agreement with Sister Aloysius, however, that child molestation is an unthinkable crime that cannot be left unpunished. She is anguished, she wants her peace of mind, and she is as disgusted by Sister Aloysius's cold heart as she is by Father Flynn's alleged behavior. Her allegiances shift, depending on who is talking to her; in short, she is just as uncertain about how to morally judge these two people as most of the open-minded audience members are inclined to be. It would be nice if she could be a voice of moderation, to make the two sides recognize each other, but, given the political structure of the Church, that clearly is not possible. Neither her mother superior nor a priest has any inclination—or need—to listen to her.

It is therefore fitting that, when the final confrontation between Father Flynn and Sister Aloysius comes in act 8, Sister James is nowhere to be found. Later, when the excitement is all over, it is explained that she was out of town visiting her sick brother, whose illness has been mentioned earlier.

(Showing concern for this brother is just one part of Father Flynn's charm offensive, to win Sister James to his side.) This absence in which she attends to other things changes the significance of Sister James in the story. Sister James avoids ending up being a junior version of either side or a combination of traits learned from Sister Aloysius and Father James, because she has a life outside the walls of St. Nicholas school and parish house. The play gives special significance to events that happen outside the insular church environment, showing separation from outer life as a direct cause of doubt and the inability to deal with it.

Each scene takes place on Church property, and the play only hints at what life is like beyond the Church's protection. Outside is a frightening world of violence and disease. One of the four onstage characters, Mrs. Muller, the mother of the boy whom Father Flynn is suspected of victimizing, lives in the secular world. She brings with her a sense of defeat that casts a cloud over the idealism of both Sister Aloysius's need for control and Father Flynn's need to love. Her son, Donald, has been beaten up, both by students at the public school he attended and by his own father, because of suspicions of homosexuality. Mrs. Muller understands that Father Flynn might be using her son sexually, but she accepts such abuse as being better than the violence of the world outside. The parish is a sanctuary for her, albeit a flawed one.

Sister Aloysius is the one member of the Church who has had significant experience with the outside world, having lived a secular life and having even been married before taking her vows. All she says about that time is that her husband fought and was killed in Italy during World War II. Her entry to the Church marked an escape from that violent world and, in itself, might be enough to explain her jaded view, her sense that such common pieces of life as ballpoint pens and sugar are luxuries that weaken the spirit. Shanley also provides a little background of her life within the Church, when, eight years earlier, at another parish, she played a part in the downfall of another sexually predatory priest. As much as life at St. Nicholas seems to be harmonious, a life like Sister Aloysius's will not let her leave appearances to speak for themselves.

Leading the life that Father Flynn has led, on the other hand, offers every encouragement to try to maintain the status quo. The priest has limited experiences to draw on: Sister James even comments on his frequent use of made-up stories for his sermons, which indicates talent and imagination but does not suggest any sort of personal history that he would care to recall. His history is with the Church, and, so far at least, it has been a successful one. If Sister Aloysius is right (and her successful bluff at the end indicates that she probably is), Father Flynn has behaved criminally before and beaten the rap, and so there is no reason to expect that he will not do so again. Perhaps he really does believe that his sexual relations with children are based in love, but, at some level at least, he knows that there is nowhere but the Church where such behavior would be protected. His past is within the Church, his future is within the Church, and in neither past nor future does his behavior earn him the sort of punishment that it would in the real world.

Having one of the key players, Sister James, go outside the Church while the other players battle each other within it is thus symbolically significant. Audiences can assume that Sister James will bring an outsider's view to the situation when she returns to it. For Sister Aloysius and Father James, though, there is nothing but symbolism to connect them to the outside world.

Sister Aloysius indulges in just one personal interest in this play: she listens to a transistor radio in act 8. Her listening is not for pleasure. She does not listen to music, she listens for news, which she relates to the time in her past when her husband was at war and she followed the news reports carefully. This curiosity about the outside world, her constant bracing for the tragedy that eventually did come in her husband's case, shows a lot about her imagination. Sister Aloysius spends her life preparing for the worst, and when she actually does find the worst in Father Flynn's actions, it seems almost a coincidence.

For Father Flynn, the outside world shows up in the form of a crow. Act 7, in which he makes the calmest and most convincing case for his innocence, is bracketed by the appearance of a crow overhead. His explanation to Sister James in that scene is entirely reasonable: he tells her how much he values the Christian principle of love and how much Sister Aloysius opposes such compassion, making it clear why she would try to distort his actions into looking like perversity. Because he apparently believes himself to be innocent, Father Flynn sounds innocent—that is, until the end of the scene, when Sister James leaves and he is left by himself. A crow, which he had accused of "complaining" at the scene's start, caws again, and Father Flynn yells at it. For a man who has just explained his innocence, he betrays himself to be conscience-stricken.

Doubt conveys how the Church creates an environment that encourages security, an environment wherein the uncertainty that rules the outside world is minimized, if not overcome. Because she can see both Father Flynn's and Sister Aloysius's points of view, Sister James is in danger, throughout the play, of becoming an adherent of one or the other extreme; instead, she escapes the trap of narrow-mindedness by renewing her connection to the world. For those who do not leave the Church grounds, there are only abstract images, such as voices on the radio or squawking birds, to remind them of the world they have shut out.

Source: David Kelly, Critical Essay on *Doubt*, in *Drama for Students*, Thomson Gale, 2006.

Stephen Phillips

In the following review, Phillips relates how Sister Margaret found out about her role in Doubt, *and provides background on the events that shaped the play.*

This season's big Broadway hit is a raw story of child abuse in the Catholic church. Stephen Phillips meets the teacher who inspired the author to speak out.

New York theatre-goers currently packing out the hit Broadway play *Doubt* would scarcely guess that the real-life inspiration for its most endearing character is still teaching at a school nearby—almost half a century on from her fictional stage representation.

It was news to Sister Margaret McEntee, too, last November, when the veteran English and religious education teacher answered a phone call at the Brooklyn convent where she lives. "Did you know you're on the first page of the New York Times arts section?" asked a former student, Geraldine Cunningham-Pare.

Come to think of it, there had been a picture of a nun wearing the old, distinctive full-length habit of her order, the Sisters of Charity, in the newspaper the other day. The play review also mentioned "Sister James," her old name before she'd switched to her baptismal name, Margaret, during the 1960s Vatican reform movement. And it mentioned a "Sister Aloysius," not a million miles from Sister Aloysia, the real-life headmistress at her old school, St Anthony's, in New York's Bronx.

"That was you," Geraldine Cunningham-Pare said. "And guess who wrote it? John Patrick Shanley." "Oh, little Johnny," Sister Margaret replied, recalling a six-year-old she'd taught as a 21-year old rookie teacher in 1956.

Geraldine Cunningham-Pare, a film critic for Catholic newspapers, had taken a keen interest in Mr Shanley's Hollywood and Broadway career. He'd won the Oscar for best screenplay in 1988 for the Cher movie, *Moonstruck*. "I think your 15 minutes of fame have begun," she told her former teacher.

It's been a rollercoaster ride ever since for Sister Margaret, aged 69 and still going strong at Greenwich Village's Notre Dame high school. *Doubt* has become one of the hottest tickets in New York. Last month it won the Pulitzer Prize for best drama, and it's tipped to land the Tony Award for best play, in Broadway's equivalent of the Academy Awards, on June 5. But the play is perhaps an unlikely box-office smash, confronting as it does the topical but still uncomfortable subject of sexual abuse in the Catholic church.

The Catholic church in the United States has been battered by stories of abuse inflicted on young people by its priests. Some parishes have been pushed to the brink of insolvency by compensation payouts to victims. And painful memories were stirred up by the spectacle of the former Boston cardinal Bernard Law—accused of presiding over the repeated reassignment of alleged paedophile priests to roles giving them access to children—officiating at Pope John Paul II's funeral last month.

In writing his fictional scenario, John Patrick Shanley, 54, drew partly on his experiences growing up in New York's Irish immigrant community. "These guys came out of the woodwork to young boys," he says. "In my case, it wasn't the clergy, but a teacher at a school subsequent to St Anthony's, who was enamoured of me but never crossed the line." A friend wasn't so lucky. After being abused he left the country. "He felt shamed, he had lost his pride."

Doubt is an intense 90-minute, one-act play, leavened by flashes of irreverent humour. Idealistic Sister James is the foil between the polarising characters of a charismatic priest with the common touch, Father Flynn, and a crusty, matriarchal headmistress, Sister Aloysius, who suspects him of abusing one of her pupils. Sister James is torn between the antagonists' clashing personalities and starkly opposing views of the Catholic ministry. Sister Aloysius conforms to an old-school view of boundaries between laity and clergy, decrying Flynn's efforts to reach out to the community.

It's a tension felt keenly by Sister Margaret, who recalls a run-in with the real-life Sister Aloysia, who reproached her as a new teacher for consorting with parents who'd come to school to pick up their children.

These days she wears civilian clothes, having shed the traditional nun's garb along with her male title.

Casting his former teacher's character in *Doubt* made perfect sense, says John Patrick Shanley, who, at 6 ft 1 in and with more than a passing resemblance to Liam Neeson, could be a leading man himself. "She was this fresh-faced young nun with this very benevolent attitude," he remembers.

Sister Margaret recalls Mr Shanley as a "loveable little kid". But she adds: "Thank God I didn't teach him in secondary school." By his own admission, Mr Shanley was no model pupil. He was banished from St Anthony's dining hall for food fighting, expelled from his secondary school, and dropped out of New York University to join the US Marines before returning to complete his studies. Despite the indelible impression left by his first teacher, he had misgivings about a meeting with her, brokered by Geraldine Cunningham-Pare, who contacted Mr Shanley via a website dedicated to their old neighbourhood. It wasn't so much the dark subject matter he'd cast her character into, but a distinctively American concern. "The word lawsuit crossed my mind," he explains. "There's the old accusation, 'You stole my life'."

A phone conversation allayed his fears. "She was so thoughtful, quoting (Holocaust survivor) Elie Weisel. I thought, 'Oh, I'm fine. This is a complex, rich, life-affirming person'." Still, Mr Shanley was nervous when Sister Margaret attended a performance as his guest in January, the first time the two had met in 48 years. He positioned himself, incognito, behind a newspaper in the theatre foyer, like a spy awaiting a secret rendezvous.

"This man got up, folded his newspaper, walked towards me and said, 'Sister James—oh my God, you don't look like I remember you'," says Sister Margaret. Inside the auditorium, staring at the mock-up of their old school (renamed St Nicholas) on stage, Mr Shanley was on the edge of his seat. "I had no idea what her reaction was going to be."

The guest was also unnerving for actress Heather Goldenhersh, who plays Sister James. "It was like having a rock star in the audience," she says.

"SISTER MARGARET RECALLS MR SHANLEY AS A 'LOVEABLE LITTLE KID'. BUT SHE ADDS: 'THANK GOD I DIDN'T TEACH HIM IN SECONDARY SCHOOL.'"

They needn't have worried. Sister Margaret was flattered by the stage depiction and thrilled to be a dramatic muse. Ms Goldenhersh has since visited her at school. Hearing Sister Margaret talk about her sense of vocation has been a refreshing antidote to the often self-absorbed world of acting, she says.

Sister Margaret's classroom at Notre Dame, a private all-girls Catholic school where she prefaces each lesson with a prayer, is a world away from the blinking brashness of New York's theatre district around Times Square.

Leading a discussion on altruism and charity, she never raises her voice in coaxing comments from the class of 16-year-olds. Walking the corridors between lessons takes some time as she stops to ask students how they're doing and greets others, eager to say hello, with a ready smile. "My approach to teaching is relational—people before content," says Sister Margaret. "But content's very important," she adds quickly. "She relates morals to real life, so it's personal and we get a higher level of understanding," says Rachel Cardero, 18. "She calls the kids, 'cupcake'," says director of advancement Robert Grote.

Sister Margaret is enjoying her new-found celebrity. On a balmy evening last month, while the curtain's up on Broadway, John Patrick Shanley is the guest speaker at the College of Mount Saint Vincent, home to her convent.

The shrill din of Manhattan is just a distant hum on this picturesque campus beside the Hudson River. Sister Margaret and her family, friends and colleagues take pride of place at the front of the hall and then cameras roll for the Today Show, America's leading breakfast television programme, capturing the local-boy-made-good. After his speech Mr Shanley is mobbed by fans.

Nevertheless, Sister Margaret says she's encountered disapproval from some quarters. Some say *Doubt* brings up an unseemly subject, publicly airing "dirty laundry". "I say, go see it," she counters. "It opened my eyes."

In the play, her devout character is chided for being too gullible by her headmistress, who counsels that innocence can be a luxury amid lurking evil. Sister James, for whom entertaining such dark suspicions about someone is anathema, is plunged into an existential crisis. Ultimately, the audience is left guessing about whether "he did it", but Sister James is the character people identify with, says Sister Margaret. "She's the voice of reality, trying to step back and make an analysis of what's going on, and it's really hurting her."

Source: Stephen Phillips, "Faith, Hope, and Doubt," in *Times Educational Supplement*, No. 4635, May 20, 2005, p. 6.

Grant Gallicho

In the following review, Gallicho calls Doubt *"remarkably balanced" and praises the play for its "lasting artistic value."*

Playwrights and screenwriters have had several years to mine the clergy sexual-abuse scandal, but it is only with John Patrick Shanley's Pulitzer Prize–winning play *Doubt* that someone has written something of lasting artistic value. *Doubt*, which recently opened on Broadway at the Walter Kerr Theater after an extended run at the Manhattan Theatre Club, is gripping. Its actors turn in riveting performances; and the play remains remarkably balanced, scrupulously avoiding caricature and moral posturing.

Shanley, who won an Oscar for his screenplay for *Moonstruck,* has cleverly wrapped the sexual-abuse crisis in the cloak of a whodunit, and set the story in 1964, at a Bronx parochial school run by the Sisters of Charity. Sr. Aloysius (Cherry Jones) is the tough-as-nails principal, whose suspicions about the character of Fr. Flynn (Brian F. O'Byrne) are confirmed when one of her young teachers, Sr. James (Heather Goldenhersh), reports that a student has been removed from her class by Flynn and returned with the smell of alcohol on his breath. Complicating the problem, the boy in question, Donald Muller, whom we never meet, is the only black student in the school.

Setting the play in the 1960s provides insights into the milieu in which clergy sexual abuse might occur—a time when deference to clerical authority was more prevalent than it is today. Shanley's choice of 1964, in the middle of the second Vatican Council—when understanding of the roles of clergy, women religious, and laity was shifting—also offers occasions for dramatic reversals and complexity. Flynn's gruff charm—straight out of Irish Catholic lore—and his easy, teasing way with boys, make clear how he might use his charisma to gain the confidence of potential victims. It is one of the play's shrewder ironies that Flynn is a proponent of the reforms of Vatican II. He regularly articulates liberal-Catholic principles—and seems to mean them. Part of the play's genius is in drawing Flynn in such sharp contrast to Sr. Aloysius, whose Catholicism is so preconciliar that she disapproves of students' singing "Frosty the Snowman" because it's "heretical" and "espouses a belief in magic." A lesser playwright would have freighted the Flynn character with all the negative and authoritarian characteristics associated with the preconciliar church, and presented Sr. Aloysius as a syrupy, saintly defender of the helpless.

Sr. Aloysius is anything but sweet. Anyone who attended Catholic schools staffed by women religious will recognize the sternly rigid yet secretly caring sister, channeled by Cherry Jones's masterly performance. Sr. Aloysius is a tough, self-assured woman who expects a toughness from her staff and fellow nuns in all matters, great and small. She admonishes Sr. James for allowing students to write with ball-point pens—"When they press down they write like monkeys"—and cautions her against being too trusting of priests, too anxious to please: "If you forget yourself and study others, you will not be fooled."

Armed with this steely resolve, Sr. Aloysius goes about the business of studying Fr. Flynn. After hearing from a fellow sister that the priest has been taking boys to the rectory for private talks about "how to be a man," she invites him to her office under the pretense of an administrative meeting, coaxing a reticent Sr. James to attend as a witness. To watch Aloysius and Flynn go through the motions of courtesy (while knowing what's boiling under the surface) is to experience an inspired moment of dramatic irony.

O'Byrne's physical performance in this scene is enormously effective. He strides into Aloysius's office and promptly takes her seat at the desk, making the power relationship perfectly clear. They make small talk. Aloysius offhandedly mentions an elderly sister who recently "fell on a piece of wood, and practically killed herself."

FLYNN: Her sight isn't good, is it?

ALOYSIUS: Her sight is fine. Nuns fall, you know.

FLYNN: No, I didn't know that.

ALOYSIUS: It's the habit. It catches us more often than not. What with our being in black and white, and so prone to falling, we are more like dominoes than anything else.

This back-and-forth, like so much of the play's dialogue, is intensified by tiny dramatic movements, even covert ones, because this exchange has a comédie bent. But they reveal something important about the characters: the hint of predatory menace in Flynn's pointed inquiry about the other nun's health (Is she fit for work at the school?), and Aloysius's protective nature—not naive, but smart enough to play to Flynn's latent misogyny by comparing nuns to falling dominoes. She has his number.

The conversation stalls once Aloysius asks Flynn why he took Donald Muller out of class. Flynn explains that he removed Donald to talk to him about having drunk the altar wine, but then recognizes the meeting is a set-up, and storms out. At a loss about how to pursue her investigation, Aloysius takes a risk by summoning Donald's mother (Adriane Lenox) to her office, but makes no headway with her either. After at first denying that Flynn has molested Donald, Mrs. Muller finally acknowledges that the abuse has taken place. But she refuses to take action against Flynn, or even remove Donald from the school, because, she explains, the priest is "the only one who pays him any attention."

Aloysius pleads with Mrs. Muller to expose Flynn, to remove Donald from his reach, pushing finally to one of the play's most powerful reversals, in which Muller offers an admonishment of her own: "You may think you're doing good, Sister, but the world's a hard place." Adriane Lenox's performance is compact, tragic, and utterly convincing. This wrenching scene is just one example of how *Doubt* turns every dramatic commonplace on its head. Even when you expect the parent of a victim to be the most scandalized, Shanley pulls the rug out from under you.

The tense last scene is a final confrontation between Flynn and Aloysius, where it's revealed that Aloysius herself has feet of clay. Flynn is at his manipulative best. Even at this point in the play, the audience can't be certain of his guilt or innocence. But Aloysius is. She threatens to expose him if he doesn't immediately request a transfer. He refuses, continuing his denials.

"IT'S GUTSY FOR SHANLEY TO WITHHOLD THE EMOTIONAL SATISFACTION OF CLOSURE IN A DRAMA FUELED BY SUCH A FRAUGHT SUBJECT."

By now, all pretense to courtesy is gone. As the conversation escalates, Aloysius makes no effort to hide her disdain for Flynn, but he will not yield. The actors never succumb to the temptation to overplay the intensity of the scene, yet they clearly convey what's at stake for Flynn and for Aloysius—his future as a cleric and her moral integrity. In the end, however, neither Flynn nor Aloysius walk away unscathed.

"In the pursuit of wrongdoing, one steps away from God," Aloysius tells Sr. James. This pillar of strength, a woman certain of herself, her convictions, her church, is broken by exposing what she's convinced is a horrific injustice. The price she pays is her certainty. "Oh, Sr. James," she sighs in the play's final sorrowful line, "I have such doubts."

The doubt in the title refers to multiple questions and betrayals. Like other Catholics confronted with clergy abuse, Sr. Aloysius comes to question and have doubts about herself. For in prosecuting the injustice she perceives, she's driven to betray her own moral code. Even in the rooting out of something as abominable as pedophilia, the play shows, other moral truths can be lost. That's the ambivalence so compellingly presented here.

Did Flynn do it? The play itself doesn't say. By not resolving the case, *Doubt* shows that its ambition extends beyond the whodunit genre. It's gutsy for Shanley to withhold the emotional satisfaction of closure in a drama fueled by such a fraught subject. And in doing so, *Doubt* reflects what the sexual-abuse crisis has been for so many Catholics: an occasion of profound grief for a church they, like Sr. Aloysius, believed in.

Source: Grant Gallicho, "The Cost of Justice," in *Commonweal*, Vol. 132, No. 8, April 22, 2005, pp. 21–22.

Robert Coe

In the following interview-essay, Coe provides background on Shanley's life and career, and

"JOHN PATRICK SHANLEY'S BRONX CHARACTERS DON'T SIDLE UP AND ASK—THEY DEMAND TO BE SEEN AND HEARD."

Shanley discusses his early plays and the experiences that inspired Doubt.

John Patrick Shanley's Bronx characters don't sidle up and ask—they demand to be seen and heard. Saying exactly what they feel, almost without appearing to think about it, they're posturing and naked at once, far-fetched, mercurial and profane, and they effortlessly own the stage. This fall theatre season in New York is offering a major revival of Shanley's electrifying first drama, *Danny and the Deep Blue Sea,* a 1984 two-hander "dedicated to everyone in the Bronx who punched me or kissed me, and to everyone whom I punched or kissed"—by a man inducted this past summer into the Bronx Walk of Fame. The play opened at Second Stage on Oct. 21. Five days later, New York audiences began catching up to Shanley's present work at the Public Theatre's Shiva Theatre, where the LAByrinth Theater Company is presenting the world-premiere production of one of the playwright's most radical stylistic experiments to date: *Sailor's Song,* a love story with dancing (to waltzes by Johann Strauss), set in an imagined seaside town, about a cynical man and a true believer battling over two beautiful women and the nature of love.

A second new play will open on Nov. 22 at Manhattan Theatre Club's New York City Center Stage I, and will play this spring at California's Pasadena Playhouse: *Doubt,* a drama set in the 1960s at a Bronx Catholic School—the story of a stern principal, Sister Aloysius (Cherry Jones), who grows suspicious of a priest who seems to be taking too much interest in a young male student. Night and day from the animal vitality of *Danny, Doubt* unfolds in a spirit of poetic restraint and deep seriousness, and it reads as Shanley's most powerful play in years.

This would seem an ideal moment to reconsider the career of an off-center playwright frequently viewed as an eccentric, vulgar provisioner for scenery-chewing actors, but who is in fact a deeply ambitious artist working through primal themes, in a language that people actually use and a voice as recognizable as David Mamet's (although less easily caricatured). An overview of his work reveals a more substantial, shapelier body than this reader had previously imagined, as well as an integrity and steadily deepening gravitas suited to a writer now nearing 54 and living comfortably in Brooklyn Heights, with a leafy school ground for a backyard, since 2000.

Formerly married, now divorced and co-parenting 12-year-olds Nick and Frank, and after two decades toiling with mixed success and failure in the killing fields of Hollywood, Shanley has settled into a solid maturity that, as he once told a journalist, leaves behind the "electric leaps" of youth in favor of "a more considered attempt to converse and discover connection."

It was slightly over 20 years ago that *Danny* burst onto the American theatre scene with two vivid characters, described by the author as "violent and battered, inarticulate and yearning to speak, dangerous and vulnerable," locked in mortal combat, longing and, eventually, a kind of love. From the beginning Shanley exhibited a seemingly effortless mastery of the rhythms of hostility and longing, along with a natural gift for instilling tremendous spiritual ambition in his characters—a willingness to leap, to let go, far more often than to hesitate and cling. Whether in doubt or rapture, Shanley's characters are unafraid of speaking in banalities or in wild poetic flight—or, when they *are* afraid of something, then the playwright confronts those fears head-on. (Courage and determination are subjects that Shanley has revisited throughout his career.)

Each of the Bronx plays that followed *Danny* would be about people wanting either IN or OUT—another way of saying that these plays are about dramatic change and a challenge to imposed definitions and boundaries, especially the ones between the Bronx/Manhattan and victimhood/liberation. Shanley's characters seek transcendence, connection and new identities, via more than words alone: They touch, sweat, spit and spray every available bodily fluid in that alternately claustrophobic and explosive atmosphere that has characterized most of the canonical mainstream of 20th-century American drama.

Shanley worked outside this atmosphere as well. *Welcome to the Moon . . . and Other Plays,* which ran in the fall of 1982 at New York's

Ensemble Studio Theatre, introduced a strain of surrealistic experimentation that established Shanley's parallel career as a radical stage formalist, not unlike that of another hard-living, essentially naturalistic Irish-American writer, Eugene O'Neill.

Shanley remained in his imagined Bronx and delivered further on his promise with *Savage in Limbo* (1985), "dedicated to all those good assassins who contributed to the death of my former self." Working with multiple characters this time, Shanley stood closest to his eponymous heroine, the pained and caustic Denise Savage: "We're on the cliff. We were born here. Well, do you wanna die on the cliff?" *Savage* was in part about the animals lurking inside human beings, just as *Danny* was, but with a caveat offered by Denise's friend in boyfriend trouble, Linda Rotunda: "It ain't the new clothes that make the man. It's what he does with his dirty things." The project of self-discovery becomes one of finding determination within the grope and flailing of tongues. As the aptly named bartender Murk opines: "The problem with people is they think they're alone. They think what they say don't do nothing. So they say every stupid thing that goes through their gourd, and they do [sh——t] they don't even know why. Which leads to what? The world looks like homemade refried [sh——t]."

Shanley could not keep working forever in this tortured Italian-American ghetto. *Women of Manhattan* (1986)—this time the inevitable and telling dedication was "to women, women, women . . . [written 23 more times] and a guy named Larry Sigman [a dying friend, now deceased]"—headed down to a lower borough, away from working-class, ethnic concerns, to address the issue and substance of self-esteem, a screaming lack in all Shanley's earlier characters. *Women of Manhattan* moved through the animal appetites to search for grown-up identities. I have probably undervalued the verbal intelligence and wit on display in these early writings, but this play, while beautifully written and complete, feels a little weightless.

Shanley wasn't through with the Bronx: His 1985 fantasia, *the dreamer examines his pillow,* dedicated, simply enough, "to my family," introduced family members for the first time—a daughter, Donna, who is unable to live with her lover, Tommy, or without him (especially after she discovers he's sleeping with her 16-year-old sister). Like *Women of Manhattan, the dreamer* pursues questions of identity, as opposed to merely coping or desperately surviving: "You are somebody," Donna tells Tommy. "Tell me who. . . . You know what it is down there inside the last Chinese box?" Dealing with their pie-in-the-sky romantic dreams, she realizes they will always find themselves "back down in this [sh——t]hole room or some other [sh——t]hole room, and I can't feature that no more." *The dreamer* is a dark attempt to chart the intellectual/emotional terrain of Shanley's imagination, leading to an ambiguous recognition that in sex we can discover identity, and escape it.

Shanley's best work simultaneously imagines and exposes the failure of "the key that lets me outta my life," as Donna puts it. Self-knowledge is far more difficult to obtain than simply escaping the past or some shithole room. In the end, *the dreamer* reaches for a deeper question: Why live at all? A didactic element entered Shanley's work for the first time: "You gotta make the big mistakes," says Donna's dad. "Remember that. It makes it easier to bear. But remember, too, that Sex does resurrect. Flyin in the face of the truly great mistakes, there is that consolation."

Shanley's constant implicit theme—the marriage of two people—became comically overt in his popular *Italian American Reconciliation* (1988), the first of his plays the author directed, with a cast including John Turturro (the original Danny), John Pankow, Laura San Giacomo and Shanley's then wife, Jayne Haynes, at Manhattan Theatre Club. *Reconciliation* had a simple, outrageous plot involving an inappropriate seduction (the commedia aspect of which was inescapable), a hilarious momentum, and an almost maudlin denouement reached when Aldo (Turturro) announces: "And this is the lesson I have to teach: The greatest, the only success, is to be able to love."

Nineteen-eighty-two to 1988 were years of extraordinary creativity for the former juvenile delinquent and NYU grad. By the time of *The Big Funk* (1990), he was arguing for the interconnectedness of everything. But an undercurrent had entered his work that was not so empathic. Shanley prefaced the published version: "And so I ask the question: Why is theatre so ineffectual, un-new, not exciting, fussy, not connected to the thrilling recognition possible in dreams? It's a question of spirit. My ungainly spirit thrashes around inside me, making me feel lumpy and sick."

The Big Funk was formally adventurous, employing nudity and direct address of the audience, while also reminding us of the Greeks by essentially being about a dinner party—a Symposium. But it also removed all recognizable contexts of time and place—as if the playwright wanted to address the interconnectedness of everything at the expense of its specificity. From this turning point, Shanley wheeled back to a theatrical beginning he never actually had and wrote a nakedly autobiographical family play: *Beggars in the House of Plenty* (1991), about how some siblings make it and others don't. *Beggars* is arguably his most successful work employing surrealistic element, while also breaking from his usual intense dramatic focus to explore a more studied irony. Out of the cauldron into what fire? (The old Shanley did periodically surface, as his stand-in "Johnny" intoned: "I look like the Bronx inside. I could vomit up a burning car.")

Inevitably, Shanley stepped back from his investigation of an increasingly distant past: *Four Dogs and a Bone* (1993) was his first play not driven by insatiable personal demons. Instead, it used bitter, excoriating comedy to limn a social world in which two actresses battle to have their parts beefed up during an indie film production. By the end of the play it's the screenwriter who grows some balls, or is corrupted (it's hard to tell which, but he does take over the show). Shanley knew something about Hollywood wish-fulfillment: Back in the early '80s, watching funds from a large NEA grant dwindling, he had decided that instead of returning to painting apartments, moving furniture or tending bar, he would write a screenplay. *Five Corners* (1987) ended up being produced by Beatle George Harrison, and was followed shortly by Shanley's signature achievement, *Moonstruck,* the Norman Jewison film and Cher vehicle that won Shanley a well-deserved Oscar for best screenplay.

Moonstruck brought together all his insights into Italian-American culture with a brilliantly funny, wise and balanced screenplay that holds up, to this day, as a masterful comedic melodrama. This was followed by *The January Man* (1989), a botched thriller; *Joe Versus the Volcano* (1990), which Shanley also directed, starring Tom Hanks and Meg Ryan, in an odd turn that died at the box office; *Alive* (1993), about a plane crash and cannibalism in the Andes; and, *Congo* (1995) a jungle-based techno-thriller about mutant apes—none of which came close to matching his early success.

Shanley returned to the stage with new aspirations: *Psychopathia Sexualis* (1996) was a clever, entertaining boulevard comedy about sexual fetishism and a loony shrink. *Cellini* (1998), his first-ever stage adaptation, drew on the notorious Renaissance autobiography; *Missing/Kissing* (1996) proved a not-particularly-engaging romantic study; *Where's My Money?* (2001), his first experience with the LAByrinth Theater Company, was a wholly satisfying dark comedic drama about a kinky affair, a cynical marriage and the loss of romantic sentiment—for my money, Shanley's best play since the '80s, although more West Side comedy of manners than raw exposé.

Then came 9/11, which inspired Shanley's topical *Dirty Story* (2003), featuring characters intended to represent the U.S., Israel and Palestine—a comedic parable so cartoonish that some critics had a hard time taking it seriously, even while the *New York Times* called it "appallingly entertaining." [Denver Center Theatre Company's production runs through Nov. 13.] Shanley was staying on a Mideast beat: *Live from Baghdad,* a 2002 film written for HBO, about CNN at the start of the Gulf War, earned an Emmy nomination for him and other co-screenwriters. (My favorite line: "If we can keep talking, then maybe we won't kill each other.") Shanley also recently completed a new script for *Moonstruck* director Norman Jewison, *The Waltz of the Tulips.* Apparently the moonstruck writer is thinking in three-four time these days.

Which brings us up to *Doubt* and *Sailor's Song*—two new plays, each a major return to form, both resounding evidence of a new confidence, maturity and economy from an artist who has always maintained that "writing is acting is directing is living your life."

We meet at his request at the SoHo Grand Hotel for tea and cookies. Shanley is grayer than the last time I saw him, back in the early '90s, strolling in a black leather jacket down Lafayette Street in Manhattan with the actress Julia Roberts. His explosive, raucous laugh and the classic Irish twinkle in his eye haven't changed; he seems eminently sane, focused, amiable and self-examined. He tells me that today is his son Frankie's birthday, and that after our interview he will be picking him up to celebrate. Both sons were adopted at birth, four-and-a-half months apart, so for the next seven-and-one-half months, Shanley laughs, "both my sons are 12." Speaking with the rhythms of his native Bronx, he is still asking ambitious questions and giving big answers, but with a new subtlety, new tools and a steady, jovial demeanor.

[*ROBERT COE*]: *When was the last time you actually saw* Danny and the Deep Blue Sea?

[JOHN PATRICK SHANLEY]: It's been a few years. Some of my plays I've never seen done by anybody since the original productions. *Danny* I've seen done maybe three times in amateur productions that somebody got me to go to. Actually, the last time I saw it was in Paris, in French.

Did you think you were watching No Exit?

[*Laughs*] No! Because *Danny* has a catharsis. Catharses build up a lot of energy, and when the energy is metabolized, it is released, and the audience is released. That can be really important! You have to legitimately achieve it. It's one of the big reasons that I would go to the theatre—in the hopes of experiencing that.

Who will be playing Danny and Roberta this year?

I don't know. Second Stage suggested Leigh Silverman for director—she had done well at the Public [*with Lisa Kron's acclaimed solo* 2.5 Minute Ride], and I met with her and thought she was smart and driven and completely unlike me. I can't explain that any more than to say she's made of different stuff. So I said, "All right, let's see what you'll do. You're free. I want the Leigh Silverman production."

You really don't want to haunt the rehearsal hall?

Nah. I'm not much for going back. You can either have a career or chase it, and I don't particularly want to chase my own shadow back through time. With the number of workshops of my plays in New York alone, it could have been my career, just going to my own shows—and how sad would that have been!

"Is Shanley here again?"

[*Raucous laughter*] That's right. "Poor guy."

So let's jump forward 20-plus years to your new play Sailor's Song. *The publicity makes it sound as if you were inspired by the two Genes: Kelly and O'Neill.*

Sailor's Song is about—just to pull a figure out of the air—35 percent dance. But it's not performed by dancers, it's very much a play. A very, very romantic play—almost a tragic-romance. I'll be very involved in this one. *Sailor's Song* and *Doubt* are only four days apart in rehearsal schedule, so I couldn't direct either one of them. Doug Hughes is directing *Doubt,* and he's great; the other show's got a much greener director, Chris McGarry, who's been an actor mostly, and who I did *Dirty Story* with. He's very intelligent and I wanted to give him a shot. The music is extant—it's waltzes, used in a very unusual way. It's almost all three-four time—"Tales of Vienna Woods," "Blue Danube," all that stuff. Johann Strauss mostly, right down the line! And it works! I did a workshop of it last fall to make sure, and it's really fun to listen to that music. All the music that's ever been written is still around, but it's amazing how pop music has pushed out everything else, for the most part, except for in formal dance. And it doesn't have to be so.

You've written so much about the nature of love and romance. I sense in Sailor's Song *a new wisdom and maturity—almost a mellowness that does not suggest complacency, just a longer overview and a deeper perspective.*

Yes. I'm savoring life now, whereas I used to just wolf it down. This play is all about savoring the moonlit moment of romantic choice—that place on the dance floor of the heart when two people could kiss but they haven't yet. You are a dancer and the music is playing like a blue river around you. Everything is on the move and yet, paradoxically, time has ceased its forward motion. And this liquid pulsing, photograph of possibilities is placed side by side in this play with mortality, with the certainty of death, with the brevity of youth, and with the importance of *now.* So *Sailor's Song* is about the almost unbearable beauty of choosing to love in the face of death. Love is the most essential act of courage, isn't it? Will you choose to love before you are swept away by oblivion? I hope so.

Now tell me about Doubt.

I went to a Catholic Church school in the Bronx and was educated by the Sisters of Charity in the '60s. That's a world that's gone now, but it was a very defined place that I was in for eight years. I realized later on when the Church scandals were breaking that the way a lot of these priests were getting busted had to be by nuns. Because nuns were the ones who were noticing the children with aberrant behavior, distressed children, falling grades, and in some cases they had to be the ones who discovered what was happening. But the chain of command in the Catholic Church was such that they had to report it not to the police but to their superior within the Church, who then covered up for the guy. This had to create very powerful frustrations and moral dilemmas for these women. It was very shortly after that that they started to leave the Church in droves.

I was not aware of that. Has this been noted elsewhere?

As far as I can make out, never. So showing this experience was one of the motivations behind *Doubt.* Another was that I saw a dark side to the Second Vatican Council's message of "go out into the community." When I was a kid, priests were not going to take boys out of church [to outside activities]. They were priests, they were in the rectory. And so I think this explosive combination of celibacy and "go out and make believe you're just one of the other folks" had a lot to do with the problems that followed.

But over and above that, the more interesting thing to me doesn't have anything to do with the scandals, and that is the cathartic, philosophical power of embracing doubt—of embracing not knowing, embracing that you may never know the truth or falsity of a story, of a scenario, and that you cannot morally stand in judgment from any place that is utterly firm in relation to another person's life. And yet actions must be taken if you feel the imperative, if you feel that you have the clarity of thought and know what should be done. And that powerful, explosive dilemma for an individual is really fraught for me. Here are these women who stumble on what may be something—and the choice is to go through the normal chain of command, which will lead to the complete exoneration and literally the *safety* of an abusive priest.

You know a member of my own family was molested by [Father John] Geoghan, the guy who was strangled in prison. And my family members went to Cardinal O'Connor, after they'd gone to everybody locally and gotten no satisfaction, and Cardinal O'Connor took them by the hands and said, "I am so sorry this happened. I will take care of it." And then he *promoted* him. Unbelievable. So they left the Church, but after 10 years they went back, and that Sunday the Monsignor got up and gave a sermon saying that these children who were abused, it was the parents' fault. That's when they left the Church again.

So this material is very close to home.

It is, but I think when you see the play you'll see that my relationship to it is very complicated. There's an even weirder level: Is what some of these guys do totally bad? That I also have doubts about. When I was growing up, at certain points I was championed by homosexual teachers who were the only people watching out for me. And why were they doing it? They were really into boys. They were really into my problems. Did they do anything *to* me? No. Did they want to? I don't know. Did they make a pass? No. Was that in the air? Somewhere yes, it was in the air. Did I take advantage of the good things they were offering me? Yes, because I needed to, because I was isolated and there was no one else. Did that make them bad people? Not to me. Not to me at all.

It's only acting out that compromises a child.

That is correct. And, even then, if it's like some guy putting his hand on my leg and me saying, "Get your hand off my leg," and that's it—frankly I wouldn't have been traumatized. But, of course, what happens is that a lot of kids who are more confused than that about their sexuality, which is perfectly natural at that age—and also out of tremendous need—can become *very* confused. So there are a lot of levels to it. I'm not interested in issue plays per se, although I'm more interested in them now than I used to be. What I'm *not* interested in is writing polemics on one side of an issue or another. Doubt does not have to dismantle passion. It can be a passionate exercise.

When you look back, do you see any arc or evolution in your career?

One of the ongoing concerns that I have is how to be intimate with another human being. Another is how to invite everybody to the party. We have to be able to find a way to communicate so that we can talk about anything. That's the one thing we should be able to do—to talk about *anything.*

We don't necessarily have to be able to do everything.

That is correct. Right now, the Democrats and the Republicans, for instance, are never able to cede anything to the other side. Everything has to be crossfire! Which can be a fun part of a play, but that's a play that never goes to catharsis. It ends up forever stuck in some kind of French existential hell! And that's not what's interesting to me. I want to find the dynamic door that leads out of the dilemma and on into the future.

I grew up in a violent place where people did not communicate well, but where there were big feelings and big longings, and I remember that some of the most interesting people were also the most doomed, because they had no tools to save themselves. In some weird way, the Palestinian character in *Dirty Story* is a descendent of those people: "If you won't solve my problem, if no one will listen to me, then I'm going to blow you and me up." I certainly knew that guy, I certainly grew up with that guy—and I've got a little bit of that guy in me. I always said that if things went well I would spend the first half of my life writing about my problems, and the second half I would write about other people's problems, and that's sort of what happened—I'm able now to start turning *out.* Maybe that's why I was able to write *Doubt,* and why I was able to write *Dirty Story.* Of course they're personal plays, but they are about larger social concerns.

Your own ethnic background provides a great example of communicating across boundaries and bridging differences.

Yes. I'm very Irish, from an Irish-Italian neighborhood in the Bronx. I grew up in a household where talk was important, music was important, clothing was not important, food was not important. Then I went over to my Italian friends' houses, where the guys were combing their hair with "Hidden Magic" which they'd stolen from their mothers and spending an hour getting dressed, and talking openly about sexuality, which was *bad* in my household! It was just a much more sensual, ebullient world, I went to their houses to soak up the sheer pleasure of it, the stimulation—and I was like, "I want what they got, *plus* what I got!"

My father came from Ireland when he was 24, had a brogue and was raised on a farm, basically in the 19th century. And my mother was first-generation—her parents were from Ireland as well. And when I went back to the farm where my father was born—he died two years ago at 96—the people on that farm spoke in poetry, and we really got along. And I thought, "This is much closer to my true family than the particular culture I grew up in!"

Most of your plays are language-driven, and yet we know movies generally aren't—the engine of a film is imagery. How do you think writing screenplays has affected your playwriting?

Actually, the influence is very much the other way around. Playwriting has continued to make my screenwriting possible. Without that constant feedback from the audience, writing can become ungrounded. Audiences show up too late in cinema; you don't get a chance to fix it after they get there. So you better have a very strong sense of what you've got, of what the music is between you and the audience. The theatre gives so much back in that way. I feel genetically born to be a playwright. When I started writing in the dialogue form, I had a complete moment of recognition, like, "Oh! This is what I do!" I'd written in many other forms before that—I started writing when I was 11 and I was a poet, exclusively, for several years. But it wasn't until I was 23, 24, that I tried the dialogue form, and it was instantaneous. I wrote a full-length play the first time I ever wrote in dialogue, and it was produced a few weeks later.

When you reflect back on your personal journey, are you ever amazed that here you are, this troublemaker from the Bronx, who ended up playwright with something to say that lots of people want to hear?

Yes. My life is both inevitable and surprising to me. But I've never had the slightest sense of future. I did not envision a fate. So I don't know why I should have any feeling of surprise.

Source: Robert Coe, "The Evolution of John Patrick Shanley," in *American Theatre*, November 2004, pp. 22–26, 97–99.

SOURCES

Brustein, Robert, "Prosecution Plays," in the *New Republic*, May 23, 2005, p. 27.

Isherwood, Charles, "Stories That Tell vs. Storytelling," in the *New York Times*, May 6, 2005, Section E, p. 1.

Zoglin, Richard, "4 Must-See Shows On (and Off) Broadway," in *Time*, April 25, 2005, p. 56.

FURTHER READING

Berry, Jason, *Lead Us Not into Temptation: Catholic Priests and the Sexual Abuse of Children*, University of Illinois Press, 2000.

This book, originally published when the abuse story was first surfacing in 1992, is considered a classic in the study of what went wrong with the priesthood in the last half of the twentieth century.

Calhoun, Ada, "Bryony Lavery and John Patrick Shanley Dish about Religion," in *New York Magazine*, September 13, 2004, p. 61.

In a joint interview, Shanley and the playwright Bryony Lavery (*Last Easter*) consider the place that religion has in their works.

Foster, David Ruel, ed., *The Two Wings of Catholic Thought: Essays on "Fides et Ratio,"* Catholic University of America Press, 2003.

In 1998, Pope John Paul II issued an encyclical, *Fides et Ratio*, proclaiming that reason and faith do not have to be considered separately but can be found together in Catholicism. The essays in this book examine the implications of that doctrine, which appears as one of the central conundrums of *Doubt*.

Wilson, Anna Victoria, and William E. Segall, *Oh, Do I Remember!: Experiences of Teachers during the Desegregation of Austin's Schools, 1964–1971*, State University of New York Press, 2001.

The authors repeat testimony of teachers and students who suffered through the awkward phases of including people of color into traditionally white school systems, giving a sense of the division that race can create in an academic setting.

Witchel, Alex, "The Confessions of John Patrick Shanley," in the *New York Times Magazine*, November 7, 2004, pp. 31–35.

This article was written at a time when three of Shanley's plays, including *Doubt*, were about to open in New York City.

Eleemosynary

LEE BLESSING

1985

Lee Blessing often focuses on family dynamics in his plays. *Eleemosynary*, one of his most acclaimed works, is no exception. The play was first performed in Minneapolis, Minnesota, in 1985 and published by the Dramatists Play Service in 1987; it forms part of the collection *Four Plays*, published by Heinemann in 1991. *Eleemosynary* won the prestigious Los Angeles Drama Critics Circle Award in 1997 for its penetrating study of the interactions among three members of the Wesbrook family. In his examination of their relationships with one another, Blessing illustrates the tensions that can stress a family to its breaking point.

Eleemosynary focuses on the lives of three Wesbrook women: seventy-five-year-old Dorothea; her middle-aged daughter, Artie; and Artie's sixteen-year-old daughter, Echo. Dorothea, an admitted New Age eccentric, has complicated the lives of the two other Wesbrook women by imposing her thwarted dreams on them, which has alienated Artie not only from Dorothea but from Echo as well. As the play begins, Echo is caring for Dorothea, who has just had a stroke. During the course of the play, Echo tries to bring the three women together. Blessing presents fragmented vignettes of the lives of the three women as they struggle to define themselves both as individuals and as part of a family unit. In this poignant and mature study of familial relationships, Blessing highlights the human need for connection and forgiveness.

AUTHOR BIOGRAPHY

Lee Blessing was born in Minneapolis, Minnesota, on October 4, 1949. He grew up in a conventional midwestern family, where, ironically, there was little attention paid to the arts. Despite his parents' lack of interest in drama, they were very supportive of Blessing's chosen career and always attended his plays. Blessing wrote his first play while he was still in high school, which was prompted by his desire to avoid a thirty-page writing assignment on a topic that held little interest for him. After graduation, he attended the University of Minnesota for two years and then transferred to Reed College in Portland, Oregon. He graduated with a bachelor's degree in English, with an emphasis on poetry. Blessing then headed back to the Midwest to attend the University of Iowa from 1974 to 1979. He obtained a master of fine arts in English in his first years; then, while working on his MFA in speech and theater, he taught playwriting. He went on to teach playwriting at the Playwrights' Center in Minneapolis from 1986 to 1988. In 1986, Blessing married Jeanne Blake and became stepfather to her two children.

Lee Blessing Photo by A. Vincent Scarano. Courtesy of Lee Blessing

Blessing's style and subject matter are often eclectic, as he focuses on public and private politics and the intricacies of human relationships. One of his most noted plays, *A Walk in the Woods* (1988), which deals with the differences between American idealism and Russian common sense, received Tony Award, Olivier Award, and Pulitzer Prize nominations. *A Walk in the Woods* also ran on Broadway, in Moscow, and in London, starring the late British actor Sir Alec Guinness, and was aired on the Public Broadcasting System's *American Playhouse*. Another of Blessing's celebrated plays, *Eleemosynary* (1987), which explores the nature of familial relationships, earned Blessing a 1997 Los Angeles Drama Critics Circle Award for Best Writing and garnered three others for production, direction, and lead performance. The play appears in a collection titled *Four Plays* (1991), along with *Independence* (1985), *Nice People Dancing to Good Country Music* (1990), and *Riches* (1991).

Blessing has written other works for stage, film, and television and has earned numerous awards and much acclaim. He has received the American Theatre Critics Award, the Great American Play Award, and the George and Elisabeth Marton Award, among others. Three of his plays have also been cited in *Time* magazine's list of the year's ten best. Blessing has received grants from the National Endowment for the Arts and the Guggenheim, Bush, McKnight, and Jerome foundations. His plays have been performed at the Eugene O'Neill National Playwrights Conference. His script *Cooperstown* was made into a film that aired on Turner Network Television and, in 1993, won Blessing the Humanitas Prize and three nominations for Cable Ace Awards. Blessing's work has been produced at the Yale Repertory Theatre, the Guthrie Theater, Arena Stage, Steppenwolf Theatre Company, Old Globe, and the Alliance Theatre Company. He moved to Manhattan in 2001 and later became head of the graduate playwriting program at Mason Gross School of the Arts at Rutgers University.

PLOT SUMMARY

Scenes 1 and 2

In the first scene of *Eleemosynary*, sixteen-year-old Echo spells the word "eleemosynary," explaining that it is her favorite word and that she once won a spelling bee by spelling it correctly. She defines it as "of or pertaining to alms; charitable." She introduces her seventy-five-year-old grandmother, Dorothea, to the audience and explains that Dorothea has suffered a stroke. Echo says that her grandmother cannot speak, but she claims that she can hear the elderly woman, as can the audience.

The first of several flashbacks begins, as Artie, Echo's mother, appears, wearing a pair of homemade wings and looking miserable. Echo explains that her grandmother believed that one could fly with the proper wings and once filmed her mother's failed attempt to do so. Dorothea says that she would like to be flying herself. During the flashback, Echo continues to speak to the audience, explaining her love of words.

As the scene shifts, Dorothea and Artie argue about the ability to fly. Echo is studying for the spelling bee, prompted by her mother, who drills her over the phone. The scene moves back to the flight film, as Echo explains that the Wesbrook women have a desire to be "extraordinary." She discusses her own outstanding scholarly aptitude, which was encouraged by her grandmother, who imparted to her a love of words. A flashback shows, however, that after she had won the spelling bee, she panicked and wondered, "What'll I do next year?" The film ends with Dorothea, embarrassed, admitting that her daughter has failed to fly, which prompts Artie's insistence that her mother is "nuts." Echo closes the scene by saying that she feels both her mother and her grandmother within her.

In scene 2, Artie admits that she has trouble touching people, including her daughter, which worries her. She notes that Dorothea, who raised Echo, was a better mother. In flashbacks, Dorothea teaches Echo the letters of the alphabet. Artie says that she never forgets anything, suggesting that there are some things she would like to forget. As Artie recalls her life, Dorothea keeps interrupting. Artie notes the irony in the fact that she became pregnant when she was eighteen: while she learned all kinds of other information, no one ever taught her about sex.

Artie and her mother argued about her future, Artie asserting that she was going to be a mother and Dorothy insisting that she get an abortion so that she could go to college and be more than "just something a child needs." Artie finally agreed to the abortion and then ran away from home. Eventually, though, Dorothea tracked her down. On the trip back home, Artie escaped and ran again, "very far away," and "stayed hidden."

Scenes 3, 4, and 5

Back in present time, Echo gives her grandmother physical therapy as she imagines what her grandmother is thinking. Dorothea recalls her childhood and her father's rejection of her, which made her feel worthless. Artie feels worthless as well. Dorothea notes her own arranged marriage and her husband's refusal to allow her to go to college, which followed her father's denial of her desire to gain an education. One day, she discovered that becoming an eccentric would allow her the freedom to do what she wanted, which, she claims, saved her life.

In scene 4, Artie visits Echo and Dorothea, curious about what the two do together. Echo notes in an aside to the audience that her mother left her when she was young. In a flashback, Dorothea says to Echo, "We all need forgiveness." Artie notes that she was on the run constantly, trying to elude her mother's reach. One day, when Artie called Dorothea and told her that she was married and pregnant, Dorothea was adamant about coming to help her. A month after Echo was born, Artie's husband died in a car accident, and Dorothea informed her daughter that the two of them, mother and grandmother, would raise Echo together.

In scene 5, Echo puts on the wings and notes that when she was a year old, the three of them moved back east to Dorothea's house. Soon after, Artie announced that she had a job offer in Europe that could be permanent if she wanted it. She wanted Dorothea to keep Echo "for good." Echo notes that, as she was growing up, she and her grandmother did not talk much about Artie.

Artie tells of an incident that took place one night when she was a child. Her mother awoke her and cut off a lock of her hair, telling Artie that she would keep it in a safe place. Artie, who, her mother claims, had "a terrible desire to want to know everything," conducted a desperate search to find it. When Dorothea came home, she discovered Artie in the middle of a scattered house and gave her the lock of hair that had been hidden in the light switch.

When Echo was seven years old, Artie came back home but told her mother that she did not want Echo back. Eventually, Artie began to call Dorothea and Echo but did not see them again for another six years, except once by accident. They bumped into each other in a bookstore, and as soon as Artie saw Echo, she ran out. Artie says to the audience, "I think a woman has a right to be irrational about her children." At night, when she thinks about her abortion, she imagines herself taking care of the child that she lost and determines that if Echo could envision this as well, she would not think that Artie is a bad mother.

Scenes 6 and 7

Soon after the incident in the bookstore, Artie suggested that Echo participate in spelling bees, "her way to apologize" for her ill treatment of her daughter. Artie spent a lot of time helping Echo practice. Echo insisted that Artie come to the spelling bee and greet Dorothea there. During the spelling bee, Echo became fiercely competitive, desperate to gain her mother and grandmother's approval. After Echo won the bee, Artie quickly greeted Dorothea and then left as Echo pleaded for her to stay.

At the start of scene 7, the action returns to the beginning of the play, when Echo notes that she won the spelling bee with the word "eleemosynary." She explains that although the word means "charitable," she "used it as a weapon" against her opponents. She admits that she is just like her mother and grandmother, no "less cruel." She says that after Dorothea had had a stroke, Artie came home. The action then jumps to the future as Echo notes that she and her mother were both asleep when Dorothea died. The next morning, they had their first fight, when Artie began to burn all evidence of Dorothea's eccentricity. Artie then suggests that Echo live with her Uncle Bill and his family, claiming that she would be "bad" for her daughter. After Echo asks why her mother keeps leaving her, Artie finally admits that she was angry that Echo seemed to prefer Dorothea over her. When Echo asks whether Artie loved her and loves her now, she replies, "Yes and no."

Within a few weeks, Echo ran away from Uncle Bill's, maintaining that she would persuade her mother to love her more of the time. She recognizes that her mother thinks that she has failed Echo, but she refuses to believe it. Echo explains that she will tend to her mother like a garden because she "need[s] work."

Dorothea admits that it is fascinating being dead and that she is beginning a project on eternal life. Artie notes that Echo persuaded her to promise that she would never leave her. As the two view Dorothea's movie of Artie's attempt to fly, Echo says that she loves watching the two of them together. The audience hears Dorothea's voice one more time, claiming that she will prove that humans can fly. The play closes with Echo's declaration that all of the Wesbrook women are in their own way, "completely . . . eleemosynary."

CHARACTERS

Artie Wesbrook

Artie, Dorothea's daughter and Echo's mother, has always had a troubled relationship with both women. She was unable to find a sense of independence from her often overbearing mother and, as a result, has withdrawn into herself. In an effort to establish her own identity, she focused her studies on hard science rather than on her mother's New Age philosophy, but she was not strong enough to hold her own ground. She admits she has trouble touching others, especially Echo. This upsets her, yet she cannot bring herself to establish true communication with her daughter.

Artie remembers everything, which, she complains, makes her mind like a memorial "with all the names of the dead etched in. No way to erase." Her inability to forget and forgive her mother caused her to move away from Dorothea and give Echo to her, who, she insisted, would be a better mother. But Artie could not stay away. She returned but was able to establish only a tentative relationship with Echo. As soon as her daughter tried to get too close, Artie withdrew into herself. The first time Artie accidentally ran into Echo, at a bookstore, Artie fled the scene without speaking to her daughter. Later, when she began to call Echo, she refused to talk about anything personal, using the spelling drills to maintain contact, but only on a limited basis. By the end of the play, she still is conflicted about her relationship with Echo, but she listens when her daughter declares that she will take care of her mother, tending her like a garden.

Dorothea Wesbrook

Dorothea is a self-proclaimed eccentric who has inadvertently made life difficult for her daughter and granddaughter. Her eccentricity became an escape from the oppressive life she led growing up in America during the 1940s and 1950s. Initially, she was not strong enough to refuse the conventional roles of wife and mother, but eventually she was able to find a way to express her individuality by embracing eccentricity.

She believed that all human beings have the ability to find a real connection with the universe if they are persistent and brave enough to try. She had complete faith in her daughter and granddaughter's abilities and encouraged their success. While Dorothea was able to forge a strong relationship with Echo, Dorothea's eccentricity and need to control alienated Artie to the point where she abandoned her own daughter.

Dorothea forced her beliefs on both Echo and Artie. She coerced Artie into dangerous activities, such as flying, to prove her theories on the connection between humans and nature. She also imposed her vision of a woman's potential on Artie when she insisted that her daughter have an abortion, explaining that Artie would be nothing more than a mother if she were to keep the baby. When Echo was born, she determined that "Barbara" was too conventional a name for her grandchild and so named the baby herself. Echo later suggests that, when she was young, she was teased because of her name.

Along with this overwhelming desire for control and insistence that her views should take precedence, Dorothea has a generous and charitable side. Believing that all of the women in her family are "extraordinary," she spent hours with both Artie and Echo when they were children, to ensure that they could have the best education possible and so be able to fight against gender-based oppression. When Echo hangs up on Artie, informing her grandmother that "a dead person" was on the phone, Dorothea stresses that "we all need forgiveness."

Echo Wesbrook

Echo, Artie's daughter and Dorothea's granddaughter, determines that all of her troubles started in 1958, when Dorothea forced her fifteen-year-old daughter to try to fly with homemade wings. She understands that her grandmother's eccentricity, coupled with her need for control, drove her mother away from home. Her generous soul will not let her condemn her grandmother, though. Her goal throughout the play is to reunite the three.

She did not always want reconciliation with her mother, however. After she came to understand that Artie had abandoned her and saw her run away at the bookstore, Echo determined that her mother was dead to her. Artie's rejection of her, coupled with her grandmother's encouragement of her education, inspired Echo to focus on the study of words, for which she developed a great love, an ironic emotion, considering the lack of communication she experienced with her mother. Still, suppressed anger toward her mother emerged in her almost monomaniacal devotion to words, to the point where she became a vicious competitor at the spelling bee. After her joyful response to her opponent's defeat and subsequent humiliation, Echo realized that she was not "any less cruel" than her mother and grandmother had been.

Ultimately, it is Echo who best becomes a reflection of the definition of "eleemosynary." She has continually tried to reconcile her mother and grandmother, insisting, for example, that the two attend the spelling bee and embrace when she won. After Dorothea has a stroke, Echo cares for her, imagining what she is thinking and moving her legs and arms to encourage circulation. When Dorothea dies, she determines that she will strengthen her relationship with her mother even though her mother gives her little encouragement.

THEMES

Loss

Each of the characters feels a sense of loss at different points in her life. Dorothea and Artie suffer from a loss of independence. Dorothea was never allowed to make choices about her future, growing up in America during the 1940s and 1950s. Her father controlled her life when she lived under his roof, refusing to let her go to college and arranging a marriage for her. When she married, she became just "a wife," since her husband limited her to that role. The only way in which she could gain a measure of independence was through her adoption of eccentricity, which, she claims, saved her life.

Ironically, this woman, who suffered so much as a result of her loss of independence, caused her daughter to experience a similar loss. Dorothea felt compelled to provide for her child the opportunities that had not been available to her. Unfortunately, that necessitated a loss of independence for Artie, since she was not allowed to make her own choices. Dorothea forced her daughter to perform tasks that would prove that she was an exceptional and freethinking woman. One, however, put her in physical danger, when she tried to fly with homemade wings. Another caused emotional turmoil when Dorothea persuaded Artie to get an abortion. The only way Artie could establish some type of independent identity was to get as far away from her mother as possible, which caused a devastating sense of loss for her daughter, Echo.

Abandonment

Artie also experienced a loss of control over her own daughter, which led to her abandonment of her. After Artie's husband had died in an accident,

TOPICS FOR FURTHER STUDY

- Another of Blessing's plays that focuses on family relationships is *Independence*. Read this play and compare in an essay its treatment of family dynamics to that of *Eleemosynary*.
- Imagine a screen version of the story of *Eleemosynary*. How would you deal with the fragmented narrative and its disrupted chronology? Write out one scene as a screenplay.
- Investigate the New Age movement in America. As you research this topic, conduct interviews with present or former adherents of this movement. How do they describe their approaches to spirituality? Explore the diversity of these approaches, the causes of this movement, and its effect on American society. Present your findings to the class.
- Write an autobiographical essay or a short story on a situation involving family members. The essay or story should focus on a specific conflict between two or more members and describe the resolution of that conflict.

Dorothea moved in and took total control of Echo, even to the point of rejecting Artie's choice of names for her. Artie's own conflicted feelings for her mother, along with her need to escape Dorothea's control, prompted her to leave Echo in her mother's care. Artie admits that she has trouble touching people, including her daughter, which appears to be a result of the disconnection she feels from her own mother. Echo's overwhelming need to establish a relationship with Artie, however, compels her to forgive her mother and insist that she will tend and cultivate her to the point that the two can establish a close and loving relationship.

STYLE

Narrative Fragmentation

The play consists of a series of sketchy plots constructed around the three women's recollections of past incidents. Blessing continually cuts back and forth from past to present as the women examine the effect that the past has had on their lives. There is little action in the play, as it juxtaposes characters' monologues spoken to the audience and short conversations with each other. The lack of action reflects the inability of the characters to move forward in their relationships with one another until the end, when Artie and Echo are forced to deal with Dorothea's death and its effect on them.

Symbolic Language

Language is used symbolically in the play, ironically pinpointing a lack of communication among the characters. Echo loves the sound of words and claims that there are some she would "give her life for." Her devotion to words becomes an escape from the reality of her unstable relationship with her mother. Still, attention to words also provides the only link between the two.

After a long absence, Artie begins to communicate over the phone with her daughter, coaching her for the spelling bee. Echo suggests that "it was probably her way to apologize" for running away from her at the bookstore. Still, Artie will go only so far in her attempts to establish a relationship with her daughter. Whenever Echo tries to make a personal connection with her, Artie returns to the spelling words, rebuffing her daughter's attempts to forge a relationship. For example, when Echo suggests they talk, instead of study, Artie ignores her request and gives her a new word to spell. By the end of the play, Echo uses the word "eleemosynary" to describe the Wesbrook women. The word becomes most appropriate for Echo, who has decided to be charitable and forgive her mother for her past mistakes.

HISTORICAL CONTEXT

The Conservative 1980s

One of the strongest influences on American culture in the 1980s was brought about by the election to the presidency of the Republican Ronald Reagan. Reagan ushered in a return to American conservatism during his two terms in office. His political ideology rejected many of the liberal attitudes that had dominated the years of the 1930s, when Franklin Delano Roosevelt was president, through the 1960s and the administration of Lyndon B. Johnson. Roosevelt faced the Depression and put in place a social and economic agenda called the New Deal. Johnson likewise helped pass progressive social programs and civil rights bills. Republicans of the 1980s proclaimed that they would undo the "welfare state" and cut the power of the central government. The result, they argued, would be a strengthening of America's capitalist economy.

An anti-Communist fervor, promoted by the Republicans, harkened back to the cold-war ideology of the 1950s. Reagan and his followers also tried to return the country to the traditional values of the 1950s, stressing middle-class family ideals and rejecting the liberal permissiveness of the counterculture 1960s. Many Americans, among them some of the "baby boomers" who had grown up in the 1950s, welcomed a return to their nostalgic view of the past, a time that appeared much simpler than the 1980s.

In the 1980s, the celebration of the ideals of the 1950s had a destructive impact on many of the gains of the social and civil rights movements of the 1960s and 1970s. Conservative Republicans felt that these movements had gone too far, negatively affecting the social fabric of the country. One of their main targets was the women's movement and the gains it had made in women's rights in the previous two decades. Republicans blocked the passage of the Equal Rights Amendment (ERA) in 1982, which contributed to the disruption of the movement's organizational structure. They also supported antiabortion groups that helped pass legislation that restricted state and federal abortion laws. Minority groups suffered as well when the Reagan administration tried to overturn affirmative action regulations and cut social programs.

Feminism

In the 1970s, the women's movement gained two important victories: the 1973 Supreme Court decision in *Roe v. Wade* to protect a woman's right to have an abortion and congressional approval of the ERA in 1972. After Reagan's election, however, these rights were threatened by the conservative Right, who promoted a return to traditional female roles. The ERA stated, "Equality of rights under the law shall not be denied or abridged by the United States or by any State on account of sex." The ratification deadline for the ERA was June 1982.

Supporters, including the National Organization for Women, insisted that this right needed to be guaranteed by law, since discrimination against women still existed throughout America. Opponents, however, voiced fears that the amendment would cause further rifts in the fabric of American society, especially within the family. The Republican administration supported the latter view; as a result, the ERA failed to gain ratification. This failure dealt a severe blow to the feminist movement, opening the door to such critics as Phyllis Schlafly, who called for women to return to more traditional roles.

The controversy over the role of women prompted Betty Friedan, one of the leaders of the feminist movement, to argue that feminists needed to find a balance between traditional and modern concerns regarding a woman's place. Even as the voices of dissent continued to be raised, women's numbers grew in the workforce during the 1980s. For some, the extra income was a necessity—especially for single mothers, whose problems were compounded by federal spending cuts for childcare.

New Age Movement

The New Age movement was less a new religion than a mixture of several Eastern philosophies brought into the modern age and the Western world. Initially a fringe organization, the movement slowly began to make its impact on mainstream American society by the beginning of the 1980s. New Age followers acknowledged the power of American consumerism and so used its forums—publishing, music, and charismatic speakers who spoke through media outlets and at seminars—to spread their philosophy and influence. Often, however, the consumer-driven aspects of the movement clashed with its teachings, which championed individuality, simplified lifestyles, communion with nature, and a counterculture sensibility.

New Age followers rejected strict adherence to religious dogma but did embrace some specific philosophical tenets, including a belief in reincarnation, spiritual healing, and astrology and in the value of practicing yoga and meditation and eating

COMPARE & CONTRAST

- **1980s:** The ERA fails to gain ratification in a decade when women are pressured to adopt more conservative roles. Conservative activists like Phyllis Schlafly argue that a woman's place is in the home since her primary role is child-bearing and child raising.

  Today: Women have made major gains in their fight for equality. Discrimination against women is now against the law, and women have the opportunity to work inside or outside the home or both. However, those who choose to have children and a career face difficult time-management choices, owing to inflexible work schedules and promotion hurdles.

- **1980s:** The New Age movement becomes a popular alternative for Americans who reject the more conservative strictures of traditional Christian denominations. While New Agers have some influence on American society, they have little impact on the political atmosphere of the country.

  Today: Right-wing Christian groups, especially evangelicals, have gained popularity in America and have had a measurable impact on the social fabric of America and even on the 2004 presidential election, helping to reelect the conservative Republican George W. Bush.

- **1980s:** The term "Me Generation" comes to represent the 1980s, an age when self-interests are encouraged.

  Today: "Family values" is the popular buzzword, in an age when many Americans try to promote traditional social mores.

"natural" foods. Many of these beliefs were taken from Native American spiritual customs and Eastern religions, especially Buddhism and Hinduism, and given a modern spin. The Gospels, along with the writings of Buddha, the Chinese philosopher Lao-tzu, and the Indian yogi Gopi Krishna, became spiritual guideposts for New Agers, especially those works that promoted a sense of unity with the universe.

One of the movement's founders, Marilyn Ferguson, explained the New Age philosophy in her 1980 book *The Aquarian Conspiracy*, which became a popular hit, especially among the baby-boom generation, some of whom rejected stricter religious practices. In the latter part of the decade, the movement grew in strength, owing in some part to the national attention given to it by the actress Shirley MacLaine, who related her personal experiences with past lives in the press, on television, and in several books.

The New Age movement, along with other self-help groups in the 1980s, gained popularity because it called for its followers to take control of their own lives, recognizing their individual capacity for spiritual and physical renewal. In this sense, the movement echoed pantheism, which taught that every human being is directly connected to the universe and to God, without the need to follow restrictive, traditional religious doctrine or to rely on spiritual mediators. The New Age movement also had an impact on American politics, helping to promote more liberal views. New Agers opposed nuclear proliferation, nationalism (excessive devotion to a nation), and environmental destruction.

CRITICAL OVERVIEW

Eleemosynary began a two-week run at the Philadelphia Festival Theatre for New Plays on April 29, 1986. Since then it has been successfully produced off Broadway and in other theaters, most notably on the West Coast. Reviews for the play have been mixed, but most have been praiseworthy. Todd Everett, writing in the *Los Angeles Times*, says it is "a strong, interesting show," nicely written. In a *Time* article, William A. Henry III writes that the play is "haunting" and "displays wit and charm." He claims that it presents an "intriguing narrative" that helps "this complex material [stay] clear."

Nancy Churnin, in her *Los Angeles Times* review, considers it "a quiet and thoughtful play that is sometimes funny and sometimes sad." She finds that "the weakest part of the show may well be the ending" and says that "it trails off more than it stops; the final words don't ring true." Still, in her closing statement, she argues that "as in so many Blessing plays, the journey is more important than the destination. This production makes it a journey well worth taking."

Some reviewers, however, find the plot contrived. Laurie Winer writes in the *Wall Street Journal* that "the controlling hand of Mr. Blessing is constantly apparent, an intrusive presence." She claims that the play "is itself like a correctly spelled word that hasn't been properly incorporated into a sentence. It doesn't add up." Winer cites instances in the play when, she argues, "Mr. Blessing lets us see him laying out his hand." In a particularly harsh review in the *New York Times*, Alvin Klein insists that the play covers "obvious, hackneyed sentimental terrain." He finds it "a pretentious, annoying play" made up of "a series of disconnected backstories, grandiloquent statements . . . and forced imagery." Henry, however, echoes most critics' assessment that the play is "Blessing's finest work, an enriching tale of sin, regret and forgiveness."

CRITICISM

Wendy Perkins

Perkins is a professor of American and English literature and film. In this essay, she examines the effects that limited roles for women can have on a family, as reflected in the play.

Echo Wesbrook, the main character in Blessing's play *Eleemosynary*, determines that all of her problems began in 1958. That is the year that her grandmother, Dorothea, forced her mother, Artie, to test her theory that humans can fly with "the proper classical training." As the reminiscence plays out, Artie, with a pair of homemade wings strapped to her back, first tries running down a steep hill. When that fails to make her airborne, her mother instructs her to jump off a water tower. Dorothea insists that Artie will be safe, since she has piled up leaves at the base of the tower. After Artie scales the tower and looks over the edge, she refuses to jump, all of which is caught on film by Dorothea. When her mother suggests that they try again the next day, Artie responds, "You are nuts! And now you're nuts on film!"

"BLESSING PROVIDES NO PANACEA AT THE END OF THE PLAY THAT NEATLY WRAPS UP THE TROUBLED RELATIONSHIP BETWEEN MOTHER AND DAUGHTER."

Many people who know Dorothea consider her "nuts." Echo notes that her grandmother was continually involved in projects: "communication with the dead, spontaneous combustion, astral projection." When she took walks, she claimed that she met famous people, like President James Monroe. Dorothea has embraced eccentricity as a response to gender restrictions placed on her throughout her life. As she puts it, "Eccentricity saved my life. It became my life." Yet her alternative behavior had a damaging effect on her family. Her unreasonable demands on her daughter caused Artie to become emotionally stunted, which resulted in a deep divide between Artie and Echo.

Dorothea recalls the oppressive conditions under which she lived, growing up in the 1940s and 1950s, which eventually drove her to embrace eccentricity. She remembers that "the only sentence of genuine interest" regarding her that her father ever spoke was "Is it a boy?" This gave her "such a feeling of worthlessness." She explains, "It was like an asthma of the soul. I could never take a deep breath of who I was." Noting her limited opportunities, Dorothea declares, "Girls really *weren't* worth much then."

After her father told her that he had arranged a marriage for her, she declared that she would rather go to college than get married, but her father only laughed at her suggestion. Her future husband

WHAT DO I READ NEXT?

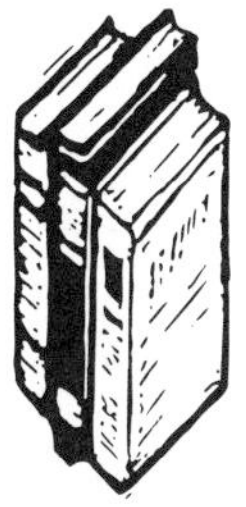

- Blessing's *Nice People Dancing to Good Country Music* (1982) is considered to be the best of his early plays. It centers on the relationship between a former nun and her aunt, who runs a bar in Houston.
- Another of Blessing's plays that focuses on family relationships is *Independence* (1984). Here Blessing follows the lives of three daughters and their mentally ill mother.
- Arthur Miller's play *Death of a Salesman* (1949) looks at the troubled relationship between a salesman and his two sons.
- The Awakening, published in 1899, is Kate Chopin's masterly novel of a young woman who struggles to find self-knowledge and inevitably suffers the consequences of trying to establish herself as an independent spirit.

made a vague promise that she could get an education after they were married, but he later refused to allow her. She explains that her husband "didn't really know what to make of [her], except a wife." Dorothea fell into a grudging acceptance of the role that had been thrust upon her until she met a spiritualist at a party, who claimed to have made "eccentric journeys," during which he enjoyed "the possibility of an entirely different world within our reach." After he told her that "*no one holds an eccentric responsible*," she breathed "a great breath of happiness" that gave her a tremendous sense of relief. She remembers, "From that day on, I never felt the need to listen to a thing my husband said—or anyone else." Finally able to break the gender-related bonds that had entrapped her, she claims, "Eccentricity solved so many problems. I could stay a wife and mother, and still converse with the souls of animals."

Dorothea insists that "the world is filled with an inner conviction. A cord of truth and power which needs only to be unsnarled and drawn taut between its center and our own." Ironically, though, as she strove to make connections between herself and the universe, she neglected the needs of her daughter, who, in turn, neglected those of her own daughter. William A. Henry III, in his review of the play for *Time*, concludes that Dorothea, "a New Age visionary," propels her daughter and granddaughter toward freedom, seeing them "as a chance to fulfill [her] own thwarted dreams." Yet the freedom she forced on them added further irony to their lives as it frustrated their own desires in much the same way that Dorothea's father had frustrated hers.

Reflecting on her relationships with her mother and her daughter, Artie warns the audience, "Never have a daughter. Never have a child, for that matter, but *never* have a daughter. She won't like you." Her statement reflects her own attitude toward her mother and what she assumes is Echo's attitude toward her.

When Dorothea discovered the benefits of eccentricity, she took control of her daughter's life, concluding that she knew best how to live. She insisted that Artie be well educated, claiming "a smart girl can hide what she knows, so there's still a chance for happiness." Nancy Churnin notes, in her review of the play for the *Los Angeles Times*, that Artie tried "unsuccessfully to escape from Dorothea by taking refuge in hard science," as a counter to her mother's New Age philosophy. Dorothea's will, strengthened through years of suppression, became too strong for Artie to fight.

Dorothea's control over her daughter reached a breaking point, however, when Artie became pregnant. After Artie announced that she wanted to keep the baby, Dorothea angrily insisted that "none of our plans, none of your potential" would then be realized. Trying to persuade Artie to get an abortion, Dorothea argued that she could be more than a mother, more than just "something a child needs." Artie eventually allowed her mother to browbeat her into getting an abortion but, soon after, ran away from home, ready to break off all ties with Dorothea.

When Artie got pregnant with Echo, however, she tried to reestablish a relationship with her mother. She called Dorothea, who immediately insisted that she would travel to California to help her. Soon after Echo was born, Artie's husband died, and Dorothea regained control over her daughter and granddaughter's lives. She named the baby Echo over Artie's objection and took over the job of raising the girl, teaching her letters before the child could speak. Dorothea established a close relationship with Echo, transferring all of her dreams to the child. Their closeness, however, damaged Artie's own relationship with Echo. She admits, "I have trouble touching my daughter" but notes that Dorothea "could touch her all day long." Understanding that Echo had come to prefer Dorothea to her and desperate to get out from under her mother's control, Artie took a job overseas, where she spent the next several years.

Dorothea doted on Echo, and, as she grew up, Echo became bitter about her mother's abandonment of her. Once, when Artie called home wanting to speak to Dorothea, Echo hung up on her. When her grandmother asked who was on the phone, Echo replied, "It was a dead person" or, at least, "nearly dead" to her. Eventually, though, as Artie attempted to make contact with her, Echo readmitted her mother into her life. Churnin writes that when the three women "pull at the ties that bind, they find that these are bonds that cannot be severed. They can, at best, be renegotiated so that the dynamics between the characters are less suffocating and lethal." Slowly, and ironically, through the study of words, Echo and Artie are able to establish a familial relationship, which Dorothea encourages as she notes, "We all need forgiveness."

Echo and Artie find common ground after Dorothea dies. Echo notes that Dorothea's control over her was difficult for her as well. When her mother sends her to live with her uncle, Echo initially feels hopeful that she "could live a whole new life" there, where she could be Barbara, not Echo. But she soon realizes that what she wants more than anything is her mother's love.

Blessing provides no panacea at the end of the play that neatly wraps up the troubled relationship between mother and daughter. Artie sometimes tries to resist Echo's efforts to be close to her, answering Echo's question about whether Artie loves her with "yes and no." But Echo insists that she will not give up on her mother, for although the Wesbrook women can be eccentric, they are also eleemosynary. She will tend to her mother and "cultivate" her, because she, like all the Wesbrook women, ultimately is charitable at heart.

Source: Wendy Perkins, Critical Essay on *Eleemosynary*, in *Drama for Students*, Thomson Gale, 2006.

Jennifer Bussey

Bussey holds a master's degree in interdisciplinary studies and a bachelor's degree in English literature and is an independent writer specializing in literature. In this essay, she explores Blessing's characterization of the matriarch Dorothea in Eleemosynary.

Blessing's *Eleemosynary* is a minimally staged play with few props. This simple presentation brings the reader's focus sharply toward the three characters, Dorothea, Artie, and Echo. By eliminating all distractions from the stage, Blessing manages to remove his three characters from the concreteness of a setting. He challenges the audience to understand these three women and how they relate to one another and the world. There are no secondary characters or context cues on which we can rely for information or perspective. Blessing's play is all about characterization, and it hinges on Dorothea.

Dorothea is Artie's mother and Echo's grandmother, but she has acted as mother to them both. The action of the play is set off by Dorothea's stroke, an event that forces Artie and Echo to meet for the first time in years. This reunion is the catalyst for telling the family history that makes up most of *Eleemosynary*. Dorothea's subsequent death triggers profound change in the relationship between Echo and her estranged mother. For years, the two have talked on the phone without ever discussing anything substantial, let alone indulging in long-overdue arguments. Dorothea's estate, however, prompts the first-ever fight between Echo and Artie. Knowing that they have only each other forces them into honesty. This is just the first of the changes in their relationship; Dorothea's death ultimately brings Artie and her daughter back together as a family. Clearly, Dorothea's role in the family has been significant, since her passing brings with it such anxiety, turmoil, and change. An examination of Blessing's characterization of Dorothea reveals why she was such a central figure in the lives of her daughter and granddaughter.

The pivotal moment in Dorothea's life was when she decided to become an eccentric. By her own admission, this was a conscious choice that liberated her from caring what her husband thought of her. As a teenager, Dorothea had dreamed of graduating from high school, attending college, and someday getting married. The news that her father had arranged for her to marry a boyfriend, however, changed her entire view of who she would become. Although she was reluctant to get married, her father had no plans to pay for her to go to college, and her husband-to-be assured her that she could be a student again someday. After having children, Dorothea realized that her husband never intended for "someday" to arrive. Her dreams would go unfulfilled. Dorothea had been unconventional (for her time) from the time she was very young, and she had difficulty finding her place within her family's and society's expectations of her. She found it impossible to reconcile her independent spirit with the life she led, so when she talked to a man who explained that nobody applies expectations to eccentrics, she had her answer. She chose to be an eccentric as a way to release herself from external expectations.

Whereas "wife" and "mother" were definable roles, "eccentric" was not. This role enabled Dorothea to create her own persona and become whatever kind of woman she wanted to be. Unfortunately, it also enabled her to use her identity as an eccentric as an excuse. She could disregard social rules, be selfish, and refuse to compromise. Further, she no longer needed her husband's approval, or anyone else's. This made her oblivious to how she made other people feel, including her sons, daughter, and granddaughter. Over time, this attitude made her insensitive to Artie. Dorothea came to value her own right to be an eccentric over her daughter's right to be understood as her own person. When Artie became pregnant at the age of eighteen, Dorothea was consumed with thoughts of how the baby would destroy her plans for Artie. Dorothea took advantage of Artie's frightened and vulnerable state to impose on Artie her own agenda about female empowerment and show her husband (Artie's father) that women can be more than mothers. Artie argued with Dorothea, but Dorothea pressured her into having an abortion, after which Artie ran away to start her own life without her mother.

Dorothea became so entrenched in her own eccentric lifestyle that she came to lack the ability to connect with her daughter in a meaningful or supportive way. As a result, her daughter ultimately escaped her domination in search of her own way. Intuitively, it would seem that Dorothea—who champions letting women define themselves—would be thrilled at her daughter's independence and desire to test her mettle in the world. In fact, Dorothea is always desperate to keep a tight hold on her daughter, directing her moves and running her life. After Artie left home, Dorothea went so far as to have a detective find Artie and then arrived uninvited in Artie's home. This only succeeded in driving a wider wedge between herself and her daughter. Dorothea allowed her self-centered eccentricity to eclipse her view of how her daughter was struggling against the same forces with which she herself had struggled.

"CLEARLY, DOROTHEA'S ROLE IN THE FAMILY HAS BEEN SIGNIFICANT, SINCE HER PASSING BRINGS WITH IT SUCH ANXIETY, TURMOIL, AND CHANGE."

Another important character trait of Dorothea's is her passive-aggressiveness. This tendency is consistent with her general approach to life, which is one of avoidance. Perhaps because she feels that all attacks on her happiness have been indirect, she is aggressive in the same way. Dorothea's happiness was attacked first by her father, who arranged for her to get married immediately after finishing high school. He never discussed it with her, just made the decision for her and then informed her of it. Her hope for future happiness was then attacked by her husband, a man she did not love but who controlled her future. He had assured her that she could go to college someday but later told her that he never really meant it. Because her experience in being attacked was never direct, Dorothea never learned how to confront issues or problems directly. For example, she had a detective find Artie and then showed up at Artie's house and criticized the house, the view, and the food instead of coming right out and criticizing Artie. Later, Artie told Dorothea that she was pregnant again, and Dorothea informed Artie that she was coming to help with the baby. She then moved into the neighborhood without consulting Artie at all. After the baby was born, Dorothea decided that although Artie had named the baby Barbara, her name instead would be Echo. These are all very intrusive and insensitive forms of behavior, carried out in nonconfrontational ways. Dorothea never budges, and Artie is left to deal with an overbearing and seemingly oblivious parent.

Dorothea is characterized as an intelligent woman who has reared her daughter and granddaughter to be intelligent women. Throughout *Eleemosynary*, Dorothea puts little emphasis on anything other than developing the girls' intellects. When we see her for the first time with her granddaughter, Echo, it is not a typical grandmotherly scene. Where we would expect to find a grandmother rocking and singing to a new baby, Dorothea is seen reviewing alphabets with the three-month-old baby. Dorothea establishes her expectations of Artie and Echo early in their lives, and she expects them to be geniuses who let nothing stand in the way of pursuing their full intellectual potential. This is what is so devastating to Dorothea when Artie becomes pregnant for the first time at the age of eighteen; all of Dorothea's plans for Artie's education and career are jeopardized by the baby. In her experience, becoming a mother is a great burden that hinders more important intellectual pursuits.

Dorothea values education; after all, she was denied going down that road. She expects the girls to be motivated to attend college and to excel when they get there. After Artie has abandoned Echo to be reared by Dorothea, Dorothea keeps Artie's memory alive by telling Echo how proud she should be of her mother, who is doing research. She places no emphasis on what kind of person Artie is but focuses solely on her intelligence and accomplishment in her field. That Artie is so accomplished in her field (science) comes as no surprise to Dorothea, just as Echo's winning the spelling bee does not surprise her. Artie is hardly surprised when Echo mentions that she may begin taking college classes at the age of thirteen. Amid Dorothea's expectations that the girls will be intellectual giants is the expectation that they will achieve great things as scholars.

Dorothea's development of Artie's and Echo's identities as intelligent women is so deeply embedded in them that they are initially able to connect only at an intellectual level. Artie suggests that Echo pursue spelling bees, and this gives them something to talk about on the phone. Once Echo starts working on being a spelling champion, Artie calls more often, so she can help Echo study her words. As superficial as it is, practicing spelling words is their only consistent link to each other. When Echo attempts to lure her mother into more personal discussions, Artie uses the passive-aggressive tactics she learned from her mother to ignore Echo and continue with spelling practice. There is also an incident before Dorothea's stroke, when Artie sees Echo at a book fair. Echo sees Artie too, and Artie drops her book and runs out of the building. Echo promptly buys the book (*Robinson Crusoe*) and reads it seventeen times. This is the only way she knows to connect with her mother. Because Dorothea never develops the other sides of their personalities (emotional, intuitive, social), the intellectual level is all they have.

As a mother to both Artie and Echo, Dorothea passes some of her own characteristics on to them. She teaches them independence, even if she fails to provide appropriate guidance for it. She teaches them that women can be respected for their intellects and that the world of academic discipline is open to them. She also teaches them to be proud of their intelligence and not hide it, as she was forced to do. Because of her own interpersonal failings, Dorothea also passes on to Artie and Echo the inability to have healthy relationships. She fails to provide them with a role model for how to forge healthy relationships with family members or men, and her relationships with them render them incapable of achieving normal emotional intimacy. After all, Dorothea chose to be the eccentric and thus free herself of obligations, but Artie and (later) Echo had to learn to coexist with her. Although they both love Dorothea, albeit differently, their relationships with her do not prepare them for a relationship with each other. Because their feelings for her differ, the two cannot even find common ground in their love for Dorothea.

At the end of the play, we see Artie and Echo determined to find a way to relate to each other and be each other's family. Dorothea's legacy, however, is a difficult one to integrate into their relationship, and it is impossible to overcome. Dorothea has shaped both of their lives and molded their identities. Because Dorothea herself was an unusual person, Artie and Echo are unusual women, too. Unlike Dorothea, Artie and Echo feel free to be themselves without having to cast off social conventions or expectations. In the final scene of the play, Artie and Echo review the tape that shows Dorothea making Artie try to fly. For Echo, the tape captures a time she never saw, when her mother and her grandmother had a life together. It represents hope that she and Artie can find a way to relate to each other. For Artie, the tape captures her mother's determination, regardless of what society or the laws of physics say. It is symbolic of her mother's approach to life. The play ends on an uncertain note. Dorothea was larger than life; now that she is gone, we hope that Artie and Echo can find their way into a well-rounded life and a healthier mother-daughter relationship.

Source: Jennifer Bussey, Critical Essay on *Eleemosynary*, in *Drama for Students*, Thomson Gale, 2006.

Neil Heims

Heims is a writer and teacher living in Paris. In this essay, he analyzes the structure of Eleemosynary *and argues that Blessing is more interested in creating a play that shows how his characters experience events than in developing action and plot.*

Having broken contact with her mother in her teens, Artie telephones her a number of years later to tell her, "I'm going to have a baby." "I'll come and stay with you," her mother says. "Where do you live now?" Artie replies, "Oh—you don't have to do that." "I want to," her mother answers. "What state do you live in? Just tell me that." Reluctantly, Artie tells her that it is "California." To which Dorothea responds, "Out there, eh? Well, I'll have to make some arrangements." But Artie interrupts her. "Mom, don't come. I don't want you to." "Nonsense," Dorothea replies. "I'll be there in a week." "Mom," Artie says, "don't you want to know what city I'm in?" "No," says Dorothea, characteristically. "I like the challenge." Artie's next line is not part of the conversation with her mother. She tells the audience, "A week later, there she was."

This dialogue toward the end of scene 4 of Blessing's *Eleemosynary* is not an actual dramatic exchange happening in real stage time. It is recollected and narrated by Artie. She is presenting it to the audience. "When I ran away the second time," she says, "I kept moving . . . Once after about three years, I called." With a change of inflection, she starts the dialogue, speaking as if into a telephone, "Mom?" When this conversation—a snapshot of their relationship and of Dorothea's temperament—ends, Dorothea, as if arriving in California, says, "Hi." She does not speak to Artie but, as the stage direction indicates, to the audience—comically, even rakishly, as if in the panel of a cartoon, framing and caricaturing herself. At that moment, Dorothea exists simultaneously within and out-side the action of the play. The actress playing her portrays her as if the character were a puppet and the actress a puppeteer. In turn, Artie resumes her stance as a narrator. Not answering her mother's greeting, she, too, speaks to the audience: "She bought a house on our block. She came over every night. My husband actually liked her." "Richard had taste," Dorothea interjects. Artie responds, telling *us*, not her mother, "He had more than that."

> "THE PLAY IS DESIGNED NOT TO DEVELOP A PLOT BUT TO MAKE THE AUDIENCE THINK ABOUT THE CHARACTERS AND THE VALUES THEY REPRESENT."

In the foregoing scene, Blessing does not present action and conversation for the sake of dramatic realism—although the conversation is realistic—but as dramatized narrative. The actors are narrating what their characters said. In *Eleemosynary*, the story is less important than the characters it serves to reveal. The play is designed not to develop a plot but to make the audience think about the characters and the values they represent. For this reason, too, it is presented on a bare stage. Blessing is not attempting to create the illusion of reality but to represent, onstage, individual consciousness.

Repeatedly, throughout the play, one of the characters tells the audience something about herself or another character, and one or both of the others step into the narrative to help *show* what she is saying. *Eleemosynary* begins with Artie's daughter and Dorothea's granddaughter, Echo, speaking to the audience. She spells "eleemosynary" and then says, "It's my favorite word. Not just because I won with it, either." With this, she establishes her character—precocious, outspoken, and brainy. She then points to another section of the stage, to a platform where a woman is lying with her eyes closed, and says, "This is my grandmother. She had a stroke." Without moving, Dorothea says, "Could you open the drapes, dear?" Echo pretends to open imaginary drapes. As she does, she tells the audience, "She can't really talk. I can hear her, though. At least I think I can." The actress playing Dorothea says, "Oh, that's nice. That's warm," and Echo continues to speak to the audience, telling more about her grandmother. The audience learns about Echo and Dorothea and also must recognize that the play is representing mental action occurring inside one character's mind as much as external interaction between characters.

Eleemosynary ends just as it began. Echo speaks to the audience. Throughout the play, too, one of the three characters always serves as the narrator, framing a dramatic scene that the three of them present. Thus, never is any of the dramatic action set in the present time. Only the narration is. Nevertheless, *Eleemosynary* is less a play about recollection than it is about defying the boundaries of time and space to represent on the stage the feeling of life as a process of consciousness and desire. Rather than dramatizing events, *Eleemosynary* dramatizes the way three women perceive events and experience living.

In *Eleemosynary*, Blessing shows the experience of experience, not just the events experienced. His concern with problems of formal exposition and dramatic structure—his technique of distancing the actors from their roles so that the audience can observe the characters and their situations and interactions rather than becoming absorbed in their melodrama—does not overwhelm his interest in representing and exploring the human matters of this unusual drama. *Eleemosynary* presents the lives of three generations of women, their influence on each other, and the ways in which each of them deals with being a woman in a society where, as Dorothea remarks, "Girls really *weren't* worth much." As she puts it, being a girl "gave me such a feeling of worthlessness. It was like an asthma of the soul. I could never take a deep breath of who I was." None of the three women is content to accept the condition of inferiority that is socially imposed upon her. Each is endowed with a particular genius. Each also represents a characteristic generational response to the treatment of women in society, as the social definitions of women, women's identities, and women's roles evolve.

Dorothea represents women of a generation who were devalued because they were not men. "As for my father," she tells us, "well, the only sentence of genuine interest he ever uttered about me was, 'Is it a boy?'" Consequently, Dorothea shows how she was defined not as herself but as a wife. "The day I graduated high school, my father smiled at me, and said he had a wonderful surprise—which turned out to be an arranged marriage between me and John Wesbrook. . . . I said, 'What about college?' And he said, 'John's going directly into his father's business.'" But Dorothea interjects, "No, no—what about college for me?" And her father laughs. "Can you imagine it?" she says. "Feeling guilty for learning?" Brilliant and thwarted, Dorothea finds refuge for herself and escapes from the limitations imposed upon her by becoming a spiritualist and an eccentric.

Artie is no less gifted than her mother, but Dorothea's eccentricity, which allowed her to escape the bondage of masculine constraints, binds Artie to her at the expense of Artie's own personality. Dorothea imposes herself upon Artie. Although she is encouraged by Dorothea in her intellectual development, Artie is stifled emotionally, her own consciousness swallowed up by her mother. Overwhelmed by the force of her mother's bohemianism, eccentricity, and ever-changing spiritual quests, she harnesses her intellectual power and suppresses her tenderness. Not only does she break with her mother, she also later leaves her daughter in the care of her mother to pursue her own career. Even when she talks to Echo—over the phone—she remains aloof, unwilling to discuss either her feelings or her actions.

Raised by Dorothea, Echo misses her mother's love and longs for it, but she is not, as her mother was, thwarted by Dorothea's eccentricities. She is nourished by them. She thrives on her grandmother's ways of sharpening her intellect and cultivating her sensibility, and she loves her grandmother as her mother never does. Echo is, therefore, the product of the clash of her grandmother and her mother. Her narrative quest is to integrate her mother and grandmother in herself. She is the principal narrator of the play and, to the degree that *Eleemosynary* has a fixed point of view, it is hers: her narration frames the others. She is, in addition, the focal point of her grandmother's and her mother's attention—however greatly the nature of each of their relationships with her differs. She tries to unite them, and they are united in her. Her particular and spectacular talent for spelling is encouraged by her mother. It is a way for Artie to be in contact with Echo as she goes over words with her, but it is also a way of avoiding intimacy with her, for she will not discuss anything else. Dorothea, however, disdains Echo's dedication to becoming a champion speller. "Why do that?" she asks. "If you already know the word, why beat someone to death with the fact?" Echo, nevertheless, pursues the championship in order to gain her mother's love and to "fly" like her grandmother. She uses the spelling bee also as an occasion to bring her mother and grandmother together, so both can be present for her.

What the three women have in common is symbolized by the metaphor of flying and, for each in her own way, by the desire to fly. The idea of flying is expressed verbally throughout the play and represented by the image of wings and by the actual pair of wings that Dorothea makes Artie wear in a film she shoots to document her attempts "to prove that man—or, in this case, woman—can fly without the aid of any motor of any kind, using only the simple pair of wings you see my daughter . . . wearing." The idea of flying represents the freedom of the spirit when it overcomes the constraints and boundaries of convention and matter and soars despite obstacles. Dorothea attempts flight through her eccentricity and imagination, undeterred by the laws of the material world. Artie attempts it by running away from her mother and daughter and pursuing scientific research, hoping to discover what is not yet known. Echo tries it by spelling words with such facility that it seems the words are revealed to her as entirely perceived objects from above, rather than agglomerations of letters. She spells as if she were a funambulist walking a tightrope, hoping to win the love of her audience.

As she competes in the spelling bee, Echo demonstrates the neediness and the fierce dedication and self-involvement each of the three women brings to whatever they pursue. "Echo was a little different than I thought she'd be. . . . She seemed so . . . desperate," Artie says. "She was frightening, is what she was," Dorothea continues. The actress playing Echo shows what they mean, speaking Echo's thoughts during the competition. "This can't go on forever, buddy. I'm going to crack you like an egg," she says mentally to her one remaining adversary. "Dear God," she prays, "please let me win! . . . I want five minutes . . . when all the lights are on me, and all the pictures are taken of me, and for five minutes I'm the most famous child in America, and Mom and Dorothea see it." When she does win, however, the focus for each of the women is not Echo but the misery of the boy she defeats.

Considering the self-reflexivity that propels each of the three women, it is perplexing that at the end of the play Echo says, "No matter what we've done—no matter how we've done it—we're all three of us, in our own way, completely . . . eleemosynary . . . 'Charitable.'" Is she deceiving herself? Or does she mean that each of them, despite and even because of her need for independence, has attempted to give to the others fully whatever she has to give? It is a depth of spiritual power and defiance of limitations in Dorothea's case. It is an unremitting pursuit of a goal in Artie's. In Echo's own case, it is loving care, which is shown both in how she tends her grandmother and in the words she says to her mother in the last moments of *Eleemosynary*. Determined to satisfy her own need for love and to repair her mother's weakened ability to love, Echo tells Artie that she chooses to love her and will work to make "you love me." She says, "I'm going to stay with you. I'm going to prepare you for me. I'm going to cultivate you. I'm going to tend you."

Source: Neil Heims, Critical Essay on *Eleemosynary*, in *Drama for Students*, Thomson Gale, 2006.

T. H. McCulloh

In the following review, McCulloh analyzes the theme of negotiation in the play.

Probably one of playwright Lee Blessing's more interior and personal plays, *Eleemosynary* is completely unlike his early baseball plays, and closer to his two-character *A Walk in the Woods,* about the intimate relationship between two international arms negotiators.

Eleemosynary, now being revived by the Pathway Theater Company at Irvine's New Community Center, also deals with negotiators. This time, the negotiations are familial, between a purposefully eccentric woman, her beleaguered and bewildered daughter, and her lucid and very logical granddaughter, who has just won a national spelling bee with the word "eleemosynary," which means charitable.

It's a good word choice, because precocious granddaughter Echo is the only one of the three who is really charitable in the shadowed relationships of this fractured family. She adores the grandmother Dorothea, who has raised her, and longs desperately for her wandering mother, Artie, to rejoin them. The play focuses on Echo's victories and defeats in this process, and it's often touching, sometimes funny, and full of Blessing's insights into the human condition.

It's a shame that Pathway isn't able to provide better production values, for the work of director John Haggard deserves them. The play is presented on a stage that is much too big for this intimate portrait, and the meager setting of three low platforms is unimaginative and distracting. Otherwise, Haggard's handling of the sensitive subject is valid, insightful and dramatically sound. He skillfully handles the relationships between the women and balances their individuality with affection.

The play's central figure is Echo, the schoolgirl who wants to be a speller for the rest of her

> "THE PLAY FOCUSES ON ECHO'S VICTORIES AND DEFEATS IN THIS PROCESS, AND IT'S OFTEN TOUCHING, SOMETIMES FUNNY, AND FULL OF BLESSING'S INSIGHTS INTO THE HUMAN CONDITION."

life; she can't believe that there aren't adult spelling bees. Young Stephanie Carrie is marvelous in the difficult role. It's the performance of a born actress, detailed with the swinging moods of her age, the joys of discovery and the rewards of accomplishment, both in her passion for spelling and her efforts to bring her mother back into her life.

Although Erika Dittner's Artie is not as varied, and not as rich, she is impressive as the mother, particularly in those dark moments when Artie tries to deny her brilliant daughter and the love from Echo that Artie feels but can't believe in.

Debbie Thoms as grandmother Dorothea gives the weakest performance, valid in its conception, but mostly on the surface, without passion and without charisma. It isn't always easy to see her avowed desire to be eccentric as a reality. Her best moments are with Echo, and fueled by Carrie's deep sense of reality.

Source: T. H. McCulloh, "A Clear View of Family Negotiation," in *Los Angeles Times*, April 23, 1999, p. 29.

Nancy Churnin

In the following review excerpt, Churnin compares Eleemosynary *with Blessing's earlier work, Cobb, which focuses on men. Churnin finds more similarities than differences, especially in character development.*

Playwright Lee Blessing has joked in the past about his tendency to separate the men and women in his plays: it keeps them out of trouble, he has said.

One would expect differences between his all-male plays like *Cobb,* the West Coast premiere that just closed at the Old Globe Theatre, and *Eleemosynary,* the San Diego premiere that just opened at the Elizabeth North Theatre under the direction of the San Diego Actors Theatre. Not the least of the differences is that the three women of *Eleemosynary* have probably never heard of the Ty Cobb in *Cobb.*

But the differences are not as striking as the similarities.

What interests Blessing in both plays is not action, so much as soul-searching. The characters address the audience. They discover that they are interconnected. When they pull at the ties that bind, they find that these are bonds that cannot be severed. They can, at best, be renegotiated so that the dynamics between the characters are less suffocating and lethal.

In *Cobb,* three actors played the same man, baseball great Ty Cobb, at different stages of his life. In *Eleemosynary,* three women play three generations of one family—grandmother, daughter-mother, granddaughter—who are so intertwined that at one they confuse their roles. The grandmother competes with her daughter to become mother to the granddaughter—and wins.

Eleemosynary did not garner raves when it had its New York debut last year. But it's not a play that lends itself to raves. It's a quiet and thoughtful play that is sometimes funny and sometimes sad.

It could be deadly in the wrong hands.

But fortunately, it is in the right hands with the San Diego Actors Theatre, a homeless local theater company that has been developing a reputation for quality productions in its five years of existence.

One of the elements that makes this production a winner is the San Diego debut of Mhari Frothingham as the granddaughter, Echo.

Frothingham, a newcomer from New Mexico, takes the vessel of her role and fills it to overflowing with energy, pathos and humor.

One could find preciousness in a child who seeks to reunite her warring mother and grandmother by getting them to watch her win a national spelling bee championship. But not in this portrayal. This child-woman is a fighter, a scrapper, a survivor. If her weapons are words (like the playwright's?), she uses them with as much ruthless determination as Cobb ever used to swing a bat.

The spelling bee, by the way, is how Blessing works the word eleemosynary, meaning "of, related to, or supported by charity," into the title.

Ann Richardson stumbles at times as the grandmother, Dorothea, but sounds, overall, perfectly and expansively at home in the part of a woman who has taken refuge in eccentricity from

"WHAT INTERESTS BLESSING IN BOTH PLAYS IS NOT ACTION, SO MUCH AS SOUL-SEARCHING. THE CHARACTERS ADDRESS THE AUDIENCE. THEY DISCOVER THAT THEY ARE INTERCONNECTED."

the disappointments of her life. Forced by her father to marry rather than to go to college, Dorothea, to the mortification of her daughter, spends all her time looking for ways to fly, to see through the earth, to talk to stones, to converse with animals.

Pamela Adams-Regan plays Artie, the daughter who tries unsuccessfully to escape from Dorothea by taking refuge in hard science. Because Artie copes by fending off intimacy, hers is the hardest character for an audience to feel close to; she does a credible job, but could do far more to suggest the emotions she has pent up inside.

The direction by Patricia Elmore, artistic director of the San Diego Actors Theatre, keeps the tension high by having these characters interact by look and gesture even when they do not address each other directly.

Elmore has also assembled a fine all-woman design team for this all-woman play—a nice touch that really goes the distance when you consider that she even housed the show in a theater that bears a woman's name.

Mary Larson's set, askew slabs with the look of concrete, suggest ancient ruins—the timelessness of this ancient battle among grandmothers, mothers and daughters. Alexandra J. Pontone's lighting keeps attention focused where it is needed. Marta Zekan's original music and sound design softens the battles with hints of lullabies. Ingrid Helton's costumes are simple, but appropriate: a buttoned up look for buttoned up Artie, bangles and flowing garments for Dorothea, jeans for Echo.

As in *Cobb,* the weakest part of the show may well be the ending. There isn't much of a sense of conclusion in *Eleemosynary* beyond an acknowledgment for a need for reconciliation. It trails off more than it stops: the final words don't ring true.

But, as in so many Blessing plays, the journey is more important than the destination. This production makes it a journey well worth taking.

Source: Nancy Churnin, "Lee Blessing Takes 3 Women on Trip," in *Los Angeles Times*, August 13, 1990, p. 1.

Laurie Winer

In the following review excerpt, Winer offers positive comment on the dialogue in Eleemosynary, *but asserts that Blessing is "an intrusive presence" as a playwright.*

Eleemosynary is the jawbreaking name of Lee Blessing's new play. It's hard to spell and I bet you didn't know it means charitable. My guess is that Mr. Blessing intended to make you feel inadequate. His play is full of premeditated gambits like that. The plot line may look free-form at first, as it floats back and forth through time to inform us about a grandmother, her daughter and her daughter, but the controlling hand of Mr. Blessing is constantly apparent, an intrusive presence.

Mr. Blessing's second trick, after the vocabulary-building title, is to make you think the play is about generosity. In fact, it's the word his young heroine, Echo (Jennie Moreau), spells correctly to win the National Spelling Bee. Formidable words are her own private "bijouterie," that is, they are "like a jewel that no one takes out of the case. . . . There are words I would give my life for," she says, but she is not a writer who exploits their precision and subtlety in pursuit of the expression of an idea or story; rather she cherishes these words for their own abstract beauty.

Logophilia is something of an escape for Echo. Her mother, Artie (Joanna Gleason), has guiltily abandoned her to the care of her eccentric grandmother Dorothea (Eileen Heckart). It's not that Artie doesn't love Echo. She keeps in touch from a careful distance, dispensing useful advice on the telephone, advice you wish Echo would follow, such as, "Some words are meant to be spelled, not used." Despite many such good lines and two compulsively watchable performances by Ms. Heckart and Ms. Gleason, *Eleemosynary* is itself like a correctly spelled word that hasn't been properly incorporated into a sentence. It doesn't add up.

Artie cannot bear to be near her mother; she gives up her own daughter rather than fight Dorothea over the naming of the child (Artie had a more normal name in mind than Echo—Barbara).

"*ELEEMOSYNARY* IS ITSELF LIKE A CORRECTLY SPELLED WORD THAT HASN'T BEEN PROPERLY INCORPORATED INTO A SENTENCE. IT DOESN'T ADD UP."

But Dorothea comes off as only slightly overbearing. Mostly (and possibly because of Ms. Heckart's abundant charm), she seems engagingly energetic, which is exactly how Echo sees her. She collects knowledge and arcane facts with equal happiness, and she has a permanent dimple in her face, which seems winsomely right. What's wrong with this picture?

Oh, yes. There was a time in 1958 when Dorothea decided that "the secret of flight lies in the assurance that we are worthy of flying," so she straps two wings on the teenage Artie and makes her run down a hill flapping her arms while she films the whole affair. "Mom, you are nuts, and now you're nuts on film," Artie tells her.

At most, this would have made an embarrassing incident, but not the kind of trauma that would provoke an almost irreconcilable break between mother and daughter. Also, it's doubtful that even the spirited Dorothea would have attempted such a ridiculous experiment. She's eccentric, not stupid.

Echo arranges a reconciliation after her victory at the spelling bee (the play's one dramatic scene), and the women learn to forgive. To underscore this, the playwright has Echo spell and define *Eleemosynary* at the start and finish of the play. Yes, indeed, the play is about generosity, after all, we wearily concede. In this and several other instances, Mr. Blessing lets us see him laying out his hand.

Source: Laurie Winer, "Theater: *Eleemosynary; Yankee Dawg*," in *Wall Street Journal*, May 23, 1989, p. 1.

SOURCES

Blessing, Lee, *Eleemosynary*, Dramatists Play Service, 1987, pp. 7–9, 11–17, 19–21, 23, 25, 26, 31, 33, 35, 41, 43, 45, 47.

Churnin, Nancy, "Lee Blessing Takes 3 Women on Trip," in the *Los Angeles Times*, August 13, 1990, p. 1.

Everett, Todd, "Three Productions with Strong Female Roles Involve Dealing with Love, Tangled Families and the Consequences of Rape," in the *Los Angeles Times*, January 20, 2000, p. 7.

Henry, William A., III, Review of *Eleemosynary*, in *Time*, May 22, 1989, p. 110.

Klein, Alvin, "Child with a Way with Words, Maybe," in the *New York Times*, April 25, 1999, p. 14CN.11.

Winer, Laurie, Review of *Eleemosynary*, in the *Wall Street Journal*, May 23, 1989, p. 1.

FURTHER READING

Coen, Stephanie, ed., *American Theatre Book of Monologues for Women*, Theatre Communications Group, 2003.

The monologues included in this text were selected from plays by authors such as Wendy Wasserstein, Edward Albee, and Sam Shepherd, published in *American Theatre* magazine.

Friday, Nancy, *My Mother / My Self*, Doubleday, 1977.

Friday explores the often complex relationship between mothers and daughters.

Heelas, Paul, *The New Age Movement: The Celebration of the Self and the Sacralization of Modernity*, Blackwell Publishers, 1996.

Heelas traces the history and explores the philosophy of the movement.

Rhodes, Ron, and Alan W. Gomes, *The New Age Movement*, Zondervan Publishing, 1995.

This study focuses on the pantheistic worldview of the movement.

The Gin Game

D. L. COBURN

1976

The Gin Game is a two-person tragicomedy in two acts that uses a card game as a metaphor for life. D. L. Coburn conceived of the play first as a conflict between a man and a woman and strictly as a tragedy. He felt that the simplicity of two people and a card game could have more impact because of its concentrated format. The setting of the old age home was not conceived until later in the development of the story, and the comedy worked its way in unintentionally through the wit of the characters. Coburn used a few models from his own life for each of the characters and was inspired by the Russian poet Aleksander Pushkin's "Elegy," which speaks to the bittersweet nature of growing old. The play premiered in 1976 and was first published by Samuel French (1977); it is also available from Drama Book Specialists.

The Gin Game was Coburn's first attempt at writing a play. He happened to know a director, who had the play produced in September of 1976 by American Theatre Arts in a very small theater in Los Angeles. *Variety* carried a review of the play that caught the attention of the Actors Theatre of Louisville. In their subsequent production, the play was introduced to the actor Hume Cronyn, who instantly wanted to act in the play and sent it to the noted director Mike Nichols. Remarkably, on October 6, 1977, only thirteen months after its debut, *The Gin Game* opened on Broadway. The play was awarded the Pulitzer Prize for Drama in 1978 and was nominated for four Tony Awards: Best Play, Best Actor, Best Actress, and Best Director. Jessica

Tandy won for her portrayal of Fonsia. The play ran for 516 performances on Broadway in its first production and then went on tour around the country with its stars, Tandy and Cronyn.

In 1997, the play had a revival on Broadway, starring Charles Durning and Julie Harris, and was nominated for a Tony for Best Revival of a Play. Harris suggested adding a dance between Weller and Fonsia, since Durning is such a wonderful dancer. At first, Coburn rejected the idea, but then he realized that a dance could bring the two characters even closer and give the audience a glimpse at how happy they might be if only they could get past their crippling faults. The dance also shows the psychological damage resulting from the physical debilitation that often comes with age. Coburn came to consider this revision essential to the play. Through the years, *The Gin Game* has been shown in dozens of countries around the world. Coburn has written several more plays, screenplays, and television scripts, but none has had anything like the success of *The Gin Game*.

AUTHOR BIOGRAPHY

D. L. (Donald Lee) Coburn was born on August 4, 1938, in East Baltimore, Maryland, to Guy Dabney and Ruth Margaret Somers Coburn. East Baltimore is an impoverished neighborhood, and Coburn's childhood was made the more difficult by his parents' divorce when he was only two. He served in the U.S. Navy from 1958 to 1960, right after graduating from high school. Coburn operated a one-person advertising agency in Baltimore from 1965 to 1968 and then worked for the Stanford Advertising Agency in Dallas, Texas. He married Marsha Woodruff Maher in 1975 and has two children, Donn and Kimberly, from a previous marriage, to Nazle Joyce French (1964–1971).

When he was thirty years old, Coburn began writing short stories for his own gratification and discovered that he had a talent for dialogue. After seeing Thomas Troupe's one-act play *Diary of a Madman* (adapted from the work of the Russian writer Nikolay Gogol), he decided to try playwriting. It took him several years to put pen to paper, and after only eight pages, he put aside his first attempt, *The Gin Game*, for two more years. At the urging of his young son, he finally went back to the project and finished the play in four months. Amazingly, the play progressed from a small Los Angeles theater to Broadway in little more than a year's time and earned Coburn a Pulitzer Prize and a Tony nomination for Best Play in 1978.

Other plays written by Coburn include *Bluewater Cottage* (1979), *Guy* (1983), *Noble Adjustment* (1985), *Return to Blue Fin* (1991), *Fear of Darkness* (1995), *Firebrand* (1997), and *The Cause* (1998). They have not gained sufficient popularity to warrant publication and are therefore not readily accessible to the reading public. In addition, Coburn has written television series pilots for two major networks and several screenplays, including *Flights of Angels* (1987), *A Virgin Year* (1991), and *Legal Access* (1994).

PLOT SUMMARY

Act 1, Scene 1

Seated on an unused, enclosed porch of the Bentley Home for Seniors, a seedy nursing home, Weller Martin is occupying himself with a game of solitaire. A new resident, Fonsia Dorsey, wanders out onto the porch, and the two become acquainted as they talk about what brought them to the home. Weller offers to teach Fonsia how to play gin rummy. It is visitor's day, and, as they sort their cards, they share the reasons that neither of them has visitors. Fonsia wins the game, claiming beginner's luck. As they continue to play, they talk about their failed marriages, their children, and Weller's business. When Fonsia wins more games, Weller starts to curse, and Fonsia declares that in her Methodist upbringing, her father never said a foul word. They discuss the cheesy entertainment that is constantly foisted upon the residents of the nursing home, until Fonsia wins another gin game and Weller throws down his cards in disgust.

Act 1, Scene 2

The next week, Fonsia seeks out Weller on the porch as they both try to escape another visitor's day. Weller asks for a rematch at cards, and Fonsia eagerly agrees. However, before they start to play, they talk about the peculiarities and problems of other residents in the home as well as their own loneliness and frustration with their situation. During the card playing, Fonsia denies that she is on welfare, but Weller admits to panic attacks. Weller excuses his belligerent attitude as frustration about the theft problem in the home, but Fonsia's continued streak of wins leads him to increased shouting and profanities that culminate in his flipping over the table in anger.

Act 2, Scene 1

The next evening, Weller seeks out Fonsia in the garden. He asks her to join him on the porch so that he can apologize for upsetting her. She tries to get him to understand how frightening his temper can be. She advises him against playing gin, since he cannot control his temper when he plays. Unfortunately, Weller interprets the comment to mean that he is not a good gin player and once again gets the cards so that he can show her his skill at the game. She refuses to play, and they pick at each other with criticisms. When Fonsia starts to go inside, Weller advises that playing cards with him is better than being distressed by the empty stares of the other patients, whose bodies have outlasted their minds. When Fonsia wins another game, she says that she wishes that Weller could win, and he warns her not to lose on purpose for his sake. When he does win the next game, he accuses her of letting him win. Fonsia gets up to leave, but Weller grabs her arm and steers her back toward the table. Fonsia expresses concern that Weller needs to see a doctor. He is determined to find an explanation for her uncanny winning streak, and he starts talking to a little man who he imagines is sitting on his shoulder. Afraid that Weller has gone crazy, Fonsia once again starts to leave but is pressured into finishing the hand, which she wins. Weller accuses her of getting the card she needed from God, and his language grows rapidly worse until she curses back at him when she again calls, "Gin!"

Act 2, Scene 2

The next Sunday, Weller tricks Fonsia into coming out onto the porch by having the nurse tell her that her sister is waiting to see her. Because she has not seen her sister in fifteen years, Fonsia knows that Weller is just trying to get her to play cards. Fonsia says that such mania is abnormal. Weller confronts her for complaining to the staff about him and suggesting that he needs a psychiatrist. In their exchange, Weller corrects Fonsia's mistaken assumption that he has money. He explains that his long convalescence after his heart attack cost him all his assets. Fonsia reiterates her concerns that he might do something awful to her in a fit of temper, and he retaliates by guessing that her son does not visit her because she was always so negatively critical. She tries to hit him in her rage and then collapses into sobs. When he comforts her, she admits that she lied and that she, too, is on welfare. However, she did have a house that she gave to the church to spite her son.

Weller reaches for the cards to get her mind off the subject, but Fonsia refuses to play, and they argue about it. Weller accuses Fonsia of manipulating him and of attempting to be as vindictive with him as she was with her son by trying to get him in trouble with the staff. He makes her sit down to play, and verbal warfare ensues about each other's excuses of bad luck for failing at business and marriage. Weller calls Fonsia rigid, self-righteous, and vicious. When she wins again, he beats his cane on the table until he cries. Then he gathers himself up and walks out silently as Fonsia realizes that she has pushed him too far, and he will not be back.

MEDIA ADAPTATIONS

- The Jessica Tandy and Hume Cronyn version of *The Gin Game* was made available on video in 1984 by RKO Home Video.
- The version of the play made for PBS and starring Dick Van Dyke and Mary Tyler Moore was released by Image Entertainment in both VHS and DVD formats in 2003.

CHARACTERS

Fonsia Dorsey

Fonsia Dorsey is a prim and proper elderly woman who has just moved into a rundown nursing home. She appears to be a fragile victim, a diabetic woman who has been abandoned by everyone she knows. No one comes to visit her. She says that her son lives too far away, in Denver, but eventually the audience learns that her friends, if she really has any, live in an upscale nursing home that Fonsia cannot afford because she is on welfare and that her son actually lives in the same town but hates his mother too much to visit her. Fonsia is only a victim when it suits her purpose. She wears a mask of charm and reticence to hide her anger and intolerance. Underneath, she is very much in control—perhaps too much in control—of her emotions and has an intense need to be right, whatever the cost.

Fonsia has reached this desolate point in her life because no one has ever been able to live up to her expectations. She is relentlessly hypercritical. Weller hits the bull's-eye when he describes her as "rigid, self-righteous, vicious." Her oft-mentioned rigidity perhaps developed from her upbringing in a strict family, where her father did not "smoke, drink or run around" and never said a curse word or approved of playing cards. Possibly because she could never find anyone who could live up to her father's stature or because she had the misfortune of a bad marriage, Fonsia is drawn into conflict with men. She is desperate to form a connection with someone, but she is unwilling to admit her own flaws and manipulative tendencies or unable to overcome them. At first, Weller gets her to laugh, forget her troubles, and enjoy playing a game. There is a chance for her to have a comfortable relationship with a friend, perhaps even a romance, but she has a need to defeat Weller in their card games and probably in everything else, too. Even though Weller becomes verbally abusive, she keeps returning to the card table because she needs to win as much as he does, and she can give as good as she gets from him.

It is impossible to tell from her behavior whether her game winning is the result of skill or very good luck. Chances are that she is hustling Weller. She acts as if she is forgetful and silly, but she is a fast study with infallible strategy and a poker face. She behaves graciously when she wins, and each win buoys her depressed spirits, but in truth her manner of winning is creating another failed relationship. She cannot help herself, even though she surely knows where her manipulations are taking her. She also cannot forgive herself for driving away her husband and son, so she takes it out on Weller, thus pushing everyone away until she has no one left.

Weller Martin

A resident of the Bentley Home for Seniors, Weller Martin is a man who sees life in terms of winning and losing, and he is deeply enraged because life has apparently defeated him. However, he gets a chance to win at something when he meets Fonsia Dorsey, a new resident at the nursing home who, like him, still has her wits about her. Here, at last, is someone with whom he can have an intelligent conversation. Furthermore, Fonsia can play cards with him, and he will have a chance to compete and win, since he considers himself an expert at gin rummy.

Weller is a man of fierce spirit and will who has to have his own way and have the last say. He is also not above resorting to low blows and hurt-filled insults. Fortunately, his sharp, sarcastic, cutting nature often translates into humor. As Richard Scholem describes him in a newspaper review, Weller Martin is a "raging bull, a volcano of a man. He sweats, snorts and sneers." Weller blasphemes, but he is, in fact, a man of faith who talks to God as if God were a man on his shoulder. His conflict with God is that he wants his own will done, not God's will.

For Weller, the gin game is a way to keep his mind sharp and avoid falling into dementia, as have the rest of the people in the nursing home. Although he has heart problems and carries a cane, Weller is energetic, but he tends to express his energy in angry outbursts and foul language. He can be charming when he wants something, however, and he wants Fonsia to play cards with him. Unfortunately, his charm quickly wears off once he starts losing game after game to this inept amateur, and he uncontrollably takes out his frustrations on Fonsia. She tries to tell him that it is just a game and not worth getting upset about, but to him the game is not just a game. It is a continuation of his life's story.

Weller blames bad luck for his business failure. His compulsion to play cards stems from his belief that he would have been able to keep his business, he would have had better partners, and he would not have had a catastrophic illness, if only he had been luckier. He cannot admit to himself that he is a loser: he has to win at something, even just a game. He cannot accept that his skills and determination are not necessarily enough to be successful, so he looks for that intervening power—that evil twist of fate—that is keeping him from winning. Just as Weller touched success in business, only to have it escape his grasp, he touches upon an enjoyable relationship with Fonsia, only to have it slip through his card-holding fingers because of his own character flaws. He sees himself as a victim, but he does not understand that he is a victim of his own temperament.

THEMES

Religion

"Yes, Weller, God gave me the card." This line from *The Gin Game* is at the heart of Weller's dilemma. He is engaged in a struggle with God about his life. Weller exhibits a universal defiance

TOPICS FOR FURTHER STUDY

- *The Gin Game* is not set in any particular geographical location or any specific time period. Conduct a small group discussion about the other plays that you know that also have no specific location or time period or both. Compare this characteristic of the play with those that must be placed in a particular time or place and with those, such as *Romeo and Juliet*, that were given a particular time and place but that have been reset in other times and places.
- The setting of *The Gin Game* is a nursing home for the elderly. Visit a few nursing homes and record your impressions. Among those you visit, choose one that will likely have residents on welfare, like Weller and Fonsia, and one that is advertised as more of an upscale "retirement residence." Write an essay explaining the differences and similarities that you saw on your visits.
- There are seventeen hands of gin played in the course of *The Gin Game*. Do a mathematical study to figure the odds of Fonsia's winning every hand.
- *The Gin Game* is a rare two-person play. Hunt for one- and two-character plays and make a list of those that you find, noting any commercial success these plays have had. Explain in an essay why you think that ensemble plays are more common.

among humans: we want to live by our own will, not God's. So far, Weller thinks that God has dealt him a rotten hand in life, and he wants to try to make it right, at least symbolically, by winning hands of gin rummy. He tries to will himself to win a game, but only a magician can bend a spoon with his mind. Thus Weller asks, as so many others have asked throughout the ages, whether there is an unseen force or presence, a divine will, that determines what happens. Weller is trying to figure out whether Fonsia's winning is a matter of luck, personal skill, or divine intervention. When her winning streak becomes uncanny, Weller cannot help but suspect that a higher power is at work, and he starts talking to the man on his shoulder; that is, he starts arguing with God. Actually, every time Weller blasphemes, he is expressing his faith in God simultaneously with his perpetual argument with God.

It is likely that Fonsia is also sincerely pious. She is not putting on an act of gentility when she says that she is offended by Weller's habit of taking the Lord's name in vain. Her beliefs were strongly ingrained by her Methodist upbringing, yet she does not treat others with the openness and forgiveness of Christian teachings. She cannot overcome her own character failings to achieve the loving self-sacrifice idealized by her religion. Fonsia, too, fails to satisfactorily answer in her life the same question with which Weller contends: Are we predestined to live as we do, or can we rise above our natures?

The Baggage We Carry

Unresolved problems, bitterness, and destructive habits are the types of things that people carry with them throughout life, even though they do not necessarily need to. It is possible to solve one's problems, set aside bitterness, and change bad habits, but most people, like Fonsia and Weller, do not manage to do so. They tend to cling to their pain-generating habits until they can no longer break them. Consequently, they keep making the same mistakes, but they justify their failures by blaming someone or something else and doing it often enough to convince even themselves that that are innocent victims. Weller still wants to win, even when it is just a game. Fonsia still wants to exercise control, even though it will drive away another man in her life. Although *The Gin Game* has many humorous moments, it is a dark, depressing story about reliving the mistakes of the past.

Wasted Opportunity

The acute sadness of this play arises from the momentary hope that Fonsia and Weller will finally find some comfort with another person, only to have that hope brutally dashed by the two characters themselves. Their own personality weaknesses are too strong to overcome, so they end up destroying a relationship that they could have built into something mutually satisfying. They could have become close. Indeed, they could have been right for each other, if they could have gotten past their self-centeredness and self-hatred. *The Gin Game* shows how easy and how tragic it is to let one's own self-serving habits get in the way of something good. Weller and Fonsia are too caught up in their personal demons to reach out to each other, and thus they perpetuate the loneliness that they have always brought upon themselves.

The Power Struggle between Men and Women

Coburn originally imagined the story of *The Gin Game* as simply a conflict between a man and a woman. It became more than that, but the core of the plot remains the competition to control the relationship. Weller wants to be a winner, at least in cards if he was not in life. He wants his skills to count for something, at least in cards if not in his business success. Fonsia wants to control the relationship, just as she tried to do with her husband and her son. Winning puts her in control and allows her to defeat a male partner in cards, even if she did not satisfactorily defeat her husband or son in her relationships with them. Both Weller and Fonsia have had lifelong problems with the opposite sex, so there is an automatic uneasiness between them that they cannot overcome.

In dramatic terms, they are perfect foils for each other, in that Weller is boisterous while Fonsia is reserved. But they are much the same when it comes to strong personalities and intense anger at fate. Both are experiencing the bitter fruits of a life of competition. They are attracted by what eventually drives them apart: a battle of wits. It is possible that Weller is a lot like Fonsia's former husband, and people tend to gravitate to what they know. This is true even when the situations are bad, as often happens with the spouses of alcoholics and abusers. It is also possible that Fonsia is rebelling against a culture that denies her intelligence and abilities and gives control of her life to the men around her. In her own subversive way, she will beat the men at their own games. She will divorce her husband and support herself, she will give her house to the church instead of to her son, and she will crush Weller in a game in which he thinks he is an expert.

The Psychological and Experiential Aspects of Old Age

The Gin Game is peppered with jokes about old age, but the psychological and physical dissipation that often comes with advanced age is no laughing matter. Hopes and goals seem pointless, because the elderly person is running out of time. Loneliness becomes a serious problem, especially for people such as Fonsia and Weller, who have been abandoned by their families in a nursing home. They are experiencing changes in their lives at a time when they are probably least tolerant of change and are subjected to further detachment from familiarity by having to live in a public facility instead of their own homes. Fonsia's diabetes and Weller's heart condition compromise their freedom, and they know there is no escape other than death.

There is a sense of isolation that is aggravated by the differences in mental and physical condition between Weller and Fonsia and the rest of the residents of the home. Although they each have health issues, they are not incapacitated in any debilitating sense. They both still have sharp mental capabilities, and that is a large part of their initial attraction to each other—they are almost unique in this nursing home, because practically everyone else is bedridden or has some form of dementia. This situation is difficult for them, as they try to maintain their dignity and sanity in, as Weller describes it, "a warehouse for the intellectually and emotionally dead." This situation is also the reason why they are the only two who ever come out on the porch. Both are angry about being on welfare and forced to live in a shabby nursing home, which reflects on the lack of accomplishments in their lives. They are embarrassed, even humiliated, by their circumstances, and they take out these feelings on each other.

STYLE

Two-Person Play

A two-person play demands special treatment to be successful. Obviously, it is difficult for only two people to hold an audience's attention for ninety minutes. To do so, the actors have to captivate the audience with rich dialogue and the sheer strength of the characters' personalities. The audience has to care about what is happening between the two people onstage. Physical actions, such as Weller's overturning of the table, and sight gags, such as Fonsia's forgetting the card stuck between her lips, help keep the audience busy watching every gesture as well as hanging on every word. In such a concentrated format, every little action carries a lot of weight.

Movements around the stage relieve the tedium, but they must be motivated, of course, by what is going on. Random movements for the sake of breaking up the scene do not fool the audience. In *The Gin Game*, the positions of Weller and Fonsia at the card table represent body language that signals the mood and becomes part of the dialogue as far as the audience is concerned. The movements can also be considered a type of choreography in a tango between these two people, as they circle each other, connect, detach, and then dance again. The set decoration, furniture, and props all take on an importance that is exaggerated compared with plays with a larger cast. In like manner, sound effects, such as the thunderstorm, actually play a part in the story; for example, the sounds of a visiting choir or the television in the background are worked into the dialogue as examples of activities at the home. Considering the elements required to make a two-person play successful, it is no wonder that this type of drama is quite rare.

A Card Game as a Structural Device

The gin game is the engine of the play. In the course of seventeen hands of gin, the layers of protection that the two characters have built around their memories and emotions are slowly peeled away to reveal their true personalities, complexities, vulnerabilities, and circumstances. Playing a game against each other causes Weller and Fonsia to drop their charming facades and expose their controlling and competitive natures. Their revealed secrets become weapons used against each other. Each hand has a different rhythm, which reflects the emotional interaction of the characters; each hand demonstrates an ebbing and renewing of tension. Fonsia's repetitive, but differentiated declaration of "Gin!" provides a moment of comedy while acting as a catalyst to Weller's anger.

The game serves as a metaphor for life in that there is an indeterminate amount of luck and skill involved in the game, just as there seems to be a certain amount of good or bad luck that offsets a person's life skills. Weller was a skilled businessman but blames his failure on the bad luck of having dishonest partners. He is also a skilled gin rummy player but cannot account for Fonsia's winning streak against him. His losses at cards are painful reminders of the seemingly unlucky events in his business career, so his bitterness and anger are aimed at Fonsia. For both of them, the game transforms into something larger than just a game.

Tragedy Mixed with Comedy

One reason for the success of *The Gin Game* is its skillful blend of light and dark. Even though Coburn's intent was to write a tragedy, he gave his characters a sharp wit that actors have been able to turn into comic moments, which every good script needs, to ease the tension. The jokes about aging are universal. (There is "no hotter topic of conversation" than funerals around the home.) However, the comedy is achieved as much visually as verbally, through facial expressions and other body language. The humor is more prevalent in the first act, and the hostility is more present in the second act—as one would expect as the tension of the conflict rises. Nonetheless, there are hints of the potential for conflict in the first act that are manifested, yet tempered by humor, in the second act. Ironically, some of the humor arises from how ludicrously people can behave when they allow their competitiveness to go to extremes.

HISTORICAL CONTEXT

The 1970s

The Gin Game was written mostly in 1976, the heart of the decade. In the 1970s, the various social movements of the turbulent 1960s, such as the Civil Rights movement and the sexual revolution, reached fruition. For example, women were admitted to the various military academies for the first time. Despite the myth that nothing much happened in the 1970s, it was a historically important time in which a vice president and a president of the United States resigned and this country found itself with a president, Gerald Ford, who had not been elected to the office. He had been appointed to the vice presidency when Spiro Agnew resigned because of scandals and then succeeded the Republican president Richard Nixon. Nixon had resigned over the Watergate scandal, a break-in at the headquarters of the Democratic National Committee during his reelection campaign in 1972 that was found to have been the work of people linked to Nixon's campaign. At the same time, an economic crisis hit the

COMPARE & CONTRAST

- **Mid-1970s:** In the mid-1970s, nursing home scandals break out across the country, demonstrating provider fraud and poor care, even though legislation was enacted several times to protect nursing home residents since the first major abuses of regulations were revealed in the 1960s.

  Today: To protect nursing home residents from elder abuse and safeguard against Medicare and Medicaid and other fraud, numerous advocacy groups have been established, further federal and state legislation has been enacted, and litigation has increased dramatically on behalf of residents and their families.

- **Mid-1970s:** Approximately twenty-five million people are sixty-five years of age or older, and life expectancy is about sixty-seven years for men and nearly seventy-five years for women.

  Today: Approximately thirty-eight million people are sixty-five years of age or older, and life expectancy is about seventy-five years of age for men and eighty years for women.

- **Mid-1970s:** People are retiring between the ages of sixty-two and sixty-five, with the expectation of living, on average, only another five to ten years after retirement.

  Today: The retirement age is being increased to sixty-seven, and it is common for people to live relatively healthy lives into their eighties and even nineties.

- **Mid-1970s:** Few people have heard of the age-related disease called Alzheimer's, even though it was identified in 1906, because it is difficult to diagnose and sometimes is confused with dementia and even short-term memory loss, which is considered more or less a normal part of aging.

  Today: With Americans living to an older age, there has been a dramatic increase in the incidence of and research into the specific dementia that is now commonly identified as Alzheimer's disease and is known to be related to a characteristic clumping of plaques and tangles in the brain.

United States, and there was a shortage of gasoline. In 1976, Ford was defeated by Jimmy Carter, whose presidency was mired in the Iran hostage crisis in 1979–1980, leading to his defeat by Ronald Reagan.

In world affairs, the war in Vietnam ended, and the United States withdrew from that country completely in 1975. The next year, North Vietnam and South Vietnam reunited to become the Socialist Republic of Vietnam. Relations between the United States and the Soviet Union, as well as China, improved. Former colonial powers continued to grant independence to the last of their colonies, and Spain once again became a democracy on the death of Francisco Franco, who had ruled the country for forty years. However, the revolution in Iran and the invasion of Afghanistan by the Soviet Union in 1979 began a period of aggressive, militant Muslim fundamentalism that has continued into the twenty-first century.

Science and technology made great strides in the 1970s, with continued lunar and interplanetary, and even interstellar, space missions. Element 107, bohrium, was discovered, and the CAT scanner was invented. While personal computers were still not universally available, pocket calculators replaced slide rules, video game arcades became popular, touch-tone phones began to replace rotary models, and digital clocks became available. Microsoft was founded in 1975, and the Apple II computer was released in 1976. The first Earth Day was held in 1970, and the environmental movement continued to grow throughout the decade.

Meanwhile, at the movies, blockbusters such as *Star Wars*, *Superman*, *Jaws*, and *Rocky* dominated.

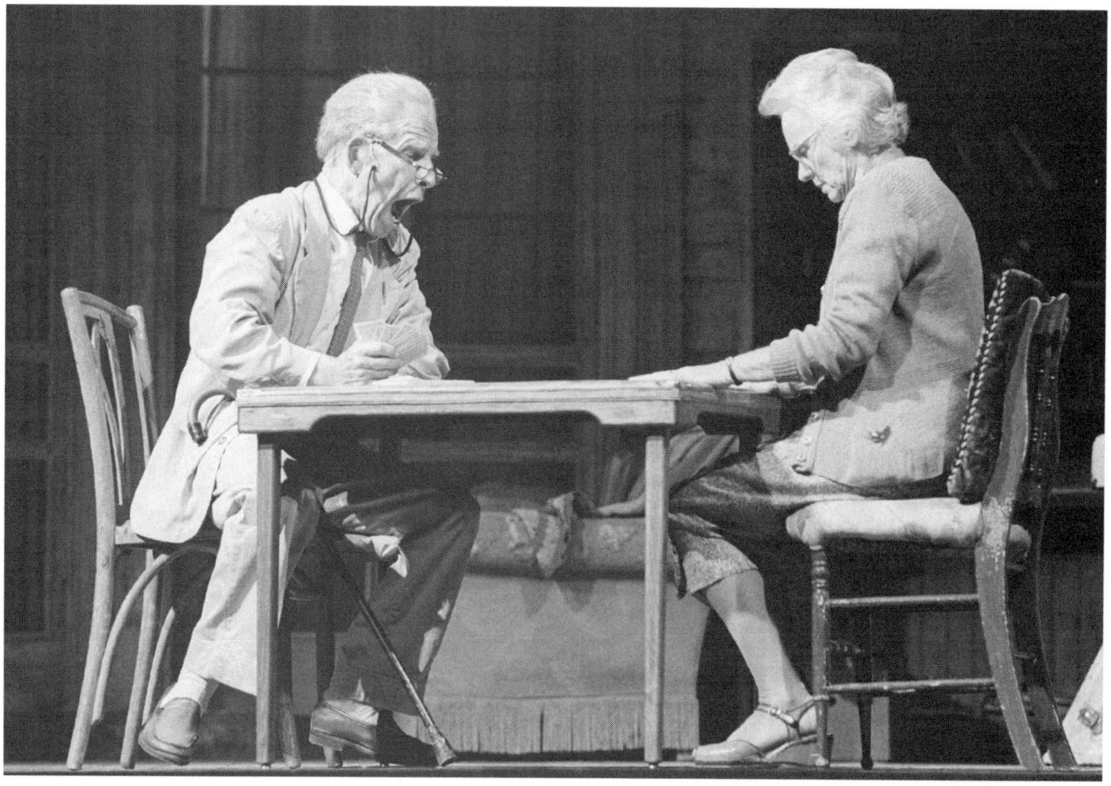

Hume Cronyn and Jessica Tandy in a 1979 production of The Gin Game © Donald Cooper/Photostage. Reproduced by permission

In music, the Beatles broke up, and Elvis passed away; rock music divided into genres, such as heavy metal and soft rock, and punk rock and disco music became the rage. On television *Saturday Night Live* premiered, and nostalgic shows such as *Happy Days* filled the channels. In sports, the tennis player Arthur Ashe in 1975 became the first black man to win at Wimbledon. Nadia Comaneci was the first Olympic athlete to garner a perfect score in gymnastics, which she received seven times at the 1976 Summer Olympics. Dorothy Hamill won the gold medal in ice skating that year.

Although the 1970s were an active time, these years were a transition period between the turbulent 1960s, which saw assassinations, demonstrations, and riots, and the rise of conservatism in the 1980s, in the wake of the Republican Ronald Reagan's election to the presidency. During the 1970s, the American people were sorting out what had happened in the 1960s, reevaluating gender roles, and attempting to overcome political and economic upheaval to come together again as a nation.

CRITICAL OVERVIEW

There could be no higher praise than to win the Pulitzer Prize for Drama, which Coburn did for *The Gin Game* in 1978. Before that award, though, the play had caught the attention and admiration of some very important people in the world of theater. When Hume Cronyn, one of the most respected stage actors of the twentieth century, read the play, he immediately wanted to take it to Broadway. The famed director Mike Nichols agreed to direct it within hours of hearing about the play, and it went on to garner a Tony nomination. When Dick Van Dyke saw the play on Broadway, he decided that he and Mary Tyler Moore had to perform it together someday; in 2003, more than twenty-five years after the play premiered, the two performed the roles of Weller and Fonsia in a PBS television production of the play.

Thomas Luddy, in a review published in *Library Journal*, remarks that "the play's brilliance lies in its simplicity and economy." He goes on to say that Coburn etches the issues of aging, loneliness, and the need for meaningful activity "clearly and devastatingly in terms that are also witty and entertaining," and declares that *The Gin Game* "will become one of the great classics of the American theater." Tony Curulla, writing for the Syracuse *Post-Standard*, echoes these sentiments with a description of the play as having "taut writing that delivers more than it promises" and a "fast-paced, smart dialogue."

A reviewer for the *Buffalo News*, Terry Doran, says: "You wouldn't imagine so much laughter could be squeezed from one little word. The word is 'gin.'" This critic comments that there is not much more to the play than Weller's dilemma of balancing his desire to play cards with Fonsia against his rage at always losing to her. On the other hand, Doran admires the way "Coburn restricts the confessionals." He comments further that "they illuminate but do not weigh down his play. The past, then, is no more than a dollop of sadness and perspective in the present." Peter Marks of the *New York Times* also declares *The Gin Game* to be "virtually plotless." In contrast, a theater critic for the *St. Petersburg Times*, Joy Davis-Platt, finds *The Gin Game* to be a "very rich story" because there is "so much drama and subtlety" within the play.

Terry Doran considers *The Gin Game* to be "a very funny play." While agreeing that the dialogue evokes laughter from the audience, Kathleen Allen, a critic for the *Arizona Daily Star*, finds *The Gin Game* "a disturbing play," because the two characters do not learn how to change their destructive behaviors and will likely die bitter and alone. In a review for the *Austin American-Statesman*, Jamie Smith Cantara likewise says that the play is "funny, yet bleak."

Among those who have given *The Gin Game* a negative review is Greg Evans, in an article for the venerable theater newspaper *Variety* on the occasion of the revival of the play in 1997. He wondered how the play had deserved a Pulitzer, because it is "at best merely decent," and he called *The Gin Game* a formulaic "one-concept play." Some critics do not find jokes about aging and the aged to be funny, nor can they tolerate the lack of a happy ending. In fact, some viewers feel that there is no ending at all. Nonetheless, *The Gin Game* continued to be a favorite of regional theaters and was still being produced around the world into the twenty-first century. Whatever its flaws may be, the play deserves its praise, because it has stood the test of time.

CRITICISM

Lois Kerschen

Kerschen is a school district administrator and freelance writer. In this essay, she suggests that the card game is a metaphor for life and that the nursing home is a metaphor for hell.

Productions of Coburn's play *The Gin Game* have been staged in numerous countries and languages on a continuous basis since its debut on Broadway. While it may seem an oddity that a two-person play could have any depth to it, *The Gin Game* has proved that a play about a man and a woman can be as rich and complex as the relationships they portray.

Billed as a tragicomedy, *The Gin Game* focuses on an elderly man and woman living in a shabby nursing home. They chat as they play a seemingly innocuous card game, but as Polly Warfield notes in a review for *Back Stage West*, the deck of cards "is *The Gin Game*'s deus ex machina and an instrument of destruction. The machinery is set in motion; it proceeds inexorably, inevitably as Greek tragedy, to a shattering conclusion." On the surface, the play is an exploration of aging and loneliness, but on a deeper level, Warfield says, it exposes "the compulsive way we sabotage ourselves" and the existence of our own personal version of hell. Life and its inevitable conclusion, it seems, are exactly what we make of them.

Weller Martin and Fonsia Dorsey are residents at Bentley, a run-down, low-rent nursing home. They meet on the sunporch, a room that collects all that is no longer useful—damaged wheelchairs, broken pianos, dead plants, and old people. Initially, Weller and Fonsia establish a welcome friendship. They dislike the other residents, who are either catatonic or complain too much, and neither of them ever has any visitors on Visitors' Day. As Weller tells Fonsia, "There's nobody to have a decent conversation with around here anyway. You're the only one I talk to." Despite living in a home full of people, they are still two lonely souls in search of companionship, and they appear to find that in each other.

This discovery of the other breeds hope, as evidenced by their change in appearance upon their second meeting. In act 1, scene 1, Weller is wearing "terry-cloth slippers, khaki pants, a pajama top and an old brown wool bathrobe," while Fonsia enters clad in "faded pink slippers, an old housecoat,

WHAT DO I READ NEXT?

- Like *The Gin Game*, *Glengarry Glen Ross* (1984), David Mamet's play about cold and calculating real estate salesmen, depicts the destructive effects of competitiveness with bitter and sarcastic humor.
- Weller Martin in *The Gin Game* is often compared to Willie Loman in *Death of a Salesman* (1948), a play by Arthur Miller. Both men are belligerent losers who blame other people for their failures.
- Lanford Wilson's play *Talley's Folley* (1979), like *The Gin Game*, involves a conflict between a man and a woman, but here prejudice provides the complication and a romance is at stake.
- *Nobody's Home: Candid Reflections of a Nursing Home Aide* (2004), by Thomas Edward Gass, reports on the author's experience of working in a nursing home as a frontline caregiver and as the social services director. His stories run the gamut of emotions, and he makes suggestions about how to preserve the dignity of the patients and make a long-term-care facility a better place to live and work.

and a cardigan sweater." However, in act 1, scene 2, Weller wears "a jacket and tie, khaki pants and loafers," and Fonsia "looks like a different woman . . . [in] a print dress, a rose-colored cardigan, and open-toed sandals." This new concern for fashion suggests anticipation, effort, and the possibility that life for them may not be over, as was previously assumed. Yet as the games of gin continue, attraction turns to competition. Slowly the vulnerabilities of both players are revealed, but these confidences do not lead to intimacy and comfort. Rather, they incite a fallback to old patterns of bitter, biting antagonisms. Just as in their card game, Weller and Fonsia are locked into roles from which they cannot, or will not, break free. Their behaviors doom them to their loneliness and decay, and the true tragedy is that, ultimately, they do it all to themselves.

It is the theme of self-sabotage that provides *The Gin Game* with layers of meaning beyond a simple examination of the complexities "of being old, poor, helpless, and rejected," as Warfield describes the pair. Weller wants to believe that he is "one of the best damn Gin players you'll ever see," but he never wins. He cannot even win when he is playing solitaire. He throws himself into horrific rages and yells at Fonsia for his losses, but he is the dealer. He is the one giving Fonsia every card she needs and ruining his own chances of winning. He wants victory, and one senses that he needs victory to redeem himself, but he does nothing but deal himself the losing hand. Still, Weller in no way takes responsibility; to him, it is all just bad luck—just as it was bad luck that he was "thrown out" of his own business or that his former wife received custody of the children and he lost touch with them. Bad luck is his excuse for all his misfortunes in life, not just in gin. As Fonsia says, "You have to be the victim of bad luck, don't you, Weller. . . . Because if it wasn't bad luck, it'd have to be something else, wouldn't it?" Weller's uncontrollable temper comes from the inner knowledge that he has created his own miserable situation, but his refusal to outwardly acknowledge his complicity allows the cycle of self-destruction to continue. He wants to win, but until he admits that he is to blame for his losses in life, he never will.

Fonsia, who initially appears to be delicate and deserving of sympathy, is really just as self-destructive as Weller. She has pushed away everyone in her family: she kicked out and divorced her husband, disowned her son (and, along with him, her two grandsons), and has not seen her sister in fifteen years (though the reason is not revealed). Fonsia is alone and on welfare, because the people she is supposed to love and who are supposed to

"IT IS CERTAINLY NOT A STRETCH TO THINK OF A DILAPIDATED OLD-AGE HOME AS A METAPHOR FOR HELL, AND THIS SEEMS TO BE EXACTLY WHERE WELLER AND FONSIA HAVE EXILED THEMSELVES."

love her are no longer allowed in her life. Then she is faced with an opportunity to establish a connection with Weller, and, like Weller, she compulsively destroys any chance to redeem herself. In the guise of a gracious, apologetic winner, she torments and criticizes Weller and eventually, inevitably, drives him away, just like every other man in her life. Also like Weller, it is everyone else's fault but her own: "When it comes to men, I've been very unlucky." Weller calls her on it, saying, "It had to be bad luck, because if it wasn't bad luck, it would've had to been the fact that maybe it was you!" He suggests that Fonsia is "rigid, self-righteous, vicious." Fonsia will never take responsibility for her own actions and thus is doomed to making the same mistakes over and over. So she is left at the end of the play, sitting by herself on the glider, saying, "Oh, no."

Weller and Fonsia's circular predicament lands them in a hell of their own making, where they are forced to examine their impoverished lives. The religious overtones in *The Gin Game* are abundant and, indeed, help to further explain the pair's situation. According to Fonsia, her "old time Methodist" father never cursed and "would never have played cards. He didn't smoke, drink or run around either." By those standards, Weller and Fonsia are both "hopeless sinner[s]," since they curse, take the Lord's name in vain, and play gin and Weller chews on an unlit cigar. They consistently use words like "[g——d——]it," "Jesus Christ," "for Christsake," and "Lord." Certainly neither one of them has treated the people in their lives with kindness or generosity. The sunporch is definitely no heaven; in fact, it seems as if heaven is taunting them from a distance. The Grace Avenue Methodist Church Choir sings offstage as Weller loses another game to Fonsia. Later, a TV evangelist can be heard in the next room, and Weller "pauses for a moment to listen. Disgusted, he 'gives the finger' to the TV." Three of the four scenes take place on a Sunday—the Sabbath as well as Visitors' Day, when Weller and Fonsia's self-imposed isolation is most acute. Thunder roars, lightning flashes, and another choir is suddenly heard offstage just as Weller and Fonsia play their last tragic hand. It is certainly not a stretch to think of a dilapidated old-age home as a metaphor for hell, and this seems to be exactly where Weller and Fonsia have exiled themselves.

In fact, even the cards in the deck seem to play by rules outside the laws of physics. Fonsia, beyond all probability, wins every game. Perhaps, as Warfield suggests, "the malevolent gods of mischief have had a hand in dealing these cards." Or, as Weller claims, it is "Divine Intervention." He asks, "God gave you that card, didn't he?" Perhaps the definition of hell for Weller and Fonsia is that all the self-sabotaging they have engaged in over the years has now trapped them in a place where they can no longer do anything except engage in self-sabotage. Thus they will never be able to leave and never have access to anything better. They are stuck in hell, and though they can hear heaven in the distance, they can never reach it. Weller and Fonsia began the gin game looking for comfort and companionship, but, ultimately, there will never be comfort, companionship, or visitors in hell.

The Gin Game not only speaks to the human condition, human frailty, and the inevitable aging process we all face but also acts as a metaphor for the lives (and possibly afterlives) we choose for ourselves and the fate we must face at the end. Just like two souls standing in front of Saint Peter, Weller and Fonsia are held accountable for their actions, which they must admit to themselves. The tragedy is not simply where they end up but the fact that it could have been different. If only Weller had kept in touch with his children or Fonsia had not been so vindictive, they could have lived out their golden years with loving relatives instead of trapped in a home full of faceless strangers. Weller and Fonsia, like the original sinners Adam and Eve, must suffer the consequences of their own actions and are destined to spend the rest of their days in exile.

Source: Lois Kerschen, Critical Essay on *The Gin Game*, in *Drama for Students*, Thomson Gale, 2006.

Scott Trudell

Trudell is a doctoral student of English literature at Rutgers University. In the following essay, he discusses Weller's inner turmoil and its sources, arguing that Coburn designs the play so that audiences are forced to experience this feeling themselves.

This essay refers to the Drama Book Specialists version of the play, while the preceding entry refers to the Samuel French version. Certain differences may be apparent.

The fascinating part of *The Gin Game* is that it creates such extraordinary tension despite its complete lack of plot action. The play cannot be classified as a straightforward comedy, because of this uncomfortable, affronting tension, all of which comes from the character of Weller. This mystifying, unstable, violent, cynical, and sexist old man intrigues and amuses audiences enough that they are able to endure a lengthy exposure to his discomforting personality. In fact, Coburn designs his play as a psychological character study in which the anger, frustration, hopelessness, and despair inside Weller extends to Fonsia and the audience as well.

The crux or mystery of the play is the cause of Weller's final fit of "madness," as it is described in the play's final stage directions. Weller voices his various gripes and alludes to his life's failures and frustrations throughout the play, but these descriptions do not add up to a clear idea of what it is that haunts Weller and ultimately causes him to go mad. His specific complaints range from the patronizing nursing home staff, to his family's desertion of him, to the other elderly people in the nursing home, to his old business partners who took his money, and to the welfare system. More broadly, he is troubled by the way that American culture treats the elderly, leaving them to die in inadequate facilities without even bothering to visit them.

Weller also seems to have a fear of death and a sense that life is pointless. He feels that he is wasting his life playing gin, but (as Fonsia points out) he has played gin his entire life. Fonsia says that this should make him think that gin is not a way of "frittering [his] life away," but it would stand to reason that the gin playing throughout his life was, in fact, a purposeless waste of time. Because gin playing is the only thing that Weller does anymore, the only thing he believes he is good at, and a metaphor for all of life's events to which he dedicated himself, this suggests that his entire life has been wasted. The paralysis Weller describes in act 1, scene 2, in which he says, "This feeling of sheer terror came over me," further suggests that he is petrified both of dying and of the idea that he has led a paralyzed, useless, and pointless existence that is about to come to an end.

Hume Cronyn in a 1979 production of The Gin Game © Donald Cooper/Photostage. Reproduced by permission

The only thing that scares Weller more than pointlessness and death is the idea that he may be personally responsible for all of it because of his own faults and bad judgment, as opposed to being a victim of bad luck. In fact, this is the central realization that Weller reaches during the play because of his interaction with Fonsia. Fonsia is no weakling, willing to submit to Weller's aggressive baiting, although he does continually manage to lure her into spending more time with him. She rejoins his aggression with perceptive and biting comments (as well as adept card playing) that enrage Weller and force him to come to terms with his own failures. When she reaches her most frustrated and aggressive point, telling Weller, "Because if it wasn't bad luck, it'd have to be something else, wouldn't it?," Fonsia severely shakes his confidence and his sense of self-worth.

On the surface, therefore, Fonsia causes Weller to go mad. Coburn suggests that this is the case in a number of places, including when Fonsia tells Weller that "Fons," an abbreviation of her name, "means 'source' in Latin." The gin game itself, which is the only rising dramatic action of the play, also suggests that Fonsia represents the cause of

"BY ARRANGING THE STRUCTURE OF THE PLAY SO THAT THE SPECTATORS FEEL THAT THEY ARE IN FONSIA'S POSITION, THE PLAYWRIGHT IS ABLE TO IMPLY THAT THE AUDIENCE ITSELF (AND, BY EXTENSION, THE PUBLIC AT LARGE) IS THE REAL SOURCE AND ROOT OF WELLER'S MADNESS."

Weller's misfortunes. This is why Weller becomes so angry at Fonsia, why he sincerely believes that divine intervention gives her the right cards, and why he is so thoroughly humiliated and infuriated by the game. However, Coburn is very careful about how he places Fonsia in the position of cause and revealer of Weller's madness. By arranging the structure of the play so that the spectators feel that they are in Fonsia's position, the playwright is able to imply that the audience itself (and, by extension, the public at large) is the real source and root of Weller's madness.

Coburn develops this agenda, first, by ensuring that the spectator experiences Weller's character from a point of view that is much like that of Fonsia's. Like Fonsia, the audience always comes upon him while he is alone and waiting on the sunporch, and, also like Fonsia, they are initially charmed by his edgy and incisive wit. As Weller begins the process of uncovering the uncomfortable and potentially threatening aspects of his personality, however, the audience and Fonsia both grow wary of being near him. Because it has only two characters and because there is no live action to distract the audience from Weller's imposing psychological presence, the play steadily builds its sense of fear and discomfort until the climax at the end of act 1, when Weller swears and furiously throws over the card table.

Although audience members may be curious about Weller or interested to see what happens to him, they feel suspicious or frightened of him after this happens. Weller has invaded their space on intimate terms, offending them, just as he has violated Fonsia's personal space and her sense of security. Like Fonsia, the audience may prefer to "be alone for a while," or withdraw from their intimacy with and sympathy for Weller's character. It is because Coburn understands this probable reaction (in fact, he carefully tries to produce it) that he places Fonsia in the audience at the beginning of the second act. This dramatic device accomplishes two important goals. First, it reminds the audience that they are in Fonsia's position: calm and reasonable observers of Weller who may seem reluctant to engage with him but are nevertheless interested in his character. Perhaps more important, however, it serves to coax the audience back into their intimacy with Weller. Weller appeals directly to them, appeases them, and draws them back into conversation and card playing, causing them to move the memory of his bout of violence to the back of their minds.

It is at this point that Weller's great inner despair begins to spread to Fonsia. Weller purposefully allows this to happen (because of his resentment of Fonsia) by prying into the reason that no one visits her on Sundays. Fonsia then alerts the audience to the fact that Weller is getting to her by suddenly exclaiming "Transferred!!!," presumably because she never could remember how to spell it but, more important, because Coburn wishes to suggest that there is a process of transference going on in the drama. Weller proceeds to thoroughly wear out, offend, threaten, and attack Fonsia as part of his defensive and bitter response to how she makes him feel. By the middle of act 3, he has uncovered the fact that Fonsia's son lives in the same city, yet never visits her. By the end of the play he has forced her to come to terms with the fact that she has some of the same qualities of bad judgment that he does, shattering her sense of security.

Because the audience feels that they are in the same position as Fonsia (again, she even sat in the audience to emphasize her proximity to them), they are also alternatively courted and frightened by Weller, and they are susceptible to his prying questions. Coburn has duped the audience into playing a sort of gin game with the play in which, like Fonsia, they submit to Weller's manipulations and engage with him because they are curious about him and feel a certain amount of sympathy for him. The play's humor is key to the success of this agenda; the audience is willing to accommodate Weller's sarcastic streaks because he is a funny old man and humor is an effective tool at diffusing uncomfortable moments. The result is a wide susceptibility in the audience that allows Coburn to make them feel shocked and afraid when Weller reaches his final explosion.

This dramatic device is effective, because Weller makes the audience feel that they are somehow implicated in the causes of his anger and terror. Weller is talented at turning around his own discomfort by becoming aggressive, which makes Fonsia feel insecure and also puts the spectators on edge. His accusations sometimes hit the mark (including his judgment about Fonsia's son), but he also throws out wild questions, such as "DIDN'T GOD GIVE YOU THAT CARD???" Such accusatory yelling goes beyond Fonsia and implicates the audience, making them feel uncomfortable and somehow party to Weller's anguish. Coburn's design is to stir up uncomfortable feelings and guilt in the audience, attacking their self-worth. The most obvious form of guilt they might feel after Weller's upsetting outbursts is over how they have treated elderly people in their own lives.

Capitalizing on the prevailing emotions of Fonsia's weariness and shock and extending them to create a sense of guilt in the audience, Coburn infects the audience with the emotions of Weller's frightening outbursts. His play is designed to manufacture deep-seated feelings of anger and terror and then force the spectator to experience them in as intimate a setting as possible. This is not just to force a reaction in the audience or to scare them; it is to demonstrate the vigorous emotion that is possible in elderly people when they have been shunned and dismissed from society. As well as a kind of emotional exploration, Coburn's play is an existential message about the futility of life, a reminder of the terrifying approach of death, and a forceful urge for audiences to appreciate the passion and vigor of the elderly and reconsider shunting them away to poorly maintained, seldom-visited nursing homes.

Source: Scott Trudell, Critical Essay on *The Gin Game,* in *Drama for Students*, Thomson Gale, 2006.

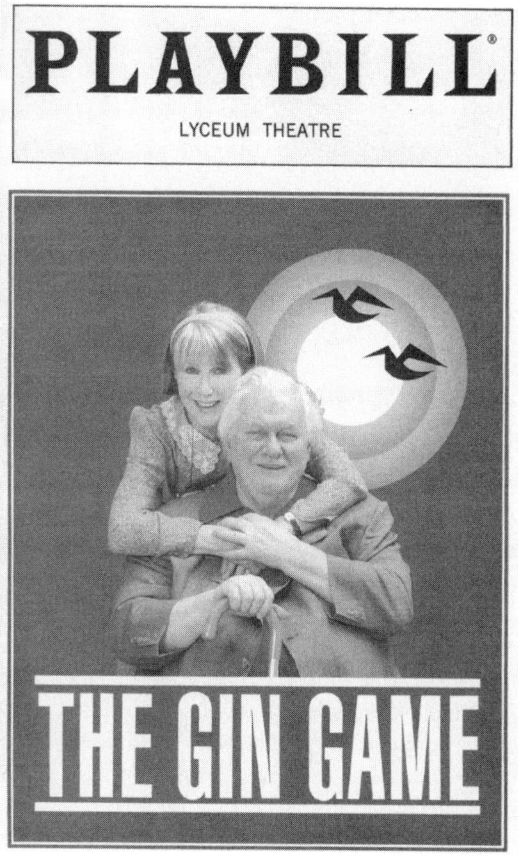

Playbill from a production of The Gin Game *at the Lyceum Theatre* Performing Arts Books, NYC. PLAYBILL ® is a registered trademark of Playbill Incorporated, N.Y.C. All rights reserved. Reproduced by permission

Neil Heims

Heims is a writer and teacher living in Paris. In this essay, he examines those aspects of The Gin Game *that make it a tragedy.*

When used in everyday speech, the word *tragedy* refers to a grave and unexpected misfortune with terrible consequences. When used in relation to drama, *tragedy* signifies a play that chronicles such a misfortune and its consequences. Tragedies can end in death or in the exclusion of the person whom the tragedy befalls from membership in the common society. But there is a particular characteristic of a tragic dramatic figure that makes her or him different from a character in a play who merely suffers misfortune or even death. While it is tragic when a character in real life is, for example, attacked and killed on the street or maimed in an automobile accident or blown up in war or the victim of a terrible loss, such events in a play, by definition and despite their horrible or heartbreaking nature, are not tragic.

For a play to be called a tragedy, the character who is the victim of misfortune and catastrophe must be, in the core of his or her being, the very agent of the terrible event. Tragedy inextricably mingles individual responsibility and fate. The tragedy reveals and results from a flaw in character that causes the tragedy. A tragic character is not an evil person, only fatally flawed. To be a tragic character, the character must have lived in ignorance

"MEETING EACH OTHER GIVES FONSIA AND WELLER THEIR LAST CHANCE TO REDEEM THEIR LIVES AND REVERSE THEIR DESTINIES, BUT SO STRONGLY ARE THEIR CHARACTERS THEIR DESTINIES THAT THE CHANCE FOR THAT REDEMPTION IS THWARTED."

of the flaw in his or her nature or character, be blind to it, and be proudly proceeding as if everything were fine. Nevertheless, he or she, innocently, must set the tragic event in motion. The blindness that hurtles the character toward disaster, not the terrible occurrence itself, is at the heart of tragedy. The terrible occurrence paradoxically provides a moment of enlightenment, of insight and revelation. It reveals truth: the existence of the flaw that the tragic character has resisted seeing. The character remains helpless in the face of the tragedy but becomes painfully enlightened.

In one of the most famous tragedies, that of Oedipus, as presented in *Oedipus the King* by Sophocles, first performed around 426 B.C.E. in Greece, Oedipus, the ruler of Thebes, is unaware of his own guilt as he sets out to find the man responsible for a plague that is devastating Thebes. The man he is searching for, whose crime is that he has murdered his father and become the husband of his mother, turns out to be Oedipus himself. In Shakespeare's *Romeo and Juliet*, written around 1595, the tragic aspect of the plot is not that the lovers die but that the cause of their death is the self-centeredness of their love and the hastiness of their actions. Similarly, in Shakespeare's *King Lear* (ca. 1605), the tragedy is not Lear's death and his daughter Cordelia's death but the fact that his own blind willfulness brings about their deaths.

The complex nature of tragedy is the result of the destruction and enlightenment simultaneously unleashed by the tragic event. Consequently, in tragedy there is an element of purgation both for the protagonist and for the audience. The reversal of fortune brings the hero down but also reveals something fundamental about the hero and humankind to the character and to the spectators. The character's blindness can also be the source of the audience's insight, and, if they pay attention to the story of the tragedy, it is less likely that they will have to undergo the experience that the tragic character has suffered. Thus, the tragic character becomes a kind of sacred sacrifice. Considered as a dramatic form, tragedy is not just an event but a process, a painful ritual with transformative power.

Tragedy is usually thought of as belonging to Greek or Shakespearean theater. It is typically associated with great, powerful, and noble figures—rulers and heroes—not with common men and women. One of the tasks that modern playwrights, like Arthur Miller in *Death of a Salesman* (1949), have set themselves is to write tragedies that involve common, ordinary people. These modern plays are about "little" people, whose lives affect few but themselves and their immediate circle, rather than leaders whose falls have wide effects. In *The Gin Game*, Coburn has attempted to write such a tragedy. Set not against a grand background involving great or even monumental figures, whose lives and deaths affect multitudes, *The Gin Game* is set in an old-age home and involves two very ordinary old people who reside there.

In a tragedy, the process of tragic revelation begins without the tragic protagonist's even knowing it—since the protagonist is figuratively blind. In *The Gin Game*, it starts with a commonplace act. Weller Martin asks Fonsia Dorsey, whom he has just met on the porch of the home for the aged where they both reside, whether she plays cards. As *The Gin Game* opens, he has been sitting there alone, playing solitaire. She comes from inside the house, obviously disturbed and crying. She excuses herself, saying "I didn't think anybody was out here." In turn, he apologizes and then asks if she is not "new here," probably assuming that is the reason for her tears and delicately referring to her sadness without intrusively inquiring. They begin to talk about their illnesses and complain about nursing homes. After they have exhausted the subject, he invites her to play gin with him. The cards are already on the table. She confesses that she has not played in years but says that she had played quite a bit in her youth, even though her parents, "old time Methodists," would have disapproved, had they known.

Once they begin to play, it becomes clear that the card game is more than a card game. Within the format of the card game, Weller and Fonsia form a relationship that mirrors and repeats all their past relationships and brings to the surface their essential personalities and the aspects of themselves that they have tried to keep hidden, even from themselves, and which they have denied existed. They encounter themselves and each other. Weller seems in control but is ineffective. He has to beg Fonsia to play, as if he were a lover seeking affection, and when he keeps losing, it rattles him, threatens the self-esteem he struggles to maintain. Fonsia withholds part of herself, is impenetrable, and has an air of being superior. She is censorious, even punitive, by nature, and she wins every game. The fact of the tragedy is that the encounter with themselves that their encounter with each other provokes is, for each of them, their final encounter with their destinies.

The two are lonely old people whose lives have been failures, as much as they first try to deny it. Meeting each other gives Fonsia and Weller their last chance to redeem their lives and reverse their destinies, but so strongly are their characters their destinies that the chance for that redemption is thwarted. It could happen only if they could become people they are not, and they are on the painful path of discovering who they unrelentingly are. Both are cut off from their families, uncared for, and indigent, and they are trying to keep up appearances. Both also explain their plight by ascribing it to bad luck, rather than accepting that their condition is a result of the flaws in their characters. In the course of the gin games, through the conversations and the behavior elicited by the games, those flaws are revealed: his pride and impotence and her self-righteous vindictiveness. The games are catalysts. For both Fonsia and Weller, the games begin to challenge the concept of luck.

Although Weller is an old hand at gin and prides himself on being an expert player, and although Fonsia seems to be an amateur to whom Weller teaches the game, from the start, she beats him at every hand. As they play, the little quirks of their characters, which suggest the possible conflicts that may arise, appear. He seems rough and his language coarse; she seems polished, refined, and genteel. He gives the impression of having been successful as a businessman, and she appears to have financial resources and a family. But the Sunday they meet, a visitors' day, they are both alone, without visitors. She explains that her son and her sister live far from the old-age home. He tells her of his divorce and of an ex-wife who turned his children away from him. As they speak, they play cards. As she keeps beating him, he is gracious at first. Soon, however, her victories and his losses begin to unnerve him, until, at the end of act 1, he throws over the card table. At the end of act 2, which is also the end of the play, he repeatedly beats the card table with his cane, crying "Gin" over and over with every blow of the cane.

After Weller becomes enraged that Fonsia is beating him, she tells him, "You take it too seriously, Weller. Lord, it's only a game." But it is not just a game for him; the game is touching on something more serious. Losing undoes him, because it reflects and confirms his failure in life. Weller has protected himself from despair and rage at his losses and failures by thinking of himself as unlucky. He explains one of the pivotal experiences of his life, the loss of his business, as a result of bad luck. When Fonsia learns that he is on welfare, she says to him, "You had your own business . . . and you did well, I thought. Flying around the country. I just assumed. . . ." He explains, "Oh hell, I did do well. You're right. I built that God-damn business. And if I'd had a little better luck with my business partners, I'd probably still have it. I was literally thrown out of my own business." When she asks him how it happened, he cannot explain but can only say, "It's too complicated."

The loss at cards, the apparent bad luck, mirrors the loss of his business and seems to indicate that it is not just luck but a fate determined by something about himself that defines and plagues him. Later, Fonsia makes him face it: "You have to be the victim of bad luck, don't you, Weller. . . . Because if it wasn't bad luck, it'd have to be something else, wouldn't it? . . . It'd have to be something like maybe you think you play this game a whole lot better than you really play it." And then she makes the connection between their game and his previous losses. "If it hadn't been bad luck with your business partners," she says, "then it would've had to been bad judgment . . . or worse yet, maybe they were simply better businessmen than you were." The fury of his response—"You shut your . . . mouth! You don't know the first thing about it"—suggests that Fonsia indeed has spoken a truth. But her acuity does not extend to herself. It is directed to the other, and, as payment for her penetration, Weller returns an indictment of her that is equally powerful, equally unwelcome, and equally accurate.

It becomes clear that the reason for Fonsia's tears at the beginning of *The Gin Game* is not that she is a new resident but that her son does not visit her on visitors' day. There has been a rupture between them, just as there was a rupture with

"THE PLAY'S BRILLIANCE LIES IN ITS SIMPLICITY AND ECONOMY."

her husband, his father, many years before. When her son, as an adult, decided to find his father, she broke with him and disinherited him. After Fonsia challenges Weller's claim that his failures stem from his being unlucky, he counters, referring to the venom that characterizes the way she has spoken of her husband and her son: "You don't have too many kind things to say about the men in your life, do you?" She answers, "I'll admit it. When it comes to men, I've been very unlucky." "You've been what?" he returns. "I haven't had much success," she says, trying to hedge, realizing that he is beating her with her own stick. "You've been unlucky!" he persists, knowing he has cornered her. "Alright!" she concedes. Then he comes in for the kill. "Sounds like you've been having the same kind of bad luck you've been telling me about. It had to be bad luck, because if it wasn't bad luck, it would've had to been the fact that maybe it was you! That maybe you're a rigid, self-righteous, vicious . . . ." She stops him, crying, "Alright! You made your point. Just be quiet and play the cards."

Their last game is an intense and angry contest, and it seals their fates and confirms their identities. She wins. He explodes in violence, raising his cane in the air and bringing it forcefully down on her chair, just after she has risen from it and walked away. Then he begins his agonized repetition of the word "gin." She cries "Don't hit me, Weller" and calls out for a nurse. He falls sobbing onto the table, realizing the falseness of his pride and the reality of his impotence, and then goes inside. She calls his name, but he does not stay. He is defeated but enlightened. She exhales the words, "Oh, no," struck not by his cane but by the realization that, without knowing she was doing it and because of her character flaws, she has wrecked a man she cared for as well as her relationship with him and finds herself once more alone.

Source: Neil Heims, Critical Essay on *The Gin Game*, in *Drama for Students*, Thomson Gale, 2006.

Thomas E. Luddy

In the following brief review of the publication of The Gin Game, *Luddy opines that "the play's brilliance lies in its simplicity and economy."*

Coburn's 1978 Pulitzer prize-winning play is now so well known and admired that the judgment on its value has been made both among the critics and in the marketplace. This publication makes the play available to those who only know its reputation. The play's brilliance lies in its simplicity and economy. The metaphor of a common card game played by two people raises universal issues of aging, loneliness and the need for meaningful activity. Coburn etches these issues clearly and devastatingly in terms that are also witty and entertaining. The play is a pleasure to read as it was a pleasure to see. This will become one of the great classics of the American theater.

Source: Thomas E. Luddy, Review of *The Gin Game*, in *Library Journal*, April 1, 1979, p. 847.

SOURCES

Allen, Kathleen, "Misdeal: Consistency Not in the Cards for 'The Gin Game,'" in *Arizona Daily Star*, April 3, 2001, Section E, p. 1.

Coburn, D. L., *The Gin Game*, Samuel French, 1977, pp. 5, 6, 8, 16, 17, 19, 22, 36, 40, 41, 43, 44, 48, 49, 55–59.

———, *The Gin Game*, Drama Book Specialists, 1978, pp. 25, 29, 39, 40, 48, 53, 69, 73.

Curulla, Tony, Review of *The Gin Game*, in the *Post-Standard* (Syracuse), March 10, 2005, p. 23.

Davis-Platt, Joy, "Playing the Cards You're Dealt," in the *St. Petersburg Times*, October 11, 2002, p. 5.

Doran, Terry, "In 'The Gin Game,' Two Lives in Merry Balance," in the *Buffalo News*, January 14, 1999, Section C, p. 3.

Evans, Greg, Review of *The Gin Game*, in *Variety*, Vol. 366, No. 12, April 21, 1997, p. 70.

Luddy, Thomas E., Review of *The Gin Game*, in *Library Journal*, April 1, 1979, p. 847.

Marks, Peter, "A Card Game as Metaphor for the Emotional Battle of Aging," in the *New York Times*, April 21, 1997, Section C, p. 11.

Scholem, Richard, "Our Man on Broadway," in *Long Island Business News*, Vol. 44, No. 21, May 26, 1997, p. 49.

Smith Cantara, Jamie, "In 'Gin Game,' Old-timers Play but Find Little Luck as Friends," in the *Austin American-Statesman*, February 13, 2002, Section E, p. 4.

Warfield, Polly, "The Gin Game at Theatre 40," in *Back Stage West*, Vol. 10, No. 20, May 15, 2003, p. 15.

FURTHER READING

Gussow, Mel, "'Gin Game' Author Lives a Miracle," in the *New York Times*, October 11, 1977, p. 43.

This article outlines the rapid success of D. L. Coburn in taking *The Gin Game* from its first reading to a Pulitzer Prize in little over a year and includes comments from an interview with the playwright.

Harrington, Joan, ed., *The Playwright's Muse*, Routledge, 2002.

This book is a collection of interviews with eleven Pulitzer Prize–winning dramatists about their inspirations and works.

Moody, Harry R., *Aging: Concepts and Controversies*, Pine Forge Press, 2000.

Although this is a textbook, Moody's clearly written discourse on aging is a good resource for questions about the social, biological, and ethical issues of aging, including demographic and Social Security data.

Sime, Tom, "Playwright Has Played His Cards Right with the Timeless 'Gin Game,'" in *Knight Ridder/Tribune News Service*, January 20, 1999, p. K.1896.

Originally an interview for the *Dallas Morning News*, this article includes several quotes from the actors who performed in the 1997 Broadway revival of *The Gin Game*. Primarily, however, the article reports Coburn's answers to questions about his most famous play, his family, and his continuing career as a playwright.

Stewart, Gail, *The 1970s*, Lucent Books, 1999.

Part of the series entitled Cultural History of the United States through the Decades, this short book has a theme-based approach and extensive photographs and sidebars that thoroughly cover the people, places, and events of the times.

Goodnight Desdemona (Good Morning Juliet)

ANN-MARIE MACDONALD

1988

The actor, playwright, and novelist Ann-Marie MacDonald has earned a reputation as one of Canada's most exciting contemporary voices. Since the production of her first solo play, *Goodnight Desdemona (Good Morning Juliet)*, she has become widely known and revered in the theatrical and literary world. In fact, the success of MacDonald's first play was key in identifying her as a socially conscious feminist as well as a witty writer with wide popular appeal.

First performed in Toronto in 1988, *Goodnight Desdemona* is the story of Constance Ledbelly, a quirky and absentminded academic who is writing a doctoral thesis about two of William Shakespeare's tragedies. Suddenly, Constance finds herself transported into the worlds of *Romeo and Juliet* and *Othello*, where she interferes with the plot, gets to know the characters, and discovers her true identity. With its witty allusions to late-sixteenth-century English culture, its use of Elizabethan dramatic conventions, and its playful reimagining of some of Shakespeare's most enduring characters, *Goodnight Desdemona* amuses its audience and brings the Elizabethan period to life. It also provides a thoughtful commentary on such issues as feminism, academia, Elizabethan values, and the nature of tragedy. The play was revised in 1990, and a revised paperback edition is available from Grove Press (1998).

AUTHOR BIOGRAPHY

Born on an army base in West Germany in 1956, MacDonald was the daughter of a Lebanese woman and a Canadian soldier of Scottish heritage. She grew up with two sisters and one brother in a strict Catholic family that moved several times before settling in Ottawa, Canada. MacDonald was a high-achieving student, and her parents encouraged her to study law, but instead she left Carleton University in Minnesota to attend the National Theatre School in Montreal. After graduation, MacDonald moved to Toronto and became involved in collaborative theater projects, including *This Is for You, Anna* (1984). While living in Toronto, MacDonald came out as a lesbian, and her family accepted this fact gradually.

MacDonald's writing career began with projects that included a libretto to the contemporary opera *Nigredo Hotel* (produced in 1992), but her first solo venture was *Goodnight Desdemona (Good Morning Juliet)* (1990). The play won the 1990 Governor General's Award for Drama, a Chalmers Canadian Play Award, and the Canadian Authors' Association Award. Her next play, *The Arab's Mouth* (1995), is set in nineteenth-century Scotland and was less successful than her award-winning first play. During and after this period, MacDonald acted and wrote for television, film, and stage, and she also worked as a broadcast journalist.

MacDonald published her first novel, *Fall on Your Knees*, in 1996, after five years of work. The story of a family from the island of Cape Breton in Nova Scotia, it delves into the racial and cultural tension on the island in the early twentieth century and then follows one of the principal characters to the jazz scene of Harlem in New York City. The novel was well reviewed and became famous after it was chosen for Oprah Winfrey's book club. MacDonald was awarded the Commonwealth Writers' Prize for Best First Book. She continued to act and write after the success of her novel, appearing in the film *Better Than Chocolate* in 1999. In 2003, she published her second novel, *The Way the Crow Flies*, which is based, in part, on the case of Steven Truscott. Truscott was convicted of murder in 1959 but has campaigned to have his name cleared since he was released in 1969. As of 2005, MacDonald continued to live and work in Toronto.

PLOT SUMMARY

Act 1

Goodnight Desdemona begins with a "dumb show," or a scene with no sound, in which three situations occur simultaneously. Othello murders Desdemona, Juliet kills herself, and Constance Ledbelly throws a pen and a manuscript into a wastebasket.

In scene 1, Constance works on her doctoral dissertation, which claims that *Romeo and Juliet* and *Othello* were originally comedies written by an unknown author and that this can be proved by decoding a manuscript written by a physicist named Gustav. Her longtime crush, Professor Claude Night, comes in, criticizes her dissertation topic, and tells her that he is taking a job at Oxford University that she had hoped to secure. Constance laments her fate and begins throwing her possessions into the wastebasket until she herself is sucked into the wastebasket.

Act 2

The second act takes place on the island of Cyprus, within the world of *Othello*. During the scene where Othello resolves to kill his wife, Constance intervenes and reveals that Iago is tricking Othello. Othello binds Iago and expresses his gratitude to Constance. Desdemona arrives and asks whether Constance may stay with them. Othello tells Constance not to make known to Desdemona that he was jealous of his wife. Constance asks Desdemona for help in her quest to discover who originally wrote Shakespeare's plays. Desdemona agrees and tells her to come to battle. Constance wonders if she has permanently changed Shakespeare's work and resolves to find the "Wise Fool," a typical Shakespearean character, who secures the happy ending of a comedy.

In scene 2, Iago discloses that he has a page from the Gustav manuscript and forms a plan to conspire against Constance. Constance bonds with Desdemona, telling of her relationship with Professor Night, while Iago eavesdrops. Constance describes the world of academia and her newfound feminist convictions. Desdemona encounters Iago carrying buckets of filth, and Iago stirs jealousy in her. Desdemona believes Iago's claims that Constance is a witch who is after Othello's heart, and she resolves to kill her.

Desdemona sees Othello give Constance a necklace, and her suspicions increase. Constance muses about what a strong woman Desdemona is.

Iago and Desdemona enter, fighting with swords, and Constance nearly kills Iago, thinking that she is saving Desdemona. Iago shows Desdemona the page from the Gustav manuscript, saying that he found it in Desdemona's underwear drawer. Desdemona shows it to Constance, who confirms that it is hers. She reads its clue that she must seek truth in Verona, Italy. Before Desdemona can kill her, Constance is dragged offstage.

Act 3

Act 3 takes place within the context of *Romeo and Juliet*. It begins with the scene in which Mercutio fights with Tybalt. Constance arrives and tackles Romeo to the ground before Tybalt can stab Mercutio under Romeo's arm. Romeo tells her, "Speak, boy," confusing her gender because Desdemona has ripped off Constance's skirt. Calling herself Constantine, Constance explains that they should stop fighting, because Romeo has married Juliet and they are all family now. They agree, and Romeo falls in love with Constance. The men make lewd jokes and go to the bathhouses. Constance wishes that she could go back home.

In scene 2, Juliet and Romeo wake up together and describe their declining interest in each other. They fight over their turtle, Hector, and end up ripping it in two; they part on bitter terms. Juliet complains to her nurse that she is dying of boredom and wishes that she could be unmarried, able to play the deadly game of love. The nurse tells her that she should cheer up, because she will enjoy the marriage festivities that night, and Juliet resolves to find another lover.

In scene 3, Constance pounces on a servant because she believes that he is the Wise Fool, but she finds instead that he is giving out invitations to a masked ball thrown by Juliet's father. In scene 4, Romeo and Juliet enter the masked ball, sulking at each other. Romeo thinks that Tybalt is Constance and puts his hand on Tybalt's bottom. Constance enters, and Romeo tells her that he loves her. Tybalt sees Romeo kiss Constance and sends Juliet to interrupt them. Romeo introduces Constance to Juliet, and Juliet falls in love with her.

Juliet dances with Constance while Romeo and Tybalt watch suspiciously. Tybalt resolves to kill Constance. Romeo decides to dress as a woman so that Constance will desire him, and he cuts in to dance with her. Juliet sees them and determines to dress as a man so that Constance will desire her. Romeo and Juliet begin to fight over Constance, and Constance tells them to apologize.

In scene 5, Juliet enters dressed in Romeo's clothing and woos Constance from below her balcony. They discover that they have the same birthday. Constance resists Juliet and tells her of her bitterness about love. Juliet tells her that she knows the name of the Wise Fool and will trade it for one kiss. Romeo then enters in Juliet's clothing, but Constance leaves before he can woo her.

Scene 6 takes place in the graveyard through which Constance walks on her way to Juliet's balcony. While she is there, she sees a ghost like that of the King in *Hamlet*, who tells her that the Wise Fool and the Author are the same "lass." The ghost disappears, and Tybalt enters, trying to kill Constance. Romeo steps between them, and Constance escapes.

In scene 7, Juliet pulls Constance up to her balcony with a rope. They share a long kiss, and then Juliet admits that she lied about knowing the name of the Wise Fool. Juliet tries to kill herself, but Constance pins her down and reveals that she is a woman. Juliet exclaims that she loves her all the more. Constance claims that she is not a lesbian, but Juliet convinces her that they should make love. Constance reaches under Juliet's shirt, where she finds a page from the Gustav manuscript.

A warp effect brings Desdemona to the scene, and she begins to smother Constance with a pillow. Juliet tries to save her and then goes to seek help. Constance holds up the necklace that Othello gave her, which has a birthday inscription to Desdemona, and Desdemona stops smothering her. Tybalt arrives, and Constance pretends to be dead, telling Desdemona to seek Juliet. In scene 8, Desdemona confuses Romeo for Juliet and tells him to meet them in the crypt.

Romeo, who is still in Juliet's clothes, has fallen for Desdemona. In scene 9, he invites her to lie with him in the crypt. Romeo confuses Tybalt for Desdemona, however, and Tybalt carries Romeo away, thinking that he is a maiden. Juliet enters and starts to stab herself out of sorrow, but Constance stops her, and they embrace. Desdemona enters and starts to stab Juliet until Constance stops her. Desdemona then urges Constance to come to Cyprus, while Juliet exhorts her to remain and die with her. Constance interrupts them and points out their faults. They promise to forgo their tragic impulses, and Constance realizes that she is both the Author of the play and the Wise Fool. Constance is then transported by warp effect back to her office at Queen's University, where she finds that her pen has turned to gold.

CHARACTERS

Author

See Constance Ledbelly

Chorus

The Chorus is the mysterious and riddling narrator of the play as well as the Ghost of act 3, scene 6. The choral tradition dates back to ancient Greece, where a group of people narrated and commented on the actions of a play. During Shakespeare's time, the chorus was often a single man who spoke during the prologue and epilogue. In the prologue of *Goodnight Desdemona*, the Chorus takes Constance's manuscript out of the wastebasket and talks mysteriously about alchemy, the mythical process of turning base metals into gold.

During the epilogue, the Chorus reveals that he played the part of the Ghost that appears to Constance in the graveyard. The Ghost tells Constance a number of jokes and riddles that hint at the solution to the play's mystery about the Wise Fool and the Author. Constance believes that the Ghost is Yorick, the family jester whom Hamlet finds dead upon his return to Denmark. As the Ghost, the Chorus serves to move along the plot and direct Constance to her discovery of herself.

Desdemona

Desdemona is Othello's wife and victim in Shakespeare's tragedy. She is generally considered a passive character who is devoted to her husband. *Goodnight Desdemona* challenges this view, however, and interprets Desdemona as a capable, headstrong, and even violent character who marries Othello because of her passion for war and conquest. In act 2, scene 2, Desdemona acknowledges that academia is wrong about her, when she shouts that the idea that she is a helpless victim is "*[b—sh——t]!!*"

Constance deeply admires Desdemona, claiming that she is "magnificent" and "capable of greatness." In fact, Desdemona serves as an inspiration for Constance to develop her own confidence and strength as well as her beliefs about feminism. The only major fault in Desdemona's character is her impulse toward tragedy. Like Othello, Desdemona is susceptible to manipulation, because she is gullible and has a tendency to become very angry and jealous. At the end of the play, however, Desdemona promises Constance that she will reform this impulse and acknowledge life's complexity.

Ghost

See Chorus

Iago

Iago is one of English literature's most famous villains. He is a bitter and crafty liar who manipulates Othello into killing his wife. In *Goodnight Desdemona*, Constance foils Iago's plans, although Iago later conspires to manipulate Desdemona into turning against Constance.

Juliet

Thirteen-year-old Juliet is known throughout the world as a symbol of young love. In Shakespeare's *Romeo and Juliet*, she falls in love with the son of a rival family and then stabs herself when she finds him dead. Her lines beginning "O Romeo, Romeo, wherefore art thou Romeo?" are among the most famous in English literature. Constance describes her as "the essence of first love— / of beauty that will never fade, / of passion that will never die."

In *Goodnight Desdemona*, Juliet is obsessed with passionate love. Her petty bickering with Romeo and the threats to tell their parents reveal that they are both immature adolescents who are inconstant in their desires. Juliet is strong and active about realizing what she wants, however. This is why she is willing to dress up as a man and vigorously woo Constance. Her views about love at first sight are idealistic and inspiring enough to persuade Constance to love her.

Juliet is also obsessed with death, and her overdramatic desire to die is a consistent joke in the play. However much she is charmed by Juliet, Constance faults her tragic impulse toward death and destruction. At the end of the play, Juliet swears that she will reform this impulse and take Constance's advice.

Constance Ledbelly

The protagonist of the play, Constance is an assistant professor at Queen's University who finds her true identity by traveling through the worlds of Shakespeare's works. She is a somewhat clumsy and absent-minded person, but she has a great talent for teaching and literary analysis. At the beginning of the play, she is a frustrated doctoral candidate in love with Professor Night. By the end, she has discovered her sexual desire for women, uncovered her true potential as a scholar, and gained a broad and substantial confidence in herself.

At the center of Constance's struggle is her lack of confidence. Rejected and manipulated by Professor Night, she believes at the outset of the play that she is a failed scholar and lover. Like Desdemona and Juliet, she has an impulse toward self-destruction and tragedy. The fact that she is a woman is crucial to this lack of confidence; Constance tells Desdemona that she is not "some kind of feminist. / I shave my legs and I get nervous in a crowd."

It is by coming to terms with her femininity that Constance begins to uncover some of her best qualities and have faith in her mind and personality. She is inspired by the strength of Juliet and Desdemona, characters that have been misinterpreted by the male-dominated academic world. Constance recognizes that women have been lied about and oppressed, and she gains confidence because these women are actually admirable and inspiring figures.

Constance's true identity, therefore, is a self-assured feminist. She remains somewhat clumsy and awkward, but this is part of her identity as the Wise Fool who is able to write and peacefully resolve comedic plays that Shakespeare turned into tragedies. She returns to the real world with a fuller knowledge of herself and an appreciation of the lessons she has learned from Juliet and Desdemona: namely, an understanding of her latent lesbian desires and a capability to practice violence.

Mercutio

Mercutio is Romeo's close friend and kinsman. In *Romeo and Juliet*, his death and dying words, "A plague a' both your houses!," set off the tragic events of the play. It is because Constance saves his life that *Goodnight Desdemona* can become a comedy.

Professor Claude Night

Charming and manipulative, Professor Night is the object of Constance's affections until she finally gets over him. He has an Oxford accent, is "*perfectly groomed*," and "*oozes confidence*." He exploits Constance by asking her to do a great deal of his work for him and receive no credit in return. His attitude toward her is sexist and dismissive, and he frustrates the audience because he gets away with everything. Instead of recommending Constance for a lecturing post at Oxford University, he takes it himself and begins a relationship with Ramona, a young student.

Nurse

As in Shakespeare's play, Juliet's nurse is a pragmatic woman who is devoted to Juliet and indulgent of her.

Othello

Othello is the tragic hero of his self-titled play, famous for his courage and strength as well as his rampant jealousy. He is a war hero of the Venetian empire, engaged in battle with the Turks on the island of Cyprus. Constance arrives during the scene in which Iago tells Othello that his lieutenant Cassio is in possession of Desdemona's handkerchief. Othello signals his readiness to be fooled with his famous lines "Had Desdemona *forty thousand lives*! / *One is too poor, too weak for my revenge*." Constance exposes Iago's lies, however, and Othello is extremely grateful.

Ramona

A young female student who is "*all business and very assertive*," Ramona competes with Constance for Professor Night's affections. She wins a Rhodes Scholarship to Oxford University and travels there with the professor, who has bought her a diamond ring.

Romeo

Romeo is the famously passionate lover of *Romeo and Juliet* who upsets his family by marrying the daughter of their rivals. In the original play, Romeo becomes embroiled in conflict after Tybalt kills Mercutio, and he eventually kills himself, believing that Juliet is dead. Constance avoids these tragic events by telling Tybalt and Mercutio of the marriage.

In *Goodnight Desdemona*, Romeo is a figure of comic relief because of his inconstant and often ridiculous passions. He falls in love with Constance, thinking that she is a boy named Constantine, and quickly becomes unhappy with his marriage to Juliet. Romeo dresses as a woman in order to win "Constantine," but he ends up falling for Desdemona and then being whisked away by Tybalt. Romeo's various homosexual and heterosexual desires suggest that he is an adolescent with shifting passions but no firm convictions.

Soldier of Cyprus

The soldier of Cyprus acts as Othello's messenger to Desdemona in act 2, scene 2.

Servant

Capulet's servant is handing out invitations to Romeo and Juliet's marriage feast when Constance pounces on him, mistaking him for the Wise Fool.

Student

The student whose name Constance confuses between "Julie" and "Jill" turns in a late paper in act 1, scene 1.

Tybalt

Tybalt is Juliet's headstrong and violent cousin. He kills Mercutio, and Romeo kills him in *Romeo and Juliet*, but Constance avoids these murders in *Goodnight Desdemona*. Throughout act 3, however, Tybalt remains a dangerous presence, ready to kill Constance and turn the play into a tragedy.

Tybalt is somewhat self-obsessed, and his sexually explicit banter suggests that he is possibly homoerotic or gay. MacDonald satirizes Tybalt's manly posing, and she emphasizes that this is one of the great dangers to the comic resolution of the play. In order to ridicule Tybalt's character, the playwright places him and Romeo in a variety of comical situations that culminate when Tybalt whisks Romeo from the crypt, believing that he is a maiden.

Wise Fool

See Constance Ledbelly

THEMES

Feminism

One of MacDonald's most important thematic goals in *Goodnight Desdemona* is to develop and explore feminist ideas. The play consistently returns to themes of women's rights, women's issues, and gender identity. MacDonald establishes a number of historical and contemporary examples of the oppression, mistreatment, or misunderstanding of women, and she explores some possibilities of addressing these problems.

Constance's experience at Queen's University is MacDonald's first example of sexism in contemporary culture. Professor Night has exploited Constance's ideas and efforts for years, securing a position for himself at Oxford University based on her writings. At the same time that he takes advantage of her hard work, however, he insults her, telling her she has an "interesting little mind" and calling her belittling names like "my little titmouse" and "pet." These names reveal that the professor is sexist and bigoted as well as exploitative and that he takes advantage of Constance on the basis of her gender.

Constance's journey into the worlds of Shakespeare's plays reveals that sexism is ingrained in the common understanding of literature and history. Tybalt seems to distrust and dislike all women, and this attitude is shared to a certain degree by Iago and Romeo. MacDonald suggests that Desdemona and Juliet, both strong-minded figures, encounter sexism in their own time and are also misunderstood by contemporary professors and readers. *Goodnight Desdemona* stresses that it is important to reevaluate historical attitudes toward women and recognize admirable female figures in history and literature.

Goodnight Desdemona also pays close attention to the feminist themes of gender identity and gender role. Many of the play's characters experience a learning process about their gender roles. When Romeo and Juliet dress in drag and when Desdemona sword fights or participates in military violence, MacDonald is commenting on the flexibility of gender identities and the importance of testing and changing their boundaries. The most important character in this regard is Constance, who discovers that her latent attraction to other women, her ambitions as a scholar, and her ability to stand up for herself are all natural and acceptable aspects of her identity as a woman.

Academia

Related to the theme of feminism is MacDonald's critique of the contemporary academic culture in Canada and Great Britain. *Goodnight Desdemona* highlights a traditional, male-dominated university system, in which older male professors are able to take advantage of intelligent females. MacDonald suggests that 1980s Canada should reform this unjust system. Ramona seems to be Professor Night's next victim in a system that is not likely to be getting any better, although it may be significant that both of them will be leaving Canada for England.

Shakespeare and Elizabethan Studies

Also important to MacDonald's thematic agenda is her treatment and analysis of Elizabethan culture and drama. *Goodnight Desdemona* reimagines some of Shakespeare's most famous characters, providing an interpretation of his texts and their historical context.

Some of MacDonald's commentary about Shakespeare's works and Elizabethan culture is deliberate satire. For example, she pokes fun at Othello's boastfulness, Tybalt's capacity for anger and violence, Romeo's inconstancy, and Juliet's death drive. All of these characteristics have strong bases in the original plays, but MacDonald exaggerates and draws attention to these faults. MacDonald also

TOPICS FOR FURTHER STUDY

- Choose a scene from *Goodnight Desdemona* that you feel is representative of a particular theme of the play and discuss, in an essay, its purpose and dramatic thrust. How does MacDonald go about achieving her goals in the scene? What are the key moments of humor, drama, suspense, or revelation? Which characters and which lines are most important? Cast the scene, choose a director, and act it out based on your observations. Then, analyze the scene you have produced, noting its successes and failures.
- Read one of Shakespeare's comedies, such as *As You Like It* or *Much Ado about Nothing*, and one of the tragedies, such as *Macbeth.* Write a paper or give a class presentation discussing the difference between tragedy and comedy in Shakespeare's time. How do the playwright's techniques differ? What do the conventions have in common? Do you think the plays are strictly divided and have necessary outcomes, or can you see the possibility of alternate endings?
- *Goodnight Desdemona* is associated with the feminist movement of the late twentieth century. Research some of MacDonald's possible influences as well as the state of feminism at the time the play was being written and produced. Write an essay discussing the key feminists of the 1970s and 1980s, focusing on how the movement changed in those two decades and how it affected the Canadian theater scene.
- Choose another of Shakespeare's plays, such as *Julius Caesar* or *Macbeth*, and read it carefully. Then write a scene in which you reinvent the play and its characters in a new way. You could include a character from the present day, add a twist in the plot, provide an extra scene between those that already exist, or engage in a parody. Make your best effort to follow the language, rhythms, and structures of Elizabethan drama, including the convention of blank verse.

---

satirizes common characteristics of Elizabethan society, such as gender bending and lewd jokes.

Not all of MacDonald's commentary is satirical, however. *Goodnight Desdemona* reinvents Shakespearean characters, particularly Desdemona and Juliet, based on the ways that MacDonald feels they should be interpreted. This process emphasizes the characters' positive and admirable characteristics as well as their faults. The play implies that Desdemona's love of violence and Juliet's strong-minded passions are important elements of Shakespeare's work that are often misinterpreted by contemporary readers and scholars.

Tragedy and Absolutism

MacDonald stresses throughout the play that it is a great problem to see no gray area between comedy and tragedy. The Shakespearean characters are nearly all inclined to a tragic worldview, and they are in continual danger of following a dark destiny. Like Othello, Desdemona is jealous and gullible enough to commit murder. Meanwhile, characters like Juliet and Tybalt seem to have a death wish, often becoming overly dramatic and deliberately entering perilous situations. Constance herself is inclined to tragedy and despair until she learns the lessons of the play.

Based on her journey of self-discovery, Constance provides an antidote to the tragic impulse by stressing that it is necessary to abandon inflexible, absolute values; acknowledge the complexity of the world; and listen to the Wise Fool. Connecting tragedy to the belief in absolute values, MacDonald emphasizes that an absolutist mindset is dangerous and perilous, and it is preferable to avoid both tragedy and absolutism.

STYLE

Blank Verse

The most important stylistic aspect of *Goodnight Desdemona* is its attention to the customs and conventions of Elizabethan drama and culture. Particularly in acts 2 and 3, inside the worlds of *Romeo and Juliet* and *Othello*, MacDonald emulates and mimics Shakespeare's style. For example, MacDonald uses blank verse, the theatrical writing style made famous by Shakespeare and his contemporaries.

Blank verse is the name for unrhymed iambic pentameter, or lines that form a meter of five two-syllable units and do not rhyme at the end. Although blank verse is normally spoken without audible line breaks, it sets the work in poetry and adds what many consider a sense of gravity and beauty. MacDonald uses this style with great dexterity, capturing the poetic personality of Shakespeare's characters and setting Constance's lines into blank verse while retaining her personality and even the tone of her late-twentieth-century Canadian accent.

Asides and Monologues

Like Shakespeare, MacDonald makes use of monologues, in which a character expresses his or her state of mind directly to the audience. She also makes use of the "aside," the dramatic convention wherein a character speaks to the audience or to himself or herself but none of the other characters can hear what is said. As in Shakespeare, asides allow the audience to be in on a particular plot without all of the characters realizing it. When Iago hatches evil plots or Romeo and Juliet express their secret passions in asides, MacDonald is joking and playing with the convention both to amuse the audience and to develop the plot.

Word Order, Spying, Cross-dressing, and More

The play is full of jokes and references to Elizabethan culture and theater, and MacDonald is careful to get these details right. MacDonald uses the typical word order and archaic language, she makes use of onstage eavesdropping, and she employs the convention of cross-dressing that is common to Shakespearean comedy. All of these elements, as well as numerous other details, are effective in establishing the setting and atmosphere of the work as well as amusing and challenging the audience.

HISTORICAL CONTEXT

Late-Twentieth-Century Canada

Canada was a former British colony and a modern democracy in the late twentieth century. Most of Canada was English speaking, but French was also an official language, and the French-speaking province of Quebec had a unique culture in which separatism was a major issue. Canada's political and social climate was strongly affected by the United States, and the two countries had close economic ties.

Toronto Theater Scene

Toronto was the center of the English-speaking theater scene in 1980s Canada, a scene that had flourished since the 1970s. A number of playwrights revitalized Canadian theater in English, including David French, David Fennario, and Carol Bolt. The city became famous for direct, realistic, and compelling theater that often addressed important social issues, and playwrights like French were known for closely collaborating with directors and actors. Although MacDonald has since become a more international celebrity, she was closely identified with the Toronto theater scene when she produced *Goodnight Desdemona.*

Late-Twentieth-Century Feminism

Broadly speaking, feminism is the advocacy of women's rights, and it is a movement that dates back centuries. It advances the rights of women by acknowledging the historical dominance of men and working to address inequalities. The feminist movement began to exert an increasing amount of influence on literary and cultural studies in the decades following World War II. In literary studies, feminism has concentrated on critiquing the male-dominated literary canon, reevaluating the role of women in literature, studying writings about women, and exploring gender identity. Writers such as Simone de Beauvoir and Kate Millet began inquiries into feminist literary studies and critics like Sandra Gilbert, Susan Gubar, and Judith Butler have continued or adjusted their focus.

Elizabethan England and William Shakespeare

The rule of Queen Elizabeth I of England forms an important context for *Goodnight Desdemona.* Although *Othello* was probably first performed after the queen's death in 1603, it and *Romeo and Juliet* are associated with Elizabethan culture and society. Elizabeth was a shrewd, able monarch who presided over a period of increased power and prosperity in England. In this environment of relative tolerance and stability, the flourishing of the arts in continental Europe spread to England, and the late sixteenth century became famous for a flowering in the arts known as the English "Renaissance."

COMPARE & CONTRAST

- **1600:** The first French settlers arrive in eastern Canada, but there will be no significant settlements in Toronto for more than one hundred years.

  1980s: Toronto is Canada's largest city. It is the capital of the province of Ontario and is the center of Canada's English-speaking artistic culture.

  Today: Toronto has suffered from the drawback in tourism after the SARS (severe acute respiratory syndrome) epidemic in 2003. The city is still known as the economic engine of Canada, however, and it continues to grow and prosper.

- **1600:** Queen Elizabeth I, one of England's shrewdest and most able monarchs, is nearing the end of her long and prosperous rule.

  1980s: Margaret Thatcher, known as the "Iron Lady" for her conservatism and inflexibility, is the prime minister of the United Kingdom.

  Today: Tony Blair, a pioneer of the "New Labor" movement intended to combine social services with privatization, is the British prime minister.

- **1600:** Drama in the English language is flourishing, as Shakespeare and other playwrights continue to produce masterpieces for the London theater.

  1980s: Drama in English is no longer centered in London but has spread to the many English-speaking cities, particularly Toronto and New York City.

  Today: With an increased emphasis on multiculturalism, drama in English involves playwrights and actors of Jamaican, Indian, South African, and many other nationalities.

William Shakespeare is probably the most important dramatist in the English language, and his plays are considered the high point of Elizabethan art. Born in 1564, Shakespeare grew up in Stratford-upon-Avon during Elizabeth's rule. At some point before 1592, he moved to London and began a successful career as a dramatist, writing comedies, histories, and tragedies for the stage. *Romeo and Juliet* was probably first performed in 1594 or 1595 and *Othello* in 1604 or 1605.

The Venetian City-State

The pertinent scenes of *Othello* are set in sixteenth-century Cyprus, which was then a part of the Republic of Venice. A powerful mercantile city of the Middle Ages and Renaissance, Venice ruled an independent empire that stretched between present-day Italy and Greece. The city of Venice established its independence in the ninth century and became very wealthy because of its extensive trade network. Venice was initially ruled by an all-powerful duke, but power was later divided between elected and appointed aristocrats. During the period in question, Venice was fighting the Ottoman Turks for control of Cyprus, which it would lose by 1571.

Fourteenth-Century Verona

Although Shakespeare does not set an exact date, *Romeo and Juliet* takes place in the city of Verona, Italy, at some point in the fourteenth century. This period was the height of Verona's power, when it was dominated by the aristocratic family of the Scaligeri. However, different aristocratic families competed for influence and control at this time, and, as in *Romeo and Juliet*, tensions ran high between bitter rivals.

CRITICAL OVERVIEW

Goodnight Desdemona was a popular and critically acclaimed play that was vital to launching MacDonald's career. Critics writing for *Canadian*

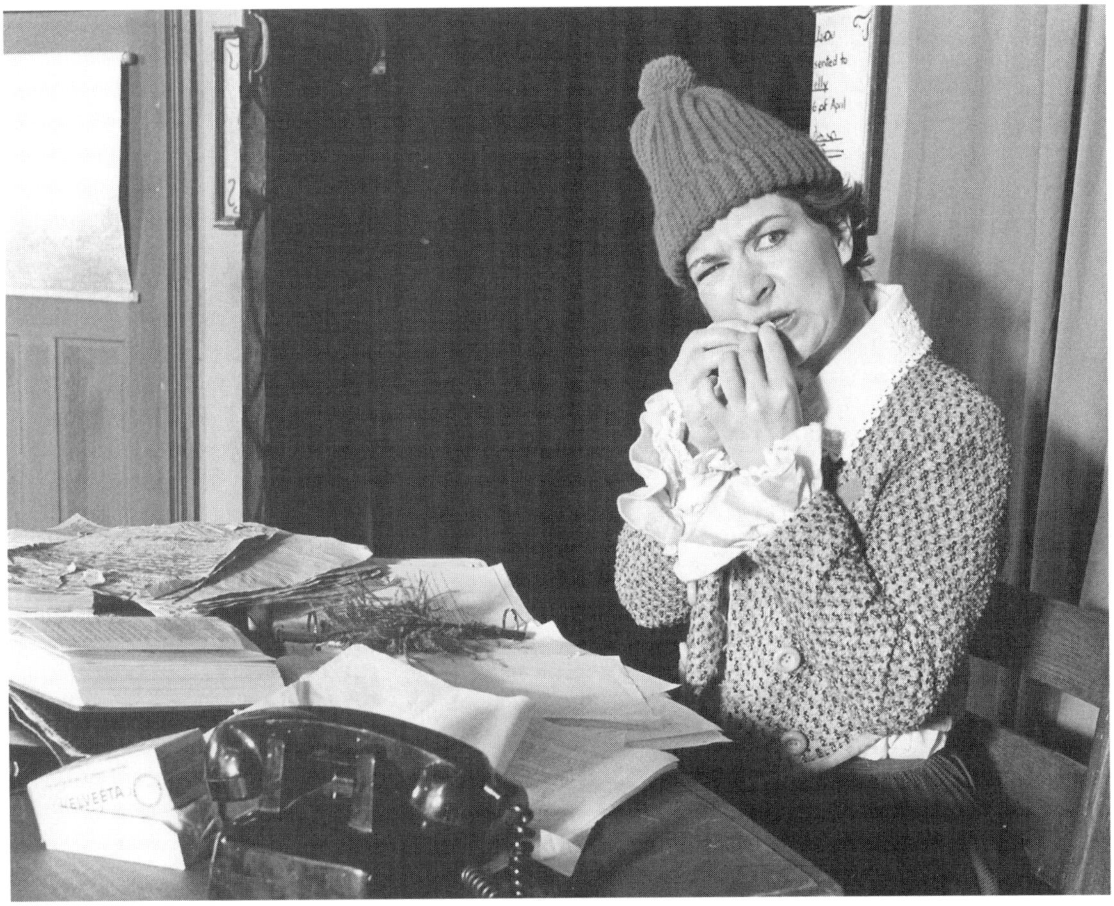

Tanja Jacobs as Constance Ledbelly in Goodnight Desdemona (Good Morning Juliet) *by Ann-Marie MacDonald, Nightwood Theatre, 1988* Photo by Cylla von Tiedemann

Literature, *Canadian Theatre Review*, *Maclean*, and *Back Stage* praised MacDonald for producing a witty and successful work. Mark Fortier, for example, writes in *Canadian Theatre Review* that the original production had its problems but that the play has great potential and that in one performance with "rare energy . . . I was given a wonderful sense of living, indigenous Shakespeare."

Most critics tend to concentrate their discussion of the play on its value as a work of feminism. Although MacDonald has resisted classifying the play as an exclusively feminist work, she is a self-proclaimed feminist, and critics argue that her analysis of Shakespearean culture and the academic world rests heavily on the feminist tradition. Shannon Hengen, for example, stresses in *Canadian Literature* that the play is a "feminist comedy" associated with "the potential for real social or political change." Similarly, Marta Dvorak writes in *Canadian Theatre Review* that the play "can be considered to exemplify contemporary 'female' artistic strategy" and that MacDonald "playfully challenges preconceptions and breaks every rule" with a "strategy of deviance" in order to realize feminist goals.

Some critics are more ambivalent about the success of *Goodnight Desdemona* as a work of feminism. In *Commonweal*, for example, Gerald Weales writes: "A feminist play, then, but it is primarily a literary game in which MacDonald makes comedies—farces, more like—out of the tragedies. . . . But the device finally defeats itself, dissolving into historical tedium." Weales is in the minority, however, with most critics praising the success and innovation of MacDonald's feminism.

CRITICISM

Scott Trudell

Trudell is a doctoral student of English literature at Rutgers University. In the following essay, he discusses MacDonald's feminist agenda, with a focus on how she uses the conventions of comedy, in the Elizabethan sense of the term, to forward this agenda.

MacDonald is a well-known feminist, and *Goodnight Desdemona* clearly brings forth a feminist agenda. In particular, it identifies the sexism and exclusion in both late-twentieth-century academic culture and historical (specifically Renaissance European) literary culture. The play then envisions an emergence of a degree of power and autonomy in its principal female characters, Desdemona, Juliet, and Constance. Desdemona represents violent female self-assertion, while Juliet represents passionate, boundary-crossing female sexuality. Constance absorbs both of these traits and emerges as a formidable literary scholar with faith in her own abilities and an independence from the male establishment.

Although MacDonald's feminist agenda is apparent and important, it is not generally considered confrontational or offensive to readers and theatergoers. Many critics have argued that the playwright goes to great efforts to disguise her political agenda as a vibrant and witty comedy. Because the play is funny, they say, audiences do not feel that they are being hit over the head with a political message. Mark Fortier, for example, comments on MacDonald's method of presenting a feminist message in his 1989 essay for *Canadian Theatre Review*:

> MacDonald is uncomfortable thinking of *Goodnight Desdemona* as a feminist work; she prefers to think of it as humanism through a woman's point of view, or through feminist language. Although MacDonald considers herself a feminist, the strongest impulses in her theatre are popular and populist, and she seems to feel that labelling her work as feminist or lesbian would jeopardize the pluralist audience that she is seeking.

The reviewer Gerald Weales goes further and suggests in his 1992 review for *Commonweal* that the witty humor of the play "defeats itself" and subverts its feminist message. Other critics, such as Marta Dvorak and Shannon Hengen, concentrate on the ways in which *Goodnight Desdemona* uses humor to produce an extremely effective and wide-reaching feminist political message. These critics disagree about the nature of the play's feminist argument and many aspects of how it is implemented. They tend to agree, however, that MacDonald packages her message in a humorous format so that it will be palatable and acceptable to an audience of wide-ranging political beliefs.

> "THE PLAY, THEREFORE, PROPOSES THAT CONTEMPORARY SCHOLARSHIP SHOULD CROSS THE LINE OF WHAT CAN BE CONSIDERED A REASONABLE INTERPRETATION OF HISTORICAL OR CANONICAL TEXTS AND BEGIN UNDERSTANDING TEXTS NOT AS RIGID FORMULAS BUT AS STARTING PLACES FOR NEW IDEAS AND POSSIBILITIES."

The danger of critical approaches that classify MacDonald's use of comedy as a humorous shroud over her political goals is that they tend to overlook a more important aspect of the play's use of comedy. These critics are inclined not to emphasize that the comic convention is important to the play's feminist subtext chiefly because it is the opposite of tragedy—in other words, because it requires a happy ending. The argument of this essay is that MacDonald may make use of humor and wit, but her main concern is to use the comic convention to underscore the nature of her positivist feminist message. *Goodnight Desdemona* is the opposite of a tragedy in the sense that it encourages women to escape from the tragic fatalism of a patriarchal world and emerge as hopeful subjects.

To develop this argument, it is first necessary to clarify the terms *comedy* and *tragedy* as they were used in Shakespearean England. The ancient Greek philosopher Aristotle and other writers contributed to the strict distinction between comedy and tragedy that was common to the Elizabethan period. While tragedies were characterized by disastrous yet necessary and unavoidable endings (according to ancient Greek and Roman models), comedies resolved

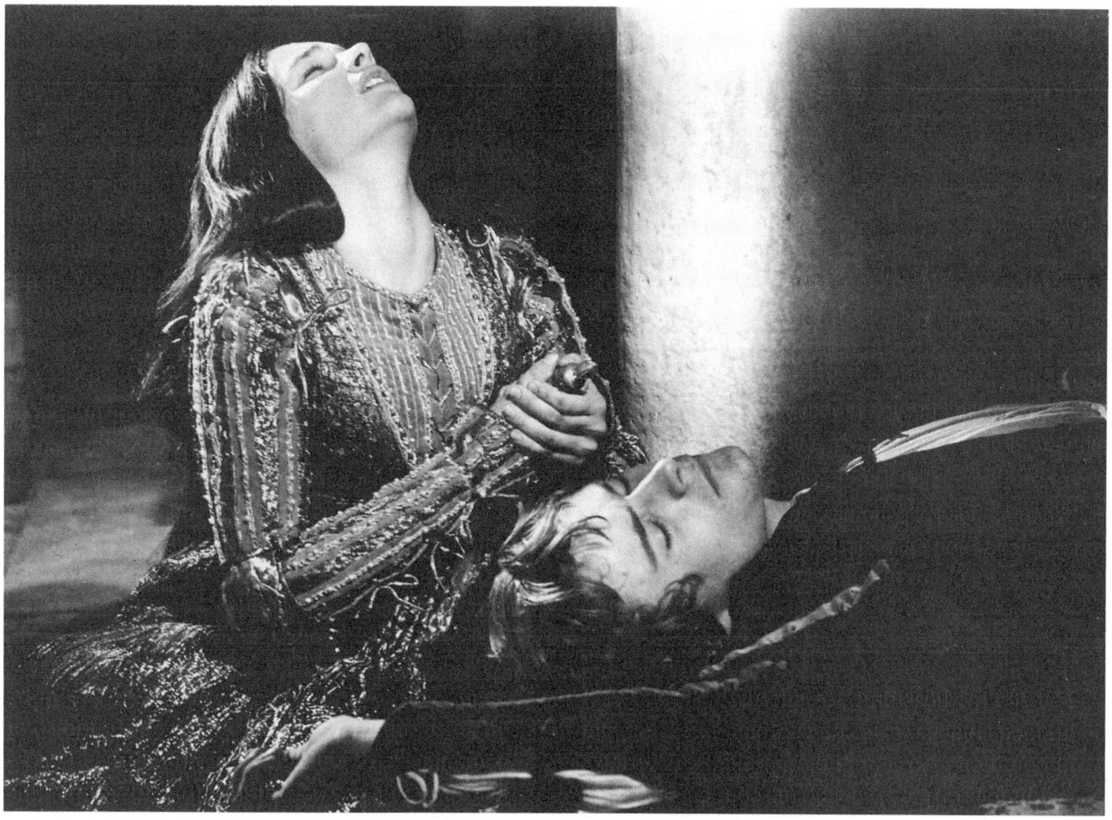

Olivia Hussey and Leonard Whiting in Franco Zeffrelli's 1968 film version of Romeo and Juliet The Kobal Collection. Reproduced by permission

in happy and hopeful conclusions. Both tragedy and comedy used humor, and a comedy could be entirely serious. *Goodnight Desdemona* is a comedy, then, primarily in the Elizabethan sense of the word: a drama with a happy ending.

Constance's chief function as the "Wise Fool" and, more important, as the "Author" and feminist literary scholar of the play is to formulate a comedy out of a tragedy. She goes about this quest by getting to know two of the most tragic and doomed female figures in English literary history. In a sense, her role is to redeem Desdemona and Juliet from four hundred years of resignation to their grim fates. She closely interacts with these characters, gaining their trust and undertaking along with them a journey toward empowerment and selfhood.

Constance's close interaction with the Shakespearean lines and characters suggests that careful readings and analyses of original texts are an important aspect of MacDonald's feminist agenda. She must throw herself down the "wastebasket" of English literature—its "Garbage" or "Sargasso Sea," a reference to Jean Rhys's novel *Wide Sargasso Sea*, which reimagines the life of Mrs. Rochester, a tragic character from Charlotte Brontë's novel *Jane Eyre*. Entering the Sargasso Sea is a metaphor for exploring the forgotten world of literature about women's issues that has been suppressed by centuries of male domination in the form of figures like Professor Night. Initially, Constance is in danger of losing herself in this Sargasso Sea, but instead she is able to find her own story and identity in a play that has been previously claimed by a patriarchal reading world.

Constance does not undergo a simple process of digging through a literary Sargasso Sea in order to find lost women's literature, however. Her journey of self-discovery is characterized by a reimagining and repossession of classic literature. As the "Author" of the original comic precursors to Shakespeare's plays, she envisions herself in a position of control and power over literary history. There are hints in *Othello* that Desdemona is interested

WHAT DO I READ NEXT?

- Shakespeare's classics *Romeo and Juliet* (c. 1594) and *Othello* (c. 1603) are absorbing plays that add a great deal to one's appreciation of *Goodnight Desdemona*. Also, Constance's journey resembles that of the Danish prince in *Hamlet* (c. 1600), which follows the story of Hamlet's revenge after the murder of his father.
- MacDonald's critically acclaimed *Fall on Your Knees* (1996) is the story of a family from the island of Cape Breton in Nova Scotia, Canada, in the early twentieth century. After delving into the island's world of cultural tension, it follows one of the main characters to Harlem, in New York City, where she becomes involved in the jazz scene.
- *Feminist Readings of Early Modern Culture: Emerging Subjects* (1996), edited by Valerie Traub, M. Lindsay Kaplan, and Dympna Callaghan, is a collection of critical essays dealing with a variety of women's issues in the Elizabethan and Jacobean periods.
- Carol Bolt's *One Night Stand* (1977) is a hit comedy-thriller by one of Canada's most influential late-twentieth-century playwrights. It tells the story of a young woman and a drifter she finds in a bar.
- *Tongue of a Bird* (1997), by Ellen McLaughlin, is a haunting and tragic play with an all-female cast that serves as a contrast to *Goodnight Desdemona* in its expression of feminist themes. Its main character is a search-and-rescue pilot named Maxine who is trying to find a young girl in the mountains.

in war and violence, and Shakespeare indicates to some degree that Juliet is strong-minded, but Constance's reimagining of these characters goes far beyond interpretation or even parody. Desdemona and Juliet are rewritten according to MacDonald's 1980s feminist values. The play, therefore, proposes that contemporary scholarship should cross the line of what can be considered a reasonable interpretation of historical or canonical texts and begin understanding texts not as rigid formulas but as starting places for new ideas and possibilities.

The play implies, further, that the audience should partake in this process of historical repossession. Marta Dvorak points out, in her 1994 essay for *Canadian Theatre Review*, that Constance changes from the role of spectator to the role of "actor and author." Therefore, "Is this not an invitation to us spectators as well to assume our share of creativity, to use well our power of participation?" The play implies that a spectator, normally someone who is forced to sit passively and absorb the message of a play, can and should actively participate and alter the implications of a particular work. This participation is a "power" indeed, because it invites contemporary readers to reinvent history outside the accepted patriarchal discourse.

In the process, contemporary spectators are offered the possibility of working out their own problems. Constance is able to escape the sexism of the literary establishment represented by Professor Night, who is not only exploitative but also manipulative and repressive. When he tells Constance that she has "such an interesting little mind" and then says, "Hand it over" (seemingly referring to her latest plagiarism for him), he implies that he wishes to own and control Constance's mind. Because they are speaking about Constance's scholarly work, he also implies that his sexism extends to his interpretation of English literature and his wish to retain control over the patriarchal norms of literary interpretation. Furthermore, it is clear from the surrounding context that he wishes to control and confine Constance's sexuality to a tragic and hopeless longing for him.

Again, MacDonald casts the power struggle that follows Constance's rejection by Professor

Night as a quest to rethink the tragic trajectories of *Othello* and *Romeo and Juliet* and transform them into comedies. Constance's main reinterpretive role is to avoid the expected outcome of the tragedies, chiefly the tragic fate of Shakespeare's female characters, and empower these women with some important nuggets of late-twentieth-century wisdom. Constance invokes a critique of the absolutist, tragic mindset of historical literary women that leaves no room for an acknowledgment of complexity. She inspires a philosophical shift in Desdemona and Juliet, opening their minds to theories of relativism and feminism and unlocking them from what they previously considered unavoidable destinies.

MacDonald opens up the possibility, therefore, that contemporary readers and scholars can overturn historical forms of sexism and repression through a process of participation and reimagination. Her principal metaphor for this process relies on the conventions of Elizabethan comedy, which are less interested in humor than in the process of redemption and positive resolution. MacDonald does not provide the conventional marriage at the end of an Elizabethan comedy, but she does rely on the refusal of comedy to submit to fatalism and inescapable female tragedy. She reconstructs a feminist happy ending and urges contemporary spectators to do the same, reinventing and repossessing history.

Source: Scott Trudell, Critical Essay on *Goodnight Desdemona (Good Morning Juliet)*, in *Drama for Students*, Thomson Gale, 2006.

Murray Bramwell

In the following review, Bramwell calls Goodnight Desdemona (Good Morning Juliet) *"tedious" and "dramatically disengaging."*

Why does all the tribulation in Shakespeare's tragedies hinge on flimsy plot devices such as stolen handkerchiefs and wrongly delivered letters? What if these plays were really meant to be comedies? These are the questions asked by Constance Ledbelly, the central character in *Goodnight Desdemona (Good Morning Juliet),* a light-hearted exploration of the female characters in Othello and Romeo and Juliet by Canadian playwright Ann-Marie MacDonald.

Low in status and self-esteem, Ledbelly is a university researcher bullied by a self-important professor and persisting with unfashionable lines of inquiry about alchemy in Shakespeare's canon.

"JUST HOW SERIOUS IS THE WRITER WITH THIS PASTICHE ELIZABETHAN VERSE? THE EFFECT IS TEDIOUS; WORSE STILL, IT IS DRAMATICALLY DISENGAGING."

She believes that there is a missing author in the plays—a wise fool who knows their true meaning. Before you can say totally implausible, Constance, like Alice down the rabbit hole, finds herself in a time warp straight into Othello's Cyprus—in time, it seems, to save Desdemona from Iago's treachery and the Moor from meltdown.

After that, it is destination Verona and our unlikely heroine, disguised as a boy, rescues Tybalt and is amorously pursued by both Romeo and Juliet, now trapped in a faltering teenage marriage.

Attentively directed by Kim Durban, the performers in this State Theatre Company production bring their best effort to MacDonald's whimsy. Sally Cooper is endearing as the ditzy but stout-hearted Constance, Margot Fenley is sporting as the bloodthirsty Desdemona and Ksenja Logos is gently comic as a sex-starved Juliet.

As Romeo, Justin Moore is amusingly gormless and Michael Habib is often hilarious as the revised Othello and Juliet's prurient nurse.

But with an over-long and dated text tottering with plot convolutions, self-conscious asides, wisecracks, undergraduate parody and needless reams of cod blank verse, the strengths of the performances are often lost.

Matters are also not helped by designer Dean Hills who, while providing a pleasingly workable set, burdens the actors with voluminous faux Elizabethan breeches and other costume follies that persistently work against the more thoughtful purposes of the play.

Which raises the question—just how serious is the writer with this pastiche Elizabethan verse? The effect is tedious; worse still, it is dramatically disengaging. And what, after all the extruded comic complication, are we to make of the banality of concluding speeches such as, "I've had it with all that tragic tunnel vision" and "Life is a mess, thank god."

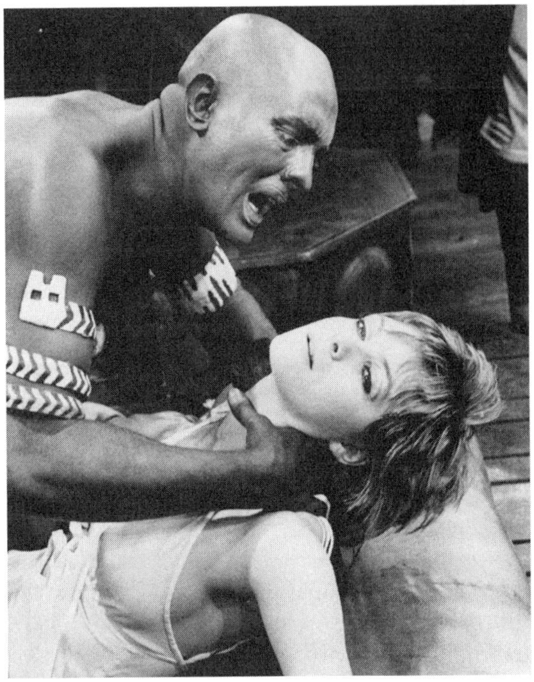

Jack Good and Sharon Gurney in a 1970 production of Othello © Hulton-Deutsch Collection/Corbis. Reproduced by permission

Constance should know that the accomplishment of Shakespeare's plays is to dramatise complexities, not reduce them to the wisdom of a Christmas cracker.

Source: Murray Bramwell, "From Bard to Worse," in *Australian*, September 23, 2004, p. 16.

Robert Crew

In the following review, Crew calls a newer production of Goodnight Desdemona (Good Morning Juliet), *in which MacDonald herself plays the role of Constance Ledbelly, a "tour de force."*

Ann-Marie MacDonald's *Goodnight Desdemona (Good Morning Juliet)* was born in a burst of high spirits; the title came to the author during some horseplay involving a pillow.

This exuberant play, which I reviewed when it premiered in 1988, is a tour de force. It manages to be serious, frivolous, intellectual, lighthearted, political and even, at times, downright silly, all in the space of two hours and 15 minutes.

The great joy of this production is that the author herself is playing the lead role of the mouse-like academic, Constance Ledbelly, for the first time.

Constance, shamelessly exploited by Professor Claude Night, is hot on the trail of a new theory about two particular Shakespearean tragedies—*Othello* and *Romeo And Juliet.* What if Shakespeare lifted them from two earlier comedies? This, she reasons, would explain why both Romeo and Othello seem to be "the unwitting victims of a disastrous practical joke rather than the heroic instruments of an inexorable Fate."

Suddenly Constance is whisked away into the worlds of the plays. First stop is Cyprus, where she thwarts the villainous Iago, only to create further knotty complications. Then it's off to fair Verona, where Constance stops Romeo from killing Tybalt, setting off a daisy chain of unexpected reactions, with both Romeo and Juliet cross-dressing to try to win her love. "Zounds, does no one in Verona sail straight?" is still one of my favourite lines in the play.

The language is an exhilarating roller-coaster ride of real Shakespearean iambic pentameters and clever imitations. It's lots of fun for anyone who has a passing acquaintance with R&J, Othello and Hamlet, which MacDonald also dips into from time to time.

It's a joyful romp with MacDonald—who looks like Minnie Mouse in her red booties and black tights—at the heart of it all.

Tanja Jacobs, the 1988 Constance, slipped at times into broad comedy and pushed the role into caricature; MacDonald's performance is more subtle and draws on clown techniques. There are little trips, spins and pirouettes, a quick roll of the eyes or sharp double take. The result is a faster, lighter production and one that only very occasionally loses steam.

Director Alisa Palmer has also fashioned some very funny visual gags; Alison Sealy-Smith is a splendidly bellicose Desdemona; Juan Choiran has declamatory fun with Othello and is a delightfully lascivious Nurse.

Forget the fact that the production feels a little raw and unfinished in places. We're ready to fall on our knees and say thank you for the return of a Canadian classic.

Source: Robert Crew, "Hello, Desdemona!" in *Toronto Star*, March 25, 2001, p. EN3.

Toronto Star

In the following essay, the critic uses a production of Goodnight Desdemona (Good Morning Juliet) *as occasion to remark on other plays built upon Shakespeare's works.*

If you're going to have a collaborator on a play, it might as well be a good one, and I suppose they don't come any better than William Shakespeare.

That thought occurred to me as I re-read Ann-Marie MacDonald's delightful *Goodnight Desdemona (Good Morning Juliet),* which opens next week at the Bluma Appel Theatre as the final show of CanStage's current season.

MacDonald takes a "coulda, woulda, shoulda" approach to a pair of Shakespeare's most intense plays (*Othello* and *Romeo And Juliet*) and manages to come up with a work that is deft, light and incisive at the same time.

Call it Postmodern or Deconstructionist if you like, but MacDonald is too clever to be pigeonholed in any such academic straightjacket. That refusal, in fact, is what her play is truly about.

But for our purposes today, MacDonald is just a jumping-off point to think about some of the other modern authors who have used Shakespeare as their blithely unknowing partner in crime.

Tom Stoppard probably heads the list, having turned to the Bard of Avon for inspiration on at least four occasions.

Most prominent is *Rosencrantz And Guildenstern Are Dead,* his inspired riff on two of the greatest nonentities in all of dramatic literature. Two Elizabethan courtiers turn into the soulmates of *Waiting for Godot's* Vladimir and Estragon—existential heroes in an Elizabethan world.

But the best part of Stoppard's work is that it sends you back to *Hamlet* to examine the originals once again, and your respect for Shakespeare's writing grows and grows.

What began as an act of mockery ends as a form of tribute to all concerned.

The next Stoppardian Shakespeare was the double bill *Dogg's Hamlet* and *Cahoot's Macbeth,* a somewhat impenetrable pairing of Wittgenstein's philosophy and Czech politics, with the original plays forming structures against which ideas can be hurled and—hopefully—bounce back again.

But it's most recently (and successfully) that Tom reunited with Will, on the screenplay of *Shakespeare in Love.*

Although a certain amount of revisionist backlash is now trashing the film as more slick than scholarly, there remains a great deal of literary as well as historical food for thought in Stoppard's imaginative hypothesis about how a real life romance dissolved the Bard of Avon's writer's block and allowed him to create *Romeo And Juliet.*

Moving on from Stoppard, there's still inspiration to be found in those Shakespearean "hills, brooks, standing lakes and groves."

"ANN-MARIE MACDONALD'S *GOODNIGHT DESDEMONA (GOOD MORNING JULIET)* WAS BORN IN A BURST OF HIGH SPIRITS; THE TITLE CAME TO THE AUTHOR DURING SOME HORSEPLAY INVOLVING A PILLOW."

Ronald Harwood's *The Dresser* takes a fictionalized version of Sir Donald Wolfit and has him performing *King Lear* while the bombs fall during World War II. The twin storms and tragedies are nicely matched, and the Shakespeare original is enhanced rather than diminished by the contact.

Plays like *Kean, Barrymore and Two Shakespearean Actors* use their thespian leads to grant them licence to appropriate large chunks of Bardic material, but that's not exactly the kind of partnership we're discussing here.

More of that type of union can be found in the unlikely world of musical theatre. Would there be a *West Side Story* without *Romeo And Juliet,* a *Kiss Me Kate* without *The Taming of the Shrew, The Boys from Syracuse* without *The Comedy of Errors?*

But not all marriages are happy ones and the same logic also led to shows like *Catch My Soul* (the musical *Othello*), *Fire Angel* (ditto for *The Merchant of Venice*), and one title that needs no further explanation, *Rockabye Hamlet.*

Even the world of teen flicks knows a good thing when it stumbles onto one, and we've recently been through *Get Over It* (*A Midsummer Night's Dream*), *Ten Things I Hate About Her* (*The Taming of the Shrew*) and *Never Been Kissed* (*As You Like It*).

So there you have it. Not only did Shakespeare write that "all the world's a stage," he saw to it that his stages went all over the literary world as well.

Goodnight, Desdemona. Good morning, Juliet. Break a leg, Ann-Marie.

Source: "Playwrights Brush up Their Shakespeare," in *Toronto Star*, March 17, 2001, p. AR1.

Laurin R. Porter

In the following essay excerpt, Porter explores how MacDonald illuminates differences between Shakespeare's tragic and comedic heroines in Goodnight Desdemona (Good Morning Juliet).

In "Feminist Thematics and Shakespearean Tragedy," Richard Levin takes to task that body of feminist critics who take a thematic approach to Shakespeare's tragedies. All of them, as he sees it, insist in one way or another that "the plays are about the role of gender in the individual and in society." While he does not deny that the worlds Shakespeare presents us with are patriarchal in nature (how could they be otherwise?), he resists the feminist tendency to single out this patriarchal aspect as the fundamental cause of the tragic events.

"They are necessary conditions of the action but are not in themselves sufficient to cause it," he argues. "Many of these critics seem to have confused these two different kinds of agency."

Be that as it may, the fact remains that, on the whole, the women in Shakespeare's tragedies do not fare well. Judith Bamber points out in *Comic Women, Tragic Men* that in the comedies Shakespeare at least takes the woman's part. "Often the women in the comedies are more brilliant than the men, more aware of themselves and their world, saner, livelier, more gay." The tragedies, she continues, present monstrous females—Goneril, Regan, and Lady Macbeth, for instance—who unnerve us precisely because their cruelty is located "on the very site of our expectations of a woman's kindness," giving as an example Lady Macbeth's infamous "I have given suck" speech.

Judging from her first solo drama, *Goodnight Desdemona (Good Morning Juliet),* Canadian playwright Ann-Marie MacDonald is acutely aware of the contrast between Shakespeare's tragic and comic heroines. In this play, Constance Ledbelly, a struggling assistant professor at Queen's University, is convinced that the sources for two of Shakespeare's most famous tragedies, *Othello* and *Romeo and Juliet,* were actually comedies and that Desdemona and Juliet, misunderstood and unappreciated by contemporary critics, were originally comic heroines. MacDonald constructs the frame story so that the timid, insecure Constance literally "falls" into the worlds of these plays and interacts with the characters, changing the outcome of the tragedies in the process. As a contemporary woman and scholar, she liberates the two heroines from their victim status and "wimp-ish" Renaissance portrayals.

The notion of tampering with Shakespeare is hardly new, of course. Other playwrights have written travesties (*I Hate Hamlet*) or parodies (such as *MacBird,* written during Lyndon Johnson's administration), while directors have transposed his plays to other milieux and historical settings. In more serious efforts, playwrights have used Shakespeare as a jumping-off point, borrowing from the text in creative ways to frame contemporary issues. Stoppard's insertion of men with twentieth-century sensibilities into Hamlet's world in *Rosencrantz and Guildenstern Are Dead,* for example, allows him to examine current questions about ontology, epistemology, and aesthetics.

Though it may seem a far cry from Stoppard, MacDonald's rollicking, bawdy, even raucous comedy operates in much the same fashion. On a superficial level, Constance's entry into Shakespeare's Cyprus and Verona merely provides the audience with comic entertainment, replete with stock characters (jealous lovers, absent-minded professors, slimy villains, and inflated windbags) as well as mistaken identities, romantic triangles, and revenge subplots. The language is also a source of delight; wit, wordplay, and outrageous puns abound. On a deeper level, however, the play raises questions about the ways in which identity is constructed and the impact of gender and societal expectations upon this process. As Constance interacts with first MacDonald's warlike Desdemona and then her erotic Juliet, she discovers aspects of her personality that had hitherto lain dormant. Ultimately, the action takes place not in Constance's office or the fictive worlds of Shakespeare's tragedies but within Constance's psyche.

Because it is a new play (first written in 1988; revised in 1990) and relatively unknown, a brief synopsis may be necessary. The action begins in the office of Constance Ledbelly, who for years has devoted herself to decoding the famous "Gustav" manuscript, which she believes will prove that the sources for *Othello* and *Romeo and Juliet* were originally comedies that Shakespeare "plundered and made over into ersatz tragedies." Part of her theory rests on the notion of a missing Fool, "conspicuous by his very absence . . . these two tragedies turn on flimsy mistakes," she argues, "a lost hanky, a delayed wedding announcement," mistakes "easily concocted" by a Wise Fool. If she can just find the Fool and discover the author of the repressed sources by decoding the manuscript, she will revolutionize the standard interpretations of these great plays.

When we first meet Constance, she hardly appears the stuff of which heroines are made. Entering her office at the beginning of Act One singing "Fairy Tales Can Come True" and carrying a Complete Shakespeare and "a stack of dog-eared loose-leaf foolscap," she appears the typical absent-minded professor (assistant professor, in this case). "She removes her coat," revealing a "crumpled tweedy skirt and jacket," but forgets to take off her red woolen toque with pom-pom (her fool's cap, one of the play's running gags), which she wears throughout the play. She nibbles absentmindedly on Vetveeta cheese and drinks a warm Coors Light, already opened, which she takes from her desk drawer. As she works aloud on her dissertation, writing on the foolscap in green ink, she is interrupted twice, first by a student named Jill, whom she mistakenly calls "Julie," and later by Ramona, a confident, attractive coed. Jill tries to slip her late paper on "The Effect of Filth on Renaissance Drama" undetected under Constance's door; the tug-of-war that ensues is a mini-version of the many battles that Constance will wage before the play is over. Ramona haughtily asks Constance to tell "Claude" (i.e., Professor Night) that she has just won the Rhodes. Both interactions reveal that Constance is not even a match for her students. Unfocused and socially inept, she is easily manipulated.

Professor Claude Night is a smooth-talking British academic who has enticed Constance to write essays and reviews that he passes off as his own, publications which he uses to become a full professor. When he arrives to pick up the articles that Constance has ghost-written for him, she is even more flustered and apologetic than before. Though she is self-deprecating, however, in her own way she refuses to back down from her belief in the importance of the Gustav manuscript, which Night ridicules. . . .

It's significant that Constance is so absorbed in her own work that she essentially sleepwalks through her conversations with Julie/Jill and Ramona. Structurally, these two bits of dialogue serve as precursors to her encounters with Juliet ("Julie") and Desdemona (Ramona). Constance is not ready to learn from these earthbound women; she must first, like the proverbial alcoholic, hit bottom.

And hit bottom she does, as Claude announces that he is marrying Ramona and moving with her to Oxford, where he will take the post for which Constance thought she was being groomed. Both her professional aspirations and her romantic daydreams are decimated within a matter of minutes. As she melodramatically discards the memorabilia on her desk, it is as if she is stripping away the layers of her past, symbolically ready at last to begin life anew, though she is not, of course, aware of this yet. . . .

"CALL IT POSTMODERN OR DECONSTRUCTIONIST IF YOU LIKE, BUT MACDONALD IS TOO CLEVER TO BE PIGEONHOLED IN ANY SUCH ACADEMIC STRAIGHTJACKET."

For all practical purposes, as the play begins Constance is a child, an innocent. Her formative experiences seem to be centered around either her fantasies about Claude Night or a long-distant past. All this is destined to change when she meets Desdemonia.

Constance's entrance into the world of Cyprus occurs in the pivotal scene in *Othello* (III, iii) where Iago finally convinces the Moor that he has been cuckolded. Believing Iago's testimony that the strawberry handkerchief he gave Desdemona is now in Cassio's possession and that this is evidence of Desdemona's infidelity, Othello declaims, "Damn her, lewd minx, O, damn her. Damn her. O. / I will chop her into messes." At this critical point, Constance sticks her head out from behind an arras and says, "No . . . Um . . . you're about to make a terrible mistake . . . m'Lord," and, plucking the handkerchief from Iago's back pocket, she averts the tragedy.

Othello, of course, thinks she is a prophet or seer, since she knows so much about his life. When Desdemona arrives on the scene shortly thereafter, Constance introduces herself, still marveling at her presence in the play:

> CONSTANCE I'm Constance Ledbelly. I'm an academic. I come from Queen's University. You're real. You're really real.
>
> DESDEMONA As real as thou art, Constance, Queen of Academe.
>
> CONSTANCE Is that my true identity? Gosh. I was just a teacher 'til today.

"THOUGH IT MAY SEEM A FAR CRY FROM STOPPARD, MACDONALD'S ROLLICKING, BAWDY, EVEN RAUCOUS COMEDY OPERATES IN MUCH THE SAME FASHION."

DESDEMONA A learned lady? O most rare in kind.
And does your husband not misprize this Knowledge?

CONSTANCE Oh I'm not married.

IAGO aside Most unnatural.

OTHELLO A virgin oracle. Thanks be to Dian.

DESDEMONA Brave ag'ed maid, to wander all alone.

Because they come to Constance with no preconceptions or stereotypes, Desdemona and Othello are able to see her value. MacDonald, of course, manipulates the plot to make this possible, using especially the character of Desdemona to turn liabilities, as Constance's culture would perceive them, into assets. The fact that she is a scholar, unmarried, traveling alone, even the fact that she is a vegetarian, which Desdemona declares "meet in vestal vows"—all these qualities are set in a new context and admired.

It is important to note that this Desdemona is not like the one we're used to. MacDonald establishes this from the outset, combining some of Shakespeare's lines with her own. When Desdemona greets Othello, he addresses her as his "fair warrior," which sets the tone. When she responds, her lines include a paraphrase of a line Shakespeare assigns to Othello which takes on a new meaning in this play. Referring to Othello, she says, "My sole regret that heaven had not made me such a man; / but next in honour is to be his wife." The implication in MacDonald's re-rendering of these lines is not that Desdemona regrets not having a man like Othello, but that she regrets not being one herself. The play embroiders on this theme, portraying her as adventurous, aggressive, even bloodthirsty, while Othello becomes a pompous windbag, fond of telling old war stories.

Desdemona and Constance are immediately simpatico. When Desdemona learns that at home in "Academe," Constance's students call her "The Mouse," she is outraged. To Constance's comment that she saw this name "carved into a lecture stand," Desdemona replies, "The sculptor dies." She assumes that Constance rules a race of Amazons who "brook no men" and immediately pledges to join the ranks of these "spiked and fighting shes." Constance enlists her aid in helping her find the mysterious Author and the Wise Fool, which Desdemona pledges on her honor to do, saying "for I do love thee. And when I love thee not, / chaos is come again." At this point, a cannon blast is heard, signaling the arrival of the Turks, and Desdemona urges Constance to join with her in the fray. When she refuses, saying she can't even kill a mosquito, Desdemona replies, "That's a fault," adding that to defend her honor, a single woman "must study to be bloody and betimes." Constance promises to go with Desdemona, who assures her, "we be women; not mice."

So begins Constance's transformation from "Mouse" to a self-confident, strong, independent woman. But the metamorphosis isn't complete until she encounters Juliet. If her encounters with Desdemona enable Constance to acknowledge her anger against Claude Night and discover her own power, her relationship with Juliet raises questions of gender and sexuality. During her rather hasty exit from Cyprus, which is prefaced by her reading in the foolscap that "Cyprus is too hot for thee. / Seek truth now in Verona, Italy" Constance's skirt is impaled on Desdemona's sword, leaving her in only her jacket, longjohns, and boots. She arrives in the midst of the Mercutio/Tybalt scene in which Romeo, intervening in their fight, ends up inadvertently contributing to Mercutio's death. This sets in motion the tragic events which will ultimately lead to both Juliet's death and his own. As in the previous act, Constance interposes in the nick of time, explaining to the hot-headed Tybalt that Romeo and Juliet have secretly wed, ending: "Tybalt, Romeo is your cousin now, / in law, and so you fellows should shake hands." After a split second's hesitation, Tybalt and Romeo turn to each other and embrace, then turn their attention to the newcomer, whom Romeo has addressed as "Boy." Ever the quick thinker, Constance lowers the pitch of her voice, changes her name to "Constan . . . tine," and concocts a story about washing up from the shores of Cyprus, "a roving pedant lad to earn my bread / by wit and by this fountain pen, my sword." This disguise will get her into trouble, but in true Shakespearean fashion, her false identity will ultimately engender insight.

Immediately after the feud is averted, Romeo, Mercutio, and Tybalt invite her to the baths to "baptize" their new friendship. Romeo, who is interested in Constantine in more than a brotherly way, urges, "Greekling, splash with us." Begging off, Constance delivers this monologue after they leave:

> How long can I avoid their locker room?
> Those guys remind me of the Stratford shows
> I've seen.
> where each production has a Roman bath:
> the scene might be a conference of state,
> but steam will rise and billow from the wings,
> while full-grown men in Velcro loin-cloths speak,
> while snapping towels at each other.
> Why is it Juliet's scenes with her Nurse
> are never in a sauna? Or "King Lear":
> imagine Goneril and Regan, steaming
> as they plot the downfall of their Dad,
> while tearing hot wax from each other's legs;
> Ophelia, drowning in a whirlpool full
> of naked women. Portia pumping iron—

The stereotypical macho images presented here are reinforced by the lewd jokes and puns that the three men exchange as they anticipate visiting the baths, full of references to the pox and maidenheads and wenches, while Constance, watching, bites her thumb-nail. Tybalt, seeing this, whirls around and says, "Do you bite your thumb at me sir?" (Constance's reply is a typical example of the play's witty use of bathos and the juxtaposition of Shakespearean language with contemporary rhetoric: "No. I just bite my nails, that's all. . . Look, I'll never bite them again. This'll be a great chance for me to quit once and for all. Thanks.") It is no accident, I think, that their bawdy jokes about what they will do to the "wenches" at Mistress Burnbottom's are followed with Tybalt's menacing threat. Both are part of the cultural norm for the "manly" behavior of Renaissance times (and all too often today): to be a man of the world one must show mastery over women and be fearless in the defense of one's honor. At the same time, the above passage suggests the valorization of male values, not only in Shakespeare's texts, but in contemporary productions of them. The prevalence of patriarchal values in today's society, as in the past, renders these cultural details invisible, until we turn them upside down and apply their female counterpart (as with Portia pumping iron), exposing them for what they are.

While Constance's male persona adds to our enjoyment, it also allows MacDonald to reveal the extent to which not only our social exchanges but our very identities are shaped by gender constructs. This fact is emphasized when both Juliet and Romeo fall in love with the "Greekling." MacDonald takes up the story of the star-crossed lovers after their wedding night together, beginning with Romeo's line, "Was that the lark?" Bathos is once again employed, as Juliet replies that it was the luncheon bell, and Romeo leaps out of bed, late for his appointment with the boys. It seems that after the newlyweds' passionate night, their affections have cooled; each looks for some new form of amusement. While Romeo makes a quick exit, hoping to meet up with Constantine again, Juliet whines to the Nurse, "I die of tedium." This Juliet, we quickly gather, is randy and adventurous, hardly the emblem of purity and innocence we're accustomed to. The confusion sets in when she, too, meets Constantine and falls madly in love.

The chaos multiplies when Romeo decides that Constantine, who rebuffs his advances, is put off because he is a man and decides to don one of Juliet's dresses to woo in. Juliet, meanwhile, concludes that Constantine favors young boys, and borrows Romeo's hose and doublet. Thus we have one man dressed as a woman and two women disguised as men (with the audience's awareness that in Shakespeare's time, all women's roles were played by males in female dress, adding a third layer to the reversals). To stir up the pot even more, the play assigns multiple roles to every actor except the one playing Constance, deliberately crossing over gender lines. The actor assigned the part of Juliet also plays Julie/Jill and a soldier; Desdemona is also Ramona, Mercutio, and a servant; and Othello, in addition to playing Tybalt and Professor Night (symbolically appropriate), also plays the Nurse. In both productions I saw, no attempt was made to play these parts "realistically"; the Nurse, for example, wore Othello's full beard and mustache. Again, while this can be seen as comedy behaving as it is wont, with exaggeration, slapstick effects, and broad humor, at the same time, it points to more serious questions of gender and identity formation.

By rendering both Romeo and Juliet in love with Constance/Constantine, with both in error about her gender, MacDonald asks us to question the assumption that heterosexuality is the norm and homosexuality a perversion. While we feel superior to this mismatched menage á trois, at the same time we are compelled to recognize, perhaps with some discomfort, the arbitrary quality of our own assumptions about gender. This point is rendered doubly ironic by the fact that MacDonald uses the quintessential young lovers of Western literature to make this point, borrowing some of Shakespeare's most romantic lines to portray the double pursuit of Constance. . . .

MacDonald uses Juliet in a more serious fashion to awaken Constance to her own sexuality. Her desires are aroused earlier by Romeo's kiss, to which she at length yields, but it is with Juliet that Constance most fully embraces her erotic potential. After first resisting Juliet's amorous advances, Constance finally kisses her with deep feeling. Shortly thereafter, she reveals that she's actually a woman and points out that she's a good deal older than Juliet. Neither fact deters Juliet. Indeed, their bond is deepened by the realization that they are both women, metaphorical sisters.

At this precise juncture Desdemona reappears on the scene, as the play progresses towards its climax. Intent on revenging the affair she thinks Constance is having with Othello, Desdemona, pulled through the time warp, leaps into the bedroom and tries to smother Constance. She is as bloodthirsty and quick to jump to conclusions as is Shakespeare's Othello. Juliet is also bent on death—her own. Histrionic and committed to a romanticized vision of suicide, she seeks out opportunities to plunge a dagger into her breast or swallow poison to prove her love.

Both have to learn from Constance, as she has learned from them. In a subsequent scene, set in a crypt reminiscent of that in Romeo and Juliet's death scene, Desdemona pursues Juliet, thinking she has killed Constance. As the two come to blows, Constance separates them, shouting, "Nay nay . . . I've had it with all the tragic tunnel vision around here . . . life is a hell of a lot more complicated than you think." She goes on to chastise Desdemona for her over-violent nature and Juliet for being in love not with life, but with death. Acceding to the truth of her vision, that one must live by questions, not solutions, and be content in confusion rather than clinging to over-simplified certainties, the two heroines are reconciled in their love for Constance. "Then I was right about your plays," she says. "They were comedies after all, not tragedies. I was wrong about one thing, though: I thought only a Wise Fool could turn tragedy to comedy."

At this point she is ready to recognize that she herself is the wise fool she has been seeking. The dialogue here turns on a series of puns which echo Hamlet, MacDonald's third primary source. A laugh comes from under the stage, which Constance identifies as belonging to Yorick, based on an earlier graveyard scene where she had encountered a ghost. "Yorick," she calls out. "Na-a-ay. You're it," the ghost replies, repeating his oracular saying of before. But this time, Constance gets the pun:

> CONSTANCE I'm it? I'm it I'm the Fool.
>
> GHOST A lass.
>
> CONSTANCE A lass.
>
> GHOST A beardless bard.
>
> CONSTANCE "The Fool and the Author are one and the same" . . . That's me. I'm the Author.

As the three women join hands, celebrating their triple birthday, a time warp occurs once again, returning Constance back to her office at Queen's. All is as it was before—the phone dangling on its cord, with Constance leaning over the wastebasket, though hatless this time. As she tentatively touches her head "as if to confirm her reality" she removes the feathered pen behind her ear and discovers that is has turned to solid gold. Her pen, mightier than the sword she learned to wield in Verona, has been transformed, as has her psyche; the alchemy is complete.

The three plots merge neatly in the final scene, uniting the transformed Desdemona and Juliet, now comic and reformed heroines—or at least aware of their tragic tendencies—and with Constance, no longer the Mouse, but the Mighty One. This satisfies our desire for closure and brings the comic narrative to completion. A closer inspection of the ways in which MacDonald effects this metamorphosis points to still another set of transformations as the contemporary playwright takes on the Bard, appropriating his voice and subsuming it into her own, which brings me to my final point.

A large part of the delight of reading or viewing this play comes from a dawning awareness of the many different strategies Macdonald employs in bending Shakespeare's plots, characters, and language to her own purposes. On the simplest level (which is not at all "simple," I might add), she combines the plots of three of Shakespeare's masterpieces into one Othello, Romeo and Juliet, and Hamlet—subsuming all of them into the metamorphosis of Constance Ledbelly. . . .

In borrowing Shakespeare's lines, MacDonald sometimes uses them as is, sometimes omits passages to abbreviate and tighten long speeches (lago's gulling of Othello, for instance), and sometimes condenses two different speeches into one. A variation on this strategy occurs when she changes the meaning of an exactly quoted line by placing it in a new context; for instance Desdemona's "Would that God had made me such a man."

MacDonald also assigns several of her Shakespearean characters lines spoken by someone else in the original version. Perhaps the clearest instance of this is in Act Two when Desdemona speaks many of Othello's lines. . . .

It is appropriate that Desdemona assumes Othello's lines, since in MacDonald's version, she takes on his characteristics (another gender reversal). . . .

Thus we, like Constance, become detectives, only instead of tracking down the author of the Gustav manuscript, as she is ostensibly doing, we're tracing the authorship of the lines we're hearing. It's a tribute to MacDonald that this isn't as easy as one might think. . . .

This detective work on the part of the audience is perhaps MacDonald's ultimate point. As we join Constance in her quest, identifying with her and becoming detectives ourselves, we can experience at least to a limited extent our own conversion, becoming our own authors. It is a transformation "most to be desired," an alchemy of the highest order, since from the outset, authorship and the authenticity of experience, female as well as male, has been the issue.

This level of meaning is reinforced by the alchemical motif which runs throughout the play. It's first mentioned in the Prologue by a character named simply "Chorus," who appears mysteriously in Constance's office and speaks the play's opening lines:

> What's alchemy? The hoax of charlatans?
> Or mystic quest for stuff of life itself:
> eternal search for the Philosopher's Stone,
> where mingling and unmingling opposites,
> transforms base metal into precious gold.

The play then presents us with a proliferation of transformations—Shakespearean characters are recast in contemporary terms with decidedly different characteristics (the passive Desdemona becomes aggressive and warlike, pure and faithful Juliet seeks new sexual experiences, Othello is a windbag, etc.); the tragedies turn into comedies; the lines are condensed, altered, added to, assigned to different characters. Most important, of course, Constance is transformed from Mouse to Owl, from "lead" (hence, "Ledbelly") to "gold" (imaged in her gold pen and associated with her pet Laurel, the symbol of victory).

MacDonald juxtaposes the Renaissance notion of alchemy with references to Jungian analysis, a twentieth-century version of a similar phenomenon: the search for a truth or process, whether internal or external, that will transform "base metal into gold." In the Chorus's opening speech, for instance, the reference to alchemy is followed immediately with these lines:

> Hence, scientific metaphor of self:
> divide the mind's opposing archetypes
> —if you possess the courage for the task—invite
> them from the shadows to the light;
> unite these lurking shards of broken glass
> into a mirror that reflects one soul.
> And in this merging of unconscious selves,
> there lies the mystic "marriage of true minds."

The play's final speech, also given to the Chorus, recapitulates this theme:

> The alchemy of ancient hieroglyphs
> has permeated the unconscious mind
> of Constance L. and manifested form,
> where there was once subconscious dreamy thought.
> The best of friends and foes exist within,
> where archetypal shadows come to light.

Both modern clinical analysis and alchemy, considered a science in its day, deal in transformations, changing what is into something better. And both, significantly, require an element of mystery, the inexplicable. A reaction between common elements produces a rare metal: the uncovering of a secret from the past transforms not just the present but one's understanding of what was: how, precisely, does this rake place?

MacDonald refuses to reduce life to a simple formula. The play insists upon a measure of magic, and a goodly measure, at that: heads popping out of wastebaskets, time warps that transpose Constance from her university office to Cyprus and from Cyprus to Verona, hieroglyphics and coded manuscripts and ghosts. It is necessary that as viewers we "suspend our disbelief," as the Chorus instructs us: "Be foolish wise." If we allow ourselves to be swept up not just by the humour but by the magic of this play, we, too, become "wise fools," the authors of our own stories.

In her classic essay "If Shakespeare Had a Sister," Virginia Woolf calls for someone to rewrite history, including women's stories along with those of men. In *Goodnight Desdemona (Good Morning Juliet),* MacDonald takes up this charge but goes Woolf one better. Woolf creates the fictitious Judith Shakespeare, William's "sister," to account for the absence of female Renaissance playwrights. MacDonald creates the fictitious Constance Ledbelly, and in this story of a timid scholar reclaiming the authorship of her own life, appropriates the plots, characters, and very lines of Shakespeare, making them her own. She becomes, if you will, the "Judith" Shakespeare that never was. As she declares her independence from the Bard, she places her faith in sisterhood: the sisterhood of Constance, Desdemona, and Juliet and that of contemporary women everywhere.

Source: Laurin R. Porter, "Shakespeare's 'Sisters': Desdemona, Juliet, and Constance Ledbelly in *Goodnight Desdemona (Good Morning Juliet)*," in *Modern Drama*, Vol. 38, No. 3, Fall 1995, p. 362.

SOURCES

Dvorak, Marta, "Goodnight William Shakespeare (Good Morning Ann-Marie MacDonald)," in *Canadian Theatre Review*, Nos. 79/80, Summer/Fall 1994, pp. 130, 133.

Fortier, Mark, "Shakespeare with a Difference: Genderbending and Genrebending in *Goodnight Desdemona*," in *Canadian Theatre Review*, No. 59, Summer 1989, pp. 50, 51.

Hengen, Shannon, "Towards a Feminist Comedy," in *Canadian Literature*, No. 146, Autumn 1995, p. 97.

MacDonald, Ann-Marie, *Goodnight Desdemona (Good Morning Juliet)*, Grove Press, 1998, pp. 11, 13, 15, 17, 19, 31, 37, 38, 50, 56, 64, 74.

Shakespeare, William, *Romeo and Juliet*, in *The Complete Works*, edited by Stanley Wells and Gary Taylor, Oxford University Press, 1987, p. 345.

Weales, Gerald, "Gender Wars," in *Commonweal*, Vol. 119, No. 21, December 4, 1992, pp. 15, 20.

FURTHER READING

Djordjevic, Igor, "*Goodnight Desdemona (Good Morning Juliet)*: From Shakespearean Tragedy to Postmodern Satyr Play," in *Comparative Drama*, Vol. 37, No. 1, Spring 2003, pp. 89–115.

Djordjevic's analysis of *Goodnight Desdemona* concentrates on the genres of tragedy and comedy as they can be applied to the play and its influences.

Honan, Park, *Shakespeare: A Life*, Oxford University Press, 1998.

Honan provides a readable, well-researched, and informative account of Shakespeare's life and career, including a description of the cultural atmosphere in Elizabethan England.

Nurse, Donna Baily, "Send in the Clowns," in *Publisher's Weekly*, Vol. 250, No. 47, November 24, 2003, pp. 37–38.

Nurse's brief interview and biography of MacDonald touches on some of the author's influences and passions.

Stevenson, Melanie A., "Othello, Darwin, and the Evolution of Race in Ann-Marie MacDonald's Work," in *Canadian Literature*, No. 168, Spring 2001, pp. 34–54.

This essay discusses the issues of race and evolution in *Goodnight Desdemona* and MacDonald's other work.

I Am My Own Wife

DOUG WRIGHT

2003

I Am My Own Wife was the first one-person show ever to win a Pulitzer Prize, which it did in 2004. The main character of Doug Wright's award-winning play is a German transvestite, who goes on to become a celebrity in his/her own right, to the point of being declared by some a national German hero. The play was published in 2004 by Faber and Faber. Wright, who is included in the more than forty characters portrayed (by one man), went to Germany in 1993 to meet and record conversations with the real Charlotte von Mahlsdorf (born Lothar Berfelde), upon whose life the play is based. The playwright struggled for several years after meeting with Charlotte, trying to conceptualize how to turn the material he had into a play. There were so many different facets of Charlotte's life, including some that were not very flattering—among them, news stories that confirmed that Charlotte had been a Nazi spy.

Wright called together two of his closest friends and brainstormed with them. Those friends were Moisés Kaufman, an award-winning director who would go on to direct the play, and Jefferson Mays, who would astonish audiences with his versatility in acting out all forty or more characters and eventually capture his own award, the Tony. *I Am My Own Wife* tells a story that spans Charlotte's childhood in the 1930s through the erection (1961) and deconstruction (1989–1990) of the Berlin wall, which separated Communist-controlled East Berlin from West Berlin. Through the eyes of Charlotte, the audience gains a glimpse into life in Germany

Doug Wright Getty Images

as it is transformed first by the Nazi regime and then by the bombings of the Allied Forces. The play opened off Broadway in May 2003 and moved to the Lyceum Theater on Broadway on December 3, 2003. It stayed on Broadway for almost a year and enjoyed 361 performances. As of the summer of 2005, it was still on national tour.

AUTHOR BIOGRAPHY

Doug Wright was born in Dallas, Texas, and it has been reported that, in 2005, he still spoke with a slight Texan twang. He received his bachelor's degree from Yale in 1985 and then went on to New York University, where he completed his master's degree in 1987. When Wright was interviewed by Gerard Raymond for the *Advocate*, after having won the Pulitzer Prize for *I Am My Own Wife*, Wright stated, "I keep calling my boyfriend every two hours and saying, 'I still have my Pulitzer!'" In fact, Wright's play won a long list of prizes that year, including the Tony Award for Best Play, the Drama Desk Award for Outstanding Play, the Outer Critics Circle Award, the Lucille Lortel Award, and the Drama League Award.

Wright should be used to winning prizes. He first captured an Obie for Outstanding Achievement in Playwriting and the Kesselring Award for Best American Play with *Quills*. This 2000 play focused on the subject of the Marquis de Sade and his time spent in prison. In this story, a friendly priest brings quills to Sade so that he can write. After the play was produced on the stage, Wright adapted this work as a screenplay. The movie version, which was Wright's motion picture debut, also won praise. It was given the Paul Selvin Award and received three Academy Award nominations. Other plays of Wright's include *The Stonewater Rapture* (1990), *Watbanaland* (1995), and *Unwrap Your Candy* (2001).

In the interview with Raymond, Wright talked about his attraction to Charlotte von Mahlsdorf, the subject of his Pulitzer Prize–winning play. Wright told Raymond that when he first met Charlotte, he thought of her as a mentor to him. She had survived so much more than Wright had. "I thought that all the negative conditioning I had endured as a young gay man growing up in Texas," Wright said, was offset by Charlotte's extraordinary experiences of survival. In the early 2000s, Wright was at work creating screenplays for Warner Brothers. When asked by one reporter if he would return to the stage, Wright answered in the affirmative. He claimed to have stored in one of his desk drawers enough material to keep him writing plays for a long time.

PLOT SUMMARY

Act 1

Wright's play, *I Am My Own Wife* opens in silence. Charlotte stares out at the audience, smiles slightly, and then disappears. The stage is empty for a short time before Charlotte reappears. She carries a large antique Edison phonograph, sets it down, admires it, and finally speaks. She proceeds to lecture the audience on the topic of the phonograph, giving a history of how it was developed and how it works.

Charlotte becomes quiet again; this time, when she speaks, she has been transformed into John Marks, the bureau chief of the Berlin office of *U.S. News & World Report*. John writes a letter (which is read) to Doug Wright, telling him of Charlotte. John changes into Doug, who is in Berlin with John and is talking into a tape recorder. The two men are heading toward Mahlsdorf, where Charlotte lives in East Berlin. On their way, they pass remnants of the Berlin wall, which has been torn down.

Doug morphs back into Charlotte. She holds some doll furniture in her hands and describes it. She continues to do the same with other antiques. She explains that after every disaster in Berlin, she would go through the rubble and save artifacts. Charlotte changes into Doug. He reads a letter that he has written to Charlotte. Doug is back in the United States but wants to revisit Charlotte and interview her if Charlotte will allow it. Charlotte writes back and agrees. Doug, now in East Berlin, asks John to translate for Charlotte his questions about her background. Charlotte waives the translations and begins to answer the questions directly in English.

She talks about her Tante Luise and how she encouraged Charlotte's cross-dressing. Through Tante Luise, Charlotte learned about a book that states that everyone has various proportions of male and female elements in their bodies. Some people do not fit in the normally defined classifications, being neither fully male nor fully female. Tante Luise gave Charlotte the book and told her to read it. Charlotte talks about World War II, when Berlin was heavily bombarded by Russian splatter bombs. The German S.S. officers were looking for boys to recruit. One officer asks whether Charlotte is a girl or a boy. As Lothar (Charlotte's given name), the audience hears the sixteen-year-old claim that he is a boy, but the officer decides Lothar is too young to shoot.

Charlotte says that her father was a Nazi and that he was brutal. In 1943, while Charlotte and her mother and siblings are living with Luise, Charlotte's father visits them. He has a revolver and threatens to kill his wife and children. Luise counters with a gun of her own, which she fires. The father leaves. Luise declares that it is a shame she missed. Charlotte is sent back to Berlin to help renovate the family home to accommodate war refugees. While she is there, Charlotte is confronted by her father, who insists that Charlotte choose between him and her mother. When Charlotte chooses her mother, her father locks her in her room. Charlotte escapes and finds her father sleeping, whereupon she beats him to death. She is sentenced to four years in prison. Charlotte is in prison when the Russians bomb it. The prisoners are told by the guards to run, which Charlotte does. The Allied Forces are approaching Berlin. Russian soldiers are handing out free food.

Doug begins another visit with Charlotte. He follows her down a series of steps that opens up to what looks like an old-fashioned tavern. Charlotte describes the tavern and tells Doug how she bought all the furniture and brought all the flooring and walls over to her house to save the tavern from being destroyed by the Nazis. The Berlin tavern, since the time of Emperor Wilhelm II, had been a favorite hangout for homosexuals and transvestites. Once the Berlin wall was constructed, homosexuals and transvestites in East Berlin had no place to gather. So Charlotte secretly opened the tavern, which was then in her basement, as a place of entertainment. Charlotte painted the windows black to keep the Stasi (Berlin secret police) from spying on them. Doug interjects the fact that when the Berlin wall fell, Charlotte had the only cabaret in all of East Germany, which she ran for almost thirty years.

The Cultural Minister of Berlin appears and gives Charlotte a medal for the work she has done in preserving historical pieces. Charlotte is thrilled not just for the honor but also at having the ceremony broadcast on national television, thus demonstrating to all of Germany that even a transvestite can work. Doug asks Charlotte what it was like to visit West Berlin after so many years of living behind the Berlin wall. Charlotte then proceeds to read from a Berlin travel guide. She mentions several bars, cafés, and bookstores that cater to homosexuals and transvestites. When she is done, Doug asks her about her reputed collaboration with the Stasi. Charlotte describes how the Stasi came to her. The Stasi insisted, Charlotte says, that she write a statement, which they dictated to her and made her sign. The signed statement confirms that Charlotte willingly agreed to work with the Stasi. She would become their spy.

Doug tries to get further details from Charlotte about why she agreed to spy. Charlotte offers little, other than to relate what Tante Luise used to tell her. In essence, Luise advised that Charlotte should do whatever was necessary to survive. John speaks next. He tells Doug that the German press has gotten hold of Charlotte's Stasi file, which confirms that she was definitely an informant. The file also reveals that Charlotte informed on one of her friends, who was subsequently sent to prison.

Act 2

The act opens with the character Alfred Kirschner. He is reading a letter he has written to Charlotte. Kirschner is in prison for having sold antique clocks to American soldiers. He also relates some of his experiences in jail. He thanks Charlotte for encouraging him to not give up.

Doug asks questions about Charlotte's Stasi file. He is confused and asks Charlotte to straighten out some of the details. Charlotte begins to tell the story of her relationship with Alfred, how they met and how they worked together to sell the old clocks. When Kirschner fears that the Stasi knows what he is doing, he stores the clocks at Charlotte's house. Kirschner tells Charlotte to deny having any connection with him, which is what Charlotte does. When the Stasi come, Charlotte tells them the clocks belong to Kirschner, and they arrest him.

Charlotte then acts out one of her visits to Kirschner while he is in jail, claiming, to the guards, that she is his wife. Charlotte explains that Kirschner named her in his will. After his release, Charlotte helps Kirschner find a place to live in a nursing home. The Nazis have taken everything from his home. He dies later, leaving Charlotte only his bills.

John and Doug briefly discuss Charlotte's Stasi file. A Stasi agent appears and reads items from the file itself, which refute Charlotte's claims. The file states that Charlotte informed on Kirschner to the Stasi over a period of at least five months. This information helped the Stasi make their arrest of Kirschner. Doug takes the file to Charlotte to confront her, but Charlotte evades all his questions. Voices from an invisible loudspeaker can be heard. Politicians and other citizens are discussing whether her medal of honor should be taken away from Charlotte now that the news of her being an informant has been made public. Some people find it disgraceful; others say the whole discussion is meaningless, since many people informed on others during the Nazi era.

Ziggy Fluss, a talk-show host, interviews Charlotte, calling her "Trannie Granny." He asks whether the rumors are true that she is moving to Sweden. Charlotte confirms this. She says that she is leaving because of the violence in Berlin. She recounts how her museum was vandalized by a group of neo-Nazis. About thirty of them scaled the wall of her backyard and terrorized her guests. A neo-Nazi talks: "Hitler forgot to shove you in an oven in Sachsenhausen!" Charlotte returns to her narration of the event, telling Ziggy that she attempted to defend herself by swinging an ax. As she explains this, she tells Ziggy that she shouted at one of the intruders: "I have met you before! When I was sixteen years old!" The police came, she says, but no one was arrested.

Charlotte talks about the atmosphere in East Berlin. She claims that anti-Semitism has returned, as has homophobia. Ziggy listens but then asks whether her leaving Germany might also have something to do with the reaction to her Stasi file. Charlotte deflects the question. As Charlotte leaves the studio, she is confronted by reporters. They ask her about her father's death, the Stasi, and all the furniture she has. The reporters suggest that she has lied about her father, has collaborated with the Stasi, and was paid for her work with stolen furniture that was taken from people who were wrongfully forced from their homes. One reporter even suggests that Charlotte has lied about her sex, that she really is a woman. Again, Charlotte does not answer any question directly. She does make one solid statement in reference to whether she is a man or a woman. She says that her mother once told her that it was time to get married. Charlotte told her mother: "I am my own wife."

A psychiatrist, Dieter Jorgensen, offers a psychiatric diagnosis of Charlotte, concluding that she is mentally ill, suffering from autism. "Her stories aren't lies, per se," Jorgensen states. "They're self-medication." Next follows a discussion between Doug and John. Doug confesses to John that he needs to believe in Charlotte, no matter what is in the Stasi files or what the media says. "I need to believe in her stories as much as she does!" Then Doug adds: "I need to believe that things like that are true. That they can happen in the world." Doug is impressed just by Charlotte's mere survival as a transvestite in a Nazi and Communist world. However, Doug admits that he does not have a clue how to put all the information that he has gathered about Charlotte into a play.

Doug turns on a tape. Charlotte is talking about the old furniture she has collected. She says that one must leave the furniture as it is, with all its marks and blemishes. And that one must show it "as is." Doug relates that Charlotte did move to Sweden, where she lived for seven years. In April 2002, she decided to return to Berlin for a visit. While she was there, she died of a heart attack in the garden of her old home. Before she died, Charlotte sent an envelope to Doug that he received after her death. There is no letter inside, but rather an old photograph of Charlotte (Lothar) as a young boy, sitting between two tiger cubs. The play ends with the sound of one of Doug's tapes. On the tape, Charlotte is talking about Thomas Alva Edison and his invention of the phonograph.

CHARACTERS

Herr Berfelde

Herr Berfelde is Charlotte's father. He was a government official in the Nazi regime and was reportedly very cruel to his wife and his children. At one point he threatens to kill his family. In retribution, Charlotte steals into his room one night and murders him. Later, when Charlotte is confronted by threats from neo-Nazis, she goes after them unafraid, remembering how her father had threatened her. Herr Berfelde thus exemplifies the brutal threats that Charlotte confronted throughout her life.

Lothar Berfelde

See Charlotte von Mahlsdorf

Cultural Minister

The Cultural Minister is one of many characters who appear briefly onstage. The Cultural Minister, however, is a pivotal character, in that he honors Charlotte, demonstrating a complete turnaround in Germany's attitude toward transvestitism, nontraditional gender roles, and homosexuality. He appears briefly to present the Bundesrepublik Deutschland, a medal of honor, to Charlotte for her efforts in conservation. Later, Charlotte discloses that on this day she was recognized for all her work. She liked this honor because it showed the country that a transvestite could also work just like any other person. Not too long afterward, however, the bestowing of this medal of honor comes into question as the news of Charlotte's having been an informant leads to an outcry from the public, protesting that Charlotte is not a good candidate for the medal.

Ziggy Fluss

Ziggy is a Euro-pop, hip talk-show host who interviews Charlotte for his program. The show begins on an upbeat note, with Ziggy referring to Charlotte as "Trannie Granny." However, as Charlotte discusses the recent invasion of her home by a neo-Nazi group, the conversation takes on a darker atmosphere. Ziggy attempts to find some validation for the neo-Nazis, trying to excuse their destructive acts based on the frustrations they have been feeling since the Berlin wall was brought down. Charlotte does not allow Ziggy to go too far in this defense.

Ziggy also calls Charlotte on one of her stories. Charlotte tells Ziggy that she is leaving Germany and moving to Sweden to get away from the violence in Germany. Ziggy is a little too hip to accept this, though. He knows that Charlotte has lost face in Berlin because of the opening and public viewing of the Stasi file, which reveals that Charlotte was an informant. Ziggy does not let Charlotte bow out gracefully.

Dieter Jorgensen

Dieter Jorgensen is a psychiatrist who studies Charlotte von Mahlsdorf's case and declares that she is autistic. It is not clear whether Jorgensen actually meets with Charlotte or if his conclusions are drawn from merely reading about her. Jorgensen's statement is added to the play's conclusion to demonstrate the variety of opinions about Charlotte and the contradictions in her stories.

Alfred Kirschner

Alfred Kirschner is a friend of Charlotte's. Some people claim that they might have even been lovers at one time. Kirschner, like Charlotte, collected antiques. He devised a plan to sell old clocks to the American soldiers, which was illegal in Germany. Although Charlotte helped Kirschner with the plan, it has been suggested that she informed on him; Kirschner was sent to jail.

In Charlotte's account, however, Kirschner told Charlotte to free herself of any connection with him so that she would not also go to jail. Charlotte's Stasi file, though, contradicts this story, making the claim that Charlotte set Kirschner up, informing on him and his activities for several months before he was imprisoned. There is little indication from Charlotte's version of events that her friend was aware of this. Rather, as Charlotte reads Kirschner's letters, nothing but friendship is indicated. Kirschner's ordeal and Charlotte's role in it become a pivotal point in the play, as Charlotte's reputation and truthfulness are challenged.

Tante Luise

Tante Luise is Charlotte's aunt, her mother's sister. She lives in East Prussia. Charlotte and her mother stay with Luise to escape Charlotte's father's brutal beatings. Luise eventually threatens the father with a gun when he appears with a shotgun. She is a lesbian and encourages Charlotte to explore her own definition of sexuality. She gives Charlotte books to read about studies that claim that female and male distinctions are not black and white.

Charlotte von Mahlsdorf

Charlotte is the main character. She was born a boy but has dressed as a woman most of her life. She is an antique collector; her home resembles a museum, and she gives tours to visitors. Charlotte is an enigma in many different ways. First, there is the question of her sex. Is she male or female? Did she inform on her friends? And, finally, there is the question of how to judge Charlotte. Is she a hero worthy of a medal of honor? Or is she a fraud?

In creating this play, Wright was torn about how to represent Charlotte. He admires her in many ways, thinking of her as his own mentor, in terms of how to live unafraid. However, he recognizes elements in Charlotte's personality and in her past that were very flawed. In Charlotte's reflections on the ways one should deal with "old furniture," Wright discovered how to portray Charlotte, flaws and all. Charlotte is a survivor, doing what she considered she had to do to stay alive.

John Marks

John Marks, the Berlin bureau chief of *U.S. News & World Report*, is a friend of Doug Wright's (in real life and in the play). John is the one who tells Doug about Charlotte and encourages him to come to Berlin to interview her. Throughout the play, the character Doug turns to John in order to reflect on some of his thoughts. John's friendship with Doug encourages him and helps him find his way when he gets lost.

Doug Wright

The author of this play is also portrayed as a character. This offers legitimacy to the play, which is presented in pseudo-documentary style. By putting himself into the play as the character Doug, the author allows the audience to take a step out of Charlotte's story and reflect on some of the things that Charlotte says. Through Doug, the audience learns about contradictions in Charlotte's story. The audience also learns of some of the challenges that the author had to face in presenting Charlotte's story. Because all characters are played by one person, the character Doug also acts, at times, as a narrator, providing background details and information about the settings.

THEMES

Oppression

The theme of oppression begins with the presentation of Charlotte's father, who bullies Charlotte's mother, aunt, and siblings. Oppression follows a course through Charlotte's life, most specifically the psychological oppression that she experiences when she realizes that she does not fit into the mold society has created for her. Once Charlotte realizes that she is different from most people around her, she is repressed in fully acting out what she believes is her true self. Is she a boy or a girl? She dresses like a girl, but when asked by the military officer, she says that she is a boy.

As an adult, Charlotte witnesses the oppression practiced by the Nazis, who were known to gather up homosexuals and transvestites and imprison them in concentration camps. The nightclubs are closed, and even though Charlotte rescues and reconstructs one in her basement, she must paint the windows black so that no government officials can see in. Whether it is fear of admitting what she feels or fear of physical punishment, oppression is the undercurrent when Charlotte must write and then sign an agreement with the Stasi to spy on her friends. The subsequent imprisonment of Kirschner is another reminder of oppression. In this case, it is severe oppression for having done something rather trivial (selling old clocks).

In the introduction to the published version of his play, Wright comments on his own sense of oppression growing up as a gay man in Texas. He admires Charlotte for dealing with far more oppression than he ever dreamed of facing. He emphasizes oppression in his play so that the opposite experience, that of freedom, can shine forth. Despite the oppression that Charlotte suffered, she was able to create a somewhat successful life. She maintained a large home, entertained, had friends, and in the end became something of a hero.

Homosexuality, Transvestitism, and the Transgendered

Wright has stated that he is interested in the history of homosexuality. So when he had the chance to interview Charlotte, he knew that she would supply him with information that was very hard to come by. Material is extremely sparse on the plight of gay people and on others like Charlotte who did not fit the standard gender roles during the Third Reich in Germany. However, Charlotte, having experienced this world, could offer Wright a living history of a moment in time that very few people know about firsthand. This play explores various questions: What was life like for homosexuals and others of nonstandard gender in Germany during the Nazi era? What did it require to stay alive as an openly gay man, lesbian, or transvestite? What were the changes in such people's private lives?

The theme of nontraditional genders runs through the first half of the play, but by the time the play reaches its conclusion, this theme is immaterial. The focus is no longer on how this particular transvestite survived but rather on who Charlotte is and on the truth of her story. In other words, by the end of the play, it makes no difference whether Charlotte is straight or gay. The

TOPICS FOR FURTHER STUDY

- Charlotte was a collector of antiques. Some of her favorite pieces were old phonographs. Read about the beginning of recorded sound. What were the first phonographs like? How has the recording of music changed over the years? Write a report and present it to your class.
- Berlin has gone through many changes since World War II. Read a history of Berlin from the mid-1930s to the present day. Make a presentation to your class about the major changes in politics, government, society, and the arts since the 1930s. Create a timeline to highlight the more significant points.
- Research three repressive societies, such as North Korea, China, and Nazi Germany. How do they compare? How were they or are they different? Pay special attention to the activities of the secret police in each country. What restrictions and punishments were or are imposed on the citizenry? How did or does repression affect the arts and culture? Write your report.
- Berlin was once known for its cabarets. What kind of entertainment was provided in cabarets? Try to uncover some of the music that might have been played in a cabaret. Watch a movie, such as *Cabaret* (1972), that portrays typical cabaret scenes. Then create your own performance to entertain your class.

---

audience is fascinated merely with Charlotte's humanity. Why does she not answer questions directly? Why does she tell untruthful stories? What need are her imaginary stories fulfilling? This, in some ways, may be the major point of the play. Whereas transvestitism appeared to be so important at the beginning of the story, when the story closes the audience is left to ponder whether the real truth is that transvestitism should be of little significance to anyone except oneself.

Mystery

There are many mysteries in this play. Wright sums them up in the introduction to the published version of the play, "Portrait of an Enigma." Then he writes about his experience of attempting to capture Charlotte's personality and life in a play. Wright has said that he was tormented by the many puzzles of Charlotte's life. He could not solve any of the riddles. He would ask Charlotte direct questions, but she always found some way to elude giving answers. Wright would research and find that the facts contradicted what Charlotte had told him. However, the records in which Wright found these outside facts were themselves suspect.

Because Wright could not solve any of the mysteries, he has to leave them unsolved. Not everything in life has an answer. He will not draw any conclusions, or at least he will not present them. Instead, he allows the mysteries to stay within the play. Audiences would have to come to their own conclusions. Mysteries, in and of themselves, cannot be solved. One has to learn to live with the uncertainty that mysteries present. Mysteries solved are no longer mysteries. Wright's play remains open-ended, which allows a wide expanse into which anyone who is curious can wander. It is as if Wright is saying through his play, "This is the story of a very interesting person's life. You can take it or leave it."

Brutality

Charlotte is both a victim and a perpetrator of brutality. Her father was very hard on her, both physically and mentally, but she herself sought revenge in a very brutal way. Brutality did not figure only in her early years. She lived in Berlin, which was almost completely demolished during World War II by the Allied Forces. By some accounts, more than 80 percent of the buildings in

Berlin were destroyed. There is also brutality at the end of the play, when Charlotte recounts her experiences with neo-Nazis who storm her garden and threaten her guests. Most of the members of her party disappear, but Charlotte recognizes the force of brutality and retaliates much in the same way that she did with her father—brutally. Like the theme of oppression that is used to highlight the ultimate freedom, brutality contrasts with Charlotte's genteel nature. Her overall demeanor is that of a gentle grandmother figure. By emphasizing the brutality that lies dormant within her, Wright displays a complex and therefore intriguing character.

STYLE

Multiple Roles, One Actor

Wright's *I Am My Own Wife* supports a forty-person cast of characters. These characters are all acted out by one man. With only minimal changes in costume (the addition of a hat or the removal of a string of pearls), the many different characters are distinguished from one another by physical mannerisms, intonation of voice, and accent. For example, the main character, Charlotte, often offers the audience what is described as a very sly smile. The audience becomes familiar with this smile, so that the actor merely has to flash this facial expression to let the audience know that the character of Charlotte has returned. The character of Doug is recognizable by his slight Texan accent. Other dialogues are presented in loud voices or through different body stances or gestures.

The constant switching from one character to another plays into the overall sense of mystery. The audience has to take an active role in keeping up with the suggestions that imply the arrival of each new character. This sense of mystery filters back to the main character too. Charlotte, to some degree, also switches from one character to another as she narrates the story of her life, presenting the audience with another challenge of trying to decipher which of Charlotte's characters (and stories) are true.

Pseudo-documentary

Wright presents his play as a pseudo-documentary, which looks as if it were all based on fact, as would be true in a real documentary, but has been manipulated so that it fits more easily into a dramatic narrative or storytelling mold. The details of the play may be as Wright experienced or heard them. However, in the retelling of his experiences, Wright must take poetic license to bring the elements of the play together in a more succinct story form. Although the details might be very close to the truth, he edited many boxes of recorded tapes made of his conversations with Charlotte. He had to choose which of the interviews best exemplified her character and tell her story in a somewhat entertaining, or at least engaging, way.

By using this form, the play takes on an element of authenticity. It appears as if Wright is presenting actual events that took place in real life. That is the documentary part. The invented element provides the play with the typical parts of a dramatic presentation, such as a beginning, middle, and end. In other words, the play tells a story. The audience is not sure which part of the play is truth and which part has been fictionalized. An author might use pseudo-documentary to bend a true story toward a particular idea, making certain implications. Or an author might choose pseudo-documentary to make a fictionalized story appear to be based on fact.

Implied Setting

Although the physical stage set for this play is one simple room, the overall setting, as created by the stories of Charlotte, conveys a feeling of what life was like in Nazi Germany and Communist-controlled East Germany. The brutality, oppressiveness, and secrecy of this wider context help illuminate the actual world in which Charlotte's life unfolded, giving the audience more material to help them understand what Charlotte's life was like and to comprehend why she felt she had to do what she did.

There is another element in the stage set that is also implied: Charlotte's large collection of antiques. The stage is not filled with furniture, as might be expected; rather, the stage directions call for doll-size furniture. Thus, the actor can talk about how a certain piece might have come into Charlotte's collection or convey a certain appreciation for the workmanship of a piece merely by holding up a small, toylike table or couch. In both cases—the world of East Germany and the antique furniture collection—the setting is an illusion in the audience's mind.

Emotional Swings

The mood of the play swings from light emotion, such as humor, to heavier and more complex feelings of despair, frustration, and anger. It could be said that the various moods of Wright's play are its strongest element. There is a sense of compassion when Charlotte retells incidents from her youth, whether it is the love and respect of a favorite old aunt or the disgust of having to deal with an unsympathetic father. However, the overall mood of the play is that of confusion. When, near the end of the play, Doug offers the information that Charlotte may not be telling the truth, all the former moods coalesce into one, or at least all the moods are overshadowed by confusion. Once doubt is introduced, the audience must go back and reevaluate what mood they might have felt earlier. This sense of doubt lingers to the end, leaving the audience in a perplexed state, which may be the whole point of the play.

HISTORICAL CONTEXT

Berlin, 1930s–1990s

Berlin is the capital of Germany and its largest city, with more than three million inhabitants. Before World War II, however, more than four million people called Berlin home. Adolf Hitler planned to reconstruct most of the buildings in Berlin during his rule (1933–1945). He found Berlin ugly and had visions of creating an entirely new city that he wanted to call Germania. When Allied Forces bombed the city, Hitler thought it was a good thing. It would save Germany the cost of demolishing the old buildings that he so disliked.

Most of Berlin was destroyed by the Allied Forces. In 1944, the city was divided four ways with the United States, the United Kingdom, France, and the Soviet Union taking control of different zones. Governance was maintained in West Berlin by the Western countries, while the Soviet Union controlled East Berlin. As the relationship with the Soviet Union deteriorated, tensions mounted in the city. At one point, the Soviet Union blocked the passage of goods to West Berlin, and food and other supplies had to be airlifted in. Then, in 1961, in an attempt to keep East Berliners (as well as people from East Germany) from escaping, the Soviet Union began to build the Berlin wall. The Berlin wall was ninety-six miles long and was first made of barbed wire. By 1975, the concrete version of the wall was fully in place. Over the years, almost two hundred people were killed trying to escape beyond the wall, but it is estimated that about five thousand people made it out successfully. In 1989, most of the wall was torn down, except for sections that remain as memorials.

Stasi

The term *Stasi* is taken from the German word *Staatssicherheit*, which means "state security." Stasi were East Germany's notorious secret police and were stationed in East Berlin. The group was founded in 1950 under the leadership of Wilhelm Zaisser. The Stasi, often referred to as one of the most effective security police forces in the world, was fashioned after similar forces in the Soviet Union. Many members of the Stasi were former Nazi S.S. officers. When the Stasi was dismantled in 1989, the police hastily attempted to destroy all their files. Their files were either shredded or torn by hand. However, these torn documents (sixteen thousand bags of them) were discovered by the new German government, which commissioned a group of people to restore them. By 2001, only three hundred bags of files had been put back together again.

Homophobia

Wright has stated that it was hard being a homosexual in the southern United States, where a fear of homosexuals is often based on a deep-seated belief that homosexuality runs counter to the teachings of the Bible. Homophobia, or the fear of homosexuality, is not limited to the South, of course, but that is where Wright grew up. When Wright, raised in a climate of homophobia, came across the story of Charlotte von Mahlsdorf, he became fascinated with it. Here was a man who dressed as a female for most of his life, and who did so under the oppressive and repressive regimes of Nazi and Communist governments. Both governments persecuted homosexuals and transvestites. It has been estimated that, during the Nazi reign, there may have been more than 100,000 homosexuals and transvestites who died in the concentration camps. Homosexual and transvestite prisoners were forced to wear pink triangle badges to identify themselves in the camps, a practice that has since been converted to a positive symbol: the pink triangle has been adopted by gay men and women as an emblem of solidarity.

Charlotte von Mahlsdorf

Charlotte von Mahlsdorf was a real person, who was born Lothar Berfelde in 1928 and lived most of her life in Berlin. Physically, Charlotte was a man, but she considered herself to belong to what she called a third sex, as described in the introduction to the published version of Wright's play about her. Charlotte felt that she was a "female spirit trapped in a male body" and always referred to herself as "she." She lived in a "mammoth stone

Jefferson Mays in a 2005 production of I Am My Own Wife © Donald Cooper/Photostage. Reproduced by permission

mansion" in what would eventually become East Berlin after the division of the city following World War II. It was in this mansion that Charlotte gathered the bounty of her passion for collecting old furniture and other relics. In a review of Charlotte's autobiography, with the same title as Wright's play, Thom Nickels, writing for the *Lambda Book Report,* states that Charlotte's philosophy about life was this: "Antiques and furniture before love, before sex, before sufficient food to feed her own face, even."

Charlotte is often described as an unusual kind of transvestite. Nickels sums up this difference: "There are no glamour wigs in her closet, no makeup in her medicine cabinet, no saucy gowns to wear in gay bars or outrageous drag queen antics or caustic comments while camping it up." Rather, Charlotte was more easily compared to a cleaning woman, dressed simply and most frequently in a very plain black dress. She did not dye her hair, and, in her later years, it was completely white. Her only extravagance was a simple pearl necklace.

CRITICAL OVERVIEW

I Am My Own Wife ran on Broadway for almost a full year. The critic Michael Feingold, in his review for the *Village Voice*, finds it to have beauty that he describes as "extraordinary," especially in the way that Wright portrays Charlotte, who was, as Feingold points out, a murderer and an informer. There are contradictions in the play and moral issues that go unanswered. Allowing Charlotte's contradictions (being both a murderer and a national hero) to coexist, however, makes the play more interesting. As Feingold puts it, "This is a play which is in some ways not a play, and a piece of drama which is in all ways a piece of theater. And its beauty . . . falls into the category of always being two things at once." Feingold says that Charlotte is "a truth that invites you not to believe it, off-putting and welcoming, utterly frank and phony sounding, in the same instant." Wright "has not hesitated to include all the worst and most discreditable information regarding the puzzle of [Charlotte's] survival."

The first line from the *New York Times* critic Bruce Weber's review of the play reads, "Of all the peculiar entries in the Broadway derby this fall, perhaps the most peculiar is Doug Wright's fascinating one-actor play." Weber wrote his review as the play was premiering on Broadway. He wonders how many of the Christmas holiday tourists would be drawn to see it. "How many visitors from the heartland of America," writes Weber, "will be eager to pass up the bling-bling of a Broadway musical for this quiet, dramatic tale about an East German transvestite played by an unknown male actor speaking in heavily accented English and wearing a black dress and a string of pearls?" Immediately following this statement, Weber goes on to invite the many New York visitors to do exactly that. Actually, Weber urges them to do so. The play tells "a terrific story," Weber writes, and he concludes by calling it "the most stirring new work to appear on Broadway this fall."

Many critics are so fascinated with the subject of Wright's play that they focus almost entirely on the character of Charlotte and forget to say much about the play. Added to the distraction is the fact that Jefferson Mays's performance (as the lone actor in the play) was so outstanding and Moisés Kaufman's direction of the play was so clever. In his review for the *New Yorker*, for instance, John Lahr manages only one line of praise for the play. "The one-man show is a notoriously intractable species of entertainment," Lahr writes, "but Wright . . . marshals his words with command." The critic praises Kaufman and commends Wright for his portrayal of "an eccentric who seems herself to have been a work of semi-fiction."

Stefan Kanfer, a writer for the *New Leader*, takes an interesting position when reviewing Wright's play. Many critics have pointed out that the play leaves many questions unanswered. Kanfer praises Wright for doing so. There is a line in the play in which Charlotte asks how anyone can evaluate her. Kanfer states that "to his credit, Wright never did. He simply recorded what he saw, organized the material into a coherent narrative, and presented it as a one-man show."

CRITICISM

Joyce Hart

Hart is a freelance writer and published author with degrees in English and creative writing. In this essay, she looks at the various mood swings in Wright's play, mapping how they change and how they might affect the audience.

> "UNTIL THE REVELATION THAT SHE HAS BETRAYED KIRSCHNER, CHARLOTTE SEEMED SWEET AND ENDEARING. NOW SHE APPEARS CUNNING AND MAYBE EVEN A LITTLE LETHAL."

In the published version of Wright's play *I Am My Own Wife*, the playwright offers an introductory essay, "Portrait of an Enigma." For the reader (as opposed to a member of a theater audience), this provides a clue to the overall mood of Wright's play. Charlotte von Mahlsdorf, the subject of the play, was indeed puzzling. Is puzzlement also the mood that Wright intended for his play?

There is a mystifying element that hovers over this play, one that is difficult to miss even if one has not read Wright's essay. Imagine sitting in the audience, watching a live performance of this play; one probably would sense a perplexing mood right from the opening moments. It would begin with Charlotte's first appearance on stage. She is, first of all, obviously a man clothed in a black dress. Even more puzzling, she stands and faces the audience for a few moments without saying a word. She just stares at the people, much as they are staring at her. This is definitely a unique and fascinating opening. Most actors avoid eye contact with audiences, because they want to give the appearance of existing in a different world from those who are sitting watching the play. Often, they quite ignore the audience.

After staring for a few seconds, Charlotte's expression changes, as "the tiniest flicker of a smile dances on her lips. Then, surprisingly, she closes the doors as quickly as she appeared, and is gone." After experiencing this opening, how could anyone not guess that the intention of this play is to make one feel a bit baffled? From the beginning, Wright has his audience members' attention, as they try to figure out what is going on. Who is this man dressed

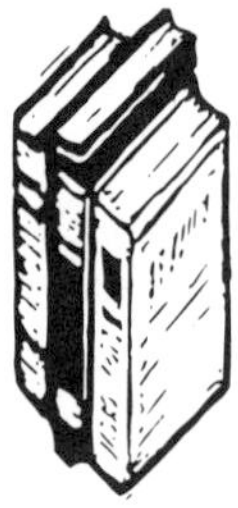

WHAT DO I READ NEXT?

- Before he wrote *I Am My Own Wife*, Wright created the play *Quills* (1996). The play is based on the story of another controversial real-life character, the Marquis de Sade (1740–1814), a French aristocrat who wrote pornography and practiced rather brutal sexual acts. His name inspired the word *sadism*.
- Charlotte von Mahlsdorf wrote her own version of her story in her autobiography, also called *I Am My Own Wife* (1995). The critics question the veracity of the story, but truth or fiction, this book has been praised as no less than a good read.
- For a different take on transvestites and a lighter read, try the pulp-fiction author Ed Wood's *Death of a Transvestite* (1999), about a murderer on death row who, as his last wish, asks to be able to dress in drag.
- Moisés Kaufman, who directed Wright's play, wrote a successful play of his own that deals with a young man who was not as lucky as Charlotte and did not survive. *The Laramie Project* (2001) is based on a true story, that of a homosexual man who was murdered.

in women's clothes? Why was she staring at us? What did that smile mean? Is she hiding a secret? Where has she gone, and when is she going to return? These questions grab the audience's attention and keep the audience involved. As all good mystery writers know, one has to keep people guessing. The mood of confusion is working well.

The mood changes throughout the play, however. When Charlotte reappears onstage, she demonstrates that she can be an educator or an entertainer, depending on how she appeals to the audience. She is definitely engaging, and so the mood of the play becomes more relaxed, lulling the audience into a more receptive state, yet not totally removing the edge of mystery. As Charlotte talks, she reveals an interesting and unique personality. She has lived through very difficult times and has gained a wealth of information and experience.

Mystery returns again when Charlotte morphs into another character, John Marks. She does so not by changing costumes but rather by standing more erect, dropping her German accent, and taking on a slight Texas twang. "What is going on?" the audience might be asking. Before they can figure it out, John transforms into Doug. Then Charlotte returns shortly thereafter and carries on a conversation with Doug. The single actor on the stage is, in fact, talking to himself, but he is pulling off a dialogue as if someone else were onstage with him. At this point, the mystery has itself transformed and spiraled, until it indeed becomes a challenge. The members of the audience are not only guessing about what is going on, they are also working hard to keep up.

Charlotte dominates the stage for the next segments, as the mood of the play settles down once more. The people watching the play sit back in their seats and enjoy the return to a relaxed mood, as Charlotte offers a tour of her museum-like mansion and a brief and intimate history of life in Berlin before World War II. Curiosity is aroused when Charlotte begins to reveal tidbits of her personal history. The mood changes once more. The curious mood, however, quickly gives way to tension. There are brutal moments in Charlotte's history. She talks about the war and about fearing for her life first when confronted by a military officer who threatens to shoot her and then when similarly confronted by her father. Charlotte speaks of the oppressive nature of living under Stasi surveillance, especially when one is gay. The mood is tinged with fear. This brings out a sense of empathy in the members of the audience, as they listen to the horrors that Charlotte has endured. The relationship between Charlotte and the audience is changing: they are

Jefferson Mays in a 2005 production of I Am My Own Wife © Donald Cooper/Photostage. Reproduced by permission

drawing closer together. Whereas she was an enigma at the beginning of the play, she is now coming closer to being someone to admire, a point that is emphasized when she is given a medal of honor. Charlotte then talks about her association with the Stasi, the secret police. She tells the audience that she was forced to become a spy. Audience concern for Charlotte's welfare increases as the mood becomes tinted with sympathy. The first act ends on this note. The mood is somber.

As act 2 opens, the audience is introduced to Alfred Kirschner, who is writing a letter to Charlotte from prison. Curiosity is again piqued. Who is this man? What is his relationship with Charlotte? Why is he imprisoned? Answers come quickly. Charlotte provides the history of her relationship with Kirschner as well as her role in putting him in prison. It is a sad tale, one of victimization. When Kirschner tells her not to become involved in his troubles with the Stasi, Charlotte says that she obeys. It makes no sense for both of them to go to jail for illegally selling old clocks. On its face, this is a simple but sad story. Charlotte believed that she had no choice. She later writes letters to Kirschner to help keep his spirits up. She even tells the prison guards, when she goes to visit, that she is Kirschner's wife. Poor Charlotte, the audience might be thinking. She may have been in love with Kirschner.

John returns to say that what Charlotte has said about Kirschner does not tally with the facts. Charlotte's Stasi file shows that she had been spying on Kirschner, gathering information in order to set him up for the arrest. What is the mood of the play now? This news is shocking, and the audience is thrown back into bewilderment. Audience members must mull over everything they have heard so far and reevaluate their feelings for Charlotte. They might again be asking, Who is this woman? What part of her story is true, if anything? How could she turn in a friend?

One can almost sense the audience pulling back. Until the revelation that she has betrayed Kirschner, Charlotte seemed sweet and endearing. Now she appears cunning and maybe even a little

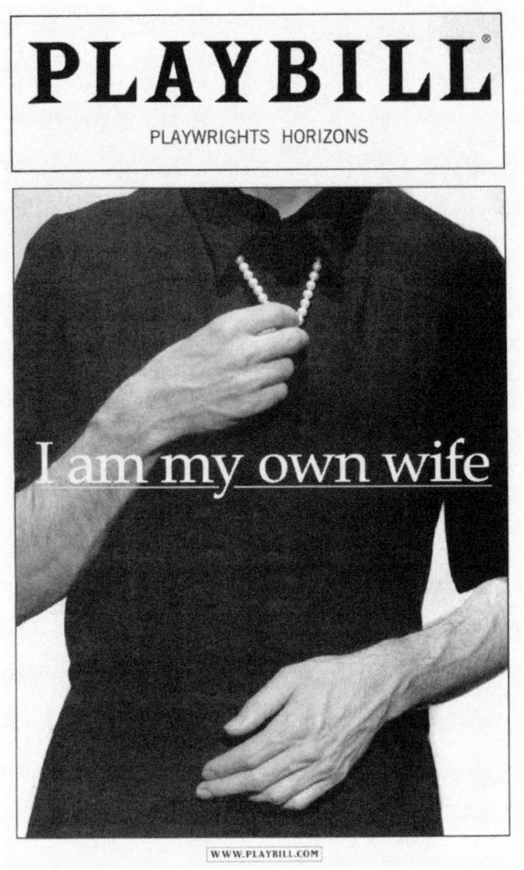

Playbill from a production of I Am My Own Wife *at Playwrights Horizons* Performing Arts Books, NYC. PLAYBILL ® is a registered trademark of Playbill Incorporated, N.Y.C. All rights reserved. Reproduced by permission

lethal. The knowledge that she has killed her father takes on a different color. A sort of gloom sets in, perhaps even a sense of disgust. After all, the audience was beginning to trust Charlotte. All the questions have returned, and now there is also a feeling of having been betrayed. But perhaps Charlotte can clear this all up. Indeed, the Stasi could be the ones who are lying. Unfortunately, Charlotte does not entirely rise to the occasion, when Doug gives her a chance to clear herself. She evades questions or offers answers that do not quite dispel the confusion. She appears to be a fallen hero. Even her fans turn against her, and a disillusioned mood prevails. There is still a hint of curiosity—Charlotte remains an enigma, but is she still interesting?

In a final attempt to bring the audience back to Charlotte's side, Wright provides a horrifying anecdote. Charlotte relates how she was attacked by neo-Nazis; for this reason, she is leaving town. The radio-talk-show host who is interviewing her, however, does not quite buy her neo-Nazi story. Are you leaving, he asks Charlotte, or are you running away? Doug states that he wants to believe Charlotte; he still admires her for what she has gone through. The play ends with a message from Charlotte that might win over certain members of the audience. Charlotte, in essence, suggests that she is only human and has weaknesses just like everyone else. Wright presents this idea to us through Charlotte's instructions on how to display and care for antique furniture. As Charlotte puts it, it is the wear and tear, the scratches and imperfections, that make a particular piece interesting. Once again, the audience is puzzled. Their mood is a little marred from the experience of the play, much like the antique furniture. In what mood does the audience leave the theater? That is another mystery.

Source: Joyce Hart, Critical Essay on *I Am My Own Wife*, in *Drama for Students*, Thomson Gale, 2006.

Allen Ellenzweig

In the following review, Ellenzweig discusses the source documents used to create I Am My Own Wife *and praises Jefferson Mays's portrayal of Charlotte and the entry of Wright as a character in the play.*

In general I don't like drag, yet there are times when a man in a dress does something transformative: he comes to embody something other than a camp cliche. Such is the case with the one-man production written by Doug Wright, *I Am My Own Wife,* currently on the boards at New York City's Playwrights Horizons. Here we have a man in a severe black dress presenting the extraordinary figure of Charlotte von Mahlsdorf, a male-to-female transvestite who survived the Nazi regime as a teenager only to live nearly all her adult life under the repressive Communist boot of East Germany.

Wright is the author of *Quills,* a play about the Marquis de Sade that he adapted for the screen in a much-lauded film starring Geoffrey Rush. With *I Am My Own Wife,* the playwright has had good fortune in his collaborators. *Wife* is directed by Moises Kaufman, whose previous credits include *Gross Indecency: The Three Trials of Oscar Wilde* and *The Laramie Project.* Both of those productions relied heavily upon an architecture made of documents—court records, contemporaneous newspaper accounts, taped interviews—to build a coherent historical text in which the drama took place. The source materials for *I Am My Own Wife,* which Kaufman has helped to shape along with Wright, include the playwright's interviews with Charlotte von Mahlsdorf, letters the two exchanged over ten years, newspaper accounts of her life, and her East German Stasi file.

None of this would have amounted to much had Wright and Kaufman not had Jefferson Mays to play Charlotte and all the other characters in the piece—including representations of the playwright himself and assorted Nazi and East German Stasi police, American soldiers, heartless homo-hustlers, an antiques-dealing conman, and Charlotte's lesbian aunt. What Mays does is nothing less than to "channel" Charlotte in her declining years and bring her to us whole: the cadences of her speech and German accent; her manner of walking and physical gesture. She is not a caricature, though she is a character. She's not a lovable old tranny, but we are cast under her spell nonetheless. All this Mays achieves with an economy of means in a performance that is at once controlled and spirited. He can go in a flash from Charlotte describing in piquant timbre the antique phonograph machines she collects, some from as far back as Thomas Edison, to assuming the innocence of a Midwestern GI on duty in Cold War Germany or the bullying presence of Charlotte's abusive father. And all this in the same black dress, with pearls.

While there are many characters in this one-person play, all of them acted by Jefferson Mays in quick incisive strokes, it is his embodiment of Charlotte von Mahlsdorff—born Lothar Berfelde—that holds us in thrall. As the owner of an antique furniture "museum" in East Berlin, Charlotte's collection of cylinders and discs from a bygone era, together with her well-stuffed and well-crafted chaises and chairs, are her witnesses to the history that fate has condemned her to survive. An early, brutal transgression committed in self-defense has forced Lothar into youth detention until a lucky escape. A lesbian aunt, conversant in the sexology theories of Magnus Hirschfeld, hands Lothar a study on transvestitism and commands him to make it his bible. A gay antiques dealer, a fellow obsessive of early Edison cylinders, enlists Charlotte in a get-rich-quick scheme involving young American soldiers eager to send elegant kitsch back home. The East German Stasi police discover his export violation and enlist Charlotte as an informer. All the while, Charlotte herself has made her basement a clandestine recreation of a Weimar-era nightclub, a venue for gay and lesbian trysts.

After the fall of the Berlin Wall, Charlotte is lauded as a national German heroine until her Stasi connections are made public. In a country where informing on one's neighbors was widespread, if not universal, the aging transvestite is now roasted over the coals in the media.

> "BY HAVING 'DOUG WRIGHT' ENTER THE NARRATIVE AS A CHARACTER, THE PLAY EXPLORES THE DRAMATIST'S EVOLVING RELATIONS WITH CHARLOTTE AND BECOMES AN INQUIRY ABOUT TRUTH AND FICTION."

By having "Doug Wright" enter the narrative as a character, the play explores the dramatist's evolving relations with Charlotte and becomes an inquiry about truth and fiction—how much of what she has told him about her past, and therefore told the audience, is verifiable? For example, we have witnessed a scene in which her dealer friend has given her permission to inform on him—as a way of saving herself. Larger questions of reality and illusion are at play here, for is not Charlotte's entire life a deeply committed performance? Is she not at all times the biological Lothar embedded in the female-gendered Charlotte?

I Am My Own Wife uses all the stagecraft at its command—kudos to its scenic and lighting design, and to its sound engineers—to awaken from a simple stage the moral complexities of one man's life intersecting with the 20th century's two worst totalitarian scourges. Wright, Kaufman, and Mays have collaborated to (re)create a compromised hero/heroine whose life was both a beacon and a shadow.

Source: Allen Ellenzweig, "One-Woman Show," in *Gay & Lesbian Review Worldwide*, Vol. 10, No. 5, September–October 2003, p. 50.

SOURCES

Feingold, Michael, "Unnerving Berlin," in the *Village Voice*, Vol. 48, No. 23, June 4–10, 2003, p. 55.

Kanfer, Stefan, "Wrong Mistakes," in the *New Leader*, Vol. 87, No. 1, January/February 2004, pp. 41–43.

Lahr, John, "Boys Won't Be Boys," in the *New Yorker*, Vol. 79, No. 15, June 9, 2003, p. 106.

Nickels, Thom, "House Frau," in *Lambda Book Report*, Vol. 13, No. 3, October 2004, pp. 25–26.

Raymond, Gerard, "His Own Pulitzer," in the *Advocate*, May 11, 2004, p. 81.

Weber, Bruce, "Inventing Her Life as She Goes Along," in the *New York Times*, December 4, 2003, Section E, p. 1.

Wright, Doug, *I Am My Own Wife*, Faber and Faber, 2004, pp. ix–xxiv, 9, 70, 75, 78.

FURTHER READING

Beck, Gad, *An Underground Life: Memoirs of a Gay Jew in Nazi Berlin*, University of Wisconsin Press, 1999.

Homosexuals were persecuted during the Nazi regime in Germany. Being both gay and Jewish, Beck had no reasonable expectation of surviving. But he did, and his story is quite remarkable.

Peukert, Detlev, *Inside Nazi Germany: Conformity, Opposition, and Racism in Everyday Life*, Yale University Press, 1989.

This book is an insider's view of life during the Nazi regime in Germany. Peukert takes a special interest in the German youths who found ways to oppose the Nazis. One of those ways was through music.

Maran, Meredith, *50 Ways to Support Lesbian and Gay Equality: The Complete Guide to Supporting Family, Friends, Neighbors—or Yourself*, Inner Ocean Publishing, 2005.

Charlotte von Mahlsdorf found a way to survive in a world that took homophobia to the extreme. In the early twenty-first century, the environment is not quite as drastic as in Charlotte's day, but adjusting to or fitting into modern society as a homosexual, transvestite, or other nontraditionally gendered person is still a challenge. This book offers essays about the gay world by people who study it and by those who not only live in it but also actively and politically support it, with timely suggestions on how to live with homophobia.

Prieur, Annick, *Mema's House, Mexico City: On Transvestites, Queens, and Machos*, University of Chicago Press, 1999.

There are not many books written about transvestites. Prieur's is one of the few. She did her studies in Mexico in a community of transvestites and homosexuals at the outskirts of Mexico City.

Life Is a Dream

PEDRO CALDERÓN DE LA BARCA

1635

La vida es sueño (*Life Is a Dream*), probably first performed in 1635 and published in 1636 in Madrid, is the best-known work in a large body of secular and religious plays by Pedro Calderón de la Barca, one of Spain's greatest dramatists, and, after Lope de Vega (1562–1635), the foremost playwright of Spain's Golden Age, a period between 1580 and 1680 when Spanish literature and painting reached their zenith. As the title suggests, in *Life Is a Dream*, Calderón plays with the problem of distinguishing between illusion and reality. Set in a mythical version of the kingdom of Poland, *Life Is a Dream* tells the story of King Basilio, who imprisons his son, Segismundo, at birth, because his astrological studies have given him reason to fear that the boy will grow up to be a tyrant and a rebel against his authority. Inside this fable, Calderón considers the power of the contrasting forces of free will and determinism to shape human character and destiny. In the subplot, in which Rosaura seeks to find Astolfo, who has dishonored her, Calderón examines the problems of honor and vengeance.

Life Is a Dream shows the influence of Lope de Vega, representing a form he perfected, the *comedia*, a three-act play written in verse, which mixes comic and serious elements in a complex plot full of mystery and derring-do. Its cast of characters was also well established—the old man, the young man, the young lady, the maid, and the clown. Rather than exerting influence on future drama, *Life Is a Dream* embodies the culmination

Pedro Calderón de la Barca © Bettmann/Corbis. Reproduced by permission

of a tradition. Spanish drama itself shows a serious decline after the end of the seventeenth century.

In the original Spanish, *Life Is a Dream* is a verse play. In translations attempting to be true to the original verse form, the qualities that add to the play's appeal—its lyricism, poetic invention, and linguistic beauty—can make the play seem stilted and more difficult and less engaging than it is. Edward and Elizabeth Huberman, in 1963, fashioned a prose translation of *La vida es sueño* that, while it does not sacrifice the beauty, wit, drama, imagery, or philosophical playfulness of the original, flows with ease and is natural and engaging. It is available in *Spanish Drama*, edited by Angel Flores and published by Bantam Books.

AUTHOR BIOGRAPHY

Pedro Calderón de la Barca was born in Madrid on January 17, 1600. His mother died when he was ten. His father, secretary of the king's treasury, died five years later. Calderón was educated at the Jesuit College in Madrid, where he prepared to take holy orders. But before his studies were completed, he enrolled in the university at Salamanca to study law. He neglected his law studies there, however, and wrote poetry instead. Between 1620 and 1622, in Madrid, Calderón participated in a literary festival held to celebrate the beatification and canonization of Saint Isidore, Madrid's patron saint, and was honored in the literary competitions that were a part of the celebration. In 1622, he became Spain's court poet.

There are conflicting accounts of how Calderón spent his next years. According to Juan de Vera Tassis y Villaroel, Calderón's contemporary, editor, literary executor, and biographer, Calderón served in Italy and Flanders in the Spanish army between 1625 and 1635. There are many extant legal documents, however, that suggest that Calderón was living in Madrid during these years. One document indicates that, in 1629, Calderón and a group of his friends broke into the convent of the Trinitarian nuns to seize an actor who had stabbed Calderón's brother Diego and had fled there for sanctuary. In a sermon preached before Philip IV, Hortensio Felix Paravincio denounced Calderón for this act. Calderón reciprocated by mocking the priest's linguistic pomposity and bombast in his play *El principe constatae* (*The Constant Prince*) and was jailed for a short time.

His imprisonment did not harm his reputation. In 1635, after the death of the great Spanish playwright and man of letters Lope de Vega, Calderón became known as Spain's greatest living playwright. In 1636, a volume of Calderón's plays, edited by another of his brothers, José, was published. *La vida es sueño* (*Life Is a Dream*) appeared in that collection. That same year (1636), Philip IV commissioned a series of plays by Calderón to be performed at the royal theater located inside the Buen Retiro, which was Philip's private park. In 1637, Philip made Calderón a knight of the Order of Santiago.

In 1640, despite recognition and popularity as a playwright, Calderón interrupted his career and became a horseman in an army raised by Philip's prime minister, Gaspar de Guzmán Olivares, to quell a secessionist rebellion in Catalonia. Because of ill health, he retired from the army at the end of 1642. In 1645, he was awarded a military pension in recognition of his valor in battle.

Calderón did not marry, but he had a mistress, with whom he had a son, Pedro José. The death of his mistress around 1648 or 1649 left him distraught, and he sought consolation in renewed religious devotion. In 1650, he became a tertiary of the Order of Saint Francis and was ordained a priest in 1651. At the time, he renounced writing for the theater.

Although Calderón continued in the priesthood until the end of his life, he began again to write plays after 1653. Most of them are *autos sacramentales*, religious allegories performed on and in celebration of Christian holy days. Some of these plays offended the Inquisition—the judicial branch of the Roman Catholic Church concerned with protecting the approved understanding of Catholic Church doctrine—and were condemned and the manuscripts confiscated. Nevertheless, Calderón was appointed honorary chaplain to Philip IV in 1663, and the condemnation of the plays was lifted in 1671. Calderón wrote his last secular play at the age of eighty-one, in honor of Charles II's marriage to Marie-Louise de Bourbon.

Calderón died on May 25, 1681, in Madrid. His executor, Vera Tassis, published an edition of his complete works between 1682 and 1691, ensuring Calderón's place in Spanish literature.

PLOT SUMMARY

Act 1, Scene 1

A figure dressed as a man enters. When the man speaks, the audience realizes that it is a woman. Transported from her home in Muscovy by a flying horse, Rosaura has been set down in the mountains of Poland, accompanied by the talkative Clarin. Without naming the cause of her grief, Rosaura complains of her unhappiness. She and Clarin stumble upon a tower and hear within the rattle of chains and then a human voice. It is Segismundo, clothed in animal skins, lamenting his wretched state.

Enraged that he has been overheard in his moment of weakness, Segismundo threatens to kill Rosaura and Clarin. Rosaura begs him for mercy. Her voice enchants him; he cannot take his eyes off her. Not knowing that she is a woman, he is, nevertheless, fascinated by her. Wretched as she thought she was, seeing Segismundo makes Rosaura realize how much worse it is for him. She asks if there is anything she can do to help him, but the jailer Clotaldo and the guards rush in and seize her and Clarin.

Segismundo struggles vainly to free himself from his chains in order to save them from the death that is the punishment for anyone who sees him. Rosaura and Clarin are blindfolded and their weapons confiscated. Rosaura tells Clotaldo to guard her sword, since it is a key to great mysteries, though she does not know what they are. She was given the sword by a woman and instructed to go to Poland to revenge an injury done to her (Rosaura). An unidentified person in Poland, she was told, would recognize the sword and protect her. Clotaldo recognizes the sword. He had given it to Violante, Rosaura's mother, whom he had seduced but not married. Violante gave the sword to Rosaura, and it signifies to Clotaldo that Rosaura is his child—his son, he thinks.

Resolving the conflict between love for his "son" and duty to his king, Clotaldo decides to take his prisoners to the king and perhaps win pardon for his "son"; if the pardon is granted, Clotaldo might then be able to help his "son" avenge the wrong done him. But Clotaldo does not reveal himself to Rosaura. Should his effort fail, his "son" will die—not knowing that it will be through the agency of his own father.

Act 1, Scene 2

Cousins contending for the throne of Poland, Astolfo, with his soldiers, and Estrella, with her ladies, confront each other. Rather than battle, Astolfo proposes that they join together in love and jointly rule Poland. Estrella is wary of his declaration of love, because he wears the portrait of another woman on a chain around his neck. Their exchange is cut short by the entrance of Basilio, king of Poland, and his entourage.

Addressing the court, Basilio explains his plan for the succession, revealing a history that had been unknown to the court and which solves some of the mysteries of the first scene. Learned in mathematics, Basilio cast the horoscope of his son, Segismundo, while the child was still in his mother's womb. In it, Basilio saw that Segismundo would overthrow him and become a tyrannical ruler. To defeat destiny, Basilio declared that Segismundo died at birth, along with his mother, and then secretly locked the infant in a tower. He made Clotaldo his tutor and jailer and decreed death to anyone who entered the tower and discovered the secret.

Before he surrenders his crown to Astolfo and Estrella, however, Basilio informs the court that he has planned an experiment to see whether Segismundo can overcome his destiny. Segismundo will be drugged, brought from prison to the court, attired and treated like a prince, and told his true history and the reason for his imprisonment. Basilio hopes that armed with this warning, Segismundo will become a good ruler. If he shows himself to be virtuous, he will be made king. Astolfo and Estrella agree to renounce their claims in that case. Should Segismundo show himself to be cruel and tyrannical, however, he will be drugged again, returned to the tower prison, and told that his experience at the court was merely a dream. Astolfo and Estrella will rule Poland.

After the court withdraws and Basilio is left alone, Clotaldo enters with Rosaura and Clarin. Because Basilio has revealed the story of Segismundo, Rosaura will not be punished for having seen him. There is still, however, her dishonor to avenge. Clotaldo returns her sword, and she tells him that Astolfo is the enemy she seeks. Clotaldo again is burdened by divided loyalties. Astolfo is his lord. He tells Rosaura that since Astolfo is the duke of Muscovy and Rosaura is his subject, Astolfo cannot have dishonored "him" (Rosaura) no matter what he did. Rosaura is then compelled to reveal that she is a woman and that the dishonor was rape.

Act 2, Scene 1

Astonished by his transformation, Segismundo appears at court, dressed like a prince. Clotaldo tells him who he is and of the dire prophecy about him, hoping that the warning will correct him. Segismundo, however, responds in rage, threatening to kill Clotaldo. Clotaldo exits; Astolfo enters and salutes Segismundo, who returns his greeting with insults. Estrella enters. Segismundo is captivated by her beauty and is rudely forward with her. When a servant points out the faults in his behavior, Segismundo grabs the man and throws him off a balcony. When Basilio learns that Segismundo has acted according to his unhappy expectations, despite warning, he is grieved. Segismundo responds to his reprimands with contempt, and Basilio leaves him angrily, advising him that although he appears to be enjoying a position of power, he ought to take heed—he may only be dreaming.

Segismundo does not heed him, however. When Rosaura, now dressed as a woman and following in Estrella's train, encounters him again, he demands she surrender to him. She tries to leave; he orders the doors shut. As Segismundo is about to force Rosaura to yield to him, Clotaldo attempts to save her. Segismundo draws his dagger, and Clotaldo seizes it. They struggle. Rosaura exits, crying for help; Astolfo runs in and comes between Segismundo and Clotaldo. Astolfo demands that Segismundo return his dagger to its sheath, but Segismundo refuses. Astolfo draws his sword, and the two duel. Basilio enters, and, following the code of chivalry, they both sheath their swords in front of the king. Basilio demands an explanation. Segismundo boasts that he has tried to kill Clotaldo and that he may be moved to kill Basilio himself in revenge for having been imprisoned. So saying, he leaves the stage. The king orders that Segismundo be returned to his prison and made to believe that all that has occurred was only a dream.

Alone with Estrella, Astolfo declares his love, but she scoffs at him and demands that he speak of love not to her but to the woman whose portrait he has been wearing. He promises to replace that portrait with Estrella's and goes to bring her Rosaura's portrait. Estrella then catches sight of Rosaura, who has entered during their conversation. Unaware that Astolfo's portrait is of Rosaura, she asks Rosaura to take it from Astolfo when he returns, because it would embarrass Estrella to do so herself.

When Astolfo returns with the portrait, expecting to find Estrella, he is shocked to find Rosaura instead. She says that she is not Rosaura but Astrea, Estrella's serving woman. He insists that she is Rosaura; denying it again, she explains that Estrella has asked her to take the portrait from him. He refuses to give it to her; she attempts to seize it, and they struggle. Estrella enters, astonished at the sight of them. Rosaura explains that as she waited for Astolfo, she remembered that she had a picture of herself and took it out to look at. Astolfo, upon seeing her, took the picture from her. Estrella sees the picture of Rosaura and gives it to her, believing the story that it is hers. Rosaura leaves, and Estrella demands the "other" portrait from Astolfo. There being no other portrait, he has none to give and cannot admit that the portrait of Rosaura was the one in his possession, for that would be admitting that he had dishonored her. Disgusted by him, Estrella says that she wants neither the portrait nor ever to see him again. She leaves, and he trails after, begging her to let him explain.

Act 2, Scene 2

Drugged, Segismundo is returned to his prison, accompanied by Clotaldo, his tutor/jailer, and by Clarin, who is imprisoned because he talks too much. Segismundo wakes, as astonished to be back in prison as he was to be a prince. Clotaldo explains he has been dreaming, but Segismundo has trouble believing it. Since his experience at court seemed so real, perhaps he might have been awake then and be dreaming now, he thinks. When Clotaldo questions him about his life at court, Segismundo recalls its glories and his own violent behavior, including his attempts to kill Clotaldo. Clotaldo reminds Segismundo that he has cared for him as his tutor and advises him that even in dreams one ought to do good. Left alone, Segismundo realizes that what Clotaldo has said is true and promises himself to restrain his fierceness and fury because—since he can never be sure when he is dreaming and when he is not—perhaps everything is a dream and life is an illusion in which we are not what we are but only what we dream we are.

Act 3, Scene 1

Clarin's reverie about what life is like in prison is interrupted by a mob, shouting that they have come to free Segismundo. They do not want to be ruled by Astolfo, a foreigner. They mistake Clarin for Segismundo, however. Segismundo enters, declares himself, and finds that he is at the head of a force that will fight to make him king. He is reluctant to believe that what is happening is real, remembering that the last time he was endowed with kingship, it was a dream. He maintains that the people freeing him are only shadows. The mob persists. A soldier argues that dreams are omens and that Segismundo's earlier dream was an omen of the reality that now appears to him. Segismundo accepts the role they impose on him, even if it is illusory; he is prepared to be disillusioned.

That Segismundo's realization that everything is illusory has tempered his spirit is clear when Clotaldo enters. He expects to be murdered and throws himself at Segismundo's feet, ready to die. Segismundo tells him to rise. He acknowledges that Clotaldo has been his teacher; that he needs Clotaldo's guidance; and that even if he is dreaming, he wishes to do good deeds. Clotaldo explains that he cannot side with him against Basilio. Segismundo flies into a momentary rage but catches himself, particularly because he is not even sure he is awake. He praises Clotaldo's courage and allows him to go to the king. Whether he is awake or asleep, Segismundo says, does not matter. All that matters is to act well and do good deeds.

Act 3, Scene 2

There is tumult and bloodshed as the people battle, some supporting Segismundo and others Astolfo. Basilio himself rides into battle to defend his crown against Segismundo. Rosaura complains to Clotaldo that although Astolfo has seen her, he still woos Estrella. She wants Clotaldo to kill Astolfo. Clotaldo explains that because Astolfo saved his life when Segismundo tried to kill him, he is in Astolfo's debt; to kill him would show an unbecoming lack of gratitude. He says that, instead, he will give Rosaura his fortune but that she must enter a convent. Rosaura refuses and declares that she will kill Astolfo herself to avenge her honor. At that point, Clotaldo agrees to help her.

Act 3, Scene 3

Leading his troops, Segismundo declares that the less he cares for victory, the less it will grieve him when he wakes to find his triumph has been only in a dream. Armed, Rosaura implores his assistance in her cause against Astolfo, recounting the story of her mother's seduction and betrayal by a man whose identity she does not know (but whom the audience knows is Clotaldo) and of her own similar seduction and betrayal by Astolfo. She speaks of the other times that she and Segismundo have seen each other—in the tower, where he was imprisoned, and at court, where he had princely power. That she has known him in both these states adds to his confusion about which was a dream and which a waking state, or if both are the same.

Whether waking or dreaming, Segismundo understands that Rosaura is in his power and that he may satisfy his lust. This momentary urge is overcome by his reflection that if he is dreaming, abandoning the way of goodness will gain him little lasting pleasure. If he is not dreaming and really awake, the case is similar, for life is like a dream from which one wakes in death, and there is little satisfaction gained from an evil action, which is as short-lived as an action in a dream and will have eternal consequences. Segismundo therefore steels himself against his lust for Rosaura and proceeds to do battle against Astolfo.

Clarin, though he is hiding, is killed in the crossfire of battle. Segismundo's forces are victorious. Basilio, urged to flee by Astolfo and Clotaldo, does not. He is resigned to the death he expects at the hands of Segismundo. But Segismundo lets his father live, renounces his own passion for Rosaura, and gives her to Astolfo to marry, thereby restoring her honor. He takes Estrella as his wife and becomes the king, virtuous and merciful, because he is aware that life is a dream and dreams are illusions that end.

CHARACTERS

Astolfo

Astolfo, the duke of Muscovy, is Basilio's nephew. Basilio has summoned him to Poland to become king if Segismundo proves unworthy. As his name suggests, there is something wolfish about him. He has seduced and abandoned Rosaura. He is presented, however, as a ludicrous, rather than villainous, figure when Estrella rejects him. There are also streaks of decency and honor in him, which become evident, for example, when he protects Clotaldo from Segismundo.

Basilio

Basilio is the king of Poland, a mathematician, and a scholar. Fearing, because of a horoscope reading, that Segismundo will grow up to overthrow him and become a tyrannical ruler, Basilio has kept Segismundo locked up in a tower since birth. Basilio's position as a ruler and a seeker of wisdom is reinforced by the celestial imagery surrounding him.

Clarin

Clarin is a chatterbox. His name suggests a clarion, or high-pitched trumpet. He accompanies Rosaura to Poland and offers witty, cynical, and philosophical comments about the action of the play. For a brief moment, a mob mistakes him for Segismundo and almost makes him king. He is killed during a battle, though he is in hiding and not fighting. He represents the impossibility of staying aloof from the action of life, as he attempts to, even if life is illusory.

Clotaldo

Clotaldo is an old man in Basilio's court who serves as a jailer and tutor to Segismundo in his tower. He is portrayed as constantly torn by divided loyalty. Still, he always acts honorably, though in his past he has been dishonorable, having seduced but not married Violante, who gave birth to his daughter, Rosaura.

Estrella

Estrella is Basilio's niece. He expects that she will marry Astolfo and rule over Poland with him if Segismundo proves unworthy to be king. Her name means *star*; when Segismundo marries her at the end of the play, after he has triumphed over the brutal aspects of himself, it signifies his reconciliation with the stars, for it was in the stars (his horoscope) that Basilio had seen Segismundo's evil destiny recorded.

Rosaura

Although she does not know it, Rosaura is the illegitimate daughter of Clotaldo. Disguised as a man and accompanied by Clarin, she has followed Astolfo to Poland to force him to marry her and restore her honor, which he had taken from her when he seduced and then left her. Her name means *rosy dawn*, and, as her name suggests, she awakens new perception in Segismundo, when, through her, he achieves enlightenment about the meaning of honor.

Segismundo

Segismundo is Basilio's son. He has lived his life unaware of his identity, imprisoned by his father because Basilio feared—after charting Segismundo's horoscope—that he would grow into a treacherous son and savage ruler. When Basilio devises a ruse to free him from his prison for a day and give him the power of a king, Segismundo's brutal behavior confirms his father's fear, and he is returned to prison. After he is liberated from the tower a second time, he overcomes his brutality and his predestined identity. Segismundo is often described by himself or by others as a beast or a force of nature. He is clothed in animal skins, and he contrasts himself with fish, snakes, streams, and volcanoes. Before Segismundo is taken to the court, Clotaldo fills his mind with the image of himself as an eagle. The meaning of his name, however, stands in contrast to the predatory imagery surrounding him and indicates his triumph over an unchangeable fate written in the stars. *Segismundo* is derived from the German words *sige*, meaning "victory," and *mund*, meaning "protector."

THEMES

Certainty

The impossibility of certainty dominates the action of *Life Is a Dream*, presenting two fundamental problems: 1) How can one be sure of anything? and 2) What are the consequences of uncertainty? Before Basilio tests Segismundo, the problem of uncertainty is introduced in the figure of Rosaura at the beginning of the play, and the audience is implicated in the problem as much as the characters of the play are. The audience cannot be certain what it is seeing or what is happening. Perception is deception. In Rosaura, spectators behold a man who soon reveals that he is a woman. The identity of Segismundo and the reason for his confinement are also mysteries, as are the nature and cause of Rosaura's confessed dishonor. She does not know who will recognize the sword she bears and protect her. Clotaldo, in turn, is tormented by

TOPICS FOR FURTHER STUDY

- Although dreams are generally thought not to be real in themselves, they have often had the power to transform reality. Choose two works from the following list and write an essay discussing the way in which dreams recounted in those works transform the course of reality when they are heeded or fail to do so when they are unheeded: the Joseph story in the book of Genesis, Chaucer's poem *The Book of the Duchess*, Shakespeare's play *Julius Caesar*, Charles Dickens's novel *A Christmas Carol*, or the original 1962 version of the film *The Manchurian Candidate*, directed by John Frankenheimer.
- The poet William Wordsworth wrote that "the Child is father of the Man." Compose a dialogue between King Basilio and his son, Segismundo, in which they argue about the truth of Wordsworth's observation.
- Read Lope de Vega's play *Fuente ovejuna* (*The Sheep Well*) and write an essay comparing and contrasting it with *Life Is a Dream.*
- Write a short story in which a dream plays a significant role in determining the attitude of at least one of the characters in the story.
- Keep a bedside journal in which you record all your dreams every day for a week. At the end of the week, write an analysis of your dreams, describing the themes, imagery, characters, settings, plots, sensations, and anything else you think is noteworthy about your dreams.
- Research the way plays were staged in Spain and in England in the late 1500s and early 1600s and write an essay in which you show the similarities and differences.

uncertainty that continues throughout the play. Where ought his loyalty lie? In the first instance, should it be with his child or with his king? Later, should it be with Rosaura or with Astolfo, the man who dishonored her?

Even as the audience learns the answers to the mysteries of scene 1, the theme of uncertainty is only strengthened as the play proceeds. The strategy Basilio employs to determine whether the destiny written in the stars is fixed and certain or can be influenced—making Segismundo believe that he has been dreaming events that have actually occurred—results in making Segismundo always uncertain as to whether he is asleep or awake. By extension, the problem the play presents regards the certainty of all experience. Is life real, or is it a dream? The resolution of the problem is achieved by the unification of the opposites. Reality, being a matter of perception, itself is a dream. Because human happiness comes to an end, experience must not be overvalued and clung to. In the play, generosity and magnanimity follow from that awareness.

Free Will and Determinism

At the heart of *Life Is a Dream* is the problem of whether destiny is fixed or if people can affect and even alter what appears to be their destiny. When Basilio studies the stars before Segismundo's birth, he learns that they show that the child will grow up to be a brutal and tyrannical prince who will dishonor his father. In an attempt to control fate, Basilio has Segismundo imprisoned. In an attempt to test the strength of individual will in the face of destiny, Basilio arranges for Segismundo's release. When Segismundo behaves as his horoscope predicted, it seems that determinism has triumphed. But in the last act, Segismundo himself, addressing the court, questions the power of determinism by noting that even if he had been a mild-mannered person, the brutal way his father had him raised would have transformed him into a beast. It was not just the stars that determined his nature but also his father's intervention. Segismundo conquers his destiny by overcoming the rage and lust within himself when he realizes that life is an illusion that will end but that actions that are just will endure.

Honor and Duty

The theme of honor, presented in Rosaura's quest to find Astolfo, determines the subplot of *Life Is a Dream.* According to the play, honor means living according to one's duty, and duty means recognizing the integrity and humanity of others and not violating them. Rosaura, in pursuit of her own honor, is the instrument that moves Segismundo to act honorably. By overcoming his self-centered desire, his lust to possess Rosaura, and by helping her to redeem her honor through ensuring that Astolfo marry her, Segismundo redeems himself and defines himself as a man, not as a beast. He is able, consequently, to forgive Basilio and spare his life.

STYLE

Comedia

Life Is a Dream is a *comedia*, a form of Spanish drama perfected at the beginning of the seventeenth century by the great Spanish playwright Lope de Vega and codified in his 1609 treatise *El arte nuevo de hacer comedias en este sieglo* (The New Art of Playwriting in This Century). *Comedia* is verse drama in three acts. In the first act, the issues are introduced. In the second, they are developed. In the third, they are resolved. *Comedia* mixes comic and serious elements and features intrigue, disguise, swordplay, and battles.

Conflict between Characters and Ideas

There are two sorts of conflicts that shape the plot of *Life Is a Dream*. There are conflicts between characters, such as the conflict between Basilio and Segismundo or Astolfo and Rosaura or Astolfo and Estrella. There are also clashes of ideas, like that between free will and determinism or between self-interest and forgiveness or between illusion and reality. These tensions, more than those between characters, determine the course of action in the play and are at the heart of the conflicts between the characters. The conflict binding Astolfo and Rosaura, for example, is one between honor and selfishness or justice and greed. The father/son conflict joining Basilio and Segismundo also serves as the vehicle that permits conflicts between free will and determinism and between illusion and reality to be represented.

Gongorism

Gongorism is the name given to the ornate style of verse in which Calderón wrote. It is named for the poet Luis de Góngora y Argote (1561–1627). This style is characterized by references to mythology, stylistic excesses, and complexity of language and thought. Readers of an English translation will not be able to experience it fully but may get a lingering sense of it in such passages as this at the opening of the play: "Wild hippogriff, running swift as the wind, flash without flame, bird without color, fish without scales, unnatural beast, where are you wildly rushing in the intricate labyrinth of these bare rocks?" Another example is in Segismundo's first speech in the play's first scene: "The bird is born, with the gaudy plumage that gives it unrivalled beauty; and scarcely is it formed, like a flower of feathers or a winged branch, when it swiftly cuts the vaulted air, refusing the calm shelter of its nest."

HISTORICAL CONTEXT

The Golden Age in Spain

The period between 1580 and 1680 is called the Golden Age in Spain, when art and literature flourished. The first part of *Don Quixote*, by Miguel de Cervantes (1547–1616), was published in 1605. In this novel, Cervantes plays with the shifting boundaries between reality and perception and introduces, in the figure of Don Quixote, a character who shows the influence of literature on consciousness. Lope de Vega's *Fuente ovejuna*, or *The Sheep Well* (performed in 1614), dramatizes a village rebellion against an authoritarian governor, in which the characters realize both a group identity and individual identities. In 1630, Tirso de Molina (ca. 1580–1648) first introduced the character of Don Juan in his play *El burlador de Sevilla*, or *The Love Rogue*. The Don is a figure who embodies the Renaissance passions, defining himself by his appetite and by his defiance of convention. During the period between 1597 and 1614, the year of his death, the artist El Greco (1541–1614) produced more than a dozen paintings that have come to be regarded as masterpieces, including the *Laocoon* and the *View of Toledo*. And between 1620 and 1660, Diego Velázquez (1599–1660) produced work of such brilliance that he is considered to be Spain's greatest painter. The paintings of El Greco and Velázquez embody the terror of being human, the struggle to be human, and the breadth of vision and depth of character humanity can achieve.

COMPARE & CONTRAST

- **1600s:** People often consult the stars to help them decide how to act and to see into the future.

  Today: Many people still consult professional astrologers or look up their horoscopes in the newspaper to find out about their love lives or to determine favorable times to travel or make business deals.

- **1600s:** Scientific discoveries and geographical exploration challenge accepted beliefs about religion, nature, the cosmos, and reality.

  Today: Technological advances in computing, virtual reality, and genetic engineering are challenging traditional values and ideas.

- **1600s:** Gender identity is clearly signified by the clothing that members of each sex wear.

  Today: Male and female fashions often overlap, although women are far more likely than men to wear attire traditionally identified with the opposite gender.

- **1600s:** In Spain, the books people read and the plays they see must be approved by ecclesiastical authorities. Failure to comply with the dictates of the Church is punished by the Inquisition, the judicial body the Catholic Church has established in Spain to enforce its doctrines.

  Today: After years of political tyranny and censorship under the government of General Francisco Franco (1892–1975), Spain is a democratic country, where freedom of thought, freedom of speech, and the unfettered right to publish and read are respected.

Politics

The hundred years between 1550 and 1650 were marked by power conflicts that combined political and religious issues and took place within and between nations. In Spain, the power of the Roman Catholic Church was enforced by the courts of the Inquisition, which could punish deviations from accepted doctrine, and by the Index, a list of books that were banned by the Catholic Church because they threatened accepted religious truth. While these measures strengthened the power of religion, they also nurtured underground Protestant and humanist opposition.

Protestant leaders like Martin Luther (1483–1546) attacked the power of the pope and the Church's practice of selling indulgences. Indulgences were supposed to lessen the time the purchaser of the indulgence would spend in purgatory after death. Protestant reformers like Luther also believed that the Bible ought to be available to each Christian, in the vernacular languages rather than only Church Latin or the original Greek. They believed that the Bible, not the Church fathers, ought to be the ultimate religious authority.

Protestant reformers were often originally closely allied with humanists. Humanists were scholars like the Dutch-born Desiderius Erasmus (1466–1536). Their philosophy grew out of the study of the Greek and Latin classics and an appreciation of their literary qualities, their grace, and their structure. Humanists sought excellence in humankind itself and focused on the study of humankind and nature rather than on the nature of God and divine phenomena, which was called Scholasticism.

Spanish influence also extended to England when, in 1553, Queen Mary I, attempting to return England to Catholicism after Henry VIII's break with Rome in 1534, married Spain's king, Philip II. She died four years later and was succeeded by her Protestant sister, who became Queen Elizabeth I and whose navy defeated the Spanish armada in 1588. Spain also at this time was defending other territories it held in Europe, including parts of Italy and the Netherlands, and it was establishing itself as a major colonial power in the New World and struggling with the Turkish Ottoman Empire for the northern coast of Africa.

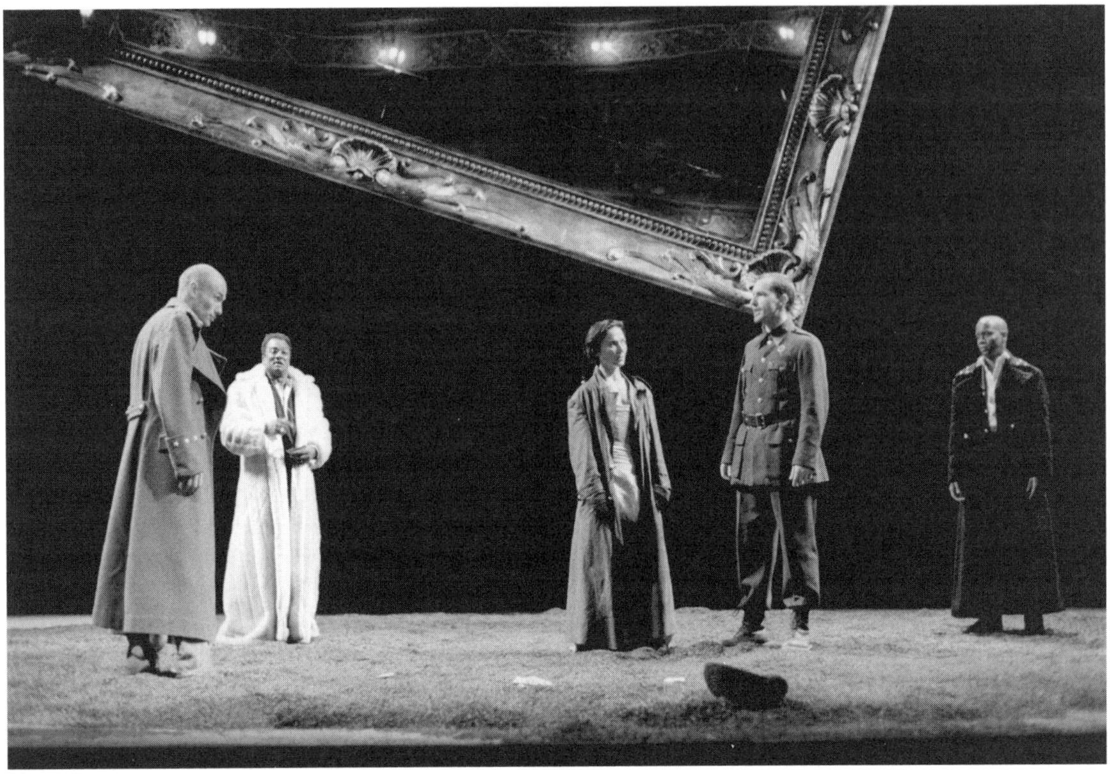

George Anton, Jeffery Kissoon, Olwen Fouere, Simon Turner, and Nicholas Bailey in a 1998 production of Life is a Dream © Donald Cooper/Photostage. Reproduced by permission

Cultural Changes

The period in which Calderón lived was particularly vital because of the encounter and contention of two ways of understanding the world. The medieval organization of society and thought essentially was formed by an adherence to doctrines of well-defined religious and secular order. The Renaissance, with the resurgence of classical learning, global exploration, individualism, and challenges to one dogmatically established religion, destabilized and threatened medieval values and truths. "Man," who lived in the Middle Ages under the yoke of authority, in the Renaissance, had become the measure of all things.

CRITICAL OVERVIEW

From its first appearance in 1635 up through the present, *Life Is a Dream* has enjoyed acclaim and popularity. It was first printed in Madrid in an edition edited by Calderón's brother José in 1636. Reprinted along with all of Calderón's work by his friend and biographer Juan de Vera Tassis y Villaroel in a reliable and readable edition in the years immediately following his death in 1681, it was readily available in Spain and to translators, even when Spanish drama itself was in decline.

One of the earliest translators of Calderón's work into English was the romantic poet Percy Bysshe Shelley, whose 1822 notebook shows translations from *La vida es sueño* as well as from other of Calderón's works. In the 1850s, the Irish poet Denis Florence MacCarthy published translations of Calderón's works, and in 1858, Edward FitzGerald, best known for his translation of *The Rubáiyát of Omar Khayyám*, freely translated *La vida es sueño* into blank verse, calling his version *Such Stuff as Dreams Are Made Of.*

During the twentieth century, the play was translated into English a number of times and was never off the stage for very long. In 2002, it was produced off Broadway and presented at Oxford. In 2005, it was produced independently at the Stage

Center Theatre at Northeastern Illinois University, at the University of Colorado in Boulder, and at the University of Massachusetts at Amherst. In 2000, Lewis Spratlan's opera of *Life Is a Dream*, with a libretto by James Maraniss, won the Pulitzer Prize in Music. In 1925, the great Austrian poet and playwright Hugo von Hofmannsthal wrote a German adaptation of it called *Der Turm* (*The Tower*) in order to reflect the chaotic pre-fascist climate in Germany.

Life Is a Dream has also been the subject of much academic criticism concerned with analyzing its structure, philosophy, and mythic quality, as Frederick A. De Armas does in *The Return of Astraea: An Astral-Imperial Myth in Calderón*. Examining its natural, animal, and celestial imagery, De Armas asserts that in *Life Is a Dream* "Calderón mirrors . . . eternal truth, revealing aspects of the heavenly text inscribed in stars and souls in a work that aims at transcending conflict through a vision of wonderment at the ways in which God's creation unfolds."

There is one aspect of *Life Is a Dream* that many critics find troublesome. "The very critics who were unanimous in placing *La vida es sueño* among the greatest of Spanish and world plays were equally unanimous in condemning its subplot, regarding it not merely as a useless adjunct, but as an action which seriously detracted from the play's unity," A. E. Sloman observes. In "The Structure of Calderón's *La vida es sueño*," he goes on to demonstrate that by representing honor and by serving as a catalyst for Segismundo's conversion, "the Rosaura episode . . . is clearly . . . no mere afterthought to fill out the required three acts" but is "linked . . . to the main episode and related . . . to the play's central theme."

CRITICISM

Neil Heims

Heims is a writer and teacher living in Paris. In this essay, he considers how Calderón uses the very uncertainty of perception that is central to the drama of Life Is a Dream *as the force that enables the human exercise of free will.*

When Rosaura appears during the first moments of *Life Is a Dream*, descending from the craggy mountains where her wild flying horse has left her, the audience is confronted by ambiguity and uncertainty. The unreliability of sense perception, one of the problems around which the entire play revolves, is presented in this scene. Rosaura appears to be a man; yet, when that man begins to talk, despite appearances, the man is a woman: "Unkindly, O Poland, do you receive a stranger; for you inscribe her arrival in your land with blood; and hardly does she arrive, but she comes to grief." As it draws the audience into the action of the drama, the opening speech of the play also burdens the audience with the same problem that the characters of the drama face. The spectators are forced to reevaluate and reconfigure their first impressions and to doubt appearances. What they saw, or rather, what they *thought* they saw, is not what is. Reality, as it is constructed in *Life Is a Dream*, is not fixed. It shifts. Things are ambiguous—and so is human possibility. The ambiguity of things that seem definite is the principal theme of *Life Is a Dream*, the idea that unifies its elements, and the condition that gives meaning to the play's other central concern—the conflict between free will and determinism.

> "WHETHER SEGISMUNDO IS A PRINCE OR A BEAST MAY BE UNCLEAR, BUT NO MATTER WHICH HE IS, HE CAN CHOOSE TO BE EITHER PRINCELY OR BEASTLY IN EITHER THE PRINCE OR THE BEAST ROLE."

Segismundo, the wild beast of a man Rosaura finds amid the mountains, imprisoned in a tower and clothed in animal skins, speaks nevertheless with the grace, facility, and learning of a Renaissance courtier and laments his condition with a poet's eloquence and passion. Wretched like her, he may also be something other than what he seems. Indeed, Basilio, the king of Poland, confirms that fact in the ensuing scene. Segismundo is a prince, his own son. Basilio imprisoned him in the tower at his birth, because in his study of the stars, it appeared to Basilio that Segismundo would grow up to be a rebellious son and a tyrannical ruler, humiliating his father and oppressing the nation. But Basilio is troubled by the sense that he may have

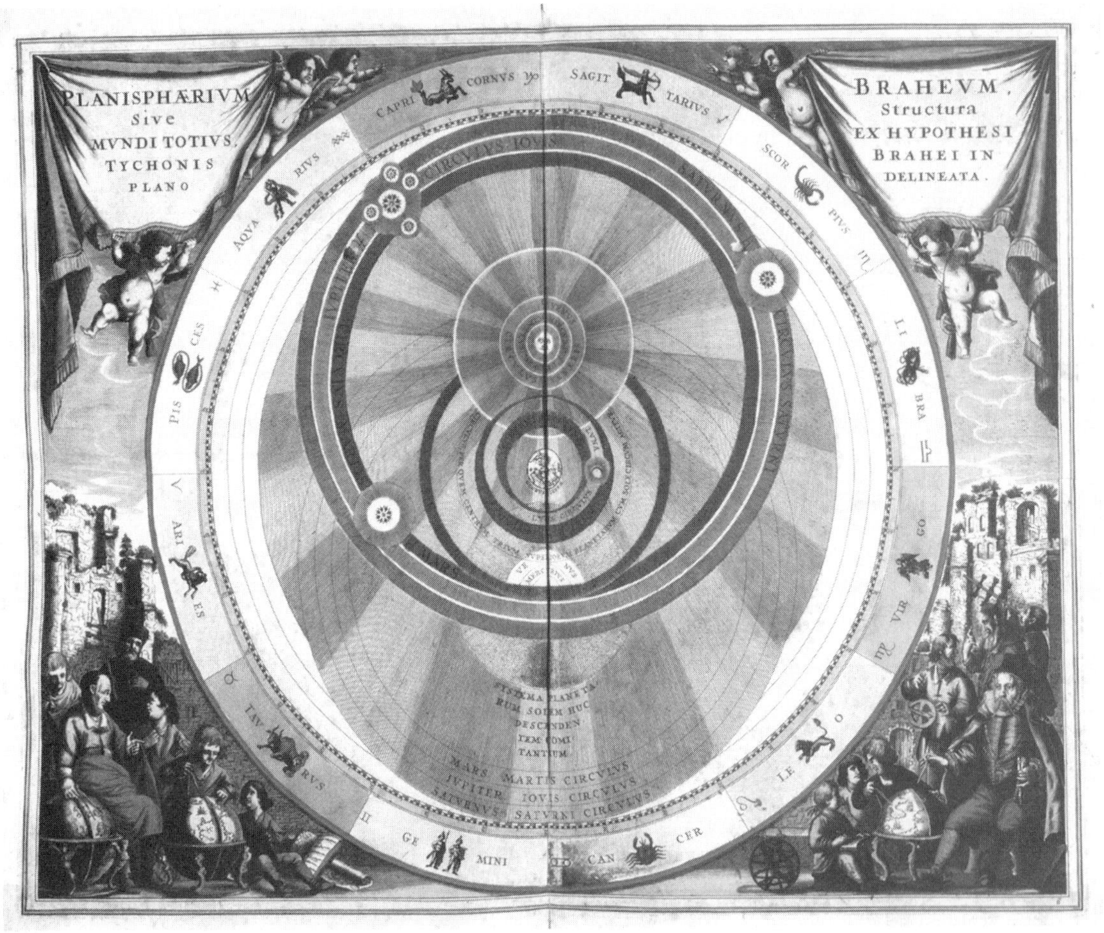

A Renaissance artist's representation of the zodiac © Archivo Iconografico, S.A./Corbis. Reproduced by permission

acted tyrannically against the threat of tyranny. To make sure that his action, even if driven by his mathematical wisdom and motivated by concern for the good, was not tyranny but a justified act of preventive punishment, Basilio has decided to release Segismundo from his prison and let him rule Poland for a day. Should he prove benevolent, Basilio will yield authority to him, happy that Segismundo can exercise a freedom of will that is stronger than cosmic predestination. Should Segismundo's behavior confirm the destiny Basilio saw written in the stars, however, Basilio will know that he was justified in imprisoning his son. Segismundo will be returned to prison, and, to prevent him from falling into despair, he will be told that he was dreaming.

After Segismundo uses his power badly and is returned to prison and told that he only dreamed he was a prince, he never again is able to be sure when he is awake and when he is dreaming. He cannot tell whether he is definitely a prisoner or definitely a prince. How can he be both? Yet he perceives that he is. Thus, taught by ambiguity and uncertainty that experience is not a proof of actuality, Segismundo realizes that he is neither prisoner nor prince in reality, for there may not be any reality. He is not defined by what he perceives but by himself no matter what he perceives—that is, by how he chooses to act. If everything is illusion and life is a dream, it is not important what Segismundo perceives or thinks is real. The only thing that matters and that he can be sure of is how he behaves.

Basilio, too, is deceived in his strategy. Contrary to his belief, when Segismundo acts like a brute on his day of trial, it does not serve as a definite proof that determinism is stronger than free will, as Basilio had feared. Segismundo himself, in

WHAT DO I READ NEXT?

- "Abu Hassan; or, The Sleeper Awakened," in *The Arabian Nights* (ca. 1000 C.E.), is the tale of a wise young man who exhausts half his inheritance on ungrateful friends and then befriends the caliph Haroon al Rashid, who is disguised as a merchant. The caliph drugs Abu Hassan and has him conveyed to the palace and made to believe that he is the caliph. When he is returned to his own home, Abu Hassan's friends think that he has become a madman, and he becomes entirely confused about what is real and what is not. The story is an obvious precursor to *Life Is a Dream.*
- *Oedipus Rex* (ca. 425 B.C.E.), the first play in Sophocles' Theban trilogy—*Oedipus Rex*, *Oedipus at Colonus*, and *Antigone*—tells the story of a man who, as an infant, survives exposure on a mountainside. His parents place him there after hearing a prophecy that when he grows up, he will kill his father and wed his mother.
- In *Oration on the Dignity of Man* (1486), Giovanni Pico della Mirandola (1463–1494) defines the human being as a creature able to ascend to the heights of heaven in nobility of character or descend to the baseness of beasts in behavior.
- Mark Twain's novel *The Prince and the Pauper* (1881) tells the story of two boys in England, one the Prince of Wales and the other a slum child, who exchange identities.
- "Rapunzel," one of the folktales collected by the brothers Jacob and Wilhelm Grimm between 1812 and 1815, tells the story of a girl kept imprisoned in a tower from birth who discovers her true identity and marries her true love only after overcoming a series of dangers.
- Shakespeare's early comedy *The Taming of the Shrew* (ca. 1593) begins with a scene in which an impoverished drunkard, Christopher Sly, is taken by a nobleman to his house while he is in a stupor, treated like a lord, and told he has suffered from an illness that has made him believe that he was a poor drunkard. The main action of the play is concerned with the difficulty sometimes involved in separating what is real from pretense and with the power of supposing.
- Theodore Dreiser's 1925 novel *An American Tragedy* recounts the story of a young man brought up in oppressive conditions and longing for escape from such a life. He reacts violently when his dreamlike illusions and the real world conflict.

the last scene of the play, makes the sound argument that it was not his star-determined destiny that was the cause of his brutality but the brutal way he was raised. It is the course his father chose, not the configuration of the stars, that has made him uncivilized. Basilio's will, influenced by his understanding of the stars, is just as likely the power that determined Segismundo's nature as the stars themselves. Segismundo is just as likely to have been taught by his experience to be brutal as his brutality was formed by destiny. His impulsive inability to exercise freedom of choice may just as likely derive from a lack of education of his will as from his inherent nature. The cause is uncertain. Destiny itself is not solely determinant: it is clear that, to be fulfilled, destiny needed Basilio's intervention. The problem that Segismundo and the play itself must confront is whether either sort of determinism—the fate written in the stars or the fate imposed by the force of human actions—can be overcome by free will. The answer in the play is that it can, through the human ability to choose. That is the power, when he exercises it, which liberates Segismundo from his fate.

What makes choice necessary and possible and marks it as an expression of free will, Calderón shows, is the fact of the ambiguity of perception and Segismundo's awareness of that ambiguity. Segismundo becomes free when he chooses, and he is able to choose because there are alternatives. Only after he is confronted with uncertainty does Segismundo realize that he can choose to act tyrannically or not. In his first encounter with power, at court, his actions explode impulsively from him. He is a force of raging desire, and what he wants seems to be palpably in front of him to take, if he would. In his second encounter with power, after the mob frees him from prison and he defeats Astolfo and Basilio, his sense of his own power has been tempered by his experience of uncertainty. Consequently, each of his actions becomes a matter for deliberation. In an apparently illusory world, Segismundo has realized that the only thing that is not illusory is the way he acts in relation to what surrounds him. By his actions, he can shape illusion. In the midst of instability, he can be the stable element. The exercise of free will, Calderón establishes in *Life Is a Dream*, is what conquers uncertainty and ambiguity. When he frees himself from his apparent destiny, Segismundo becomes the one who shapes destiny.

Ambiguity's defining characteristic is that it is all-encompassing. It contains alternatives and takes in mutually exclusive and opposing phenomena. Ambiguity suggests that there are fixed and yet distinct categories and, simultaneously, that something may not be what it seems. For a woman to be mistaken for a man, as Rosaura is, those two categories—male and female—must exist independently of each other. For a man to be in doubt as to whether he is a prisoner or a prince, a beast or a man, those categories must exist independently of each other. Still, it must be possible for them to be confused with each other and, consequently, to be determined by behavior. Whether Segismundo is a prince or a beast may be unclear, but no matter which he is, he can choose to be either princely or beastly in either the prince or the beast role. The very ambiguity inherent in perception forces him to reject the power of perception and to rely on the authority of his own action.

In themselves, the characters in *Life Is a Dream* contain all possibilities, by virtue of their humanity, which is itself defined by ambiguity. Rosaura embodies the masculine in the first act, the feminine in the second, and both when she appears dressed like a woman but armed like a man in the third. Being at the center of ambiguity gives Segismundo the power to determine himself, to deliberate. This is a common Renaissance idea. It is expressed most unambiguously by Giovanni Pico della Mirandola (1463–1494), a scholar who combined Neoplatonic Renaissance humanism and medieval Roman Catholic theology in his *Oration on the Dignity of Man* (ca. 1486), when he imagined God "taking man . . . this creature of indeterminate image," and saying to him:

> We have given you, O Adam, no visage proper to yourself, nor endowment properly your own, in order that whatever place, whatever form, whatever gifts you may, with premeditation, select, these same you may have and possess through your own judgement and decision. The nature of all other creatures is defined and restricted within laws which We have laid down; you, by contrast, impeded by no such restrictions, may, by your own free will, to whose custody We have assigned you, trace for yourself the lineaments of your own nature. I have placed you at the very center of the world, so that from that vantage point you may with greater ease glance round about you on all that the world contains. We have made you a creature neither of heaven nor of earth, neither mortal nor immortal, in order that you may, as the free and proud shaper of your own being, fashion yourself in the form you may prefer. It will be in your power to descend to the lower, brutish forms of life; you will be able, through your own decision, to rise again to the superior orders whose life is divine.

In *Life Is a Dream*, the problem is this: In a world shaped by ambiguity and instability and governed by perception, what can determine how to act, if action, rather than perception or desire, is the only possible stabilizing force? How can humankind recognize what Pico della Mirandola shows as the divine stability and, by action, achieve something enduring rather than temporary? For Segismundo, it is by an act that achieves victory over himself. He has been "a man among wild beasts, and a beast among men." He becomes a man when he recognizes the otherness and humanity in Rosaura. Her power to bestow this gift on him is inherent in her situation and in what she represents. She is the abused maiden who seeks justice. As she seeks justice, so, too, does she represent Justice. The very name she takes in her conversation with Astolfo is Astrea, the heavenly Roman goddess of Justice, and through her person she brings the awareness of justice to Segismundo.

Segismundo realizes that the nature of his relationship to Rosaura is a matter of his choice and that it is not his perception of her that matters but his behavior toward her. In his first encounter with her, he responds to some overwhelming quality in her by a kind of animal tropism. He does not know why, but the sound of her voice fascinates him. His first impulse, to kill her because she had overheard him grieving, is overtaken by the stronger and mystifying impulse of attraction. His second encounter with her at the royal court, when he is a prince,

Laocoon *by El Greco, 1610–14* The Art Archive/National Gallery of Art Washington/Joseph Martin

shows him as bestial and rapacious, blinded by lust. But in their third encounter, he becomes self-defining and deliberating—a man, not a beast—when he triumphs over himself and, choosing to champion her honor rather than gratify his own lust, turns his head away from her so that he cannot look at her. By this action, he shows that he will not be guided by perception but by will. Recognizing her and his obligation to her, Segismundo also recognizes the force of Justice and, in doing so, brings into an unstable and uncertain world an absolute principle that cannot be undermined by the alterations that attend being alive. It is steady in the face of them, because of the free ability people have to will the good, which is eternal, by their actions.

Source: Neil Heims, Critical Essay on *Life Is a Dream*, in *Drama for Students*, Thomson Gale, 2006.

Wojciech Sadurski

In the following essay excerpt, Sadurski considers Life Is a Dream *as "a treatise on line drawing," exploring where Calderón draws lines separating life and dream, and essential human qualities and contingent ones.*

Life can be seen as an enterprise of line drawing. Everything we do relies upon drawing lines between the spheres within which we act. Indeed, an action which does not rely upon separating objects and phenomena into spheres which inform the action is not conceivable. What is less obvious is that the lines, once drawn, have a tendency toward petrification. They become, in our minds, axiomatic rather than dependent upon the purposes for which they were drawn in the first place. While there can be no social (or personal) life without drawing lines, the location of particular lines is inherently controversial. All radical challenges to social order can be seen as postulates about the change of demarcation lines, even though the rhetoric employed often suggests that what is demanded is the outright abolition of the lines.

> "CALDERON'S OWN ANSWER SEEMS TO BE AN AGNOSTIC ONE: THE INTRUSION OF 'REALITY' INTO 'THE DREAM' SUGGESTS THAT IT IS NOT IN HUMAN POWER TO DRAW THE LINE BETWEEN DREAMS AND REALITIES."

Challenging conventionally accepted lines forces us to rethink the bases of lines drawn, not merely their position. Michael Walzer has suggested that we could "think of liberalism as a certain way of drawing the map of a social and political world." We could say the same of any ideology, and also of our private beliefs. One benefit of looking at the way lines are drawn is that the inherent instability of this phenomenon (lines are drawn by reference to reasons, which themselves rely upon some other lines, etc.) makes us consider the foundations of various forms of social (and private) action.

This function of challenging lines can be illustrated by *Life's a Dream* (La vida es sueno), a play by Pedro Calderon de la Barca written around 1631 and first published in Madrid in 1636. The main protagonist is Segismundo, a royal heir who is kept from a very early age in a tower in the mountains because his father, Basilio, King of Poland, was foretold of a violent son who would wage a war against him. Once Segismundo is grown up, however, Basilio in a moment of doubt about the wisdom of his earlier decision asks Clotaldo, the keeper of his son, to drug Segismundo and have him wake in the palace and waited on as a prince. The strategy is to drug him again and take him back to the tower—in order to avoid risks should the astrological reading prove true—and then tell him that his palace experience was only a dream. When this plan is carried out, Basilio's worst fears are confirmed by the outrageous behavior of Segismundo during his one day in the palace. When Segismundo finds himself in prison again, he is convinced by Clotaldo that he only dreamt about being a prince.

At the same time a parallel plot develops: a young woman, Rosaura, disguised as a man and accompanied by her servant Clarion, proceeds to Poland to find Astolfo, an aristocrat who has a claim to the succession of the Polish throne, and who had abandoned Rosaura after having seduced her. Rosaura (who, it is later revealed, is Clotaldo's illegitimate daughter) meets Segismundo in his tower, and is soon recognized by Clotaldo who takes her to the court. The truth about Segismundo's identity spreads throughout the country, and a rebellion against the king breaks out: mutinous soldiers free Segismundo from his jail and ask him to lead them against the king. Rosaura offers to join Segismundo's army if he will assist her in her attempt to regain Astolfo who, along with Clotaldo, sides with the king. Segismundo defeats his father in battle but decides generously not to take vengeance. In the last scene Basilio crowns his son who in turn makes Astolfo marry Rosaura, despite his own passionate love for her.

What is Calderon's "point" in *Life's a Dream?* The tragedy of uncertainty, contingency and interchangeability of human existence? The continuous and yet never successful pursuit of one's own real identity, a destiny which is hidden from us? The ultimate solitude of every individual for whom other people, and the world, are as illusory as a dream? The burden and also the exhilaration of the "self" which is its own author, which writes its own story, which constructs itself through its free choice in the world in which human stories are as unpredictable as they are pre-determined? The conflict of two great moral codes, honor and commitment, in a world which makes us choose one and sacrifice the other? The absurdity of life not imbued with objective values and necessarily ending with death? The mortal risks which accompany the manipulation of destiny? Certainly, Calderon's play addresses all these themes, but my specific concern is with the work as a treatise on line drawing.

The title of the play in itself draws attention to a basic conventional distinction—that between life and dream. "What is life? A frenzy. What is life? An illusion, a shadow, a fiction, and the greatest good is very little because all life is a dream and dreams are only dreams" says Segismundo. In this observation we can see the way that the life/dream distinction overlaps with the reality/illusion distinction, and the essence/appearance distinction. This latter distinction is, however, in turn undermined because the "dream" is no less real than "real life": (what we know to be) a reality intrudes upon (what we know to be) a dream. From Segismundo's perspective the whole day he spends in the Palace is as real as his life in the Tower. Yet having been persuaded by Clotaldo that the Palace episode was only a dream, he is forced to place a dream and real life on par. Indeed, his "dream" in the Palace seems to him, if anything, more "real" than his real life in the Tower; having woken up, in his jail again, he confides to Clotaldo: "If the things which I saw when I was dreaming were palpable and certain, what I see now must be uncertain."

As if this were not enough to undermine the "dream/reality" distinction, the "reality" intrudes physically into "the dream." In Act 3, in a scene crucial to the entire drama, Rosaura meets Segismundo and recalls scenes from the Palace episode which Segismundo has in the meantime confined to the "dream" realm. His response to her recollection is to ask: "If I dreamed that greatness, in which I saw myself, how is it possible that this woman can recount it all to me?" One interpretation available to Segismundo would be a reversal of the order of the "dream/reality" distinction: to validate the Palace episode as "real" (because certified as such by Rosaura) and to recognize the Tower life and current events on the battlefield as dream. This would be unintelligible, however, because the only basis for doing so is Rosaura's testimony given on the battlefield—that is, in the context that he would be relegating to a dream. If the testimony is only a dream, it cannot be relied upon as a basis for un-dreaming the Palace episode.

Calderon's own answer seems to be an agnostic one: the intrusion of "reality" (personified here by Rosaura) into "the dream" (the Palace episode) suggests that it is not in human power to draw the line between dreams and realities. "Is the copy so similar to the original that we cannot tell which is real?" asks Segismundo. The conundrum here is: if all our life is a dream, and if the line between dreams and reality cannot be drawn, then possibly the "We" is also a dream. If the dream-ness attribute applies to everything, then it must also apply to the subject who does the dreaming. Yet in whose dreams does the dreamer appear? And is the one who does the dreaming about the dreamer, also a character in someone else's dreams? Where does this regress end? One answer could be God, but Calderon's own agnosticism as to the human capacity of drawing the line between reality and dream sits uneasily with this hypothesis.

Even if Segismundo can imagine that everything he sees in the Tower, in the Palace, on the battlefield, is but a dream, he cannot think that he is but a dream. For if he were to be an object of his own dreams, he would have to exist (as the dreamer), while if he were to be the object of someone else's dreams, it would be tantamount to saying that he was deceived by that other person as to the fact of his existence (the deception stemming from the fact that he falsely thinks he exists). Yet to be deceived, he must exist in the first place. This merely paraphrases the proof given by Descartes in his Second Meditation: "Even though there may be a deceiver of some sort, very powerful and very tricky, who bends all his efforts to keep me perpetually deceived, there can be no slightest doubt that I exist, since he deceives me; and let him deceive me as much as he will, he can never make me be nothing as long as I think that I am something." So that is where the regress must stop: even if we only dream, there must be the WE to do the dreaming; even if we are only dreamt about, there must be the WE for someone to dream about.

The second distinction Calderon draws is that between those attributes of human beings which are of an essential nature and those which are merely contingent. Up to a point, this is simple: there is the line which divides those properties without which we would not have existed qua ourselves and those which are fortuitous, and which do not belong to our "essence." One of Calderon's concerns seems to involve debunking the illusion that various properties of our everyday existence—power, money, personal fortunes and misfortunes—are "essential" rather than "contingent." He does this by reducing those contingencies to dreams: "The king dreams that he is king, and living under that delusion he rules, governs and disposes, and all the applause that he receives is written in the wind. . . . The rich man dreams of his wealth. . . . The poor man dreams that he suffers misery and poverty."

Yet there is an irony here: for precisely those features which are illusory or contingent are those same ones which we have the power to control. What can be more "human" (more of the essence of one's identity, which makes him or her a separate human being) than these things which we can affect through our own intentional and deliberate action? The King can modify the way he exercises his power, or even surrender it—thus showing that royal power is a thoroughly human attitude, that it belongs to those properties which make the King what he is, rather than an open and neutral repository of contingent and fortuitous features.

Calderon, however, undermines the line between the essence and contingencies of humaneness by relegating features such as power and wealth to the dream category. Or, as Mircea Eliade would say, by showing the "false identification of Reality with what each one of us appears to be or to possess." As Eliade continues, in a very Calderonian vein, "A politician thinks that the only true Reality is political power, a millionaire is convinced that wealth alone is real, a man of learning thinks the same about his studies, his books, laboratories and so forth."

By characterizing those attributes which make us distinct, separate and unique as purely fortuitous (or illusory), Calderon may well be saying that there is no objective basis for drawing a line between the fortuitous and the essential, and that while we often believe that only the essential is important, the better way is to say that something is essential because antecedently it is important. Conversely, our characterization of something as fortuitous is a consequence, not a premise, of denying any moral worth to it.

E. M. Wilson says that the soliloquy by Segismundo in which the worldly attributes of power, wealth, etc., are equated with a dream, relies upon a Stoic distinction between "the things that are in our power and those that are not." The lesson seems to be that "If we live only for the things that are not in our power we are no more free than is the dreamer in his dream who cannot exercise his powers of choice, for the outside things, things not in his power, rule him." Yet how can this assertion be reconciled with the view that the dream is at least as "real" as the reality?

In my opinion, Calderon does not assert the Stoic line between the things that are in our control and those that are not: he undermines it. And he does so in two ways: not merely by challenging our freedom to affect things in "reality" (if we are only dreaming, we are acted upon rather than acting) but also, conversely, by challenging (even if only en passant) our lack of freedom to affect things in our dreams. Annoyed by Segismundo's story about his violent behavior in the Palace episode, Clotaldo gives him this piece of advice: "Even in dreams it would be better to honor those who brought you up, Segismundo, because even in dreams good deeds are not wasted." It is only against the background of a subversion of the line between freedom and lack of freedom (consequent on the subversion of the line between the contingent and the essential) that we can view this extraordinary suggestion by Clotaldo as neither sarcastic nor cruel.

"Now Segismundo's a prince and I a lady," says Rosaura in the English "adaptation" of the play by Adrian Mitchell. This sentence does not appear in the original but it grasps well a central concern of the play: to parallel the development of Rosaura and Segismundo—the former in terms of gender, the latter in terms of social position. As the male-disguised Rosaura evolves from (apparent) manhood to womanhood, Segismundo evolves from a beast in the Tower to the prince in the Palace. And just as Rosaura's evolution by the end of Act 2 is not complete (it is not until Act 3 that she will achieve a synthesis of manhood and womanhood), neither is Segismundo's: he will find himself in the tower once again, only to reach a synthesis of "nature" and "civilization" on the battlefield in Act 3. As William Whitby has noted, Rosaura is "the key to Segismundo's conversion"; indeed, her conversions are catalysts in Segismundo's development. Their interconnected transformations inform the structure of the play because, as Frederick de Armas observes, Segismundo's final conversion in Act 3, brought about by the third appearance of Rosaura, "alters the process of destruction that had been set in motion and leads to a peaceful and harmonious denouement." These two quests for identity are parallel (with Rosaura always a step ahead of Segismundo), and it is a consideration of this parallelism—rather than an examination of either character in isolation—which may provide us with some clues as to the conundrum about the "real self" in *Life's a Dream.*

At first glance, the parallel journeys to identity undertaken by Rosaura and Segismundo would seem to call for an "essentialist" reading, whereby one would discern in both these characters' evolutions a move toward the discovery of their real selves. Rosaura is not truly "herself" when she appears in the beginning of the play disguised as a boy and is forced to play a male role; neither is Segismundo truly "himself" in the Tower, when as a human being he is kept as a wild beast. They will both have a tortuous journey to make. Rosaura will not simply shed her disguise and appear as her "true" self (note that her quest for identity does not end in Act 2 when she finally appears as a woman), nor will Segismundo easily convert from a creature of nature into a man of civilization. Both will attain their real selves the hard way; through a three-stage synthesis (man-woman-man/woman in the case of Rosaura; beast-prince-statesman in the case of Segismundo) rather than through a simple reversal. They have no choice but to go through this process because, as Ruth El Saffar suggests, they "struggle . . . for definition—to recover for themselves, out of the ever-impending threat of erasure, a solid sense of place and meaning."

On the way to this ultimate self-discovery they will find out things about themselves which they had not known at the beginning of their journey, very much in the way Joseph Conrad's Marlow says of Kurtz: "[the wilderness] whispered to him things about himself which he did not know, things of which he had no conception till he took counsel with this great solitude. . . ."

Source: Wojciech Sadurski, "Calderon's Conundrums, Or: Where Do You Draw the Line," in *Mosaic*, Vol. 28, No. 2, June 1995, pp. 23–42.

Edwin Honig

In the following essay excerpt, Honig comments on the complex and changing themes in Life Is a Dream *and how Calderón treats such concepts as honor, authority, and vengeance.*

The appeal of *Life Is a Dream* can never be wholly accounted for. From one point of view it seems incomplete, even fragmentary, like Marlowe's *Doctor Faustus.* From another, the play powerfully condenses in its enacted metaphor of living-and-dreaming an overwhelming perception about life's worth together with man's failure to make much if it. The play is many-faceted: it keeps changing as one holds it up to scrutiny so that its real theme seems impossible to pin down. It has the appeal of a mystery, but one in which the living energy that makes up the mystery is withheld, and while being withheld gets transformed into something different from the rigid terms and structure meant to contain it. . . .

In this play honor is seen in its broadest possible sense as related to the whole of life, interwoven with the very substance and meaning of life. The title implies the question, Is life worth living? By a further implication, if honor is an illusion, so is life, and if this is true, how does one cope with such a vast and fearful discovery?

Another related and basic problem is the question of how to deal with the violent and secret crimes of the older generation. Since Rosaura as well as Segismundo have been dishonored by their fathers, how can they redress their personal grievances without rupturing the relationship of one generation with the next, the succession of life itself? The old myths stir beneath the surface: Zeus dethroned Cronus, as Calderón fully showed in another play, *La estatua de Prometeo* 1669 (Prometheus's Statue); Zeus raped Leda as a swan and Europa as a bull; Aeneas abandoned Dido. All the actions pertain here to the sexual crimes of worldly men as fathers and lovers. Clotaldo raped and abandoned Violante, Rosaura's mother, and the rapist duke Astolfo abandoned Rosaura. In political terms, Segismundo will swear to overcome his father and trample on his beard.

"ANOTHER RELATED AND BASIC PROBLEM IS THE QUESTION OF HOW TO DEAL WITH THE VIOLENT AND SECRET CRIMES OF THE OLDER GENERATION."

Rosaura and Segismundo both have good cause to seek vengeance. They have been brutalized. Rosaura has been raped, deprived of her sexual honor, and rejected as a woman, without explanation. And, as far as he knows, also without explanation, Segismundo has been spiritually assaulted, deprived of his liberty, his free will, his honor as a man, and left since birth in a prison tower, like his father's guilty rotting dream. Deprived of his power as a man and as a prince, Segismundo has also been left ignorant of the existence of women, of love, of social communion.

To regain her honor (since there is no one to act for her), Rosaura must pretend to be a man—dress and act like one—so that she may have the sexual and political freedom needed to force the issue. To redress his grievances, Segismundo must seek power by revolution, imitate a tyrant in order to dethrone one, so that when he triumphs he can accomplish three things: rectify the misuse of power and dispense justice; restore his own freedom and gain the power proper to him as a man and as a prince; destroy the opposing vision: his father's self-rotting dream.

No other course is possible since, as the situation of the play proposes, even if *la vida es sueño, vida infame no es vida*—a life disgraced is no life at all.

Segismundo must be twice awakened and have Rosaura's help before he attains to consciousness. . . . In the darkness of the prison tower, in the open doorway waiting to emit him, Rosaura sees the womb and tomb of life:

> The front door
> stands open to . . . what is it,

a mausoleum? And pitch darkness
like the night itself comes
crawling out as from a womb.

It is life, unaware of itself as yet, for it has been buried in death, a light in the darkness at first, followed by the clanking of chains as the prisoner, man himself, emerges in animal pelts. Can it be that Rosaura is privileged to witness this birth scene because she is Segismundo's "twin"—that at this moment she, too, is being born into consciousness through her recognition of his birth?. . .

It is not often seen that the mysterious interdependence between Rosaura and Segismundo has directly to do with the moral realism of their claims in a male-dominated, autocratic society. They need each other not only to regain their womanhood and manhood, respectively, but also because what they have to face is an extremely adverse and unpromising set of circumstances, not least because they are going against the rule of custom and law as represented by guilty, well-meaning, and unjust men: Basilio, the King; Clotaldo, his chief counsellor and Rosaura's father; and the duke, Astolfo. And so the act of restoring the human integer of magnanimity in the face of its thorough brutalization by well-intentioned, civilized men is nothing short of saintly. And this is what Segismundo proceeds to do.

If the life of consciousness is the only life worth living, then Segismundo is clearly the only character in the play who succeeds in attaining it. . . .

The stages of his regeneration are marked off by certain of his speeches and soliloquies which other characters overhear and by actions which they then witness. But these characters, often like figures in a dream, do little or nothing to show that they have been personally affected by his behavior in the narrative sequence of the play. Through his soliloquies and what he says to others, Segismundo seems constantly to be setting up rationales for acting the way he does as he goes along. The other characters, Rosaura especially, are there to feed him with the possibilities of experience which will turn out, when he understands it, to confirm his own gradual acquisition of moral consciousness. This sort of procedure, involving both being-there and not-being-there at the same time, resembles what happens in dreams and in dream allegories. There is an unalterable line to be followed which only the consciousness of a single actor may pursue, since it is essentially from his actions leading to his awareness that the real business of the play takes its meanings.

The ambiguous creature wearing animal pelts and lying chained in the tower is the prince of mankind. This is how Segismundo begins. Thereafter we are obliged to judge the moral and psychological distance he traverses in the course of the play in order to become consciously human. He must go from the lowest form of human life, the equivalent of the cave man, to the highest—the human being who learns to be civilized by responding to everything around him while doubting it all and believing in nothing. (How could someone who has scarcely even been born believe in anything?) Others may say life is a dream; Segismundo must find out whether this is true or not by living his own life. He must fight for the power he has been denied, but once it is achieved he must also wear it lightly, pardoning his enemies and renouncing his love. . . .

The precise virtue, then, which Segismundo will attain is magnanimity, the quality of the highest civilized behavior. Battle in a just cause, the pursuit of one's honor, the achievement of knowledge and intellectual pride, and the unswerving course of loyalty are other virtues embodied by characters in the play. But none of these saves them from suffering desperation, an unresolved moral dilemma. Only Segismundo's attainment frees the others; or—since they frequently seem to be little more than figures revolving in Segismundo's orbit—enables the lesser virtues they represent to be seen against his fundamental moral evolution.

Like honor, of which it is part, his magnanimity means nothing in itself; it must be won by experience, past which, as he himself says,

If my valor is destined
for great victories, the greatest
must be the one I now achieve
by conquering myself.

This is no mere rephrasing of the familiar Greek adage; coming nearly at the end of the play, the sentence rings out as a momentous renunciation of power politics, the life of tooth and claw, the deceptions of intellectual and sexual pride, the blandishments of romantic appetite, and even the ambiguities of filial piety. We see that to achieve magnanimity Segismundo has had fully to recognize who and what he is, through a series of acts which includes one murder and several attempts at murder as well as threats of parricide and rape. He has had to learn to love and then to undo his love, to overcome himself, and to vanguish his father. It is not an easy formula at all. His career is a paradigm of several millennia of human history.

For magnanimity to arise it must contend with the brute in man as well as the brute in society. Half man and half beast as Segismundo recognizes himself to be at the beginning, his first understanding is that though he has an intellect which makes him superior to animals, he lacks the freedom to use it, a freedom which even the animals have.

A brute is born, its hide all covered
in brightly painted motley,
which, thanks to nature's brush, is lovely
as the sky in star-strewn panoply,
till learning man's cruel need
to lunge and pounce on prey
when it becomes a monster
in a labyrinth. Then why should I,
with instincts higher than a brute's,
enjoy less liberty?

. . .

I dream that I am here
manacled in this cell,
and I dreamed I saw myself
before, much better off.
What is life? A frenzy.
What is life? An illusion,
fiction, passing shadow,
and the greatest good the merest dot,
for all of life's a dream, and dreams
themselves are only part of dreaming.

What we do, what we become through what we do, is the substance of our dream which is our life. . . . Having accepted the dream of life, Segismundo is ready to act; he is ready to deal as a prince with the chance and irrational events of experience. He has begun to control his impulses.

The gift of life Rosaura has stirred up in Segismundo is what Basilio has all the time been zealously withholding from him. And subsequently, when Segismundo's experience teaches him how to understand the caution that "life is a dream," the prince is ready to accede to the soldiers' invitation to rebel against his father and actively wrest the power which Basilio has been hoarding.

To do so Segismundo must first break the conspiracy which prevents him from acting, surrounded as he is, like a bull, by baiters cautioning him to accept the illusion of life as self-explanatory. . . .

To effect these transformations Calderón employs the *gracioso* Clarín and the rebellious soldier in the final act. . . . Clarín is incapable of illusion or disillusionment; he stands outside the course of events in order to comment on them from a non-moral point of view. But now in the third act it is just such a point of view which Calderón finds especially useful: first, to underscore the folly and taint of the power drive, and second, to provide a victim for another substitute sacrifice, one that must now be made for Segismundo's taboo crime of a son overcoming a father, and worse, overcoming him as the divinely appointed king in an act of rebellion.

So Clarín's fate—to be shot to death while hiding from the battle—accomplishes two things. It shocks King Basilio into understanding his own vainglory in opposing the designs of heaven, hence preparing him to succumb to Segismundo; it also releases Segismundo from the crime of rebellion. And when the dissident soldier is sent to the tower, we recognize that the order of constituted authority has been restored by Segismundo. Chaos and anarchy have been consigned to the house of illusion, sleep, and death. The tower itself is preserved; it is not destroyed. What Segismundo suffered in it others will continue to suffer. Segismundo himself points to this condition in the closing words of the play:

Why are you surprised? What's there
to wonder at, if my master in this
was a dream, and I still tremble
at the thought that I may waken
and find myself again locked in a cell?
Even if this should not happen,
it would be enough to dream it,
since that's the way I've come to know
that all of human happiness
must like a dream come to an end.

. . . Stressing the nature of the play as a waking dream vision with the leading thematic concern it expresses for the triumph of consciousness indicates how Calderón essentializes thought and action while giving both the widest possible applicability in a strict dramatic form. Though *Life Is a Dream* is Calderón's best-known play, it is not, like his *auto* of the same title, a religious but a metaphysical drama. Yet it shares with a good many of his plays a basically antiauthoritarian bias. What is more, it is aligned with such a variety of other plays as *Devotion to the Cross, The Wonder-Working Magician, The Mayor of Zalamea,* and *The Phantom Lady* by its persistent exploration of the humane virtues of clemency, love, and magnanimity, held up against the combative principle of the strict honor code—the power drive, vengeance, absolute law. In *Life Is a Dream,* perhaps uniquely among Calderón's plays, a metaphysical problem is supported not by appeals to faith or insistence on ideality but from the proofs of experience itself. For the virtue of magnanimity to emerge in Segismundo it must be shown to overcome the lesser virtues breeding the brutalization of experience—false pride, rape, murder, and perverted sexuality. By implication the play is a criticism of inflexible rule, of self-deceptive authoritarianism masquerading as benevolent justice, and of all abuses to the individual arising from it.

Appropriate to such criticism are Calderón's disclosures of the life of impulse which underlies the motivations of his characters. Such disclosures often lead typically to a formula whereby compulsive action, moral desperation, and distraught behavior must issue from sidetracked and guilty consciences: the pursuit of vengeance and the expression of doubt from the fear of infidelity, perverted love, and incest. But from this and other examples of his psychological realism, we see that Calderón at his best is never merely a preacher or an upholder of an abstract morality. He essentializes in order to identify; he dramatizes in order to characterize; and he particularizes experience in order to show that relation of misguided motives to the espousing of false ideals and the necessity of earned perception for the attainment of practicable ideals. This still seems a lesson worth having.

Source: Edwin Honig, "The Magnanimous Prince and the Price of Consciousness: *Life Is a Dream*," in *Calderon and the Seizures of Honor*, Harvard University Press, 1972, pp. 158–75.

SOURCES

Calderón de la Barca, Pedro, *Life Is a Dream*, translated by Edward and Elizabeth Huberman, in *The Golden Age*, selected and introduced by Norris Houghton, Dell, 1963, pp. 86–89.

De Armas, Frederick A., *The Return of Astraea: An Astral-Imperial Myth in Calderón*, University Press of Kentucky, 1986, p. 122.

Pico della Mirandola, Giovanni, *Oration on the Dignity of Man*, available online at http://cscs.umich.edu/~crshalizi/Mirandola (August 31, 2005).

Sloman, A. E., "The Structure of Calderón's *La vida es sueño*," in *Critical Essays on the Theatre of Calderón*, edited by Bruce W. Wardropper, New York University Press, 1965, pp. 90–91.

FURTHER READING

Cascardi, Anthony J., *The Limits of Illusion: A Critical Study of Calderón*, Cambridge University Press, 1984.

Cascardi studies Calderón's work with regard to the literary and philosophical currents of his time and probes his treatment of illusion and skepticism in all his plays.

Freud, Sigmund, *The Interpretation of Dreams*, edited and translated by James Strachey, Avon Books, 1980.

Freud's dream book, first published in 1900, is one of the most important and influential books of the twentieth century. In it, Freud advances the theory that dreams are essentially wishes that are represented in a mystifying manner in order to evade the censorship of internalized social constraints.

Fulton, J. Michael, "In Defense of Clotaldo: Reconsidering the Secondary Plot in Calderón's *La vida es sueño*," in *Rocky Mountain Review of Language and Literature*, Vol. 56, No. 1, Spring 2002, pp. 11–23.

Citing the body of criticism that brands Rosaura's father as cowardly, deceptive, and self-serving, Fulton argues that, by contrast with Basilio, Segismundo's father, Clotaldo represents the type of an honorable and loyal father.

Hofmannsthal, Hugo von, *Der Turm*, translated by Michael Hamburger, in *Hugo von Hofmannsthal: Poems and Verse Plays*, Bollingen Foundation, 1961.

The Tower is a German adaptation of *La vida es sueño*. Published in 1925 and first performed in 1927, it reflects the chaotic situation of Germany at the time of its composition. Sigismund is freed from his tower prison at the age of twenty-one, defeated in his rebellion against his father, and sentenced to death. On the day of his execution, however, the nobility overthrows Basilius and makes Sigismund king, but he is assassinated during a peasant uprising.

Honig, Edward, "The Magnanimous Prince and the Price of Consciousness: *Life Is a Dream*," in *Calderón and the Seizure of Honor*, Harvard University Press, 1972.

Honig studies the nature of the relationship between Segismundo and Rosaura in *Life Is a Dream*, not only discussing their common concerns with seeking vengeance and gaining honor but also regarding precursor figures in some of Calderón's earlier plays.

Parker, Alexander A., *The Mind and Art of Calderón: Essays on the Comedias*, Cambridge University Press, 1988.

Parker's volume is a survey and a study of Calderón's secular dramas, concentrating on how social and political life as well as myths are reflected in those works. In his discussion of *Life Is a Dream*, Parker considers the father-son conflict, the meaning of the tower, the power of horoscopes, and the conflict between fate and responsibility.

Strother, Darci L., *Family Matters: A Study of On- and Off-Stage Marriage and Family Relationism in Seventeenth-Century Spain*, Peter Lang Publishing, 1999.

In the context of works by Calderón and other seventeenth-century Spanish playwrights, Strother studies family relations in seventeenth-century Spain and the way the family was presented on the stage. Strother focuses on consensual and arranged marriages, women's roles, child rearing, and alternatives to marriage.

Necessary Targets

EVE ENSLER

1996

Eve Ensler's *Necessary Targets*, first produced in 1996 (and later published by Villard Books in 2001), was inspired by the author's trip to the former Yugoslavia. Ensler went there to interview Bosnian women war refugees. It was from Ensler's experience with these women that *Necessary Targets* was born. "When we think of war," Ensler writes in the introduction to her published play, "we think of it as something that happens to men." The focus is on bombs and the immediate destruction that they wreak. Little media attention or conscious thought on the part of people living in other countries is focused on the aftermath of war. "But after the bombing," Ensler continues, "that's when the real war begins." Ensler wrote *Necessary Targets* in an attempt to change this focus.

In Bosnia, Ensler met women who were forced to deal with the aftermath of war, and it was their stories that inspired her. "It was their community, their holding on to love, their insane humanity in the face of catastrophe, their staggering refusal to have or seek revenge," Ensler writes, "that fueled me and ultimately moved me to write this play." The outstanding performances of many actresses have paid tribute to *Necessary Targets*. In 1996, Meryl Streep and Anjelica Huston read the play at a benefit performance in the United States; Vanessa Redgrave did the same in London. In Sarajevo, the capital of Bosnia, Glenn Close and Marisa Tomei performed the play.

Ensler, who won international fame for her award-winning play *The Vagina Monologues*

Eve Ensler © Nicolas Guerin/Azimuts Production/Corbis

(1996), has stated that she dreams of building a world in which women are safe and free. *Necessary Targets* is one of the first steps toward that goal. It is the story of two American women who go to Bosnia in the hope of teaching five female survivors of war how to cope with their trauma. By the end of the play, it is one of the American women who has learned the more valuable lesson. After Ensler won an Obie in 1997 for *Vagina Monologues*, *Necessary Targets* gained renewed interest and, in 2001, was performed in Connecticut and Washington, D.C. The following year, it opened off Broadway at the Variety Arts Theatre in New York.

AUTHOR BIOGRAPHY

Eve Ensler was born on May 25, 1953, in New York City. Her childhood was not a happy one. She has revealed that she was sexually and physically abused by her father. After her father's death, Ensler told her mother about the abuse. Ensler has stated that it was this revelation to her mother that set her free. "At that moment," Ensler told Cora Llamas, a writer for the *Philippine Daily Inquirer*, "my entire life changed. I went from a depressed, self-hating person to a free one." Llamas went on to write in the same interview that it was because of these difficult experiences that Ensler has been able to empathize with women around the world who also have suffered abuse.

In 1975, Ensler graduated from Middlebury College in Vermont. Later, she worked as an editor for *Central Park Magazine*. The first of her plays to gain media attention was *Floating Rhoda and the Glue Man* (1995), about a dysfunctional relationship between a man and a woman. Ensler's stepson, Dylan McDermott, played the male protagonist, whose character often stepped back from the action of the play to dissect his feelings.

Ensler's next play, *Necessary Targets* (1996), enjoyed public readings by such famous actresses as Meryl Streep, Vanessa Redgrave, and Glenn Close, to raise money for Bosnian war refugees. The play garnered little media attention, however, until Ensler gained international fame for her successful 1996–1997 production of *The Vagina Monologues*, in which she performed all the roles. This play won her an Obie Award for playwriting and launched her career not only as a dramatist but also as an activist for women's rights. Jack Helbig describes *The Vagina Monologues* in *Booklist* as a "witty, wildly popular meditation on female sexuality." The play also is referred to, in an article by Marc Peyser for *Newsweek*, as "one of the biggest theater successes in years."

The success of *The Vagina Monologues* caused quite a strong reaction around the world. China, at first, banned it. According to one newspaper headline, Japan braced for it. Many women, however, wrapped their arms around the play. As a result of the enthusiasm, Ensler founded the V-Day movement to stop violence against women. From the founding of the movement on, Ensler has been a political activist. She travels around the globe, raising people's awareness about the plight of women subjected to violence. The V-Day movement is so powerful that many people credit Ensler with stimulating a new wave of feminism.

In 2003, Ensler produced the film documentary *What I Want My Words to Do to You: Voices from Inside a Woman's Maximum Security Prison. The Good Body*, in which she also starred, premiered in 2004. In addition, Ensler published the book *Vagina Warriors* (2005) and, as of 2005, had begun writing two new works, *I Am an Emotional Creature* and *V-World*. Other plays include *When I Call My Voices* (1979) and *Rendezvous* (1983).

Ensler was married for a brief period to Richard McDermott. During their marriage, Ensler adopted McDermott's son, Dylan. Dylan, only a few years younger than Ensler, has gone on to become an accomplished actor, crediting Ensler for his success. In 2005, Ensler was sharing her life with Ariel Orr Jordan, a psychotherapist.

PLOT SUMMARY

Scene 1

Necessary Targets is not broken down into acts, only into scenes. It begins in a plush apartment somewhere in New York City. Two women are onstage. The first to speak is Melissa, who is described as "a young, strong woman who sits awkwardly on the sofa." The second woman, called J.S., is a "reserved woman near fifty." Through the conversation, the audience can tell that Melissa is very laid back, whereas J.S. is just the opposite.

J.S. is a psychiatrist, but Melissa refers to her as a "shrink" and becomes self-conscious about the questions J.S. asks her. She senses that every time she offers an answer, J.S. is analyzing her. This is especially apparent when Melissa makes the comment, "Well, I've been through a lot." Melissa offers this information to make the point that she is older than her calendar years. Melissa has come to J.S.'s apartment for an interview. Melissa is a trauma counselor and a writer, and the two women are planning to travel together to meet with Bosnian women who are refugees from the war. Melissa has worked in other countries, with other victims of war. J.S., on the other hand, has never been to a war-torn country. This is why J.S. has asked Melissa to go with her to Bosnia.

Melissa challenges J.S. about her lack of experience. J.S., however, states that "trauma is trauma," indicating that her background in dealing with such problems as anorexia should qualify her to work with women who are suffering from the violence of war. Melissa expresses doubts about this. She also objects to being called J.S.'s assistant. She is used to working alone.

Scene 2

The setting is a refugee camp in Bosnia. J.S. complains of the filthy conditions in the bathroom. She would prefer to stay in a hotel. Melissa points out that the distance and the dissimilarities between the camp and the hotel would foster resentment among the women they have come to interview.

Scene 3

The third scene opens with J.S. and Melissa in a room with Jelena (a middle-aged woman), Zlata (a sophisticated older woman), Nuna (a teenager), Seada (a young adult), and Azra (an elderly woman). The Bosnian women are a bit testy, and they make fun of the American women. One woman refers to J.S. as a "loony doctor." Then the Bosnian women talk among themselves, kidding one another and appearing not to listen to J.S., who is trying to set up the guidelines for their sessions together. The Bosnian women are reluctant participants. Instead of responding to J.S.'s questions, they ask their own questions, including questions about the process of the counseling. J.S. attempts to keep the conversation on course, but the Bosnian women point out the irrelevance of J.S.'s questions. Melissa, too, is impatient. When J.S. asks whether one of the women is from Bosnia, Melissa is the first to respond, and the words she has chosen—"Of course she's from Bosnia."—reflect her irritation at J.S.'s seeming lack of awareness.

Zlata then says, "We're all from Bosnia. What do you think we're doing here?" This comment adds to the tension, as the women gang up on J.S., mocking her as a way of pointing out how ridiculous it is that she is there. Jelena steps in at this point and subtly reminds the other women of their manners. "We are very honored that you Americans came all the way here," she says; then she proceeds to introduce the other Bosnian women. The Bosnian women ask why the Americans have come. Melissa tries to explain. First, she tells the women that they have come to help them talk. The Bosnian women scoff at this. All they have been doing is talking, they say.

J.S. tries to make it clearer. She tells them she has come to help them talk about the war, in particular. This makes even less sense to the refugees. Several of them make condescending remarks before Zlata says: "You flew all the way here for that?" She asks J.S. what she thinks they have spent most of their days talking about since they arrived at the camp: "Our lingerie, our dinner parties . . . ?" The Bosnian women are tired of talking. They are tired of people coming from the outside and wanting to hear their stories.

Melissa tells the women that she wants to record their stories so that the whole world knows about them. Even Jelena, who had been supportive of the Americans up to this point, finds this difficult to swallow. At the end of the third scene, Nuna says,

"So this is American therapy?" To this, Azra responds: "It just feels like another terrible day to me."

Scene 4

Scene 4 begins in J.S.'s room at the camp. She has given up and is packing her suitcase. She says that she feels embarrassed and ludicrous. She does not believe she has anything to offer the women. Melissa tries to talk her out of this. She reminds J.S. that the women are only taking out their frustration, anger, and fear on the two of them. It is here that the title of the play is explained. Melissa tells J.S. that the women are attacking them because she and J.S. are "necessary targets." But Melissa and J.S. are interrupted when Nuna runs into their room. "Baby Doona won't stop crying," she says. Melissa leaves the room. Nuna tells J.S. that the women are not as bad as they first appear. When Melissa comes back with the baby, she tells J.S. that one of the Bosnian women is ready to talk to the Americans. Melissa does not say which one.

Scene 5

Jelena opens the next scene, talking about her husband and the awful changes in his personality since the war. Jelena is talking to Azra, but Azra is not really connecting with her. Rather, Azra is lost in her own world. She wants her goats and her cow.

Scene 6

It is nighttime when scene 6 opens. Someone creeps into J.S.'s room. It is Seada, who refers to J.S. as "mama." Seada wants to sleep with J.S. and climb into her bed. J.S. feels awkward and tries to talk Seada out of it, to no avail.

Scene 7

A rainstorm begins scene 7. All the women are sitting around a table. Some of the women are willing to talk, but Zlata continues to refuse. Jelena says that everyone knows everyone else's story, but no one knows Zlata's story. Azra is the first to tell her story. When she starts to cry, Zlata wants to know how this is helping anyone. Coffee is poured for all the women, but J.S. does not drink hers. When she is asked why, she tells the women that she has given up caffeine. The Bosnian women think that this sounds like an American thing to do. Nuna takes offense at J.S.'s not drinking coffee with them. She thinks it means J.S. does not like them. When Jelena explains this to her, J.S. hesitates but finally sips the coffee.

Scene 8

Zlata is sitting in a room by herself, crying, when J.S. walks in. J.S. feels awkward about her intrusion and, to cover her awkwardness, starts up a conversation about the weather. Zlata quickly switches the topic to J.S.'s wealth and profession. J.S. refuses to answer Zlata's questions, explaining that she is trained to pose questions, not answer them. Zlata confronts her on this, asking whether J.S. is even able to hold a normal conversation. The women start talking about the war. Zlata says she used to blame the leaders for the war, but now she thinks that there is a monster in all human beings that waits for an opportunity to come out. They each laugh at themselves when they try to describe the monster inside of them. And when Zlata's body begins to shake, J.S. becomes concerned, wanting to help. She tells Zlata that she wants to be her friend.

Scene 9

In scene 9, J.S. confronts Melissa. She asks Melissa to stop using her tape recorder. J.S. thinks the recorder makes the women feel uncomfortable. Melissa does not believe this. J.S. is warming up to the women, but Melissa is standing back, seeing it as the way to help the women as quickly and efficiently as possible and allowing her to move on to the next assignment.

Scene 10

In scene 10, the women are sitting by a river. A French company has sent skin cleansers, and the women are having facials. The women start talking about what they miss. Nuna tells how she is of mixed heritage and belongs to neither side of this ethnic conflict. Then Jelena produces a bottle of booze. The women sing, drink, and dance. J.S. notices that Zlata is missing. She goes to find her.

Scene 11

In scene 11, J.S. finds Zlata and talks about how she can no longer sing. J.S. is a professional woman, she says, who cannot allow herself to be sloppy. Zlata urges J.S. to sing. The other women join J.S. and Zlata, singing and dancing.

Scene 12

At the start of scene 12, J.S. finds Azra lying in a large hole in the earth. Azra says she wants to die. She is in her grave. J.S. persuades Azra to talk to her cow. This cheers Azra up, and she crawls out of the hole.

Scene 13

Seada's story unfolds in the next scene. Zlata is mending Jelena's black eye, the work of Jelena's husband. Melissa blames this injury on the drinking from the night before. But the Bosnian women claim that it was one of the best nights they have had in a long time. J.S., however, is concerned that she has crossed a line and needs to be more professional. Melissa keeps pushing for the women to open up. Zlata resists. Their stories belong to them, she tells Melissa. Seada is not in the room, but Nuna begins to tell Seada's story. Soldiers came into their village and were threatening to rape all the women. Seada's husband hides her, but the soldiers find her. When her husband tries to protect Seada, the soldiers shoot him in the head. Seada starts running with her baby. In her panic, she drops the baby but does not realize she has done so until too late.

Seada walks into the room. The women are unaware that she is hearing her story told. When Nuna talks about Seada's having dropped her baby, Seada unwraps the rags she has been cradling and realizes there is no baby there. She starts screaming and running. The women go after her. J.S. and Melissa are told to stay behind. J.S. berates Melissa for pushing the women too hard to open up and tell their stories. J.S. fears that Seada was not ready to face reality. Nuna runs in and yells that they have found Seada and she is hurting herself badly.

Scene 14

Seada is eating dirt and pulling out her hair. She is crying for her mother. She thinks J.S. is her mother. J.S. holds Seada but tells her she is not her mother. Seada offers details of the rape that she suffered after losing her baby. J.S. holds her and sings a lullaby to soothe her. Melissa tells everyone that she did not mean to hurt anyone. She was just doing her job.

Scene 15

When scene 15 opens, Melissa is packing her bags. She tells J.S. that she is going to Chechnya to gather material for the final chapter of her book. Melissa suggests that she herself suffered some kind of trauma when she was young. She tells J.S. that she used to have terrible nightmares. When she started traveling to war-torn countries and dealing with the problems of other women, the nightmares went away. Melissa takes her bag and leaves.

Scene 16

Scene 16 focuses on J.S. and Zlata. The women are sitting outside, under the stars. Zlata opens up to J.S. and tells her about the massacre of her parents. They were beheaded. Then Zlata recounts the beauty that once was Bosnia. With its friendliness and openness, Bosnia was once a paradise, she says.

Scene 17

J.S. is back in her apartment in the United States in the final scene. She is talking into a recorder. She directs her thoughts to Melissa. J.S. tells Melissa that she feels empty but happy. She says that the women in Bosnia have changed her forever. She cannot return to what she once was. She wants only to be with the women in Bosnia.

CHARACTERS

Azra

Azra is the oldest woman of the group. She is from the countryside and is known for repeating her stories, especially stories about her cow. Azra complains a lot. She wants to go home. She wants a doctor to look at her and ease her pains. Azra stands for the traditional Bosnian woman, a woman tied to the earth and her country ways. She exists at one end of the spectrum, while Nuna, who is described as a very Westernized teenager, is positioned at the other.

Azra is one of the first women upon whom J.S. has an effect. J.S. talks Azra out of a so-called grave that Azra has discovered and climbed into. Azra wants to die. She feels as if she has nothing more to live for. J.S. uses Azra's pleasant memories of her cow to bring Azra back into the world of the living. Although Azra is the oldest woman of the group, she does not necessarily represent wisdom. She does, however, have Old World charm. At one point, she tells everyone that talking about Seada behind her back is bad luck. In some ways, this turns out to be true, as Seada hears the women talking about her and is thrown into a desperate fit of anxiety. Azra is not among the women who later soothe Seada, however. Her character does not exhibit any nurturing or mothering skills. The exception is the loving way that Azra talks about her cow. Azra has apparently never been married and has never experienced sex, which, someone suggests, is the reason she is so grumpy.

Doona

Doona is the name of Seada's baby. Throughout most of the play, the women talk about Doona as if she were present in their midst. They talk about her being cold and about her crying, which is so loud that they become annoyed and worried. However, at the end of the play, the audience discovers that the bundle that Seada has been carrying around is merely a bunch of wrapped rags. Doona was lost during the time when Seada was running away from men who wanted to rape her. Seada dropped her baby and did not realize it until it was too late. There is no mention of the real Doona's fate, whether she is still alive or not.

Jelena

Jelena is described as an earthy woman. She is in her forties, and it is she who calms the group of Bosnian women and reminds them to be respectful of the American women rather than continually mocking them. While the other women respond to the American women in sarcastic tones, Jelena takes a more nurturing attitude, as she attempts to understand why J.S. and Melissa are there and then to explain it to the Bosnian women.

Jelena has the only connection to a man in this play. Her husband fought in the war and suffers psychologically from his memories. He takes out his pain on Jelena, who appears one day with a black eye. The rest of Jelena's story remains untold. She is the most optimistic of the refugee women, however, and continually tries to represent hope for the future. She finds things to feel good about, despite her hardships, and encourages the other women to do the same. She is the most down-to-earth character and the most resilient.

J.S.

J.S. is a well-established and successful psychiatrist, living a comfortable life in New York City. She has been appointed by the president to go to Bosnia to help war refugees there. J.S. has never been in a war zone and is very uncomfortable when she arrives at the camp. She dislikes the filthy conditions and wants to stay in a hotel rather than live with the refugees.

At first, the refugees mock J.S.'s attempts at therapy. They feel her separateness and try to bring her down from her pedestal. It almost defeats her. J.S. comes close to giving up and returning home. She gives it one more try, however, and slowly drops the walls she has built around herself. She does this first with Seada, whom she allows to sleep in her bed and to pretend that J.S. is her mother. Then J.S. drinks with the women one night and talks about personal aspects of her life. For instance, she tells Zlata that she has not been able to sing as an adult, although she loves singing. This is Ensler's way of demonstrating that the most pleasurable things J.S. enjoyed have been locked away inside her, because she has donned what she believes is the mask of professionalism. She hides behind this mask until Zlata challenges her to take it off.

Of the two American women, J.S. is the one who is transformed by her experiences in Bosnia. She is the opposite of Melissa in many ways. The most telling of these is that she is able to see who she is and what she does not like about herself, and then she is able to alter her life's course.

Melissa

Melissa, a young woman in her twenties, is a writer and a trauma therapist. She has traveled all over the world trying to help women who have suffered from war. She is in the process of collecting stories from these women so that she can write a book about their experiences. Melissa stands in diametric opposition to J.S., the American psychiatrist. Melissa, too, is an American, but she is much more experienced in international settings and war-torn circumstances. Melissa is also very wary of psychiatrists. Her sensitivity and defensiveness in response to J.S.'s questions suggest that Melissa herself might have been in therapy.

Still, Melissa is somewhat in awe of J.S., as well as being disdainful of her. While visiting J.S. in her posh apartment, Melissa feels uneasy and admits that comfort unsettles her. However, in Bosnia, Melissa demonstrates her strength. There seem to be fewer barriers between herself and the other women, despite their differences. She mocks J.S.'s need to keep a distance between herself and the refugees.

Melissa, though, has troubles of her own. She is trying to run away from an ugly past. She does not stand still and take stock of her life, as she strongly suggests that the other women do. Instead, when she is confronted and challenged by J.S. for being too harsh with the women, Melissa packs her bags and rushes off to yet another country. She fulfills the Bosnian women's definition of her: Melissa turns out to be just another journalist trying to capture a story.

Nuna

Nuna is the youngest of the Bosnian women. She likes everything American, and the other women tease her about watching too many American movies. Nuna is fascinated with J.S. and asks her many questions about American culture. Nuna is lost in a fantasy of what she thinks America is, and it has become her escape. As a character, Nuna provides an occasional break in the tension by saying something that is entirely bizarre or by displaying a rather comical view of Americans. Her character also shows the Western influence on the people of Bosnia before the war.

Seada

Seada is the second-youngest Bosnian woman, referred to as the "gorgeous one." Seada's story is the most tragic. Her character draws the strongest emotional response from the audience. She has lost a husband and a mother. She dropped her baby somewhere along the path while running from the soldiers. She was raped unmercifully by them. And she is the character who is most caught in denial. She is the catalyst that brings J.S. out of her objective, professional stance. She is also the character around whom all the other Bosnian women come together. Seada's abrupt and brutal awakening is caused by Melissa's sharp and possibly heartless demands. Seada's healing process, on the other hand, begins with J.S., who soothes her and even rocks her in her arms and sings a lullaby to her.

Zlata

Zlata is a medical doctor and a Bosnian refugee, and she relates to J.S. better than the other women do. This could be because of their similar education, knowledge, and experience. But it is also because of Zlata's background that she dislikes what J.S. and Melissa are doing. Of all the women, it is Zlata who knows that the American women really have nothing at stake and will one day leave. This barrier of awareness is difficult for Zlata to break down. She does not want to be treated as if she were sick. She does not feel that there is anything wrong with her. If there were, she believes that she could heal herself, so she closes herself off to the Americans and their desires to do good.

It is through Zlata, more than any other character, that Ensler develops the concept of the "other." Ensler portrays what she believes is a general notion among Americans that people who are not Americans are different. Taken to an extreme, some people remove their sense of humanity from specific groups of people and think of them as the "other." Zlata confronts J.S. with this. She tells J.S. that before the war, she and her family and friends were just like a typical American family. They had wealth, comfort, and leisure time. J.S. sees them after the war has utterly destroyed their way of life, but that does not mean that the Bosnian women are any different from the Americans.

By the end of the play, Zlata has undergone a certain transformation. She is one of the few characters that experience change. She can put down her barriers after she sees J.S. dropping hers, and the two women become friends.

THEMES

Isolation

The theme of isolation is apparent in many of the characters in *Necessary Targets*. First, there is the overall environment of the war in Bosnia, which isolated one ethnic group from another. People in villages were cut off from people who lived in cities, as neighbor fought neighbor. There is also the isolation that the victims of war, the female refugees of the play, suffer in its aftermath. The Bosnian women are not the only ones who feel isolated from their past, from their families, and from themselves. The American women also suffer from isolation.

J.S., the American psychiatrist who travels to Bosnia, has built for herself what she once considered a safe haven. She lived within the psychological walls of her castle, believing that this was the proper way to conduct her life. She was a professional, and her job was to maintain an objective distance between herself and her patients. It was not until she arrived in Bosnia and was confronted by the women there that she realized that the so-called safe haven she had constructed kept her isolated and alone.

J.S. was able to break through this isolation. Melissa, J.S.'s American counterpart, is not so fortunate. The nature of Melissa's suffering is not fully explained, but some trauma in her childhood made Melissa build walls around herself also. Melissa's walls are more transparent, more fluid. They are easily penetrated, so she must keep moving in order to keep everyone and everything outside herself from touching her. Despite her efforts to get the Bosnian women to break through the walls that keep them in isolation, Melissa cannot stand still long enough to allow anyone to help her deconstruct her own psychological barriers. In the end, Melissa is the most isolated character in the play.

Trauma

The aftermath of trauma is one of the main themes of Ensler's play. As a result of the war in

TOPICS FOR FURTHER STUDY

- Think about the title of this dramatic work. Read the passage in scene 4 in which Melissa states that she and J.S. are the necessary targets. What does she mean by this? Write a paper focusing on your interpretation of the title. To demonstrate your understanding and interpretation, use an extended example from your own life or from the life of someone you know that would demonstrate how a person could be a necessary target. If you do not have a real example, make up a situation to use as a model.
- Research the human rights violations that occurred during the Bosnian civil war. Then read accounts about segregation and human rights abuse in the South during the first half of the twentieth century in the United States. How were the circumstances in the two countries different? How were they the same? Write a paper about your findings.
- Take a poll of people's knowledge and understanding of the war in Bosnia and its aftermath. First make a list of five to ten questions, such as these: Do you remember the war in Bosnia? Do you know what the war was about? Do you know who the Serbs were? Then go to three different locations in your vicinity (for example, the grocery store, the post office, or the library). Tell the people you encounter that you are taking a survey for a study project and ask if they could answer a few questions. Ask at least fifteen people at each location. Keep a record of how many people you talked to and how many questions they were able to answer. Present your results to your class.
- Pretend that Nuna is your pen pal. Write her a long letter, telling her about your life in the United States. You might want to describe two different days, a school day and a weekend day. Next, imagine that you are Nuna. Research life in a refugee camp and compose a letter as if she were responding to your correspondence, telling you what her life is like.
- Write a scene, at least three pages long, between two characters that do not have much interaction in this play. You might focus on Seada and Melissa or Nuna and Azra. Write your scene as if it were a part of the play. Be careful not to let the dialogue bring either of your characters out of sync with what is happening in the play.

Bosnia, hundreds of thousands of war victims poured into refugee camps. These masses of people are represented by the five Bosnian women characters. These women all suffer from similar traumas, but each manifests her trauma differently. Nuna, the young girl who is fascinated by all things American, does not speak of her trauma but rather fantasizes about what life in America, a safer world, is like. Azra, the oldest woman, had to abandon her animals, while Seada cannot face having abandoned her baby. Seada has lost all touch with reality because of her shock. Zlata is forced into silence and bitterness, after seeing her parents beheaded in front of her. She is a trained physician, and yet she could do nothing to save their lives. She reacts in anger toward anyone who attempts to save her.

The American women travel to Bosnia to help alleviate the trauma the Bosnian people have been through, but these Americans also suffer from trauma. It is a more subtle form, one that they do not completely face until their confrontations with the Bosnian women force them to do so. J.S. has never dealt with people who have suffered through a war. She believes that trauma is trauma, whether it is produced by the debilitating mental stress her American patients suffer or the devastating ordeals that war victims experience. She learns, through her visit to Bosnia, that there are different kinds of trauma. The challenges she faces in Bosnia shake her so completely that she wakes up to a new vision of herself. Melissa, the victim of another kind of trauma, is not so fortunate. Possibly, as Melissa states in the play, her trauma came at too early an age and, therefore, has become a part of her that she cannot shed. Instead, she continually tries to run away from it.

Therapy

There are two therapists in the play: J.S., who is a psychiatrist, and Melissa, who has been trained as a trauma counselor. These two are at odds with each other in their therapeutic techniques. J.S. uses a soft, even subtle approach, while Melissa is in a hurry and, therefore, is very blunt. She throws psychological punches at the Bosnian women, in attempts to get them to open up. It is not clear whether (as the Bosnian women suspect) Melissa wants to obtain her stories quickly and then travel to another country to gather more, so she can complete her book, or if (as Melissa believes) she is a focused therapist who wants to get to the heart of an issue instead of tiptoeing around it.

Despite the fact that both the American women have been trained as therapists, they have failed to apply their knowledge to themselves. It is Zlata who acts as J.S.'s therapist; trained as a medical doctor, she uses her bedside skills to help J.S. work through her own issues. Jelena, on the other hand, uses alcohol as therapy one night, encouraging the women to drink, dance, and sing their cares away, at least for a few hours. Although alcohol offers Jelena a short reprieve from her worries, drinking only worsens her husband's condition. Alcohol, J.S. and Melissa both agree, is not an effective therapy for trauma.

Therapy is often criticized or mocked in the play. Melissa rejects J.S.'s attempts to figure her out, and so do the Bosnian women. Zlata accuses J.S. of hiding behind her therapy techniques and encourages her to embrace their interactions, not as a trained, objective asker of questions but as one person communicating with another. Toward the end of the play, J.S. seems to follow Zlata's advice and wraps her arms around Seada, rocking her, while singing a lullaby. It is implied that this is not what J.S. had learned in school or in all her years as a therapist. J.S. finds her way to her own cure through the therapy of friendship.

Empathy

The theme of empathy weaves through the play, in stark contrast to the accounts of the lack of empathy that existed during the war, when whole throngs of men were massacred, women were raped, and villages and cities were destroyed. Despite that horrifying lack, the women in this play, for the most part, find or recover their empathetic natures. One of the strongest illustrations of this can be seen in the way the Bosnian women play along with Seada's need to believe that she is carrying her baby in her arms. Although Seada merely holds on to a bundle of rags, the women complain of the baby's loud crying. They worry that the baby might be sick, and they hold the so-called baby in their arms to make Seada comfortable. In the face of this, J.S.'s objective stance breaks down for Seada's sake, and, finally, she empathizes with the young woman's need to be cuddled by her mother. J.S. takes on the maternal role out of empathy for a woman who needs to be loved. She allows Seada to sleep with her in her bed.

The Bosnian women stand up for one another in various empathetic ways. They protect one another from intrusions from the American women, and yet Jelena, in particular, also empathizes with J.S. and Melissa and goes to them, telling the Americans that the Bosnian women are not as unfriendly as they seem. Again, it is Melissa who stands out in the group. She is so hardened by her personal trauma that she appears to have no room in her heart or no understanding of how to empathize with anyone else. Still, she is drawn to their situation and wants to help. Taking a broad view, perhaps Melissa feels empathy too.

STYLE

Character Arcs of Growth

A character arc charts the change that a character goes through in the course of a work of dramatic fiction. In *Necessary Targets*, many of the characters experience change in the form of growth—some more than others. First there is Azra, who is coaxed back into the world of the living after she is found lying in a hole in the ground that she calls her grave. This is a significant change for Azra, who had until that moment not felt that she had any reason to live.

The most dramatic growth is exemplified by Seada, who has created an imaginary world, because she could not face the fact that her husband and mother are gone, as is her baby. Seada's growth happens in a piercing moment when she hears Nuna recounting the truth of her life. In one clashing confrontation, all of Seada's pretenses are shattered. She tries to hurt herself, wanting to physically manifest the emotional pain she is suffering from. Although, by the end of the play, Seada is not depicted as a fully healed person, the audience can anticipate her recovery, or at least partial recovery, and that is growth.

Zlata does not, for most of the play, tell anyone her story. She is bitter and angry and often lashes out at or completely excludes herself from the group of other women. She is particularly upset with the two Americans, whom she looks upon as yet another intrusion into her life. However, Zlata grows through her encounters with J.S. and finally reveals the trauma she has suffered. She also is able to find a way, through their shared training, education, and past experiences, to make friends with J.S. In reaching out, Zlata demonstrates her willingness to change, a willingness that she knows is necessary if she wants to grow.

J.S. returns to the United States so completely changed that she cannot go back to doing anything she once did. In her friendship with Zlata, J.S. has found a new center. She finds happiness in friendship, where once she would not allow anyone to come close to her. Melissa is portrayed as a flat character, one who seems not to change. Many critics of the play point this out as a weakness. When a character does not transform in any way, it is difficult for the audience to empathize with her. Without some indication of growth, the character appears less real and becomes something of a stereotype, standing only for a certain sentiment or one-sided belief.

Symbols of Hopelessness and Frivolity

The most poignant symbol in this play is the bundle of rags that Seada carries in her arms, pretending that it is her baby. When the bundle is unfolded and there is no baby inside, the tragedy of war suddenly becomes that much more apparent to the audience. The moment is designed to elicit a gasp from a live audience, as the truth of Seada's trauma is revealed. The baby (or the lack of baby) signifies the hope that is lost, the dreams that are shattered. The women's talk of the atrocities they have endured has had a significant impact on the audience, but the overwhelming need of the women to pretend that Seada's baby is not only alive but also well protected and cared for pierces the hearts of those watching the play.

Other symbols include the journalists, who personify the outside world. In the minds of the Bosnian women, at least, the journalists do not seem to really care about the Bosnian people. They come to Bosnia to capture stories and images but do nothing to stop the war and suffering. In the play, the journalists represent everyone who has come to Bosnia and who, after seeing what is happening, leave and return to their comfortable lives, forgetting the pain and anguish they have witnessed. The journalists have collected their stories, and that is all they wanted.

Nuna, in some ways, also represents the outside world, at least in all its frivolous aspects. Nuna is a young teenager who is fascinated by American culture, mostly the surface glitz and glitter. She focuses on things like clothes and makeup rather than on deeper, psychological topics. Although Nuna is typical of teenagers all over the world, it is through her character that the play makes fun of Americans. In contrast to what the Bosnian women are living through, Americans, as seen through the play, appear frivolous.

Insignificant Plot

Unlike many plays, Ensler's *Necessary Targets* has an insignificant plot. The American women go to Bosnia to help war victims; in exchange, one of them is transformed by the experience. Although this is enough of a plot to make the play interesting, it is the dialogue and development of the characters that make the play worth seeing. In other words, a major plot or dramatic action is not required to stir the interests of an audience. People may be interested in this play for a variety of other reasons, including wanting to know about the sufferings of Bosnian women during the war, how these experiences have affected them psychologically, and whether the American women will be able to help them. The development or changes of the characters drive the play, rather than a well-thought-out line of action.

Conflict: World Events and Personal Lives

The conflict in this play comes, for the most part, through the accounts of the challenges of life after a war and how people deal with them. But there is also the internal conflict that all the characters face. Melissa suffers from nightmares, so she constantly keeps herself on edge by surrounding herself with the conflicts that other people are facing. J.S. wants to sing, but she believes that by acting out her own emotions, such as the joy she might express in singing, she is coming into conflict with her image of what a psychiatrist should be—a stoic, objective receiver of information. Jelena wants to love her husband for what he once was and yet has to deal with the present reality of his abuse. Zlata, who has been trained to help other people, must face the fact that there are many thousands of people she cannot help. The conflict in this play builds, as all the forces come together when the characters help Seada face the strongest conflict in the play: that between her fantasy world and the world of reality.

Opposing Forces

Opposing forces are represented by the disputing characters, J.S. and Melissa. Their theories of how to conduct their therapy sessions differ quite drastically. Their lifestyles are at opposite ends of the spectrum, with J.S. living in luxurious comfort and controlled organization and Melissa living out of her suitcase in war-torn countries. J.S. wants to work slowly with the Bosnian women, while Melissa wants to hit them over their heads and crack their stories open. Despite the fact that they are in opposition, for the sake of the play and its development, these opposing forces work together, providing tension that eventually erupts, stimulating a catharsis, or at least a partial resolution.

HISTORICAL CONTEXT

Bosnia: The Land and the People

Bosnia is located in south-central Europe, east of the Adriatic Sea, and shares borders with Croatia, Serbia, and Montenegro. The country, about the size of Missouri, is officially called the Republic of Bosnia and Herzegovina, with the capital at Sarajevo. The country's geography features both mountains (with the highest point being Maglic in Herzegovina) and plains, which spread out from the Sava River. The people at lower altitudes enjoy moderate weather (cold and snowy, but bearable, winters and humid, but tolerable, summers). Most areas of Bosnia are under constant threat of powerful earthquakes.

Bosnia is a land of many different cultures, most based on the population's religious beliefs, which include Catholicism, Orthodox Christianity, Judaism, Islam, and Protestantism. Although outlying villages tend to be homogeneous, the cities (this was especially true before the war) have populations that are quite diversified, and people of different backgrounds and beliefs accept one another. The majority of the population in Bosnia is made up of Bosnian Serbs (Orthodox Christians), Croats (Catholics), and Bosniaks (Muslims). Despite the fact that the three different groups have chosen different names for the language they speak, it is basically the same, differing only in a few mutually understandable dialects and individual alphabets.

War and Its Aftermath in Bosnia

Trouble for Bosnians began in 1990 with the breakup of Yugoslavia, of which Bosnia was a part. Bosnia officially became independent the following year and was ruled by Croat and Muslim political parties, which had come together to defeat the Serb nationalists. This angered the Serbs, who were adamant about creating a so-called greater Serbia by uniting the Serbs in Bosnia with those in Serbia. Serbs in Bosnia began to worry about rumors of mass killings, despite the fact that parliament had declared equal rights for all ethnic groups. Tensions exploded during a demonstration in Sarajevo in 1992, when Serb gunmen shot into the crowds. At that point, civil war broke out.

Serbs were committed to their plan of a greater Serbia and began to expel all Muslims from northern and eastern Bosnia. Homes and mosques were destroyed. Thousands of Muslim men were massacred, and women were raped. In the summer of 1992, Croats took up arms against the Bosniaks (Muslims). The killings in this war culminated in 1995 with a massacre of an estimated six thousand Muslim men in Srebrenica. It has been estimated that at least two hundred thousand people died during the conflict. The city of Banja Luka (which is mentioned in the play) became the provisional capital of the Serbian Republic of Bosnia during the war in the 1990s. One of the largest concentration camps was built there, and it has been estimated that the city suffered the most extreme of the war's ethnic cleansings, a term that arose out of this conflict and refers to forced deportation and even genocide.

For three weeks, from November 1 to November 21, 1995, the Serbian president Slobodan Milošević, the Croatian president Franjo Tuđman, the Bosnian president Alija Izetbegović, the chief American negotiator Richard Holbrooke, and General Wesley Clark met in Dayton, Ohio, to work out a peace agreement that would end the civil war in Bosnia. Through what has become known as the Dayton Accord, the country was divided into two parts, the Muslim-Croat Federation and a Serb state, called the Republika Srpska. Despite the seeming success of the Dayton Accord in stopping the fighting, the country struggled in the aftermath

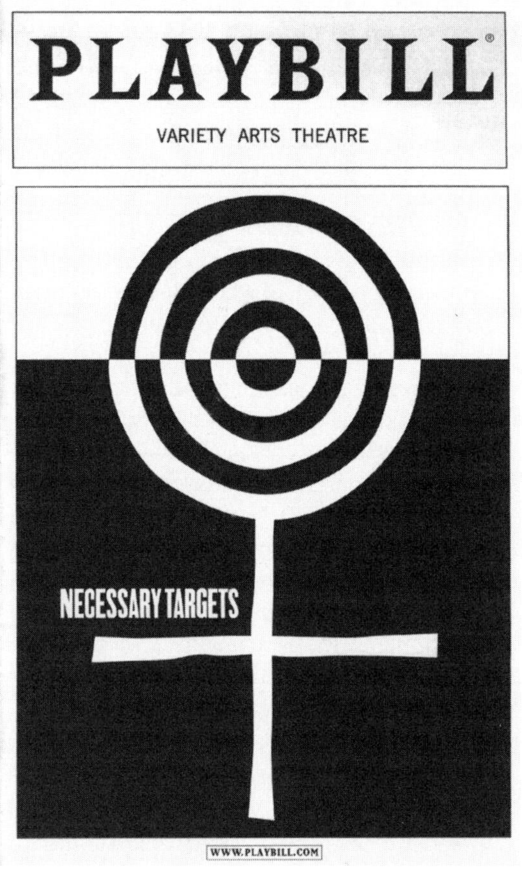

Playbill from a production of Necessary Targets *at the Variety Arts Theatre* Performing Arts Books, NYC.

of the war. Cities were destroyed and families were torn apart and murdered. The psychological scars remain to contribute to tensions. War tribunals have tried and convicted many of the war criminals, but peace is not assured. In 2005, the European Union Force, an international military group, continued to police the towns and cities. There were no plans for removal of these troops in the foreseeable future.

American Theater, 1990s

Large, extravagant musicals with corporate backing prevailed among the productions that were staged on Broadway in the 1990s. Mainstream plays that could pull a large audience became the mainstay. More provocative plays were often seen off Broadway and in regional theaters. Low budgets curtailed the building of lavish sets in these smaller productions, and many of these off-Broadway plays had only a handful of characters at best.

There was concern, among critics and others who study drama, that the gap was widening between the entertaining, extravagant productions on Broadway, such as the Walt Disney Company's *Lion King*, and the somewhat radical, small-audience dramas produced in regional theaters. Although the second category of plays might be thought-provoking, very few people had the chance to see them. There was seldom enough money in the budget for these plays to travel around the country, and only if the play was adapted to a film script and made into a movie did anyone outside the region have a chance to experience it.

This does not mean that there were not big successes in the production of serious plays. For example, Tony Kushner was not daunted by the prevalence and popularity of musicals. His *Angels in America: Millennium Approaches* and *Angels in America: Perestroika* (1993), a two-part work, won two Tony Awards and a Pulitzer Prize. The plays deal with the very serious topic of the epidemic of AIDS. Other thought-provoking plays that were successful in the 1990s included two by the elder statesmen—dramatists Edward Albee, author of *Who's Afraid of Virginia Woolf?* (1962), and Arthur Miller, author of *Death of a Salesman* (1949). Both of these playwrights are considered masters of American drama. Albee's *Three Tall Women*, a play that looks back at three stages in the life of an elderly woman, won the Pulitzer Prize in 1994. That same year saw the production of Miller's *Broken Glass*. Prompted by the civil war in Yugoslavia, Miller wrote a play concerning the troubled marriage of a Jewish couple, set in 1930s Brooklyn at the time when Nazi mistreatment of Jews was beginning to make headlines around the world.

CRITICAL OVERVIEW

Necessary Targets went through several public (and celebrated) readings before it was staged as a play in the United States. Movie stars read the play in benefits to raise money for war refugees. Ensler then gained fame, even world recognition, with the successful run of her Obie-winning *Vagina Monologues*. This brought interest in her earlier play, and *Necessary Targets* was staged.

The first staging in the United States took place in Connecticut in 2001. Despite the many previous readings the play had received, Markland Taylor, writing for *Variety*, finds that Ensler's work still needs some polishing. "If it's ever to be the shattering cri de coeur [protest] it seemingly intends," Taylor writes, "more work is needed." Taylor faults the writing, stating that Ensler's characters need more depth. In the end, however, Taylor offers an oblique word of praise when he says that "Ensler must deliver the assured theatrical sophistication the play needs if it is to live up to its admirable intentions."

The *New York Times* critic Alvin Klein also has trouble with the play. Klein recognizes the play's "transparent manipulation" but then goes on to write that "it takes an ingrate to lack appreciation for ensemble acting so fine, and a curmudgeon to think that there is nothing here that cannot be fixed." Another *New York Times* critic, Ben Brantley, finds *Necessary Targets* to be "more artistically introspective" than Ensler's more famous play, *The Vagina Monologues*. However, he also finds weaknesses. "Yet while 'Targets' bristles with enough tantalizing topics to fuel a year's worth of symposiums, it never shapes its themes into a seductive dramatic structure," he writes.

Joy Press of the *Village Voice* mentions the fact that the audience appreciated the play by honoring it with a standing ovation, but Press does not find that much to applaud. She finds that the play tends to stray "into cliched territory once or twice too often" and that Ensler's vision was often "clouded by ambivalence." Charles Isherwood, writing for *Variety*, finds the play to be "awkwardly structured, chopped up into brief scenes that meander around and seem to end just when they should be beginning."

Although Karen Bovard, for *Theatre Journal*, also notes the play's weaknesses, she praises Ensler for her focus on the American women in the play. "By centering on the American psychiatrist's story, Ensler avoids the most egregious kind of speaking for 'the other' and thereby committing an arrogant act of imagined empathy," Bovard writes. Instead, Ensler is concerned about the "changes in consciousness" that the Americans experience, the effect that the war refugees have on the foreigners, who come from a "position of privilege and relative safety." It is this focus that Bovard thinks produces "some of the most telling lines" in the play.

Tricia Olszewski, writing for the *Washington Post*, takes just the opposite position from Bovard's. Olszewski finds that the focus on the American women "prevents anyone from being terribly sympathetic" with any of the characters. Although "Ensler takes a few satisfying jabs at American culture," Olszewski writes, "in a play allegedly about the atrocities of war, the sharpest commentary shouldn't be about the absurdity of the States."

Looking at the play through a director's eye, the *Washington Post* reporter Dan Via quotes Cornelia Pleasants, who directed *Necessary Targets* at the Olney Theatre in Maryland. Pleasants readily admits that the play presents challenges but had this to say: "I think it's a play worth discussing and it's a time in the world's history that we need to look at closely."

CRITICISM

Joyce Hart

Hart is a freelance writer and published author with degrees in English and creative writing. In this essay, she examines what Ensler refers to as the "death of trust" and what Ensler suggests that it takes to bring trust back into life.

In her introduction to the published version of *Necessary Targets*, Ensler refers to the difference between the loud and obvious catastrophes that occur while a war is in progress and the less observable psychological wounds that the victims must endure after a ceasefire has been proclaimed. "It is the bombing, the explosions in the dark," she writes, "that keep us watching." She refers here to the media coverage that is sent out to television stations around the world. People are often glued to their TV sets while the bombs are falling, but then, when the streets of the war-torn countries become quiet, the journalists and their cameras disappear. All that is left is the physical rubble of the buildings, along with the terrible destruction of people's lives. A camera can broadcast pictures of the buildings, but how does one capture images of a person's shattered mind and soul? How can one depict the trauma that a victim of war has suffered? And yet it is when the impoverished victims face the horrors they must live with in the aftermath that "the real war begins," Ensler writes.

"When we think of war, we do not think of women," Ensler continues, "because the work of survival, of restoration, is not glamorous work." Ensler is referring to the fact that the media is not interested in this type of story. It is too difficult to

> "She does not want her life, yet again, to be captured and then forced, slavelike, to reveal itself not in the intimate connection between one person and another but broadcast by a camera into the square eye of a television set, so that strangers she will never meet can watch it while eating dinner."

pinpoint, to dramatize in a single shot. But this "real war," Ensler believes, can be found "in the broken-down fabric of community, in the death of trust, in the destruction of the everyday patterns of living." Ensler wrote her play to dramatize what she felt the media had skipped over and ignored. In this play, she portrays one element of the psychological wounds the Bosnian women have suffered, the death of trust, and what they do in an attempt to resurrect trust.

Ensler describes several variants of the destruction of trust. Some of the women who survived the war are so badly wounded that they distrust their own versions of reality. Others are suspicious of outsiders, those who have come merely to talk about the war but have not suffered from it. But the American women, who admittedly are not survivors of a war, also suffer from lack of trust. Their wars are more personal and internal. All of these women appear to suffer from the same affliction. Some are more deeply wounded than others and are unable to heal. A few have buried their trust deep within themselves, yet it is not quite dead. They may not be fully aware of it, but they appear to reach out, hoping that someone will come along and help them learn to trust again.

Ensler, who based the writing of her play on interviews she conducted with real victims of the war in Bosnia, has the war refugees mock the American women when they first arrive at the refugee camp. J.S. and Melissa want to help them, but the Bosnian women are suspicious of the therapists' motives. The Bosnians accuse the Americans of being no more empathetic to their condition than the journalists who once crawled all over their country, gathering stories so they could send their reports to their respective publications and other media. The journalists invaded the victims' lives, stole the grimy details of their circumstances, and disappeared unscathed. As a group, the Bosnian women no longer trust anyone who has not suffered through the war and who can leave all the destruction behind and return to a cozy life somewhere else. Their trust in outsiders has been broken. The words of outsiders hold little meaning for them, because the refugees found that words were empty. The journalists did nothing to improve the Bosnian women's lives. They did not stop the war; they did not save their families. Now that the war victims have nothing left, why should they trust these American women?

Death of trust does not mean, however, that the women have lost their sense of humanity, despite the horrendous crimes they have both survived and witnessed. One brave woman, Jelena, is not entirely broken. She still has hope, and therefore a little trust, left in her. She steps forward and tries to build a bridge between her comrades and the American women. Jelena's trust, though shattered, is amazingly strong. It is through her example, her willingness to try yet one more time to breathe life into the fragile remnants of her trust, that some of the other women gain the strength to piece together, slowly but surely, their own sense of faith in humanity.

Standing in opposition to Jelena's willingness to trust is Zlata, the physician, who is the least trusting of the Bosnian women. She turns her back on the American women, literally, and walks away from them. She will have nothing to do with their attempts at therapy, which she finds lack any personal involvement. She is vehemently opposed to Melissa's use of a tape recorder, which too obviously reminds her of the journalists. She does not want her life, yet again, to be captured and then forced, slavelike, to reveal itself not in the intimate connection between one person and another but broadcast by a camera into the square eye of a television set, so that strangers she will never meet can watch it while eating dinner.

Zlata, if she answers the therapists' questions at all, does so sarcastically, mocking their insensitivity.

WHAT DO I READ NEXT?

- *The Vagina Monologues* (1999) has caused a stir throughout the world. This play made Ensler a celebrity and inspired her to organize what is referred to as the V-Day movement, to stop violence against women. Ensler performed all the roles and was awarded an Obie for her writing. In the play, women talk about their bodies and their sexual experiences. The women represent just about every age group, from a six-year-old to a septuagenarian.
- As with her other plays, Ensler gathered material from interviews with women from around the world to write *The Good Body* (2004). The focus in this play is on women's stomachs. The dialogue is often funny, and the subject matter reveals women's different cultural attitudes about their bodies.
- David Rieff's *Slaughterhouse: Bosnia and the Failure of the West* (1996) provides a journalist's point of view of the war in Bosnia. Although the details are terrifying, Rieff relays the story through an objective eye. In this account, he tells of ethnic cleansing, the efforts of the UN forces, and the systematic murder of Muslim leaders.
- Some of Ensler's peers are represented in the collection *Women Playwrights: The Best Plays of 1998*, published in 2000. This book contains plays by Erin Cressida Wilson, Wendy Weiner, Val Smith, Jill Morley, Wendy MacLeod, Jessica Goldberg, Aviva Jane Carlin, and Jocelyn Beard.
- Another collection, *Feminist Views on the English Stage: Women Playwrights 1990–2000*, was published in 2003. It offers the changing perspective of feminist views through the eyes of British playwrights during the last decade of the twentieth century.

She is in no way taken in by the Americans. She wants to know why they are there, what they intend to do, and how they plan on doing it. She takes a logical stance, as if she were mirroring the objective stance she sees the American women taking. When she is dissatisfied with their answers, she tells them that she and the other women are "sick of talking." She does not, in other words, trust their intentions. Why should she? All the other outsiders came and took what they wanted. What do the Bosnian women get from the exchange?

Ironically, it is Zlata who finally makes the deepest connection with the Americans, or at least with J.S. After confronting J.S. about her own inability to open up to anyone, Zlata slowly begins to reveal herself. She does so after watching J.S. help Seada. Seeing J.S. break down her own barriers, stepping out of the role of psychiatrist and allowing Seada to sleep with her, causes Zlata to reevaluate her perception of J.S. Maybe this outsider is not just like the journalists. Maybe J.S. has real compassion for these women. With these thoughts, Zlata begins to mend her broken trust, one small step at a time.

Zlata's trust grows when she and J.S. are sitting alone. Zlata notices that J.S. has scrubbed her face and is in a natural state. "You look different without your makeup," she says. Her statement has symbolic meaning, demonstrating that Zlata feels as if J.S. has taken off her mask; she is now more like the Bosnian women. Without her makeup, J.S.'s true emotions are revealed. Zlata sees sadness in J.S.'s clean face, something that Zlata can relate to. Even though J.S. is not a victim of the Bosnian war, J.S.'s sadness probably indicates to Zlata that J.S. has been wounded by some other kind of war. This is important to Zlata—not that J.S. is wounded, but that, because of her wound, J.S. might actually have real compassion.

Melissa, on the other hand, does not express any recognizable compassion. She appears to be in Bosnia for herself. She wants to write a book, and

Yugoslavian refugees fleeing civil war © David Turnley/Corbis

she wants to put herself in the midst of other people's tragedies so that she can forget her own. Melissa does not trust any of the women, including J.S., and none of the women trust her. Melissa is, indeed, like the journalists of whom the Bosnian women speak—journalists who got what they wanted and then left as soon as they could.

By comparing J.S. to Melissa, in terms of their relationships with the refugees, audiences grasp Ensler's message. They see that in some ways, both American women came to Bosnia without any trust. They both arrived with the impression that they were doing a job. They both had personal problems of their own that diminished their ability to trust. The circumstances that ravaged the American women's trust remain undefined. J.S. mentions locking herself up in a very conservative and objective suit of armor, which she thought was required by her profession. Melissa hints that something awful happened to her when she was young. Whatever originally caused these two women to close themselves off from others is not the issue. The issue is that J.S. changes and Melissa does not. The change in J.S. occurs when she allows her compassion to lead her. Thus, Ensler dramatizes with J.S. that it is through compassion that trust is rebuilt. The implication of this statement might be that if trust is rebuilt, perhaps there will be no reason for future wars.

Source: Joyce Hart, Critical Essay on *Necessary Targets*, in *Drama for Students*, Thomson Gale, 2006.

Karen Bovard

In the following review, Bovard describes the plot of Necessary Targets *and praises Ensler's "naturalistic, character-based drama."*

The world premiere of Eve Ensler's play about women managing the aftermath of war-time atrocities in Bosnia opened in the early days of active US military involvement in Afghanistan. Traditional and chronological in structure, the play follows two American therapists who go to Bosnia to help refugee women recover from trauma. One is a wealthy New York psychiatrist in mid-life, well known for her work with eating disorders, who lacks all experience with refugee populations and—with her designer nightgown and pampered hygienic habits—seems initially quite ill-suited to the work at hand. Played by Shirley Knight, the character J.S. is the most changed by ensuing events. The other American citizen is a young trauma specialist and expatriate who never stays long in any given location but has considerable experience with international crises. At first her hard-nosed practicality renders her sympathetic, but it quickly emerges that Melissa (Catherine Kellner) is a "story vulture" whose highest priority is tape-recording traumatic personal accounts for a book she is writing. The pressure she exerts precipitates a crisis, and her own volatile feelings about her exploitation of the women she is supposed to be helping induces her to leave the camp abruptly, headed for the latest crisis in Chechnya.

The five other characters are all refugees, living together and doing their best to look after one another. Nuna (Maria Thayer) is a hip urban teenager of mixed ethnic heritage; Seada (Marika Dominczyk) is a young mother who refuses to accept her baby's death; Jelena (Alyssa Bresnahan) is deeply in love with her husband, who has been undone by her rape. She accepts his beating her as a reaction to his own impotence. Azra (Sally Parrish) is an elderly woman displaced from a rural village; and Zlata (Diane Venora), a doctor in her own right, is the most skeptical about outside intervention. The play moves from a framing scene in New York where the two therapists size each other up to the refugee camp in Bosnia, where they are to conduct group therapy. A series of ensemble scenes are punctuated by two-person confrontations. It is Zlata who refuses to accept the role of victim and who, despite her resistance, praises J.S.'s handling of the crisis that develops. Once J.S. acknowledges the limitations to the do-gooder posture she initially held, a real relationship of mutual respect is possible between the two physicians, but J.S. recoils from the intimacy of touch and returns to her Park Avenue life, changed, confused, and challenged by her encounter with the refugees.

Music provides the bridge for the most genuine contact between characters. In one case, this is a Madonna song on cassette that Melissa shares with young Nuna; in another, it is a lullaby that J.S. sings in an attempt to comfort Seada when she has a breakdown. The most joyous and transcendent scene involves the women drinking and dancing together. Michael Wilson's direction of the all-female cast won him high praise in local reviews and captured the kind of abandon into physical release that women sometimes share outside the gaze of men. John Gromada's sound design effectively incorporated ethnic music, helicopter sounds, Bach (important symbolically as the source of J.S.'s name), and urban cacophony. Scenic designer Jeff Cowie used the thrust space in predictable ways to indicate multiple locations and Susan Hilferty's costume designs flirted with stereotype but provided significant character information. This may have been unavoidable, given the somewhat typed nature of the roles as written.

"IN THE ARRAY OF OPTIONS ABOUT HOW TO MAKE ART ABOUT TRAUMA WITHOUT EXPLOITATION OR RETRAUMATIZATION, *NECESSARY TARGETS* REPRESENTS A MAINSTREAM CHOICE: NATURALISTIC CHARACTER-BASED DRAMA."

It is only in the final moments of the Hartford production that the imaginative, non-literal potential of the theatre as a form is activated. *Necessary Targets* is very much in the tradition of the well-made play, centered around one character's arc, in a method-based acting style that involves limited direct address to the audience and precludes an actor stepping out of role. Given this stylistic choice, the play might work as well or better on film or television. This could suit Ensler's interest in reaching a mass audience and promoting activism, as she has with V-Day and the website www.vday.org, dedicated to preventing violence against women worldwide.

In the array of options about how to make art about trauma without exploitation or retraumatization, *Necessary Targets* represents a mainstream choice: naturalistic character-based drama. It is not an adaptation of interviews (as Ensler's *Vagina Monologue* is, or *The Good Body,* her work in progress on women's body image), nor does it depend on heightened language and stylistic innovation to add artistic value. By centering on the American psychiatrist's story, Ensler avoids the most egregious kind of speaking for 'the other' and thereby committing an arrogant act of imagined empathy, but focuses instead on the changes in consciousness that traumatic events have on Americans from our position of privilege and relative safety. Some of the most telling lines in *Necessary Targets* provide this kind of pointed cultural critique.

Ensler actively revised the play during its Hartford run and also after the production transferred to the Variety Theater in New York, where it ran from 28 February to 21 April 2002. Simultaneously, she was engaged in political action around the breaking news in Afghanistan. An incognito visit to Kabul in 2000 gave her connections to underground women's organizations there. From 4–5 December 2001, Ensler attended the Afghan Women's Summit for Democracy in Brussels. V-Day was one of the sponsoring organizations of this gathering of fifty Afghan women, which authored the Brussels Proclamation in support of women's participation in the reconstruction and governance of post-Taliban Afghanistan. Ensler accompanied a delegation of six of these women as they addressed the European Parliament on December 16th, and then flew with them to the U.S. to address Secretary of State Colin Powell and members of Congress before bringing the group to Hartford on December 16th to see *Necessary Targets* and conduct a well-attended public talkback. They addressed the United Nations the following day. After the production transferred to New York, Ensler traveled to Kabul to participate in a roundtable with thirty prominent Afghan women leaders on 9–10 March 2002, as a follow-up to the Brussels conference.

New York reviews of *Necessary Targets* were generally lukewarm, though some praised aspects of the production or individual actors. Hartford reviewers tended to focus more on political context than on the play itself. To my eye there were two outstanding performances: Alyssa Bresnahan as Jelena, who projected a luminous sensuality that was never manipulative, and Diane Venora, who brought great physical precision and piercing intelligence to the pivotal role of Zlata. Whether the play will have a life beyond the immediate political situation is unclear.

Source: Karen Bovard, "*Necessary Targets*," in *Theatre Journal*, Vol. 54, No. 4, December 2002, pp. 642–43.

Giselle P. Kasilag

In the following essay-interview, Ensler describes to Kasilag her organization of V-Day and her reaction to the experiences of women in the Bosnian conflict, which inspired Necessary Targets.

> Fact no. 1: There are 300,000 women in prostitution and 75,000 prostituted children in the Philippines. (*The Factbook on Global Sexual Exploitation,* 1999)
>
> Fact no. 2: At least one in three women and girls has been beaten or sexually abused in her lifetime. (*UN Report on the Commission on the Status of Women,* February 2000)
>
> Fact no. 3: At least 60 million girls who would otherwise be expected to be alive are "missing" from various populations, mostly Asia, as a result of sex-selective abortions, infanticide or neglect. (*United Nations Study on the Status of Women,* 2000)

The list goes on and on and it is likely that a computer capable of storing all the horror stories regarding the abuse of women has yet to be invented. And even if one can come up with a list of the top 10 atrocities against women, always, a new one is bound to come up more horrifying than the last.

It may therefore seem like a miracle that playwright Eve Ensler has kept her sanity since the "vagina revolution" she spearheaded with her play/book *The Vagina Monologues.*

Three years after her first performance in the basement of the Cornelia Street Cafe in New York, and after hearing one story of abuse after another from women who saw her performance and were moved by it, Ms. Ensler made a decision to play a more active role in the crusade to end the violence against women. Thus, VDay was born.

"It never grows tiring," said Ms. Ensler in a press conference for the VDay celebration in Manila held last Saturday at Powerbooks Makati. "I never get to the point wherein I don't feel (affected). I really believe that the desecration of women on this planet is the desecration of the human species. And it really doesn't matter if you are in Manila or in Africa or in Louisiana. When you see women being violated to the degree that they are violated on this planet—being raped and sold and beaten and mutilated—you know that if you don't change this in a radical way and we don't do it soon, we're not going to be here much longer."

VDay, she explained, started in 1998 in New York but the organizers never dreamed that a "vagina revolution"—a growing awareness of women's rights and an active campaign to end violence against women—would come about five years later. This year, 800 VDay events were scheduled in 550 colleges worldwide and 250 venues.

VDay is Valentine's Day which the organizers proclaimed as "Victory Day." It was the day when a group of women in New York, headed by Ms. Ensler, banded together demanding the end of violence against women. It has become a global movement for which annual theatrical and artistic events are staged to raise funds in support of international organizations and programs that work to end rape, battery, incest, female genital mutilation and sexual slavery.

Their vision is simple and clear. They would like to "see a world where women live safely and freely. We believe women should spend their lives creating and thriving rather than surviving or recovering from terrible atrocities. We will work as long as it takes. We will not stop until the violence stops," states an official pamphlet promoting VDay.

VDay, Ms. Ensler proudly announced, has penetrated all continents and all cultures with the exception of the Muslim world. But Ms. Ensler predicted that this would not be the case for long. They are actively working on a project to reach the Muslim community as well.

The Vagina Monologues, a series of monologues based on interviews with a wide variety of women on their experiences and attitudes towards their bodies, won for Ms. Ensler the Obie Award in 1997 and the Elliot Norton Award in 2001 as well as nominations for the Drama Desk and the Helen Hayes Award.

Ms. Ensler is also a poet, a screenwriter and an activist. She was a recipient of the 1999 Guggenheim Fellowship Award in Playwriting, the Berilla-Kerr Award for Playwriting, and the Jury Award for Theatre at the 2000 U.S. Comedy Festival.

Among her other works for the stage are *The Depot, Floating Rhonda and the Glue Man, Extraordinary Measures, Lemonade, Ladies* and *Scooncat.*

Her newest play, *Necessary Targets,* which is based on women's plight in Bosnia, opened in New York last weekend—an event that she skipped in favor of the VDay celebration in Manila. It was previously performed at the National Theatre in Sarajevo, the Kennedy Center, the Alley Theatre and the Hartford Stage.

"My new play (*Necessary Targets*) is about two Americans who go to Bosnia during the war and hear stories," she explained. "When I first went to Bosnia in 1994 during the conflict, I thought I would go as a detached writer, listen to things and have an answer. What happened is that I was destroyed. I sat for hours listening to stories of women who have been raped and abused. There were

"IT WAS THE DAY WHEN A GROUP OF WOMEN IN NEW YORK, HEADED BY MS. ENSLER, BANDED TOGETHER DEMANDING THE END OF VIOLENCE AGAINST WOMEN. IT HAS BECOME A GLOBAL MOVEMENT."

horrible, horrible stories. And what I did was cry. I sat and I cried, and I cried, and I cried. I realized that if I showed up as I am, as I lived, as I feel in this body, that I don't get numb. And when I try to be somebody I'm not—like this detached journalist or this writer—then I get into trouble.

"I feel very inspired by Monique Wilson and Rosanna Abueva (producers of the local staging of *The Vagina Monologues*). I am very inspired by the thousands and thousands of people in Manila who clearly care about women and are rising up to say that they care. And I know that we are going to win and we are going to end violence otherwise this species isn't going to be here anymore. And I like being alive. And I like human beings. And I think we should keep going."

There is no reason that can justify violence, she continued. The events of Sept. 11, she admitted, led her to wonder about how her country and her government have been handling the situation in Afghanistan. According to her, today, despite the intervention of the rest of the world, the women in Afghanistan are experiencing a more difficult life than ever before.

"When people resort to violence, it often means that they have been humiliated and ashamed to the point wherein they have no alternatives. There is a need to look at why people are willing to fly airplanes through buildings. What does that mean? Why are people raging at the United States?

"Somebody asked me if I think Laura Bush is a feminist and I said I think there is a burning feminist in every woman and if Laura Bush's moment has come, more power to Laura Bush. I think the wave of feminism never ends. For whatever reason, *The Vagina Monologues* connected with people's psyches, I think, because it is based on real women's stories and because women have such a desire to think about their vaginas and talk about their vaginas and reclaim their vaginas and feel good about their vaginas, and protect their vaginas that suddenly the world just grabbed a hold of this."

She dismissed as false perceptions that she is a man-hater. She is, in fact, happily living with her partner, Ariel Orr Jordan, who accompanied her to Manila. There are many men, she added, who have seen *The Vagina Monologues* and have become "vagina-loving men"—men who are supportive of the movement and have actively participated in ensuring that violence does not happen to women.

She confided how a sniper who was part of a protection firm hired for her trip to Kabul in Afghanistan saw her performance about a Bosnian woman who was gang-raped by soldiers. The sniper approached her after the show weeping—"Something is shifting in the world when you see a sniper cry!" said Ms. Ensler.

The biggest problem, however, lies in the silence among women who have been abused. The reluctance to speak up, according to Ms. Ensler, is something she has seen everywhere she has been. Women tend to take the blame, believing that they brought the abuse upon themselves rather than feeling they were victimized.

She said it has become a tradition on VDay performances to ask the members of the audience who have been victims of abuse to stand up. And every year, half the audience gets on their feet. But Ms. Ensler believes many opt to remain seated because of the shame. The challenge is to free the women of the shame and give that shame back to the abusers. And the first step is to break the silence and stop feeling that it is their fault.

"You can wear whatever you want to wear, and walk anyway you want to walk . . . and you can get drunk, and no one has the right to touch you unless you invite them to touch you . . . We still believe that if we had not been wearing that, if we hadn't said that, if we hadn't been friendly, that it would not have happened. And the answer to that is that it would have happened! If someone makes a decision to rape you or beat you, they are going to rape you or beat you whatever you are wearing. You can be wearing a burqua and men would rape you because it happens all the time. So it is really important for women to understand that it's not their fault and that they have power."

At one point, in an attempt to challenge *The Vagina Monologues,* a play *The Penis Response* was staged but the production did not last long. Though she has been asked many times to write a play about penises, Ms. Ensler dismissed the idea saying it would be redundant. "We are, after all, living in a 'Penis Monologue' and the world does not need any more of that," she quipped.

No, she reiterated, she is not anti-penis or anti-men. A line in the monologue, "My Short Skirt," reads that "My short skirt is about provication and initiation. But mainly, my short skirt has nothing to do with you."

"I love men and I adore men. But *The Vagina Monologues* is not against men or for men. It does not hate men. It just does not address men. It is about women. Get used to it!"

Source: Giselle P. Kasilag, "All about Eve," in *Business World* (Philippines), February 26, 2002.

Pamela Grossman

In the following interview, Grossman talks to Ensler about reaction to The Vagina Monologues, *her own body image, and her other projects, including* Necessary Targets.

"'Vagina.' Doesn't matter how many times you say it, it never sounds like a word you want to say." That's Eve Ensler in the prologue to her immensely popular play *The Vagina Monologues,* which began as a one-woman show performed by Ensler off-off-Broadway four years ago. The play is currently in production off-Broadway, with rotating three-woman casts. Alanis Morissette, Julie Kavner and Marlo Thomas were recent performers; Claire Danes is among those onstage now.

The play condenses 200 interviews Ensler conducted with women about their vaginas into a series of character-driven monologues. The research process transformed Ensler from a woman who hesitated to say the word "vagina" to a performer who said it 128 times per show. Ensler has taken advantage of the play's success, using it as a political vehicle and in fund-raisers for international women's charities. "V-Day" benefits, staged by celebrity actors on Feb. 14 for the last three years, have routinely sold out; one show in Los Angeles alone raised approximately $250,000. Meanwhile, college students across the country are eagerly staging the show, and HBO will tape Ensler performing it in August.

I recently met Ensler for breakfast at City Bakery in New York, days before she left on a four-month worldwide trip to research her next project. I found her confident and hugely enthusiastic, amazed and overjoyed about recent self-discoveries—physical and emotional. "Through the course of doing the show," Ensler said at one point in our interview, "I feel like I've reentered my vagina. And that has completely changed my life."

[*Pamela Grossman*]: *The New York Times said that many people think of you as "the Messiah heralding the second wave of feminism."*

[Eve Ensler:] [*Laughing*] Yes. I call myself "messiah" every day, and I'm making everyone refer to me as that.

How do you feel, hearing that kind of thing?

I try not to think about what people think of me. You can't, because then you get hung up in all the people who *love,* you, and you've also got all the people who *hate* you, because of what you're doing. What I feel excited about is the work. And I feel that with *Vagina Monologues* and V-Day, we are, in fact, creating a huge movement. And if I have contributed to that in any small way, it is my deepest privilege and honor.

I really want to help stop violence toward women. I feel I'm here to do that, to work on making that happen. I think that anytime you get clear about what your mission is or what your focus wants to be, things start to come together in your life. Lack of clarity—which I think plagues women particularly, so much of our lives—to me is very connected to lack of desire. We don't get to understand what our desires are. Doing *The Vagina Monologues* was, for me, reconnecting to my desire, allowing myself to know what I wanted. That just made me so happy. And then to get to actually do it—to have the clarity, to know my desire and then to get to manifest it—you know, life doesn't get better.

Humor feels very important in the show. What role do you think it plays?

When people are laughing, they process things in ways they're not conscious of. And a lot of times, places where they're closed up, where they have a limited way of thinking, open up. So I really believe in laughter. There is enormous community that happens around it. When I was younger, I was more didactic and more polemical. I was insecure, and I didn't really believe that my message would come through. And now, after writing for a long time, I have more of a security that what I'm saying will be heard, and I don't have to beat people over the head with it.

When did you feel like you wanted to create The Vagina Monologues? *Was there any sort of an epiphany?*

"WHEN PEOPLE ARE LAUGHING, THEY PROCESS THINGS IN WAYS THEY'RE NOT CONSCIOUS OF. AND A LOT OF TIMES, PLACES WHERE THEY'RE CLOSED UP, WHERE THEY HAVE A LIMITED WAY OF THINKING, OPEN UP."

It was all very accidental. I just stumbled upon questions and started asking people casually, and before I knew it, I was down the vagina trail. I don't think I consciously set out to do this. I mean, who would have done that? It would have been such a weird thing to do. It was more that it took me. And I have to tell you, I feel the last five years I have been hostage, in a very good way, to this thing. When I did it off-Broadway for months and months, I really felt like my job was to keep my body in shape—that it was a much bigger thing than me and that I just had to stay in shape, but it didn't really have a lot to do with me, ironically.

The intro to the show mentions the difficulty of saying "vagina." I had to laugh because, going to the theater, I had this very courtly, polite cabdriver. I told him where I was going, which theater, and he asked what was playing, and I couldn't tell him. I said it was a one-woman show, and he said, "Oh, really, it's called 'One-Woman Show'"? But I felt like I would horrify him if I said it, and I just couldn't.

[*Nodding*] At the beginning of this, it was like, "What am I doing?" But I don't have issues with vaginas anymore.

Has writing or doing the show changed how you feel about your body?

It's completely changed that. I think when I began doing the show, I was completely disengaged from my vagina, disconnected. I lived in my head. Now I feel right with myself. I'm in my body, and I really like it in there, and it's the motor of my life. You know, before, I was kind of living—I was hanging onto the car door, and a lot of times it was throwing me off. And now I feel like I'm in the car, and it's my car, and I determine where it goes. And that's the best thing that's ever happened in my life. As I said to you at the beginning, I know what I desire. I don't feel apologetic. When you feel insecure, you either beg people to let you in or you demand to be let in. But when you are in your body, you just know that you're in. You don't ask permission, and you don't hurt people.

It's a long journey. You have to do a lot of work, particularly if you've been raped or violated, because the degree to which you are disassociated and leave yourself is profound, and it takes a long time to come back. But you can come back, and that's the good thing.

I think a lot of times, what we're told is that if we've been raped or violated, we'll never come back. Sex will never be good again; we'll never feel good again. I think that you can fully recover; you can totally get your body back; you can totally get your sexuality back. You just have to do work, and you have to go through fire. And then, when it's over, it's over, and you move on. But you have to make a decision, too, not to live as a victim anymore, and not to see yourself as a victim, and not to be treated as a victim. And that's a huge thing to give up. Huge.

That mind-set can take so many forms: anger, fear, guardedness.

Mm-hmm. And also, there are all of the people you've gotten to take care of you on some level or another because you are a victim. There's the fear of not being taken care of if you stop being a victim. You know what? People don't take care of you when you're not a victim. [*Laughing*] They don't. Things change. But that's OK. You take care of yourself.

I wonder if you'd like to address something I read [*in Salon*] *recently. Camille Paglia called* The Vagina Monologues *"ravingly anti-male" and said it represents a "painfully outmoded brand of feminism." Any comment?*

I'll be happy to respond to that. First of all, I don't think any brand of feminism is outmoded. I think the world is so desperate for feminism at this point, for the liberation of women, it's mad to even think about how deep that need is. There are a few other people who have said, too, that the play is anti-male. I don't really know what they mean. Is an examination of the condition of women anti-male?

I'm looking at the facts of rape and incest by men against women; I'm saying this is a serious issue that we need to deal with. If you want to call that "anti-man," that's one perception. I'm calling for an end to violence. I'm asking men and women to take responsibility for the eradication of women that's going on in the planet right now, the amount of battery, burning, shooting, suffocating and annihilating of women in every country in the world that is so out of control. If calling attention to it and if demanding an end to it is seen as anti-male, I don't know what to say.

I do know that the men I know who come to see *The Vagina Monologues* do not seem to think so. In fact, most men come up and say, "Thank you—I had no idea; I knew nothing about vaginas; thank you for inviting me into this world." Also, I'd like to point out that there are many "Vagina Monologues" that treat men very lovingly—and to say that I have never been attacked by a man, in the press, for being anti-male. So that's a fascinating thing. I believe that most men are embarrassed and ashamed of the amount of violence that's happening, and when it's talked about or dealt with, they feel relieved. In the college initiative all around the country, young men are deeply involved in productions of the show. And men have produced it everywhere I've been.

Your current director is a man.

My director's a man; my producer in New York is a man.

What's the college initiative?

In '98, we did it in 65 colleges, and in '99 it was 150. These are all kinds of schools—some conservative, even Jesuit. Next year, we think it's going to be at between 250 and 300 colleges. Of all the things we're doing, this is one of the most exciting to me, because young women are being revolutionized and are standing up. And just the process of putting this on on their campuses—producing it, directing it, publicizing it, rehearsing it—is a political act.

Are you surprised by all of this?

[*Nodding vigorously*] The last years of my life have been a huge shock. I'm just beginning to get my bearings. I'm surprised at the widespread success of *The Vagina Monologues*—completely surprised—and I'm surprised at how it keeps expanding. You know, out of this run of *The Vagina Monologues,* $10 out of every ticket goes to V-Day. So we can raise a lot of money—I mean, a lot of money! The fact that it's become this politically activating piece of theater, it's just shocking—that we're off-Broadway, that we're getting all these fabulous women to do it for the cause, that we can do more events for the cause. And, you know, I'm happy, I'm really happy, because it allows me to keep doing more work like this.

Tell me about V-Day.

Our mission with that is to create cultural events, mainly using my work, that will be a catalyst for energy to end violence. And we want to bring existing groups together, to unify them, so that they're more focused in their purpose. We have three paid consultants, who do the producing; besides that, everything is volunteer. And for V-Day 2001, we have booked Madison Square Garden for a huge event. So far Glenn Close has agreed, Jane Fonda, Alanis is going to do it, Melissa Etheridge, Joan Osborne. All the women who have ever performed *The Vagina Monologues* have been invited to come back as the Vulva Choir. Audra McDonald is singing. It's going to be truly fabulous—that will be the evening. During the day, we're going to have an international symposium on all the groups in the world that work to stop violence toward women. And there'll be chats and videos and talk backs, so women can come all day long.

You're also working on some newer things. There's Necessary Targets, *a new play.*

I wrote it during the Bosnian war. It's *about Bosnians,* the Bosnian refugees, but it's actually about two Americans who go to Bosnia, as so-called help, and in the process are radically transformed. It's had all these amazing, kind of star-studded readings, where we've raised a lot of money for Bosnian refugees. Meryl Streep did a reading on Broadway, and Glenn Close did a reading at the National Theater in Sarajevo, with a group of Bosnian actors, for 400 Bosnian refugees. So it's had this remarkable life. And now, finally, I'm one step away from it coming to New York. You know, things always take longer than you think they will. I really thought this play would be done about three years ago, but now is the right moment for it. I trust on some fundamental level that things find their way into the world at the right time and place, and you can't force them. If *Vagina Monologues* had happened a day earlier, it wouldn't have had the life it's had.

So the play is very dear to my heart. And then *Points of Reentry* is the new project that I'm starting, going around the world for four months. I'm interviewing women all around the world about their bodies—how they mutilate, change, transform, hide their bodies in order to fit in with their particular culture.

Where will you be going?

Everywhere. I'm going to Rio, to L.A., to Moscow, to Afghanistan and Turkey, to Paris, to the Bahamas, to Nigeria, to South Africa, to India, to Thailand and to Tokyo! And then we'll spend a lot of time next year in the States.

And how did the Bosnian cause in particular end up striking you, being so dear to you?

It started with a photograph I saw on the cover of Newsday of six young girls who had just been returned from a rape camp in Bosnia. I couldn't believe there were rape camps in the middle of Europe in 1993. It's one of those things: You go, "What?!" So I just knew I had to go there, had to go and see what it was. There are certain events in history you have no protection from. They just come into you, and you have to do something about it or you'll go insane.

The beautiful thing is, at that point in your career, you were able to do what you wanted to do.

Of course it meant not doing a lot of other things that were commercial—whatever. But, so what, you know? You make the decisions you make. It was an amazing opportunity, going there and being there, and staying for months in refugee camps with Bosnian refugees. It was very profound.

What are some things you're looking forward to, personally or otherwise?

Well, I'm looking forward to going around the world. I'm looking forward to spending more time with my granddaughter [*the child of Dylan McDermott, Ensler's son through adoption*]. I love that girl, love her, she's an angel. I'm looking forward to the HBO thing. I'm really looking forward to V-Day. And I'm looking forward mainly to the day when women aren't being raped or beaten. That's it. Then we can all relax a little.

Source: Pamela Grossman, "Down the Vagina Trail," in *Salon.com*, April 19, 2000.

SOURCES

Bovard, Karen, Review of *Necessary Targets*, in *Theatre Journal*, Vol. 54, No. 4, December 2002, pp. 642–43.

Brantley, Ben, "Exploring the Pain of Bosnian Women," in the *New York Times*, March 1, 2002, Section E.1, p. 3.

Ensler, Eve, *Necessary Targets*, Villard Books, 2001, pp. xiii, xiv, 3, 4, 7, 9, 23, 28, 29, 31, 36, 39, 58, 78, 79.

Helbig, Jack, Review of *Necessary Targets*, in *Booklist*, Vol. 97, No. 11, February 1, 2001, p. 1034.

Isherwood, Charles, Review of *Necessary Targets*, in *Variety*, Vol. 386, No. 3, March 4–10, 2002, pp. 42–43.

Klein, Alvin, "Melding Drama with Politics," in the *New York Times*, December 9, 2001, p. 14CN.13.

Llamas, Cora, "And God Created Eve," in the *Philippine Daily Inquirer*, March 4, 2002.

Olszewski, Tricia, "'Necessary Targets,' a Little Off the Mark," in the *Washington Post*, June 3, 2004, Section C, p. 5.

Peyser, Marc, "Eve Ensler Uses the V Word," in *Newsweek*, Vol. 139, No. 7, February 18, 2002, pp. 66–67.

Press, Joy, "The Words of War," in the *Village Voice*, Vol. 47, No. 10, March 12, 2002, p. 58.

Taylor, Markland, Review of *Necessary Targets*, in *Variety*, Vol. 385, No. 4, December 10–16, 2001, p. 38.

Via, Dan, "Wide of the Target, Still on the Mark," in the *Washington Post*, June 18, 2004, Section T, p. 27.

FURTHER READING

Malcolm, Noel, *Bosnia: A Short History*, New York University Press, 1996.

Noel Malcolm wrote this short history to provide a background for the conflicts that took place in Bosnia in the 1990s. Malcolm, a columnist for London's *Daily Spectator*, gives a politically interesting perspective on how Bosnia's civil war was fueled.

Manuel, David, *Hope in the Ashes*, Paraclete Press, 1996.

David Manuel traveled to Bosnia many times during the conflict there to gather information on how such atrocities could happen. In the process of talking to Serbs, Croats, and Bosniaks, he discovered that despite the fighting, everyone was hopeful for a peaceful future for their children. This book relates stories of people who lived through the war.

McLaughlin, Buzz, *The Playwright's Process: Learning the Craft from Today's Leading Dramatists*, Backstage Books, 1997.

McLaughlin spent time interviewing members of the Dramatists Guild to come up with enlightening tips for writing plays. Step by step, he takes his reader through the process, offering many examples and strategic materials that illustrate the process.

Sudetic, Chuck, *Blood and Vengeance: One Family's Story of the War in Bosnia*, Penguin, 1999.

Chuck Sudetic, a writer for the *New York Times*, has family members living in Bosnia. He covered stories for the *Times*, written in a journalist's objective voice. For this book, however, Sudetic writes from the heart, telling the story of the events that led up to the massacre in which more than six thousand Muslim men were killed in the town of Srebenica, in one of the worst massacres of the war.

On Golden Pond

ERNEST THOMPSON

1978

Themes of mortality, family relationships, marriage, and generations all play out at Norman and Ethel Thayer's small lake house in Maine beside Golden Pond. Ernest Thompson's *On Golden Pond* has been embraced by theatergoers since its first off-Broadway run in 1978 and by moviegoers since its 1981 adaptation. The play's believable characters are engaging and flawed, and the curmudgeonly Norman Thayer achieves personal growth despite his advanced age and slow mental decline. The play has successfully played onscreen (adapted by Thompson himself) and stage, with a white cast and a black cast (in 2005's Broadway revival). By all accounts, the play seems to have universal appeal.

Thompson wrote *On Golden Pond* at the age of twenty-eight. While he had been able to support himself as a working actor, he had gone a year without landing any work. This dry spell allowed him to pursue his interest in writing. Although he cannot say exactly what inspired the play, he credits his boyhood summer lake trips to Maine with his family as a source of special memories. Through a series of lucky opportunities, *On Golden Pond* was produced off Broadway in 1978. It was published the following year by Dramatists Play Service. Within six months, the play was in production on Broadway and soon in theaters across the United States. It was Thompson's first play to be produced. The film version earned him an Academy Award and opened numerous career doors for the young playwright. Thompson continues to

Ernest Thompson AP/Wide World Photos

write plays and television scripts as of 2005, but his reputation rests largely on the success of *On Golden Pond.*

AUTHOR BIOGRAPHY

(Richard) Ernest Thompson was born on November 6, 1949, in Bellows Falls, Vermont. His parents were Theron, a college professor and administrator, and Esther, a teacher. Esther played the piano and the violin, instilling the importance of music in their home. Thompson spent his early childhood in New Hampshire and Massachusetts and his teenage years in Maryland. His family often visited a lake in Maine during the summers.

Thompson attended the University of Maryland (1967–1968), Colorado College (1969), and Catholic University (1970) and received his bachelor's degree in 1971 from American University. After graduating, Thompson worked as a stage and television actor before becoming a playwright in 1977. Over the course of his career, Thompson has worn various hats in the television and film industry. His television work included two years spent acting on the NBC daytime drama *Somerset.* Although Thompson enjoyed acting, his desire to write scripts emerged early in his career. When he approached the producers of the television series *Emergency,* he was told that his talents were better suited to acting than writing. But in 1977, Thompson had gone a year without finding acting work, and he turned his attention back to writing. While some of his writing caught the attention of the networks, it would be a year before real success came.

At the surprisingly young age of twenty-eight, Thompson wrote *On Golden Pond.* The off-Broadway Hudson Guild Theatre produced the play in September 1978. Only five months later, it went to Broadway's New Apollo Theatre. *On Golden Pond* was the first of Thompson's plays to be produced, and it has remained his best-known work. In 1979, it won the Broadway Drama Guild's Best Play Award. In 1980, Jane Fonda saw *On Golden Pond* performed in Los Angeles. Sure that she had finally found the right script to give her the chance to act with her father, Henry Fonda, she bought the film rights and hired Thompson to adapt it. Only a year later, the movie was released. Starring the Hollywood luminaries Jane Fonda, Henry Fonda, and Katharine Hepburn, the movie garnered popular and critical praise. Thompson won a Golden Globe Award, a Writers Guild Award, and an Academy Award for his screen adaptation. Hepburn and Henry Fonda won the Best Actress and Best Actor Academy Awards, respectively. *On Golden Pond* was also nominated for an Oscar for Best Picture. In 2001, a television version was made. Directed by Thompson, it starred Julie Andrews and Christopher Plummer.

Thompson received the first and what would be the only George Seton Grant for Playwrights, which enabled him to write *The West Side Waltz: A Play in ¾ Time.* Hepburn starred in the 1981 Broadway production. Her appearance in this play came before the filming of *On Golden Pond* and marked the beginning of Thompson's relationship with her. Critics praised Hepburn's performance, though they were not as dazzled by the play as they had been by *On Golden Pond.* In 1995, Thompson went a step further when he wrote, directed, and acted in the film version of *The West Side Waltz,* an adaptation of his stage play. In 1983, an altogether different play, *A Sense of Humor,* was produced in Los Angeles, starring Jack Lemmon. The story is about a grocery store manager whose daughter has committed suicide. He tries to handle his anger and guilt with harsh jokes and a very dark sense of humor. The response from the audience was so negative that Thompson actually rewrote some passages so that the humor would be less offensive, dark, and shocking. But Thompson maintained that the spirit of the play was not negotiable; despite the controversy surrounding the play, he and Lemmon defended its importance.

In 1988, Thompson's screenplay *Sweet Hearts Dance* was produced and released, and he directed one of his own teleplays, *1969*. *Out of Time*, a 2000 television movie, was cowritten and directed by Thompson. Between writing and directing, Thompson also took acting roles in such films as *Star 80* (1983) and *Next Stop Wonderland* (1998). Thompson is strongly associated with *On Golden Pond*, despite his years of work in the industry. While he is proud of his other accomplishments, he still discusses his most famous plays in interviews and lectures. He continues to develop new ideas for plays and teleplays. In 2005, Thompson was residing in New Hampshire.

PLOT SUMMARY

Act 1, Scene 1

On Golden Pond opens in May with Norman and Ethel Thayer returning to their lake house in Maine. Norman is content to sit and read a book, but Ethel is busily moving furniture back in place, dusting, and generally getting the house ready for their summer stay. Through their conversations, the audience learns that they have been married a long time, love each other very much, and have different dispositions. They will be celebrating Norman's eightieth birthday, and he makes frequent jokes about his own mortality. Ethel is not amused, not so much because it upsets her as because she refuses to allow her husband to act like a victim.

Act 1, Scene 2

It is now June, and as she putters around the house, Ethel tries to give Norman updates about their neighbors. While she is very interested in the lives of her casual friends, Norman does not care enough to remember most of their names. He is more interested in reading the local wants ads in search of an easy part-time job. This seems to be more of a fun exercise for him than an actual job search. Later, Charlie stops by with the mail. He is a local man in his forties who has known the Thayers for many years. He asks about the Thayers' daughter, Chelsea, who is only a few years younger than he is. Their conversation reveals that he still harbors feelings for Chelsea.

In the mail, Ethel receives a letter from Chelsea, letting Ethel know that she will be visiting them for Norman's birthday. She will bring her new boyfriend, a dentist named Bill Ray. Norman responds with his usual sarcasm, but the audience can tell that there is a rift between him and his daughter.

Norman is also having bouts of memory loss, a reality he struggles to accept. Ethel sends him to pick strawberries, but when he returns early with an empty basket, he confesses that he did not know where the road was. It was a road nearby, and they had been to it numerous times over the years. His fears about his mental decline are exposed, and Ethel responds with compassion and reassurance.

Act 1, Scene 3

It is now July, and Chelsea arrives for her father's birthday. She brings her boyfriend and his thirteen-year-old son, Billy Ray. The unexpected arrival of the teenager delights Ethel, but Norman is initially unimpressed. After Billy has a tour of the house, Bill enters with the luggage and meets Ethel and Norman. Not interested in making Bill feel welcome, Norman gives him a chilly reception.

Ethel, Chelsea, and Billy go for a quick canoe ride, and Billy asks Norman if it is acceptable for him to share a bed with Chelsea while they are there. Norman responds with sarcasm and makes the conversation even more difficult for Bill. When Bill asserts himself and tells Norman that he will not tolerate being treated that way, Norman warms up to him. He says he likes him and that it is okay for him to share a bed with Chelsea. Billy returns, excited about the canoe ride, and sends Bill down

MEDIA ADAPTATIONS

- *On Golden Pond*, adapted as a film by Ernest Thompson and starring Katharine Hepburn and Henry Fonda, was produced and distributed by Universal Pictures (1981)

to be with Ethel and Chelsea, who reportedly are skinny-dipping.

Norman asks Billy questions about his interests, his posture, and his reading. He comes to like the spunky, outspoken boy and sends him to his room to read the first chapter of *Swiss Family Robinson*. Ethel returns, and Norman pretends to be surprised that she has clothes on. She tells him that Chelsea has asked her whether Billy can stay at the lake house for a month while she and Bill go to Europe. Ethel likes Bill and wants to give her daughter a chance at happiness, so she asks Norman to do this for Chelsea. Norman agrees with surprisingly little reluctance.

Act 2, Scene 1

It is August. Norman and Billy have become very close friends, and they are getting ready to go fishing, even though Ethel warns them that it looks as if it will rain. Billy invites her to come with them, but she declines the offer. As she looks over her knickknacks and sings and dances alone, Chelsea enters. Ethel is surprised to see her, thinking that she has returned early, but it actually is the day Billy is supposed to return home.

Alone with her mother, Chelsea begins to complain about her difficult childhood. She feels that she tried very hard to please Norman but could never be what he wanted her to be. She also feels that Ethel was not there to protect and defend her. Ethel has had enough and says so; she believes that Chelsea should stop complaining about the past and live her life as an adult now. Chelsea announces that she and Bill got married during their trip overseas, and Ethel is thrilled.

It is now raining, and Norman and Billy return from their fishing excursion. Billy is excited to see Chelsea, but Ethel sends him to take a warm shower before he can hear her news. Then Ethel leaves Chelsea and Norman alone, and Chelsea tells him that she wants them to have a normal father-daughter relationship. He is caught off-guard, but agrees that they can try. He asks whether that means she will visit more often, and when Chelsea says it does, he says that it will make Ethel happy. Norman goes to take a shower, and Charlie stops by to deliver the mail and see Chelsea. They reminisce with Ethel.

Act 2, Scene 2

Now that it is September, Ethel and Norman are preparing to go back home. They have repacked their things at the lake house and replaced the dust covers on all the furniture. The phone rings, and it is Chelsea. She talks to both of her parents, and they make tentative plans for another visit. Trying to carry a heavy box, Norman strains himself and feels as if he is having a heart attack. Ethel panics but finds his medicine; as she is trying to call a hospital, he begins to feel better. She tells him how scared she was to feel that she was actually losing him. Together, they go to bid farewell to Golden Pond.

CHARACTERS

Charlie Martin

Charlie is a local man who has known the Thayers most of his life. He is described as big and round with a weathered face from spending so much time on the lake, and he has been the mailman for many years. Only two years older than Chelsea, he has been harboring feelings for her since their youth. Charlie is helpful, sincere, and sociable, but he has never married. Charlie laughs a little too often and does not understand the subtlety of Norman's sarcasm, although he is drawn to Ethel's hospitality.

Bill Ray

Chelsea's fiancé, Bill Ray, is a dentist from California. He is father to thirteen-year-old Billy. Bill is an honest person who confronts issues in a straightforward way. When Norman tries to intimidate him, Bill stands up to him. This shows a great deal of maturity and self-confidence, and it wins Norman's approval and respect.

Billy Ray Jr.

Billy Ray is the thirteen-year-old son of Bill Ray. Billy is short, smart, and struck by the awkwardness that comes with his age. Like Norman, Billy masks his self-doubt by appearing confident and comfortable with himself. Billy is unusual in that he is not intimidated by Norman, as many people are. He is adaptable, open-minded, and expressive. As his friendship with Norman deepens, he becomes wiser and more sensitive. The friendship helps him mature, and it teaches him how to be a caregiver and a true friend.

Ethel Thayer

Ethel is Norman's sixty-nine-year-old wife. She is energetic, loving, and sociable. She is good at handling Norman's crankiness and fatalistic outlook, and she challenges his negative behaviors and attitudes. She is also decisive and calm under pressure. When she thinks Norman is having a heart attack, she panics but finds and administers medicine to him. Ethel is also very compassionate with Norman's health problems and memory loss. Her nurturing attitude extends to the rest of her family and friends, and she likes to make their lake house feel like a home. Among her favorite things about the lake are the loons. She looks for them, listens to them, and watches what they do all summer.

Unlike Norman, Ethel is very interested in maintaining relationships with her neighbors and extends her warmth and welcoming to them. When Charlie first visits, she is delighted to see him and wants him to stay and have coffee, so they can talk about the other people on the lake and recall old memories. Ethel is nonjudgmental, good-natured, and encouraging.

Norman Thayer Jr.

Norman is an eighty-year-old retired college professor who is spending the summer with his wife at their lake house in Maine. He has many of the ailments common to people his age, including arthritis and palpitations, but his most pressing health issue is his slow mental decline. He is described as a white-haired man with glasses who dresses comfortably. Although Norman's pace has slowed, Thompson tells the reader that he retains his humor and boyishness. At the same time, he is distinguished and respectable. Despite his curmudgeonly attitude, his wife, Ethel, adores him and likes spending time with him. Norman enjoys solitary activities, such as reading and fishing. He is not a sociable person, and he has little interest in the lives of his neighbors. He has a sarcastic sense of humor, and he can be impatient, insensitive, and intolerant. Norman's tough exterior intimidates most people, so when someone stands up to him (like Bill) or answers sarcasm with sarcasm (like Billy), Norman shows respect.

Norman has a strained relationship with his adult daughter, Chelsea. According to Chelsea, the strain has come because she tried so hard to please him when she was a child and never felt that she met his expectations. Norman does not seem to understand this, and so he never apologizes or explains his parenting. As Norman spends the summer grappling with issues of aging and mortality, he makes a surprising friend in Billy, Chelsea's boyfriend's teenage son. Softened by this unlikely friendship, Norman is more open to the idea of trying to mend his relationship with his daughter.

Chelsea Thayer Wayne

Chelsea is the only child of Ethel and Norman. She is forty-two and divorced, and she has a strained relationship with her father. Chelsea is described as pretty, tan, and athletic-looking, but slightly heavy. She calls Ethel "Mommy," but calls Norman "Norman." At the request of her mother, she has come to the lake house to celebrate her father's birthday, but she has also brought her fiancé (whom she marries by the end of the play) and his teenage son. She wants her parents to watch the son for a month, but because she knows her parents so well, she brings up the subject to Ethel. In this way, the reader sees that despite her age, Chelsea still feels a bit like a little girl around her parents. She talks to her mother openly about her own resentment toward her father, and although she complains that Norman never really talks to her, she is reluctant to talk to him about matters of substance, too. Chelsea takes a great stride toward maturity when she tells her father outright that the two of them have been mad for long enough and that she wants a healthy father-daughter relationship with him.

THEMES

Facing Mortality

Early in the play, Norman starts making references to his own mortality in jokes and offhand comments. He talks about living on borrowed time and preparing to celebrate his last birthday. In one way, he seems to have a healthy attitude about his mortality, but, in another, his incessant joking makes one wonder whether he is trying too hard to maintain that facade. Cleaning the living room, Ethel finds that her old doll, Elmer, has fallen into the fireplace. Because it is a sentimental item for her, she is sad to find it in such a place, but Norman speculates that Elmer threw himself into the fireplace. He then says that when it is time for him to die, Ethel should prop him up on the mantel so that he can do what Elmer did. Ethel tries to get Norman to stop, but he is having too much fun making jokes about his mortality. Making jokes not only enables him to make light of a serious subject but also offers him the opportunity to push Ethel's buttons.

Ethel endures Norman's morbid comments, but she tries to get him to stop. If she were really upset by them, however, her reaction would be intense and emotional. Instead, her tone is more like a reprimand. When, in the second scene of act 1, he says,

TOPICS FOR FURTHER STUDY

- After reading the play, watch the 1981 movie adaptation of *On Golden Pond.* Was the director's vision of the play the same as yours, or did you picture some of the scenes and characters differently? As you watch the film, think about how different a stage production is from a movie. Make note of these differences and the ways in which you think they alter the presentation of the story. For example, a theater script does not call for close-ups, but a movie director can use them. How does this affect the actors' expressions and, in turn, the audience's experience? What about other issues, such as lighting, sets, and the presence (or absence) of a live audience? Write a review of the movie focusing on the fact that it is a stage adaptation. Compare the movie to the script you have read and decide whether you think it works well as a movie.
- Alzheimer's disease and other forms of mental decline are devastating for sufferers and their families. Research Alzheimer's disease to find out about common experiences of people in the beginning stages of the disease and the types of available support for families of sufferers. Prepare a presentation for your class that will encourage awareness, compassion, and discussion.
- Many people find lake homes to be relaxing getaways. What is it about this particular setting that is both calming and rejuvenating? Write a poem or essay expressing your thoughts on this subject.
- What do you think the Thayers were doing the summer after the events of *On Golden Pond*? Write a plot summary of a sequel, along with one scene from any part of your play.
- Throughout the play, Ethel is fascinated by the loons on the lake. What purpose do the loons serve in the play? Do they reveal something about Ethel's character? Lead a group discussion about Ethel's personality and perspective, including a consideration of the loons. Introduce passages from the play in your discussion. Encourage the people in your group to think of other literary characters to whom particular animals have special meaning.
- The relationship between Norman and Billy suggests that younger generations not only accept but also fully embrace the older generation. What do you think American society's attitude is toward the elderly? More specifically, what do you think teenagers' attitudes are? Facilitate a discussion among your peers on this topic.

"I'm on borrowed time as it is," she replies, "Would you please take your cheery personality and get out of here?" And at the end of his Elmer rant, she tells him, "Your fascination with dying is beginning to frazzle my good humor." She is reacting more to his flippant attitude than to the reality that she will have to go on without him. She knows that he is older than she is and that his health is beginning to decline, so she is aware that she will be a widow at some point in the future. But she will not indulge Norman's self-pity masked as humor. She also does not like him to interrupt a nice moment with the suggestion that their time at Golden Pond may be drawing to a close. At the end of the first scene, she says, "Our forty-eighth summer on Golden Pond," to which he responds, "Probably be our last." She tells him, "Oh, shut up." This exchange has a slightly more serious tone, because Norman is only half-kidding. Given his declining health, he thinks it may be their last summer in the house. Her response is directed at the part of him that is kidding, as well as to the part that is not.

Generation Gap

Thompson first introduces the theme of the generation gap in the conversation between Bill and Norman about the sleeping arrangements. Bill is a straightforward man who asks Norman whether he and Chelsea can sleep in the same bed while they are staying at the lake house. When Norman seems somewhat confused and asks whether Bill is referring to a moral issue, Bill responds, "Well, it's just that we're of different generations." To Bill, the moral issue stems from the generational issue, and he assumes that there is a difference in their thinking. As he soon learns, however, Norman does not object to his daughter's sleeping with her boyfriend at the lake house. The generation gap was only perceived by Bill, but he quickly discovers that there is no gap. The gap that exists between Norman and Chelsea is a result of their particular relationship, not generational issues.

The most obvious illustration of the generation gap is in the friendship between Billy and Norman. Here, Thompson's approach is to show that the idea of a generation gap is false, at least among these characters. An eighty-year-old man whose mind is slipping has nothing in common with a bright, feisty thirteen-year-old, and yet in *On Golden Pond*, these two are best friends. Not only do they find that they enjoy each other's company, but they also begin to take on each other's characteristics. The second act opens with Norman livelier than he has been: the screen door is fixed, and he is getting his equipment to go fishing, even though at the beginning of the play, he had told Ethel that he was not sure if he would do any fishing this year. Billy is then heard using Norman's expressions while wearing one of his hats. He is as anxious to go fishing as Norman is. This unlikely pair has formed a bond that demonstrates that there actually is no generation gap.

Marriage

In depicting the relationship between Norman and Ethel, Thompson makes it very clear that they are still completely in love after almost fifty years. Their interactions are realistic enough for the reader to understand that they have certainly had difficulties, but their marriage has been strong enough to withstand their trials. Norman and Ethel are two very different people. Where she is gregarious, he is standoffish; where she is energetic, he is still; and where she wants everyone to be happy, he is more concerned about his own happiness. Ironically, it is because of their differences that they have a strong marriage. They counterbalance each other and create stability.

As Norman's memory continues to decline, Ethel provides much-needed reassurance and security for him. His future must frighten her terribly, but she remains positive and compassionate toward her husband. Thompson provides a very poignant picture of marriage in the way Ethel and Norman interact in these circumstances. Readers and audiences have the comfort of knowing that whatever happens to Norman, he will be cared for by his loving and devoted wife.

STYLE

The Lake House as Setting

Thompson keeps all the action of the play in the setting of the lake house. Every scene is played out in the same set of rooms, with the only changes showing in what is packed or unpacked, based on what time of the summer it is. Setting the play in a place that is so familiar and comfortable for Norman and Ethel communicates a sense of who they are and what their history is. Their house by Golden Pond has been a home to them for decades, and it reflects their personalities and their life together. Everything of importance that happens in the play—Chelsea's return to their lives, Billy's introduction to the family, Chelsea's attempt to make amends with her father, and all of the interactions between Ethel and Norman—happens in the setting that is most comfortable for them.

The Lake House as Symbol

Thompson uses the lake house as a symbol of Ethel and Norman's aging. The house was built in 1914, and Thompson's stage directions say that "it has aged well." The house has the character and patina of an old, well-loved house, just as the Thayers are advanced in years but are still doing well. Their marriage has lasted close to fifty years, and they are healthy enough to make another annual trip to the lake. At the same time, they are showing signs of age. Norman walks slowly and suffers from a variety of ailments.

The aging couple feels completely at home at the lake house. Toward the end of the first scene of the play, Ethel gazes out the window and says, "It's so good to be home, isn't it?" This remark lends insight into the way the couple feels about the house. They have presumably left their regular home to come to the lake for the summer, but her comment indicates that it is actually the lake house that feels like home to them. Ethel and Norman feel a special kinship with the house and recognize the parallels between it and themselves. Norman makes an interesting comment in the first scene, when Ethel complains about the mouse tracks in the kitchen. She does not like the thought of the "little

COMPARE & CONTRAST

- **1970s:** Although the medical community can recognize and diagnose Alzheimer's disease, treatment options are very limited and do not yet include medications. Patients and families are encouraged to seek support as doctors monitor the disease's progression.

  Today: Since 1993, doctors have been able to add medication to their treatment plans for Alzheimer's patients. While the disease is still not reversible, the constantly improving medications make it possible to slow down the mental degeneration.

- **1970s:** The traditional family structure is challenged by increasing divorce rates and acceptance of couples living together. During the 1970s, premarital sex becomes more common, and more women are making the decision not to have children.

  Today: Divorce rates remain high (over 50 percent), and the decision to live together is very common among couples who date seriously. Premarital sex is also common and is starting at younger ages than ever before. Many women still feel comfortable choosing not to become mothers, though more women now decide to become mothers later in life.

- **1970s:** As a result of the large number of college professors hired in the 1960s and early 1970s, college faculties are relatively young. In fact, in 1977, the median age of college professors is forty. Until 1978's Age Discrimination in Employment Act raises the age of mandatory retirement to seventy (from sixty-five), college professors tend to retire in their early to mid-sixties. Retiring at this point in their lives gives professors many more healthy, productive years to pursue personal interests, traveling, guest speaking engagements, and second careers.

  Today: College professors are, on average, older than they were in the 1970s. In 1996, the median age of college professors is forty-eight. Over the course of the 1990s, the percentage of professors who are fifty-five or older rises from 24 percent to 32 percent. This aging of college faculties is due in part to the fact that in 1993, the mandatory retirement age for college professors was eliminated.

---

rascals" settling into their house, but Norman replies, "It's nice to think there was life here. Keeps the house company, it doesn't get lonely."

Chelsea responds to the house in an emotional way, too. When she arrives at the house, she surveys it and concludes that it looks the same. Norman responds, "The old house is exactly the same. Just older. Like its inhabitants." Later, in the first scene of act 2, Chelsea comments on the house again, but this time she acknowledges the emotional presence of the house. After reflecting on how frustrating it was for her to grow up trying to please Norman, she says, "This house seems to set me off. . . . I act like a big person everywhere else. I do. I'm in charge of Los Angeles. I guess I've never grown up on Golden Pond. . . . There's just something about coming back here that makes me feel like a little fat girl." Chelsea does not have the same warm, homey feelings about the house, but she somehow equates it to her parents, or at least to Norman. That her first comment about the house was that it looked the same indicates that, in her mind, nothing about Norman changes over the years.

HISTORICAL CONTEXT

New York Newspaper Strike of 1978

In 1978, a prolonged newspaper strike meant there were no issues of the *New York Times*, *Post*, or *Daily News* being published. Theater producers

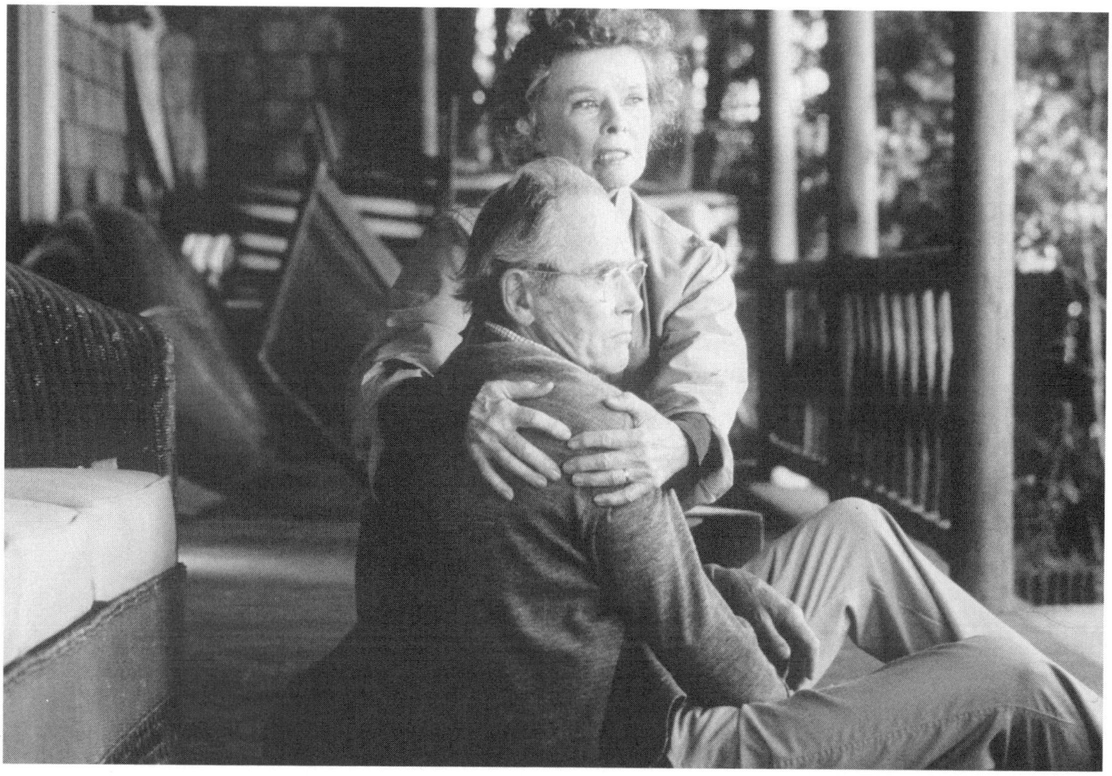

Katharine Hepburn and Henry Fonda in the 1981 film version of On Golden Pond Universal/The Kobal Collection

turned to television and other media to promote their plays, but reviews of those plays were not available. As a result, theatergoers had no way of reading new reviews and had to rely on chance and word of mouth to find good productions. It was during this time that *On Golden Pond* opened off Broadway and began building its base of support from theater enthusiasts. The strike ended in early October, and by then Thompson's play already had a solid reputation. Whether the reviews would have helped or hindered its success will never be known. Regardless, *On Golden Pond* did well and was soon moved to a theater on Broadway, where it continued to enjoy success.

Broadway in the 1970s

Many of the nonmusical plays in the 1970s reflected the cynicism of the era, which made *On Golden Pond* unique. In an era so dominated by youth culture and music, musicals seemed to characterize theatrical expression. Broadway in the 1970s saw various styles of musicals vie for the attention of theatergoers. There was the new brand of musical called the rock opera, which included shows such as *Jesus Christ, Superstar*, *Godspell*, and *The Me Nobody Knows*. Other shows, such as *Grease* and *The Wiz*, proved that rock music was a popular element in modern musicals. Broadway also saw the rise of concept musicals. A concept musical is a musical based on an idea or theme (such as love, finding a job, or dying) rather than being driven by a plot. While concept musicals often have story lines, they are secondary to the presentation of the main idea. Such musicals included productions like *A Little Night Music*, *Pippin*, *A Chorus Line*, and Bob Fosse's sexy dance masterpiece, *Chicago*. In the midst of these new approaches to the Broadway musical were revivals of traditional musicals, including *Hello, Dolly*!, *Man of La Mancha*, *My Fair Lady*, and *The King and I*.

CRITICAL OVERVIEW

In the "Author's Note" to the Dramatists Play Service edition of *On Golden Pond*, Thompson recalls an early performance of the play that was attended by the acclaimed American playwright Tennessee Williams. Thompson says that Williams loved the play but hated to see the characters go, adding, "Let them stay the winter." While there is little critical commentary on the script of *On Golden Pond*, theater critics often comment on it in their reviews of productions of the play. The play has remained a critics' favorite, even though it was written in the 1970s. Reviewers find that the characters are believable and likeable and that the themes are both worthwhile and relevant. In the *Sarasota Herald Tribune*, Kay Kipling writes, "Familiarity is what makes Ernest Thompson's play work," adding that "the dramatic situation—an aging couple faces mortality—[is] familiar to just about all of us on a personal level."

Reviewers often praise Thompson's use of humor and sensitivity in the play. In the *New York Amsterdam News*, Linda Armstrong deems *On Golden Pond* a "very funny and sometimes moving play." She describes it as "a play about what all people can go through when they become old," adding that "it deals with the love that lasts over decades between a couple." Armstrong praises Thompson for writing "a piece that is filled with human frailty as well as laughter. Norman becomes a very sympathetic character." She concludes her review by declaring the play "a flawless piece of theater" with a "fabulous script." One reviewer, Paul Harris of *Variety*, recalls the impressive cast members who have acted in *On Golden Pond* over the years. Harris notes, "Ernest Thompson's touching *On Golden Pond* has always been a perfect vehicle for star turns."

A few reviewers over the years have noted flaws in the play. *Daily Variety*'s Joel Hirschhorn, for example, remarks, "Some of the staging by Ernest Thompson is almost bizarre," citing the scene in which Norman falls to the floor with chest pains, and Ethel does not first call a doctor. Recalling the entire scene, Hirschhorn writes, "The events flash by with no logic." In *Back Stage*, Julius Novick criticizes the play's lack of action or emotional depth. He comments, "Instead of plot, Ernest Thompson's sentimental comedy offers a beloved way of summertime life and the pathos of old age encroaching on it. Nostalgia flourishes and cuteness abounds."

CRITICISM

Jennifer Bussey

Bussey holds a master's degree in interdisciplinary studies and a bachelor's degree in English literature and is an independent writer specializing in literature. In the following essay, she explores the tense relationship between Norman and his daughter, Chelsea, in On Golden Pond.

Thompson's play *On Golden Pond* portrays various kinds of family relationships, some healthy and some not. Norman and Ethel Thayer have been married for almost fifty years, and their marriage represents enduring love and respect. Their daughter, Chelsea, gets married in the course of the play, and her union represents the hope of a new marriage. Norman's relationship to Chelsea's new stepson is both friendly and grandfatherly. All of these relationships are generally healthy and satisfying, but Norman's relationship with Chelsea is an altogether different story. This is the only relationship in *On Golden Pond* that is hurtful and destructive.

From the first words they say about each other in the play, Norman and Chelsea communicate that their relationship is fraught with tension. Norman barely acknowledges Chelsea's pictures on the mantel in the lake home by Golden Pond, and the few comments he makes are negative. In the first act, he notices a picture and says, "Here's Chelsea on the swim team at school. She wasn't exactly thin." Ethel reminds him that Chelsea joined the team only to please him. Norman's tendency is to find something to criticize about Chelsea, rather than to see a picture of his daughter doing something for the sole purpose of winning his approval. When Chelsea arrives for a visit at the lake house, she calls Ethel "Mommy," and she calls Norman "Norman." When Bill, Chelsea's boyfriend, asks Norman about it, he merely states enigmatically that there are reasons for it. Chelsea's attitude toward Norman is courteous but devoid of emotion, at least in his presence. The reader will notice that Ethel quietly defends Chelsea and Norman to each other and that she obviously wishes that they would make amends. Chelsea is guilty of putting Ethel in the middle of her conflict with her father, as when she asks her mother privately about leaving Billy at the lake house for a month. This kind of behavior shows the audience that Chelsea is not willing to address her father directly about potentially volatile subjects, much less about the root of their problem.

In her conversation with her mother in the first scene of act 2, Chelsea reveals the source of her problems with her father. As a child and a teenager, Chelsea always felt that she did not measure up to her father's expectations. She chased after his approval by joining the diving team and going fishing

"THE RELATIONSHIP BETWEEN NORMAN AND CHELSEA IS DEFINED BY THEIR HURT, ANGER, AND INDIFFERENCE TOWARD EACH OTHER."

with him, but her heart was in neither activity. The sting of his criticism has not healed after all these years. As she puts it, "He always makes me feel like I've got my shoes on the wrong feet." She also tells Ethel that being at the lake house still makes her feel like "a little fat girl." Chelsea feels as if she is so far removed from what her father wanted that she wonders if he really wanted a son. When she returns from Europe to pick up Billy and finds him out fishing with Norman, she remarks, "Billy reminds me of myself out there, way back when. Except I think he makes a better son than I did."

Chelsea and Norman are very similar in their passive-aggressive way of dealing with their broken relationship. They both make snide remarks and act uninterested. Even when Chelsea vents her anger about Norman's overbearing parenting style and her mother's failure to do anything about it, she does so in front of Ethel, not Norman. This scene reveals, however, how angry Chelsea still is about her childhood. Norman appears to be apathetic or, at most, inconvenienced, but his feelings lack the passion that Chelsea's outburst expresses. When she finally talks to him, she tells him that she is sorry, adding, "We've been mad at each other for too long." He is slightly confused, stating that he just thought they did not like each other. Again, their experiences of the relationship are completely different, which makes reconciliation even more difficult.

Thompson could have used a flashback technique to show the audience exactly what Norman was like when Chelsea was a child, but he seems to have known that it would not be necessary. Although the audience can assume that Chelsea's memories are colored by her emotional pain, the audience can also suppose that the younger Norman was probably at least as insensitive and sarcastic as the older Norman is. The objective truth about who was wrong, and how wrong he or she was, is irrelevant. The relationship between Norman and Chelsea is defined by their hurt, anger, and indifference toward each other.

The unlikely friendship between Norman and Billy, Bill's son, has a great deal of relevance to the difficult relationship between Norman and Chelsea. It reveals that Norman is capable of change, even though he is not a man who embraces it, as evidenced by his well-worn hats, familiar books, and tendency toward routine. So when Billy arrives unannounced, he is not pleased at the prospect of hosting a teenager. When Billy shows that he can handle, as well as return, Norman's sarcasm and irreverent attitude, he wins Norman over. Norman senses in this thirteen-year-old boy, of all people, a kindred spirit. He warms up to Billy in short order, and, when given the chance to have him stay at the lake house for a whole month, he agrees without hesitation. From what is known about Norman, his agreeable attitude is unexpected. His decision is the turning point in the play.

Norman's willingness to watch Billy for a month while Chelsea and Bill go to Europe is fascinating. That Ethel wants to have the boy stay with them is no surprise at all, but Norman is a different story. Because he is not emotionally demonstrative or expressive, one is compelled to consider why he is so willing to embrace this major change in his summer plans. There are three possibilities. First, Norman, like Ethel, may genuinely want to help Chelsea. This is her chance to go to Europe with the man she loves and to pursue long-term happiness. As it happens, she and Bill get married in Europe. Perhaps Norman wants to do something to help Chelsea and support her chance for stability and happiness, but, because of their relationship, he feels that he can make only an indirect gesture. If that is the case, then agreeing to host Billy at the lake house accomplishes it. The second possibility is that Norman really likes the boy and feels that spending time with him will not be a burden at all. Billy is bright, receptive, and spunky. This means that he will probably be teachable and enliven the lake house during his stay. Norman may recognize a second chance to do a better job with a child than he did with Chelsea. Second chances are rare and unexpected; in Norman's fatalistic state of mind, it is too valuable to let pass.

Billy tells Ethel that sometimes when he and Norman are fishing, Norman calls him by Chelsea's name. Ethel explains that Billy probably just reminds Norman of Chelsea, but there is more that she is not telling him. On one hand, Norman is

WHAT DO I READ NEXT?

- Thomas DeBaggio offers a firsthand account of his slow descent into Alzheimer's disease in *Losing My Mind: An Intimate Look at Life with Alzheimer's* (2003). DeBaggio shares his fears, hopes, regrets, and joys, along with memories from his distant and recent past. The daily challenges and disappointments are described honestly in an effort to help readers understand better what life with Alzheimer's disease is really like.
- Harvey and Myrna Katz Frommer's *It Happened on Broadway: An Oral History of the Great White Way* (2004) offers an extensive oral history of Broadway. The Frommers include interviews and musings by actors, producers, writers, composers, set designers, and critics, to name a few. Their combined experiences give a unique understanding of the history of Broadway.
- Professor Roger Hall teaches playwriting and captures his lessons in *Writing Your First Play* (1998). Hall covers the basics of characterization, plot development, setting, and other important elements, along with examples and writing exercises for students new to the process.
- Pete Hamill's 1998 novel *Snow in August* tells the story of a friendship between an eleven-year-old Catholic boy and an elderly rabbi who is new to the United States. The rabbi learns to speak English and love baseball, and the boy learns to deal with his difficulties with greater maturity and insight.
- Edited by David Savran, *In Their Own Words: Contemporary American Playwrights* (1999) presents the reader with interviews of some of the foremost playwrights of the American stage. Savran inquires about their inspirations, their processes, and their techniques for writing great plays. Although Thompson is not included here, among the playwrights featured are David Mamet, Stephen Sondheim, and August Wilson.
- Thompson's *The West Side Waltz: A Play in $\frac{3}{4}$ Time* (1981) is his second-best-known play, after *On Golden Pond*. It is about an aging piano teacher who mentors a young actress, only to find that she might be better off reconnecting with an old friend.

losing his memory and becoming easily confused. On the other, he may be trying to do a better job of being a father to Chelsea through Billy. In a sense, Norman is proving to himself that he now knows how to be a better father, even though it is too late to take Chelsea fishing. It may be healing for him to feel as if he is being a good father to Chelsea.

The third possibility is that Norman wants to draw Chelsea closer to him by being a grandfather to Billy. After the frank discussion with Chelsea's boyfriend, Norman could reasonably assume that Bill is going to marry his daughter. That would make Chelsea a mother for the first time in her life, at the age of forty-two. And it would make Norman a grandfather at last, at the age of eighty. The play takes place during the summer that Norman worries may be his last (or at least the last one with all his faculties), so being a grandfather to Billy for himself and for the sake of Chelsea would be a gratifying experience.

Another way in which Billy's friendship with Norman is relevant to Chelsea's relationship with Norman is that it brings about their reconciliation. After all, Chelsea has to come back to the lake house to get Billy, and it is during this visit that she finally tells Norman that she wants the relationship to be better. Her motivation for trying to make amends with her father, however, is less clear. She seems a bit more mature when she returns from Europe, presumably because her relationship with Bill requires more maturity from her. She has found love with Bill, and she has also found a family. At the age of forty-two, it is time for her to learn what it is to be a parent. This realization, along with the realization that Norman has already forged a grandfatherly bond with Billy, leads her to make an effort to repair her relationship with Norman. Clearly, she is still angry (as evidenced by her tirade in front of her mother), but she has come to the end of that part of her life when she can justify her anger with blame. She realizes that living far away from her parents will no longer be a good enough reason not to see her father. She has a stepson who needs a family and likes hers.

The reconciliation scene is a bit awkward, but then so are the characters. Chelsea struggles to express herself to her father in a way that will enable him to see her point of view, but he is emotionally detached, as he always has been. She characterizes their relationship in one way, and he characterizes it in another. It is important to note that the reason Chelsea's offer of reconciliation is accepted by Norman is that she does not attack him with her anger and put him on the defensive. Instead, she adopts his calm disposition (probably unknowingly) in her approach, making him more receptive to what she has to say. Given the years of tension, the brevity of this scene is a bit surprising and even unsatisfying. But it is consistent with Norman's way of doing things, and so it is believable. He and Chelsea are not sure what their new relationship will mean to them, but they know it will be friendlier. Thompson shows that Norman and Chelsea struggle a bit to become accustomed to the new arrangement; when she calls at the end of the summer, her conversation with her mother comes much easier to her than the one with her father. Still, they are working to overcome the awkwardness in the interest of the relationship.

The problem of strained relationships between parents and their adult children is very common, and Thompson's handling of it is believable and hopeful. Norman and Chelsea are alike in many ways, and they do love each other, but the years of destructive patterns have weathered away their motivation to treat each other better. This play is about coming to terms with change—aging, mental deterioration, marriage, the possibility of saying goodbye, and entering into a family. Both Norman and Chelsea face change, and these changes make them willing to find each other's humanity and see whether they can discover a loving father-daughter relationship in the process. Thompson gives a message of encouragement that it is never too late to make a significant relationship right.

Source: Jennifer Bussey, Critical Essay on *On Golden Pond*, in *Drama for Students*, Thomson Gale, 2006.

Bryan Aubrey

Aubrey holds a PhD in English and has published many articles on twentieth-century literature. In this essay, he discusses the changes made to the play in the 1981 movie version.

Since its first appearance as a play on Broadway in 1978, *On Golden Pond* has been made into a film, a television show, and a musical as well as being revived on Broadway, with some dialogue rewritten, in 2005. In a review of the revival in *Variety*, Thompson was quoted as saying that none of these versions were very different from each other. While this is certainly true in terms of the major themes and characters, readers of the play (or those fortunate enough to be able to see a live theater performance) might note a few significant differences between the play and the 1981 movie version starring Henry Fonda, Katharine Hepburn, and Jane Fonda. Thompson, who wrote the screenplay for the film, used the opportunity to sharpen the dramatic conflicts and resolutions to meet the expectations of a mass audience accustomed to the conventions of Hollywood.

Translating a play into a movie is not as simple a task as it might at first appear. A film appeals more to the eye than to the ear, so the visual element in a movie is as important as the spoken word, and often even more so, whereas in a play, language dominates. There are a number of scenes (or sequences, to use the language of film) in the movie version of *On Golden Pond* that exploit the visual opportunities of the medium, such as when young Billy Ray, in a purely visual scene, goes out on his own and joyfully drives the Thayers's boat in large circles and figure eights all over the lake; or the action sequence that takes place in Purgatory Cove, which was created especially for the movie; or Chelsea's backflip from the diving board near the end, which adds a visual dimension, not present in the play, to her reconciliation with her father. Another visual symbol is the second shot in the movie's opening sequence, which shows in long shot (a shot taken from a considerable distance) the sun setting over Golden Pond, the water shimmering in the golden light. This is a perfect metaphor for the relationship between Norman and Ethel Thayer, which has stood firm for a long day of forty-eight years and is now, because of Norman's age and ill health, probably approaching its end. A similar shot of a sunset on Golden Pond returns at the end of the film, just as the credits begin to roll. It effectively frames the film as a tale of human lives in the "sunset" years. It is a touching, if sometimes sentimental story, which shows that even near

"THE CHARACTER WHO IS MOST IN NEED OF CHANGE IS ALSO THE ONE WHO APPEARS TO BE THE LEAST INCLINED TO MAKE THE EFFORT THAT CHANGE REQUIRES. THIS, OF COURSE, IS NORMAN."

the end of life, there are still possibilities for growth and change and the healing of old hurts. It is never too late.

The character who is most in need of change is also the one who appears to be the least inclined to make the effort that change requires. This, of course, is Norman. The opening scene of both play and film brings out the contrast between Norman and Ethel in this respect. Ethel is fully alive, open to the beauty of nature on Golden Pond, and still able to make new friends. She may be in her late sixties, but she has lost none of her zest for life. Norman, the old curmudgeon, is locked into his small, rigid world, verbally sparring with Ethel while frequently giving expression to his morbid thoughts about approaching death. Many of his comments in this respect are meant to be facetious, a way to keep his fears at bay. Still, to the devoted Ethel, they are not funny, although she understands her husband well and either ignores his provocations or gives as good as she gets.

In the play, much of the dialogue in the first scene conveys memories and reminiscences—Charlie as a boy; Elmer, the doll that Ethel has had since she was four—that express how long the Thayers have been together and how much of their lives is in the past. In the film, this dialogue is cut, the director Mike Rydall opting instead for a couple of telling shots of Norman peering at photographs, the first of which is of himself as a younger man. (Beside it is a newspaper clipping dated 1966, with the headline "Professor Thayer Retires.") The second is of himself and Ethel when they were much younger. It seems that the past stretches back as far as memory can reach, but the future beckons hardly at all. Although, in many ways, *On Golden Pond* is a light, sentimental play and film, the shadow of approaching death hangs over it.

This theme is presented even more strikingly in the film than in the play. The film adds a scene in which Norman and Ethel refuel their boat, and one of the teenagers at the gas station makes fun of Norman's old age. Norman berates them both in a poignant outburst that conveys the infirmities and indignities of age: "You think it's funny being old? My whole goddam body's fallin' apart. Sometimes I can't even go to the bathroom when I want to." The film also shows directly the frightening incident that the play can only describe—when Ethel sends Norman out to the woods to pick strawberries, and he quickly becomes disoriented and has to come home. Quick cuts and rapidly shifting camera angles suggest his confusion and fear. At one point, a low angle shot looks up at a big tree with a gnarled pattern that resembles a face. The effect is menacing and even spooky, and the whole sequence reduces the gruff, combative Norman to a frightened and frail old man.

Old age may be advancing rapidly, but Norman has unfinished business to take care of before he dies. Unfortunately, he does not realize this until the issue is forced upon him. The issue, of course, is his failed relationship with Chelsea and the anger and frustration that she feels on account of it. In the film, Chelsea expresses her anger at her father in a far more direct, overt manner—if only to her mother—than she does in the play, and Norman is also supplied with a reason to be angry with her, which he does not have in the play.

In the screen version, the moment when Chelsea arrives and awkwardly hugs Norman is a telling one. In the play, the stage directions state that Norman "hesitates only the briefest instant" before hugging Chelsea, but Henry Fonda's Norman actually flinches as Chelsea goes to kiss him, pulling his head back before recovering himself and responding to her. This is clearly a man who is deeply uncomfortable with receiving affection from his daughter, perhaps from anyone except his wife. He then alienates Chelsea immediately with his comment about "this little fat girl." He does not mean it unkindly, but Chelsea (Jane Fonda in the movie) is not fat, and she is humiliated by this thoughtless reference to her younger self. It is as if the relationship between them has frozen in time. Although she is now forty-two years old, her father still makes her feel like a child, and an unwanted child at that, since the clear implication is that Norman would have preferred to have had a son rather than a daughter.

Given the emotional impasse between them, it is not surprising that Chelsea seldom visits her parents, and it is this that supplies Norman with his resentment toward his daughter. The filmmakers obviously thought that Norman should have a grievance against Chelsea to match hers against him, so lines not in the play are added to the movie dialogue. "I'm frankly surprised Chelsea could find the way," Norman says sarcastically, after Bill Ray comments on how pleased he is that Chelsea has brought him and Billy to Golden Pond. Just in case anyone in the audience misses the point, Norman then quizzes Bill Ray about whether he visits his own parents. None of this dialogue is in the play. For her part, when Chelsea talks to Ethel, she explodes in anger and resentment, several times using profanities to describe her father, none of which occurs in the play. She goes so far that Ethel is forced to slap her face and rebuke her, and this also takes place only in the screen version.

The effect of all these changes in the film version is to sharpen the tensions all round, the purpose being to set up more effectively the final emotional reconciliation. In real life, of course, such longstanding blocks and resentments in family relationships are hard to overcome, but in a Hollywood movie, usually all it takes is some straight talking and a hug or two for everything to be magically transformed. And so it is with Norman and Chelsea. Chelsea tells him that it is time that they had a real father-daughter relationship; she finally manages the backflip that she could not do to please him as a child; he says what she had always wanted to hear, that it does not matter whether she can do the backflip; and, in a final embrace, she calls him Dad rather than Norman. The reconciliation between father and daughter is therefore more smooth and complete (if more sentimental and less convincing) in the film than in the play. In the play, Chelsea and Norman do make progress but remain somewhat wary of each other, and the more oblique dialogue leaves much to the interpretation of director and actors.

Another theme that is expanded on the screen, when compared with the stage, is the relationship between Norman and Billy. This is largely because film gives the opportunity to show their fishing expeditions on the lake directly, whereas onstage they can only be described. The theme is hardly an original one. Young people reinvigorate tired old hearts in works as diverse as the British novelist George Eliot's *Silas Marner* (1861), in which an old miser finds new purpose in life when he adopts an orphaned two-year-old girl, and the movie *Secondhand Lions* (2003), starring Michael Caine and Robert Duvall, in which a fourteen-year-old boy stays for the summer on the Texas farm of his two eccentric great-uncles and duly softens them up with his youthful innocence. This is close to what happens in *On Golden Pond*, as Norman, for a short while, gets the son he always secretly wanted, and Billy, an initially disgruntled and sometimes rude young teenager who is angry at being left behind by his parents when they go to Europe, grows affectionate toward the cantankerous old man who becomes his fishing companion. Billy's comment "I'll miss you," made after Norman says that he will not be around much longer, typifies the sentimental way in which the film develops the relationship. (That line is not in the play.)

If, on occasion, the film provides enough Hollywood-style syrup to fill up Golden Pond, it also has its moments, as the play does, of insight, wisdom, and genuine feeling. Indeed, it would be hard not to be moved by the final shot, of Ethel and Norman standing still on the shores of Golden Pond, saying goodbye to it, perhaps for the last time, as the camera pulls back and up, making them smaller and smaller and revealing more and more of the natural world to which, as human beings whose stay on earth can only be brief, they will soon return.

Source: Bryan Aubrey, Critical Essay on *On Golden Pond*, in *Drama for Students*, Thomson Gale, 2006.

Neil Heims

Heims is a writer and teacher living in Paris. In this essay, he argues that On Golden Pond *is an actors' play.*

Whenever Norman Thayer, the eighty-year-old protagonist of *On Golden Pond*, speaks, he camouflages the expression of his thoughts and feelings using clever and evasive verbal tricks and riffs of language. These contrivances allow him simultaneously to express and to avoid confronting unpleasant realities, such as his disquiet at aging or his anxiety about death. Likewise, he can avoid making direct contact with other people, like his daughter—which he finds embarrassing. These verbalizations serve to distance him from his real emotions and to permit him to stand aloof and apparently unaffected, as if with an academic detachment—he is a retired college English professor—above and outside everything, offering wry commentary.

"THE WORDS THAT NORMAN AND ETHEL SPEAK MUST SERVE TO EXPRESS THINGS THAT ARE NOT BEING SAID BUT WHICH ARE PALPABLY PRESENT."

The behavior is so characteristic of him that it is impossible to know whether it is deliberate—that he is aware he is doing it and aware of the feelings he is camouflaging—or whether it has become so ingrained in him that he is unaware of it or of the feelings he is avoiding. Is it so deeply his manner that, in fact, one identity has usurped another and his "real" meanings are hidden from even himself? Perhaps they have actually been obliterated so thoroughly that they exist beneath the surface of the self he seems to be, like unburied ghosts condemned to wander disembodied among the living. The actor playing Norman must be able to convey two simultaneously interconnected and alienated personalities moving, as it were, in opposite directions. One is expressed and seen, and the other is repressed and invisible. The antecedent, submerged personality or self, however, suffuses everything about him and covers him like a shadow or an aura.

It is just this tension between what is expressed and what is withheld, yet suggested in Norman Thayer's character and the profound challenge it presents to the actor playing him that give *On Golden Pond* a subdued emotional force and make it an actors' play. A similar challenge, indeed, confronts the actress playing Ethel Thayer, Norman's wife of forty-six years. She must portray a woman who sees the man beneath the man Norman presents to the world and even, frequently, to her. She must portray a strongly independent woman who is beset, even irritated, by the frustration of his flinty and distracted character but who has a deep, abiding, and even submissive love for him, just because she can understand the language he speaks and, in a sense, translate it. She must convey Ethel's ability to see what is admirable in Norman when he appears foolish and what is generous about him when he appears cranky. The words that Norman and Ethel speak must serve to express things that are not being said but which are palpably present. The dramatic tension that gives *On Golden Pond* vibrancy depends on the actors' subtle portrayal of the characters much more than on the plot, for there is really very little plot. Without virtuoso performances by charismatic actors who can command a stage and hold an audience, what plot there is can come across as relatively hackneyed, sentimental, and even manipulative.

Much of the "action" of *On Golden Pond* is concerned with conveying the local color of rural Maine and, more significantly, establishing Norman and Ethel as endearing characters, despite everything, characters with whom the audience is supposed to bond. If the audience does not become fond of their environment and enchanted by these characters and is not indeed seduced by them, what little plot there is will go by, leaving no impression. So Norman is shown in his bumbling interactions with the telephone, the want ads in the newspaper, a rack of hats, and a broken screen door. He is made to deliver gently bigoted observations about the neighbors and wry comments about the past and the landscape. He is given a verbal dexterity that shows that while he may be forgetful, he is still intellectually sharp. Ethel's ongoing battle with spiders, blackflies, and mosquitoes takes up a fair share of her dialogue, as do her reminiscences about her childhood on the pond, her "conversations" with the loons that live there, and her affection for her childhood doll. If the actors can establish a convincing relationship with each other and a rapport with the audience, then the three elements that constitute the plot—Norman's failed relationship with his daughter, his April-December friendship with his daughter's thirteen-year-old stepson-to-be, and his confrontation with his own approaching death—will resonate with the audience. It will cause a catch in the throat, a tear in the eye, and a melancholy smile.

Despite its reliance on characters, *On Golden Pond* is not a deeply psychological play. It simply presents what is. Norman, for example, is ill at ease with his forty-two-year-old daughter, Chelsea, it seems certain, because she is not male. Joie de vivre is restored to his life because young Billy Ray, who spends the summer with him, *is* a boy and can, therefore, be the son Chelsea never was. Chelsea is angry with her father and has made only infrequent visits to the family, because she has never been cherished as a girl or a woman and, consequently, as a person. She has been kept at a distance by her disappointed father, whose only topic

James Earl Jones and Leslie Uggams in a 2005 production of On Golden Pond Photo by Scott Suchman

of conversation with her has always been baseball, as if he were ignoring the fact that she is not male. As an adult, she has kept herself at a distance, infrequently visiting her parents.

Very little in the script seems to motivate Chelsea and Norman's reconciliation toward the end of *On Golden Pond*, except her sense, encouraged by her mother, that if she does not make peace with her father now, there will not be much time left in his life for her to do so. Perhaps her own aging and the need to be "normal" are also factors. Her meeting Bill Ray, the decent, successful, straightforward dentist with the son who brightens her father's summer and brings verve to his life, may also have given her the strength to give up needing her father's approval and to let go of the anger that has resulted from getting so little of it.

Their reconciliation, consequently, is much more the result of Chelsea's capitulation to the reality of her need to love her father and her accepting that she wishes him to love her than it is of a dramatically developed, mutual realization of each other or a recognition on his part that she is a person. To make contact with him, she apologizes to her father, "I just wanted to say . . . that I'm sorry." His response—"Fine. No problem."—seems to show no more interest in her than he has ever shown. But she persists, "Don't you want to know what I'm sorry about?" He ventures, "I suppose so." And she tells him, "I'm sorry that our communication has been so bad. . . . That I've been walking around with a chip on my shoulder." He says only, "Oh." When she continues, apologizing for not attending his retirement dinner, he only talks about what a funny speech he gave.

She persists in searching for some traction: "I think it would be a good idea if we tried . . . to have the kind of relationship we're supposed to have." He asks, "What kind of relationship are we supposed to have?" "Like a father and a daughter," she replies. "We've been mad at each other for too long." He answers in a telling fashion, "I didn't realize we were mad. I thought we just didn't like each other." The audience may infer from this exchange that she was "mad" at him because he did not like her. In view of the close and mutually gratifying relationship Norman has forged with Billy, the reason for his dislike of Chelsea seems quite simply to be because, being a daughter, she frustrated his wish for a son. Despite her father's apparently cool response, she forges ahead. "I want to be your friend," she says. Rather than yielding verbally, he retorts with what seems like a passive reproach: "Does this mean you're going to come around more often?" She says yes, and he responds, still remaining distant, at least on the surface, "It would mean a lot to your mother," overtly saying nothing about himself. She answers, "Okay," and the stage direction reads "*They look at each other a moment, nothing more to say.*" She picks up the dialogue where he left off before her intervention, "Now you want to tell me about the Yankees?"

In print, Norman comes off as rather cold and unsympathetic in this exchange and Chelsea as perhaps more generous than she ought to be. Many in the audience might think that she has a valid grievance, rather than a chip on her shoulder. But the written text itself is only scaffolding, something like a musical score that must be brought to life through the interpretation of performers. The meaning and intensity of the confrontation depend on how the actors play it and what they bring to it. Norman's dialogue is hardly Shakespearean, but all of what Norman says can be delivered by an actor in such a way as to suggest everything that he might feel but is unable to say. What comes across on the page as dry, detached, and cold may be used onstage to show desperate struggle, inner turmoil, the conflict between love and embarrassment, and quiet self-conquest. Thus, when Chelsea finally tells Norman that she has married Bill, his elaborate but familiar ritual of teasing, evasion, and punning can signify a real connection with her rather than withdrawal. The one word, "Yes," he directs at her, in response to Ethel's rhetorical, "Isn't that wonderful?" in the midst of his usual verbal high jinks, can be fraught with an immensity of acceptance. The revelation that the actor playing Norman can bring to the scene is that the reason Norman longed for a son, rather than a daughter, was not that he valued a boy more but that he was unable to tolerate the emotion having and loving a daughter might provoke in him. He was too embarrassed by his love for her to express it or even to permit it. The strength of his evasion, then, can serve to indicate, in inverse ratio, the strength of his love, a love too strong for him to express, a current too powerful for the wire. Even his expressions of love for Ethel, after all, are often tinged with protective irony.

One further challenge is given to the actor playing Norman. His characteristic evasiveness and witty digressive tangents, his professorial absent-mindedness, might no longer be only what they seem but instead indications of an incipient senility and the approach of death. Death does pay a warning visit in the last scene of the play, when Norman suffers a minor heart attack. The combination of the real awareness of mortality, contact with Billy, and reconciliation with his daughter creates in him a renewed desire for life, which he expresses with his familiar ironic reserve. But through Norman's characteristic understatement, cynicism, and detachment, the actor playing him can clearly signify his connection with life and his family, instead of evasion. Indeed, Ethel's closing words of the play—"Hello, Golden Pond. We've come to say goodbye."—are moving because they encapsulate in one utterance the melancholy awareness at the core of the play, which Norman, too, has come to realize and accept, that greeting and parting are inextricably implicated in each other.

Source: Neil Heims, Critical Essay on *On Golden Pond*, in *Drama for Students*, Thomson Gale, 2006.

Linda Armstrong

In the following review of a 2005 production of On Golden Pond, *Armstrong calls the play "a flawless piece of theater," and praises Thompson for creating "a piece that is filled with human frailty as well as laughter."*

On Golden Pond is a very funny and sometimes moving play. James Earl Jones is delightful, rude, amusing and vulnerable in the lead role of Norman Thayer. Leslie Uggams is spirited, funny and charming as his wife and co-star, Ethel.

These characters staying at their summer lakeside home on Golden Pond have a vacation that everyone who sees this production will remember. *On Golden Pond* is really a play about what all people can go through when they become old, no matter their ethnic background. It deals with the love that lasts over decades between a couple, but also shows the ornery side of a person who is being affected by growing old—losing his memories and losing his train of thought. Norman is turning 80 and can't remember which people are in various pictures displayed in their lakeside home. This is also a story about the strained relationship that can happen between a father and daughter.

Although there are a few emotional scenes in this magnificent production, most of the play is filled with humor. Norman has a quick, often sarcastic or rude reply to anything he hears, and Ethel doesn't shy away from letting him know he's an "old poop." Norman, however, tends to be the source of humor, with his saucy comments. In one scene his daughter Chelsea (powerfully performed by Linda Powell) comes to the family's home with Bill (well done by Peter Francis James), her fiancé, and his 13-year-old son, Billy (marvelously played by Alexander Mitchell). When the boy meets Norman he tells him he's old. Norman says, "You should meet my father." When Billy asks if his father is still alive, Norman replies with a straight face, "No, but you should meet him."

Anyone who comes in contact with Norman is fair game. When Bill is left alone to talk with Norman and asks if it's o.k. to sleep with Chelsea while they spend the week with them, Norman puts him through the ringer. Then he tells him, "I would be delighted to have you abusing my daughter—upstairs. Do you want to violate her in the same bedroom I did Ethel?"

Playwright Ernest Thompson, who also wrote the original movie and past Broadway stage version of this play, has created a piece that is filled with human frailty as well as laughter. Norman becomes a very sympathetic character, in a scene in which Ethel asks him to pick some strawberries. She names the location and when he comes back within moments with an empty basket, she is livid. As she questions him, he has to painfully admit that he didn't know how to find the place where the strawberries were. When he walked away from the house, nothing looked familiar. He had to run home to see her pretty face and to reassure himself that he was himself. As Norman shares his fears, Ethel is moved to comfort him. She holds him and promises to show him where the strawberries are and pick them.

In this scene, as well as others in the production, Uggams and Jones simply shined.

Uggams has such a warm and loving presence on the stage, and Jones is a gem.

Thompson also presents Norman as someone who had a difficult relationship with his daughter when she was growing up. Chelsea could never please him and has grown to dislike and resent him. Anytime they are together they go at each other. Powell is captivating as Chelsea. She is vulnerable to her father's mean-spirited comments and easily able to fire back. Powell clearly demonstrates the deep emotions that this character goes through, from being hurt and feeling inadequate to being angry and then allowing herself to be vulnerable and extend the olive branch to begin mending their relationship.

"PLAYWRIGHT ERNEST THOMPSON, WHO ALSO WROTE THE ORIGINAL MOVIE AND PAST BROADWAY STAGE VERSION OF THIS PLAY, HAS CREATED A PIECE THAT IS FILLED WITH HUMAN FRAILTY AS WELL AS LAUGHTER."

On Golden Pond is a flawless piece of theater, from the phenomenal acting performances of the cast to the fabulous script by Thompson and the precious direction by Leonard Foglia.

This incredible production is playing at the Cort Theater, where I had the pleasure of attending the opening night. The theater was full of celebrities, including Tony Award winners Lillias White, Audra McDonald, and Brian Stokes Mitchell; singer Dionne Warwick; and former Mayor David Dinkins.

"This is an event. Anytime you see a great play with great actors, it's always a plus," said dancer/choreographer/actor Maurice Hines.

Referring to Uggams and Jones, actor/writer/composer Lee Summers said, "They are theatrical royalty. No finer actors of any color could have been chosen for this production." Former Secretary of State Colin Powell, Linda Powell's father, also attended opening night with her mother and sister.

Commenting on Linda's performance, Powell said, "It's always a delight to watch her on stage. We saw the show in Washington. It's just so polished. When she's on stage, I'm more nervous than she is."

Source: Linda Armstrong, "*On Golden Pond* Shimmers with Spectacular Performances," in *New York Amsterdam News*, Vol. 96, No. 16, April 14, 2005, pp. 22–23.

Kevin Kelly

The following interview finds Thompson amid the buzz of his Oscar win for On Golden Pond. *He shares with Kelly background on his beginnings as a playwright and discusses some of his newer works.*

[*KEVIN KELLY*]: *Hello . . . Ernest Thompson?*

[ERNEST THOMPSON]: You got him.

How does it feel to be a rich, famous, handsome, Oscar winner?

I've felt worse before in my life. (*Taut laughter whips the cables from LA to Boston.*) A whole lot worse. But let me tell you, sitting through the Oscars was an agony. The three hours seemed like a year. Before it started I thought—maybe—I had a good shot at winning, but as the evening wore on and *Golden Pond* didn't win anything, I thought it was all over. Then when the guy in front of me won for *Chariots of Fire,* that came as such a surprise, I was sure *Golden Pond* was going to lose out. I started to think I'd be like the California Angels, for the rest of my life saying, "Next season . . . next season we're really gonna do it all, for sure."

When you thought your Golden Pond *script might not win, were you rooting for anything else?*

I thought *Reds* and *Golden Pond* would split the vote. At least that's one of the theories I had going in. *Chariots of Fire* would have been my second choice.

After?

After mine! *Golden Pond* as best film. Listen, I don't want to sound like sweet grapes or anything, but I have to tell you—in my book—all those Academy voters are geniuses. Except I keep having this nightmare that the Oscars are really the Miss America Contest and next April I have to crown a new winner and give back the trophy.

(*Buzzing muffles his words.*)

Hold on, OK? My phone's been crazy since the Oscars. The whole world seems to be calling me, a lot of people I didn't even know I knew. (*Long pause*) Sorry. Let me say this, to be given the kind of endorsement the Oscar represents, for me, right now, is just a lucky break. It's like someone has suddenly said to me, It's OK, Ernest, it's OK, you're good, you're good. . . .

[Narrative:] Then Ernest Thompson explains *Golden Pond's* on-again/off-again history. He wrote the play in 1978 when he couldn't find work as an actor, the first script he says he ever "really finished." After a promising start Off-Broadway at the Hudson Guild Theater, *Golden Pond* transferred to the New Apollo where it closed after a rocky 107 performances, only to reopen three months later at the Century. Since then it has become a staple in regional theaters. Even before the runaway success of the movie adaptation—which won additional Oscars for Henry Fonda, Katharine Hepburn—Thompson had made a fortune from the script. He is expecting further royalties between "$1.5 to $2 million as *Golden Pond* hits the international market." Thompson says that his producers estimate "something like 10,000 productions over the next five years."

How does it feel to be a millionaire?

"I'm 32 and it feels pretty rich, except money's pretty fickle and you never know, you just never know! The best part is that it frees me to work. I've finished another play, *A Sense of Humor,* about parents dealing with their 25-year-old daughter's suicide. And I'm cooking with a movie to be called *Kidstuff,* about a relationship between a bachelor and a divorced mother with two kids. *Sense of Humor,* I guess, developed from the anger and confusion that struck me after my father died. *Kidstuff* is about me and my relationship with my ex-girlfriend of seven years, Patty McCormack. Oh yah, and in the trunk were three one-act plays which are going to be done next winter on CBS cable next winter, under the title, *Answers.*"

[Narrative:] Ernest Thompson was born in Bellows Falls, Vt., near what is now the Thompson family home in Walpole, N.H. He grew up in Mansfield, Mass., lived for a time in North Brookfield. His family used to summer at a cottage bought by his grandparents in 1903 on Great Pond, part of the Belgrade Lakes in Maine: Great Pond is the actual site of the fictionalized Golden Pond. Thompson's father, who died three years ago (and whom he mentioned in his Oscar acceptance), was a New England public school administrator and, later, a professor at Western Maryland College. The family includes two brothers, Paul and David, who live in Washington and work for the government; an unmarried sister Esther, who manages a hotel in Kingfield, Maine; and a married sister Bettina, a school teacher in New Jersey. Thompson's mother Esther "winters in Florida and summers on Golden Pond." Thompson says that the two eldery protagonists in his play "were ripped-off my parents, not biographically, really, but in their spirit and their eccentricities."

"I went to American University in Washington. I had a teacher who told me I was handsome and had good speech and should be an actor. Which I never questioned. So I decided to become an actor. I'd always been interested in writing, too, but I never seemed to finish anything I started. I played Dick Dudgeon in a Catholic U production of *The Devil's Disciple* directed by Cyril Ritchard. I simply took a course at Catholic U to get into the play, which was a great way to win the alienation of the rest of the students. Incidentally, that kind of alienation has followed me all my life. Do you remember what some of the critics did to *Golden Pond?* Two months after I graduated from American U, Cyril Ritchard signed me for a tour of *The Pleasure of His Company,* then, later, I did a soap, *Somerset.*"

[Narrative:] Thompson credits his interest in playwriting to a teacher, Arthur Bean, who assigned him, in his senior year at American U, to read all the plays of Eugene O'Neill, followed "by all of Tennessee Williams, William Inge, Arthur Miller, Edward Albee, the Realists of the 1940s and 1950s, those were my influences." Ernest Thompson's second play, *The West Side Waltz,* which opens Tuesday at the Shubert, had a considerable success on the road prior to Broadway, then a limited run on Broadway. It stars, of course, Katharine Hepburn. Like *On Golden Pond, West Side Waltz* was poorly received by some influential New York critics, although with wreathed smiles to Katharine Hepburn's performance. Similarly, the movie version of *Golden Pond* drew steam from the headier critics like Pauline Kael and David Denby although, here, with a dismissal of Katharine Hepburn for overacting. Does Ernest Thompson remember? Ernest Thompson remembers!

I gotta say that I just don't get it! I didn't get any respect at all when *West Side Waltz* opened in New York. The critics are a force, and eventually I suppose one learns to navigate through them without being upset. But, hell, I was upset. I am upset. I mean from time to time. I don't sit around brooding about it. But I get upset when a bum on the street tells me he doesn't like my shoes; I stop and think about my shoes for five minutes; but I probably won't go home and change them. I don't know what I can do about the critics, other than flash my Oscar and my sterling good looks in their faces!

(*Hostility crackles the wire. I have an image of vultures eavesdropping on telephone posts from LA to Boston.*)

Hepburn, my dear friend Katharine Hepburn, warned me about some of this. We're soul mates, she and I. She tells me every time I meet her to

> "TO BE GIVEN THE KIND OF ENDORSEMENT THE OSCAR REPRESENTS, FOR ME, RIGHT NOW, IS JUST A LUCKY BREAK. IT'S LIKE SOMEONE HAS SUDDENLY SAID TO ME, IT'S OK, ERNEST, IT'S OK, YOU'RE GOOD, YOU'RE GOOD. . . ."

watch it, to be careful. She's been getting it all her life. You know that! I know that! And I guess I'm going to be getting it all my life, too. It's crazy. There's some kind of resentment about success in this country. You're nothing without it, then when you get it you're still told you're nothing.

And, by the way, I'd like to clear up something about Hepburn and *West Side Waltz.* I refused to do any interviews before the play opened in New York. Just couldn't imagine myself sitting around pontificating about the art of playwriting. I'm sorry now. It could have been an educative process.

For you?

For me?! Naw, for the critics. I mean, for one thing, they would have learned that *Waltz* was categorically and absolutely NOT WRITTEN AS A VEHICLE FOR KATHARINE HEPBURN! When I was writing it I sometimes imagined it for Eileen Heckart. I knew nothing about Hepburn, nothing at all. It was widely reported that I wrote *West Side Waltz* as a vehicle for Hepburn. Had I agreed to interviews, I would have quashed that and said that it was a pretty lousy vehicle play. I'll tell you something: I still don't know why Hepburn is doing it in that regard. I know 5 percent of why she's doing it. It's because the artist in her wants to be accepted as a real actress beyond her celebrity, which is greater now than ever. She wanted to play the character in my play and become that character for the audience.

Anyway, the truth is: to date I've seen only one Katharine Hepburn movie. . . .

(*Suspense hums cross-country through a long dramatic pause.*)

Which Katharine Hepburn movie?

Why mine, *On Golden Pond,* Ernest Thompson says. (*In the distance I imagine his glistening smile as vultures topple from telephone posts coast to coast.)*

Well thanks, Ernest.

Nice talking . . . Damn, there goes my other phone. . . . Goodby.

Source: Kevin Kelly, "The Importance of Being Ernest," in *Boston Globe*, April 11, 1982, p. 1.

SOURCES

Armstrong, Linda, "*On Golden Pond* Shimmers with Spectacular Performances," in the *New York Amsterdam News*, Vol. 96, No. 16, April 14, 2005, pp. 22–23.

Harris, Paul, Review of *On Golden Pond*, in *Variety*, Vol. 396, No. 8, October 11, 2004, p. 68.

Hirschhorn, Joel, Review of *On Golden Pond*, in *Daily Variety*, Vol. 271, No. 44, May 1, 2001, p. 12.

Hofler, Robert, "Return to 'Pond,'" in *Variety*, Vol. 398, No. 7, April 4, 2005, p. 79.

Kipling, Kay, "A Pleasant Reverie Awaits *On Golden Pond*," in the *Sarasota Herald Tribune*, May 23, 2000, Section E, p. 2.

Novick, Julius, Review of *On Golden Pond*, in *Back Stage*, Vol. 46, No. 16, April 21, 2005, p. 48.

On Golden Pond, Universal Pictures, 1981.

Thompson, Ernest, *On Golden Pond*, Dramatists Play Service, 1979, pp. 3, 5, 13, 15, 18, 20–21, 35, 43, 58, 60, 62.

———, *On Golden Pond*, Dodd, Mead, 1979, p. 79.

FURTHER READING

Bigsby, C. W. E., ed., *Modern American Drama, 1945–2000*, Cambridge University Press, 2000.

This book provides comments and insights from America's best-loved modern playwrights, including Tennessee Williams, Eugene O'Neill, Edward Albee, and Arthur Miller. Plays, biographies, and essays make this an important volume for anyone wanting to understand the breadth and importance of modern drama.

Mamet, David, *Three Uses for the Knife: On the Nature and Purpose of Drama*, Vintage, 2000.

David Mamet, one of the foremost playwrights of the contemporary stage, offers three essays about the centrality of drama to human nature. He discusses the theory of drama and gives experienced insights into the craft of writing plays.

Nielsen, Linda, *Embracing Your Father: How to Build the Relationship You Always Wanted with Your Dad*, McGraw-Hill, 2004.

This how-to book provides daughters with the support, awareness, and encouragement they need to reach out to their fathers and build stronger, healthier relationships. She reviews the importance of the father-daughter relationship, along with a review of the common conflicts.

O'Reilly, Evelyn M., *Decoding the Cultural Stereotypes about Aging: New Perspectives on Aging Talk and Aging Issues*, Garland Publishing, 1997.

O'Reilly presents the results of her study about the aging process and the place of the elderly in American culture. Considering aging issues from the perspective of the elderly, she explores issues such as language, conflict, and social engagement.

Rent

JONATHAN LARSON

1996

When the musical *Rent* first appeared off Broadway in 1996, it immediately became a hit. Tragically, Jonathan Larson could not appreciate the overwhelming success of his play, since he had died on the evening of the final dress rehearsal. His death made the play that much more poignant in its focus on the diseased and drug-addicted young people of New York City's East Village. Still, in its examination of the lifestyles of the young men and women who inhabit the slums of the Village, the play becomes a celebration of life and the heroic struggle to survive. It was published by William Morrow in 1997.

Rent is loosely based on the Italian composer Giacomo Puccini's *La bohème*, an opera that focuses on the experiences of bohemian artists living in Paris at the end of the nineteenth century. Larson places his play in New York City a century later than Puccini's work. It opens on Christmas Eve and chronicles the characters' lives over the course of one year. The fast-paced production moves through a collection of vignettes that are united by a rent strike against the landlord of the run-down tenement where some of the characters live. During the course of the play, the characters protest the landlord's plans to evict them and face other obstacles that are more difficult to fight, including drug addiction, AIDS, and troubled relationships. The characters do not overcome all their problems, but those that they do overcome provide them with a sustaining sense of community and the will to endure.

Jonathan Larson AP/Wide World Photos

AUTHOR BIOGRAPHY

Jonathan Larson was born in Mount Vernon, New York, on February 4, 1960, to Allan and Nanette Larson. His family loved the arts, and Larson received much support and encouragement from them. The house was often filled with music, including his piano playing, which he was able to pick up by ear. In high school, Larson was called the "piano man" by his fellow students. While attending White Plains High School, Larson was very active in the music and drama departments. He became friends with a fellow student named Matt O'Grady, who would later be the inspiration for many of his characters as well as for the writing of *Rent*, Larson's most notable and only published work. In 1978, Larson attended the acting conservatory at Adelphi University on Long Island, New York, on a four-year, full-tuition merit scholarship. At Adelphi, he wrote his first musical, Sacrimoralimmortality, an unpublished work that attacked the hypocrisy of the Christian Right. He also began a relationship with Victoria Leacock, a woman who later worked on the production of two of his (unpublished) plays, tick . . . tick . . . BOOM! (an adaptation of his one-man show, 30/90) and Superbia.

After receiving a BFA with honors from Adelphi, Larson moved to New York City under the advisement of his mentor, the composer Stephen Sondheim, who told Larson that there are more starving actors than starving composers in the world. Larson lived a bohemian lifestyle in New York, where he took jobs waiting tables and gathered material for his works. He had a series of roommates, more than thirty different people, to help him pay the rent. He later incorporated these roommates into his works as characters. Paula Span, in her biographical notes on Larson for the *Washington Post*, notes that Larson "harbored a serious, soaring ambition." James Nicola, artistic director of the New York Theatre Workshop, where Larson developed and staged *Rent*, called this the need "to somehow reunite popular music and theater, which divorced somewhere back in the '40s." As Nicola put it, "This might be the guy who could do it."

In 1989, Larson was approached by the playwright Billy Aronson, who asked him to collaborate on a new version of Giacomo Puccini's *La bohème*, an opera depicting the lives of struggling artists trying to cope with poverty and disease. The collaboration did not last long, however, and the two men parted ways. In 1991, after Larson had seen many of his friends diagnosed as HIV-positive, he decided to take up the project again, this time on his own. He named the new version of the play *Rent*.

Larson died of an undiagnosed aortic aneurysm on January 25, 1996, the night before *Rent* was to premiere. *Rent* became a huge success, posthumously winning Larson the 1996 Pulitzer Prize for Drama and four Tony Awards. His other works have earned him six Drama Desk Awards and three Obies.

PLOT SUMMARY

Act 1

Rent opens on Christmas Eve at Mark and Roger's apartment. They are freezing, since there is no heat in the building. The landlord has turned it off. Mark is filming with a movie camera, and he explains that he is shooting without a script, to see if anything comes of it. He notes that Roger has not played his guitar for a year and that he has just gone through drug withdrawal. Roger's dream is to write one great song.

Mark's mother leaves a message on the telephone answering machine, expressing sorrow over the fact that Mark's girlfriend, Maureen, has left him. Mark and Roger's friend Collins rings the doorbell, but before he is let in, two thugs mug him. Benny, their landlord, then calls, asking when Mark and Roger will be paying him rent, which they have not paid for a year. After Benny inquires about Maureen, Mark tells him that she has left him for a woman named Joanne. Benny warns that if Mark and Roger do not pay the rent, he will evict them.

Mark wonders how anyone can "document real life / When real life's getting more / Like fiction each day." Roger asks how a person can write a song when he has lost his creativity, and Mark adds that they are hungry and cold. They both wonder how they will pay the rent. Mark, along with half the actors, asks how a person can "leave the past behind / When it keeps finding ways to get to your heart." With the other half of the company, Roger asks how someone can "connect in an age / Where strangers, landlords, lovers / Your own blood cells betray." Both Mark and Roger note that one way to connect is through artistic expression, Mark using his camera and Roger his guitar. The entire company then declares that they are "not gonna pay rent."

Angel appears on the street and offers to help Collins after he is mugged. When the two discover that they both have AIDS, they decide to go together to a support group meeting. Upstairs, Roger declares that he has wasted opportunities in the past and is determined to write one good song "that rings true." Mimi, a neighbor, enters, shivering, with a candle. As they talk, she insists that she dropped a bag of heroin somewhere in the apartment. Mimi tells Roger that she is a stripper, and Roger admits that he used to be a junkie. He finds the bag and puts it in his pocket, but Mimi grabs it on her way out.

After returning from the support meeting, Collins introduces Angel to Mark and Roger on the street. Angel is dressed up in Santa drag and clutching twenty-dollar bills in each hand. Benny appears and tells a homeless man to get out of his way, the very sort of callous attitude that Maureen will soon be protesting in her performance demonstration outside his building, where she, Mark, Roger, and Mimi live. Benny tries to bribe Roger and Mark, insisting that he will help their careers if they can get Maureen to stop her protest. Later, after Joanne reveals that Maureen has not been faithful to her, Mark and Joanne sympathize with each other for loving someone who is too egocentric to return their affections.

MEDIA ADAPTATIONS

- In 1996, Dreamworks produced an audio compact disk of the play, featuring the original Broadway cast.
- A film version of *Rent*, featuring almost all of the original Broadway cast, was released by Columbia Pictures in 2005.

When Mimi returns to Roger's apartment, he tells her that if she's "looking for romance," she should "come back another day." He explains, "Long ago—you might've lit up my heart / But the fire's dead—ain't never gonna start." Angel tells Collins that he will be Collins's "shelter," and they pledge their love to each other.

Maureen enacts a protest performance, criticizing Benny, who, she claims, has abandoned his principles "to live as a lapdog to a wealthy daughter of the revolution." After Benny insists that the bohemian lifestyle that they have all been living is dead, the cast sings "La Vie Bohème," an anthem to that lifestyle. Roger invites Mimi to a party after the performance but then ignores her. When Mimi asks whether she has done something wrong, Roger apologizes, explaining that he has "baggage" and that he is a "disaster." Maureen's performance triggers a riot, which Mark captures on film as Mimi and Roger embrace. In response to the protest, Benny locks them out of the apartment building.

Act 2

On New Year's Eve, Mimi announces that she is going to get off drugs and go back to school. Later that night, Maureen tries to persuade Joanne, who has broken off their relationship, to come back. Maureen insists that she will "learn to behave" and asks for "one more chance." That same night, after seeing some of the footage of the riot, a representative from a television newsmagazine leaves a message on Mark's answering machine, offering him a job. He says that the show is "*so sleazy*" but considers the offer anyway.

Benny apologizes for locking them out of the building, hinting that Mimi influenced his decision to let them back in by seducing him, which Mimi angrily denies. The main characters conclude that friendship depends on love and trust and on "not denying emotion," and Mimi and Roger embrace. When Roger goes back into his apartment, Mimi's dealer appears on the street and hands her a bag of heroin.

By Valentine's Day, Roger and Mimi have been living together for two months, and Maureen and Joanne are back together. When Joanne accuses Maureen of flirting with another woman, Maureen insists that Joanne take her as she is. The two argue and decide they will split up once again. That spring, Roger determines to break off his relationship with Mimi and go to Santa Fe to write his one great song before he dies of AIDS. In the fall, Angel dies, and the cast mourns his death.

On Halloween, Mark meets the producer for the TV newsmagazine, after he has signed a contract to work for them. He is conflicted about his new job, admitting that he has sold out to corporate America. After Angel's memorial service that day, Roger tells Mimi that he is leaving for Santa Fe. Later, Mimi and Joanne discuss their troubled relationships, and each wishes that she had someone who would truly love her for who she is. In the next scene Mark quits his job and plans to finish his film.

On Christmas Eve, Roger returns, declaring that he has written his song at last. Maureen and Joanne appear in the apartment, carrying Mimi, who is dying of AIDS. As Roger begins to play his song, "Your Eyes," which Mimi inspired, her fever breaks, and the two declare their love for each other.

CHARACTERS

Benjamin Coffin III

Their former roommate and present rent-gouging landlord, Benjamin Coffin III, wants to raze the building in which Roger, Mark, Mimi, and Maureen live. His aim is to gentrify the neighborhood by pushing out the bohemian element. He tries to appear generous when he tells Roger and Mark that he let their rent slide for one year, but his mercenary side soon emerges.

After Benny married into a wealthy, upper-class family, his father-in-law sold him the building and the neighboring lot, which he hopes to turn into a cyberstudio. Roger points out his callous materialism by declaring, "You can't quietly wipe out an entire tent city / Then watch 'It's a Wonderful Life' on TV." But Benny responds that if they want to write songs and produce films, as they claim, they will understand, and if they do not, he will kick them out. When Benny tries to bribe Mark and Roger into persuading Maureen to stop her protest, he reveals that he will do anything to succeed. By the end of the play, he has softened, as evidenced when he decides to pay for Angel's funeral.

Mark Cohen

Mark, an aspiring filmmaker, narrates the play as he films the lives of his friends. He insists that he can survive the bleakness of his environment through his art. It soon becomes apparent, though, that he is more comfortable viewing the world through his lens than in actively engaging in it. At the beginning of the play, the audience discovers that Maureen has left him for Joanne, which has made him bitter.

Mark, along with Roger, becomes defiant and declares that he will not pay the rent when Benny presses them, insisting instead that he will fight the system. However, when his film of the riot caused by Maureen's protest performance garners him a lucrative job offer with a sleazy network television newsmagazine, he briefly joins the system he criticizes to ensure himself financial stability. By the end of the play, however, he regains his values and gives up the job.

Tom Collins

Tom Collins, a black computer genius, teacher, and anarchist who has been expelled from MIT, is the intellectual voice of the company. In the opening scene, he is mugged, reflecting the harsh reality of the world in which the characters live. He is brave enough to allow himself to fall in love with Angel, knowing that since both of them are infected with HIV, their relationship will not have much of a future.

Roger Davis

Roger has been off heroin for six months, but he is infected with HIV. His main goal in life is to write one great song before he dies, but he has not been able to play his guitar in a year, fearing that he has lost his creative energy. He falls in love with Mimi but is too afraid to commit to her, knowing that she also is infected with HIV.

Roger has already lost the woman he loved to the disease, after she committed suicide. He tells

Mimi, "Long ago—you might've lit up my heart / But the fire's dead—ain't never gonna start." In an effort to protect himself and to find the spark he needs to write his song, he leaves. He eventually returns, however, with a song of which he is proud, saying that Mimi has inspired his creativity. As he sings the song to Mimi, her fever breaks, and the two are reunited.

Joanne Jefferson

Joanne, a lawyer from an upper-class New York family, is in love with Maureen, who is unable to commit to her. Her character, which does not develop during the play, serves as a complication for Mark after Maureen leaves him for her.

Maureen Johnson

Maureen, a bisexual performance artist and rock singer, protests Benny's renovation of the building with a performance piece that highlights his insensitivity toward the homeless. Her performance rallies the tenants, but her selfishness is displayed in her relationships with others. Maureen is a self-involved hedonist who resists anyone's attempts to persuade her to commit to a relationship. She has cheated on both Mark and Joanne. Although she and Joanne reconcile at the end of the play, there is no evidence to suggest that her character has changed enough to ensure that the two will be able to work out their problems in the long term.

Mimi Marquez

Mimi Marquez works in a strip club and struggles with her addiction to heroin, which has resulted in her contraction of HIV. She falls in love with Roger, who is unable to commit to a relationship with her. Still, she is sympathetic to his reluctance, as she expresses when she sings to him: "So let's find a bar / So dark we forget who we are / And all the scars from the / Nevers and maybes die." When she declares to Roger after he rebuffs her, "I live this moment / As my last / There's only us / There's only this," she voices the ultimate spirit of the play.

Angel Dumont Schunard

The most generous and selfless character, Angel hands out money to the neighborhood while dressed in Santa drag. He first offers comfort to Collins by inviting him to an AIDS support group and later gives his love to Collins, along with all that he has, while declaring, "today for you—tomorrow for me." His death, brought about by complications from AIDS, is mourned by all of the characters and inspires them to live each day to the fullest.

THEMES

Betrayal

The characters must deal with an overwhelming sense of betrayal—by their bodies, by the materialistic society in which they live, and by people they have trusted. Their bodies betray them after they contract HIV, slowly shutting down as their immune systems weaken and allow them to fall prey to various illnesses. Their society has let them down in its promotion of its vision of the American dream, which depends solely on upward social mobility and financial gains. The artists of the East Village are ignored in this system, unless they sell out to soulless corporations, such as the sleazy television newsmagazine that hires Mark to exploit the plight of the homeless for profit. One of the homeless people whom Mark films makes him realize that he has compromised his art when he angrily declares, "I don't need no [g—— d——] help / From some bleeding heart cameraman / My life's not for you to / Make a name for yourself on!" He notes that Mark is just trying to use him "to kill his guilt." He has bought in to the same system as has Benny, who heartlessly pushes the homeless out of his way in his plans to change the neighborhood so that he can profit.

The most damaging betrayals come from individuals once trusted, like Benny, who exploits his friendship with Mark and Roger to gain success. After he marries into a rich, upper-class family, he becomes caught up in the materialistic system that measures success only through monetary gain. He tries to get Mark and Roger to persuade Maureen to stop her protest performance, enlisting their help in his capitalistic vision, and he threatens to evict them if they do not comply. Other betrayals are more personal. Roger feels betrayed by his girlfriend, who, unable to face life with AIDS, kills herself. He, in turn, betrays Mimi's trust when he leaves her, unable to allow himself to open up to another possibility of loss. Maureen betrays Mark and Joanne as the pressures of living in the East Village turn her into a self-serving hedonist.

La Vie Bohème

The characters lead a bohemian lifestyle as an escape from the harsh realities of their lives and as

TOPICS FOR FURTHER STUDY

- Read the libretto for Puccini's *La bohème*, on which *Rent* is based, and compare and contrast its characters and themes. In a short presentation to the class, discuss these comparisons and contrasts and say why you think Larson made the changes that he did in his play.
- The film *A Chorus Line* is a screen version of a Broadway musical that focuses on the experiences of a group of actors. The narrative is similar to that of *Rent*, in that it weaves the stories together as they relate to one main event. Watch the film versions of both plays and analyze how the various stories are depicted on the screen. Stage a scene from each film that reflects a similar theme and one from each that illustrates two different themes.
- *Rent* has often been called "the *Hair* of the 1990s." *Hair* was a Broadway hit that illustrated the "hippie" generation that came of age during the 1960s. Explore how *Rent* depicts the Generation Xers who came of age during the 1990s. Write an essay that determines whether or not the play is an accurate reflection of American youth during this decade.
- Read biographical accounts of Larson's life. What elements of *Rent* are autobiographical? Develop a PowerPoint presentation of your findings and present it to the class.

a form of artistic expression and individual style. Angel expresses himself by dressing as a woman, Maureen through performance art, Mark through documentary film, and Roger through rock music. They define their bohemian attitude by rejecting convention and pretension. They scorn the materialistic society in which they live and replace it with a strong sense of individuality.

Mark expresses this sensibility when he sings, "Playing hooky, making something / Out of nothing, the need / To express— / To communicate, / To going against the grain." They align themselves with the avant guard, "To Absolut [Vodka]—to choice— / To the *Village Voice* [a counterculture newspaper]— / To any passing fad / To being an us—for once— / Instead of a them—."

STYLE

Musical Narrative

The narrative is driven by some thirty-five songs sung by fifteen cast members. The songs present the characters' poignant, emotional responses to their experiences. The most notable are Mark and Joanne's lament on having an egoist as a lover in "Tango Maureen"; Roger's struggle for artistic expression in "One Song Glory"; and his and Mimi's duets in "Light My Candle" and "I Should Tell You," which express their tentative love for each other. The songs communicate the characters' reactions to thwarted artistic expression, unrequited love, illness, and death. The lyrics and arrangements of the songs also reflect the ethnic diversity of the characters.

Fast Pacing

The play is fast paced, as it juxtaposes vignettes of the various characters' struggles to survive. This pacing reflects the energy and exuberance of the characters and reinforces their motivations: their desperate efforts to exist one more day with the threat of poverty and disease hanging over their heads and to live each day to the fullest. The fast cuts from scene to scene and from character to character underscore the sense that time is running out for them. Angel's death, placed in the middle of act 2, adds to the tension and helps force the characters to make important decisions about their futures.

HISTORICAL CONTEXT

Giacomo Puccini

Giacomo Puccini was born in Lucca, Italy, on December 22, 1858, and lived until 1924. He began his musical career at age fourteen, when he became an organist at local churches in Lucca, the same time that he began to work on his own compositions. *Manon Lescaut*, his first successful opera, for which he gained worldwide recognition, was produced at Turin in 1893. His next opera, *La bohème*, is considered to be his masterpiece. However, its unique conversational style, which includes a mixture of gaiety and tragedy, was not well received when it was first produced at Turin in 1896. A later opera, *Tosca*, gained much more favorable reviews when it was staged in 1900. Puccini continued his success with the production of *Madame Butterfly* in 1904. His operas, known for their beautiful melodies and intermingling of passion and tenderness, tragedy and despair, have cemented his reputation as one of Italy's finest composers.

AIDS

The promotion of traditional values in the 1980s received unexpected support as a result of the emergence of AIDS (acquired immune deficiency syndrome). The American public became aware of AIDS in the early 1980s, but the disease did not take center stage as a serious issue until the film star Rock Hudson died from an AIDS-related illness in 1985. By the beginning of the 1990s, the disease had spread rapidly, generating tremendous public fear, since no effective treatment had been discovered. Most of the early cases emerged in the homosexual population and among intravenous drug users, but by the 1990s, it had spread throughout the American populace. Racial and ethnic minorities have been hardest hit, representing approximately three-quarters of all new AIDS cases.

Because sexual contact is a primary method of infection, the sexual revolution that had begun in the 1960s was threatened. Still, abstention was not a guarantee of safety. The disease can lay dormant in the body for several years before symptoms become apparent. People can become infected long before they know that they have the disease. The rights that homosexuals had started to gain also were put in jeopardy as a result of the spread of AIDS. The conservative right wing blamed gays for the spread of the epidemic, some insisting that AIDS was God's punishment for their immoral lifestyles.

Since the 1980s, the incidence of AIDS has grown rapidly, and the spread of the disease shows no signs of slowing down. By 1994, an estimated half a million Americans had been infected with HIV, the virus that causes AIDS, and the same number had died from AIDS. About forty thousand people are infected each year, and some twenty thousand people die from complications associated with the disease. The epidemic is worse in developing countries such as Africa, where people have little access to medications that can help combat the disease. The major factor in the reduction of the transmission of AIDS is education. The public needs to be aware of the risks and learn about methods to prevent disease transmission. Sexual abstention, condom use, and needle-exchange programs have all proved to be effective preventive methods.

CRITICAL OVERVIEW

Laurie Winer, in her review for the *Los Angeles Times*, notes that "Larson garnered the kind of rave reviews that young, struggling composer-lyricists pray and dream for." She calls the play "muscular, chilling and energizing" and argues that "what would have been merely moving in *Rent* is made almost unbearable bittersweet" by Larson's untimely death following a lifelong struggle to realize his artistic vision. She concludes, "*Rent* is a memorial service as a work of art, clearly and authentically created in love."

In his review for the *Wall Street Journal*, Donald Lyons adds to the chorus of praises for the play, claiming, "It's the best new musical since the 1950s." He declares that it presents itself with "clarity," "force," and "crisp definition." Commenting on the play's construction, he writes that it appears that "we're about to see a rehearsal, and what we do experience has the raw, ragged, slightly unfinished, excited, urgent feel of a late but coalescing run-through: This seeming artlessness is a sophisticated achievement."

Patrick Pacheco, in the *Los Angeles Times*, concludes that the play is "a raw and exuberant celebration of bohemian East Village artists . . . living on the edge." He claims that the topical subject matter, focusing on "the prevalence of violence and HIV . . . suffuses the musical with the fragility of life, the theme of Puccini's opera."

Anthony Rapp and Adam Pascal in a 1998 production of Rent © Donald Cooper/Photostage. Reproduced by permission

In his review of the play for the *Washington Post*, Chip Crews declares, "Bristling with energy and assurance, *Rent* roars across the stage like an urban brush fire." This show, he states, "leads with its heart—an angry heart, taking up the cause of street people, AIDS patients, the young disaffected of a society that [in Larson's view] has no place for them." Crews, however, finds fault with the development of the plot, saying that "the emotions here are very raw, so raw that they're never fully articulated." He insists that the fragmented narrative in the second act "begins to seem arbitrary and capricious. The breakups are too easy, the battles too melodramatic." He adds, "It's a fast, muzzy conclusion that does no justice to the pain they have suffered."

James Gardner, in his article for the *National Review*, also finds fault with the plot, writing that the play is "pretty much the same old showbiz fare, though with almost formulaic inversions. Instead of boy meets girl, you now have girl meets girl and boy meets drag queen." The play, he says, "wants desperately to be taken as the anthem of some nonexistent youth movement. But the bohemian life glorified in *Rent* looks no more vital than it did before," in the 1960s production of the rock musical *Hair*.

In his mixed review of the play for *New Republic*, Robert Brustein writes that the play is "good-natured, fully energized, theatrically knowing and occasionally witty." At the same time, he concludes that "it is also badly manufactured, vaguely manipulative, drenched in self-pity and sentimental." Its characters, he argues, are "poorly constructed," and it fails "to penetrate very deeply beneath a colorful and exotic surface." While "*Rent* has a lot to say about the need for human communication," Brustein determines that this "warm-hearted" book "is basically superficial and unconvincing."

CRITICISM

Wendy Perkins

Perkins is a professor of American and English literature and film. In this essay, she examines the theme of survival in the play.

The nineteenth-century American writer Stephen Crane's celebrated short story "The Open Boat," which focuses on four men in a small dinghy struggling against the current to make it to shore, is often quoted as an apt expression of the tenets of naturalism, a literary movement in the late nineteenth and early twentieth centuries in France, the United States, and England. Writers included in this group, such as Crane, the Frenchman Émile Zola, and the American Theodore Dreiser, expressed in their works an environmental determinism that prevented their characters from exercising their free will and thus controlled their destinies. These authors wrote of a world beset by poverty and war at the beginning of the industrial age.

Environmental forces also threaten to rob individuals of their free will in Larson's celebrated play *Rent*, as they struggle to overcome grinding poverty and a new kind of war at the turn of the twentieth century: the war on AIDS. Yet Larson does not adopt the same naturalistic bleakness as do his predecessors at the previous *fin de siecle* (end of the century). While the play's vignettes present a grim portrait of inner-city life in the age of AIDS, its vision is tempered by the heroic endurance of its characters, who ultimately choose not only to survive but also to embrace each day.

Chip Crews, in his review for the *Washington Post*, declares that the play "bristl[es] with energy and assurance" as it "roars across the stage like an urban brush fire." This show, he claims, "leads with its heart—an angry heart, taking up the cause of street people, AIDS patients, the young disaffected of a society that [in Larson's view] has no place for them." The characters' most immediate fear is being thrown out of their tenement by their former friend and current landlord, Benny, who has traded his friendships for success. Even Mark is tempted by the lure of money when he is offered a job by a television newsmagazine and must decide whether to abandon his artistic principles for a secure economic future. AIDS, however, is the most devastating threat hanging over their lives. Four of the eight main characters have the disease, and all have mourned the loss of loved ones to it. Roger lost his girlfriend, and in the course of the play, Angel, who has just established a loving relationship with Collins, succumbs to the disease.

Drug addiction is another force that threatens to control the characters' futures. They are surrounded by dealers, who feed on their need to find solace from the harsh realities of their lives; some characters, like Mimi, are not strong enough to resist. Mimi, who is forced to work as a stripper in order to survive, turns to heroin to escape and is unable to break her addiction to it, especially since Roger is unable to allow her to get close to him. Commenting on Roger's inability to establish a relationship with Mimi, the company sings, "How do you leave the past behind / When it keeps finding ways to get to your heart?" His only goal now is to write one good song "that rings true," but his creative energies have been blocked by the pain he has suffered. He rejects Mimi's love for the same reason, declaring, "Looking for romance? / Come back another day."

The company warns him, "Give in to love / Or live in fear," but he cannot open himself to the possibility of more loss. The company expresses the difficulty that all of the characters have in allowing themselves to establish real connections with one another, knowing that these relationships will most likely not last, when they sing, "How can you connect in an age / Where strangers, landlords, lovers / Your own blood cells betray." Ultimately, however, the characters do connect with each other, as they realize that their relationships with others and the expression of their creativity are the only things that provide meaning. In her review for the

"THE CHARACTERS' MOST IMMEDIATE FEAR IS BEING THROWN OUT OF THEIR TENEMENT BY THEIR FORMER FRIEND AND CURRENT LANDLORD, BENNY, WHO HAS TRADED HIS FRIENDSHIPS FOR SUCCESS."

Los Angeles Times, Laurie Winer praises Larson's focus on "people clinging fiercely together while living a difficult, exhilarating existence on the brink of poverty." His characters unite in their distain for convention and pretension and in their celebration of their bohemian lifestyle, which enables them to freely express themselves. Winer concludes, "the Bohemians of *Rent* wear their youth, poverty and creativity like a cloak around them, shielding them from judgment by the enemy—anyone who has 'sold out' and has money."

The characters also come to understand that friendship "depends on true devotion" and "on not denying emotion." Collins and Angel had been brave enough to accomplish this, refusing to let the future determine how they will live their lives in the present. The selfless Angel, whose anthem is "today for you—tomorrow for me," initiates his union with Collins when he declares that he will be Collins's shelter, wrapping him in love. Collins reciprocates, knowing that their relationship will provide them with "a new lease" on life.

Love also ultimately proves to be an inspiration for Roger, who returns and declares that he has found his song, inspired by Mimi. His declaration of love enables her to find the strength to survive at the end of the play, which ends with a call to *carpe diem* (live for today). In the closing scene, the company sings "No other road no other way / No day but today." In the final moments of the play, Larson reveals to the audience the way in which seemingly overwhelming environmental forces can be checked through the saving power of faith: faith

WHAT DO I READ NEXT?

- *Hair* (1968), with book and lyrics by Gerome Ragni and James Rado, is considered to be the youth anthem of the 1960s, just as *Rent* is considered to be an expression of the 1990s. The play is a rock musical that communicates the attitudes and behavior of young Americans who became caught up in the counterculture atmosphere of the age.
- *Bright Lights, Big City* (1984), by Jay McInerney, chronicles the lives of young New Yorkers who have become caught up in the corporate world and subsequently discover the meaninglessness of their existence.
- James Joyce's classic coming-of-age novel *A Portrait of the Artist as a Young Man* (1925) follows a young Dublin man's quest for artistic expression.
- *AIDS in the Twenty-First Century: Disease and Globalization*, by Tony Barnett and Alan Whiteside (2002), provides a detailed study of how the disease has spread not only in America but all over the world.

in self, faith in the creative spirit, faith in love, and faith in the present. As Winer concludes, "'Rent' is a rousing anthem to living each day as it comes."

Source: Wendy Perkins, Critical Essay on *Rent*, in *Drama for Students*, Thomson Gale, 2006.

John Istel

In the following essay-interview, Istel looks back one year previous to when Larson was alive and enjoying the fruits of his labor. In Larson's interview with Istel, Larson expounds on musical theater and his musical influences and style.

Some 525,600 minutes ago, Jonathan Larson was listening to a sing-through rehearsal of *J.P. Morgan Saves the Nation* in a gutted, empty floor of a New York City Financial District office building. He was there by the confluence of talent, accident and perseverance that typifies most theatrical endeavors. Larson was offered the assignment—to compose music for En Garde Arts's outdoor production of Jeffrey M. Jones's postmodern pageant detailing the life of the famous financier of the title—only a few months before, after Jones's longtime collaborator, Dan Moses Schreier, dropped out. Artistic director Annie Hamburger suggested Larson as a replacement composer, after seeing (and hearing) the workshop production of *Rent* at New York Theatre Workshop.

For Larson it was the best of times. *Rent,* his rock version of *La Boheme,* was now scheduled for a full production in NYTW's upcoming season, and Anne Bogart had just commissioned a new composition for her next project. His children's video, *Away We Go,* was scheduled to be released in 1996. And here I was, a freelance writer for the *Village Voice,* invited to attend rehearsals, check in on a rainy tech dress and visit the recording studio where, with his arranger Steve Skinner, Larson mixed his music. He was clearly a man with a plan, bicycling around town to drop off the latest version of the finale he'd written for *J.P. Morgan*, calling to sing the latest addition to the score, written in a frenzy the night before the first preview. He fed me demo tapes and scripts like food. And in our interviews, he detailed his life's mission.

Last summer was Larson's 13th out of college, and after several modest but essential grants, awards and workshops, *J.P. Morgan* would be the first opportunity for large numbers of theatregoers and (especially important to Larson) critics to hear his practicum on how he planned to save the American musical theatre. The score for *J.P. Morgan* contains Larson's musical recipe: employ a full-range of pop vernaculars, from Sousa to soul to Seattle-flavored, electric-guitar-heavy grunge, mix them carefully with Skinner's help, and have them sung,

Full-cast shot from Rent © Jack, Robbie/Corbis

with gusto, by voices that haven't been unnecessarily vacuumed of emotion by excessive conservatory training.

In the "Notes on Design" to *Superbia,* an as-yet-unproduced futuristic parable which predates *Rent,* Larson states his goals succinctly: "The sound design is as important a factor as costumes and sets. The music mix must be clean, current and digitally enhanced—reflecting today's standards in pop music rather than 'Broadway' sound." However, as he himself made clear in our discussions, these stylistic concerns must at all times be in service of the story's narrative and the emotional development of each character.

Anyone who can manipulate multiple integers can do the math. Multiply the 60 minutes in an hour times the 24 in a day. Multiply that figure, 1,440, by 365 days. Whether you did it on a napkin in your kitchen at two a.m. or in your head on the subway to work, you've just done what Jonathan Larson did in the process of creating "Seasons of Love," the second-act song, quoted above, that serves as the heart and soul *Rent.* But as Larson asked, how do you calculate the ineffable—the worth of a person's life? And to extend the implications of his question: On what Richter Scale do we measure the impact of a work of art?

You can certainly tally the Pulitzer, Tony, Obie, Drama Desk and other awards. The trade magazines update the number of performances, the box-office gross, the amounts offered by Hollywood for the film rights, the sum David Geffen paid to produce the cast recording. You can measure the column inches of newsprint and front covers that *Rent* has inspired. But such calculations have been tragically complicated by Larson's death the night before *Rent*'s first preview in January.

In the last few months, I have often wondered what the audience and critical reception of *Rent* would have been if that aneurysm hadn't developed in Larson's aorta. Were that the case, you obviously wouldn't be reading a year-old interview with him—Larson would have been more than willing to give an update on his mission.

More important, the whole endeavor of *Rent*—which most theatregoers now know relocates

"I'M A ROCK-AND-ROLLER AT HEART AND I'M INFLUENCED BY CONTEMPORARY MUSIC. THERE IS A JONATHAN LARSON STYLE, BUT I CAN'T TOTALLY DESCRIBE IT."

Puccini's famous doomed romance to the East Village of New York, with its two main love interests, Roger and Mimi, straggling against the ticking of their HIV-positive clocks—would have been treated as Larson intended it to be, as a work of art, a stage drama, a fiction, a compelling critique of traditional definitions of "family values." It may have been dismissed as facile, derivative and exploitative of its subject matter, or it may have been seen as a vital, innovative rock opera that heralded a bright future for the composer. Either way, or somewhere in between, the composer's literal presence would have forced critics to actually listen to what he had to say.

But in article after article, Larson's real-life tragedy is inextricably linked to the onstage drama. A typical review details the circumstances of Larson's death, mentions the "important" entertainment industry people who were spotted in the audience, and ends with a cursory examination of the musical itself, commenting on the parallels with Puccini or the structural flabbiness of the second act. Peter Marks in a *New York Times* article in February, shortly after *Rent*'s debut at New York Theatre Workshop, made this conflation clear: "Until a few weeks ago, hardly anyone had heard of the musical. Then its 35-year-old composer and librettist, Jonathan Larson, died suddenly of an aortic aneurysm on the night of the final dress rehearsal. And now, buoyed by waves of glowing reviews and strong word of mouth, *Rent* is the hottest show in town."

The paper of record was particularly prone to hyperbole, devoting practically an entire Sunday arts section to the musical. Frank Rich even used his op-ed column to stand in as musical theatre champion and lift the victorious arm of the latest contender: "*Rent* is all the critics say it is.... It takes the very people whom politicians now turn into scapegoats for our woes—the multicultural, the multisexual, the homeless, the sick—and, without sentimentalizing them or turning them into ideological symbols or victims, lets them revel in their joy, their capacity for love . . . all in a ceaseless outpouring of melody."

Larson, so eager to share his passion and music with the critics, would have appreciated this enthusiasm and validation of his life's work. Yet, I'd venture, he'd be troubled by the fact that few tried to really listen—to hear what he was trying to say. And as he says in the interview, he felt that writing a play or musical without a burning need to articulate some important concern was a waste of time.

While some lauded the grittiness and the authenticity of his musical, it's clear Larson was a severe romantic and shameless sentimentalist. After all, his answer to his own question:—"How do you measure the life of a woman or a man?"—was simple: love. His East Village Romantics are Rodgers and Hammerstein versions—they forsake their death wish and dissipation, join support groups and find love in the unlikeliest circumstances. And, in the most notable departure from Puccini, Mimi rises up from her death bed, her fever broken, her recovery assured. Ah, the American musical ending! This is pure art, as in artifice, and Larson, so well-versed in the musical and structural materiel of the genre in which he worked, knew it. How can Rich claim that Larson doesn't "sentimentalize" the characters? Of course, they're sentimentalized. Sentimentality is at the heart of every Rodgers and Hammerstein hit, and it's the pulse behind all the characters in *Rent.*

Larson's ability to infuse lyrical, wide-eyed optimism into the darker realities of contemporary life—homelessness, AIDS, dog-eat-dog capitalism—is exactly what helped move the musical uptown. In the past three decades, many films and plays have dealt with such themes with far higher levels of credibility—the Living Theater's 1959 production of *The Connection* comes immediately to mind. *The Normal Heart* conveyed the anger and frustration of living with AIDS more powerfully. *Angels in America* gave it a deeper, more insightful socio-historical context.

In his *New Republic* review, Robert Brustein perceived some of these criticisms, as he decried what he saw as sloppy sentimentalism and the way AIDS was used for "mawkish purposes." However, when he wrote, "Larson has been hailed for creating the downtown equivalent of Bohemian life. I fear he has only created another fashion. . . . Larson's New Age Bohemians display nothing but their lifestyles," Brustein was aiming at the wrong target. It was *Rolling Stone, Time Out* and the *Voice,* not Larson, that reduced *Rent* to fashion spreads. Tamed by the proscenium frame, these "lifestyles"—which existed before *Rent*—were suddenly ripe for the co-opting.

Personally, watching a chorus line of homeless people shuffling in a dance step on Broadway was acutely disturbing to me. However, it's clear Larson did have a vision with social and political implications. He was deeply disturbed by a society that could become obsessed with an exclusionary notion of "family values" while alienating itself from the fundamental human values of community, caring and love. Society's embrace of superficiality and the power of mass media are the culprits.

But Larson was faced with a profound paradox: how to condemn the pervasiveness of the media and the alienating effects of technology while exploiting their dramatic possibilities. *Rent,* like his early work *Superbia,* is a constant comment on how technology can alienate us. Take the phone messages from Mom that we hear punctuating the score; the way Mark, a documentary film maker, continually puts his camera between himself and those closest to him; the irony of his ex-girlfriend Maureen's performance art piece. Solo work like hers has been traditionally one of the most potent tools in postmodern theatre to burst the isolating media bubble we live in. Yet Maureen's piece can't take place until Mark fixes the sound system.

Larson's concerns about the society's slide into superficiality were evident in *Superbia* (the only other musical he'd written book, music and lyrics for), which he was still pushing to get produced when I talked to him (it had received a workshop production at Playwrights Horizons in 1988).

The futuristic setting is populated by two classes of people—the Ins and Outs. This Brave New World was founded by Mick Knife, a rock star, and is now controlled by the Master Babble Articulator, or MBA. It all seems a *Tommy*-like metaphor for how rock music becomes co-opted and audiences become slaves to fashion. Act 2 opens (ironically, considering the fate of *Rent* in the media) with an Award Show to name the new "Face of the Year." And at the heart of his musical, of course, is a romantic Romeo-and-Juliet like love affair between an In and an Out. Their one-night fling, however, is televised, like everything in this world. As Larson writes in his own synopsis, "The result is instant celebrity."

Larson's awareness of the perils of fame didn't ease his hunger for recognition. After my *Voice* piece was published a year ago he called to express appreciation for describing his one-man manifesto. I had made one mistake, though, that he corrected. I implied that Mimi died in *Rent.* "She doesn't die in my version," he reminded me. And that's the ultimate tragedy: that we can't rewrite his story to make a happy ending. The sad fact that Larson's demise is irreversible highlights just how far his art diverged from his life.

An Interview with Jonathan Larson On Pop Music in the Theatre

[*John Istel*]: *Do you see your music as part of the American musical theatre tradition?*

[Jonathan Larson]: My whole thing is that American popular music used to come from theatre and Tin Pan Alley, and there's no reason why contemporary theatre can't reflect real contemporary music, and why music that's recorded or that's made into a video cannot be from a show. Popular music being a part of theatre ended with *Jesus Christ Superstar* and *Hair* and rock musicals in the late 1960s. A number of things happened. One was that there had been singers in the '40s, '50s, even early '60s, who would sing anybody's material—Frank Sinatra, what have you. Then, beginning with the Beatles, you had songwriters and bands who were singing only their own material. So you didn't have that venue for theatre music to be popular.

What do you think about Randy Newman's latest musical project [Faust] *and other pop stars working in the theatre?*

New York magazine ran this article [about what was killing Broadway]. The last part had a 12-step program—12 ways to renovate Broadway. Number 12 was bringing new music to Broadway. They were getting all excited about Randy Newman, and Prince evidently is thinking about it, and Paul Simon is working on a new musical. That's exciting if they're successful and if they bring younger people to the theatre who wouldn't normally go. But it's almost going backwards to have a musical that is songwriter-generated because of the traps they can fall into.

They're used to a number of things: not collaborating, not making changes and writing in their own voice. There's so much that Rodgers and Hammerstein and Sondheim have taught us about how to advance plot and character and theme in a song. Often, you get contemporary pop writers who know how to write a verse and a chorus, but they don't necessarily know how to write an inner monologue where a character goes through a change by the end of the song so the plot and story continues.

On those messy concept albums like the Who's Tommy *or the Kinks's* Soap Opera *there's so much left to the imagination or that isn't spelled out because you don't have to physicalize it.*

Right. And that was the problem with *Tommy.* At least Pete Townshend knew he had to work with a book writer, Des McAnuff, who was a theatre person. Even if I don't agree with the story they chose to tell in *Tommy,* which was this sort of return-to-family-values thing at the end, at least he understood the concept of collaborating. It's easy to write 18 songs, but it's not easy to write a two-and-a-half hour piece that has an arc.

On the Maturation of a Musical Writer

What's Jonathan Larson's *style?*

I'm a rock-and-roller at heart and I'm influenced by contemporary music. There is a Jonathan Larson style, but I can't totally describe it.

Who were your favorite composers?

Well, I loved Pete Townshend growing up, and I loved the old Police and Prince—or whatever his name is—he's brilliant. I love Kurt Cobain and Liz Phair. Beatles. And in the theatre—Leonard Bernstein, Sondheim. I absolutely love them.

Were you a theatre major in college?

Yeah. I was an actor, too. I had a four-year acting scholarship to Adelphi. Adelphi was a lousy place to go to school in the sense that it's in suburbia and that's where I grew up. But it was run by a disciple of Robert Brustein's named Jacques Burdick, who basically made an undergraduate version of Yale Drama School. And I was mature enough coming out of high school to appreciate it. I got to do everything from Ionesco to Shakespeare to original plays or musicals.

The best thing, though, was that, like Yale, they had four original cabarets a year, and they were always looking for people to write them. So by the end of my time there I had written eight or ten shows. And I found that I liked it as much as performing. I had a skill doing it. When I came to New York, I had gotten my Equity card because I had done summer stock. I started going to cattle calls, but at the same time I had my first musical which was a really bad rock version of *1984,* based on Orwell. It was getting a lot of attention and serious consideration—basically because the year was 1982. We came close to getting the rights, but it was a good thing we didn't because it was not a very good show. But it was my first real attempt to write a big show.

At Adelphi we wrote the original Nick and Nora Charles musical—it was called *The Steak Tartar Caper*—10 years before they did it on Broadway. We did *ShoGun Cabaret*—we were way ahead of our time.

Then, when I came to New York, Sondheim was always a big mentor. He encouraged me to be a writer as opposed to being an actor, and suggested that I join ASCAP and do the musical theatre workshop. ASCAP was sort of a 12-step meeting for people who write musicals, but you get to show your work to top-notch professionals in the field.

Two things amazed me at ASCAP: One was that I had written 100 songs by then, had seen them in productions, and had seen them work or not work with audiences. If Peter Stone, head of the Dramatists Guild, or Sondheim, said something that I disagreed with, I said, "I disagree and I'll tell you why." Some of my peers, and those even older, had never had their work performed. And they would be like, "Okay, I'll just throw out my project. You're right—it sucks."

On the Genesis of 'Rent'

Ira Weitzman put me in touch with Billy Aronson who had an idea—years ago—to do a modern-day *La Boheme.* Billy's done stuff at Ensemble Studio Theatre and with Showtime and TV, and he's a sort of Woody Allen type and he wanted to do a modern-day *La Boheme,* set it on the Upper West Side, and make it about Yuppies and funny. I said, "That doesn't interest me, but if you want to set it in Tompkins Square Park and do it seriously, I like that idea a lot." He had never spent any time in the East Village, but he wrote a libretto. He wanted to write the book and lyrics, and I was to set a few of the songs to music and see what everyone's response was. I also came up with the rifle of *Rent.* So I wrote "Rent," "Santa Fe" and "I Should Tell You."

I found different types of contemporary music for each character, so the hero [*Roger*] in Rent sings in a Kurt Cobain-esque style and the street transvestite sings like De La Soul. And there's a Tom Waits-esque character. The American musical has always been taking contemporary music and using it to tell a story. So I'm just trying to do that.

We made a demo tape and everyone loved the concepts, loved the music—but when they read the

Most of the original Broadway cast appeared in the 2005 film version of Rent Sony Pictures/The Kobal Collection/Bray, Phil

accompanying libretto, they weren't too strong on it. So we just put it on hold. I loved the concept, but I didn't have a burning reason to go back to it. And then I did.

Two years later a number of my friends, men and women, were finding out they were HIV-positive. I was devastated, and needed to do something. I decided to ask Billy if he would let me continue by myself, and he was very cool about it.

I am the kind of person that when I write my own work, I have something I need to say. It surprises me that in musicals, even plays today, sometimes I don't see what the impetus was, other than thinking it was a good smart idea or it could make them some money or something.

On Composing in the American Musical Theatre

What's it like making a living as a composer in the theatre these days?

Well the old thing about how you can make a killing but you can't make a living is absolutely true. I'm proof of that. Now, I have the ability to compete trying to write jingles, trying to do other kinds of music that makes money, and I haven't put myself out there. My feeling is that it's not what I want to do, and I would be competing with guys who do want to. So I'm just working on musicals—it's like this huge wall, and I'm chipping away at it with a screwdriver. I just keep making a little more headway. I've had a lot of very generous grants, but they all go to the play. I get a little stipend, but I can't live off the commissions.

I work two days a week waiting tables at Moondance in Soho. I've been there for eight-and-a-half years but I don't mind it. In fact, I love the customers—the regulars are fantastic. The management and the owner totally support me. I can take a couple of months off when I need to do a show, come back, and I've actually gotten work there twice. There was a little piece on me in *New York* magazine a few years ago, and one of the regular customers who I'd known for years, Bob Golden, brought it up and said, "I saw that you were in *New York* magazine and that you wrote for *Sesame Street.*" I said, "Yeah, it was mostly freelance." He said, "Have you ever considered making a children's video yourself? You can make a lot of money." I said, "I'd love to but I don't have the capital to put up." He said, "Well, I do."

And the next week I brought in a five-page budget and concept, and handed it to him with his eggs, and he totally went for it. It's a half-hour video called *Away We Go.* It stars a puppet called Newt the Newt. (Unfortunately, we came up with that name before it took on other connotations.) It's for very young kids—*Sesame Street* age. The great thing about that—besides that someone was trusting me and putting up the money—was I had something tangible that that no one could take away from me. Theatre is so ethereal. You have programs, and you have maybe a recording of the show, but that's it. It's such a weird medium.

Source: John Istel, "*Rent* Check," in *American Theatre,* Vol. 13, No. 6, July–August 1996, pp. 12–16.

Thomas J. Carroll

In the following review, Carroll reflects on Rent*'s social criticism and its depiction of modern Bohemian culture.*

The power of any work of art is in its telling of the truth. At its best moments, the American musical theater tradition has done that well. The grappling with racial prejudice in *South Pacific,* for example, remains both effective and relevant, as does the biting critique of militarism in *Hair.* The flaws of either of those shows, or of many another significant musical, notwithstanding, American musical theater has often become a teacher of our hearts, dating to tell us truths we have needed to know, or to know again or to know more deeply.

As I flew to New York at the end of January for Jonathan Larson's memorial service, I did not realize that he had left for us just such a legacy in his new rock opera, *Rent.* When I had dinner with him a couple of summers ago at Manhattan's Ear Inn, Jonathan shared with me his enthusiasm over the progress of this new show he was writing. As he guided me around SoHo after our meal, he was giving me, I now realize, an introduction to many of the themes and issues that straggle toward resolution in *Rent.*

The initial preview performance of *Rent* was scheduled for Friday, Jan. 26, at the New York Theater Workshop in Manhattan. Only a few hours after the final dress rehearsal ended on the 25th, Jonathan died at age 35 of an aortic aneurism. A stunned and grieving company gathered that Friday evening to sing the score for the Larson family and many of Jon's friends. The memorial

"RENT EXTENDS AN OPPORTUNITY: TO SEE TODAY'S BOHEMIAN PHENOMENON WHOLE, IN ALL ITS ATTRACTIONS AND SORROW."

service for Jonathan at the Minetta Lane Theater on Feb. 3, even as it mourned his death, celebrated an artist's life.

Jonathan Larson pursued such a life, working year after year at a SoHo diner to make ends meet while he composed songs and crafted lyrics, producing a series of innovative shows. His creative efforts won him professional encouragement and support from Stephen Sondheim and the Richard Rodgers Foundation, among others. Passion for life, devotion to his work and a goofy and optimistic sense of humor kept Jon on the path that has led to the critical and popular success of *Rent.*

Based on a concept by Billy Aronson, *Rent* translates the story of Puccini's *La Boheme,* from the Left Bank in 1860's Paris to the East Village in today's New York. In the setting of that contemporary bohemian world Larson knew and loved, a company of 15 young actors explores the mysteries of life and love, of loss and death. The threat of tuberculosis has been replaced by the specter of AIDS. The relative simplicity of another century's bohemian life has given way to contemporary complexity.

Directly and poignantly *Rent* faces the effects of addiction and alienation, of dysfunction and co-dependency, of homelessness and gentrification, of sexual liberation and enslavement to habits and passions. The story is told through a succession of varied and well-crafted songs, each evocative and many moving. Together these songs vividly portray interwoven lives marked by desire and the hope for relationship, by shame and the quest for integrity, by despair and the yearning for glory, by suffering and the search for meaning.

Rent extends an opportunity: to see today's bohemian phenomenon whole, in all its attractions and sorrow. Larson pointedly ends Act I with a conjunction of two songs: "La Vie Boheme," which shouts the satisfactions of life on the edge, and "I Should Tell You," which finds two fearful characters trying to reveal to each other that they both are H.I.V. positive. *Rent* draws us into the humanity of each straggling character and allows us to see that their pains and fears are not so different from our own.

Rent tenders an invitation: to find good in all things, even in the outcasts of society. Larson begins Act II with a stirring gospel anthem, "Seasons of Love," reminding us that the one appropriate measure of any person's life is love. That message may seem banal, but the challenge to us remains: It is only with the eyes of love that we can see love for what it is. *Rent* opens to our view the attempts of a few souls on the fringe of society to discover how to love. If learning to love and choosing love are, for each of them, ongoing tasks, we must admit that they are the tasks of our everyday lives as well.

Rent yields a truth: that for each of us each day is a judgment day, a proof of who we are. The inestimable value of that opportunity in each day is affirmed in *Rent*'s final refrain, "No day but today." In the course of "Rent," each of Larson's characters is brought face to face with the finality of each moment and with the precariousness of life. As each character chooses between evasion and love, stagnation and creation, hatred and forgiveness, death and life, we encounter again the challenge of the Book of Deuteronomy: "Choose life."

Larson's is not the strident voice of a "fundamentalist liberal" who approves of everything avant-garde while repudiating everything traditional, nor is *Rent* dominated by rage or bitterness. It is instead a thoughtful voice, asking us to have reverence for all of creation, even for those we feel certain we can justly criticize. And *Rent* overflows with positive energy, with confident affirmation of the good that is to be found in life and in people.

Larson intended to win a younger audience to the tradition of musical theater and was confident that, with its vital cobination of contemporary music and issues, attitude and wit, *Rent* would lure them in. The enthusiastic response to *Rent* in these past months suggests that his hope was not in vain. *Rent* has left its first home at the New York Theater Workshop and made the move up to Broadway. The Nederlander Theater has once again opened its doors, welcoming a new voice, a new optimism, a new word of truth. Another mark of approval has just come to Larson with the posthumous award of the Pulitzer prize for playwriting.

Thanks, Jonathan.

Source: Thomas J. Carroll, "Legacy," in *America*, Vol. 174, No. 16, May 11, 1996, pp. 22–23.

John Sullivan

In the following review, Sullivan explores parallels and differences between Rent *and* La Boheme.

Once upon a time—a time of intellectual and political ferment—disaffected youth abandoned their parents, their studies and their comfortable middle-class surroundings to congregate in low-rent districts, shun social convention and imbibe as freely as possible life, love and other intoxicants, devoting themselves loudly and explicitly to the creation of new Art and a new Age. You could call it San Francisco in the '60s, or New York and Paris in the '20s, or you could locate the source of the myth of Bohemia, as many have, in the Paris of the 1830s. Henri Murger popularized that myth in his autobiographical novel, *Scenes de la vie de Boheme* (1845), and the legend found further expression, and has lived on for subsequent generations, in theatrical variations: Puccini's durable opera *La Boheme* (1896) and, 100 years later, Jonathan Larson's musical phenomenon *Rent.*

With the driving energy of its musical throughline and a glorious ensemble of vibrant young actors, Larson's Broadway hit has a lot going for it. But as John Istel details in this issue's cover story, "Rent Check," most of the show's press has revolved around the poignant life-meets-art tragedy of composer/lyricist/librettist Larson's death on the eve of his show's success, obscuring the serious issues Larson intended to address. One of those issues was the reduction of contemporary life to a basic level of economic exchange—rent.

While the parallels between *La Boheme* and *Rent* have been widely discussed, the divergence of the two stories may better illuminate Larson's meaning. For instance Benoit, the landlord in *La Boheme,* is a relatively minor comic character, but Benny, the landlord and developer in *Rent,* drives the plot. Though he once shared Bohemian digs with the filmmaker and songwriter at the heart of Larson's story, Benny has married rich and has bought their building and the adjacent vacant lot with its "tent city" of the homeless. Now he wants back rent and something more: To clear the tent city so he can build a state-of-the-art "cyber studio."

Gentrification is a familiar story for Bohemians. Small, undervalued enclaves reclaimed by

> "IT IS IMPRESSIVE THAT JONATHAN LARSON'S MESSAGE HAS TRAVELED FROM THE MARGINS OF SOCIETY TO THE CENTER OF BROADWAY'S POPULAR CULTURE."

artists are often ripe for picking. But Larson's *Rent* is concerned with more than the depletion of physical space: He warns of commercial encroachment to what we may refer to as our Bohemia of the mind—the private domain in which personal character and style are defined. There's a knowing concern in Larson's phrase, "You'd find an old tablecloth on the street and make a dress—and the next year, sure enough, they'd be mass-producing them at the Gap," particularly when juxtaposed with the pointed fatalism in his lyric, "Bohemia, Bohemia, a fallacy in your head. This is Calcutta, Bohemia's dead." When Larson's alter ego, the filmmaker Mark, says "How do you document real life, when real life's getting more like fiction each day?", he poses a central challenge for artists living and creating in consumerized world, and a terribly perplexing question for young people searching for identity.

Puccini's Bohemians, while economically marginalized, were bold and playful, confidently flouting social convention by creating for themselves determinedly distinctive personalities. *Rent,* on the other hand—its frenetic pace in sync with America in the accelerating '90—depicts the coming generation's often desperate attempts to create a vision of themselves before the masters of market segmentation appropriate, pertect and sell it back to them.

It is impressive that Jonathan Larson's message has traveled from the margins of society to the center of Broadway's popular culture. Some will say the meaning of *Rent* is affected by the change of venue, and there is probably some truth in that, but to explore how ideas are assimilated into American culture is a subject for another day. For now, two facts seem clear: *Rent's* success reflects the momentum of a huge young talent; and, as Stephanie Coen's article "Not Out of Nowhere" shows, this young talent was encouraged and nurtured along the way. While Larson lived and absorbed the contemporary Bohemian ethos, *Rent* exalts, artistic director James Nicola and the staff of New York Theatre Workshop played an essential role in helping Larson flesh out his tale. (*Rent* represents the fullest expression to date of Nicola's vision of integrating New York Theatre Workshop with the community in which it resides, New York's Lower East Side.) Equally important, the early boost given Larson by his mentor Stephen Sondheim, and the recognition given *Rent* by the Richard Rodgers Award from the American Academy of Arts and Letters, serve in retrospect as harbingers of the production's spectacular move.

With an increasing number of Broadway shows such as *Bring in 'Da Noise, Bring in 'Da Funk, Seven Guitars, Master Class* and *Rent*—having benefited from development in nonprofit venues, this has been Broadway's best year in the last 15. Even Broadway's self-celebrating Tonys bear out the importance of our theatres, with six of eight productions nominated for best play or revival of a play, and five of eight nominated for best musical or revival of a musical, having originated in the American nonprofit sector.

The nonprofit theatre knows how to provide the Bohemia of the mind most young talents like Jonathan Larson need to create. While innovative approaches to development and cost containment, like the Broadway Alliance, may keep creative commercial producers on Broadway, alliances between the nonprofit and commercial sectors will increasingly be the route taken by new ideas and new impulses as they travel from the hearts of theatre artists to the center of American culture. Every day, as the physical and mental boundaries of Bohemia contract, threatening the very future of independent thought, those of us committed to an expanding nonprofit culture must appreciate and meet the needs of artists, and keep alive the Bohemian in us all.

Source: John Sullivan, "Bohemians of the Moment," in *American Theatre*, Vol. 13, No. 6, July–August 1996, p. 3.

Robert Brustein

In the following review, Brustein laments the "messianic fervor," due largely to Larson's sudden death, surrounding Rent. *Brustein finds fashion, but a lack of real art, in the play.*

The American theater chases after a new musical sensation with all the messianic fervor of a religious sect pursuing redemption. And when the composer/librettist dies the day before his show begins previews, we have all the conditions required for cultural myth-making—a martyred redeemer, a new gospel, hordes of passionate young believers and canonization by *The New York Times,* which devoted virtually all the theater columns of a recent Arts and Leisure section to *Rent,* the "rock opera for our time."

Jonathan Larson's premature death at the age of 35 from an aortic aneurism was a misfortune from many points of view. He was a young man on the brink of a strong career who did not live to enjoy the early fruits of his talents, a promising artist who would undoubtedly have gone on to write much more finished works. I hope it will not be construed as coldhearted when I say that his death was also a sad day for contemporary criticism, being another instance of how it can be hobbled by extra-artistic considerations.

Rent (now playing at the New York Theatre Workshop before it moves to Broadway) is an updated version of *La Bohème,* substituting the multicultural denizens of New York's East Village for Puccini's Latin Quarter Bohemians. It is good-natured, fully energized, theatrically knowing and occasionally witty. It is also badly manufactured, vaguely manipulative, drenched in self-pity and sentimental in a way that makes Puccini and his librettists (Illica and Giacosa) look like cynics.

Rent is being advertised as "*Hair* for the '90s," and there are indeed certain similarities between the two musicals. Both idealize their socially marginal characters, both are poorly constructed, and both fail to penetrate very deeply beneath a colorful and exotic surface. Larson was a sophisticated librettist, if a somewhat sloppy architect (there is twice as much incident in his brief second act as in the much longer section that precedes it). But his score for *Rent* struck me as the musical equivalent of wallpaper, the rock version of elevator music ("tame and second hand," as Bernard Holland wrote in the only *Times* dissent). Compared to Galt McDermott's exhilarating compositions for *Hair,* Larson's songs—except for the moving "Another Day"—show little lyric genius. Their impact derives less from intrinsic inspiration than from extrinsic amplification. Whenever the show begins to flag, the appealing cast lines up downstage to holler into microphones.

The cast, in fact, is highly amplified throughout the entire evening, often leaving us in bewilderment over whose lips are issuing the sounds. The principals wear head mikes, which not only makes them look like telephone operators but makes any physical contact between them (such as a hug or a kiss) sound more like a scrape. *Rent* has a lot to say about the need for human communication, but nothing very human is allowed to emerge from all this acoustical racket. "You're living in America where it's like the Twilight Zone," notes one character, while another (cribbing from Philip Roth) asks, "How do you document real life when real life is getting more like fiction every day?" What isn't probed is how these people also contribute to a sense of the American unreality, especially when they are so superficially examined.

Although warm-hearted, Larson's book is basically superficial and unconvincing. In this piggyback *Bohème,* the painter Marcello becomes Mark, a documentary filmmaker; Rudolfo the poet turns into Roger, a rock composer; Colline the philosopher emerges as Tom Collins, a black anarchist expelled from MIT for his work on "actual reality"; and Schaunard, the musician, metamorphoses into Angel, a black sculptor by profession and transvestite by disposition. As for the women, Musetta evolves into a bisexual rock singer named Maureen who has left Mark for Joanne (Puccini's Alcindoro transformed into a black lawyer from Harvard), while Mimi, the mignonette, has turned into Mimi Marquez, a Latino strip dancer and heroin user (when she enters Roger's apartment with frozen hands, carrying a candle, she's looking for her stash).

The background for all this interracial, intersexual character grunge is a rent strike. Blacks, Latinos and whites alike, whether gay, bisexual or straight, all stand in common opposition to the uptight Benjamin Coffin III, who, though also black, is, like his Puccini prototype Benoit, a grasping landlord and rent gouger. What they protest is his hardheartedness toward the homeless ("Do you really want a neighborhood where people piss on your stoop every night?") and his desire to gentrify the surroundings ("This is Calcutta. Bohemia's dead").

Aside from this easy mark, and similar simplistic oppositions, what virtually all these people have in common is AIDS (an analogy for Mimi's tuberculosis in *La Bohème*). Some have contracted the disease from sexual activity, some from drug use, but in *Rent* it seems to be an East Village epidemic. During an AZT break, the entire cast pops pills. Most of them are dying. Angel, minus his wig and connected to an IV, is provided with a protracted death scene, after which Mimi memorializes him as "so much more original than any of us."

"I HOPE IT WILL NOT BE CONSTRUED AS COLDHEARTED WHEN I SAY THAT HIS DEATH WAS ALSO A SAD DAY FOR CONTEMPORARY CRITICISM, BEING ANOTHER INSTANCE OF HOW IT CAN BE HOBBLED BY EXTRA-ARTISTIC CONSIDERATIONS."

(Following Kushner's *Angels in America,* Phyllis Nagy's *Weldon Rising,* the PBS documentary *The Time of Our Dying* and other such theatrical artifacts, it is doubtful how "original" black drag queens really are any more.)

The death of Angel (the angel of death?) sets the stage for Mimi's demise. She and Roger have finally consummated their love after discovering they are both HIV positive and therefore can't contaminate each other. Still, Roger decides to leave for Santa Fe to write one great song before he dies. Upon his return, he learns that Mimi has been living on the street, in deteriorating health. Maureen carries the dying girl into Roger's apartment, and all the comrades gather round for the obligatory death scene. Roger declares his love in song ("Who do you think you are, leaving me alone with my guitar"), Mimi falls back on the couch, and the concluding strains of *La Bohème*—the most powerful music of the evening—swell up over the sobs and groans.

Fear not. Unlike bel canto opera, American musicals allow resurrections and require happy endings. Mimi awakes. Her "fever has broken." Love has triumphed over immune deficiency. And the show concludes with the lovers in each other's arms, as movie memories are projected onto an upstage screen.

We don't ask our musicals to be like real life unless they pretend to be: *Rent* is offered to us as an authentic East Village *tranche de vie.* This pretense makes the final Puccini musical quotation seem cheap and the ending sentimental. George Meredith once defined the sentimentalist as "He who would enjoy without incurring the immense debtorship for the thing done." He accurately describes the emotions forced upon the audience in *Rent:* a ghastly disease is exploited for mawkish purposes.

Michael Greif's highly charged production employs a host of gifted young performers: Daphne Rubin-Vega as a dejected Mimi in skin-tight Spandex pants; Adam Pascal as the rock-and-rolling Roger; Anthony Rapp as the camera-toting Mark; Wilson Jermaine Heredia as the transvestite sculptor Angel; Idina Menzel (a Sandra Bernhard look-alike) as the sexually ambivalent Maureen; and Taye Diggs, Fredi Walker and Jesse L. Martin in other roles. The energy of the entire cast is prodigious. I hope that energy can be sustained over what promises to be a long Broadway run.

Larson has been hailed for creating the downtown equivalent of 13 Bohemian life. I fear he has only created another fashion. Bohemia used to be celebrated not just for flamboyant life-styles but also for artistic innovation. Many Bohemian artists (Ibsen, Manet) dressed like burghers and lived exemplary lives. It was Flaubert who famously said that he was peaceful and conservative in his life in order to be violent and radical in his work. Alas, Larson's New Age Bohemians display nothing but their life-styles. As for their art, it's just a little daunting to note that most of them have no greater ambition than to dominate the rock charts.

Source: Robert Brustein, "The New Bohemians," in *New Republic*, April 22, 1996, pp. 29–31.

James Gardner

In the following review of Rent, *Gardner comments on "the essential bad faith of the musical," finding nothing new in the play or its concept despite the hype.*

I have this theory: in any given musical after 1970, there will come a moment in which the protagonist is on stage alone and sings the words, "Who am I?" This may be called the hokey-identity-crisis moment, when the character is torn between his principles and his self-interest, and tempted to take the easy way out, which threatens to damn his soul and shave twenty minutes off the second act.

In *Rent,* the new great hope of the American musical theater, this does not happen—or at least not quite. The protagonist, Mark, an aspiring video artist who cannot pay his rent and has no electricity or food in his house, is offered a lucrative assignment from some cheesy network news magazine. Will he take the job and end his financial plight, or will he preserve his principles—though we never quite learn what those are—and turn the job down? At this point, Mark, on the verge of accepting, turns to the audience and says, "What am I doing?" Then his roommate, Roger, an equally insolvent rock poet, comes on stage and asks, "Who are you?" Now since he has known Mark for years and is not suffering from any psychotic disorder, despite a healthy drug habit, we assume that this question is meant metaphorically.

My point: there seems to have been a tacit agreement among twenty or thirty powerful people on Broadway that *Rent* is to be the Next Big Thing and everyone else is docilely toeing the line. And yet, despite its studied hipness and its aspirations to be the voice of the Nineties, *Rent,* which is an updating of *La Boheme,* is pretty much the same old showbiz fare, though with almost formulaic inversions. Instead of boy meets girl, you now have girl meets girl and boy meets drag queen. The audience is almost explicitly invited to say, "Look at that! Lesbians. Say!" And whereas earlier generations acknowledged the archetype of the annoying mother-in-law, as in *Barefoot in the Park,* here one is beset with the Annoying Jewish Mother archetype who endeavors to stifle with self-centered affection the young hero's artistic ambitions. Then there's the overbearing landlord with the heart of gold, who, in a cutesy reversal of type, is a black yuppie. Combine that with myriad references to AZT, Prozac, and Pee Wee Herman and you can positively hear the Generation Xers in the audience as they "relate." The low point in this process comes in the form of Mark's nutty ex-girlfriend, Maureen. Protesting the landlord's desire to transform their tenement into a studio space, she does a performance piece which we know we are supposed to find silly, though in fact it is not much sillier than the rest of the musical. Well, at one point Maureen imitates a cow (I forget why) and delivers what is perhaps the one genuinely funny line in the play, "C'mon. Moo with me!" This would be fine except that then, sure enough, the majority of the terminally hip audience started lowing like a stable of prize Guernseys.

As for the music, it is standard rock fare of the sort that pleases some people more than me. For what it's worth, I found myself enjoying *Hair* and *Jesus Christ Superstar,* also rock operas, far more than I did this, which means that I am not totally averse to the art form. The staging, furthermore, seems surprisingly drab and lifeless, an impression that the dull, vaguely industrial set does little to mitigate.

Like most people who saw *Rent,* I was expecting a great deal, since the musical had won the Pulitzer Prize and had been praised by all and sundry. Furthermore, knowing the genuinely tragic circumstances of the life and death of the author, Jonathan Larson, his having waited on tables in obscurity for years while struggling in vain to get his musical produced, and then dying at age 35 of an aortic aneurysm the day it was supposed to open—I wanted to like the play. And I was and remain sincerely happy for the author that all these people, who probably wouldn't even have tipped him properly if he had waited on their tables, were now clamoring to get the few remaining tickets, not to mention the few remaining *Rent* T-shirts and *Rent* buttons that were being hawked at the entrance.

> "THERE SEEMS TO HAVE BEEN A TACIT AGREEMENT AMONG TWENTY OR THIRTY POWERFUL PEOPLE ON BROADWAY THAT *RENT* IS TO BE THE NEXT BIG THING AND EVERYONE ELSE IS DOCILELY TOEING THE LINE."

But I found that I could never get past what seemed to be the essential bad faith of the musical, its trying to be the *Hair* of the Nineties. You just know that the chorus that ends the first act, "La Vie Boheme," wants desperately to be taken as the anthem of some nonexistent youth movement. But the bohemian life glorified in *Rent* looks no more vital than it did before, and Broadway itself, whose fortunes this musical was said to revive, appears about as moribund as ever.

Source: James Gardner, "Lowering the *Rent,*" in *National Review*, Vol. 48, No. 10, June 3, 1996, pp. 56–57.

SOURCES

Brustein, Robert, "The New Bohemians," in the *New Republic*, April 22, 1996, pp. 29–30.

Crews, Chip, "'Rent': Electricity Included; Raw Emotion Keeps Musical on Track," in the *Washington Post*, April 30, 1996, Section E, p. 1.

Gardner, James, "Lowering the *Rent*," in the *National Review*, June 3, 1996, pp. 56–57.

Larson, Jonathan, *Rent*, William Morrow, 1997.

Lyons, Donald, "'Rent,' New Musical Is Deserved Hit," in the *Wall Street Journal*, March 6, 1996, Section A, p. 18.

Pacheco, Patrick, Review of *Rent*, in the *Los Angeles Times*, April 14, 1996, p. 4.

Rich, Frank, "East Village Story," in the *New York Times*, March 2, 1996, Section A, p. 19.

Span, Paula, "The Show Goes On; Reeling from Triumph and Tragedy, 'Rent' Rockets onto Broadway," in the *Washington Post*, April 18, 1996, Section C, p. 1.

Winer, Laurie, "'Rent' Goes Up—to Broadway; Pulitzer Prize–Winning Musical Celebrates Life, Even under Specter of Death," in the *Los Angeles Times*, April 30, 1996, p. 1.

FURTHER READING

Bordman, Gerald, and Thomas S. Hischak, *The Concise Oxford Companion to American Theatre*, Oxford University Press, 1987.

The comprehensive guide to American theater includes articles on relevant topics, such as "AIDS and the American Theatre."

Galvin, Peter, "How the Show Goes On: An Interview with 'Roger,' 'Mimi,' and 'Mark,'" in *Interview*, Vol. 20, March 1996, p 105.

This interview with three of the original cast members—Adam Pascal, Daphne Rubin-Vega, and Anthony Rapp—focuses on the cast's reaction to Larson's death.

London, Herbert, *Decade of Denial: A Snapshot of America in the 1990s*, Lexington Books, 2001.

London charts the decade, which he considers to be a media-driven age, consumed by greed.

Shilts, Randy, *And the Band Played On: Politics, People, and the AIDS Epidemic*, Stonewall Inn Editions, 2000.

The authors trace the impact of social and political forces on the development of the AIDS epidemic.

Tommasini, Anthony, "The Seven-Year Odyssey That Led to 'Rent,'" in the *New York Times*, March 17, 1996, Section 2, pp. 7, 37.

Tommasini traces Larson's creation and development of *Rent*.

This Is Our Youth

KENNETH LONERGAN

1998

In 1993, the MET in New York City produced Kenneth Lonergan's one-act play "Betrayal by Everyone" during their festival of short plays. Lonergan then expanded the play and renamed it *This Is Our Youth.* The new version opened off Broadway in 1998 to rave reviews that continued when the play moved the following year to the Douglas Fairbanks Theater on Broadway. The play was published by Overlook Press in 2000.

The entire play takes place in an Upper West Side apartment in New York City in 1982 and centers on two friends: twenty-two-year-old Dennis, whose father pays for his rent, and nineteen-year-old Warren, who has just stolen fifteen thousand dollars from his father. Both are college dropouts who have been caught up in the excesses of the "Me Generation" of the 1980s yet, at the same time, reject the elitist world of their parents. The plot is complicated by a young woman who, along with Dennis, introduces Warren to the complexities of human relationships, especially concerning issues of loyalty and betrayal. As Lonergan focuses on the efforts of Dennis and Warren to return the cash to Warren's father, he presents an acerbic look at this generation in its ironic struggle both to resist and to attain adulthood.

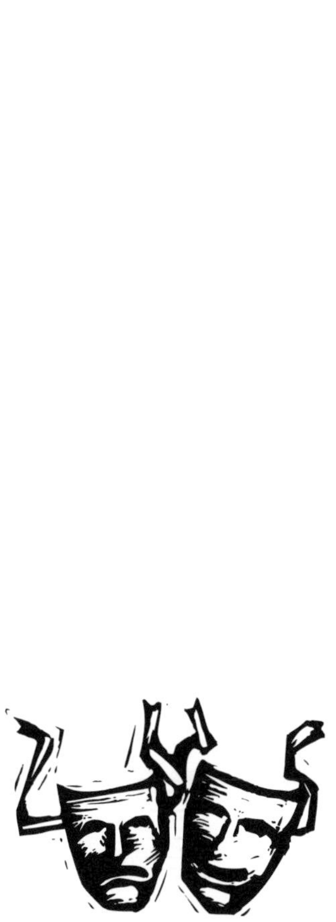

Kenneth Lonergan Getty Images

AUTHOR BIOGRAPHY

Kenneth Lonergan was born in New York City in 1963 to parents who were both psychiatrists. His father was also a retired doctor and medical researcher. Lonergan attended Walden School, a progressive private school in Manhattan, where he began writing in the ninth grade. His interest in playwriting was sparked when his drama teacher asked him to collaborate on a play. The characters in *This Is Our Youth* are loosely based on his Walden friends and himself. After graduation, Lonergan attended Wesleyan University in Connecticut and took classes at the HB Studio in Greenwich Village, New York City. He eventually earned a degree from New York University's drama writing program. While he was attending New York University, he wrote his first play, *The Rennings Children*, which was chosen for the Young Playwright's Festival of 1982.

Lonergan supported himself after college by writing speeches for the Environmental Protection Agency and Weight Watchers, creating video presentations for Grace Chemicals, and writing comedy sketches for Fuji Films sales meetings. During his time as a speechwriter, he never abandoned his love of writing for the theater; he often participated in readings and workshops with the Naked Angels, an off-Broadway theater troupe.

The fact that Lonergan's parents were both psychiatrists seems to have influenced much of his writing, including *The Rennings Children*, a play about a family's struggle to avoid mental disintegration, and the screenplays for both *Analyze This* (1999) and *Analyze That* (2002), films that explore the psychiatric problems of a member of the Italian mafia. Lonergan's play *This Is Our Youth* gained much attention at the 1993 festival of short plays at the MET in New York City. *Waverly Gallery*, another semi-autobiographical work, is based on the life of his grandmother. The play received critical acclaim, including a Pulitzer Prize nomination in 2001, but it was not a commercial success. Another of Lonergan's works, *Lobby Hero*, made the top-ten list in *The Best Plays of 2000–2001*.

Lonergan also wrote the screenplay for *The Adventures of Rocky and Bullwinkle* (2000) and wrote, directed, and costarred in *You Can Count on Me*, a film that won the Grand Jury Prize at its premiere at the 2000 Sundance Film Festival and an Oscar nomination for Best Original Screenplay and earned Lonergan the Waldo Salt Screenwriting Award. Lonergan has also worked with the director Martin Scorsese on writing for some of Scorcese's films. He was nominated for an Oscar for Best Original Screenplay for his "on-the-set" rewrites for Scorsese's film *Gangs of New York* (2002).

PLOT SUMMARY

Act 1

This Is Our Youth takes place in Dennis Ziegler's one-room apartment on the Upper West Side of Manhattan, in New York City. It opens on a Saturday night in March, after midnight. His friend Warren appears at Dennis's door, lugging a large suitcase and a backpack. Dennis begins rolling a joint, after he discovers that Warren has brought some marijuana with him. Warren admits that his father has kicked him out because he smokes too much of it.

Warren pulls two hundred dollars out of his backpack and gives it to Dennis, in payment of a loan. He admits that he stole fifteen thousand dollars from his father, who, he guesses, got it from a shady business deal with gangsters. He explains that he wanted to make his father pay for kicking him out. Dennis tells Warren that he is stupid for stealing the money and is afraid that his father and his associates will come after Warren and find him at Dennis's apartment. He wants Warren to take the money somewhere else, but Warren insists that there is nowhere else he can go.

Dennis tells Warren that no one likes him, because he is always provoking people and he is an idiot. He then analyzes everything that is wrong with Warren's life—that his father continually beats him, that he owes Dennis money, that he is "an annoying loudmouthed little creep," and that now he is "some kind of fugitive from *justice*." Close to tears, Warren says that he does not know what to do or where to go. Warren talks Dennis into letting him stay until he figures out what to do about the money.

Warren asks whether Dennis has seen Jessica, a friend of Dennis's girlfriend, Valerie, but Dennis tells him that Jessica is out of his league. Warren suggests that they take some of the money, get a hotel room, and have a party with Jessica and Valerie. After he accidentally breaks Valerie's sculpture, Dennis explodes.

As a way to replace the missing money, the two think about selling some of the vintage toys that Warren is carrying around in the suitcase, but Dennis comes up with a plan to sell cocaine instead. The plan involves partying with Jessica and Valerie. Dennis insists that Warren will do fine with Jessica if he does not talk about his dead sister. When Jessica arrives, Dennis goes downstairs (offstage) to meet Valerie, and the two leave to get the drugs and some champagne.

After some awkward conversation, Warren and Jessica talk about their plans for the future and argue about environmental influences and personality development. They then have more amicable conversations about their families and Warren's toy collection, which Jessica admires. He tells her that he considers the 1914 Wrigley Field Opening Day baseball cap that his grandfather gave him his most valuable piece. After she inquires about his sister, he reluctantly tells her how she was murdered by her boyfriend. They smoke pot and begin to dance to the vintage albums Warren has. They begin to kiss, but Jessica soon breaks it off, asking Warren whether he really likes her. He insists that he does and invites her to share a room with him at the Plaza Hotel.

Act 2

In the early afternoon of the next day, Warren arrives at Dennis's apartment. Dennis tells him that he got the cocaine and that Valerie stormed out after she saw her broken statue. When Dennis asks what happened with Jessica, Warren says that they had sex at the Plaza. Dennis says that the Plaza is a dump and that they should have gone to the Pierre instead. Warren is worried that Jessica was too quiet before she left in the morning.

When Warren says that he spent about a thousand dollars for the night, Dennis explodes, claiming that they will not be able to make up the money by selling the cocaine and that Warren's father will come after him. The two decide to sell Warren's toys to make up the difference, but Warren keeps the baseball cap. When the door buzzer rings, Dennis panics, thinking that it is Warren's father, but he calms down when he finds that it is Jessica. She comes up, and Dennis makes innuendos about her and Warren.

After Dennis leaves, Jessica tells Warren that she cannot go out to brunch with him because her mother is upset that she stayed out all night without calling. When Warren inquires whether he can see her later in the week, she declines and asks whether he told Dennis that they had slept together. After Warren admits that he did, she becomes angry, and the two get into an argument. Warren tries to explain that he really likes her and that what he told Dennis was very respectful. When he asks what he can do to make it up to her, she tells him that she would like him to give her his grandfather's baseball cap. He immediately hands it to her, insisting that he wants her to have it, but he cannot hide his distress.

They argue about the hat; Jessica tries to give it back to him, but he refuses. When she asks about seeing him later in the week, he replies, "I don't think we can. I'm all out of baseball hats." As she takes it off her head, he threatens to burn it if she tries to give it back again. Jessica leaves it on the table and departs.

Just after Warren pours out on a plate the cocaine that Dennis has bought, the phone rings, and he knocks over the plate. When Warren realizes that it is his father, he admits that he took the money. They discuss his sister and his own bad judgment and end the conversation with each telling the other, "I hate you."

Dennis returns, apparently devastated by the discovery that the person he bought the drugs from the previous night has died of an overdose. When he tells Warren how much he got for the toys, Warren says that Dennis was cheated. At first, Dennis explodes, but then he apologizes, explaining that he is upset by his friend's death. As he starts talking about it, he determines that he will get off drugs, because he has become "high on fear." He considers how he can try to make something of himself, insisting that he could be an excellent chef, film director, or sports star.

Warren and Dennis then argue about the money and the spilled cocaine, and Dennis again tells Warren that he is a loser. Fed up, Warren complains that Dennis is not on his side, which causes Dennis to sob. Warren tries to calm him down by telling him to drop the subject. They then discuss the overdose, and Warren goes into a long monologue about how alone his father is after his sister's death. Dennis, obviously not listening, cuts in with the comment "I can't *believe* you don't think I'm on your *side*." To placate him, Warren insists that he knows Dennis is and then decides to go home. The play ends with Dennis smoking pot and Warren just sitting there.

CHARACTERS

Jessica Goldman

Nineteen-year-old Jessica Goldman is a "cheerful but very nervous girl" who displays "a watchful defensiveness that sweeps away anything that might threaten to dislodge her, including her own chances at happiness and the opportunity of gaining a wider perspective on the world." She uses this defensiveness to help her project her own image of herself as a hip, intelligent, independent young woman who cannot be taken advantage of, yet her actions suggest that she is not as self-assured as she appears.

On first meeting Warren, Jessica tries to convince him that she is in control, when she insists that she will not let others play matchmaker for her. But her defensiveness immediately becomes apparent when she does not recognize that Warren is teasing her about his sexual intentions. She ironically reveals her own fragile sense of self when she tells Warren, "Like right now you're all like this rich little pot-smoking burnout rebel, but ten years from now you're gonna be like a plastic *surgeon* reminiscing about how wild you used to be." Jessica's vision of their futures as successful doctors or fashion designers suggests that she will follow the same path as their parents, proving that she does not recognize the meaninglessness and moral vacuity of their lives. She insists that this inevitable transition "just basically invalidates whoever you are right now." "So," she says, "it's like, what is the point?" This view also provides her with easy excuses for her present behavior, such as trying to persuade Warren to give her his most prized possession, a vintage baseball cap given to him by his grandfather.

Jessica reveals her shallowness in her obvious attraction to Dennis and his famous father and beautiful mother and in her excitement when Warren suggests that they get a penthouse room at the Plaza Hotel. The most blatant example of this quality emerges after she becomes worried about telling Dennis's girlfriend, Valerie, that she and Warren did not sleep together, after Warren told Dennis that they had. Even when Warren insists that he talked about her with a great deal of respect, she still needs him to validate her worth by asking him to give up his most important possession. She clearly shows no concern for how valuable the baseball cap is to Warren and how difficult it would be for him to give it away. Her only concern is proving her own merit, through Warren's offer of a treasured possession.

Warren Straub

Warren is "a strange barking-dog of a kid" who finds himself in a great deal of trouble at the beginning of the play. After he steals his father's money, he turns to the only person he can; unfortunately, that is Dennis, who continually makes him feel like a loser. Although that description fits Warren in many respects, he has more thoughtfulness and "a dogged self-possession" that gives him more authenticity than his friends exhibit.

Unlike his friends, Warren understands that he is wasting his time in New York. He reveals his desire to move on when he talks about the pleasure of being out west in the mountains, in contrast to what he considers the trash heap of the city. He notes that he is not getting any intellectual stimulation and that all he is doing is getting high, which he can do anywhere.

Warren is also more able to express his vulnerability and his sense of loss, especially concerning the death of his sister. Although he is reluctant to talk about her, he admits that he is dealing with her death by keeping pictures of her in his room. He later tells his father that he thinks about her "all the time" and sees her in his imagination. Warren's compassionate nature emerges when he recognizes how much his father has also suffered. Even though his father has physically and mentally abused him, Warren shows sympathy for the fact that he is "totally by himself." He also exhibits compassion for Dennis, even though he recognizes how self-involved his friend is. When Dennis practically begs Warren to reassure him that he feels that Dennis is on his side, Warren agrees.

Valerie

We never meet Valerie, Dennis's girlfriend, but Dennis speaks to her on the phone. Her function in the play is to reinforce Dennis's character flaws, specifically, his inability to control his anger and his self-centeredness. He screams at her when she voices anger at the fact that Warren has broken the sculpture she made for Dennis, never acknowledging to her the time and effort that she put into it. She also helps generate conflict for Jessica, who has to admit to Warren that she lied to Valerie about her night with him.

Dennis Ziegler

Dennis is "a very quick, dynamic, fanatical, and bullying kind of person; amazingly good-natured and magnetic, but insanely competitive and almost always successfully so." He had been "a dark cult god of high school" and still appears to have a great deal of influence over his circle of friends, whom he frequently verbally abuses. He takes great pride in this authority, insisting to Warren, "I'm like providing you with precious memories of your *youth*" and "I'm like the basis of half your personality." Dennis has learned that when he breaks down his friends' egos, they become grateful to him for agreeing to allow them to be in the company of what they consider to be a superior person.

Dennis has no compassion for anyone, including Warren, who appears on his doorstep with nowhere else to turn after he steals his father's money. Dennis shows him no mercy, continually criticizing and belittling him, goading him to tears at one point. He tries to take advantage of Warren's predicament by planning a drug deal to replace the lost money but figuring in a large cut for himself.

Others besides Warren suffer from Dennis's abuse, always doled out in an effort to maintain a complete sense of control over them. He berates his drug supplier for being overweight and greedy when the supplier dares to increase the selling price of some cocaine Dennis wants to buy, and he screams obscenities at Valerie when she expresses anger over Warren's breaking the sculpture that she had made for Dennis. In an effort to get back in Valerie's good graces, he blames his behavior on his mother, who, he claims, taught him to lash out as viciously as he can when he feels that he is being attacked.

At one point in the play, Dennis expresses a sense of vulnerability, but it takes a cowardly form. After he learns that his drug supplier has overdosed, he shows no compassion for his friend, concerned only with his own welfare. Realizing that if he does not change his current lifestyle, he could meet a similar fate, he admits to Warren, "I'm like, high on fear." He assumes that whatever choice he makes would bring him great success and considers that he could "go to *cooking* school in *Florence* or like go into *show* business." His overly inflated ego prompts him to declare, "I could so totally be a completely great chef it's like ridiculous." When he considers a career directing films, he insists, "I'd be a genius at it."

At the end of the play, however, Dennis reveals that his inflated ego is just a sham. When Warren questions whether Dennis is really a true friend to him, Dennis cannot deal with his friend's doubts about his character and breaks down in tears. Only after Warren reaffirms his friend's worth can Dennis calm down and recreate the illusion of confidence.

THEMES

Coming of Age

All three main characters are on the brink of adulthood but are having difficulties with the transition. They have been living in a state of stasis, supported by their wealthy parents, who demand only that their children leave them alone. None of them has been forced to examine his or her empty life or to determine the future. Their days are spent thinking only about how they can fulfill their immediate desires: drugs, alcohol, and sex. Only Warren shows any development toward maturation, as he begins to realize the meaninglessness at the heart of their existence.

When Jessica determines that she wants Warren's baseball cap, his most prized possession, Warren recognizes her self-centeredness and her lack of respect for what is important to him. He rejects her offer of getting together later in the week, because he no longer wants to spend time with someone who cannot acknowledge the needs of others. He becomes impatient with Dennis at the end of the play for these same qualities, when he tells his friend that he does not believe that Dennis is on his side. Jessica's and Dennis's lack of sensitivity ironically encourages the sensitivity in Warren, who begins to think about what his father must have suffered after his sister died.

TOPICS FOR FURTHER STUDY

- Lonergan's dialogue in the play has been praised for its realism. Write your own dialogue of a conversation between you and a friend that reveals an important quality of your friendship.
- Read J. D. Salinger's novel *The Catcher in the Rye* and compare the depiction of a teenager in 1950s America with the depiction of young people in the early 1980s in *This Is Our Youth.* Are the struggles involved in the coming-of-age process the same or different in these works? Write an essay comparing and contrasting the two works.
- Imagine what might have happened to Warren after the end of the play. Would he have given his father back the money and reconciled with him? Would he have continued his friendship with Dennis? Write a character analysis of Warren ten years after the play ends. Use details from the play to back up your views.
- Interview four people who have experienced death in their families. Take notes, focusing on the effect of death on the family members. Report your findings to the class and lead a discussion, asking the class to compare your findings with the effects of Warren's sister's death on him and his father.

Identity

Each of the main characters must find a clear sense of identity in order to make the transition into adulthood. The two who appear to have accomplished this are Dennis and Jessica, yet during the course of the play, they reveal the illusory nature of their images of self. While Warren has not established a firm sense of his own self by the end of the play, he has been able to see the true nature of those around him, which suggests that he will then eventually be able to gain a clearer vision of himself.

Dennis and Jessica exhibit a confidence that is easily shaken when tested. Dennis continually promotes himself as a role model for all those who know him. As he tells Warren, "I'm providing you schmucks with such a crucial service" (as their drug supplier) as well as supplying "precious memories of your *youth*." He claims that he is "like the basis of half your personality." Dennis notes that his friends all imitate him and so should thank God they met him. Still, when Warren, who has grown tired of Dennis's constant criticism of him and his lack of support, declares that he cannot tell whether Dennis is on his side, Dennis crumbles and begins to sob. He cannot face the fact that he may not be the heroic figure he thought he was, since he has based his entire identity on this assumption.

We do not gain as clear a picture of Jessica as we do of Dennis, since she appears in only two scenes. However, Lonergan's acute ear for dialogue effectively presents a penetrating snapshot of Jessica's own struggles with her identity. Initially, she seems self-confident; she is not as arrogant as Dennis but is just as self-assured in her opinions, of which she has many. She immediately declares that she does not want Warren to assume that she will agree to any matchmaking scheme that he and Dennis may have planned. She insists that she alone makes any decisions about whom she will date.

Jessica also has strong opinions about the maturation process, insisting that all of them will undergo radical personality changes, which will "basically invalidate whoever you are right *now*." Yet this becomes an ironic statement of her own tentative identity, since, as the stage directions suggest, Jessica's sense of herself is continually undercut by "a watchful defensiveness that sweeps away anything that might threaten to dislodge her." She is obviously shaken when she discovers that Warren has been discussing with Dennis his night with her, becoming increasingly agitated to the point that she declares that she does not care what others think of her because she can make more new friends if she has to. Her insecurities lead her to ask for Warren's most prized possession, the hat his grandfather gave him, as a way to try to reestablish her self-worth; she assumes that she must have value if he would give her something so precious to him.

Warren has not built up a false persona, as have the other two characters. He sees himself more realistically, even though that means he must recognize the more negative aspects of his personality. This insight into his own identity provides him with the capacity to discover the illusory concepts of self that his friends have constructed. Lonergan suggests that Warren's ability to recognize this reality will help him establish a truer sense of himself in the future.

STYLE

Dialogue-Driven Plot

The plot advances through dialogue rather than action, which occurs offstage. The dialogue reinforces the sense of the characters' self-absorption, especially in the case of Dennis, who pays little attention to what the others are saying. This occurs most notably at the end of the play, when Warren has just delivered a heartfelt monologue about his father's reaction to his sister's death. Dennis's response to Warren's question about his father being "totally by himself" is "I guess," followed quickly by his attempt to shift the focus back to himself and his fear that Warren thinks ill of him.

Symbols

The sparse setting becomes an important symbol in the play, which takes place entirely in Dennis's studio apartment, an appropriately confined space for the limited lives of the two main characters, Dennis and Warren. Only three characters appear in the play; three others are spoken to by Dennis and Warren on the phone, but Lonergan does not include their words, which reflects and underscores the self-centeredness of the main characters.

The dominant symbol in the play, however, is Warren's suitcase full of toys, which he calls "the proceeds from my unhappy childhood." They are a symbol of a lonely youth spent gathering "authentic" artifacts that gave him pleasure. One item in his suitcase, however, provides a happy memory, because it reflects a strong familial link: the Wrigley Field Opening Day baseball cap that his grandfather gave him. This item is the most precious to him, and it becomes an important catalyst for change when Jessica asks him for it.

HISTORICAL CONTEXT

Consumerism

In the 1980s, the government's political and economic agenda, with its championing of American capitalism, triggered a promotion of self-interest. The decade of the 1980s was ushered in with Ronald Reagan's presidential inauguration in 1981 and was heavily influenced by Reagan's economic philosophy. "Reaganomics," as this philosophy was termed, proposed that the encouragement of the free-market system, which depends on the individual pursuit of wealth, would strengthen the economy. This vision included the theory of trickle-down economics: as businesses were freed from governmental regulation, their profits would eventually trickle down to the American public through the creation of jobs and strengthening of wages. Americans would then be able to spend more money, which would further bolster the economy.

Republicans argued that the welfare programs implemented in the 1960s had turned Americans into government dependents and that only the reality of poverty would inspire lower-class Americans to adopt an independent spirit of enterprise. This championing of the free-market system focused the country's attention on the amassing of wealth and material possessions, fostering a dramatic escalation in consumerism and a new zeitgeist for the age. Reagan's own inauguration cost eleven million dollars. Soon after entering the White House, the first lady, Nancy Reagan, continued the spending spree with expensive renovations at the White House, which included a new set of china that cost more than two hundred thousand dollars. Initially, this lavish spending was criticized, but eventually, the entire country became caught up in the attraction of wealth.

In the 1987 film *Wall Street*, the New York financier Gordon Gekko insists that "greed is good," which became the mantra of the 1980s for many American consumers as well as for investors on Wall Street. During this decade, American goods were more plentiful than ever, and Americans began to feel that they had the right to acquire them. This age of self-interest was promoted by the media through periodicals like *Money* magazine, which taught Americans how to dramatically increase their earnings and glorified entrepreneurs like Steven Jobs, the founder of Apple Computers, and the real-estate tycoon Donald Trump. One of the most popular television shows of the time was *Lifestyles of the Rich and Famous*, which brought viewers into the lavish homes of the superrich.

Casey Affleck, Summer Phoenix, and Matt Damon in a 2002 production of This is Our Youth © Donald Cooper/Photostage. Reproduced by permission

Shopping became Americans' favorite pastime during the 1980s. Apart from going to malls, consumers could also satisfy their shopping urges by accessing the mall from home. With the advent of the shopping television network QVC and the steady stream of catalogues and telemarketing pitches from a wide range of mail-order companies, such as Sears and L. L. Bean, consumers could purchase a variety of goods over the phone.

Voices of Dissent

Some voices critical to the promotion of America's consumer appetites were emerging in the early 1980s and became stronger at the end of the decade, when evidence of insider trading on Wall Street resulted in prison terms for greedy speculators. Economists noted that the unemployment rate reached its highest point in more than forty years in 1982, which helped raise the number of Americans living in poverty to the highest level in seventeen years. Sociologists warned of the effects of homelessness and drug abuse and insisted that more governmental programs were needed.

Writers like Tom Wolfe (*Bonfire of the Vanities*, 1987) and Jay McInerney (*Bright Lights, Big City*, 1984) chronicled the empty lives of Wall Street's elite. Musicians made political statements by organizing concerts and recording music to help a variety of social and political problems. In 1984, Bob Geldof, for example, put together a band of Irish and British musicians, called Band Aid, to cut a single to raise money for famine relief in Ethiopia. Geldof went on to organize multivenue charity concerts, called Live Aid, in London and Philadelphia for the same cause. Elizabeth Taylor took up fundraising activities for the awareness and treatment of AIDS.

CRITICAL OVERVIEW

The critical response to *This Is Our Youth* has been overwhelmingly positive. Many critics, like Robert Brustein, in his review for the *New Republic*, have applauded the play's realism and praised Lonergan as a "penetrating cultural historian."

Brustein characterizes the play as a "sharp [x-ray] of social abscess and moral atrophy," noting its "tough-minded, almost clinical examination of the aimlessness, the vacuity, and the emotional deadness" of its privileged main characters. He concludes, "Lonergan's capacity to evoke these qualities without moralizing about them is the mark of a significant writer."

Stefan Kanfer, in a review for the *New Leader*, echoes Brustein's assessment of Lonergan's talent when he writes, "A lesser playwright might have been content to let [the initial conflict] occupy the evening." But while Dennis and Warren are trying to decide what to do about the money, "Lonergan introduces a third party and takes the play to another level." Kanfer insists that "the star of the evening is the playwright, who summons up a world much larger than the three actors onstage" and who has "a gift for character analysis, dramatic tension and the kind of wry, ironic dialogue that jump-starts the Off-Broadway season."

In his review for *Variety*, Matt Wolf claims that Lonergan is "a playwright blessed with an ear so finely attuned to slacker-speak that every 'um' and 'man' seemed to encapsulate an era." Wolf comments that this "master dramatist" "clearly and cleanly sets forth" the play's "jumble of emotions." He notes "how seamlessly orchestrated the play feels, its landscape encompassing burgeoning romance and long-abiding friendship alongside sudden and brutal ache." In a closing note, he praises the "numerous perceptions so piercingly captured by a play that could not seem more adult."

Richard Ouzounian, in his review for *Variety*, has a darker vision of the play, concluding that it is "a deeply disturbing look at the moral emptiness of a generation." However, in her review for *American Theatre*, Pamela Renner calls it an "acerbic comedy" and says that "the transitional self of adolescence is hard to pin down in writing, but *Youth* draws urgency and propulsive strength from its presence."

CRITICISM

Wendy Perkins

Perkins is a professor of American and English literature and film. In this essay, she traces the development of one of the central characters in the play as he takes the first steps toward adulthood.

At the beginning of Lonergan's play *This Is Our Youth*, twenty-one-year-old Dennis Ziegler tells his nineteen-year-old friend Warren Straub, who has just stolen fifteen thousand dollars from his father, "Nobody can stand to have you around because you're such an annoying loudmouthed little creep, and now you're like some kind of fugitive from *justice*? What is gonna happen to you, man?"

"BY THE END OF THE PLAY . . . WARREN WILL EMERGE FROM HIS SELF-INDUCED FOG, AS HE BEGINS TO MAKE A THOUGHTFUL ASSESSMENT OF THE CHARACTERS OF THOSE AROUND HIM. THIS NEW AWARENESS OF HIS WORLD AND HIS PLACE IN IT WILL MARK THE BEGINNING OF HIS TRANSITION INTO ADULTHOOD."

Although Dennis's assessment of his friend is characteristically harsh, Warren often proves himself to be quite annoying, a trait intensified by his decision to hole up in Dennis's apartment until he can figure out what to do about his father's money. He also wonders what will happen to him when his father finds out that his money is missing. Warren, along with Dennis, never thinks much beyond the next few days, which are often viewed through a haze of marijuana smoke. By the end of the play, however, Warren will emerge from his self-induced fog, as he begins to make a thoughtful assessment of the characters of those around him. This new awareness of his world and his place in it will mark the beginning of his transition into adulthood.

Both Warren and Dennis are the spoiled, rootless offspring of Upper West Side elitist parents who have written them off as essentially worthless members of society. Robert Brustein, in his review for the *New Republic*, writes that Lonergan is a "penetrating cultural historian" who has realistically depicted "the aimlessness, the vacuity, and the emotional deadness" of these youths.

WHAT DO I READ NEXT?

- Lonergan's 1982 play *The Rennings Children* focuses on the psychological problems and tensions within a family.
- Arthur Miller's play *Death of a Salesman* (1949) looks at the troubled relationship between a salesman and his two sons.
- J. D. Salinger's 1951 novel *The Catcher in the Rye*, celebrated as an acute expression of the cynical adolescent zeitgeist, chronicles a teenaged boy's maturation into adulthood.
- Jonathan Larson's play *Rent* (1996) presents eight different stories of young adults in New York City in the 1990s as they struggle to cope with poverty, drugs, and AIDS.

In her review for *American Theatre*, Pamela Renner notes an important difference, however, between the two main characters and their parents. Renner notes that Warren and Dennis "both know that they are running out of excuses." And, she says, "they don't mistake their own disaffection for moral authenticity; it's just a way of gaining some breathing room until they figure out what they want." They are determined not to become just like their parents. They reject the false philanthropy of Dennis's mother, who, Warren insists, is "a bleeding-heart dominatrix with like a *hairdo*," and the greed of Warren's father, who is involved in business deals with the mob.

At the beginning of the play, Warren has no idea what he wants, other than the money that he has just stolen from his father. He steals it initially to make his father "pay" for kicking him out of the house and for emotionally and physically abusing him for so many years. Once he has it, he is not sure what to do with it, other than to buy a few bottles of champagne and some drugs and, he hopes, lure girls to an expensive suite at the Plaza Hotel for a night of partying.

Warren knows that without the money, he is not likely to get a date. He illustrates his penchant for disaster not only when he steals money that his father most likely got from gangsters but also when he destroys Dennis's girlfriend's sculpture. Dennis underlines this trait when he asks, "How emblematic of your personality is it that you walk into a room for *ten minutes* and break the *exact item* calculated to wreak the maximum possible amount of havoc?" He determines Warren to be "a total troublemaker."

Warren has a long list of other faults, as Dennis continually points out. Dennis notes that Warren is not very bright, which he has proved by stealing his father's money, and has little to say unless he is asked a direct question. Warren's inability to establish his own identity has prompted him to adopt Dennis's habits and style, which others, including Dennis, recognize as blatant hero worship. These traits have prevented him from attracting girls, a fact to which Dennis often calls attention, until Warren has fifteen thousand in cash ready to spend on a night of partying.

Warren soon discovers, however, that the money is not a guarantee of success. When Jessica appears to have lost interest in him the morning after their stay at the Plaza, Dennis inquires, "What kind of talent for misery do you have, man?" Warren replies, "I don't know. I guess I'm pretty advanced." Warning him that his destructive lifestyle may eventually ruin him as it does other less advantaged youths, his father has insisted that "the only difference between you and them is my money. . . . It's like a big . . . safety net, but you can't stretch it too far, man, because your sister fell right through it."

For all of his faults, however, Warren has—as Lonergan's stage directions suggest—"large tracts of thoughtfulness in his personality." Still, at this point in his life, they "are not doing him much good." He exhibits "beneath his natural eccentricity a dogged self-possession" that suggests a certain core of inner strength. Brustein comments, "Warren seems at first to be slightly brain-dead—restless, easily bored, always asking 'What's up?'—but the closer we get to him, the more sharply focused he becomes."

Renner writes, "It's a testament to Lonergan's slyness and restraint as a writer that one comes to care powerfully about his hapless Warren—who has a way of reminding you instinctively how much the empty spaces inside your heart ached at his age." We note his painful self-consciousness as he tries to impress Jessica enough to encourage her to give him a chance. We glimpse his heartache in his

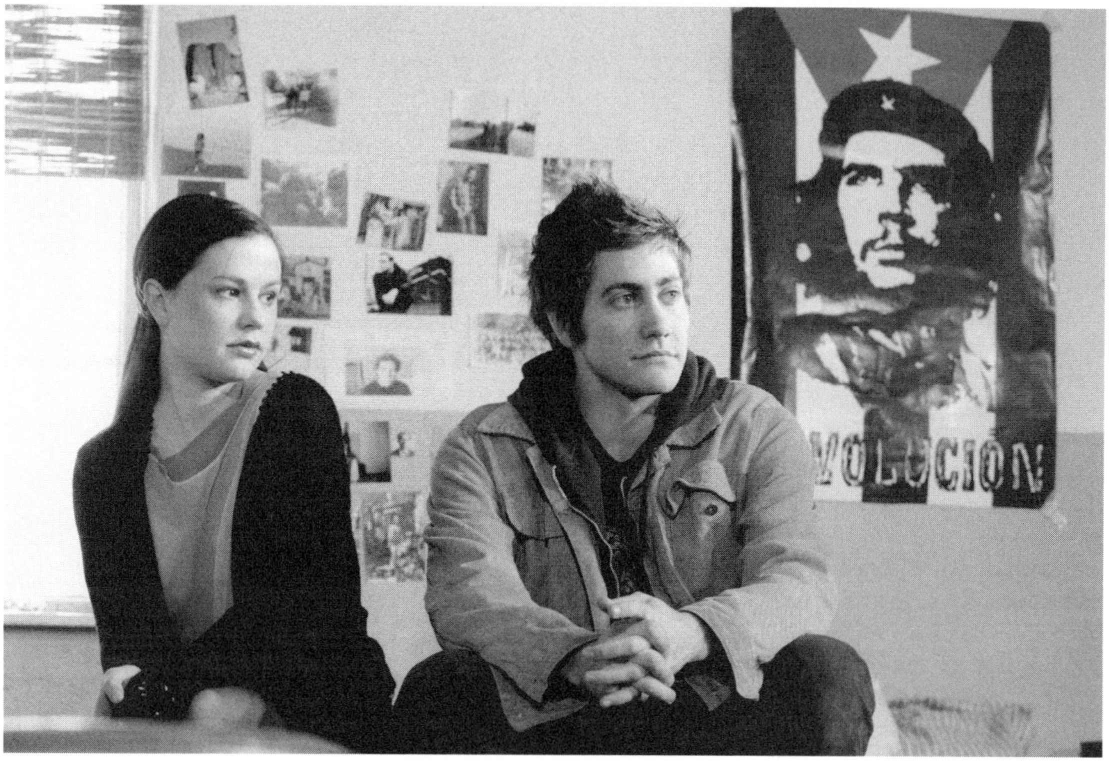

Anna Paquin and Jake Gyllenhaal in a 2002 production of This Is Our Youth

attachment to his suitcase full of toys, "the proceeds from my unhappy childhood" as he calls them. These toys are "authentic" artifacts to Warren of moments when he could escape the loneliness of a childhood that offered him little comfort. We recognize the importance of the baseball cap given to him by a grandfather who apparently provided him with moments of attention and affection that he did not often experience. Finally, we observe the painful loss of his murdered sister, a loss with which he has not been able to come to terms. Never, though, does he succumb to self-pity.

Warren's thoughtfulness emerges in his interaction with Jessica. In an effort to prove to her that he cares about helping others, he insists, "I'm a total Democrat." His actions support his contention, revealing that he has a kinder heart than does Dennis, who repeatedly screams obscenities at his girlfriend when she expresses anger about her smashed sculpture. Warren is truly concerned about Jessica's self-consciousness when she discovers that he has discussed with Dennis their night together at the Plaza, and he does everything he can to put her at ease.

Jessica, however, does not prove worthy of his concern, as she illustrates when she asks for his grandfather's baseball cap as payment for his telling Dennis about their night together. This event forces Warren to stop worrying about how he appears to Jessica and to pay attention to her true character. He tests her shallowness when he hands over the cap that she knows means so much to him. When she accepts it, noting his distress, she fails the test. Warren subsequently rejects her suggestion that they see each other later that week with the appropriate amount of irony, declaring, "I don't think we can. I'm all out of baseball hats." He stands his moral ground when she tries to return it, threatening, "You try to give me that hat back one more time, I swear to God I'll . . . *burn* it."

The incident with Jessica appears to have lessened Warren's self-consciousness and increased his awareness of others, which becomes evident when he speaks on the phone with his father. After admitting that he stole the money, he engages in a conversation with his father about his sister, admitting, "I think about her all the time." He says that he sees her "in my imagination." That conversations ends on an ugly note when he declares to his father, "Do whatever you want. . . . I hate you too." But Warren soon displays a true sense of compassion for his father. He explains to Dennis, "For the last nine years he's been trying to literally *pound* his life back into shape. But it's not really going too well, because he's totally by himself. . . . You know?"

By the end of the play, his compassion extends even to Dennis, who has taken every opportunity to criticize and belittle him during the past twenty-four hours. Recognizing Dennis's overwhelming need to envision himself as a role model to his friends, Warren calms him with false assurance, "All right, all right. You're on my side." The stage directions in this final scene note that Warren looks at Dennis "as if from a very great distance." Warren, in fact, has distanced himself, by the end of the play, from Dennis, who is still caught up in the same destructive self-absorption that Warren displayed when he first arrived at the apartment. Unlike Dennis, however, Warren has been able, through his capacity for introspection and insight into the character of others, to take his first steps toward maturation and a clearer sense of selfhood.

Source: Wendy Perkins, Critical Essay on *This Is Our Youth*, in *Drama for Students*, Thomson Gale, 2006.

Myles Weber

In the following review excerpt, Weber identifies Lonergan as an exception to the dearth of talent in current American theater, and praises the characters and dialogue in This Is Our Youth.

"Our American theater sucks," declared Michael Cunningham in an interview with Tony Kushner at the height of *Angels in America*'s popularity. Kushner had to agree that there probably was, in percentage terms, more bad drama produced in our culture than bad prose fiction, bad poetry, or even bad film. And playwright Suzan-Lori Parks makes the same point in her essay "Elements of Style": in no other genre these days, she laments, is the writing so awful.

Why should this be? Kushner offered the plausible explanation that money lures the talented away to other fields; only the chronically unemployable continue to plug away in theater. But Parks faults the slim intentions of the artists: the entire institutional apparatus of theater encourages works intended not to delight, fascinate, or awe the audience but rather to elicit a safe political reaction—"to discuss some issue," as Parks puts it. The buzz from a topical play can catapult the work, the playwright, the production, even the theater company involved, out of obscurity. There is every professional reason, then, to write bad drama of this particular issue-oriented sort.

> "THOUGH I CAN'T SAY LONERGAN REALLY BELONGS IN THE THEATER, I WOULD BE DELIGHTED IF HE SHOULD CHOOSE TO REMAIN THERE."

Rebecca Gilman, a successful Chicago playwright, is riding a national wave of buzz generated by two recent works—*Spinning into Butter* and *Boy Gets Girl* (both published by Faber and Faber in 2000)—that each discuss an approved contemporary issue: liberal racism in the first case, violence against women in the second. By way of contrast, Kenneth Lonergan took a different route from obscurity, and I believe it spared him the necessity of writing bad plays. Lonergan worked with various theater companies in New York—Second Stage, the New Group, Naked Angels—but finally rose to prominence by following the money trail to film. His screenplay credits include the Hollywood comedy *Analyze This* and the independent feature *You Can Count on Me,* which he also directed, and which deservedly won him wider praise than any single stage production could.

Like Gilman, Lonergan has two plays currently published in trade paperback editions. Both works display the acumen and modesty of a truly gifted artist. *The Waverly Gallery* (Grove, 2000) chronicles the final undignified months in the life of Gladys Green, who—hard of hearing and losing her memory—just likes to yammer. "Everyone needs someone to talk to," she explains, "otherwise you'd just go nutty. I love to talk to people." A one-time lawyer, but now the naive proprietress of a money-losing art gallery in Greenwich Village, Gladys is provided with the gratuitous resume of a political radical who found herself in Germany just as the Nazis were consolidating power. But there is an aura of the playwright's autobiography clinging to Gladys and her family that may account for stock elements of her personal history.

A basically endearing woman, Gladys alarms those with responsibility for her wellbeing when she invites an unknown artist to sleep in the back-room of her gallery. She compounds that error, in the eyes of her daughter Ellen and grandson Daniel, by imposing her hospitable inclinations on them and also, for good measure, misplacing Ellen's Vermont cabin in a neighboring state.

ELLEN: She's getting worse.

DANIEL: OH, she's definitely getting worse, Mom.

A play about a character with a frustratingly disordered mind, who is in a frustrating and combative relationship with her family, could have been itself a frustrating experience. But *The Waverly Gallery* is not frustrating—it's an unusually pleasurable juggling act of overlapping, misdirected dialogue. The grandson, Daniel, addresses the audience at regular intervals. That works to good effect, in part because we need some order imposed on the narrative, but also because the author's language is precise and deft. This is the case in his stage directions and character descriptions as well. Don, the possibly talentless artist, is described as "a careful, hardworking and detail-fixated person who devotes a lot of his mental energy to very slowly and carefully arriving at the wrong conclusion." As much an author surrogate as grandson Daniel, Don feels compelled to reproduce on canvas the image of a macrame decoration his mother once made, to preserve for posterity the domestic details of his family history.

With its gestures toward autobiography, its painfully humorous representations of dementia, and Daniel's apt if obvious conclusion—"it must be worth a lot to be alive"—*The Waverly Gallery* reminded me of Christopher Durang's *The Marriage of Bette and Boo,* as well as Thornton Wilder's *Our Town,* a stark, horrific play dismissed as soft by those with faulty memories. Like those works, *The Waverly Gallery* confronts honestly the unpleasant aspects of its subject matter. Gladys, with her fumbled insulin injections and incessant word salad, ends up completely alienating her grandson, who lives in the same building and wishes to preserve memories of an unfaded, robust Gladys. "She rang my doorbell so much I stopped answering it all the time," Daniel confesses. "Instead I'd just go to the door and look through the peephole to make sure she was okay, and then I'd watch this weird little convex image of her turn around in the hallway and go back into her apartment." For her part, Daniel's mother, Ellen, wishes her own eighty-five-year-old mother peacefully dead. "[B]ut Dr. Wagner says there's nothing wrong with her physically," she tells Daniel. "She could go on like this for another ten years."

It is the strongest praise I can give the playwright that these acts of disloyalty, hurtful and selfish as they are, can be read as tragic signs of both hpelessness and, ultimately, love.

Like *The Waverly Gallery,* Lonergan's previous play, *This Is Our Youth* (Overlook Press, 2000), features characters trying to evoke a less corrupted, more energetic past. But, aged nineteen to twenty-one, they are only just embarking on the young adulthood they are trying to reclaim. Their current misadventures are self-conscious attempts to manufacture fond memories before they ineluctably mature into the roles currently held by their impeccably responsible, upper-middle-class parents.

The characters themselves are completely aware of their impending metamorphoses. Warren, the younger of two male characters, is told by his mentor and abusive friend Dennis, "I'm like a one-man youth culture for you pathetic assholes. You're gonna remember your youth as like a gray stoned haze punctuated by a series of beatings from your [f——]in' dad, and like, my jokes. God damn!" Jessica, whom Warren has designs on, offers an equally clear appraisal: "[R]ight now you're all like this rich little pot-smoking burnout rebel, but ten years from now you're gonna be like a plastic surgeon reminiscing about how wild you used to be."

The story is this: Warren has stolen $15,000 from his estranged father who, though not a criminal himself, is in business with criminals. Dennis hatches a plot to use the stolen money to finance a quick drug-selling scheme, return the stolen cash before the theft is detected, and walk away with a neat profit. (Even as they stall at becoming their parents, it is clear that they already are their parents.) As the plot unfolds, Lonergan includes a few half hearted nods to nihilism:

DENNIS: What is gonna happen to you, man?

WARREN: What is gonna happen to anybody? Who cares?

But the more prominent authorial tone is caution: characters play with fire, hoping not to get burned. Still, some do. Dennis's dealer friend, Stuey, dies of a drug overdose, and we are told that Warren's older sister was murdered years before at about this same age, as she passed through her own rebellious stage.

Set in 1982, *This Is Our Youth* owes a lot to *Less Than Zero,* Bret Easton Ellis's novel from that era. Both feature a set of young, privileged characters whose self-inflicted injuries are only as severe as they themselves permit. Family wealth acts as a safety net but, alas, some characters choose to stretch the weave too far and slip through.

Lonergan's play also pays homage to *American Buffalo,* David Mamet's own three-character drama involving petty theft, the pawning of useless goods, and other vague dealings in a half-assed criminal underworld. And like *American Buffalo,* Lonergan's play concludes with a consideration of male friendship, which trumps family as the major concern of characters caught in this Peter Pan world of extended adolescence.

The play's theme gets punctuated perhaps a bit too hard when Warren, to cover his debts when the drug deal falls apart, is forced to sell his collection of mint-condition toys; Dennis's panicked conversion to sobriety after Stuey's death also seems to me too easy (I thought the author might have been setting up a joke—that Dennis resolves to "totally stop" with drugs every month or so); and the ghost of Warren's sister, meant to provide depth and poignancy to her brother's antics a la *The Catcher in the Rye,* is a bit too convenient. But the play's most basic elements are sturdy. And regardless of how pleased David Mamet claims to be with the structure of *American Buffalo,* it is actually the characters and his famous dialogue that form the strength of that play. The same is true here, whether it is Warren explaining to Jessica that he's never been into the cigarette scene himself ("But I hear great things about it") or Dennis putting Warren in his place: "Listen. You're a [f——]in' idiot. You never have any money. Nobody can stand to have you around. And you can't get laid. I mean, man, you cannot get laid. You never get laid."

Dennis is, in fact, a rare creation: a powerful, confident, amoral personality who doesn't seem too precious or too much adored by the playwright for his naughtiness. Lonergan gives Dennis significant blind spots that undercut his slacker bravado and slyly reflect on the playwright's own hubristic forays away from theater. "I should totally direct movies, man, I'd be a genius at it," Dennis brags. "Like if you take the average person with the average sensibility or sense of humor or the way they look at the world and what thoughts they have or what they think, and you compare it to the way I look at [sh——t] and the [sh——t] I come up with to say, or just the slant I put on [sh——t], there's just like no comparison at all. I could totally make movies, man, I would be like one of the greatest movie makers of all time."

As it turns out, *You Can Count on Me* established Lonergan as one of the most intelligent movie makers of recent years. And his two published plays suggest he is one of the few prominent contemporary playwrights worthy of significant notice. Though I can't say Lonergan really belongs in the theater, I would be delighted if he should choose to remain there. Still, if he can continue to produce films of a quality equal to his plays, and for a much larger audience, more power to him. . . .

Source: Myles Weber, "Two Times Two: Some Notes on Our Contemporary Theater," in *New England Review,* Vol. 23, No. 2, Spring 2002, pp. 179–86.

Robert Brustein

In the following review, Brustein calls Lonergan "a significant writer" and praises his "tough-minded, almost clinical" approach to his subject matter.

Two Sharp x-rays of social abscess and moral atrophy are currently playing in New York theaters. *Closer* (The Music Box) follows the purposeless sexual adventures of four London professionals. *This Is Our Youth* (Douglas Fairbanks Theater) focuses on the directionless lives of three young middle-class New Yorkers. Both demonstrate that playwrights can sometimes be among our most penetrating cultural historians.

The American play, written by the gifted Kenneth Lonergan, has a misleading title. Rather than being a cautionary sociological study of wayward teenagers, *This Is Our Youth* is a tough-minded, almost clinical examination of the aimlessness, the vacuity, and the emotional deadness of a trio of privileged kids in their twenties. Set in 1982, at the beginning of the Reagan era, the play takes place in the West Side studio apartment of Dennis Ziegler (Mark Rosenthal), who is discovered lying in an unmade bed, surrounded by newspapers and magazines strewn carelessly around the floor. His dazed eyes are fixed upon an Abbott and Costello movie.

The apartment is a gift from his parents, out of gratitude for the fact that he has no desire to live with them. Dennis has festooned the place with recruitment posters and basketball trivia. Into this squalid den comes another figure estranged from his parents, Warren Straub (Mark Ruffalo), a

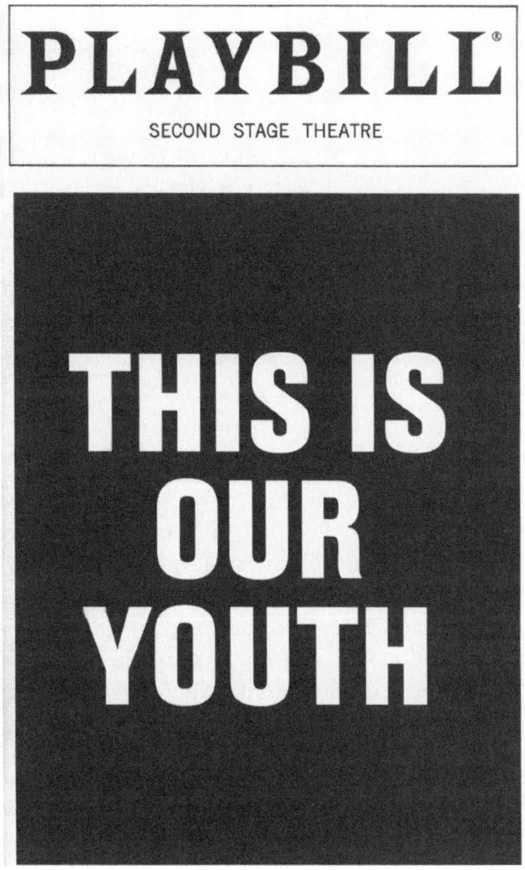

Playbill from a production of This Is Our Youth *at the Second Stage Theatre* Performing Arts Books, NYC. PLAYBILL ® is a registered trademark of Playbill Incorporated, N.Y.C. All rights reserved. Reproduced by permission

zonked-out airhead wearing a parka and backpack. Following a fight with his father, Warren has fled the house with $15,000 of his dad's ill-gotten gains. These two characters, both of them wholly concerned with sex, drugs, and rock and roll, resemble the kind of affectless druggies usually played in the movies by Robert Downey Jr. Indeed, the action of the play revolves around a burgeoning cocaine deal that begins to acquire some of the intensity of the quest for the Holy Grail.

Warren seems at first to be slightly brain-dead—restless, easily bored, always asking "What's up?"—but the closer we get to him, the more sharply focused he becomes. He clearly has "an advanced talent for misery." His sister has been murdered in California for no apparent reason. His father has no use for him. And he is always breaking things or knocking them over—most calamitously for him, the hefty stash of coke that he has managed to obtain from a pusher with his father's money. His other major passions are for "retro" objects such as toasters manufactured in the 1960s and a Wrigley Field Opening Day baseball cap, though he seems to have a little feeling for a young woman named Jessica Goldman (Missy Yager), who has come to the apartment to share his bag of blow. After an awkward bit of foreplay, he books a room in the Plaza Hotel ("I happen to be extremely liquid at the moment"), where the two manage a perfunctory kind of sexual consummation.

As for Dennis, his rich mother is a big-city social worker, "a bleeding-heart dominatrix" devoted to installing swimming pools for the poor and lording her liberal sentiments over the rich husband who supports her. His offstage girlfriend Valerie is a sculptress, one of whose pieces—two lesbians making out—is carelessly smashed by the hapless Warren, thus leading to a major fight between her and Dennis. The two young men move in and out of their various sexual relationships with the same bored indifference they bring to their sense of the future. Dennis contemplates maybe going to cooking school in Venice, or maybe "I'll totally direct movies (get the best actors in the world and let them improvise)." Warren will probably return to his parents with what is left of the stolen money.

These are young people with no belief in themselves, and even less faith in their hypocritical parents or their disillusioned peers. For them, Reagan's America is populated with people once passionately eager to change the face of civilization, who eventually said, "You know what? Maybe I'll just be a lawyer." What gives these creatures some life is their personal style, perfectly captured by the director, Mark Brokaw, and by the three actors, particularly Mark Ruffalo, his brows knitted, his shoulders hunched, a carpenter ant trying to disappear into the woodwork. Although the play sometimes reproduces the drug-dazed atmosphere of David Rabe's *Hurlyburly,* it also reminded me of *Ivanov.* The male characters have the same flabby characteristics, the same elegiac sense of loss as Chekhov's superfluous man. Kenneth Lonergan's capacity to evoke these qualities without moralizing about them is the mark of a significant writer.

Patrick Marber is an even more exciting young talent. His *Closer* is the most interesting new English play I have seen since Pinter's *Betrayal,* a work it somewhat resembles. Indeed, as an anatomy of adultery, *Closer* may be even more impressive. It is certainly a more compassionate piece of

> "KENNETH LONERGAN'S CAPACITY TO EVOKE THESE QUALITIES WITHOUT MORALIZING ABOUT THEM IS THE MARK OF A SIGNIFICANT WRITER."

theater—Pinter with heart, however bitter at the root. As both a writer and a director, and with the aid of a fine, functional design by Vicki Mortimer and a score by Paddy Cunneen that sounds like modern Bach, Marber has composed a piece of music himself, a classical string quartet in which the various players keep exchanging their parts and their instruments.

Put another way, *Closer* is a contemporary version of *Les Liaisons Dangereuses,* where the four lovers, though less predatory than those of Choderlos de Laclos, are equally obsessed with erotic conquest and immediate gratification. Throughout the play, Alice, a young striptease *artiste,* Dan, a would-be novelist reduced to writing obituaries, Larry, a dermatologist, and Anna, a photographer, keep moving in and out of each other's lives with the regularity of commuter trains picking up passengers at a station. These characters change partners as if they were the only four people in the world, satisfying their compulsive sexual needs with very little restraint, though with occasional pangs of conscience.

At times, this process becomes extremely manipulative. A justly celebrated scene in the play shows Dan online, pretending to be a woman, exchanging hot sex talk with Larry in an Internet chat room (their hilarious typed messages are projected onto a screen). Pretending to be Anna, Dan entices Larry into a rendezvous with her at the Aquarium, a meeting that eventually leads to their marriage. Sex-obsessed, these characters are also, most of them, obsessed with the truth. Larry informs Anna that he visited a whore in New York. "Why did you tell me?" she asks. "Because I love you," he replies. Anna, in turn, informs Larry that she's leaving him for Dan. It's not enough for Larry to learn she's betrayed him. He has to know all the details. "Is he a good [f——]?. . . Better than me?" ("Gentler," she replies.) Later, it is not enough for Dan to hear Anna admit that she went to bed with her ex-husband. He also has to know the details. "Did you enjoy it?" "Did you come?" "Did you fake it?" "Do you fake it with me?" *Closer* is extremely explicit about the rituals of sexual transactions, and extremely provocative in the way it demonstrates how for some people the act of cuckoldry can itself be a form of erotic pleasure.

If the absolute value among these people is honesty, their prime mover is not love but lust. The characters try to trick out their infidelities with romantic inventions, but these are easily exposed. "Stupid expression. 'I fell in love'," muses Alice, when Dan says he's leaving her for Anna. "As if you had no choice. . . . You didn't fall in love. You gave in to temptation." Toward the end, she sadly concludes, "They spend a lifetime [f——]ing and they never learn how to make love." *Closer* explores the vanishing line between conscience and temptation, treating adultery like some unmanageable habit, similar to smoking. Smoking, in fact, is the play's parallel metaphor. Those able to kick the habit are the ones most likely to be faithful. But don't count on it.

The major victim of these amoral sexual exchanges is Alice, the only one who has managed to give up smoking. Returning to her old profession after having been abandoned by Dan, she is visited by Larry, who stuffs her stockings with money in the hope of getting her to sleep with him. But although she is willing to show him every orifice of her body, she will not, at first, let him use her for his purposes. Significantly, she is the only character who is not passionate about veracity. ("Lying," she says, "is the most fun a girl can have without taking her clothes off.") Finding her again, Dan demands that she tell him the truth about her relations with Larry, "because I'm addicted to it, because without it we are animals." She doesn't want to lie, but she can't tell the truth. Forced to admit that she had relations with Larry, she sacrifices what is left of her identity ("I'm no one"), confesses to Dan that she no longer loves him, and spits in his face.

It is because she is unable to live with truth that Alice commits suicide. At the end, it is revealed that she has been living the most spectacular lie of all, having taken her name and her biography off a memorial tablet belonging to someone else. The three survivors gather around her fake memorial at the end permeated by an enormous sense of remorse.

Memorial blocks constitute the backdrop of the set—a design that gradually accumulates all the scenic pieces used in the play, as if these four lives were a detritus of props and furniture. Marber's writing is reinforced by his stagecraft, his remarkable sense of space and time, and especially his impeccable cast: Natasha Richardson's cool and reserved Anna; Rupert Graves's anguished, driven Dan; Anna Friel's plucky if vulnerable Alice; and Ciaran Hinds's authoritative, somewhat barky Larry.

From the 1930s to the 1960s, the theater was usually much more explicit about sex than the movies, a medium forced to ban four-letter words and to limit lovemaking to a chaste kiss before a fade-out. Following Bertolucci's breakthrough in *Last Tango in Paris,* the movies became so sexually explicit they made the theater look priggish by contrast. One of the virtues of *Closer* is the way it prods the stage into joining the sexual revolution. The play tells us more about the tragic consequences of this revolution than almost any other work I know.

Source: Robert Brustein, "Two Moral X-rays," in *New Republic*, June 28, 1999, pp. 36–38.

"THE TEEN-AGED LOSER DIDN'T BECOME A SURGEON AFTER ALL. HE BECAME A PLAYWRIGHT WITH A GIFT FOR CHARACTER ANALYSIS, DRAMATIC TENSION AND THE KIND OF WRY, IRONIC DIALOGUE THAT JUMP-STARTS THE OFF-BROADWAY SEASON."

Stefan Kanfer

In the following review, Kanfer remarks on the accurate and realistic portrayal of setting, characters, and plot in This Is Our Youth.

Remittance men are dubious characters whose families pay them to live elsewhere. In the 1880s they could be found in the backwaters of Southeast Asia or the trading posts of Africa. There, the checks arrived by packet boat. A hundred years later they tended to set down roots on the West Side of Manhattan. There, the money came by plastic—credit cards, underwritten by Daddy.

The Second Stage production of Kenneth Lonergan's discerning tragicomedy. *This Is Our Youth,* examines the life of one such figure, and another in the making. The 20-year-old Dennis Ziegler (Mark Rosenthal) would be an ideal model for the "Before" in a Just Say No commercial. This bipolar windbag not only takes drugs, he pushes them—as well as himself, ceaselessly booming about his gifts for persuasion and leadership. In fact, only one person is naive enough to fall under his sway: Warren Straub (Mark Ruffalo), 18, a hunched, gangling shlemozzle whose father has just exiled him for substance abuse. What Straub Sr. does not know is that his son, on the way out the door, purloined $15,000 in cash. Now that Warren has committed the crime, he has second thoughts. Could he hole up in Dennis' apartment while he ponders his next move?

Dennis is in no mood for him. As he sees it, his place is too small and his life too big. Besides, what if Warren's father finds out about the theft? The lingerie manufacturer is a Mafioso. Who knows what he'll do when he misses the money? "My father is not a criminal," Warren protests. "He just does business with criminals." But Dennis is not mollified. Between refusals he keeps dialing numbers and yelling into the phone, attempting to bring off another deal or raging at an obviously bewildered girlfriend. With such a crowded schedule how can he possibly accommodate Warren? Still, he does need a sounding board for his egomania . . .

Negotiations between pusher and acolyte occupy most of Act I, with close attention paid to their backgrounds. The former schoolmates met at a West Side progressive academy where, according to Dennis, "they think it's going to cripple you for life if you learn how to spell." Dennis' father is a celebrated artist, embittered by his losing battle with cancer. His mother is a "bleeding heart dominatrix"—her son's definition of a social service administrator. Warren's father also suffers from an incurable malady: He remains traumatized by the murder several years ago of his 19-year-old daughter, Warren's sister. In the aftermath his ex-wife fled to California, where she and her new boyfriend do "volunteer work for some sort of grape-picking civil liberties organization." Clearly, both young men are grieving in one way or another, beseeching their parents for attention that will always be lavished on others.

Lonergan has given his characters little indulgence, but plenty to do and much to talk about.

Warren, for example, has brought with him a valise full of old toys ("the proceeds from my unhappy childhood"). Some are worth serious money. Should he sell, or hang on to them in case his father closes in and reclaims the 15 grand? As for Dennis, how long will it take the narcs to catch up with this middleman between the Colombian cartel and students who want a line of coke? A lesser playwright might have been content to let these questions occupy the evening. But Dennis is never allowed to be still; he sets up an elaborate scam, planning to use the stolen loot to buy and sell some cocaine. If the deal comes off, Warren can return all of his father's money, and Dennis can pocket a handsome profit. While all this is transpiring, Lonergan introduces a third party and takes the play to another level.

Unlike her acquaintances, Jessica Goldman (Missy Yager) hopes to make something of herself. An occasional user, she has dropped by to palaver and maybe buy a little something for the weekend. She swiftly develops a thing for Warren, but he is so inept that she practically has to draw a blueprint for his next moves. Still, the ungainly youth is not without his own kind of wit. When they begin to dance, stepping all over each other's feet, he mutters, "If only society would give us a chance" in a perfect parody of James Dean in *Rebel Without a Cause.*

Jessica's political views are emblematic of the '80s West Side. Ronald Reagan has recently been elected President, and therefore, "I definitely feel evil has, like, triumphed in our time." Suddenly assuming the role of Cassandra, she informs Warren, "Right now you're a rich little pot-smoking burnout, but 10 years from now you'll be a plastic surgeon." This is a depressing thought, "because it just basically invalidates whoever you are right now." Never mind that whoever he is right now is rudderless and emotionally immature. After all, he can always make her laugh. As he courts Jessica, for example, Warren notes, "Chivalry isn't dead. It just smells funny."

The young woman's aim in life is to graduate from the Fashion Institute of Technology. Until then, Jessica wouldn't mind a little romance in her life, and when Warren flashes his bankroll she agrees to follow him to the destination of his choice: the Plaza Hotel for a night of carousal. The next morning Dennis expresses shock: They should have gone to the Carlyle, the Plaza is tacky. And he returns to the phone, detailing the schemes that cannot lead anywhere but down.

If Dennis' detritus-filled apartment is anything like my old one on the West Side, it has an oversized bathtub with three faucets labeled "Hot," "Cold" and "Waste." These are the prevalent themes of the evening, with an accent on the third indicator. Anomie is not the liveliest of subjects, and these are not the most likable of people. Yet the cast makes them compelling, credible and in a strange way, sympathetic. When the curtain descends, the trio of actors gives the impression that Dennis, Warren and Jessica are very much alive, slackers taking one step forward and two steps back until something—maturity, jail, whatever—comes along to deal them a new hand.

At the McGinn-Cazale Theater, Allen Moyer's set is accurate down to the smudges around the doorknob and the framed pictures of the Honeymooners over the sink; and Michael Krass' costumes cannily evoke the period of thrift shop chic. Under Mark Brokaw's strong direction, Rosenthal provides a heady mix of swagger and distress; Ruffalo fully inhabits his role of Holden Caulfield redivivus, the wisecracks never quite covering the catch in his throat; and Yager hilariously conveys the kind of sexual insecurity that did not end with the '80s.

But the star of the evening is the playwright, who summons up a world much larger than the three actors onstage. Lonergan has stated, unsurprisingly, that there is a great deal of autobiography in the play—first: presented in a short run back in 1996—and that as a student at the late progressive Walden School he and his friends were very much like the credit-card mutineers of *This Is Our Youth.* He has gone so far as to suggest that there is a bit of himself in Warren. If so, then Jessica's prediction has turned out to be incorrect. The teenaged loser didn't become a surgeon after all. He became a playwright with a gift for character analysis, dramatic tension and the kind of wry, ironic dialogue that jump-starts the Off-Broadway season.

Source: Stefan Kanfer, "Trio and Quintet," in *New Leader*, Vol. 81, No. 13, November 30, 1998, pp. 22–23.

SOURCES

Brustein, Robert, Review of *This Is Our Youth*, in the *New Republic*, June 28, 1999, pp. 36–38.

Kanfer, Stefan, "Trio and Quintet," in the *New Leader*, Vol. 81, No. 13, November 30, 1998, pp. 22–23.

Lonergan, Kenneth, *This Is Our Youth*, Overlook Press, 2000, pp. 5, 6, 14, 17, 31, 49, 57, 65, 73, 79, 111, 112, 117, 118, 119, 120, 127, 128.

Ouzounian, Richard, Review of *This Is Our Youth*, in *Variety*, October 6, 2003, p. 95.

Renner, Pamela, "Rites of Passage," in *American Theatre*, January 1999, pp. 54–56.

Wolf, Matt, Review of *This Is Our Youth*, in *Variety*, April 1–7, 2002, p. 40.

FURTHER READING

Camardella, Michele L., *America in the 1980s*, Facts on File, 2005.

Camardella explores the cultural history of America in the 1980s.

Frosch, Mary, ed., *Coming of Age in America: A Multicultural Anthology*, New Press, 1995.

The essays in this collection offer different multicultural views of the maturation process.

Kushner, Rachel, "Kenneth Lonergan," BOMB, Vol. 76, Summer 2001, pp. 40–45.

Kushner discusses Lonergan's writing process and the main themes in his plays and screenplays.

Schaller, Michael, *Right Turn: America in the 1980s*, Oxford University Press, 2005.

Schaller focuses on politics in the 1980s and America's reversion to the conservatism of the 1950s.

Twelve Angry Men

REGINALD ROSE

1954

Twelve Angry Men, by the American playwright Reginald Rose, was originally written for television, and it was broadcast live on CBS's show *Studio One* in 1954. The fifty-minute television script can be found in Rose's *Six Television Plays*, published in 1956 (out of print in 2005). Rose expanded the play for the stage, and a new version was published in 1955 (Dramatic Publishing Company; in print). Two years later, in 1957, Rose wrote the screenplay for a film version, which he coproduced with the actor Henry Fonda. The play has subsequently been updated and revived; for example, in a production at the American Airlines Theater in New York City in 2004.

The play was inspired by Rose's own experience of jury duty on a manslaughter case in New York City. At first, he had been reluctant to serve on a jury, but, he wrote, "the moment I walked into the courtroom . . . and found myself facing a strange man whose fate was suddenly more or less in my hands, my entire attitude changed." Rose was greatly impressed by the gravity of the situation, the somber activity of the court, and the "absolute finality" of the decision that he and his fellow jurors would have to make. He also thought that since no one other than the jurors had any idea of what went on in a jury room, "a play taking place entirely within a jury room might be an exciting and possibly moving experience for an audience" ("Author's Commentary" on *Twelve Angry Men* in *Six Television Plays*). The result is a taut, engrossing drama in which eleven jurors believe the defendant in a capital murder trial is guilty, while one juror stands up courageously for what he believes is justice and tries to persuade the others to his way of thinking.

AUTHOR BIOGRAPHY

Reginald Rose was born on December 10, 1920, in New York City, the son of William (a lawyer) and Alice (Obendorfer) Rose. Rose attended City College (now of the City University of New York) from 1937 to 1938 but did not graduate. During World War II and shortly after, he served in the U.S. Army, from 1942 to 1946, ending his army career as a first lieutenant. In 1943, Rose married Barbara Langbart, and they had four children.

After the war and continuing into the early 1950s, Rose worked as a clerk, publicity writer for Warner Brothers Pictures, and advertising copywriter. He also wrote short stories and novels, but he never had any luck selling his work until he turned to writing plays for television. CBS bought the first script he wrote, called *The Bus to Nowhere*, and it aired live in 1951. He then became a regular writer for CBS's *Studio One*, a weekly show that produced live drama. His plays for *Studio One* included *Dino*, *The Death and Life of Larry Benson*, *The Remarkable Incident at Carson Corners*, and *Thunder on Sycamore Street*, all of which aired in 1954. In the same year, Rose wrote *Twelve Angry Men*, the work for which he is best known. The play, which was inspired by his experience of jury service, was broadcast on September 20, 1954. It won an Emmy Award for best-written drama and a Writer's Guild of America Award. The teleplay was published in Rose's *Six Television Plays* in 1956.

Twelve Angry Men was published in an expanded form as a stage play in 1955 and made into a successful film in 1957, starring Henry Fonda and coproduced by Fonda and Rose. The film garnered Academy Award nominations for Best Picture, Best Director, and Best Writing, Screenplay Based on Material from Another Medium, and an Edgar Allan Poe Award for Best Motion Picture Screenplay from Mystery Writers of America.

Rose continued to write television scripts during the 1960s and beyond. One of his best-known shows was the series *The Defenders* (1961–1965), about a father-and-son team of defense lawyers. Other shows included *A Quiet Game of Cards* (1959), the *Studs Lonigan* miniseries (1979), *Escape from Sobibor* (1987), and made-for-television movies of *Twelve Angry Men* and *The Defenders: Taking the First* in the 1990s.

Reginald Rose AP/Wide World Photos

Rose wrote five plays for the stage, including *Black Monday* in 1962 and *This Agony, This Triumph* in 1972, as well as several rewrites of *Twelve Angry Men* (1960, 1964, and 1996). He also wrote eleven screenplays besides *Twelve Angry Men*, including *Somebody Killed Her Husband* (1978), *The Wild Geese* (1978; based on a novel by Daniel Carney), and *Whose Life Is It Anyway?* (1981), starring Richard Dreyfuss.

Rose's first marriage ended in divorce. He married his second wife, Ellen McLaughlin, in 1963; they had two children. He died on April 19, 2002, in Norwalk, Connecticut.

PLOT SUMMARY

Act 1

Twelve Angry Men takes place in a jury room in the late afternoon on a hot summer's day in New York City. After the curtain rises, the judge's voice is heard offstage, giving instructions to the jury. He says that the defendant is being tried for first-degree

MEDIA ADAPTATIONS

- In 1957, *Twelve Angry Men* was made into a film starring Henry Fonda and Lee J. Cobb and directed by Sydney Lumet, with a screenplay by Rose (produced by Orion-Nova Productions/ United Artists). It is available on DVD through MGM/UA Video.
- In 1997, the cable channel Showtime released the made-for-television movie of *Twelve Angry Men*, directed by William Friedkin and starring Jack Lemmon as Juror Eight, with George C. Scott, Hume Cronyn, James Gandolfini, and Tony Danza. Rose produced an updated screenplay for this production. The videotape, put out by MGM/UA Video, has limited availability.

murder, which carries a mandatory death penalty. The judge adds that if the jury has reasonable doubt about the guilt of the accused, they must acquit him. The verdict must be unanimous.

The jurors, all men, file into the jury room and sit in straight-backed chairs around a long conference table. The weather is hot, and there is no air-conditioning; some of the men are irritable. From the initial chitchat, it is clear that most members of the jury regard the man as guilty. Jurors Seven and Ten ridicule the defendant's story. Apparently, a young man has stabbed his father to death with a knife. He admits that he bought a knife that night but claims that he lost it.

The jury takes a vote. Eleven jurors vote guilty, and one juror, Juror Eight, votes not guilty. Jurors Three, Seven, and Twelve criticize him, but Juror Eight says that he does not know whether the man is guilty or not but that it is not easy for him to send a boy to his death without discussing it first. After some argument, they agree to discuss the facts of the case. Juror Three reviews what they know. An old man who lives underneath the room where the murder took place heard loud noises just after midnight. He heard the son yell at the father that he was going to kill him. Then he heard a body falling and moments later, saw the boy running out of the house. Juror Four says the boy's story is flimsy. He said that he was at the movies at the time of the murder, but no one remembers seeing him there. Also, a woman living opposite looked out of her window and saw the murder through the windows of a passing elevated train. During the trial, it was verified that this was possible. Further facts emerge: the father regularly beat his son, and the son had been arrested for car theft, mugging, and knife fighting. He had been sent to reform school for knifing someone.

Juror Eight insists that, during the trial, too many questions were left unasked. He asks for the murder weapon to be brought in and says that it is possible that someone else stabbed the boy's father with a similar knife. Several jurors insist the knife is a very unusual one, but then Juror Eight produces from his pocket a switchblade that is exactly the same. He says that it is possible the boy is telling the truth. The other jurors scoff at this, but Juror Eight calls for another vote, a secret one this time. He says that he will abstain. When the votes are counted, there are ten guilty votes and one not guilty.

Act 2

Juror Three is angry with Juror Five because he thinks that Juror Five is the one who changed his vote. It transpires that the not-guilty vote was cast by Juror Nine. This juror says that he wants to hear more discussion of the case, even though there is still a strong feeling among the other jurors that the defendant is guilty. Jurors Three and Twelve start to play a game of tic-tac-toe to pass the time, but Juror Eight angrily snatches the piece of paper away, saying that jury deliberations are not a game. Pressured by Juror Eight, the jury agrees that it would take about ten seconds for the train to pass by the apartment. Juror Eight also establishes that the train is noisy, so the old man could not have heard the boy yell that he was going to kill his father, as the old man testified. Juror Nine suggests that the old man may have convinced himself that he heard the words because he has never had any recognition from anyone and has a strong need for attention. Juror Three responds to this with hostility, but Juror Eight argues additionally that even if the boy had said he was going to kill his father, that does not mean he intended to do so, since people often use that or similar phrases without meaning them. Convinced by these arguments, Juror Five changes his vote to not guilty, making the vote nine to three.

Juror Eight then questions the old man's testimony that he took only fifteen seconds to get downstairs, open the front door, and see the boy fleeing. He says that bearing in mind that the man cannot walk well, it probably took longer. Using a diagram of the apartment, Juror Eight acts out the old man's steps and is timed at thirty-nine seconds. He says that the old man must have heard, rather than seen, someone racing down the stairs and assumed it was the boy. An argument erupts between Jurors Three and Eight, as Juror Three insists the boy is guilty and must be executed. Juror Eight accuses him of being a sadist. Juror Three lunges at him, screaming that he will kill him. Juror Eight replies softly, suggesting that perhaps Juror Three does not really mean what he is saying.

Act 3

The jurors take another vote, this time an open one, which is evenly split, six to six. Jurors Two, Six, and Eleven have switched their votes, to the annoyance of Jurors Three and Ten. The possibility of being a hung jury is brought up, but Juror Eight refuses to accept the possibility. They take a vote on that, too. Six jurors vote in favor of declaring themselves a hung jury; six vote against. Juror Four changes his vote, so it is seven to five against declaring a hung jury. Juror Four then argues persuasively for a guilty verdict, based on the evidence. He raises the possibility that although the old man may have taken longer to get to the door than he testified, the murderer might also have taken longer to escape. Reenacting the actions of the murderer, the jurors time it at twenty-nine and a half seconds. This suggests that the old man's testimony that he saw the boy fleeing may be correct after all. As a result, three jurors change their votes back, leaving the tally at nine to three in favor of guilt.

Juror Two raises a question about the fact that the fatal wound was caused by a downward thrust of the knife. How could that be, since the son is six inches shorter than his father, which would make such an action very awkward? Juror Three demonstrates on Juror Eight how it could be done, crouching down to approximate the boy's height and then raising the knife and making a downward stabbing motion. But Juror Five, who has witnessed knife fights, says that anyone using a switchblade would use it underhand, stabbing upward, thus making it unlikely that the boy, who was an experienced knife fighter, could have caused the fatal wound. Another vote is taken, and it is nine to three in favor of acquittal. Juror Ten goes off on a prejudiced rant about how all people from the slums are liars and violent and have no respect for human life. Disgusted with his views, most of the other jurors get up and walk to the window, where they turn their backs on Juror Ten.

Juror Four still insists that the boy is guilty. He says the most important testimony is that of the woman who says she saw the murder. She was in bed, unable to sleep, when she looked out the window and saw the boy stab his father. Juror Eight reminds them that the woman wears glasses, but she would not wear them in bed and would not have had time to put them on to see what she claims to have seen. He contends that she could have seen only a blur. At this, Jurors Four and Ten change their votes to not guilty, leaving the tally at eleven to one. Only Juror Three insists on a guilty verdict, but when he sees that he stands alone and cannot change anyone else's opinion, he begrudgingly votes not guilty. The jury has reached a unanimous decision, and the defendant is acquitted.

CHARACTERS

Foreman

The foreman is described in the author's notes to the play as "a small, petty man who is impressed with the authority he has." The foreman tries to run the meeting in an orderly fashion, but in the film he is too sensitive and sulks when his attempt to stick to the way they had agreed to proceed is questioned. His contribution to the deliberations comes when they are discussing how long the killer would have taken to get downstairs. The foreman points out that since the killer wiped his fingerprints off the knife, he would also have done so off the doorknob, which would have taken some time. He votes guilty several times, but in act 3 he switches his vote, along with two others, to make the total nine to three for acquittal.

Juror Two

Juror Two is a quiet, meek figure who finds it difficult to maintain an independent opinion. In the 1957 film, he is a bank clerk. Juror Two does, however, make one useful contribution to the jury deliberations. He mentions that it seems awkward that the defendant, who was six inches shorter than his father, would stab him with a downward motion, as the fatal wound indicates. Although this is not a conclusive point, it does jog Juror Five's memory of how a switchblade is used and so helps to induce doubt in the minds of a number of jurors. Juror Two changes his vote to not guilty at the beginning of act 3, along with Jurors Eleven and Six.

Juror Three

Juror Three is a forceful, intolerant man who is also a bully. In the 1957 film, he runs a messenger service called Beck and Call. He believes that there is no point in discussing the case, since the defendant's guilt is plain, and he is quick to insult and browbeat anyone who suggests otherwise. At one point, Juror Three describes how he fell out with his son. He raised his son to be tough, but when the boy was fifteen, he hit his father in the face, and Juror Three has not seen his son for three years. He condemns his son as ungrateful.

As the play develops, it becomes clear that Juror Three is the principal antagonist of Juror Eight. This is brought out visually when Juror Three demonstrates on Juror Eight how he would use a knife to stab a taller man. His animosity to Juror Eight comes out in the aggressive way he makes the demonstration, which shocks some of the jurors. Also, when Juror Eight calls him a sadist, Juror Three is incensed and threatens to kill him.

Juror Three is the last to hold out for a guilty verdict. For a few moments after it becomes apparent that he stands alone, he sticks to his guns, saying there will be a hung jury, but he finally gives in to the pressure and votes not guilty. In the film, he pulls out his wallet to produce some facts of the case—perhaps notes he has made—and a photograph of himself with his son falls out. He stares at it for a few moments and then tears it up and begins to sob. He recognizes that his desire to convict and punish the defendant is bound up with his feelings of anger and betrayal in regard to his own son.

Juror Four

Juror Four is described in the author's notes as seeming to be "a man of wealth and position, and a practiced speaker who presents himself well at all times." In the 1957 film, he is a stockbroker, a well-dressed man in an expensive suit who, unlike the others, does not remove his jacket and shows no signs of distress in the heat. He is an arch rationalist who insists that the jury should avoid emotional arguments in deciding the case. He has a good grasp of the facts and an excellent memory, and he presents the case for guilt as well as it can be done. He is extremely skeptical of the defendant's story that he was at the movies on the night of the murder. However, his pride in his memory is shaken when, under questioning from Juror Eight, he discovers that he cannot accurately recall the title of one of the movies he saw only a few days ago, nor can he remember the names of the actors. (This incident is not in the play, but it appears in the film.) However, he still believes strongly in the defendant's guilt and is the last juror but one to change his vote. This occurs when it is demonstrated that the piece of evidence on which he places greatest value—the woman's eyewitness testimony that she saw the murder take place—is undermined. He then admits that he has a reasonable doubt.

Juror Five

Juror Five is described in the author's notes as "a naive, very frightened young man who takes his obligations in this case very seriously but who finds it difficult to speak up when his elders have the floor." When, at the beginning, jurors are asked to speak in turn, Juror Five declines the opportunity. Later, he protests when Jurors Four and Ten speak disparagingly of kids from slum backgrounds, saying that he has lived in a slum all his life. Juror Five's main contribution is in pointing out that an experienced knife fighter would use a switchblade underhand, stabbing upward rather than down. He knows this because he has witnessed such fights. Juror Five is the second juror to switch his vote to not guilty. He acquires a reasonable doubt when it is shown that, because of the noise from the train, the old man could not have heard the boy yell that he would kill his father.

Juror Six

Juror Six is a housepainter, a man who is used to working with his hands rather than analyzing with his brain. He is more of a listener than a talker. In the film version, he suggests early in the debate that the defendant had a motive to kill his father, because there was testimony in the trial about an argument between father and son earlier in the evening. But Juror Eight dismisses this as a possible motive. Juror Six stands up for Juror Nine when Juror Three speaks rudely to him, threatening to strike Juror Three if he says anything like that again. Juror Six also speaks up for himself when he changes his vote, succinctly explaining why he did so. In the film version, he talks to Juror Eight in the washroom, asking him how he would feel if he succeeded in getting the defendant acquitted but later found out that he was guilty.

Juror Seven

Juror Seven is a salesman. He assumes that the defendant is guilty and has no interest in discussing it. His only concern is that the deliberations should be over quickly, so that he does not miss the Broadway show he has tickets for. (In the film version, he has tickets for a baseball game.) At no time does he make any serious contribution to the debate, other than to point out that the defendant has a record of arrests. In the film, he is a baseball fan and uses baseball allusions in almost everything he says. At one point, he gets into an argument with Juror Eleven about why Juror Eleven changed his vote, and he makes some prejudiced remarks about immigrants. He favors declaring a hung jury, because that will mean he will get out of the jury room quickly. Eventually, he changes his vote to not guilty, for the same reason. In the film version, Juror Eleven harshly rebukes him for caring only about ending the proceedings as quickly as possible, rather than whether the man is guilty or not.

Juror Eight

Juror Eight is a quiet, thoughtful man whose main concern is that justice should be done. In the film, he is an architect. Although he is usually gentle in his manner, he is also prepared to be assertive in the search for truth. He is the only juror who, in the initial ballot, votes not guilty. He does not argue that the man is innocent but says that he cannot condemn a man to death without discussing the case first. As he probes the evidence, he manages to cast reasonable doubt on many aspects of the testimony given at the trial. He is resolute in suggesting that although, on its face, the evidence may suggest guilt, it is possible that there are other explanations for what happened that night. Juror Eight is a natural leader, and one by one he persuades the other jurors to accept his arguments. A telling moment comes when he produces a knife from his pocket that is exactly the same as the murder weapon; when he says that he bought it cheaply in the neighborhood, he disproves the jury's belief up to that point that the knife is a very unusual one.

Juror Eight remains calm throughout the deliberations. The only times (in the film version) that he becomes heated is when he stops the game of tic-tac-toe that Jurors Ten and Twelve have started and when he calls Juror Three a sadist. The latter incident serves his purpose, however, because it goads Juror Three into saying that he will kill Juror Eight, thus proving Juror Eight's earlier point that when such expression are used, they are not always meant literally.

Juror Nine

Juror Nine is an old man. In the author's notes, he is described as "long since defeated by life, and now merely waiting to die." In the film version, however, he is given more strength and dignity, and other jurors insist that he be heard. It is Juror Nine (in both play and film) who is the first to switch his vote to not guilty, saying that he wants a fuller discussion of the case, as Juror Eight has requested. It is Juror Nine who offers an explanation of why the old man might have lied about hearing the boy yell that he was going to kill his father. Juror Nine's explanation is that, because the old man has led an insignificant life and no one has ever taken any notice of him, this is his one chance for recognition. Juror Nine is also extremely observant, and the film version amplifies his role in the final discussion, when he is the one to point out that the female witness at the trial, in an effort to look younger, omitted to wear the glasses that she habitually wore, as shown by the marks on either side of her nose. This is the key point that results in the discrediting of the woman's testimony.

Juror Ten

Juror Ten is described in the author's notes as "an angry, bitter man—a man who antagonizes almost at sight. He is also a bigot." He is automatically prejudiced against anyone who comes from a slum. He believes strongly that the defendant is guilty, argues the case forcefully, and is one of the last three to hold out for a guilty verdict. But he loses credibility with the other jurors when he makes a long speech near the end of the play that reveals his bigotry in full. He insists that people from slums are drunks and liars who fight all the time. The other jurors repudiate him, and Juror Four tells him not to say another word; he does not, other than to finally admit that there is a reasonable doubt in the case.

Juror Eleven

Juror Eleven is an immigrant from Europe, a refugee from persecution. He is possibly Jewish, although this is not stated explicitly. In the film, he is a watchmaker. Juror Eleven feels fortunate to be living in a country known for its democracy, and he has great respect for the American judicial system. He takes his responsibility as a juror very seriously. He is one of three jurors who change their minds, to make the vote split six to six. He further expresses reasonable doubt about the old man's ability to recognize the son in a dimly lit tenement building. In the author's notes, he is described as "ashamed, humble, almost subservient to the people around him," but in the film his character is strengthened. He rebukes Juror Seven for not taking the trial more seriously, and he is prepared to stand up for what he believes. Also in the film version, he questions whether the son would have returned to his father's house at three o'clock in the morning if he had been the murderer.

Juror Twelve

Juror Twelve works for an advertising agency. He is clever, but as the author's notes point out, he "thinks of human beings in terms of percentages, graphs and polls, and has no real understanding of people." When Juror Three presses him, near the end of the play, to explain his not-guilty vote, he finds it very hard to do so, since he does not, in fact, have strong opinions one way or the other. He is reduced to mumbling about the complexity of the evidence.

THEMES

The Triumph and the Fragility of Justice

The play is, in one sense, a celebration of justice, showing the workings of the American judicial system in a favorable light. Although initially the jury is inclined to wrongly convict a man without any discussion of the case, the persistence of Juror Eight ensures that the right verdict is reached in the end.

Three key elements of the judicial system are demonstrated in the play. The first is one that almost everyone knows, although Juror Eight has to remind Juror Two of it: According to the law, the defendant does not have to demonstrate his innocence. He is innocent until proved guilty. The second element is that the verdict must be unanimous, since unanimity guards against a miscarriage of justice. Third, the defendant can be convicted only in the absence of reasonable doubt on the part of the jury. If there is reasonable doubt, he must be acquitted. The underlying principle is that it is better that a guilty man be set free than an innocent man be convicted. In the film versions and at least one revival of the play, Juror Six, speaking to Juror Eight in the washroom, shows that he does not understand this principle, since he asks Juror Eight how he would feel if he managed to get the defendant acquitted and later found out that he was guilty (which he may be, since nothing that happens in the jury room proves his innocence). The system is as much about protecting the innocent as it is about convicting the guilty.

The play is also a warning about the fragility of justice and the forces of complacency, prejudice, and lack of civic responsibility that would undermine it. Several jurors show that they are virtually incapable of considering the matter fairly and listening to opposing points of view. Juror Seven, whose only desire is to get out of the room quickly, is clearly unfit for jury service. Juror Three insists that there is nothing personal in his negative comments about the defendant and that he is merely sticking to the facts. He denounces the arguments put forward by Juror Eight as emotional appeals. But there is an irony here, since the truth of Juror Three's position is the opposite of what he claims. He is dominated by his own emotions arising from his bad relationship with his son. Because of this, he cannot look at the case dispassionately. He harbors an unconscious desire to vicariously punish his son by convicting the defendant, who is of similar age. Juror Eight, on the other hand, refuses to let emotions interfere in the case. Unlike Juror Three and Juror Ten, the bigot, he brings no personal agenda to the deliberations and is solely interested in ensuring there is no miscarriage of justice. Whether the play is regarded as a celebration of justice or a warning about how easily justice can be subverted depends on one's views about the likelihood of a juror similar to Juror Eight being present in every jury room.

Overcoming Class and Race Prejudice

In the play, Juror Ten is violently prejudiced against anyone who comes from a slum. "You can't believe a word they say," he says early in act 1. Note that he does not say "he," meaning the defendant, but "they," the group as a whole, which shows that he cannot make a fair judgment about individual guilt. Juror Nine, the old man with much experience of life, sees this immediately and rebukes Juror Ten ("Since when is dishonesty a group characteristic?"). But Juror Ten's bigotry continues to smolder before finally erupting in a long speech near the end that leads the other jurors to reject him. The message is clear that such irrational prejudice is incompatible with justice. Juror Four also shows signs of such prejudice, though he couches it in more acceptable words: "The children who come out of slum backgrounds are potential menaces to society."

In the play, the defendant comes from a slum, but there is nothing to suggest that he is not white, as all the jurors are. In the 1957 film version, however, the defendant is shown in a fairly lengthy shot at the beginning. He is clearly Hispanic, perhaps

TOPICS FOR FURTHER STUDY

- Most states in the United States insist on a unanimous jury in criminal cases, but two states accept majority verdicts. Write an essay discussing the advantages and disadvantages of each method.
- Is a jury of ordinary people the best way to reach a correct verdict in a trial? Would a panel of judges or other legal experts be a better way? Research a trial in which the jury reached a controversial verdict and write a letter to the editor of your local newspaper discussing these issues.
- In what ways do Jurors Eight, Nine, and Eleven embody the ideal of active citizenship in a democracy? What kinds of threats to the success of democracy through active citizen participation are posed by Jurors Three, Seven, Ten, and Twelve? Team up with two other classmates and make a class presentation in which you discuss these issues.
- In the play and the 1957 film, the jury is all-white and all-male. In the 1997 remake of the film, four jurors are African American. There are no women in any versions of the play. Should race and gender play a part in jury selection? Would female jurors or Hispanic jurors have been less willing to convict the defendant in *Twelve Angry Men*? Set up a classroom debate in which one person argues in favor of taking race and gender into account and the other person argues against it.
- Watch the 1957 and the 1997 film versions of *Twelve Angry Men*. Give a class presentation, with clips from the movies if possible, outlining the major differences between the two versions. Do you prefer Henry Fonda's performance as Juror Eight, or Jack Lemmon's? Compare and contrast the ways at least two other jurors are presented.

Puerto Rican, and looks sad and vulnerable, rather different from the thug the jury initially believes him to be. The defendant as a member of an ethnic minority gives an entirely new, racial dimension to the notion of prejudice. The positive message is that in the end, prejudice is overcome in the light of reason, and perhaps those who express such prejudice are left to ponder how foolish and bigoted they have made themselves look. However, there is another, less positive way of seeing this issue. The ideal of the judicial system is that a person is judged by a jury of his peers, but the cross-section of white males on the jury can hardly be considered peers of the boy whose fate they are called upon to decide. It might also be argued that in showing the jurors almost to a man rejecting the blatant racial prejudice of Juror Ten (in a scene that is visually powerful onstage and onscreen), the playwright presents a rosy view of American society in the 1950s, which could hardly be said to be free of such prejudice against minorities or even to be willing to face up to the existence of it. Another view would argue that the playwright is aware of such social problems and is trying to educate his audience, encouraging them to see and reject attitudes that he has reason to believe many of them may hold.

Democracy and Social Responsibility

The play suggests that not only must class and race prejudice be overcome, so must political differences. Juror Eight adopts a classic liberal position. He tries to understand the social background from which the defendant came, explaining the boy's anger as a reaction to his social conditions: "You know why slum kids get that way? Because we knock 'em over the head once a day, every day." Jurors Three, Four, and Ten adopt a more conservative position. They have no sympathy with examining the social causes of crime and simply want to get tough on the criminal. But the play shows that both liberal and conservative positions are essentially irrelevant in deciding whether the boy is guilty. The jurors must transcend their political differences and work together to find out the truth. In this sense, the play is a microcosm of democracy at work. Everyone has their say, and everyone works together to further the common good, which, in this case, is the administration of justice. It is Juror Eleven who makes this connection between the American judicial system and the democracy that, as an immigrant, he loves and respects because it is so different from what he knew in his home country. He emphasizes that everyone must play their part in it: "We have a responsibility. This is a remarkable thing about democracy. . . . We have nothing to gain or lose by our verdict. This is one of the reasons why we are strong."

STYLE

Limited Setting, Claustrophobic Atmosphere

The play has only one setting, the jury room, though both films and later stage productions added a washroom. Props are minimal, consisting mainly of a long conference table and twelve chairs. The room is hot and humid, since there is no air-conditioning and the fan does not work. The atmosphere is claustrophobic, and the men are understandably short-tempered. This confined setting helps produce the basic rhythm of the play: a juror or several jurors will provide exposition, reviewing some of the details of the case, and this will be followed by a flare-up, in which jurors express sharp disagreements and engage in bad-tempered exchanges. These, in turn, are followed by a quieter phase as tempers calm, before more exposition sets the rhythm in motion again. In this way, the static setting, in which no one comes or goes, is overcome by the dramatic rhythm inherent in the dialogue. The static setting is also mitigated by the way the director has the actors move around the stage as the arguments ebb and flow.

In the 1957 film version, the heat of the room is conveyed by the jurors shown with their shirts visibly stained with sweat. This also contributes to characterization, since Juror Four, who remains calm and rational throughout, does not sweat. After the thunderstorm cools the room a little, the sweat dries up, except in the case of Juror Three, which conveys something about his tense, emotional state of mind.

Film provides opportunities a stage director does not have; in the film, the director Sidney Lumet achieves movement and variety by frequently varying the camera angles. The changes in camera angles multiply as the dramatic tension increases. Also, Lumet progressively lowers the level from which the movie is shot. The first third is shot from above eye level, the second third at eye level, and the last third from below eye level. In the last third, the ceiling of the room begins to appear, giving a sense that the room is getting smaller.

Lumet's use of progressively longer lenses also contributes to the seeming diminishment of the room. Lumet began with normal-range lenses of 28 to 40 millimeters and then progressed to 50-, 75-, and 100-millimeter lenses. (The length of the lens refers to the focal length, or the distance from the focal point to the lens.) The longer lens alters the relationships of subject and background, giving the impression in the film that the walls are closing in and also making the table look more crowded, thus adding to the atmosphere of claustrophobia.

HISTORICAL CONTEXT

Live Television Drama in the 1950s

The decade of the 1950s is sometimes known as the golden era of television, largely because thousands of live dramas were broadcast during that time. These dramas supplemented the standard television fare of variety shows, westerns, and soap operas. It was during this period that television replaced radio and film as the chief medium of entertainment for the American family.

The live programs were in the form of drama anthologies, such as NBC's *Kraft Television Theater* and *Goodyear Television Playhouse* and CBS's *Studio One*. It was *Studio One*, which ran from 1948 to 1958, that aired *Twelve Angry Men* and other plays by Rose. Rose recalled in an interview the challenging but rewarding nature of television drama in the 1950s: "It was a terrifying experience, but very exhilarating. But there were always mistakes. . . . I don't recall a show I ever did when something didn't go wrong" (quoted in "Reginald Rose: A Biography," in *Readings on "Twelve Angry Men,"* edited by Russ Munyan). Rose recalls cameras breaking down and shows that ran either too long or too short to fill the exact time slot allocated.

There was great variety in the content of these dramas. Some were adaptations of stage plays by such playwrights as Eugene O'Neill and Arthur Miller as well as Shakespeare. Most, however, were

COMPARE & CONTRAST

- **1950s:** In 1953, 55 percent of American households possess a television set. In 1955, the figure jumps to 67 percent. In this year, 7,421,084 television sets are sold in the United States. NBC is the first network to have a regularly scheduled color program on the air (*Bonanza*, starting in 1959).

  Today: More than 98 percent of households have television sets, and many have more than one. In 1999, 68 percent of households with television have cable television. On average, Americans watch four hours of television a day.

- **1950s:** Support for the death penalty in the United States drops. In the 1940s, there were, on average, nearly 130 executions a year, but in the 1950s this figure falls to an average of 71.5 executions. The most famous cases are those of Julius and Ethel Rosenberg, who are put to death in New York in 1953 for passing atomic secrets to the Soviet Union. In New York in 1954, the year *Twelve Angry Men* is first televised, nine people are executed. Two of the condemned are teenagers; a total of three more teenagers die in New York's Sing Sing in 1955 and 1956.

  Today: Although the United States is one of the few countries to retain the death penalty, the number of executions is falling, from 71 in 2002 to 65 in 2003 and 59 in 2004. In New York, Governor George Pataki reinstates the death penalty in 1995, but, as of 2005, New York had not executed anyone since 1963. In 2005, the Supreme Court abolished the death penalty for those who commit murder when younger than age eighteen. This decision affects not only future sentencing but also approximately seventy prisoners on death row who were under eighteen when they committed their crimes.

- **1950s:** The cold war between the United States and the Soviet Union dominates global politics in the era, as does the Korean War, from 1950 to 1953. Fear of Communism leads to the McCarthy era in the United States. Television drama during this period often includes patriotic sentiments, such as those expressed by Juror Eleven in *Twelve Angry Men*. There is a perceived need to reinforce U.S. citizens' belief in the virtues of American democracy in contrast to the totalitarian Communist states of China and the Soviet Union.

  Today: The cold war is over, leaving the United States as the sole superpower. U.S. and, to an extent, global politics are dominated by the "war on terror." The Islamic terrorist group al Qaeda has replaced the Soviet Union in the minds of Americans as the prime source of evil in the world. Politicians regularly exploit people's fear of terrorism to gain support for their policies.

original dramas. The constant demand for new plays provided a fruitful creative outlet for writers, directors, and actors in the new medium. Television drama offered actors who were not well known in movies their first national exposure. In 1949, Marlon Brando, then only twenty-four years old, starred in *I'm No Hero*, a television drama produced by the Actors Studio. Paul Newman and Steve McQueen made appearances on the *Goodyear Television Playhouse*. Directors such as John Frankenheimer, Robert Altman, Sidney Lumet, and Sidney Pollack, who would later become known for their work in film, began their careers directing television dramas in the late 1940s and 1950s. Live drama died out in the early 1960s, because new technology enabled productions to be filmed. This produced higher-quality technical work, since mistakes could be edited out and scenes could be reshot, but many of the pioneer actors, writers, and directors bemoaned the loss of the excitement and intimacy of live drama.

E. G. Marshall, Henry Fonda, Lee J. Cobb, Edward Binns, George Voskovec, Jack Klugman, and Joseph Sweeney in the 1957 film version of Twelve Angry Men United Artists/The Kobal Collection

McCarthyism and Fear of Communism

In the 1950s, during the cold war between the United States and the Soviet Union, Americans were apprehensive about the spread of Communism around the world and at home. The Communist takeover of China in 1949, as well as the U.S.S.R.'s first test explosion of an atomic bomb that same year, followed by the Communist invasion of Korea in 1950, had all intensified these fears. In the late 1940s, the House Un-American Activities Committee (HUAC) began to investigate people who were suspected of being Communists. Their focus was on Hollywood and the entertainment industry. In October 1947, nineteen witnesses called before HUAC refused to cooperate with the committee; as a result, ten of them, who became known as the Hollywood Ten, were sentenced in 1950 to between six and twelve months in prison. During the 1950s, many people who worked in film, theater, radio, and television were blacklisted for alleged ties to Communism. They were prevented from working again in the entertainment industry.

The 1950s also saw the rise of Joseph McCarthy, a Republican senator from Wisconsin and a fierce anti-Communist. In 1950, McCarthy claimed that he had a list of 205 Communists who worked in the U.S. State Department. The following year, McCarthy became chairman of the Senate Subcommittee on Investigations, which gave him even greater authority to pursue suspected Communists. Many people lost their jobs as a result of admitting that they were members of the Communist Party. Some, in order to show they had renounced their left-wing views, gave information about others who were Communist Party members.

Having created an atmosphere of hysteria regarding Communist infiltration and conspiracies, McCarthy overreached himself when he began to investigate Communist infiltration of the U.S. military, which angered military leaders as well as President Dwight Eisenhower, a retired general. From April to June 1954, the Army-McCarthy hearings were televised and watched by an estimated twenty million viewers. When *Twelve Angry Men* was shown only three months later, on September 20, 1954, viewers could hardly fail to see the contrast in the play's theme of fairness and justice with the witch hunt led by McCarthy. In December 1954, McCarthy was censured by the U.S. Senate, and the McCarthy era essentially came to an end.

CRITICAL OVERVIEW

When *Twelve Angry Men* was first shown as a live television drama on CBS in 1954, Leonard Traube, in *Variety*, wrote one of the first of the many positive reviews the play was to receive. As he puts it, "Seldom in TV history has a story been able to achieve so many high points with such frequency and maintain the absorbing, tense pace."

When Rose revised the play and coproduced a movie version with Henry Fonda in 1957, critical response was also positive. The reviewer for *Newsweek* calls the film a "hard, emphatic, single-minded drama of extraordinary drive and fascination." In *America*, Moira Walsh describes it as "continuously absorbing. . . . It is well constructed and abounds in forceful and abrasive characterizations." However, the film was not an immediate popular success and was quickly withdrawn from large theaters. Subsequently, it was shown at the Berlin Film Festival, where it won first prize. It also won prizes in Japan, Italy, Australia, and other countries. Since then, it has established a reputation as one of the significant films of the 1950s and an all-time American classic film.

Revised by Rose, the play was revived in 1996 at the Comedy Theatre in London, directed by the noted British playwright and director Harold Pinter. The reviewer Matt Wolf, in *Variety*, finds the play a "startlingly innocent work in its belief in a fundamental integrity to the legal process." He contrasts this with the disillusionment felt by many in the United States in the mid-1990s, after the controversial acquittal of O. J. Simpson on double-murder charges in 1995.

The play was revived again at the American Airlines Theater in New York in 2004. John Simon, writing in *New York*, praises the strong writing and the characterization and the "underlying faith in democratic procedure not neutralizing the frightful precariousness of its realization." He concludes:

> This superficially dated but fundamentally self-renewing play is more than a lesson in civics and shrewd analysis of a cross-section of psyches. It is a nudge toward our leaving the theater a bit better than we entered it.

CRITICISM

Bryan Aubrey

Aubrey holds a PhD in English and has published many articles on twentieth-century literature. In this essay, he discusses the play in the context of jury behavior, the unreliability of eyewitness testimony, and the inadequacy of defense counsel in many capital cases in the United States.

There must be many playgoers or moviegoers who come away from a performance or showing of *Twelve Angry Men* filled with images of themselves acting as the heroic Juror Eight. They, too, when their time came, would be calm and rational in the jury room and motivated only by a desire for justice, and they would gradually, through their integrity and persistence, persuade the other eleven jurors to adopt their viewpoint. It is, of course, natural for the audience to identify with the hero, but people may not realize that this aspect of *Twelve Angry Men*, in which one juror persuades eleven others to change their positions, is fiction, not reality. The truth is that in real life, no one would be able to act out the admirable role of Henry Fonda (or Jack Lemmon, who played Juror Eight in the 1997 remake of the movie).

The dynamics of group behavior simply do not work that way. In the 1950s, a study of 255 trials by the Chicago Jury Project turned up no examples of such an occurrence. The study, in which microphones were placed in the jury room to record deliberations, found that 30 percent of cases were decided, either for conviction or acquittal, on the first ballot. In 95 percent of cases, the majority on the first ballot persuaded the minority to their point

"MANY EXPERTS BELIEVE THAT MISTAKEN IDENTITY BASED ON EYEWITNESS TESTIMONY IS A LEADING CAUSE OF WRONGFUL CONVICTIONS IN THE UNITED STATES."

of view. In other words, the way a jury first casts its vote preferences is the best predictor of the final verdict. This conclusion has been confirmed by much research in jury behavior over the past half-century. So if *Twelve Angry Men* had been true to life, the defendant would almost certainly have been convicted. In group situations such as jury deliberations, there is simply too much pressure on a lone individual to conform to the view of the majority. The Chicago Jury Project showed that in the 5 percent of cases in which the original minority prevailed, there were always three or four jurors who held their minority views from the start of deliberations. (The results of the Chicago Jury Project are reported in "*Twelve Angry Men* Presents an Idealized View of the Jury System," by David Burnell Smith.)

In cases where one juror persists in maintaining his or her view against the majority, the result will be a hung jury, although research on juries suggests that hung juries are more common when there is a sizable minority rather than a minority of one. There is also a body of opinion within the legal profession that indicates that in cases where a lone juror opposes the majority, the holdout is unlikely to resemble Juror Eight in *Twelve Angry Men*, who is devoted to justice and acts with integrity. In fact, such a juror is more likely to be the opposite, a stubborn and antisocial person who, for some reason, feels driven to oppose the majority, sticking to his or her opinion when there is no evidence to support it. In a review of the play in the *Michigan Law Review*, Phoebe C. Ellsworth summarizes this view:

> The juror who opposes the majority is seen as essentially unreasonable.... The majority jurors, on the other hand, are seen as reasonable, willing to spend time sifting through the issues and listening carefully to the arguments of the minority even if the initial verdict is 11–1 and they have enough votes to declare a verdict.

If this aspect of *Twelve Angry Men* is more fiction than truth, the play does raise other issues that are as relevant for the criminal justice system today as they were in the 1950s. The most important of them is the nature of eyewitness testimony. At first, the jurors in *Twelve Angry Men*, with one exception, accept the eyewitness testimony at the trial at face value. This testimony is crucial to the case for the prosecution, and the jurors do not think to question the old man's claim that he saw the murdered man's son fleeing or the testimony of the woman across the street, who said that she actually saw the murder being committed. The jurors repeatedly refer to this testimony as the "facts" of the case, and near the end of the play, Juror Four even says that the woman's account of what she saw is "unshakable testimony." Juror Three adds, "That's the whole case."

The jurors in the play are conforming to what most people, when called to jury duty, believe—that eyewitness testimony is extremely reliable. The truth is rather different. Many studies have shown that eyewitness testimony is often unreliable, with an accuracy rate of only about 50 percent. Some experiments have shown even lower percentages for accurate identification, such as the 41.8 percent reported in Brian Cutler and Stephen Penrod's *Mistaken Identification: The Eyewitness, Psychology, and the Law*.

It seems that despite what people believe, humans do not have a good ability to identify people they may have seen for only a few seconds. Eyewitnesses have been shown to be especially poor at making interracial identification (in the film, a white man and a white woman identify a Hispanic individual). Research has also shown that people in stressful situations have less reliability of recall than those in nonstressful situations. Obviously, witnessing a murder is almost by definition a stressful situation. In addition, people find it harder to recall information about a violent event than about a nonviolent one.

Many experts believe that mistaken identity based on eyewitness testimony is a leading cause of wrongful convictions in the United States. In her book *Eyewitness Testimony*, Elizabeth F. Loftus discusses the issue in depth. She analyzes the famous and controversial Sacco and Vanzetti case in the 1920s, in which two men, Nicola Sacco and Bartolomeo Vanzetti, were convicted and executed for murder. It appears that eyewitnesses initially

WHAT DO I READ NEXT?

- Arthur Miller's play *The Crucible* (1955) is about the Salem witch trials in the seventeenth century and the hysteria that resulted in the persecution of innocent people. The play was written during the McCarthy era, in which fears about Communism led to witch hunts and many people were condemned as Communists or Communist sympathizers without evidence.
- In *The Run of His Life: The People Versus O. J. Simpson* (reprint edition, 1997), Jeffrey Toobin analyzes one of the most sensational trials of the twentieth century. Toobin argues that O. J. Simpson was guilty of the murder of his wife, Nicole, and her friend Ron Goldman, and much of the book is devoted to analysis of why Simpson was acquitted at the trial in 1995, despite the strong evidence against him. The reason, according to Toobin, was the racial divide in America that made the jury mistrust the evidence presented by the prosecution.
- *Great American Trials: 201 Compelling Courtroom Dramas from Salem Witchcraft to O. J. Simpson*, edited by Edward W. Knappman (2004), contains descriptive accounts of America's most historically significant trials as well as those that fascinated the general public. Accounts range from the Boston Massacre in 1770 to the "Boston Strangler" trial in 1967 and include the notorious nineteenth-century trial of Lizzie Borden for the murder of her parents.
- *Live Television: The Golden Age of 1946–1958 in New York* (1990), by Frank Sturcken, tells the story of television's golden age, a period in which more than five thousand dramas were broadcast live. Sturcken has done much original research, and the book is enhanced by interviews with many executives, producers, and actors from the period.

failed to identify either man as the perpetrator of the crime but later testified that they were certain of their identifications. (Loftus raises the possibility that they were improperly influenced by repeated questioning.) The jurors believed the eyewitnesses, despite plausible alibis presented by both defendants establishing that they were elsewhere at the time of the murder.

Loftus describes another case in which eyewitness testimony against the accused was accepted by a jury, even when evidence pointing to the man's innocence far outweighed it. (The conviction was later reversed.) Loftus also discusses an experiment in which subjects were asked to play the role of jurors trying a criminal case. When eyewitness testimony was included in the experiment, establishing that someone saw the murder, the percentage of the fifty jurors voting for conviction rose from 18 percent to 72 percent. Then a variation in the case was introduced that has some relevance for *Twelve Angry Men.* The defense established that the witness had not been wearing his glasses on the day of the crime and had very poor vision. Therefore he could not have seen the robber's face. Even with this variation, 68 percent of jurors still voted for conviction. In *Twelve Angry Men,* it is a juror's realization that an eyewitness who wears glasses could not have been wearing them at the time she witnessed the crime that is the decisive factor in swinging the final three jurors to a vote of not guilty.

The legal system does have safeguards against misidentification by eyewitnesses. Since *Twelve Angry Men* was written, there has been a trend toward accepting expert testimony on the reliability of eyewitness identification. In such cases, an expert would advise the jurors on how much weight they should attach to the eyewitness testimony presented at the trial. Another legal safeguard is the right of the defense attorney to cross-examine an eyewitness. The attorney may ask questions about how long the eyewitnesses saw the defendant, what the lighting was like, how much stress they were under, the degree of certainty in their identification, and other relevant questions.

Such cross-examination requires a competent attorney. In *Twelve Angry Men*, the defense attorney's cross-examination of the witnesses is weak, according to Juror Eight, who says, "Somehow I felt that the defense counsel never really conducted a thorough cross-examination. Too many questions were left unasked." Juror Four agrees with him that the defense attorney was bad. In the 1957 film, this point is expanded. Juror Eight points out to Juror Seven that since the defense attorney was court appointed, he may not have wanted to take the case. There would have been neither money nor glory in it for him. In addition, he probably did not believe in the innocence of his client and so did not mount a vigorous defense. Thus, in *Twelve Angry Men*, the jury ends up doing the defense attorney's job for him, which is hardly an ideal situation.

Unfortunately, the inadequacy of defense counsel in death penalty cases is a persistent problem in the criminal justice system in the United States. On its website, the American Civil Liberties Union (ACLU) summarizes several death penalty cases in which inadequate representation has led to wrongful or dubious convictions. The reason for this is that capital cases are extremely complex and require expertise and experience on the part of the defense counsel, who must devote large amounts of time to the case. Because most defendants cannot afford a lawyer, the court provides them with one, but few states offer adequate compensation in such cases. The result, according to the ACLU, is that "capital defendants are frequently represented by inexperienced, often over-worked, and in many cases incompetent, lawyers." The ACLU cites one egregious example of a court-appointed lawyer in Alabama who was so drunk during a capital trial in 1989 that he was held in contempt and jailed.

The facts as presented by the ACLU suggest that the ability of the jurors in *Twelve Angry Men* to reach a just verdict despite the failures of the defense counsel is not replicated in real life. Although some playgoers and moviegoers may feel that *Twelve Angry Men* vindicates the criminal justice system—because the right verdict is reached—it seems more accurate to view the play as an indictment of the system, since had it not been for the presence of the larger-than-life Juror Eight, justice would most certainly not have been served. The system was saved by one man, and that, sadly, is the stuff of fiction, not reality.

Source: Bryan Aubrey, Critical Essay on *Twelve Angry Men*, in *Drama for Students*, Thomson Gale, 2006.

"ROSE MANAGES TO MAKE THE DOZEN JURORS BOTH UNIVERSAL, BY REFUSING SO MUCH AS TO NAME THEM, AND SHARPLY INDIVIDUAL WITH REMARKABLY FEW BUT SUBTLE STROKES."

John Simon

In the following review, Simon calls Twelve Angry Men *"a classic in the making" and praises Rose's characterization and economy.*

We must not in disheveled pursuit of the radically different neglect or minimize the achievements of the past. The commercial theater has yielded hits that, upon acquiring the patina of repeated exposure, attained the status of art. Think of the Kaufman and Hart comedies, which, polished through countless productions, became enshrined as literature. Such a fate may overtake Reginald Rose's *Twelve Angry Men,* which began as a teleplay, was expanded into a movie, underwent several stage versions, and now takes flight at the American Airlines Theater as a classic in the making.

It tells of how a lone holdout at a murder trial, Juror 8, staunchly standing by his reasonable doubt in face of underwhelming evidence, confronts eleven other jurors who, convinced that a 16-year-old boy is guilty of killing his father, are ready to condemn him to what in 1954 was a mandatory death sentence. Slowly, without hectoring rhetoric or even firm belief in the boy's innocence, he argues the case for further questioning; very gradually and in different ways, the others' positions begin to change.

Though seemingly naturalistic, the play in some ways departs from reality. I do not refer to the improvements wrought in half a century—juries no longer all-white and all-male, death sentences

Lee J. Cobb, E. G. Marshall, Jack Klugman, John Fiedler, and Edward Binns in the 1957 film version of Twelve Angry Men United Artists/The Kobal Collection

no longer mandatory even in states that still allow them. Rather, I refer to certain lapses in logic or credibility that are, however, outweighed by the strong writing, with slight predictability not slackening the suspense, underlying faith in democratic procedure not neutralizing the frightful precariousness of its realization.

Rose manages to make the dozen jurors both universal, by refusing so much as to name them, and sharply individual with remarkably few but subtle strokes—by their vocabulary, by some idiosyncratic character trait, by their laconism or volubility. What in the hands of a lesser writer might court cliché here retains the pungency of the closely observed or meticulously overheard particular. Take, for example, "I mean, everybody's heart is starting to bleed for this punk little kid like the president just declared it 'Love Your Underprivileged Brother Week' or something." This precise blend of originality and banality aptly characterizes Juror 3.

Of course, for this to work, the mounting has to be as right as the Roundabout's revival. On Allen Moyer's letter-perfect jury-room set, which makes cunning lateral shifts to reveal the goings-on in the washroom, Scott Ellis, a director I have sometimes found uneven, delivers a stunning piece of staging. He has devised a kind of choreography whereby the jurors move around much more, and more dramatically, than real-life jurors would, yet keep each move believable. And I salute every single performance: Boyd Gaines's Juror 8, conveying inner uncertainties not allowed to undermine the pursuit of reasoned inquiry; Tom Aldredge's old Juror 9, his undimmed mind sturdily defying his enfeebled body; Philip Bosco's most close-minded Juror 3, neither overdoing nor shortchanging his unlikability, and riveting in his final pathos; Kevin Geer's tongue-tied Juror 2, unused to self-assertion, yet, when it counts, rising drolly to the occasion; Michael Mastro's seeming simpleton Juror 5, endearingly revealing sound instincts;

Larry Bryggman's unerringly accented European immigrant (No. 11), meeting raucous challenge with poise.

And close on their heels the Jury Foreman of Mark Blum, judiciously patient but not imperturbable; the Sixth Juror of Robert Clohessy, a tough guy but far from a brute; James Rebhorn's Fourth Juror, methodical, buttoned-up but unsweaty in this hot room, coolly yet unimaginatively reasoning; John Pankow's Seventh Juror, a loudmouth and baseball addict full of crudely funny remarks; Peter Friedman's No. 10, working up vehemently spewed-out prejudices by well-judged increments; and twelfth, Adam Trese, glibly girded with ad-agency phrases, yet easily buffeted this way or that. A solid ensemble, unerringly costumed by Michael Krass and searchingly lighted by Paul Palazzo, in performances your memory won't easily shake off.

How subtly Rose refuses to label the alleged killer as African-American, and the immigrant as Jewish, letting us fill in the blanks and, in the process, test our own possible prejudices, racial, religious, or xenophobic. How economically he strips off masks, as when seven quiet words from Juror 8 reveal Juror 3's personal bias posturing as impersonal justice. In the final analysis, this superficially dated but fundamentally self-renewing play is more than a lesson in civics and shrewd analysis of a cross-section of psyches. It is a nudge toward our leaving the theater a bit better than we entered it.

Source: John Simon, "No Doubt," in *New York*, Vol. 37, No. 39, November 8, 2004, pp. 71–72.

Thomas J. Harris

In the following essay, Harris provides an overview of the plot and characters in the film version of Twelve Angry Men, *taking issue with Juror 8's omniscience and some of the story's simplistic philosophies, but praising it as "exhilarating drama."*

Credits

An Orion/Nova Production, released through United Artists, 1957. Coproducers: Henry Fonda and Reginald Rose. Director: Sidney Lumet. Story and Screenplay: Reginald Rose. Director of Photography: Boris Kaufman, A.S.C. Editor: Carl Lerner. Art Director: Robert Markell. Music: Kenyon Hopkins. Assistant Producer: George Justin. Assistant Director: Donald Kranze. Operative Cameraman: Saul Midwall. Sound: James A. Gleason. Script Supervisor: Faith Elliott. Makeup: Herman Buchman. Black-and-white. Running time: 96 minutes.

Cast: Henry Fonda (Juror 8), Lee J. Cobb (Juror 3), Ed Begley (Juror 10), E. G. Marshall (Juror 4), Jack Warden (Juror 7), Martin Balsam (Juror 1), John Fiedler (Juror 2), Jack Klugman (Juror 5), Joseph Sweeney (Juror 9), Edward Binns (Juror 6), George Voskovec (Juror 11), Robert Webber (Juror 12), Rudy Bond (Judge), James A. Kelly (Guard), Bill Nelson (Court Clerk), John Savoca (Defendant).

It is convenient that the first chapter of this book on courtroom cinema should center on the most pivotal aspect of a trial—the jury: with a thorough understanding of its intricacies, the reader will be able to appreciate better the statements made by the writers and directors of the films to come regarding the reliability of the judicial system in general.

Strangely enough, as of 1957 the subject of the jury had only received one serious treatment in all of world cinema—by French writer-director Andre Cayette in his 1950 film *Justice est Faite* (Let Justice Be Done), which explored the extent to which the personal lives of the jury members in a mercy killing affected their verdict. Its main point was that the attainment of absolute impartiality is impossible in a jury situation, to which people unavoidably carry with them deep-seated prejudices and convictions.

Some three years after the release of the Cayette film in France, a young American TV writer named Reginald Rose found himself confronting precisely the same dilemmas that had plagued Cayette's characters when he was asked to serve on a New York jury. Rose was so affected by his experience that he fashioned a teleplay from it. When *12 Angry Men,* as it was called, aired in early 1954, it proved an immediate critical and commercial hit—its potency of theme appearing all the more credible due to its basis on actual events.

Two years later, in 1956, Rose was asked by Henry Fonda, who had seen the TV production of *12 Angry Men* and who was looking for a commercial property over which he could serve as producer as well as a starring vehicle for himself, to expand his teleplay to feature length. This practice had become fairly common during the 1950s, what with the number of original story ideas for motion pictures steadily declining. Producers had begun to turn to their greatest rival, television, for new material. Paddy Chayefsky's TV plays *Marty* and *The Bachelor Party* were both transferred to the screen in 1955 and 1957, respectively, by their original director, Delbert Mann. Since television was primarily a writer's (although to a great extent an actor's) medium, it was wisely decided that the screen adaptations of these teleplays would rely heavily on dialogue, in addition to the other fundamentals of television: "a narrative style based on medium close-ups . . . a highly mobile camera enclosed within a limited space and the intimate quality of . . . situations."

These films were also made at low costs, because they utilized television crews instead of motion picture crews (Alfred Hitchcock was to discover just how cheaply a feature film could be made in 1960 when, using the crew from his TV show, he produced and directed *Psycho,* his top-grossing film of all time, for a mere $800,000).

"IN ADDITION TO THE ISSUE OF THE OMNISCIENCE OF THE FONDA CHARACTER, THE SCRIPT ESCHEWS REALISM FOR DRAMATIC CONVENIENCE IN OTHER RESPECTS ALSO."

The man chosen to direct the screen version of *12 Angry Men* was Sidney Lumet, who was still a novice to movies (hard to believe from today's standpoint) but who was well-experienced in TV, having directed episodes for such popular series as *You Are There, Playhouse 90, Kraft Television Theatre,* and *Studio One.* In addition, most of the acting ensemble was drawn from among the ranks of TV performers: E. G. Marshall, Jack Warden, Edward Binns, John Fiedler, Martin Balsam, among others.

12 Angry Men opens on a steamy summer afternoon in a courtroom inside Manhattan's Court of General Sessions. A judge is wearily grumping his charge to an equally dog-tired and heat-soaked jury: first-degree manslaughter with a death penalty mandatory upon a guilty verdict. However, he reminds them, to send the defendant (a slum boy) to the chair their verdict of guilty must be unanimous; if there exists in any juror's mind a reasonable doubt as to the guilt or innocence of the accused, a vote of not guilty must be entered. As the jury remove themselves from the box, the viewer is shown a lingering close-up of the frightened boy. Kenyon Hopkins' grim, sympathetic theme (which will recur each time a life-or-death situation is faced) continues until the credits fade as the jury—and the audience—settle themselves in that sweltering broom closet for the next hour and a half. Already Rose has established the contrast between the slum kid of a minority race and the white, middle-class males who have been selected to determine his fate. We will soon discover that the defendant in the case is not only the boy on trial but also the jury and, in a broader sense, the judicial system itself.

Once inside the jury room, the men are introduced to the viewer as they talk among themselves about how "open-and-shut" the case against the boy seems. Assuming the airs of the intelligent, respectable citizens they presume themselves to be, they never for a moment doubt the validity of their convictions, but instead speak of how "exciting" the trial was or of the stifling atmosphere of the room (they are unable to get the fan to work) or of how the proceedings have rudely interrupted their daily routines (one is anxious to get to the ball park). They act as though they've seen it all before; in fact, one of them later says to Henry Fonda, who casts the only vote for not-guilty, "You couldn't change my mind if you talked for a hundred years." However, by the end of the film all eleven of them will have been persuaded by Fonda to open their minds to the possibility of the existence of a reasonable doubt in the case.

Juror 1 (Martin Balsam) is chosen to be the foreman. He is a high-school gym teacher, about 30, somewhat dumb and weak-willed, and extremely sensitive—when someone objects to one of his decisions, he says, "All right, then do it yourself. See how you like being in charge." His opinions will be overlooked while the other eleven take over. In short, he is a foreman by name only.

Juror 2 (John Fiedler) is a wimpy bank teller of about 35. He (like some of the others) is used to having decisions made for him and enjoys going along with the majority so he'll look good and won't have to stand up for himself. Whatever views he has are usually silenced by the more aggressive types in the group. However, he does make an effort to maintain the level of interpersonal contact among the men when arguments ensue by offering cough drops.

Juror 3 (Lee J. Cobb) is a husky, loud-mouthed, domineering bully who runs a messenger service. He states in the beginning that he has no personal feelings about the case, but we eventually learn that his own teenaged son has deserted him and for that reason he is taking out his anger on the defendant. His blind desire to side with anyone who is ready to convict the boy allows Fonda and the others on his side to come up with new evidence to support the theory that there exists a reasonable doubt concerning the boy's guilt.

Juror 4 (E. G. Marshall), the stockbroker, is a cold-blooded (so much so that he says he never sweats) rationalist who treats the whole case as if it were a detective puzzle and not a question of whether a human being is going to live or die. "Studies confirm that slum kids are potential criminals," he declares. He is conceited and stuffy and does not hesitate to tell the others what he thinks of them whenever the opportunity arises. He is, however, obviously a good producer of information and has excellent recall, and is helpful in that respect at least.

Juror 5 (Jack Klugman) is an insecure victim of a slum upbringing. He is not a mean man, but would vote in favor of the boy's guilt simply because discussing the details of a case with many parallels to his own childhood is too much for his conscience to bear. However, once he has come to grips with his past, he is eager to assist Fonda and the others in reevaluating the case against the boy.

Juror 6 (Edward Binns) is a working-class "Joe" more inclined toward using his hands than his brains. "I'm not used to supposing," he tells Fonda. "My boss does that for me." He provides a facilitation function in the group—that is, he tries to make things go smoothly—as when he badgers the bully for silencing Juror 9, the old man: "You say stuff like that to him again, and I'll lay you out."

Juror 7's (Jack Warden) only desire is to get out of his seat in the jury room and into one at the ball park. In fact, he is so completely obsessed with baseball that he makes unconscious references to it in virtually everything he says; he calls Juror 5 "Baltimore" because of his attachment to the Orioles; he tells the foreman to "just stand there and pitch" when he says something irritating; he recites the ratio of guilty to not-guilty votes as if it were a player's hit-and-miss record. He is perhaps the most alarming figure in the whole group because he has absolutely no concern for the defendant's welfare. He preoccupies himself with cracking jokes and performing stupid acts like throwing paper balls at the fan. When Fonda finally secures a majority of not-guilty votes, he switches his vote to not-guilty simply to facilitate the establishment of a unanimous verdict; he has no convictions either way. That he appears amusing on the surface seems all the more appalling when one reflects upon the seriousness of the situation which he's making light of.

Juror 9 (Joseph Sweeney), the old man, needs moral support, for he has an inferiority complex. Fortunately, Fonda, the working man, and some of the others manage to see to it that he gets the floor once in a while despite the dominance of the loudmouths in the group. In spite of his years, however, he is extremely perceptive, and some of his observations—unseen by any of the others—result in altering the opinions of a few of the more stubborn among the men.

Juror 10 (Ed Begley) is a garage owner who is absolutely seething with racial prejudice. "They're all the same—can't trust any of 'em—know what I mean?" is his recurrent statement with regard to the boy's ethnic background. He is nasty and quick to accuse (when Fonda is the only one to vote not-guilty at the beginning, he immediately snickers, "Boyoboy, there's always one"). Although he acts tough, it becomes increasingly clear that his rantings and ravings last only as long as there are supporters to urge him on.

Juror 11 (George Voskovec), a German-American, is an immigrant watchmaker who initially votes guilty simply because his reverence for the principles of American justice has blinded him into believing that the system is infallible: the boy *seems* guilty, therefore he must be. He is somewhat arrogant but is rightfully angered at the baseball fan's indifference and the bully's rudeness. By standing up for his beliefs he gives direction to the group.

Juror 12 (Robert Webber) is an ad man accustomed to making decisions for appearance's sake. He has no deep-seated convictions regarding the guilt or innocence of the boy and as a result has difficulty making up his mind when his opinion is needed to break a tie vote.

From an examination of these men it becomes clear that Rose has chosen a pretty fair cross-section of society to fill his jury. After they are certain that they've given the case a thorough evaluation (they've talked for all of five minutes), one calls to the man (Juror 8, Henry Fonda) who has been standing alone by the window. Fonda has been thinking the case over in his mind, not worrying about his own problems. The contrast between him and his fellow jurors is firmly established when a vote is taken and he is the only one who raises his hand for not-guilty. After the others have somewhat tempered their initial hostility, they agree to explain to him why they think he should change his mind. It must be pointed out that he has not voted not-guilty because he is sure the boy is innocent, but because there exists in his mind a reasonable doubt as to guilt. The law states that this is all that is necessary for acquittal.

After a once-around-the-table, it becomes obvious that no one has given the case much thought. "I just think he's guilty . . . the evidence all seemed to point in that direction," are the empty generalizations spouted by these eleven men who are prepared to send a boy to the chair without even a second thought.

Since it is evident that they would rather ignore Fonda and wait for him to "come to his senses" than try to help him see their point of view, Fonda realizes that it is up to him to convince them that there is room for reasonable doubt. He has his work cut out for him, though, for he must contend with the hostility of the others in the group—the garage mechanic in particular—who are growing more and more impatient.

It is already clear to the viewer that Fonda is the only man present who is not indifferent and who has not allowed personal prejudice to obscure his perception of the case. He is also apparently the only one with a lucid understanding of the judicial process—and the one with the most common sense. He has to remind the bank teller that the burden of proof is on the prosecution, not the defense. He cleverly makes the ad man contradict his belief that witnesses who say things under oath cannot be wrong by getting him to admit, "This isn't an exact science."

Nevertheless, for all his effort, Fonda elicits nothing but jeers from those to whom he points out shortcomings in reasoning. Discouraged, but secretly hoping that he has penetrated the stubborn veneer of at least one of the other jurors, he agrees to another vote—but this time on secret ballot, with himself abstaining. He says that if the outcome is a unanimous guilty vote, he will not stand in their way; however, if there is one vote for not-guilty among them, then they must stay and talk it out. He is taking a great risk by placing his confidence in this largely ignorant and biased bunch.

Fortunately, there is one vote for not-guilty (we later discover that it came from the old man). Reluctantly, the other members of the jury set out to reexamine the case. Fonda's task from this point on will be to convince the other ten that there is a question of doubt regarding the case of the defendant. Because he is a keen judge of character, he avoids pleading his cause directly to the most seemingly intractable types—the baseball fan, the garage owner, and the messenger-service operator—and instead concentrates on the more reasonable types—the working man, the slum kid, the bank teller, etc. He knows that once they begin to accept him as a leader, he will be able to break down the stronghold of personal prejudice that the others possess. It should be mentioned at this point that there are many temporary leaders in the group; practically everyone gets the floor once in a while. Leadership is a function, not a position. However, Fonda becomes the strongest and most influential leader because he manages to gain the support of the others in the group; lasting leadership demands followers. Fonda's unfaltering independence of judgment will gradually strengthen the independence of judgment of the others. One by one, the other jurors will begin to realize how close they came to sending a boy to die due to their indifferent attitudes.

Fonda begins to introduce pieces of evidence that throw doubt upon the so-called "open-and-shut" appearance of the case against the boy. He confounds the other jurors when he produces a knife identical to the one with which the boy allegedly stabbed his father. His point is that someone else could have bought the knife, as he did, at a store in the boy's neighborhood and used it to kill the boy's father. "It's possible, but not very probable," declares the stockbroker in his usual perfunctory tone. Nevertheless, it is still to Fonda's credit that he was concerned enough to give up some of his free time to search the boy's area, whereas the others never gave the knife a second thought because it was an unusual-looking instrument and seemed to be one of a kind.

Fonda also brings up the crucial question of the accuracy of the testimony of the lame old man who said that he got up from his seat in his bedroom after hearing what he thought were screams, went to the front door immediately, opened it, and saw the boy running past. Using a diagram of the man's apartment and imitating his movements while clocking them, Fonda shows that it would have been impossible for the handicapped witness to walk forty feet from his bedroom to the door in the twelve seconds he said it took him to do so. It would have taken him at least three times that long. Therefore, it is highly probable that the man merely heard someone running past and assumed it was the boy. Earlier, Fonda had reasoned that the old man's statement that he heard the boy say he was going to kill his father would have meant that the shouts were picked up over the deafening roar of an

L-train. When Juror 3 asked what difference it made how many seconds it took before the old man heard the screams, that no one could be that positive, Fonda had replied, "I think that testimony that could send a boy to the chair *should be* as accurate as seconds." This points up another major concern of the film—the reliability of the testimony of people who are, after all, only human and therefore prone to making mistakes. Just because someone says something under oath does not necessarily signify that it is unquestionable. Sometimes people say things for appearance's sake—as Juror 9 points out when he says that the old man on the stand may have been making an effort to look distinguished for possibly the first time in his life and that as a result he may have deliberately twisted the facts. Even the persons with superior recall—and there are not many in the group—are not totally reliable—as we will discover later with regard to the stockbroker. However, the other jurors' excessive faith in the accuracy of the judicial process would have them believe that human error somehow becomes nonexistent once a person enters a court of law. The question of what motivates a witness' testimony will be explored again in *Witness for the Prosecution* and most extensively (and realistically) in *Anatomy of a Murder.*

Apparently Fonda's efforts have not gone unrewarded, for the next vote finds the count 8 guilty to 4 not-guilty, as opposed to the original 11 to 1; the watchmaker has now changed his mind. It is at this point that Juror 3, who has been castigating those who have sided with Fonda ("You bunch of bleedin' hearts . . . what is this—Love Your Underprivileged Brother Week or something?") allows all his latent hostility with regard to his runaway son to surface:

Juror 3: You're letting him slip through our fingers!

Fonda: Slid through our fingers?! Who are you, his executioner?

Juror 3 (clenching his fist): I'm one of 'em.

Fonda: Perhaps you'd like to pull the switch.

Juror 3: For this kid, you bet I would.

Fonda (contemptuously): I feel sorry for you. What it must feel like to want to pull the switch. Ever since you came in here you've been acting like a self-appointed public avenger. . . . You're a sadist.

During this exchange all the other jurors have gathered around Fonda and have been staring, astonished, at Juror 3; he has been singled out, just as Fonda was the first time we saw him. These two are clearly the most diametrically opposed individuals in the room. Juror 3 lunges at Fonda, declaring, "I'll kill him." Fonda, defiantly: "You don't really mean you'll kill me, do you?" And Juror 3 realizes that Fonda is right. From this point on, Juror 3 appears more introspective—he speaks out less often—but still retains his angry facade. His outburst has also caused the other jurors who voted guilty to ask themselves whether they have similar prejudices which are preventing them from changing their perspectives. They are again given pause to reflect after the watchmaker's awe-inspired speech about the merits of the American jury process: "We have nothing to gain or lose by our verdict. We don't know the boy" (even though Juror 10 would contend, "They're all the same"). The next vote is a tie: 6–6.

At about this time the frustrated and exhausted men are given relief by a downpour. The rain acts to reduce the tension: it cools the intense emotional atmosphere of the room as well as the men themselves. By the next vote, Fonda has secured a majority: 9 not-guilty to 3 guilty. The three dissenters are the bully, the stockbroker, and the bigot. Fonda demands that they state their reasons for holding onto their conviction. The stockbroker's smug attitude is finally broken down by Fonda and the old man. The rationalist had refused to believe that the boy couldn't remember the names of the films he allegedly saw the night his father was murdered. However, when Fonda confronts the stockbroker with a similar question, the latter finds his usually infallible memory failing him; he cannot name all the stars in the double-feature he saw three nights ago. Fonda: "And *you're* not under emotional stress [as the boy was], are you?" The old man notices the stockbroker rubbing the marks on the sides of his nose and remembers that the woman who testified against the boy had been doing the same thing: in both cases the marks were caused by glasses (and nothing else, as the stockbroker himself admits), but the woman on the stand, in an effort to look younger, was not wearing hers. It is also deduced by the stockbroker that she would not have been wearing them to bed on the night she heard screams in the boy's apartment. Therefore, in the split second she said it took her to jump out of bed and look out the window through the cars of a passing L-train (at which point she said she saw the boy knife his father) it is highly unlikely that she took time to put on her glasses (her neglecting to wear them to court confirms that she is not in the habit of using them). Fonda concludes that she couldn't have been certain about what she saw under those circumstances. Finally, the stockbroker admits that there is room for reasonable doubt and changes his vote to not-guilty.

Next, the bigot, who is absolutely fed up with the "soft hearts" of the other jurors, launches his longest tirade against minorities. Everyone demonstrates how intolerant they have grown of his attitudes when they get up from the table and turn their backs to him, leaving him babbling in vain in the middle of the room. Evidently without others to fuel the fire of his racism, it soon dies out. When the stockbroker tells him, "Sit down and don't open your mouth again," he obsequiously complies. For the remaining period, he sits quietly by himself in a corner of the room, most likely contemplating for the first time the ludicrousness of his prejudiced views.

Finally the vote is reversed: 11 not-guilty to 1 guilty. Now the Angry Man stands alone. He tries desperately to get others to support him, but it is clear that his personal problems are the only things keeping him from going along with them. "You're trying to turn this into a contest," says the stockbroker. Reginald Rose drops his final comment on the unreliability of witness testimony when Juror 3, having resorted to bringing up the presumably settled issue of the vain woman who testified against the boy, shouts, "You can talk all you want, but you can't *prove* she wasn't wearing glasses. This woman *testified in court.*" After all of Fonda's efforts over the past hour and a half to illustrate the fact that human weakness is present everywhere—even, perhaps especially in court—and that things are not always what they seem, the words "testified in court" have virtually lost all their meaning. Realizing that he is getting nowhere, Juror 3 pulls out his wallet to show the others some "facts" that he has presumably scribbled down—and out flies a picture of him and his son together. He stares at it for a moment, then uses all his pent up rage to tear it to shreds. Having finally come to grips with his conscience, he sobs, "Not guilty."

The final moments show Fonda exiting the courthouse. The old man stops him and asks him what his name is. "Davis," he replies. "Well, so long," says the old man. Here is another of Rose's subtle points: these men have been sitting in a courtroom for ninety minutes without knowing much personal data about the others in the group outside of their emotional temperaments and intellectual capacities (they've all accepted each other as "normal"—all of them being white males), but they have judged the boy as though they understood him completely, when in fact they know less about him than they do about each other. The racist assumed he was untrustworthy because he was "one of *them,*" and the bully envisioned him as having the same characteristics as his rebellious son. Unfortunately, oftentimes people are more inclined to let their emotions govern their decisions than to use unbiased logical reasoning.

We realize that the final exchange between Fonda and the old man is a meaningless formality: they will probably never see each other again. Looking back, we see that in the beginning this group of diverse individuals was prepared (with the exception of Fonda) to send a boy to the chair and then go home and forget all about it. It is frightening to consider just how close they came to doing so. It must be stated, however, that the jury's final verdict of not-guilty does not prove conclusively that the boy did not murder his father; rather, the script shows that the case against the boy is not as strong as the case for him—the presence of reasonable doubt is Rose's concern. What if there had been no Juror 8? Rose may be praised for his convincing account of how a liberal man who is devoted to his cause is able to sway the ignorant and prejudiced minds of his peers. However, at the same time it may be said that the script relies too heavily upon the chance presence of such a man; if he had not been there to point out evidence that no one else had been able to produce, the boy would presumably have been sent to the chair. It is also questionable whether such a man, even if he happened to be present, would have the stamina to enable him to ignore the incessant badgering of his colleagues—as one character in the film remarks, "It isn't easy to stand up to the ridicule of others." Indeed, because the story "is based on the dramatically convenient but otherwise simplistic assumption that people's prejudices can be traced to specific occurrences in their past and can thereby be accounted for and removed . . . the Fonda character had to come on as a combination Sherlock Holmes and Perry Mason, as well as double as confessor, catalyst, and instant psychiatrist to a number of the jurors." Also, due to the great reliance upon Fonda's presence, details are exposed and clarified much too smoothly. It is only Fonda who employs logical reasoning most of the time, and even when someone else brings up a point it usually comes as the result of Fonda's questioning. It may also be stated that, as Adam Garbicz and Jacek Klinowski remark in their article on the film in *Cinema: The Magic Vehicle,* "the actors are hardly a team, but rather a group of diverse individuals against whom Henry Fonda shines with all the more brightness." The subordination of details to suit a single star role would also mar the effectiveness of another courtroom drama of the 50s, Robert Wise's *I Want to Live!* (1958), as we shall see in Chanter 3.

In addition to the issue of the omniscience of the Fonda character, the script eschews realism for dramatic convenience in other respects also. Juror 3's sudden emotional breakdown, for example, remains largely unconvincing because it is triggered by the chance appearance of a photo of him and his son when he throws the wallet down on the table. Since all the others have sided with Fonda, Rose is left with no alternative but to find a quick and easy method for getting Juror 3 to do the same.

Nevertheless, Rose does manage to point out ironic truths abouth the judicial system on a reasonably frequent basis. There is, for example, the bigot's complaint that the old man is "twisting the facts" when he says that the elderly gentleman on the stand gave testimony mainly to look distinguished. Since the jurors are not the people on the stand, they cannot know what the witnesses are thinking; hence, the truth is often never revealed. The best the jury can do is try to read between the lines and make intelligent guesses; however, we have seen that initially no one except Fonda even considered the possibility of testimony being inaccurate.

There is also the fact that the presence of certain individuals in the jury room can alter the course of events. No one except Juror 5, who was once a slum kid, knows how a switchblade is handled. He demonstrates how awkward it would have been for the boy, who was much shorter than his father, to stab upward into the chest. The old man, preoccupied with studying people his own age, deduces from his observations of the vain woman in the witness box that she wasn't wearing her glasses.

Rose leaves it up to the viewer whether the experience of being a jury member has changed the characters of the men who have been shown their true selves as a result. It appears as though the bigot and the bully have confronted deep-seated personal conflicts for the first time in their lives. One wonders, however, whether the lessons they learned in court will have a long-term effect on their perceptions of the world.

Although Rose's script has its shortcomings, there is no denying that it is brilliantly tight, that it makes for exhilarating drama, and that it is food for thought. However, it is director Lumet who deserves credit for bringing Rose's words to life. For his success in overcoming the otherwise inevitable static quality of such an enclosed situation enough cannot be said. His camera probes those four walls relentlessly; of the 375 shots of the film, almost all were taken from a different angle. Throughout, he heightens dramatic tension and creates suspense by using extreme (and often grotesque) close-ups and by illuminating subtle nuances of character. For instance, after Juror 3 finishes telling the others about his runaway son the first time, the camera continues to keep him in the right foreground, alone and in silent meditation, as the proceedings continue. The stockbroker early on tells Juror 5 that he never sweats; yet, after listening to the old man's revealing speech about the woman's glasses, we see him quickly take out a handkerchief and wipe his brow.

Lumet and his cinematographer, Boris Kaufman, constantly emphasize the claustrophobic atmosphere of the drab, cramped, stuffy jury room. The sound of someone coughing or sneezing often blocks out another's dialogue. The uncomfortable physical environment matches the emotional tensions generated by the discussion. Kaufman, by the way, was by this time well-accustomed to shooting in real locations (*12 Angry Men* was shot in an actual jury room): he had photographed Elia Kazan's *On the Waterfront* (1954) on the docks of Hoboken and *Baby Doll* (1956) in the decaying Southern atmosphere of Benoit, Mississippi. Kaufman would later assist Lumet on *That Kind of Woman* (1959), *The Fugitive Kind* (1960), *Long Day's Journey into Night* (1962), *The Pawnbroker* (1965), *The Group* (1966) and *Bye Bye Braverman* (1968).

Finally, there are the performances. The whole ensemble is expert and thoroughly credible (indeed, this could be said for most of the films of Lumet's early career, characterized as it was by group situations), but the more prominent players must be singled out. Lee J. Cobb brought his muscular Johnny Friendly presence from *On the Waterfront* to his portrayal of the vengeful bully and again seemed singularly suited for his role. Ed Begley made a thoroughly repellent racist. Henry Fonda once again proved himself to be the epitome of the decent, honest, soft-spoken liberal. Lumet would return Fonda's favor by using him in two subsequent features, *Stage Struck* (1958) and *Fail-Safe* (1964).

In terms of cinematic execution, *12 Angry Men* was clearly a film of its time. It is probable that if it were made today under the same conditions (with a TV crew and at TV speed), audiences who have since come to accept motion pictures and television as two unique forms of entertainment—with much higher standards for films—would dismiss it as a laughable "gimmick" film despite the gravity of its messages.

Nevertheless, after nearly thirty years *12 Angry Men* remains one of the most absorbing exposés of the workings of the judicial process. This is due mainly to Rose's penetrating indictment of the reliability of the jury system. Lumet's contribution was pretty much technical (although his direction of the actors was superlative); indeed, what with the challenge of having to complete the shooting in a mere twenty days, he could hardly have been expected to develop any sort of personal philosophy. Although the film ends on a happy note, the viewer (as mentioned before) is inescapably reminded of the more serious implications of the previous ninety minutes: the extent to which personal biases can taint a juror's perceptions of the real issues and as a result endanger the lives of the (presumably innocent) parties on trial. Even though Rose, like Cayette in *Justice est Faite,* does not offer alternatives to the present system of trial by jury, his screenplay is, on the whole, a more fervent and angered denunciation of the American public's idealistic approach to the reliability of the system. His message, that "the law is no better than the people who enforce it, and that the people who enforce it are all too human," is just as pertinent today as it was in 1957.

Source: Thomas J. Harris, "*12 Angry Men,*" in *Courtroom's Finest Hour in American Cinema*, Scarecrow Press, 1987, pp. 1–21.

Hollis Alpert

In the following review of the original movie version of Twelve Angry Men, *Alpert asserts that the story "pins too much faith on the presence . . . of the open-minded man," but calls it "a tight, absorbing drama," nonetheless.*

Henry Fonda has a most reassuring face. Something about the set of the jaw, the leanness of the cheeks, the moodiness of the eyes, inspires respect and confidence. The parts he has played in films and on the stage have made him close to an American symbol of the unbiased, uncorrupted man, and he is just about perfect for the role of Juror #8 in Reginald Rose's *Twelve Angry Men.* Fonda, in this study of a jury's intimate deliberations, must stand alone, at first, against eleven men who are convinced that a tough boy of the slums has killed his father. They're ready, all except Juror #8, to wrap up the case, send the boy to the chair, and then go home and forget about it. Out of this situation Reginald Rose makes a tight, absorbing drama.

One of the jurors is anxious to get it over with and get on to the ballgame; another remembers a boy of his own, who at just about the same age escaped his authority; a third is a crowd-pleaser—he wants to be part of the majority; and a fourth is a man of reason who has added up all the evidence in his own mind and has found no reasonable doubt of the boy's guilt. If *Twelve Angry Men* does nothing else, it reminds us, like a catechism, of the function and responsibility of the people of the jury. It is also a primer in the definition of those important words, "a reasonable doubt." The entire action is concerned with establishing it.

> "*TWELVE ANGRY MEN* IS REMARKABLY SUCCESSFUL AT ESTABLISHING ITS ATMOSPHERE."

With so single a notion, the story is bound to be limited. Sidney Lumet, however, has given it some sharp, restless direction—what might be called a maximum of movement in a minimum of space. Since practically all the action takes place in the small jury room, there's not much chance for vistas and scenery. Thus, the emphasis was placed on the actors; their faces and movements provide the mobility and, surprisingly, it is enough. This is because they're all—those who play the twelve jury men—exceedingly capable and playing at peak ability. From E. G. Marshall's calculating but reasonable businessman to Lee J. Cobb's study of a neurotic sadist they are remarkable performances. It's unfair to single any of them out; Ed Begley is fine as an elderly man shot through with prejudice, so is Jack Warden as the guy in a hurry to get out to the ballpark. And there's Fonda's own sensitive work.

The French picture, *Justice Is Done,* explored some of the same ground, and left the audience seeing an almost visible question mark on the screen at the end. It probed more, it was perhaps more vital. And perhaps the thesis of *Twelve Angry Men* pins too much faith on the presence in a jury of the open-minded man, the one who looks at all the evidence and even comes up with evidence that neither the lawyers nor the judge suspected existed during the course of the trial. If this man had not been on the jury, if he hadn't deduced facts that no one else during the course of the trial, nor in the jury room, had been able to deduce, then, presumably, the boy would have been sent to his death. It is this stacking of the story that gives it its weakness.

Beyond that, *Twelve Angry Men* is remarkably successful at establishing its atmosphere, from the sultriness of the room on a hot summer day to the tension created by the clash of overheated minds. Reginald Rose's screenplay is considerably improved and developed over its original version seen a few seasons ago on TV; Sidney Lumet's direction (his first in the movie medium) is expert enough to qualify him as an important new talent; and it looks as though Henry Fonda, in his first time out as a producer, has come up with a winner.

Source: Hollis Alpert, "Gentlemen of the Jury," in *Saturday Review*, April 20, 1957, pp. 29–30.

SOURCES

American Civil Liberties Union (ACLU), "Inadequate Representation," http://www.aclu.org/DeathPenalty/DeathPenalty.cfm?ID=9313&c=62 (posted October 8, 2003).

Cutler, Brian L., and Stephen D. Penrod, *Mistaken Identification: The Eyewitness, Psychology, and the Law*, Cambridge University Press, 1995, p. 12.

Ellsworth, Phoebe C., Review of *Twelve Angry Men*, in *Michigan Law Review*, Vol. 101, No. 6, May 2003, pp. 1387–1407.

"Inside the Jury Room," in *Newsweek*, April 15, 1957, p. 113.

Loftus, Elizabeth F., *Eyewitness Testimony*, Harvard University Press, 1979, pp. 1–7, 9–10, 171–74.

"Reginald Rose: A Biography," in *Readings on "Twelve Angry Men,"* edited by Ross Munyan, Greenhaven Press, 2000, p. 19.

Rose, Reginald, "Author's Commentary," in *Six Television Plays*, Simon and Schuster, 1956, p. 156.

———, *Twelve Angry Men: A Play in Three Acts*, Dramatic Publishing Company, 1955, pp. 4–5, 15, 16, 21, 22, 44, 45, 60.

Simon, John, "No Doubt," in *New York*, Vol. 37, No. 39, pp. 71–72.

Smith, David Burnell, "*Twelve Angry Men* Presents an Idealized View of the Jury System," in *Readings on "Twelve Angry Men,"* edited by Ross Munyan, Greenhaven Press, 2000, pp. 97–101.

Traube, Leonard, "The 1954 Production Was Excellent Television Drama," in *Readings on "Twelve Angry Men,"* edited by Ross Munyan, Greenhaven Press, 2000, p. 108; originally published in *Variety*, September 24, 1954.

Walsh, Moira, Review of *Twelve Angry Men*, in *America*, April 27, 1957, p. 150.

Wolf, Matt, "The 1996 London Stage Version Is Timely," in *Readings on "Twelve Angry Men,"* edited by Ross Munyan, Greenhaven Press, 2000, p. 122; originally published in *Variety*, May 20–26, 1996.

FURTHER READING

Abramson, Jeffrey, *We the Jury: The Jury System and the Ideal of Democracy*, with a new preface, Harvard University Press, 2000.

Abramson, who is a former prosecutor, describes the history and function of juries in democratic society. He discusses such issues as mandatory cross-section representation for juries and scientific jury selection and advocates mandatory unanimous verdicts. He concludes that the jury system works well and serves the interests of democracy.

Burnett, D. Graham, *A Trial by Jury*, Vintage, 2002.

Burnett, a historian of science, was the foreman of the jury in a murder trial in New York City, and in this book he discusses the responsibilities and frustrations of jury duty. The result is an excellent account of what really goes on in a jury room. Reviewers made comparisons between this book and *Twelve Angry Men*.

Hans, Valerie P., and Neil Vidmar, *Judging the Jury*, Perseus, 2001.

The authors discuss the performance of juries and conclude that on the whole, they do a competent job. Other issues discussed in the book include jury selection, the effects of prejudice, and the significance of whether the verdict is unanimous or a majority decision. They also cover the history and development of the jury system.

Yarmey, A. Daniel, *The Psychology of Eyewitness Testimony*, Free Press, 1979.

Yarmey presents the psychological and legal aspects of eyewitness identification. He also discusses the implications for criminal justice of the scientific literature on memory, perception, and social perception.

Glossary of Literary Terms

A

Abstract: Used as a noun, the term refers to a short summary or outline of a longer work. As an adjective applied to writing or literary works, abstract refers to words or phrases that name things not knowable through the five senses. Examples of abstracts include the *Cliffs Notes* summaries of major literary works. Examples of abstract terms or concepts include "idea," "guilt" "honesty," and "loyalty."

Absurd, Theater of the: See *Theater of the Absurd*

Absurdism: See *Theater of the Absurd*

Act: A major section of a play. Acts are divided into varying numbers of shorter scenes. From ancient times to the nineteenth century plays were generally constructed of five acts, but modern works typically consist of one, two, or three acts. Examples of five-act plays include the works of Sophocles and Shakespeare, while the plays of Arthur Miller commonly have a three-act structure.

Acto: A one-act Chicano theater piece developed out of collective improvisation. *Actos* were performed by members of Luis Valdez's Teatro Campesino in California during the mid-1960s.

Aestheticism: A literary and artistic movement of the nineteenth century. Followers of the movement believed that art should not be mixed with social, political, or moral teaching. The statement "art for art's sake" is a good summary of aestheticism. The movement had its roots in France, but it gained widespread importance in England in the last half of the nineteenth century, where it helped change the Victorian practice of including moral lessons in literature. Oscar Wilde is one of the best-known "aesthetes" of the late nineteenth century.

Age of Johnson: The period in English literature between 1750 and 1798, named after the most prominent literary figure of the age, Samuel Johnson. Works written during this time are noted for their emphasis on "sensibility," or emotional quality. These works formed a transition between the rational works of the Age of Reason, or Neoclassical period, and the emphasis on individual feelings and responses of the Romantic period. Significant writers during the Age of Johnson included the novelists Ann Radcliffe and Henry Mackenzie, dramatists Richard Sheridan and Oliver Goldsmith, and poets William Collins and Thomas Gray. Also known as Age of Sensibility

Age of Reason: See *Neoclassicism*

Age of Sensibility: See *Age of Johnson*

Alexandrine Meter: See *Meter*

Allegory: A narrative technique in which characters representing things or abstract ideas are used to convey a message or teach a lesson. Allegory is typically used to teach moral, ethical, or religious lessons but is sometimes used for satiric or political purposes. Examples of allegorical works include Edmund Spenser's *The Faerie Queene* and John Bunyan's *The Pilgrim's Progress.*

Allusion: A reference to a familiar literary or historical person or event, used to make an idea more easily understood. For example, describing someone as a "Romeo" makes an allusion to William Shakespeare's famous young lover in *Romeo and Juliet.*

Amerind Literature: The writing and oral traditions of Native Americans. Native American literature was originally passed on by word of mouth, so it consisted largely of stories and events that were easily memorized. Amerind prose is often rhythmic like poetry because it was recited to the beat of a ceremonial drum. Examples of Amerind literature include the autobiographical *Black Elk Speaks,* the works of N. Scott Momaday, James Welch, and Craig Lee Strete, and the poetry of Luci Tapahonso.

Analogy: A comparison of two things made to explain something unfamiliar through its similarities to something familiar, or to prove one point based on the acceptedness of another. Similes and metaphors are types of analogies. Analogies often take the form of an extended simile, as in William Blake's aphorism: "As the caterpillar chooses the fairest leaves to lay her eggs on, so the priest lays his curse on the fairest joys."

Angry Young Men: A group of British writers of the 1950s whose work expressed bitterness and disillusionment with society. Common to their work is an anti-hero who rebels against a corrupt social order and strives for personal integrity. The term has been used to describe Kingsley Amis, John Osborne, Colin Wilson, John Wain, and others.

Antagonist: The major character in a narrative or drama who works against the hero or protagonist. An example of an evil antagonist is Richard Lovelace in Samuel Richardson's *Clarissa,* while a virtuous antagonist is Macduff in William Shakespeare's *Macbeth.*

Anthropomorphism: The presentation of animals or objects in human shape or with human characteristics. The term is derived from the Greek word for "human form." The fables of Aesop, the animated films of Walt Disney, and Richard Adams's *Watership Down* feature anthropomorphic characters.

Anti-hero: A central character in a work of literature who lacks traditional heroic qualities such as courage, physical prowess, and fortitude. Anti-heros typically distrust conventional values and are unable to commit themselves to any ideals. They generally feel helpless in a world over which they have no control. Anti-heroes usually accept, and often celebrate, their positions as social outcasts. A well-known anti-hero is Yossarian in Joseph Heller's novel *Catch-22.*

Antimasque: See *Masque*

Antithesis: The antithesis of something is its direct opposite. In literature, the use of antithesis as a figure of speech results in two statements that show a contrast through the balancing of two opposite ideas. Technically, it is the second portion of the statement that is defined as the "antithesis"; the first portion is the "thesis." An example of antithesis is found in the following portion of Abraham Lincoln's "Gettysburg Address"; notice the opposition between the verbs "remember" and "forget" and the phrases "what we say" and "what they did": "The world will little note nor long remember what we say here, but it can never forget what they did here."

Apocrypha: Writings tentatively attributed to an author but not proven or universally accepted to be their works. The term was originally applied to certain books of the Bible that were not considered inspired and so were not included in the "sacred canon." Geoffrey Chaucer, William Shakespeare, Thomas Kyd, Thomas Middleton, and John Marston all have apocrypha. Apocryphal books of the Bible include the Old Testament's Book of Enoch and New Testament's Gospel of Peter.

Apollonian and Dionysian: The two impulses believed to guide authors of dramatic tragedy. The Apollonian impulse is named after Apollo, the Greek god of light and beauty and the symbol of intellectual order. The Dionysian impulse is named after Dionysus, the Greek god of wine and the symbol of the unrestrained forces of nature. The Apollonian impulse is to create a rational, harmonious world, while the Dionysian is to express the irrational forces of personality. Friedrich Nietzche uses these terms in *The Birth of Tragedy* to designate contrasting elements in Greek tragedy.

Apostrophe: A statement, question, or request addressed to an inanimate object or concept or to a nonexistent or absent person. Requests for inspiration from the muses in poetry are examples of apostrophe, as is Marc Antony's address to Caesar's corpse in William Shakespeare's *Julius Caesar*: "O, pardon me, thou bleeding piece of earth, That I am meek and gentle with these butchers! . . . Woe to the hand that shed this costly blood! . . ."

Archetype: The word archetype is commonly used to describe an original pattern or model from which all other things of the same kind are made. This term was introduced to literary criticism from the psychology of Carl Jung. It expresses Jung's theory that behind every person's "unconscious," or repressed memories of the past, lies the "collective unconscious" of the human race: memories of the countless typical experiences of our ancestors. These memories are said to prompt illogical associations that trigger powerful emotions in the reader. Often, the emotional process is primitive, even primordial. Archetypes are the literary images that grow out of the "collective unconscious." They appear in literature as incidents and plots that repeat basic patterns of life. They may also appear as stereotyped characters. Examples of literary archetypes include themes such as birth and death and characters such as the Earth Mother.

Argument: The argument of a work is the author's subject matter or principal idea. Examples of defined "argument" portions of works include John Milton's *Arguments* to each of the books of *Paradise Lost* and the "Argument" to Robert Herrick's *Hesperides.*

Aristotelian Criticism: Specifically, the method of evaluating and analyzing tragedy formulated by the Greek philosopher Aristotle in his *Poetics.* More generally, the term indicates any form of criticism that follows Aristotle's views. Aristotelian criticism focuses on the form and logical structure of a work, apart from its historical or social context, in contrast to "Platonic Criticism," which stresses the usefulness of art. Adherents of New Criticism including John Crowe Ransom and Cleanth Brooks utilize and value the basic ideas of Aristotelian criticism for textual analysis.

Art for Art's Sake: See *Aestheticism*

Aside: A comment made by a stage performer that is intended to be heard by the audience but supposedly not by other characters. Eugene O'Neill's *Strange Interlude* is an extended use of the aside in modern theater.

Audience: The people for whom a piece of literature is written. Authors usually write with a certain audience in mind, for example, children, members of a religious or ethnic group, or colleagues in a professional field. The term "audience" also applies to the people who gather to see or hear any performance, including plays, poetry readings, speeches, and concerts. Jane Austen's parody of the gothic novel, *Northanger Abbey,* was originally intended for (and also pokes fun at) an audience of young and avid female gothic novel readers.

Avant-garde: A French term meaning "vanguard." It is used in literary criticism to describe new writing that rejects traditional approaches to literature in favor of innovations in style or content. Twentieth-century examples of the literary *avant-garde* include the Black Mountain School of poets, the Bloomsbury Group, and the Beat Movement.

B

Ballad: A short poem that tells a simple story and has a repeated refrain. Ballads were originally intended to be sung. Early ballads, known as folk ballads, were passed down through generations, so their authors are often unknown. Later ballads composed by known authors are called literary ballads. An example of an anonymous folk ballad is "Edward," which dates from the Middle Ages. Samuel Taylor Coleridge's "The Rime of the Ancient Mariner" and John Keats's "La Belle Dame sans Merci" are examples of literary ballads.

Baroque: A term used in literary criticism to describe literature that is complex or ornate in style or diction. Baroque works typically express tension, anxiety, and violent emotion. The term "Baroque Age" designates a period in Western European literature beginning in the late sixteenth century and ending about one hundred years later. Works of this period often mirror the qualities of works more generally associated with the label "baroque" and sometimes feature elaborate conceits. Examples of Baroque works include John Lyly's *Euphues: The Anatomy of Wit,* Luis de Gongora's *Soledads,* and William Shakespeare's *As You Like It.*

Baroque Age: See *Baroque*

Baroque Period: See *Baroque*

Beat Generation: See *Beat Movement*

Beat Movement: A period featuring a group of American poets and novelists of the 1950s and 1960s—including Jack Kerouac, Allen Ginsberg, Gregory Corso, William S. Burroughs, and Lawrence Ferlinghetti—who rejected established social and literary values. Using such techniques as stream of consciousness writing and jazz-influenced free verse and focusing on unusual or abnormal states of mind—generated by religious ecstasy or the use of drugs—the Beat writers aimed to create works that were unconventional in both form and subject matter. Kerouac's *On the Road* is perhaps the best-known example of a Beat Generation novel, and Ginsberg's *Howl* is a famous collection of Beat poetry.

Black Aesthetic Movement: A period of artistic and literary development among African Americans in the 1960s and early 1970s. This was the first major African-American artistic movement since the Harlem Renaissance and was closely paralleled by the civil rights and black power movements. The black aesthetic writers attempted to produce works of art that would be meaningful to the black masses. Key figures in black aesthetics included one of its founders, poet and playwright

Amiri Baraka, formerly known as LeRoi Jones; poet and essayist Haki R. Madhubuti, formerly Don L. Lee; poet and playwright Sonia Sanchez; and dramatist Ed Bullins. Works representative of the Black Aesthetic Movement include Amiri Baraka's play *Dutchman,* a 1964 Obie award-winner; *Black Fire: An Anthology of Afro-American Writing,* edited by Baraka and playwright Larry Neal and published in 1968; and Sonia Sanchez's poetry collection *We a BaddDDD People,* published in 1970. Also known as Black Arts Movement.

Black Arts Movement: See *Black Aesthetic Movement*

Black Comedy: See *Black Humor*

Black Humor: Writing that places grotesque elements side by side with humorous ones in an attempt to shock the reader, forcing him or her to laugh at the horrifying reality of a disordered world. Joseph Heller's novel *Catch-22* is considered a superb example of the use of black humor. Other well-known authors who use black humor include Kurt Vonnegut, Edward Albee, Eugene Ionesco, and Harold Pinter. Also known as Black Comedy.

Blank Verse: Loosely, any unrhymed poetry, but more generally, unrhymed iambic pentameter verse (composed of lines of five two-syllable feet with the first syllable accented, the second unaccented). Blank verse has been used by poets since the Renaissance for its flexibility and its graceful, dignified tone. John Milton's *Paradise Lost* is in blank verse, as are most of William Shakespeare's plays.

Bloomsbury Group: A group of English writers, artists, and intellectuals who held informal artistic and philosophical discussions in Bloomsbury, a district of London, from around 1907 to the early 1930s. The Bloomsbury Group held no uniform philosophical beliefs but did commonly express an aversion to moral prudery and a desire for greater social tolerance. At various times the circle included Virginia Woolf, E. M. Forster, Clive Bell, Lytton Strachey, and John Maynard Keynes.

Bon Mot: A French term meaning "good word." A *bon mot* is a witty remark or clever observation. Charles Lamb and Oscar Wilde are celebrated for their witty *bon mots.* Two examples by Oscar Wilde stand out: (1) "All women become their mothers. That is their tragedy. No man does. That's his." (2) "A man cannot be too careful in the choice of his enemies."

Breath Verse: See *Projective Verse*

Burlesque: Any literary work that uses exaggeration to make its subject appear ridiculous, either by treating a trivial subject with profound seriousness or by treating a dignified subject frivolously. The word "burlesque" may also be used as an adjective, as in "burlesque show," to mean "striptease act." Examples of literary burlesque include the comedies of Aristophanes, Miguel de Cervantes's *Don Quixote,* Samuel Butler's poem "Hudibras," and John Gay's play *The Beggar's Opera.*

C

Cadence: The natural rhythm of language caused by the alternation of accented and unaccented syllables. Much modern poetry—notably free verse—deliberately manipulates cadence to create complex rhythmic effects. James Macpherson's "Ossian poems" are richly cadenced, as is the poetry of the Symbolists, Walt Whitman, and Amy Lowell.

Caesura: A pause in a line of poetry, usually occurring near the middle. It typically corresponds to a break in the natural rhythm or sense of the line but is sometimes shifted to create special meanings or rhythmic effects. The opening line of Edgar Allan Poe's "The Raven" contains a caesura following "dreary": "Once upon a midnight dreary, while I pondered weak and weary. . . ."

Canzone: A short Italian or Provencal lyric poem, commonly about love and often set to music. The *canzone* has no set form but typically contains five or six stanzas made up of seven to twenty lines of eleven syllables each. A shorter, five- to ten-line "envoy," or concluding stanza, completes the poem. Masters of the *canzone* form include Petrarch, Dante Alighieri, Torquato Tasso, and Guido Cavalcanti.

Carpe Diem: A Latin term meaning "seize the day." This is a traditional theme of poetry, especially lyrics. A *carpe diem* poem advises the reader or the person it addresses to live for today and enjoy the pleasures of the moment. Two celebrated *carpe diem* poems are Andrew Marvell's "To His Coy Mistress" and Robert Herrick's poem beginning "Gather ye rosebuds while ye may. . . ."

Catharsis: The release or purging of unwanted emotions—specifically fear and pity—brought about by exposure to art. The term was first used by the Greek philosopher Aristotle in his *Poetics* to refer to the desired effect of tragedy on spectators. A famous example of catharsis is realized in Sophocles' *Oedipus Rex,* when Oedipus discovers that his wife, Jacosta, is his own mother and that the stranger he killed on the road was his own father.

Celtic Renaissance: A period of Irish literary and cultural history at the end of the nineteenth century. Followers of the movement aimed to create a romantic vision of Celtic myth and legend. The most significant works of the Celtic Renaissance typically present a dreamy, unreal world, usually in reaction against the reality of contemporary problems. William Butler Yeats's *The Wanderings of Oisin* is among the most significant works of the Celtic Renaissance. Also known as Celtic Twilight.

Celtic Twilight: See *Celtic Renaissance*

Character: Broadly speaking, a person in a literary work. The actions of characters are what constitute the plot of a story, novel, or poem. There are numerous types of characters, ranging from simple, stereotypical figures to intricate, multifaceted ones. In the techniques of anthropomorphism and personification, animals—and even places or things—can assume aspects of character. "Characterization" is the process by which an author creates vivid, believable characters in a work of art. This may be done in a variety of ways, including (1) direct description of the character by the narrator; (2) the direct presentation of the speech, thoughts, or actions of the character; and (3) the responses of other characters to the character. The term "character" also refers to a form originated by the ancient Greek writer Theophrastus that later became popular in the seventeenth and eighteenth centuries. It is a short essay or sketch of a person who prominently displays a specific attribute or quality, such as miserliness or ambition. Notable characters in literature include Oedipus Rex, Don Quixote de la Mancha, Macbeth, Candide, Hester Prynne, Ebenezer Scrooge, Huckleberry Finn, Jay Gatsby, Scarlett O'Hara, James Bond, and Kunta Kinte.

Characterization: See *Character*

Chorus: In ancient Greek drama, a group of actors who commented on and interpreted the unfolding action on the stage. Initially the chorus was a major component of the presentation, but over time it became less significant, with its numbers reduced and its role eventually limited to commentary between acts. By the sixteenth century the chorus—if employed at all—was typically a single person who provided a prologue and an epilogue and occasionally appeared between acts to introduce or underscore an important event. The chorus in William Shakespeare's *Henry V* functions in this way. Modern dramas rarely feature a chorus, but T. S. Eliot's *Murder in the Cathedral* and Arthur Miller's *A View from the Bridge* are notable exceptions. The Stage Manager in Thornton Wilder's *Our Town* performs a role similar to that of the chorus.

Chronicle: A record of events presented in chronological order. Although the scope and level of detail provided varies greatly among the chronicles surviving from ancient times, some, such as the *Anglo-Saxon Chronicle,* feature vivid descriptions and a lively recounting of events. During the Elizabethan Age, many dramas—appropriately called "chronicle plays"—were based on material from chronicles. Many of William Shakespeare's dramas of English history as well as Christopher Marlowe's *Edward II* are based in part on Raphael Holinshead's *Chronicles of England, Scotland, and Ireland.*

Classical: In its strictest definition in literary criticism, classicism refers to works of ancient Greek or Roman literature. The term may also be used to describe a literary work of recognized importance (a "classic") from any time period or literature that exhibits the traits of classicism. Classical authors from ancient Greek and Roman times include Juvenal and Homer. Examples of later works and authors now described as classical include French literature of the seventeenth century, Western novels of the nineteenth century, and American fiction of the mid-nineteenth century such as that written by James Fenimore Cooper and Mark Twain.

Classicism: A term used in literary criticism to describe critical doctrines that have their roots in ancient Greek and Roman literature, philosophy, and art. Works associated with classicism typically exhibit restraint on the part of the author, unity of design and purpose, clarity, simplicity, logical organization, and respect for tradition. Examples of literary classicism include Cicero's prose, the dramas of Pierre Corneille and Jean Racine, the poetry of John Dryden and Alexander Pope, and the writings of J. W. von Goethe, G. E. Lessing, and T. S. Eliot.

Climax: The turning point in a narrative, the moment when the conflict is at its most intense. Typically, the structure of stories, novels, and plays is one of rising action, in which tension builds to the climax, followed by falling action, in which tension lessens as the story moves to its conclusion. The climax in James Fenimore Cooper's *The Last of the Mohicans* occurs when Magua and his captive Cora are pursued to the edge of a cliff by Uncas. Magua kills Uncas but is subsequently killed by Hawkeye.

Colloquialism: A word, phrase, or form of pronunciation that is acceptable in casual conversation but not in formal, written communication. It is considered more acceptable than slang. An example of colloquialism can be found in Rudyard Kipling's *Barrack-room Ballads:* "When 'Omer smote 'is bloomin' lyre He'd 'eard men sing by land and sea;

An' what he thought 'e might require 'E went an' took—the same as me!"

Comedy: One of two major types of drama, the other being tragedy. Its aim is to amuse, and it typically ends happily. Comedy assumes many forms, such as farce and burlesque, and uses a variety of techniques, from parody to satire. In a restricted sense the term comedy refers only to dramatic presentations, but in general usage it is commonly applied to nondramatic works as well. Examples of comedies range from the plays of Aristophanes, Terrence, and Plautus, Dante Alighieri's *The Divine Comedy,* Francois Rabelais's *Pantagruel* and *Gargantua,* and some of Geoffrey Chaucer's tales and William Shakespeare's plays to Noel Coward's play *Private Lives* and James Thurber's short story "The Secret Life of Walter Mitty."

Comedy of Manners: A play about the manners and conventions of an aristocratic, highly sophisticated society. The characters are usually types rather than individualized personalities, and plot is less important than atmosphere. Such plays were an important aspect of late seventeenth-century English comedy. The comedy of manners was revived in the eighteenth century by Oliver Goldsmith and Richard Brinsley Sheridan, enjoyed a second revival in the late nineteenth century, and has endured into the twentieth century. Examples of comedies of manners include William Congreve's *The Way of the World* in the late seventeenth century, Oliver Goldsmith's *She Stoops to Conquer* and Richard Brinsley Sheridan's *The School for Scandal* in the eighteenth century, Oscar Wilde's *The Importance of Being Earnest* in the nineteenth century, and W. Somerset Maugham's *The Circle* in the twentieth century.

Comic Relief: The use of humor to lighten the mood of a serious or tragic story, especially in plays. The technique is very common in Elizabethan works, and can be an integral part of the plot or simply a brief event designed to break the tension of the scene. The Gravediggers' scene in William Shakespeare's *Hamlet* is a frequently cited example of comic relief.

Commedia dell'arte: An Italian term meaning "the comedy of guilds" or "the comedy of professional actors." This form of dramatic comedy was popular in Italy during the sixteenth century. Actors were assigned stock roles (such as Pulcinella, the stupid servant, or Pantalone, the old merchant) and given a basic plot to follow, but all dialogue was improvised. The roles were rigidly typed and the plots were formulaic, usually revolving around young lovers who thwarted their elders and attained wealth and happiness. A rigid convention of the *commedia dell'arte* is the periodic intrusion of Harlequin, who interrupts the play with low buffoonery. Peppino de Filippo's *Metamorphoses of a Wandering Minstrel* gave modern audiences an idea of what *commedia dell'arte* may have been like. Various scenarios for *commedia dell'arte* were compiled in Petraccone's *La commedia dell'arte, storia, technica, scenari,* published in 1927.

Complaint: A lyric poem, popular in the Renaissance, in which the speaker expresses sorrow about his or her condition. Typically, the speaker's sadness is caused by an unresponsive lover, but some complaints cite other sources of unhappiness, such as poverty or fate. A commonly cited example is "A Complaint by Night of the Lover Not Beloved" by Henry Howard, Earl of Surrey. Thomas Sackville's "Complaint of Henry, Duke of Buckingham" traces the duke's unhappiness to his ruthless ambition.

Conceit: A clever and fanciful metaphor, usually expressed through elaborate and extended comparison, that presents a striking parallel between two seemingly dissimilar things—for example, elaborately comparing a beautiful woman to an object like a garden or the sun. The conceit was a popular device throughout the Elizabethan Age and Baroque Age and was the principal technique of the seventeenth-century English metaphysical poets. This usage of the word conceit is unrelated to the best-known definition of conceit as an arrogant attitude or behavior. The conceit figures prominently in the works of John Donne, Emily Dickinson, and T. S. Eliot.

Concrete: Concrete is the opposite of abstract, and refers to a thing that actually exists or a description that allows the reader to experience an object or concept with the senses. Henry David Thoreau's *Walden* contains much concrete description of nature and wildlife.

Concrete Poetry: Poetry in which visual elements play a large part in the poetic effect. Punctuation marks, letters, or words are arranged on a page to form a visual design: a cross, for example, or a bumblebee. Max Bill and Eugene Gomringer were among the early practitioners of concrete poetry; Haroldo de Campos and Augusto de Campos are among contemporary authors of concrete poetry.

Confessional Poetry: A form of poetry in which the poet reveals very personal, intimate, sometimes shocking information about himself or herself. Anne Sexton, Sylvia Plath, Robert Lowell, and John Berryman wrote poetry in the confessional vein.

Conflict: The conflict in a work of fiction is the issue to be resolved in the story. It usually occurs between two characters, the protagonist and the antagonist, or between the protagonist and society or the protagonist and himself or herself. Conflict in Theodore Dreiser's novel *Sister Carrie* comes as a result of urban society, while Jack London's short story "To Build a Fire" concerns the protagonist's battle against the cold and himself.

Connotation: The impression that a word gives beyond its defined meaning. Connotations may be universally understood or may be significant only to a certain group. Both "horse" and "steed" denote the same animal, but "steed" has a different connotation, deriving from the chivalrous or romantic narratives in which the word was once often used.

Consonance: Consonance occurs in poetry when words appearing at the ends of two or more verses have similar final consonant sounds but have final vowel sounds that differ, as with "stuff" and "off." Consonance is found in "The curfew tolls the knells of parting day" from Thomas Grey's "An Elegy Written in a Country Church Yard." Also known as Half Rhyme or Slant Rhyme.

Convention: Any widely accepted literary device, style, or form. A soliloquy, in which a character reveals to the audience his or her private thoughts, is an example of a dramatic convention.

Corrido: A Mexican ballad. Examples of *corridos* include "Muerte del afamado Bilito," "La voz de mi conciencia," "Lucio Perez," "La juida," and "Los presos."

Couplet: Two lines of poetry with the same rhyme and meter, often expressing a complete and self-contained thought. The following couplet is from Alexander Pope's "Elegy to the Memory of an Unfortunate Lady": 'Tis Use alone that sanctifies Expense, And Splendour borrows all her rays from Sense.

Criticism: The systematic study and evaluation of literary works, usually based on a specific method or set of principles. An important part of literary studies since ancient times, the practice of criticism has given rise to numerous theories, methods, and "schools," sometimes producing conflicting, even contradictory, interpretations of literature in general as well as of individual works. Even such basic issues as what constitutes a poem or a novel have been the subject of much criticism over the centuries. Seminal texts of literary criticism include Plato's *Republic,* Aristotle's *Poetics,* Sir Philip Sidney's *The Defence of Poesie,* John Dryden's *Of Dramatic Poesie,* and William Wordsworth's "Preface" to the second edition of his *Lyrical Ballads.* Contemporary schools of criticism include deconstruction, feminist, psychoanalytic, poststructuralist, new historicist, postcolonialist, and reader-response.

D

Dactyl: See *Foot*

Dadaism: A protest movement in art and literature founded by Tristan Tzara in 1916. Followers of the movement expressed their outrage at the destruction brought about by World War I by revolting against numerous forms of social convention. The Dadaists presented works marked by calculated madness and flamboyant nonsense. They stressed total freedom of expression, commonly through primitive displays of emotion and illogical, often senseless, poetry. The movement ended shortly after the war, when it was replaced by surrealism. Proponents of Dadaism include Andre Breton, Louis Aragon, Philippe Soupault, and Paul Eluard.

Decadent: See *Decadents*

Decadents: The followers of a nineteenth-century literary movement that had its beginnings in French aestheticism. Decadent literature displays a fascination with perverse and morbid states; a search for novelty and sensation—the "new thrill"; a preoccupation with mysticism; and a belief in the senselessness of human existence. The movement is closely associated with the doctrine Art for Art's Sake. The term "decadence" is sometimes used to denote a decline in the quality of art or literature following a period of greatness. Major French decadents are Charles Baudelaire and Arthur Rimbaud. English decadents include Oscar Wilde, Ernest Dowson, and Frank Harris.

Deconstruction: A method of literary criticism developed by Jacques Derrida and characterized by multiple conflicting interpretations of a given work. Deconstructionists consider the impact of the language of a work and suggest that the true meaning of the work is not necessarily the meaning that the author intended. Jacques Derrida's *De la grammatologie* is the seminal text on deconstructive strategies; among American practitioners of this method of criticism are Paul de Man and J. Hillis Miller.

Deduction: The process of reaching a conclusion through reasoning from general premises to a specific premise. An example of deduction is present in the following syllogism: Premise: All mammals are animals. Premise: All whales are mammals. Conclusion: Therefore, all whales are animals.

Denotation: The definition of a word, apart from the impressions or feelings it creates in the reader. The word "apartheid" denotes a political and economic policy of segregation by race, but its connotations—oppression, slavery, inequality—are numerous.

Denouement: A French word meaning "the unknotting." In literary criticism, it denotes the resolution of conflict in fiction or drama. The *denouement* follows the climax and provides an outcome to the primary plot situation as well as an explanation of secondary plot complications. The *denouement* often involves a character's recognition of his or her state of mind or moral condition. A well-known example of *denouement* is the last scene of the play *As You Like It* by William Shakespeare, in which couples are married, an evildoer repents, the identities of two disguised characters are revealed, and a ruler is restored to power. Also known as Falling Action.

Description: Descriptive writing is intended to allow a reader to picture the scene or setting in which the action of a story takes place. The form this description takes often evokes an intended emotional response—a dark, spooky graveyard will evoke fear, and a peaceful, sunny meadow will evoke calmness. An example of a descriptive story is Edgar Allan Poe's *Landor's Cottage,* which offers a detailed depiction of a New York country estate.

Detective Story: A narrative about the solution of a mystery or the identification of a criminal. The conventions of the detective story include the detective's scrupulous use of logic in solving the mystery; incompetent or ineffectual police; a suspect who appears guilty at first but is later proved innocent; and the detective's friend or confidant—often the narrator—whose slowness in interpreting clues emphasizes by contrast the detective's brilliance. Edgar Allan Poe's "Murders in the Rue Morgue" is commonly regarded as the earliest example of this type of story. With this work, Poe established many of the conventions of the detective story genre, which are still in practice. Other practitioners of this vast and extremely popular genre include Arthur Conan Doyle, Dashiell Hammett, and Agatha Christie.

Deus ex machina: A Latin term meaning "god out of a machine." In Greek drama, a god was often lowered onto the stage by a mechanism of some kind to rescue the hero or untangle the plot. By extension, the term refers to any artificial device or coincidence used to bring about a convenient and simple solution to a plot. This is a common device in melodramas and includes such fortunate circumstances as the sudden receipt of a legacy to save the family farm or a last-minute stay of execution. The *deus ex machina* invariably rewards the virtuous and punishes evildoers. Examples of *deus ex machina* include King Louis XIV in Jean-Baptiste Moliere's *Tartuffe* and Queen Victoria in *The Pirates of Penzance* by William Gilbert and Arthur Sullivan. Bertolt Brecht parodies the abuse of such devices in the conclusion of his *Threepenny Opera.*

Dialogue: In its widest sense, dialogue is simply conversation between people in a literary work; in its most restricted sense, it refers specifically to the speech of characters in a drama. As a specific literary genre, a "dialogue" is a composition in which characters debate an issue or idea. The Greek philosopher Plato frequently expounded his theories in the form of dialogues.

Diction: The selection and arrangement of words in a literary work. Either or both may vary depending on the desired effect. There are four general types of diction: "formal," used in scholarly or lofty writing; "informal," used in relaxed but educated conversation; "colloquial," used in everyday speech; and "slang," containing newly coined words and other terms not accepted in formal usage.

Didactic: A term used to describe works of literature that aim to teach some moral, religious, political, or practical lesson. Although didactic elements are often found in artistically pleasing works, the term "didactic" usually refers to literature in which the message is more important than the form. The term may also be used to criticize a work that the critic finds "overly didactic," that is, heavy-handed in its delivery of a lesson. Examples of didactic literature include John Bunyan's *Pilgrim's Progress,* Alexander Pope's *Essay on Criticism,* Jean-Jacques Rousseau's *Emile,* and Elizabeth Inchbald's *Simple Story.*

Dimeter: See *Meter*

Dionysian: See *Apollonian and Dionysian*

Discordia concours: A Latin phrase meaning "discord in harmony." The term was coined by the eighteenth-century English writer Samuel Johnson to describe "a combination of dissimilar images or discovery of occult resemblances in things apparently unlike." Johnson created the expression by reversing a phrase by the Latin poet Horace. The metaphysical poetry of John Donne, Richard Crashaw, Abraham Cowley, George Herbert, and Edward Taylor among others, contains many examples of *discordia concours.* In Donne's "A Valediction: Forbidding Mourning," the poet compares the union of himself with his lover to a draftsman's compass: "If they be two, they are two so, As stiff twin compasses are two: Thy soul, the fixed foot, makes no show To move, but doth, if the other do; And though it in the center sit, Yet when the other far doth roam, It leans, and hearkens after it, And grows erect, as that comes home."

Dissonance: A combination of harsh or jarring sounds, especially in poetry. Although such combinations may be accidental, poets sometimes intentionally make them to achieve particular effects. Dissonance is also sometimes used to refer to close but not identical rhymes. When this is the case, the word functions as a synonym for consonance. Robert Browning, Gerard Manley Hopkins, and many other poets have made deliberate use of dissonance.

Doppelganger: A literary technique by which a character is duplicated (usually in the form of an alter ego, though sometimes as a ghostly counterpart) or divided into two distinct, usually opposite personalities. The use of this character device is widespread in nineteenth- and twentieth-century literature, and indicates a growing awareness among authors that the "self" is really a composite of many "selves." A well-known story containing a *doppelganger* character is Robert Louis Stevenson's *Dr. Jekyll and Mr. Hyde,* which dramatizes an internal struggle between good and evil. Also known as The Double.

Double Entendre: A corruption of a French phrase meaning "double meaning." The term is used to indicate a word or phrase that is deliberately ambiguous, especially when one of the meanings is risque or improper. An example of a *double entendre* is the Elizabethan usage of the verb "die," which refers both to death and to orgasm.

Double, The: See *Doppelganger*

Draft: Any preliminary version of a written work. An author may write dozens of drafts which are revised to form the final work, or he or she may write only one, with few or no revisions. Dorothy Parker's observation that "I can't write five words but that I change seven" humorously indicates the purpose of the draft.

Drama: In its widest sense, a drama is any work designed to be presented by actors on a stage. Similarly, "drama" denotes a broad literary genre that includes a variety of forms, from pageant and spectacle to tragedy and comedy, as well as countless types and subtypes. More commonly in modern usage, however, a drama is a work that treats serious subjects and themes but does not aim at the grandeur of tragedy. This use of the term originated with the eighteenth-century French writer Denis Diderot, who used the word *drame* to designate his plays about middle-class life; thus "drama" typically features characters of a less exalted stature than those of tragedy. Examples of classical dramas include Menander's comedy *Dyscolus* and Sophocles' tragedy *Oedipus Rex.* Contemporary dramas include Eugene O'Neill's *The Iceman Cometh,* Lillian Hellman's *Little Foxes,* and August Wilson's *Ma Rainey's Black Bottom.*

Dramatic Irony: Occurs when the audience of a play or the reader of a work of literature knows something that a character in the work itself does not know. The irony is in the contrast between the intended meaning of the statements or actions of a character and the additional information understood by the audience. A celebrated example of dramatic irony is in Act V of William Shakespeare's *Romeo and Juliet,* where two young lovers meet their end as a result of a tragic misunderstanding. Here, the audience has full knowledge that Juliet's apparent "death" is merely temporary; she will regain her senses when the mysterious "sleeping potion" she has taken wears off. But Romeo, mistaking Juliet's drug-induced trance for true death, kills himself in grief. Upon awakening, Juliet discovers Romeo's corpse and, in despair, slays herself.

Dramatic Monologue: See *Monologue*

Dramatic Poetry: Any lyric work that employs elements of drama such as dialogue, conflict, or characterization, but excluding works that are intended for stage presentation. A monologue is a form of dramatic poetry.

Dramatis Personae: The characters in a work of literature, particularly a drama. The list of characters printed before the main text of a play or in the program is the *dramatis personae.*

Dream Allegory: See *Dream Vision*

Dream Vision: A literary convention, chiefly of the Middle Ages. In a dream vision a story is presented as a literal dream of the narrator. This device was commonly used to teach moral and religious lessons. Important works of this type are *The Divine Comedy* by Dante Alighieri, *Piers Plowman* by William Langland, and *The Pilgrim's Progress* by John Bunyan. Also known as Dream Allegory.

Dystopia: An imaginary place in a work of fiction where the characters lead dehumanized, fearful lives. Jack London's *The Iron Heel,* Yevgeny Zamyatin's *My,* Aldous Huxley's *Brave New World,* George Orwell's *Nineteen Eighty-four,* and Margaret Atwood's *Handmaid's Tale* portray versions of dystopia.

E

Eclogue: In classical literature, a poem featuring rural themes and structured as a dialogue among shepherds. Eclogues often took specific poetic forms, such as elegies or love poems. Some were written as the soliloquy of a shepherd. In later centuries, "eclogue" came to refer to any poem that was in the pastoral tradition or that had a dialogue or monologue structure. A classical example of an eclogue is Virgil's *Eclogues,* also known as *Bucolics.* Giovanni Boccaccio, Edmund Spenser, Andrew Marvell, Jonathan Swift, and Louis MacNeice also wrote eclogues.

Edwardian: Describes cultural conventions identified with the period of the reign of Edward VII of England (1901–1910). Writers of the Edwardian Age typically displayed a strong reaction against the propriety and conservatism of the Victorian Age. Their work often exhibits distrust of authority in religion, politics, and art and expresses strong doubts about the soundness of conventional values. Writers of this era include George Bernard Shaw, H. G. Wells, and Joseph Conrad.

Edwardian Age: See *Edwardian*

Electra Complex: A daughter's amorous obsession with her father. The term Electra complex comes from the plays of Euripides and Sophocles entitled *Electra,* in which the character Electra drives her brother Orestes to kill their mother and her lover in revenge for the murder of their father.

Elegy: A lyric poem that laments the death of a person or the eventual death of all people. In a conventional elegy, set in a classical world, the poet and subject are spoken of as shepherds. In modern criticism, the word elegy is often used to refer to a poem that is melancholy or mournfully contemplative. John Milton's "Lycidas" and Percy Bysshe Shelley's "Adonais" are two examples of this form.

Elizabethan Age: A period of great economic growth, religious controversy, and nationalism closely associated with the reign of Elizabeth I of England (1558–1603). The Elizabethan Age is considered a part of the general renaissance—that is, the flowering of arts and literature—that took place in Europe during the fourteenth through sixteenth centuries. The era is considered the golden age of English literature. The most important dramas in English and a great deal of lyric poetry were produced during this period, and modern English criticism began around this time. The notable authors of the period—Philip Sidney, Edmund Spenser, Christopher Marlowe, William Shakespeare, Ben Jonson, Francis Bacon, and John Donne—are among the best in all of English literature.

Elizabethan Drama: English comic and tragic plays produced during the Renaissance, or more narrowly, those plays written during the last years of and few years after Queen Elizabeth's reign. William Shakespeare is considered an Elizabethan dramatist in the broader sense, although most of his work was produced during the reign of James I. Examples of Elizabethan comedies include John Lyly's *The Woman in the Moone,* Thomas Dekker's *The Roaring Girl, or, Moll Cut Purse,* and William Shakespeare's *Twelfth Night.* Examples of Elizabethan tragedies include William Shakespeare's *Antony and Cleopatra,* Thomas Kyd's *The Spanish Tragedy,* and John Webster's *The Tragedy of the Duchess of Malfi.*

Empathy: A sense of shared experience, including emotional and physical feelings, with someone or something other than oneself. Empathy is often used to describe the response of a reader to a literary character. An example of an empathic passage is William Shakespeare's description in his narrative poem *Venus and Adonis* of: the snail, whose tender horns being hit, Shrinks backward in his shelly cave with pain. Readers of Gerard Manley Hopkins's *The Windhover* may experience some of the physical sensations evoked in the description of the movement of the falcon.

English Sonnet: See *Sonnet*

Enjambment: The running over of the sense and structure of a line of verse or a couplet into the following verse or couplet. Andrew Marvell's "To His Coy Mistress" is structured as a series of enjambments, as in lines 11–12: "My vegetable love should grow/Vaster than empires and more slow."

Enlightenment, The: An eighteenth-century philosophical movement. It began in France but had a wide impact throughout Europe and America. Thinkers of the Enlightenment valued reason and believed that both the individual and society could achieve a state of perfection. Corresponding to this essentially humanist vision was a resistance to religious authority. Important figures of the Enlightenment were Denis Diderot and Voltaire in France, Edward Gibbon and David Hume in England, and Thomas Paine and Thomas Jefferson in the United States.

Epic: A long narrative poem about the adventures of a hero of great historic or legendary importance. The setting is vast and the action is often given cosmic significance through the intervention of supernatural forces such as gods, angels, or demons. Epics are typically written in a classical style of grand simplicity with elaborate metaphors and allusions that enhance the symbolic importance of a hero's adventures. Some well-known epics are Homer's *Iliad* and *Odyssey,* Virgil's *Aeneid,* and John Milton's *Paradise Lost.*

Epic Simile: See *Homeric Simile*

Epic Theater: A theory of theatrical presentation developed by twentieth-century German playwright Bertolt Brecht. Brecht created a type of drama that the audience could view with complete detachment. He used what he termed "alienation effects" to create an emotional distance between the audience and the action on stage. Among these effects are: short, self-contained scenes that keep the play from building to a cathartic climax; songs that comment on the action; and techniques of acting that prevent the actor from developing an emotional identity with his role. Besides the plays of Bertolt Brecht, other plays that utilize epic theater conventions include those of Georg Buchner, Frank Wedekind, Erwin Piscator, and Leopold Jessner.

Epigram: A saying that makes the speaker's point quickly and concisely. Samuel Taylor Coleridge wrote an epigram that neatly sums up the form: "What is an Epigram? A Dwarfish whole, Its body brevity, and wit its soul."

Epilogue: A concluding statement or section of a literary work. In dramas, particularly those of the seventeenth and eighteenth centuries, the epilogue is a closing speech, often in verse, delivered by an actor at the end of a play and spoken directly to the audience. A famous epilogue is Puck's speech at the end of William Shakespeare's *A Midsummer Night's Dream.*

Epiphany: A sudden revelation of truth inspired by a seemingly trivial incident. The term was widely used by James Joyce in his critical writings, and the stories in Joyce's *Dubliners* are commonly called "epiphanies."

Episode: An incident that forms part of a story and is significantly related to it. Episodes may be either self-contained narratives or events that depend on a larger context for their sense and importance. Examples of episodes include the founding of Wilmington, Delaware in Charles Reade's *The Disinherited Heir* and the individual events comprising the picaresque novels and medieval romances.

Episodic Plot: See *Plot*

Epitaph: An inscription on a tomb or tombstone, or a verse written on the occasion of a person's death. Epitaphs may be serious or humorous. Dorothy Parker's epitaph reads, "I told you I was sick."

Epithalamion: A song or poem written to honor and commemorate a marriage ceremony. Famous examples include Edmund Spenser's "Epithalamion" and e. e. cummings's "Epithalamion." Also spelled Epithalamium.

Epithalamium: See *Epithalamion*

Epithet: A word or phrase, often disparaging or abusive, that expresses a character trait of someone or something. "The Napoleon of crime" is an epithet applied to Professor Moriarty, arch-rival of Sherlock Holmes in Arthur Conan Doyle's series of detective stories.

Exempla: See *Exemplum*

Exemplum: A tale with a moral message. This form of literary sermonizing flourished during the Middle Ages, when *exempla* appeared in collections known as "example-books." The works of Geoffrey Chaucer are full of *exempla.*

Existentialism: A predominantly twentieth-century philosophy concerned with the nature and perception of human existence. There are two major strains of existentialist thought: atheistic and Christian. Followers of atheistic existentialism believe that the individual is alone in a godless universe and that the basic human condition is one of suffering and loneliness. Nevertheless, because there are no fixed values, individuals can create their own characters—indeed, they can shape themselves—through the exercise of free will. The atheistic strain culminates in and is popularly associated with the works of Jean-Paul Sartre. The Christian existentialists, on the other hand, believe that only in God may people find freedom from life's anguish. The two strains hold certain beliefs in common: that existence cannot be fully understood or described through empirical effort; that anguish is a universal element of life; that individuals must bear responsibility for their actions; and that there is no common standard of behavior or perception for religious and ethical matters. Existentialist thought figures prominently in the works of such authors as Eugene Ionesco, Franz Kafka, Fyodor Dostoyevsky, Simone de Beauvoir, Samuel Beckett, and Albert Camus.

Expatriates: See *Expatriatism*

Expatriatism: The practice of leaving one's country to live for an extended period in another country. Literary expatriates include English poets Percy Bysshe Shelley and John Keats in Italy, Polish novelist Joseph Conrad in England, American writers Richard Wright, James Baldwin, Gertrude Stein, and Ernest Hemingway in France, and Trinidadian author Neil Bissondath in Canada.

Exposition: Writing intended to explain the nature of an idea, thing, or theme. Expository writing is often combined with description, narration, or argument. In dramatic writing, the exposition is the introductory material which presents the characters, setting, and tone of the play. An example of dramatic exposition occurs in many nineteenth-century drawing-room comedies in which the butler and the maid open the play with relevant talk about their master and mistress; in composition, exposition relays factual information, as in encyclopedia entries.

Expressionism: An indistinct literary term, originally used to describe an early twentieth-century school of German painting. The term applies to almost any mode of unconventional, highly subjective writing that distorts reality in some way. Advocates of Expressionism include dramatists George Kaiser, Ernst Toller, Luigi Pirandello, Federico Garcia Lorca, Eugene O'Neill, and Elmer Rice; poets George Heym, Ernst Stadler, August Stramm, Gottfried Benn, and Georg Trakl; and novelists Franz Kafka and James Joyce.

Extended Monologue: See *Monologue*

F

Fable: A prose or verse narrative intended to convey a moral. Animals or inanimate objects with human characteristics often serve as characters in fables. A famous fable is Aesop's "The Tortoise and the Hare."

Fairy Tales: Short narratives featuring mythical beings such as fairies, elves, and sprites. These tales originally belonged to the folklore of a particular nation or region, such as those collected in Germany by Jacob and Wilhelm Grimm. Two other celebrated writers of fairy tales are Hans Christian Andersen and Rudyard Kipling.

Falling Action: See *Denouement*

Fantasy: A literary form related to mythology and folklore. Fantasy literature is typically set in nonexistent realms and features supernatural beings. Notable examples of fantasy literature are *The Lord of the Rings* by J. R. R. Tolkien and the Gormenghast trilogy by Mervyn Peake.

Farce: A type of comedy characterized by broad humor, outlandish incidents, and often vulgar subject matter. Much of the "comedy" in film and television could more accurately be described as farce.

Feet: See *Foot*

Feminine Rhyme: See *Rhyme*

Femme fatale: A French phrase with the literal translation "fatal woman." A *femme fatale* is a sensuous, alluring woman who often leads men into danger or trouble. A classic example of the *femme fatale* is the nameless character in Billy Wilder's *The Seven Year Itch,* portrayed by Marilyn Monroe in the film adaptation.

Fiction: Any story that is the product of imagination rather than a documentation of fact. Characters and events in such narratives may be based in real life but their ultimate form and configuration is a creation of the author. Geoffrey Chaucer's *The Canterbury Tales,* Laurence Sterne's *Tristram Shandy,* and Margaret Mitchell's *Gone with the Wind* are examples of fiction.

Figurative Language: A technique in writing in which the author temporarily interrupts the order, construction, or meaning of the writing for a particular effect. This interruption takes the form of one or more figures of speech such as hyperbole, irony, or simile. Figurative language is the opposite of literal language, in which every word is truthful, accurate, and free of exaggeration or embellishment. Examples of figurative language are tropes such as metaphor and rhetorical figures such as apostrophe.

Figures of Speech: Writing that differs from customary conventions for construction, meaning, order, or significance for the purpose of a special meaning or effect. There are two major types of figures of speech: rhetorical figures, which do not make changes in the meaning of the words, and tropes, which do. Types of figures of speech include simile, hyperbole, alliteration, and pun, among many others.

Fin de siecle: A French term meaning "end of the century." The term is used to denote the last decade of the nineteenth century, a transition period when writers and other artists abandoned old conventions and looked for new techniques and objectives. Two writers commonly associated with the *fin de siecle* mindset are Oscar Wilde and George Bernard Shaw.

First Person: See *Point of View*

Flashback: A device used in literature to present action that occurred before the beginning of the story. Flashbacks are often introduced as the dreams or recollections of one or more characters. Flashback techniques are often used in films, where they are typically set off by a gradual changing of one picture to another.

Foil: A character in a work of literature whose physical or psychological qualities contrast strongly with, and therefore highlight, the corresponding qualities of another character. In his Sherlock Holmes stories, Arthur Conan Doyle portrayed Dr. Watson as a man of normal habits and intelligence, making him a foil for the eccentric and wonderfully perceptive Sherlock Holmes.

Folk Ballad: See *Ballad*

Folklore: Traditions and myths preserved in a culture or group of people. Typically, these are passed on by word of mouth in various forms—such as legends, songs, and proverbs—or preserved in customs and ceremonies. This term was first used by W. J. Thoms in 1846. Sir James Frazer's *The Golden Bough* is the record of English folklore; myths about the frontier and the Old South exemplify American folklore.

Folktale: A story originating in oral tradition. Folktales fall into a variety of categories, including legends, ghost stories, fairy tales, fables, and anecdotes based on historical figures and events. Examples of folktales include Giambattista Basile's *The Pentamerone,* which contains the tales of Puss in Boots, Rapunzel, Cinderella, and Beauty and the Beast, and Joel Chandler Harris's Uncle Remus stories, which represent transplanted African folktales and American tales about the characters Mike Fink, Johnny Appleseed, Paul Bunyan, and Pecos Bill.

Foot: The smallest unit of rhythm in a line of poetry. In English-language poetry, a foot is typically one accented syllable combined with one or two unaccented syllables. There are many different types of feet. When the accent is on the second syllable of a two syllable word (con-*tort*), the foot is an "iamb"; the reverse accentual pattern (*tor*-ture) is a "trochee." Other feet that commonly occur in poetry in English are "anapest", two unaccented syllables followed by an accented syllable as in inter-*cept*, and "dactyl", an accented syllable followed by two unaccented syllables as in *su*-i-cide.

Foreshadowing: A device used in literature to create expectation or to set up an explanation of later developments. In Charles Dickens's *Great Expectations,* the graveyard encounter at the beginning of the novel between Pip and the escaped convict Magwitch foreshadows the baleful atmosphere and events that comprise much of the narrative.

Form: The pattern or construction of a work which identifies its genre and distinguishes it from other genres. Examples of forms include the different genres, such as the lyric form or the short story form, and various patterns for poetry, such as the verse form or the stanza form.

Formalism: In literary criticism, the belief that literature should follow prescribed rules of construction, such as those that govern the sonnet form. Examples of formalism are found in the work of the New Critics and structuralists.

Fourteener Meter: See *Meter*

Free Verse: Poetry that lacks regular metrical and rhyme patterns but that tries to capture the cadences of everyday speech. The form allows a poet to exploit a variety of rhythmical effects within a single poem. Free-verse techniques have been widely used in the twentieth century by such writers as Ezra Pound, T. S. Eliot, Carl Sandburg, and William Carlos Williams. Also known as *Vers libre.*

Futurism: A flamboyant literary and artistic movement that developed in France, Italy, and Russia from 1908 through the 1920s. Futurist theater and poetry abandoned traditional literary forms. In their place, followers of the movement attempted to achieve total freedom of expression through bizarre imagery and deformed or newly invented words. The Futurists were self-consciously modern artists who attempted to incorporate the appearances and sounds of modern life into their work. Futurist writers include Filippo Tommaso Marinetti, Wyndham Lewis, Guillaume Apollinaire, Velimir Khlebnikov, and Vladimir Mayakovsky.

G

Genre: A category of literary work. In critical theory, genre may refer to both the content of a given work—tragedy, comedy, pastoral—and to its form, such as poetry, novel, or drama. This term also refers to types of popular literature, as in the genres of science fiction or the detective story.

Genteel Tradition: A term coined by critic George Santayana to describe the literary practice of certain late nineteenth-century American writers, especially New Englanders. Followers of the Genteel Tradition emphasized conventionality in social, religious, moral, and literary standards. Some of the best-known writers of the Genteel Tradition are R. H. Stoddard and Bayard Taylor.

Gilded Age: A period in American history during the 1870s characterized by political corruption and materialism. A number of important novels of social and political criticism were written during this time. Examples of Gilded Age literature include Henry Adams's *Democracy* and F. Marion Crawford's *An American Politician.*

Gothic: See *Gothicism*

Gothicism: In literary criticism, works characterized by a taste for the medieval or morbidly attractive. A gothic novel prominently features elements of horror, the supernatural, gloom, and violence: clanking chains, terror, charnel houses, ghosts, medieval castles, and mysteriously slamming doors.

The term "gothic novel" is also applied to novels that lack elements of the traditional Gothic setting but that create a similar atmosphere of terror or dread. Mary Shelley's *Frankenstein* is perhaps the best-known English work of this kind.

Gothic Novel: See *Gothicism*

Great Chain of Being: The belief that all things and creatures in nature are organized in a hierarchy from inanimate objects at the bottom to God at the top. This system of belief was popular in the seventeenth and eighteenth centuries. A summary of the concept of the great chain of being can be found in the first epistle of Alexander Pope's *An Essay on Man,* and more recently in Arthur O. Lovejoy's *The Great Chain of Being: A Study of the History of an Idea.*

Grotesque: In literary criticism, the subject matter of a work or a style of expression characterized by exaggeration, deformity, freakishness, and disorder. The grotesque often includes an element of comic absurdity. Early examples of literary grotesque include Francois Rabelais's *Pantagruel* and *Gargantua* and Thomas Nashe's *The Unfortunate Traveller,* while more recent examples can be found in the works of Edgar Allan Poe, Evelyn Waugh, Eudora Welty, Flannery O'Connor, Eugene Ionesco, Gunter Grass, Thomas Mann, Mervyn Peake, and Joseph Heller, among many others.

H

Haiku: The shortest form of Japanese poetry, constructed in three lines of five, seven, and five syllables respectively. The message of a *haiku* poem usually centers on some aspect of spirituality and provokes an emotional response in the reader. Early masters of *haiku* include Basho, Buson, Kobayashi Issa, and Masaoka Shiki. English writers of *haiku* include the Imagists, notably Ezra Pound, H. D., Amy Lowell, Carl Sandburg, and William Carlos Williams. Also known as *Hokku.*

Half Rhyme: See *Consonance*

Hamartia: In tragedy, the event or act that leads to the hero's or heroine's downfall. This term is often incorrectly used as a synonym for tragic flaw. In Richard Wright's *Native Son,* the act that seals Bigger Thomas's fate is his first impulsive murder.

Harlem Renaissance: The Harlem Renaissance of the 1920s is generally considered the first significant movement of black writers and artists in the United States. During this period, new and established black writers published more fiction and poetry than ever before, the first influential black literary journals were established, and black authors and artists received their first widespread recognition and serious critical appraisal. Among the major writers associated with this period are Claude McKay, Jean Toomer, Countee Cullen, Langston Hughes, Arna Bontemps, Nella Larsen, and Zora Neale Hurston. Works representative of the Harlem Renaissance include Arna Bontemps's poems "The Return" and "Golgotha Is a Mountain," Claude McKay's novel *Home to Harlem,* Nella Larsen's novel *Passing,* Langston Hughes's poem "The Negro Speaks of Rivers," and the journals *Crisis* and *Opportunity,* both founded during this period. Also known as Negro Renaissance and New Negro Movement.

Harlequin: A stock character of the *commedia dell'arte* who occasionally interrupted the action with silly antics. Harlequin first appeared on the English stage in John Day's *The Travailes of the Three English Brothers.* The San Francisco Mime Troupe is one of the few modern groups to adapt Harlequin to the needs of contemporary satire.

Hellenism: Imitation of ancient Greek thought or styles. Also, an approach to life that focuses on the growth and development of the intellect. "Hellenism" is sometimes used to refer to the belief that reason can be applied to examine all human experience. A cogent discussion of Hellenism can be found in Matthew Arnold's *Culture and Anarchy.*

Heptameter: See *Meter*

Hero/Heroine: The principal sympathetic character (male or female) in a literary work. Heroes and heroines typically exhibit admirable traits: idealism, courage, and integrity, for example. Famous heroes and heroines include Pip in Charles Dickens's *Great Expectations,* the anonymous narrator in Ralph Ellison's *Invisible Man,* and Sethe in Toni Morrison's *Beloved.*

Heroic Couplet: A rhyming couplet written in iambic pentameter (a verse with five iambic feet). The following lines by Alexander Pope are an example: "Truth guards the Poet, sanctifies the line,/ And makes Immortal, Verse as mean as mine."

Heroic Line: The meter and length of a line of verse in epic or heroic poetry. This varies by language and time period. For example, in English poetry, the heroic line is iambic pentameter (a verse with five iambic feet); in French, the alexandrine (a verse with six iambic feet); in classical literature, dactylic hexameter (a verse with six dactylic feet).

Heroine: See *Hero/Heroine*

Hexameter: See *Meter*

Historical Criticism: The study of a work based on its impact on the world of the time period in which it was written. Examples of postmodern historical criticism can be found in the work of Michel Foucault, Hayden White, Stephen Greenblatt, and Jonathan Goldberg.

Hokku: See *Haiku*

Holocaust: See *Holocaust Literature*

Holocaust Literature: Literature influenced by or written about the Holocaust of World War II. Such literature includes true stories of survival in concentration camps, escape, and life after the war, as well as fictional works and poetry. Representative works of Holocaust literature include Saul Bellow's *Mr. Sammler's Planet,* Anne Frank's *The Diary of a Young Girl,* Jerzy Kosinski's *The Painted Bird,* Arthur Miller's *Incident at Vichy,* Czeslaw Milosz's *Collected Poems,* William Styron's *Sophie's Choice,* and Art Spiegelman's *Maus.*

Homeric Simile: An elaborate, detailed comparison written as a simile many lines in length. An example of an epic simile from John Milton's *Paradise Lost* follows: "Angel Forms, who lay entranced Thick as autumnal leaves that strow the brooks In Vallombrosa, where the Etrurian shades High over-arched embower; or scattered sedge Afloat, when with fierce winds Orion armed Hath vexed the Red-Sea coast, whose waves o'erthrew Busiris and his Memphian chivalry, While with perfidious hatred they pursued The sojourners of Goshen, who beheld From the safe shore their floating carcasses And broken chariot-wheels." Also known as Epic Simile.

Horatian Satire: See *Satire*

Humanism: A philosophy that places faith in the dignity of humankind and rejects the medieval perception of the individual as a weak, fallen creature. "Humanists" typically believe in the perfectibility of human nature and view reason and education as the means to that end. Humanist thought is represented in the works of Marsilio Ficino, Ludovico Castelvetro, Edmund Spenser, John Milton, Dean John Colet, Desiderius Erasmus, John Dryden, Alexander Pope, Matthew Arnold, and Irving Babbitt.

Humors: Mentions of the humors refer to the ancient Greek theory that a person's health and personality were determined by the balance of four basic fluids in the body: blood, phlegm, yellow bile, and black bile. A dominance of any fluid would cause extremes in behavior. An excess of blood created a sanguine person who was joyful, aggressive, and passionate; a phlegmatic person was shy, fearful, and sluggish; too much yellow bile led to a choleric temperament characterized by impatience, anger, bitterness, and stubbornness; and excessive black bile created melancholy, a state of laziness, gluttony, and lack of motivation. Literary treatment of the humors is exemplified by several characters in Ben Jonson's plays *Every Man in His Humour* and *Every Man out of His Humour.* Also spelled Humours.

Humours: See *Humors*

Hyperbole: In literary criticism, deliberate exaggeration used to achieve an effect. In William Shakespeare's *Macbeth,* Lady Macbeth hyperbolizes when she says, "All the perfumes of Arabia could not sweeten this little hand."

I

Iamb: See *Foot*

Idiom: A word construction or verbal expression closely associated with a given language. For example, in colloquial English the construction "how come" can be used instead of "why" to introduce a question. Similarly, "a piece of cake" is sometimes used to describe a task that is easily done.

Image: A concrete representation of an object or sensory experience. Typically, such a representation helps evoke the feelings associated with the object or experience itself. Images are either "literal" or "figurative." Literal images are especially concrete and involve little or no extension of the obvious meaning of the words used to express them. Figurative images do not follow the literal meaning of the words exactly. Images in literature are usually visual, but the term "image" can also refer to the representation of any sensory experience. In his poem "The Shepherd's Hour," Paul Verlaine presents the following image: "The Moon is red through horizon's fog;/ In a dancing mist the hazy meadow sleeps." The first line is broadly literal, while the second line involves turns of meaning associated with dancing and sleeping.

Imagery: The array of images in a literary work. Also, figurative language. William Butler Yeats's "The Second Coming" offers a powerful image of encroaching anarchy: "Turning and turning in the widening gyre The falcon cannot hear the falconer; Things fall apart. . . ."

Imagism: An English and American poetry movement that flourished between 1908 and 1917. The Imagists used precise, clearly presented images in their works. They also used common, everyday speech and aimed for conciseness, concrete imagery, and the creation of new rhythms. Participants in the Imagist movement included Ezra Pound, H. D. (Hilda Doolittle), and Amy Lowell, among others.

In medias res: A Latin term meaning "in the middle of things." It refers to the technique of beginning a story at its midpoint and then using various flashback devices to reveal previous action. This technique originated in such epics as Virgil's *Aeneid.*

Induction: The process of reaching a conclusion by reasoning from specific premises to form a general premise. Also, an introductory portion of a work of literature, especially a play. Geoffrey Chaucer's "Prologue" to the *Canterbury Tales,* Thomas Sackville's "Induction" to *The Mirror of Magistrates,* and the opening scene in William Shakespeare's *The Taming of the Shrew* are examples of inductions to literary works.

Intentional Fallacy: The belief that judgments of a literary work based solely on an author's stated or implied intentions are false and misleading. Critics who believe in the concept of the intentional fallacy typically argue that the work itself is sufficient matter for interpretation, even though they may concede that an author's statement of purpose can be useful. Analysis of William Wordsworth's *Lyrical Ballads* based on the observations about poetry he makes in his "Preface" to the second edition of that work is an example of the intentional fallacy.

Interior Monologue: A narrative technique in which characters' thoughts are revealed in a way that appears to be uncontrolled by the author. The interior monologue typically aims to reveal the inner self of a character. It portrays emotional experiences as they occur at both a conscious and unconscious level. images are often used to represent sensations or emotions. One of the best-known interior monologues in English is the Molly Bloom section at the close of James Joyce's *Ulysses.* The interior monologue is also common in the works of Virginia Woolf.

Internal Rhyme: Rhyme that occurs within a single line of verse. An example is in the opening line of Edgar Allan Poe's "The Raven": "Once upon a midnight dreary, while I pondered weak and weary." Here, "dreary" and "weary" make an internal rhyme.

Irish Literary Renaissance: A late nineteenth- and early twentieth-century movement in Irish literature. Members of the movement aimed to reduce the influence of British culture in Ireland and create an Irish national literature. William Butler Yeats, George Moore, and Sean O'Casey are three of the best-known figures of the movement.

Irony: In literary criticism, the effect of language in which the intended meaning is the opposite of what is stated. The title of Jonathan Swift's "A Modest Proposal" is ironic because what Swift proposes in this essay is cannibalism—hardly "modest."

Italian Sonnet: See *Sonnet*

J

Jacobean Age: The period of the reign of James I of England (1603–1625). The early literature of this period reflected the worldview of the Elizabethan Age, but a darker, more cynical attitude steadily grew in the art and literature of the Jacobean Age. This was an important time for English drama and poetry. Milestones include William Shakespeare's tragedies, tragi-comedies, and sonnets; Ben Jonson's various dramas; and John Donne's metaphysical poetry.

Jargon: Language that is used or understood only by a select group of people. Jargon may refer to terminology used in a certain profession, such as computer jargon, or it may refer to any nonsensical language that is not understood by most people. Literary examples of jargon are Francois Villon's *Ballades en jargon,* which is composed in the secret language of the *coquillards,* and Anthony Burgess's *A Clockwork Orange,* narrated in the fictional characters' language of "Nadsat."

Juvenalian Satire: See *Satire*

K

Knickerbocker Group: A somewhat indistinct group of New York writers of the first half of the nineteenth century. Members of the group were linked only by location and a common theme: New York life. Two famous members of the Knickerbocker Group were Washington Irving and William Cullen Bryant. The group's name derives from Irving's *Knickerbocker's History of New York.*

L

Lais: See *Lay*

Lay: A song or simple narrative poem. The form originated in medieval France. Early French *lais* were often based on the Celtic legends and other tales sung by Breton minstrels—thus the name of the "Breton lay." In fourteenth-century England, the term "lay" was used to describe short narratives written in imitation of the Breton lays. The most notable of these is Geoffrey Chaucer's "The Minstrel's Tale."

Leitmotiv: See *Motif*

Literal Language: An author uses literal language when he or she writes without exaggerating or embellishing the subject matter and without any tools of figurative language. To say "He ran very quickly down the street" is to use literal language, whereas to say "He ran like a hare down the street" would be using figurative language.

Literary Ballad: See *Ballad*

Literature: Literature is broadly defined as any written or spoken material, but the term most often refers to creative works. Literature includes poetry, drama, fiction, and many kinds of nonfiction writing, as well as oral, dramatic, and broadcast compositions not necessarily preserved in a written format, such as films and television programs.

Lost Generation: A term first used by Gertrude Stein to describe the post-World War I generation of American writers: men and women haunted by a sense of betrayal and emptiness brought about by the destructiveness of the war. The term is commonly applied to Hart Crane, Ernest Hemingway, F. Scott Fitzgerald, and others.

Lyric Poetry: A poem expressing the subjective feelings and personal emotions of the poet. Such poetry is melodic, since it was originally accompanied by a lyre in recitals. Most Western poetry in the twentieth century may be classified as lyrical. Examples of lyric poetry include A. E. Housman's elegy "To an Athlete Dying Young," the odes of Pindar and Horace, Thomas Gray and William Collins, the sonnets of Sir Thomas Wyatt and Sir Philip Sidney, Elizabeth Barrett Browning and Rainer Maria Rilke, and a host of other forms in the poetry of William Blake and Christina Rossetti, among many others.

M

Mannerism: Exaggerated, artificial adherence to a literary manner or style. Also, a popular style of the visual arts of late sixteenth-century Europe that was marked by elongation of the human form and by intentional spatial distortion. Literary works that are self-consciously high-toned and artistic are often said to be "mannered." Authors of such works include Henry James and Gertrude Stein.

Masculine Rhyme: See *Rhyme*

Masque: A lavish and elaborate form of entertainment, often performed in royal courts, that emphasizes song, dance, and costumery. The Renaissance form of the masque grew out of the spectacles of masked figures common in medieval England and Europe. The masque reached its peak of popularity and development in seventeenth-century England, during the reigns of James I and, especially, of Charles I. Ben Jonson, the most significant masque writer, also created the "anti-masque," which incorporates elements of humor and the grotesque into the traditional masque and achieved greater dramatic quality. Masque-like interludes appear in Edmund Spenser's *The Faerie Queene* and in William Shakespeare's *The Tempest.* One of the best-known English masques is John Milton's *Comus.*

Measure: The foot, verse, or time sequence used in a literary work, especially a poem. Measure is often used somewhat incorrectly as a synonym for meter.

Melodrama: A play in which the typical plot is a conflict between characters who personify extreme good and evil. Melodramas usually end happily and emphasize sensationalism. Other literary forms that use the same techniques are often labeled "melodramatic." The term was formerly used to describe a combination of drama and music; as such, it was synonymous with "opera." Augustin Daly's *Under the Gaslight* and Dion Boucicault's *The Octoroon, The Colleen Bawn,* and *The Poor of New York* are examples of melodramas. The most popular media for twentieth-century melodramas are motion pictures and television.

Metaphor: A figure of speech that expresses an idea through the image of another object. Metaphors suggest the essence of the first object by identifying it with certain qualities of the second object. An example is "But soft, what light through yonder window breaks?/ It is the east, and Juliet is the sun" in William Shakespeare's *Romeo and Juliet.* Here, Juliet, the first object, is identified with qualities of the second object, the sun.

Metaphysical Conceit: See *Conceit*

Metaphysical Poetry: The body of poetry produced by a group of seventeenth-century English writers called the "Metaphysical Poets." The group includes John Donne and Andrew Marvell. The Metaphysical Poets made use of everyday speech, intellectual analysis, and unique imagery. They aimed to portray the ordinary conflicts and contradictions of life. Their poems often took the form of an argument, and many of them emphasize physical and religious love as well as the fleeting nature of life. Elaborate conceits are typical in metaphysical poetry. Marvell's "To His Coy Mistress" is a well-known example of a metaphysical poem.

Metaphysical Poets: See *Metaphysical Poetry*

Meter: In literary criticism, the repetition of sound patterns that creates a rhythm in poetry. The patterns are based on the number of syllables and the presence and absence of accents. The unit of rhythm in a line is called a foot. Types of meter are classified according to the number of feet in a line. These are the standard English lines: Monometer, one foot; Dimeter, two feet; Trimeter, three feet; Tetrameter, four feet; Pentameter, five feet; Hexameter, six feet (also called the Alexandrine); Heptameter, seven feet (also called the "Fourteener" when the feet are iambic). The most common English meter is the iambic pentameter, in which each line contains ten syllables, or five iambic feet, which individually are composed of an unstressed syllable followed by an accented syllable. Both of the following lines from Alfred, Lord Tennyson's "Ulysses" are written in iambic pentameter: Made weak by time and fate, but strong in will To strive, to seek, to find, and not to yield.

Mise en scene: The costumes, scenery, and other properties of a drama. Herbert Beerbohm Tree was renowned for the elaborate *mises en scene* of his lavish Shakespearean productions at His Majesty's Theatre between 1897 and 1915.

Modernism: Modern literary practices. Also, the principles of a literary school that lasted from roughly the beginning of the twentieth century until the end of World War II. Modernism is defined by its rejection of the literary conventions of the nineteenth century and by its opposition to conventional morality, taste, traditions, and economic values. Many writers are associated with the concepts of Modernism, including Albert Camus, Marcel Proust, D. H. Lawrence, W. H. Auden, Ernest Hemingway, William Faulkner, William Butler Yeats, Thomas Mann, Tennessee Williams, Eugene O'Neill, and James Joyce.

Monologue: A composition, written or oral, by a single individual. More specifically, a speech given by a single individual in a drama or other public entertainment. It has no set length, although it is usually several or more lines long. An example of an "extended monologue"—that is, a monologue of great length and seriousness—occurs in the one-act, one-character play *The Stronger* by August Strindberg.

Monometer: See *Meter*

Mood: The prevailing emotions of a work or of the author in his or her creation of the work. The mood of a work is not always what might be expected based on its subject matter. The poem "Dover Beach" by Matthew Arnold offers examples of two different moods originating from the same experience: watching the ocean at night. The mood of the first three lines—"The sea is calm tonight The tide is full, the moon lies fair Upon the straights. . . ." is in sharp contrast to the mood of the last three lines—"And we are here as on a darkling plain Swept with confused alarms of struggle and flight, Where ignorant armies clash by night."

Motif: A theme, character type, image, metaphor, or other verbal element that recurs throughout a single work of literature or occurs in a number of different works over a period of time. For example, the various manifestations of the color white in Herman Melville's *Moby Dick* is a "specific" *motif,* while the trials of star-crossed lovers is a "conventional" *motif* from the literature of all periods. Also known as *Motiv* or *Leitmotiv.*

Motiv: See *Motif*

Muckrakers: An early twentieth-century group of American writers. Typically, their works exposed the wrongdoings of big business and government in the United States. Upton Sinclair's *The Jungle* exemplifies the muckraking novel.

Muses: Nine Greek mythological goddesses, the daughters of Zeus and Mnemosyne (Memory). Each muse patronized a specific area of the liberal arts and sciences. Calliope presided over epic poetry, Clio over history, Erato over love poetry, Euterpe over music or lyric poetry, Melpomene over tragedy, Polyhymnia over hymns to the gods, Terpsichore over dance, Thalia over comedy, and Urania over astronomy. Poets and writers traditionally made appeals to the Muses for inspiration in their work. John Milton invokes the aid of a muse at the beginning of the first book of his *Paradise Lost:* "Of Man's First disobedience, and the Fruit of the Forbidden Tree, whose mortal taste Brought Death into the World, and all our woe, With loss of Eden, till one greater Man Restore us, and regain the blissful Seat, Sing Heav'nly Muse, that on the secret top of Oreb, or of Sinai, didst inspire That Shepherd, who first taught the chosen Seed, In the Beginning how the Heav'ns and Earth Rose out of Chaos. . . ."

Mystery: See *Suspense*

Myth: An anonymous tale emerging from the traditional beliefs of a culture or social unit. Myths use supernatural explanations for natural phenomena. They may also explain cosmic issues like creation and death. Collections of myths, known as mythologies, are common to all cultures and nations, but the best-known myths belong to the Norse, Roman, and Greek mythologies. A famous myth is the story of Arachne, an arrogant young girl who challenged a goddess, Athena, to a weaving contest; when the girl won, Athena was enraged and turned Arachne into a spider, thus explaining the existence of spiders.

N

Narration: The telling of a series of events, real or invented. A narration may be either a simple narrative, in which the events are recounted chronologically, or a narrative with a plot, in which the account is given in a style reflecting the author's artistic concept of the story. Narration is sometimes used as a synonym for "storyline." The recounting of scary stories around a campfire is a form of narration.

Narrative: A verse or prose accounting of an event or sequence of events, real or invented. The term is also used as an adjective in the sense "method of narration." For example, in literary criticism, the expression "narrative technique" usually refers to the way the author structures and presents his or her story. Narratives range from the shortest accounts of events, as in Julius Caesar's remark, "I came, I saw, I conquered," to the longest historical or biographical works, as in Edward Gibbon's *The Decline and Fall of the Roman Empire,* as well as diaries, travelogues, novels, ballads, epics, short stories, and other fictional forms.

Narrative Poetry: A nondramatic poem in which the author tells a story. Such poems may be of any length or level of complexity. Epics such as *Beowulf* and ballads are forms of narrative poetry.

Narrator: The teller of a story. The narrator may be the author or a character in the story through whom the author speaks. Huckleberry Finn is the narrator of Mark Twain's *The Adventures of Huckleberry Finn.*

Naturalism: A literary movement of the late nineteenth and early twentieth centuries. The movement's major theorist, French novelist Emile Zola, envisioned a type of fiction that would examine human life with the objectivity of scientific inquiry. The Naturalists typically viewed human beings as either the products of "biological determinism," ruled by hereditary instincts and engaged in an endless struggle for survival, or as the products of "socioeconomic determinism," ruled by social and economic forces beyond their control. In their works, the Naturalists generally ignored the highest levels of society and focused on degradation: poverty, alcoholism, prostitution, insanity, and disease. Naturalism influenced authors throughout the world, including Henrik Ibsen and Thomas Hardy. In the United States, in particular, Naturalism had a profound impact. Among the authors who embraced its principles are Theodore Dreiser, Eugene O'Neill, Stephen Crane, Jack London, and Frank Norris.

Negritude: A literary movement based on the concept of a shared cultural bond on the part of black Africans, wherever they may be in the world. It traces its origins to the former French colonies of Africa and the Caribbean. Negritude poets, novelists, and essayists generally stress four points in their writings: One, black alienation from traditional African culture can lead to feelings of inferiority. Two, European colonialism and Western education should be resisted. Three, black Africans should seek to affirm and define their own identity. Four, African culture can and should be reclaimed. Many Negritude writers also claim that blacks can make unique contributions to the world, based on a heightened appreciation of nature, rhythm, and human emotions—aspects of life they say are not so highly valued in the materialistic and rationalistic West. Examples of Negritude literature include the poetry of both Senegalese Leopold Senghor in *Hosties noires* and Martiniquais Aime-Fernand Cesaire in *Return to My Native Land.*

Negro Renaissance: See *Harlem Renaissance*

Neoclassical Period: See *Neoclassicism*

Neoclassicism: In literary criticism, this term refers to the revival of the attitudes and styles of expression of classical literature. It is generally used to describe a period in European history beginning in the late seventeenth century and lasting until about 1800. In its purest form, Neoclassicism marked a return to order, proportion, restraint, logic, accuracy, and decorum. In England, where Neoclassicism perhaps was most popular, it reflected the influence of seventeenth-century French writers, especially dramatists. Neoclassical writers typically reacted against the intensity and enthusiasm of the Renaissance period. They wrote works that appealed to the intellect, using elevated language and classical literary forms such as satire and the ode. Neoclassical works were often governed by the classical goal of instruction. English neoclassicists included Alexander Pope, Jonathan Swift, Joseph Addison, Sir Richard Steele, John Gay, and Matthew Prior; French neoclassicists included Pierre Corneille and Jean-Baptiste Moliere. Also known as Age of Reason.

Neoclassicists: See *Neoclassicism*

New Criticism: A movement in literary criticism, dating from the late 1920s, that stressed close textual analysis in the interpretation of works of literature.

The New Critics saw little merit in historical and biographical analysis. Rather, they aimed to examine the text alone, free from the question of how external events—biographical or otherwise—may have helped shape it. This predominantly American school was named "New Criticism" by one of its practitioners, John Crowe Ransom. Other important New Critics included Allen Tate, R. P. Blackmur, Robert Penn Warren, and Cleanth Brooks.

New Negro Movement: See *Harlem Renaissance*

Noble Savage: The idea that primitive man is noble and good but becomes evil and corrupted as he becomes civilized. The concept of the noble savage originated in the Renaissance period but is more closely identified with such later writers as Jean-Jacques Rousseau and Aphra Behn. First described in John Dryden's play *The Conquest of Granada,* the noble savage is portrayed by the various Native Americans in James Fenimore Cooper's "Leatherstocking Tales," by Queequeg, Daggoo, and Tashtego in Herman Melville's *Moby Dick,* and by John the Savage in Aldous Huxley's *Brave New World.*

O

Objective Correlative: An outward set of objects, a situation, or a chain of events corresponding to an inward experience and evoking this experience in the reader. The term frequently appears in modern criticism in discussions of authors' intended effects on the emotional responses of readers. This term was originally used by T. S. Eliot in his 1919 essay "Hamlet."

Objectivity: A quality in writing characterized by the absence of the author's opinion or feeling about the subject matter. Objectivity is an important factor in criticism. The novels of Henry James and, to a certain extent, the poems of John Larkin demonstrate objectivity, and it is central to John Keats's concept of "negative capability." Critical and journalistic writing usually are or attempt to be objective.

Occasional Verse: Poetry written on the occasion of a significant historical or personal event. *Vers de societe* is sometimes called occasional verse although it is of a less serious nature. Famous examples of occasional verse include Andrew Marvell's "Horatian Ode upon Cromwell's Return from England," Walt Whitman's "When Lilacs Last in the Dooryard Bloom'd"—written upon the death of Abraham Lincoln—and Edmund Spenser's commemoration of his wedding, "Epithalamion."

Octave: A poem or stanza composed of eight lines. The term octave most often represents the first eight lines of a Petrarchan sonnet. An example of an octave is taken from a translation of a Petrarchan sonnet by Sir Thomas Wyatt: "The pillar perisht is whereto I leant, The strongest stay of mine unquiet mind; The like of it no man again can find, From East to West Still seeking though he went. To mind unhap! for hap away hath rent Of all my joy the very bark and rind; And I, alas, by chance am thus assigned Daily to mourn till death do it relent."

Ode: Name given to an extended lyric poem characterized by exalted emotion and dignified style. An ode usually concerns a single, serious theme. Most odes, but not all, are addressed to an object or individual. Odes are distinguished from other lyric poetic forms by their complex rhythmic and stanzaic patterns. An example of this form is John Keats's "Ode to a Nightingale."

Oedipus Complex: A son's amorous obsession with his mother. The phrase is derived from the story of the ancient Theban hero Oedipus, who unknowingly killed his father and married his mother. Literary occurrences of the Oedipus complex include Andre Gide's *Oedipe* and Jean Cocteau's *La Machine infernale,* as well as the most famous, Sophocles' *Oedipus Rex.*

Omniscience: See *Point of View*

Onomatopoeia: The use of words whose sounds express or suggest their meaning. In its simplest sense, onomatopoeia may be represented by words that mimic the sounds they denote such as "hiss" or "meow." At a more subtle level, the pattern and rhythm of sounds and rhymes of a line or poem may be onomatopoeic. A celebrated example of onomatopoeia is the repetition of the word "bells" in Edgar Allan Poe's poem "The Bells."

Opera: A type of stage performance, usually a drama, in which the dialogue is sung. Classic examples of opera include Giuseppi Verdi's *La traviata,* Giacomo Puccini's *La Boheme,* and Richard Wagner's *Tristan und Isolde.* Major twentieth-century contributors to the form include Richard Strauss and Alban Berg.

Operetta: A usually romantic comic opera. John Gay's *The Beggar's Opera,* Richard Sheridan's *The Duenna,* and numerous works by William Gilbert and Arthur Sullivan are examples of operettas.

Oral Tradition: See *Oral Transmission*

Oral Transmission: A process by which songs, ballads, folklore, and other material are transmitted by word of mouth. The tradition of oral transmission predates the written record systems of literate society. Oral transmission preserves material sometimes over generations, although often with variations. Memory plays a large part in the recitation and preservation of orally transmitted material. Breton lays, French *fabliaux,* national epics (including the Anglo-Saxon *Beowulf,* the Spanish *El Cid,* and the Finnish *Kalevala*), Native American myths and legends, and African folktales told by plantation slaves are examples of orally transmitted literature.

Oration: Formal speaking intended to motivate the listeners to some action or feeling. Such public speaking was much more common before the development of timely printed communication such as newspapers. Famous examples of oration include Abraham Lincoln's "Gettysburg Address" and Dr. Martin Luther King Jr.'s "I Have a Dream" speech.

Ottava Rima: An eight-line stanza of poetry composed in iambic pentameter (a five-foot line in which each foot consists of an unaccented syllable followed by an accented syllable), following the abababcc rhyme scheme. This form has been prominently used by such important English writers as Lord Byron, Henry Wadsworth Longfellow, and W. B. Yeats.

Oxymoron: A phrase combining two contradictory terms. Oxymorons may be intentional or unintentional. The following speech from William Shakespeare's *Romeo and Juliet* uses several oxymorons: "Why, then, O brawling love! O loving hate! O anything, of nothing first create! O heavy lightness! serious vanity! Mis-shapen chaos of well-seeming forms! Feather of lead, bright smoke, cold fire, sick health! This love feel I, that feel no love in this."

P

Pantheism: The idea that all things are both a manifestation or revelation of God and a part of God at the same time. Pantheism was a common attitude in the early societies of Egypt, India, and Greece—the term derives from the Greek *pan* meaning "all" and *theos* meaning "deity." It later became a significant part of the Christian faith. William Wordsworth and Ralph Waldo Emerson are among the many writers who have expressed the pantheistic attitude in their works.

Parable: A story intended to teach a moral lesson or answer an ethical question. In the West, the best examples of parables are those of Jesus Christ in the New Testament, notably "The Prodigal Son," but parables also are used in Sufism, rabbinic literature, Hasidism, and Zen Buddhism.

Paradox: A statement that appears illogical or contradictory at first, but may actually point to an underlying truth. "Less is more" is an example of a paradox. Literary examples include Francis Bacon's statement, "The most corrected copies are commonly the least correct," and "All animals are equal, but some animals are more equal than others" from George Orwell's *Animal Farm.*

Parallelism: A method of comparison of two ideas in which each is developed in the same grammatical structure. Ralph Waldo Emerson's "Civilization" contains this example of parallelism: "Raphael paints wisdom; Handel sings it, Phidias carves it, Shakespeare writes it, Wren builds it, Columbus sails it, Luther preaches it, Washington arms it, Watt mechanizes it."

Parnassianism: A mid nineteenth-century movement in French literature. Followers of the movement stressed adherence to well-defined artistic forms as a reaction against the often chaotic expression of the artist's ego that dominated the work of the Romantics. The Parnassians also rejected the moral, ethical, and social themes exhibited in the works of French Romantics such as Victor Hugo. The aesthetic doctrines of the Parnassians strongly influenced the later symbolist and decadent movements. Members of the Parnassian school include Leconte de Lisle, Sully Prudhomme, Albert Glatigny, Francois Coppee, and Theodore de Banville.

Parody: In literary criticism, this term refers to an imitation of a serious literary work or the signature style of a particular author in a ridiculous manner. A typical parody adopts the style of the original and applies it to an inappropriate subject for humorous effect. Parody is a form of satire and could be considered the literary equivalent of a caricature or cartoon. Henry Fielding's *Shamela* is a parody of Samuel Richardson's *Pamela.*

Pastoral: A term derived from the Latin word "pastor," meaning shepherd. A pastoral is a literary composition on a rural theme. The conventions of the pastoral were originated by the third-century Greek poet Theocritus, who wrote about the experiences, love affairs, and pastimes of Sicilian shepherds. In a pastoral, characters and language of a courtly nature are often placed in a simple setting. The term pastoral is also used to classify dramas, elegies, and lyrics that exhibit the use of country settings and shepherd characters. Percy Bysshe Shelley's "Adonais" and John Milton's "Lycidas" are two famous examples of pastorals.

Pastorela: The Spanish name for the shepherds play, a folk drama reenacted during the Christmas season. Examples of *pastorelas* include Gomez Manrique's *Representacion del nacimiento* and the dramas of Lucas Fernandez and Juan del Encina.

Pathetic Fallacy: A term coined by English critic John Ruskin to identify writing that falsely endows nonhuman things with human intentions and feelings, such as "angry clouds" and "sad trees." The pathetic fallacy is a required convention in the classical poetic form of the pastoral elegy, and it is used in the modern poetry of T. S. Eliot, Ezra Pound, and the Imagists. Also known as Poetic Fallacy.

Pelado: Literally the "skinned one" or shirtless one, he was the stock underdog, sharp-witted picaresque character of Mexican vaudeville and tent shows. The *pelado* is found in such works as Don Catarino's *Los effectos de la crisis* and *Regreso a mi tierra.*

Pen Name: See *Pseudonym*

Pentameter: See *Meter*

Persona: A Latin term meaning "mask." *Personae* are the characters in a fictional work of literature. The *persona* generally functions as a mask through which the author tells a story in a voice other than his or her own. A *persona* is usually either a character in a story who acts as a narrator or an "implied author," a voice created by the author to act as the narrator for himself or herself. *Personae* include the narrator of Geoffrey Chaucer's *Canterbury Tales* and Marlow in Joseph Conrad's *Heart of Darkness.*

Personae: See *Persona*

Personal Point of View: See *Point of View*

Personification: A figure of speech that gives human qualities to abstract ideas, animals, and inanimate objects. William Shakespeare used personification in *Romeo and Juliet* in the lines "Arise, fair sun, and kill the envious moon,/ Who is already sick and pale with grief." Here, the moon is portrayed as being envious, sick, and pale with grief—all markedly human qualities. Also known as *Prosopopoeia.*

Petrarchan Sonnet: See *Sonnet*

Phenomenology: A method of literary criticism based on the belief that things have no existence outside of human consciousness or awareness. Proponents of this theory believe that art is a process that takes place in the mind of the observer as he or she contemplates an object rather than a quality of the object itself. Among phenomenological critics are Edmund Husserl, George Poulet, Marcel Raymond, and Roman Ingarden.

Picaresque Novel: Episodic fiction depicting the adventures of a roguish central character ("picaro" is Spanish for "rogue"). The picaresque hero is commonly a low-born but clever individual who wanders into and out of various affairs of love, danger, and farcical intrigue. These involvements may take place at all social levels and typically present a humorous and wide-ranging satire of a given society. Prominent examples of the picaresque novel are *Don Quixote* by Miguel de Cervantes, *Tom Jones* by Henry Fielding, and *Moll Flanders* by Daniel Defoe.

Plagiarism: Claiming another person's written material as one's own. Plagiarism can take the form of direct, word-for-word copying or the theft of the substance or idea of the work. A student who copies an encyclopedia entry and turns it in as a report for school is guilty of plagiarism.

Platonic Criticism: A form of criticism that stresses an artistic work's usefulness as an agent of social engineering rather than any quality or value of the work itself. Platonic criticism takes as its starting point the ancient Greek philosopher Plato's comments on art in his *Republic.*

Platonism: The embracing of the doctrines of the philosopher Plato, popular among the poets of the Renaissance and the Romantic period. Platonism is more flexible than Aristotelian Criticism and places more emphasis on the supernatural and unknown aspects of life. Platonism is expressed in the love poetry of the Renaissance, the fourth book of Baldassare Castiglione's *The Book of the Courtier,* and the poetry of William Blake, William Wordsworth, Percy Bysshe Shelley, Friedrich Holderlin, William Butler Yeats, and Wallace Stevens.

Play: See *Drama*

Plot: In literary criticism, this term refers to the pattern of events in a narrative or drama. In its simplest sense, the plot guides the author in composing the work and helps the reader follow the work. Typically, plots exhibit causality and unity and have a beginning, a middle, and an end. Sometimes, however, a plot may consist of a series of disconnected events, in which case it is known as an "episodic plot." In his *Aspects of the Novel,* E. M. Forster distinguishes between a story, defined as a "narrative of events arranged in their time-sequence," and plot, which organizes the events to a "sense of causality." This definition closely mirrors Aristotle's discussion of plot in his *Poetics.*

Poem: In its broadest sense, a composition utilizing rhyme, meter, concrete detail, and expressive language to create a literary experience with emotional and aesthetic appeal. Typical poems include sonnets, odes, elegies, *haiku,* ballads, and free verse.

Poet: An author who writes poetry or verse. The term is also used to refer to an artist or writer who has an exceptional gift for expression, imagination, and energy in the making of art in any form. Well-known poets include Horace, Basho, Sir Philip Sidney, Sir Edmund Spenser, John Donne, Andrew Marvell, Alexander Pope, Jonathan Swift, George Gordon, Lord Byron, John Keats, Christina Rossetti, W. H. Auden, Stevie Smith, and Sylvia Plath.

Poetic Fallacy: See *Pathetic Fallacy*

Poetic Justice: An outcome in a literary work, not necessarily a poem, in which the good are rewarded and the evil are punished, especially in ways that particularly fit their virtues or crimes. For example, a murderer may himself be murdered, or a thief will find himself penniless.

Poetic License: Distortions of fact and literary convention made by a writer—not always a poet—for the sake of the effect gained. Poetic license is closely related to the concept of "artistic freedom." An author exercises poetic license by saying that a pile of money "reaches as high as a mountain" when the pile is actually only a foot or two high.

Poetics: This term has two closely related meanings. It denotes (1) an aesthetic theory in literary criticism about the essence of poetry or (2) rules prescribing the proper methods, content, style, or diction of poetry. The term poetics may also refer to theories about literature in general, not just poetry.

Poetry: In its broadest sense, writing that aims to present ideas and evoke an emotional experience in the reader through the use of meter, imagery, connotative and concrete words, and a carefully constructed structure based on rhythmic patterns. Poetry typically relies on words and expressions that have several layers of meaning. It also makes use of the effects of regular rhythm on the ear and may make a strong appeal to the senses through the use of imagery. Edgar Allan Poe's "Annabel Lee" and Walt Whitman's *Leaves of Grass* are famous examples of poetry.

Point of View: The narrative perspective from which a literary work is presented to the reader. There are four traditional points of view. The "third person omniscient" gives the reader a "godlike" perspective, unrestricted by time or place, from which to see actions and look into the minds of characters. This allows the author to comment openly on characters and events in the work. The "third person" point of view presents the events of the story from outside of any single character's perception, much like the omniscient point of view, but the reader must understand the action as it takes place and without any special insight into characters' minds or motivations. The "first person" or "personal" point of view relates events as they are perceived by a single character. The main character "tells" the story and may offer opinions about the action and characters which differ from those of the author. Much less common than omniscient, third person, and first person is the "second person" point of view, wherein the author tells the story as if it is happening to the reader. James Thurber employs the omniscient point of view in his short story "The Secret Life of Walter Mitty." Ernest Hemingway's "A Clean, Well-Lighted Place" is a short story told from the third person point of view. Mark Twain's novel *Huck Finn* is presented from the first person viewpoint. Jay McInerney's *Bright Lights, Big City* is an example of a novel which uses the second person point of view.

Polemic: A work in which the author takes a stand on a controversial subject, such as abortion or religion. Such works are often extremely argumentative or provocative. Classic examples of polemics include John Milton's *Aeropagitica* and Thomas Paine's *The American Crisis.*

Pornography: Writing intended to provoke feelings of lust in the reader. Such works are often condemned by critics and teachers, but those which can be shown to have literary value are viewed less harshly. Literary works that have been described as pornographic include Ovid's *The Art of Love,* Margaret of Angouleme's *Heptameron,* John Cleland's *Memoirs of a Woman of Pleasure; or, the Life of Fanny Hill,* the anonymous *My Secret Life,* D. H. Lawrence's *Lady Chatterley's Lover,* and Vladimir Nabokov's *Lolita.*

Post-Aesthetic Movement: An artistic response made by African Americans to the black aesthetic movement of the 1960s and early '70s. Writers since that time have adopted a somewhat different tone in their work, with less emphasis placed on the disparity between black and white in the United States. In the words of post-aesthetic authors such as Toni Morrison, John Edgar Wideman, and Kristin Hunter, African Americans are portrayed as looking inward for answers to their own questions, rather than always looking to the outside world. Two well-known examples of works produced as part of the post-aesthetic movement are the Pulitzer Prize-winning novels *The Color Purple* by Alice Walker and *Beloved* by Toni Morrison.

Postmodernism: Writing from the 1960s forward characterized by experimentation and continuing to apply some of the fundamentals of modernism, which included existentialism and alienation. Postmodernists have gone a step further in the rejection of tradition begun with the modernists by also rejecting traditional forms, preferring the anti-novel over the novel and the anti-hero over the hero. Postmodern writers include Alain Robbe-Grillet, Thomas Pynchon, Margaret Drabble, John Fowles, Adolfo Bioy-Casares, and Gabriel Garcia Marquez.

Pre-Raphaelites: A circle of writers and artists in mid nineteenth-century England. Valuing the pre-Renaissance artistic qualities of religious symbolism, lavish pictorialism, and natural sensuousness, the Pre-Raphaelites cultivated a sense of mystery and melancholy that influenced later writers associated with the Symbolist and Decadent movements. The major members of the group include Dante Gabriel Rossetti, Christina Rossetti, Algernon Swinburne, and Walter Pater.

Primitivism: The belief that primitive peoples were nobler and less flawed than civilized peoples because they had not been subjected to the tainting influence of society. Examples of literature espousing primitivism include Aphra Behn's *Oroonoko: Or, The History of the Royal Slave,* Jean-Jacques Rousseau's *Julie ou la Nouvelle Heloise,* Oliver Goldsmith's *The Deserted Village,* the poems of Robert Burns, Herman Melville's stories *Typee, Omoo,* and *Mardi,* many poems of William Butler Yeats and Robert Frost, and William Golding's novel *Lord of the Flies.*

Projective Verse: A form of free verse in which the poet's breathing pattern determines the lines of the poem. Poets who advocate projective verse are against all formal structures in writing, including meter and form. Besides its creators, Robert Creeley, Robert Duncan, and Charles Olson, two other well-known projective verse poets are Denise Levertov and LeRoi Jones (Amiri Baraka). Also known as Breath Verse.

Prologue: An introductory section of a literary work. It often contains information establishing the situation of the characters or presents information about the setting, time period, or action. In drama, the prologue is spoken by a chorus or by one of the principal characters. In the "General Prologue" of *The Canterbury Tales,* Geoffrey Chaucer describes the main characters and establishes the setting and purpose of the work.

Prose: A literary medium that attempts to mirror the language of everyday speech. It is distinguished from poetry by its use of unmetered, unrhymed language consisting of logically related sentences. Prose is usually grouped into paragraphs that form a cohesive whole such as an essay or a novel. Recognized masters of English prose writing include Sir Thomas Malory, William Caxton, Raphael Holinshed, Joseph Addison, Mark Twain, and Ernest Hemingway.

Prosopopoeia: See *Personification*

Protagonist: The central character of a story who serves as a focus for its themes and incidents and as the principal rationale for its development. The protagonist is sometimes referred to in discussions of modern literature as the hero or anti-hero. Well-known protagonists are Hamlet in William Shakespeare's *Hamlet* and Jay Gatsby in F. Scott Fitzgerald's *The Great Gatsby.*

Protest Fiction: Protest fiction has as its primary purpose the protesting of some social injustice, such as racism or discrimination. One example of protest fiction is a series of five novels by Chester Himes, beginning in 1945 with *If He Hollers Let Him Go* and ending in 1955 with *The Primitive.* These works depict the destructive effects of race and gender stereotyping in the context of interracial relationships. Another African American author whose works often revolve around themes of social protest is John Oliver Killens. James Baldwin's essay "Everybody's Protest Novel" generated controversy by attacking the authors of protest fiction.

Proverb: A brief, sage saying that expresses a truth about life in a striking manner. "They are not all cooks who carry long knives" is an example of a proverb.

Pseudonym: A name assumed by a writer, most often intended to prevent his or her identification as the author of a work. Two or more authors may work together under one pseudonym, or an author may use a different name for each genre he or she publishes in. Some publishing companies maintain "house pseudonyms," under which any number of authors may write installations in a series. Some authors also choose a pseudonym over their real names the way an actor may use a stage name. Examples of pseudonyms (with the author's real name in parentheses) include Voltaire (Francois-Marie Arouet), Novalis (Friedrich von Hardenberg), Currer Bell (Charlotte Bronte), Ellis Bell (Emily Bronte), George Eliot (Maryann Evans), Honorio Bustos Donmecq (Adolfo Bioy-Casares and Jorge Luis Borges), and Richard Bachman (Stephen King).

Pun: A play on words that have similar sounds but different meanings. A serious example of the pun is from John Donne's "A Hymne to God the Father": "Sweare by thyself, that at my death thy sonne Shall shine as he shines now, and hereto fore; And, having done that, Thou haste done; I fear no more."

Pure Poetry: poetry written without instructional intent or moral purpose that aims only to please a reader by its imagery or musical flow. The term pure poetry is used as the antonym of the term "didacticism." The poetry of Edgar Allan Poe, Stephane Mallarme, Paul Verlaine, Paul Valery, Juan Ramoz Jimenez, and Jorge Guillen offer examples of pure poetry.

Q

Quatrain: A four-line stanza of a poem or an entire poem consisting of four lines. The following quatrain is from Robert Herrick's "To Live Merrily, and to Trust to Good Verses": "Round, round, the root do's run; And being ravisht thus, Come, I will drink a Tun To my *Propertius."*

R

Raisonneur: A character in a drama who functions as a spokesperson for the dramatist's views. The *raisonneur* typically observes the play without becoming central to its action. *Raisonneurs* were very common in plays of the nineteenth century.

Realism: A nineteenth-century European literary movement that sought to portray familiar characters, situations, and settings in a realistic manner. This was done primarily by using an objective narrative point of view and through the buildup of accurate detail. The standard for success of any realistic work depends on how faithfully it transfers common experience into fictional forms. The realistic method may be altered or extended, as in stream of consciousness writing, to record highly subjective experience. Seminal authors in the tradition of Realism include Honore de Balzac, Gustave Flaubert, and Henry James.

Refrain: A phrase repeated at intervals throughout a poem. A refrain may appear at the end of each stanza or at less regular intervals. It may be altered slightly at each appearance. Some refrains are nonsense expressions—as with "Nevermore" in Edgar Allan Poe's "The Raven"—that seem to take on a different significance with each use.

Renaissance: The period in European history that marked the end of the Middle Ages. It began in Italy in the late fourteenth century. In broad terms, it is usually seen as spanning the fourteenth, fifteenth, and sixteenth centuries, although it did not reach Great Britain, for example, until the 1480s or so. The Renaissance saw an awakening in almost every sphere of human activity, especially science, philosophy, and the arts. The period is best defined by the emergence of a general philosophy that emphasized the importance of the intellect, the individual, and world affairs. It contrasts strongly with the medieval worldview, characterized by the dominant concerns of faith, the social collective, and spiritual salvation. Prominent writers during the Renaissance include Niccolo Machiavelli and Baldassare Castiglione in Italy, Miguel de Cervantes and Lope de Vega in Spain, Jean Froissart and Francois Rabelais in France, Sir Thomas More and Sir Philip Sidney in England, and Desiderius Erasmus in Holland.

Repartee: Conversation featuring snappy retorts and witticisms. Masters of *repartee* include Sydney Smith, Charles Lamb, and Oscar Wilde. An example is recorded in the meeting of "Beau" Nash and John Wesley: Nash said, "I never make way for a fool," to which Wesley responded, "Don't you? I always do," and stepped aside.

Resolution: The portion of a story following the climax, in which the conflict is resolved. The resolution of Jane Austen's *Northanger Abbey* is neatly summed up in the following sentence: "Henry and Catherine were married, the bells rang and every body smiled."

Restoration: See *Restoration Age*

Restoration Age: A period in English literature beginning with the crowning of Charles II in 1660 and running to about 1700. The era, which was characterized by a reaction against Puritanism, was the first great age of the comedy of manners. The finest literature of the era is typically witty and urbane, and often lewd. Prominent Restoration Age writers include William Congreve, Samuel Pepys, John Dryden, and John Milton.

Revenge Tragedy: A dramatic form popular during the Elizabethan Age, in which the protagonist, directed by the ghost of his murdered father or son, inflicts retaliation upon a powerful villain. Notable features of the revenge tragedy include violence, bizarre criminal acts, intrigue, insanity, a hesitant protagonist, and the use of soliloquy. Thomas Kyd's *Spanish Tragedy* is the first example of revenge tragedy in English, and William Shakespeare's *Hamlet* is perhaps the best. Extreme examples of revenge tragedy, such as John Webster's *The Duchess of Malfi,* are labeled "tragedies of blood." Also known as Tragedy of Blood.

Revista: The Spanish term for a vaudeville musical revue. Examples of *revistas* include Antonio Guzman Aguilera's *Mexico para los mexicanos,* Daniel Vanegas's *Maldito jazz,* and Don Catarino's *Whiskey, morfina y marihuana* and *El desterrado.*

Rhetoric: In literary criticism, this term denotes the art of ethical persuasion. In its strictest sense, rhetoric adheres to various principles developed since classical times for arranging facts and ideas in a clear, persuasive, appealing manner. The term is also used to refer to effective prose in general and theories of or methods for composing effective prose. Classical examples of rhetorics include *The Rhetoric of Aristotle,* Quintillian's *Institutio Oratoria,* and Cicero's *Ad Herennium.*

Rhetorical Question: A question intended to provoke thought, but not an expressed answer, in the reader. It is most commonly used in oratory and other persuasive genres. The following lines from Thomas Gray's "Elegy Written in a Country Churchyard" ask rhetorical questions: "Can storied urn or animated bust Back to its mansion call the fleeting breath? Can Honour's voice provoke the silent dust, Or Flattery soothe the dull cold ear of Death?"

Rhyme: When used as a noun in literary criticism, this term generally refers to a poem in which words sound identical or very similar and appear in parallel positions in two or more lines. Rhymes are classified into different types according to where they fall in a line or stanza or according to the degree of similarity they exhibit in their spellings and sounds. Some major types of rhyme are "masculine" rhyme, "feminine" rhyme, and "triple" rhyme. In a masculine rhyme, the rhyming sound falls in a single accented syllable, as with "heat" and "eat." Feminine rhyme is a rhyme of two syllables, one stressed and one unstressed, as with "merry" and "tarry." Triple rhyme matches the sound of the accented syllable and the two unaccented syllables that follow: "narrative" and "declarative." Robert Browning alternates feminine and masculine rhymes in his "Soliloquy of the Spanish Cloister": "Gr-r-r—there go, my heart's abhorrence! Water your damned flower-pots, do! If hate killed men, Brother Lawrence, God's blood, would not mine kill you! What? Your myrtle-bush wants trimming? Oh, that rose has prior claims—Needs its leaden vase filled brimming? Hell dry you up with flames!" Triple rhymes can be found in Thomas Hood's "Bridge of Sighs," George Gordon Byron's satirical verse, and Ogden Nash's comic poems.

Rhyme Royal: A stanza of seven lines composed in iambic pentameter and rhymed *ababbcc.* The name is said to be a tribute to King James I of Scotland, who made much use of the form in his poetry. Examples of rhyme royal include Geoffrey Chaucer's *The Parlement of Foules,* William Shakespeare's *The Rape of Lucrece,* William Morris's *The Early Paradise,* and John Masefield's *The Widow in the Bye Street.*

Rhyme Scheme: See *Rhyme*

Rhythm: A regular pattern of sound, time intervals, or events occurring in writing, most often and most discernably in poetry. Regular, reliable rhythm is known to be soothing to humans, while interrupted, unpredictable, or rapidly changing rhythm is disturbing. These effects are known to authors, who use them to produce a desired reaction in the reader. An example of a form of irregular rhythm is sprung rhythm poetry; quantitative verse, on the other hand, is very regular in its rhythm.

Rising Action: The part of a drama where the plot becomes increasingly complicated. Rising action leads up to the climax, or turning point, of a drama. The final "chase scene" of an action film is generally the rising action which culminates in the film's climax.

Rococo: A style of European architecture that flourished in the eighteenth century, especially in France. The most notable features of *rococo* are its extensive use of ornamentation and its themes of lightness, gaiety, and intimacy. In literary criticism, the term is often used disparagingly to refer to a decadent or over-ornamental style. Alexander Pope's "The Rape of the Lock" is an example of literary *rococo.*

Roman a clef: A French phrase meaning "novel with a key." It refers to a narrative in which real persons are portrayed under fictitious names. Jack Kerouac, for example, portrayed various real-life beat generation figures under fictitious names in his *On the Road.*

Romance: A broad term, usually denoting a narrative with exotic, exaggerated, often idealized characters, scenes, and themes. Nathaniel Hawthorne called his *The House of the Seven Gables* and *The Marble Faun* romances in order to distinguish them from clearly realistic works.

Romantic Age: See *Romanticism*

Romanticism: This term has two widely accepted meanings. In historical criticism, it refers to a European intellectual and artistic movement of the late eighteenth and early nineteenth centuries that sought greater freedom of personal expression than that allowed by the strict rules of literary form and logic of the eighteenth-century neoclassicists. The Romantics preferred emotional and imaginative expression to rational analysis. They considered the individual to be at the center of all experience and so placed him or her at the center of their art. The Romantics believed that the creative imagination reveals nobler truths—unique feelings and attitudes—than those that could be discovered by logic or by scientific examination.

Both the natural world and the state of childhood were important sources for revelations of "eternal truths." "Romanticism" is also used as a general term to refer to a type of sensibility found in all periods of literary history and usually considered to be in opposition to the principles of classicism. In this sense, Romanticism signifies any work or philosophy in which the exotic or dreamlike figure strongly, or that is devoted to individualistic expression, self-analysis, or a pursuit of a higher realm of knowledge than can be discovered by human reason. Prominent Romantics include Jean-Jacques Rousseau, William Wordsworth, John Keats, Lord Byron, and Johann Wolfgang von Goethe.

Romantics: See *Romanticism*

Russian Symbolism: A Russian poetic movement, derived from French symbolism, that flourished between 1894 and 1910. While some Russian Symbolists continued in the French tradition, stressing aestheticism and the importance of suggestion above didactic intent, others saw their craft as a form of mystical worship, and themselves as mediators between the supernatural and the mundane. Russian symbolists include Aleksandr Blok, Vyacheslav Ivanovich Ivanov, Fyodor Sologub, Andrey Bely, Nikolay Gumilyov, and Vladimir Sergeyevich Solovyov.

S

Satire: A work that uses ridicule, humor, and wit to criticize and provoke change in human nature and institutions. There are two major types of satire: "formal" or "direct" satire speaks directly to the reader or to a character in the work; "indirect" satire relies upon the ridiculous behavior of its characters to make its point. Formal satire is further divided into two manners: the "Horatian," which ridicules gently, and the "Juvenalian," which derides its subjects harshly and bitterly. Voltaire's novella *Candide* is an indirect satire. Jonathan Swift's essay "A Modest Proposal" is a Juvenalian satire.

Scansion: The analysis or "scanning" of a poem to determine its meter and often its rhyme scheme. The most common system of scansion uses accents (slanted lines drawn above syllables) to show stressed syllables, breves (curved lines drawn above syllables) to show unstressed syllables, and vertical lines to separate each foot. In the first line of John Keats's *Endymion,* "A thing of beauty is a joy forever:" the word "thing," the first syllable of "beauty," the word "joy," and the second syllable of "forever" are stressed, while the words "A" and "of," the second syllable of "beauty," the word "a," and the first and third syllables of "forever" are unstressed. In the second line: "Its loveliness increases; it will never" a pair of vertical lines separate the foot ending with "increases" and the one beginning with "it."

Scene: A subdivision of an act of a drama, consisting of continuous action taking place at a single time and in a single location. The beginnings and endings of scenes may be indicated by clearing the stage of actors and props or by the entrances and exits of important characters. The first act of William Shakespeare's *Winter's Tale* is comprised of two scenes.

Science Fiction: A type of narrative about or based upon real or imagined scientific theories and technology. Science fiction is often peopled with alien creatures and set on other planets or in different dimensions. Karel Capek's *R.U.R.* is a major work of science fiction.

Second Person: See *Point of View*

Semiotics: The study of how literary forms and conventions affect the meaning of language. Semioticians include Ferdinand de Saussure, Charles Sanders Pierce, Claude Levi-Strauss, Jacques Lacan, Michel Foucault, Jacques Derrida, Roland Barthes, and Julia Kristeva.

Sestet: Any six-line poem or stanza. Examples of the sestet include the last six lines of the Petrarchan sonnet form, the stanza form of Robert Burns's "A Poet's Welcome to his love-begotten Daughter," and the sestina form in W. H. Auden's "Paysage Moralise."

Setting: The time, place, and culture in which the action of a narrative takes place. The elements of setting may include geographic location, characters' physical and mental environments, prevailing cultural attitudes, or the historical time in which the action takes place. Examples of settings include the romanticized Scotland in Sir Walter Scott's "Waverley" novels, the French provincial setting in Gustave Flaubert's *Madame Bovary,* the fictional Wessex country of Thomas Hardy's novels, and the small towns of southern Ontario in Alice Munro's short stories.

Shakespearean Sonnet: See *Sonnet*

Signifying Monkey: A popular trickster figure in black folklore, with hundreds of tales about this character documented since the 19th century. Henry Louis Gates Jr. examines the history of the signifying monkey in *The Signifying Monkey: Towards a Theory of Afro-American Literary Criticism,* published in 1988.

Simile: A comparison, usually using "like" or "as", of two essentially dissimilar things, as in "coffee as cold as ice" or "He sounded like a broken record." The title of Ernest Hemingway's "Hills Like White Elephants" contains a simile.

Slang: A type of informal verbal communication that is generally unacceptable for formal writing. Slang words and phrases are often colorful exaggerations used to emphasize the speaker's point; they may also be shortened versions of an often-used word or phrase. Examples of American slang from the 1990s include "yuppie" (an acronym for Young Urban Professional), "awesome" (for "excellent"), wired (for "nervous" or "excited"), and "chill out" (for relax).

Slant Rhyme: See *Consonance*

Slave Narrative: Autobiographical accounts of American slave life as told by escaped slaves. These works first appeared during the abolition movement of the 1830s through the 1850s. Olaudah Equiano's *The Interesting Narrative of Olaudah Equiano, or Gustavus Vassa, The African* and Harriet Ann Jacobs's *Incidents in the Life of a Slave Girl* are examples of the slave narrative.

Social Realism: See *Socialist Realism*

Socialist Realism: The Socialist Realism school of literary theory was proposed by Maxim Gorky and established as a dogma by the first Soviet Congress of Writers. It demanded adherence to a communist worldview in works of literature. Its doctrines required an objective viewpoint comprehensible to the working classes and themes of social struggle featuring strong proletarian heroes. A successful work of socialist realism is Nikolay Ostrovsky's *Kak zakalyalas stal* (*How the Steel Was Tempered*). Also known as Social Realism.

Soliloquy: A monologue in a drama used to give the audience information and to develop the speaker's character. It is typically a projection of the speaker's innermost thoughts. Usually delivered while the speaker is alone on stage, a soliloquy is intended to present an illusion of unspoken reflection. A celebrated soliloquy is Hamlet's "To be or not to be" speech in William Shakespeare's *Hamlet.*

Sonnet: A fourteen-line poem, usually composed in iambic pentameter, employing one of several rhyme schemes. There are three major types of sonnets, upon which all other variations of the form are based: the "Petrarchan" or "Italian" sonnet, the "Shakespearean" or "English" sonnet, and the "Spenserian" sonnet. A Petrarchan sonnet consists of an octave rhymed *abbaabba* and a "sestet" rhymed either *cdecde, cdccdc,* or *cdedce.* The octave poses a question or problem, relates a narrative, or puts forth a proposition; the sestet presents a solution to the problem, comments upon the narrative, or applies the proposition put forth in the octave. The Shakespearean sonnet is divided into three quatrains and a couplet rhymed *abab cdcd efef gg.* The couplet provides an epigrammatic comment on the narrative or problem put forth in the quatrains. The Spenserian sonnet uses three quatrains and a couplet like the Shakespearean, but links their three rhyme schemes in this way: *abab bcbc cdcd ee.* The Spenserian sonnet develops its theme in two parts like the Petrarchan, its final six lines resolving a problem, analyzing a narrative, or applying a proposition put forth in its first eight lines. Examples of sonnets can be found in Petrarch's *Canzoniere,* Edmund Spenser's *Amoretti,* Elizabeth Barrett Browning's *Sonnets from the Portuguese,* Rainer Maria Rilke's *Sonnets to Orpheus,* and Adrienne Rich's poem "The Insusceptibles."

Spenserian Sonnet: See *Sonnet*

Spenserian Stanza: A nine-line stanza having eight verses in iambic pentameter, its ninth verse in iambic hexameter, and the rhyme scheme ababbcbcc. This stanza form was first used by Edmund Spenser in his allegorical poem *The Faerie Queene.*

Spondee: In poetry meter, a foot consisting of two long or stressed syllables occurring together. This form is quite rare in English verse, and is usually composed of two monosyllabic words. The first foot in the following line from Robert Burns's "Green Grow the Rashes" is an example of a spondee: "Green grow the rashes, O"

Sprung Rhythm: Versification using a specific number of accented syllables per line but disregarding the number of unaccented syllables that fall in each line, producing an irregular rhythm in the poem. Gerard Manley Hopkins, who coined the term "sprung rhythm," is the most notable practitioner of this technique.

Stanza: A subdivision of a poem consisting of lines grouped together, often in recurring patterns of rhyme, line length, and meter. Stanzas may also serve as units of thought in a poem much like paragraphs in prose. Examples of stanza forms include the quatrain, *terza rima, ottava rima,* Spenserian, and the so-called *In Memoriam* stanza from Alfred, Lord Tennyson's poem by that title. The following is an example of the latter form: "Love is and was my lord and king, And in his presence I attend To hear the tidings of my friend, Which every hour his couriers bring."

Stereotype: A stereotype was originally the name for a duplication made during the printing process; this led to its modern definition as a person or thing that is (or is assumed to be) the same as all others of its type. Common stereotypical characters include the absent-minded professor, the nagging wife, the troublemaking teenager, and the kind-hearted grandmother.

Stream of Consciousness: A narrative technique for rendering the inward experience of a character. This technique is designed to give the impression of an ever-changing series of thoughts, emotions, images, and memories in the spontaneous and seemingly illogical order that they occur in life. The textbook example of stream of consciousness is the last section of James Joyce's *Ulysses.*

Structuralism: A twentieth-century movement in literary criticism that examines how literary texts arrive at their meanings, rather than the meanings themselves. There are two major types of structuralist analysis: one examines the way patterns of linguistic structures unify a specific text and emphasize certain elements of that text, and the other interprets the way literary forms and conventions affect the meaning of language itself. Prominent structuralists include Michel Foucault, Roman Jakobson, and Roland Barthes.

Structure: The form taken by a piece of literature. The structure may be made obvious for ease of understanding, as in nonfiction works, or may obscured for artistic purposes, as in some poetry or seemingly "unstructured" prose. Examples of common literary structures include the plot of a narrative, the acts and scenes of a drama, and such poetic forms as the Shakespearean sonnet and the Pindaric ode.

Sturm und Drang: A German term meaning "storm and stress." It refers to a German literary movement of the 1770s and 1780s that reacted against the order and rationalism of the enlightenment, focusing instead on the intense experience of extraordinary individuals. Highly romantic, works of this movement, such as Johann Wolfgang von Goethe's *Gotz von Berlichingen,* are typified by realism, rebelliousness, and intense emotionalism.

Style: A writer's distinctive manner of arranging words to suit his or her ideas and purpose in writing. The unique imprint of the author's personality upon his or her writing, style is the product of an author's way of arranging ideas and his or her use of diction, different sentence structures, rhythm, figures of speech, rhetorical principles, and other elements of composition. Styles may be classified according to period (Metaphysical, Augustan, Georgian), individual authors (Chaucerian, Miltonic, Jamesian), level (grand, middle, low, plain), or language (scientific, expository, poetic, journalistic).

Subject: The person, event, or theme at the center of a work of literature. A work may have one or more subjects of each type, with shorter works tending to have fewer and longer works tending to have more. The subjects of James Baldwin's novel *Go Tell It on the Mountain* include the themes of father-son relationships, religious conversion, black life, and sexuality. The subjects of Anne Frank's *Diary of a Young Girl* include Anne and her family members as well as World War II, the Holocaust, and the themes of war, isolation, injustice, and racism.

Subjectivity: Writing that expresses the author's personal feelings about his subject, and which may or may not include factual information about the subject. Subjectivity is demonstrated in James Joyce's *Portrait of the Artist as a Young Man,* Samuel Butler's *The Way of All Flesh,* and Thomas Wolfe's *Look Homeward, Angel.*

Subplot: A secondary story in a narrative. A subplot may serve as a motivating or complicating force for the main plot of the work, or it may provide emphasis for, or relief from, the main plot. The conflict between the Capulets and the Montagues in William Shakespeare's *Romeo and Juliet* is an example of a subplot.

Surrealism: A term introduced to criticism by Guillaume Apollinaire and later adopted by Andre Breton. It refers to a French literary and artistic movement founded in the 1920s. The Surrealists sought to express unconscious thoughts and feelings in their works. The best-known technique used for achieving this aim was automatic writing—transcriptions of spontaneous outpourings from the unconscious. The Surrealists proposed to unify the contrary levels of conscious and unconscious, dream and reality, objectivity and subjectivity into a new level of "super-realism." Surrealism can be found in the poetry of Paul Eluard, Pierre Reverdy, and Louis Aragon, among others.

Suspense: A literary device in which the author maintains the audience's attention through the buildup of events, the outcome of which will soon be revealed. Suspense in William Shakespeare's *Hamlet* is sustained throughout by the question of whether or not the Prince will achieve what he has been instructed to do and of what he intends to do.

Syllogism: A method of presenting a logical argument. In its most basic form, the syllogism consists of a major premise, a minor premise, and a conclusion. An example of a syllogism is: Major premise:

When it snows, the streets get wet. Minor premise: It is snowing. Conclusion: The streets are wet.

Symbol: Something that suggests or stands for something else without losing its original identity. In literature, symbols combine their literal meaning with the suggestion of an abstract concept. Literary symbols are of two types: those that carry complex associations of meaning no matter what their contexts, and those that derive their suggestive meaning from their functions in specific literary works. Examples of symbols are sunshine suggesting happiness, rain suggesting sorrow, and storm clouds suggesting despair.

Symbolism: This term has two widely accepted meanings. In historical criticism, it denotes an early modernist literary movement initiated in France during the nineteenth century that reacted against the prevailing standards of realism. Writers in this movement aimed to evoke, indirectly and symbolically, an order of being beyond the material world of the five senses. Poetic expression of personal emotion figured strongly in the movement, typically by means of a private set of symbols uniquely identifiable with the individual poet. The principal aim of the Symbolists was to express in words the highly complex feelings that grew out of everyday contact with the world. In a broader sense, the term "symbolism" refers to the use of one object to represent another. Early members of the Symbolist movement included the French authors Charles Baudelaire and Arthur Rimbaud; William Butler Yeats, James Joyce, and T. S. Eliot were influenced as the movement moved to Ireland, England, and the United States. Examples of the concept of symbolism include a flag that stands for a nation or movement, or an empty cupboard used to suggest hopelessness, poverty, and despair.

Symbolist: See *Symbolism*

Symbolist Movement: See *Symbolism*

Sympathetic Fallacy: See *Affective Fallacy*

T

Tale: A story told by a narrator with a simple plot and little character development. Tales are usually relatively short and often carry a simple message. Examples of tales can be found in the work of Rudyard Kipling, Somerset Maugham, Saki, Anton Chekhov, Guy de Maupassant, and Armistead Maupin.

Tall Tale: A humorous tale told in a straightforward, credible tone but relating absolutely impossible events or feats of the characters. Such tales were commonly told of frontier adventures during the settlement of the west in the United States. Tall tales have been spun around such legendary heroes as Mike Fink, Paul Bunyan, Davy Crockett, Johnny Appleseed, and Captain Stormalong as well as the real-life William F. Cody and Annie Oakley. Literary use of tall tales can be found in Washington Irving's *History of New York,* Mark Twain's *Life on the Mississippi,* and in the German R. F. Raspe's *Baron Munchausen's Narratives of His Marvellous Travels and Campaigns in Russia.*

Tanka: A form of Japanese poetry similar to *haiku.* A *tanka* is five lines long, with the lines containing five, seven, five, seven, and seven syllables respectively. Skilled *tanka* authors include Ishikawa Takuboku, Masaoka Shiki, Amy Lowell, and Adelaide Crapsey.

Teatro Grottesco: See *Theater of the Grotesque*

Terza Rima: A three-line stanza form in poetry in which the rhymes are made on the last word of each line in the following manner: the first and third lines of the first stanza, then the second line of the first stanza and the first and third lines of the second stanza, and so on with the middle line of any stanza rhyming with the first and third lines of the following stanza. An example of *terza rima* is Percy Bysshe Shelley's "The Triumph of Love": "As in that trance of wondrous thought I lay This was the tenour of my waking dream. Methought I sate beside a public way Thick strewn with summer dust, and a great stream Of people there was hurrying to and fro Numerous as gnats upon the evening gleam, . . ."

Tetrameter: See *Meter*

Textual Criticism: A branch of literary criticism that seeks to establish the authoritative text of a literary work. Textual critics typically compare all known manuscripts or printings of a single work in order to assess the meanings of differences and revisions. This procedure allows them to arrive at a definitive version that (supposedly) corresponds to the author's original intention. Textual criticism was applied during the Renaissance to salvage the classical texts of Greece and Rome, and modern works have been studied, for instance, to undo deliberate correction or censorship, as in the case of novels by Stephen Crane and Theodore Dreiser.

Theater of Cruelty: Term used to denote a group of theatrical techniques designed to eliminate the psychological and emotional distance between actors and audience. This concept, introduced in the 1930s in France, was intended to inspire a more intense theatrical experience than conventional theater allowed. The "cruelty" of this dramatic theory signified not sadism but heightened actor/audience involvement in the dramatic event. The theater of cruelty was theorized by Antonin Artaud in his *Le Theatre et son double* (*The Theatre and Its Double*), and also appears in the work of Jerzy Grotowski, Jean Genet, Jean Vilar, and Arthur Adamov, among others.

Theater of the Absurd: A post-World War II dramatic trend characterized by radical theatrical innovations. In works influenced by the Theater of the absurd, nontraditional, sometimes grotesque characterizations, plots, and stage sets reveal a meaningless universe in which human values are irrelevant. Existentialist themes of estrangement, absurdity, and futility link many of the works of this movement. The principal writers of the Theater of the Absurd are Samuel Beckett, Eugene Ionesco, Jean Genet, and Harold Pinter.

Theater of the Grotesque: An Italian theatrical movement characterized by plays written around the ironic and macabre aspects of daily life in the World War I era. Theater of the Grotesque was named after the play *The Mask and the Face* by Luigi Chiarelli, which was described as "a grotesque in three acts." The movement influenced the work of Italian dramatist Luigi Pirandello, author of *Right You Are, If You Think You Are.* Also known as *Teatro Grottesco.*

Theme: The main point of a work of literature. The term is used interchangeably with thesis. The theme of William Shakespeare's *Othello*—jealousy—is a common one.

Thesis: A thesis is both an essay and the point argued in the essay. Thesis novels and thesis plays share the quality of containing a thesis which is supported through the action of the story. A master's thesis and a doctoral dissertation are two theses required of graduate students.

Thesis Play: See *Thesis*

Three Unities: See *Unities*

Tone: The author's attitude toward his or her audience may be deduced from the tone of the work. A formal tone may create distance or convey politeness, while an informal tone may encourage a friendly, intimate, or intrusive feeling in the reader. The author's attitude toward his or her subject matter may also be deduced from the tone of the words he or she uses in discussing it. The tone of John F. Kennedy's speech which included the appeal to "ask not what your country can do for you" was intended to instill feelings of camaraderie and national pride in listeners.

Tragedy: A drama in prose or poetry about a noble, courageous hero of excellent character who, because of some tragic character flaw or *hamartia*, brings ruin upon him- or herself. Tragedy treats its subjects in a dignified and serious manner, using poetic language to help evoke pity and fear and bring about catharsis, a purging of these emotions. The tragic form was practiced extensively by the ancient Greeks. In the Middle Ages, when classical works were virtually unknown, tragedy came to denote any works about the fall of persons from exalted to low conditions due to any reason: fate, vice, weakness, etc. According to the classical definition of tragedy, such works present the "pathetic"—that which evokes pity—rather than the tragic. The classical form of tragedy was revived in the sixteenth century; it flourished especially on the Elizabethan stage. In modern times, dramatists have attempted to adapt the form to the needs of modern society by drawing their heroes from the ranks of ordinary men and women and defining the nobility of these heroes in terms of spirit rather than exalted social standing. The greatest classical example of tragedy is Sophocles' *Oedipus Rex.* The "pathetic" derivation is exemplified in "The Monk's Tale" in Geoffrey Chaucer's *Canterbury Tales.* Notable works produced during the sixteenth century revival include William Shakespeare's *Hamlet, Othello,* and *King Lear.* Modern dramatists working in the tragic tradition include Henrik Ibsen, Arthur Miller, and Eugene O'Neill.

Tragedy of Blood: See *Revenge Tragedy*

Tragic Flaw: In a tragedy, the quality within the hero or heroine which leads to his or her downfall. Examples of the tragic flaw include Othello's jealousy and Hamlet's indecisiveness, although most great tragedies defy such simple interpretation.

Transcendentalism: An American philosophical and religious movement, based in New England from around 1835 until the Civil War. Transcendentalism was a form of American romanticism that had its roots abroad in the works of Thomas Carlyle, Samuel Coleridge, and Johann Wolfgang von Goethe. The Transcendentalists stressed the importance of intuition and subjective experience in communication with God. They rejected religious dogma and texts in favor of mysticism and scientific naturalism. They pursued truths that lie beyond the "colorless" realms perceived by reason and the senses and were active social reformers in public education, women's rights, and the abolition of slavery. Prominent members of the group include Ralph Waldo Emerson and Henry David Thoreau.

Trickster: A character or figure common in Native American and African literature who uses his ingenuity to defeat enemies and escape difficult situations. Tricksters are most often animals, such as the spider, hare, or coyote, although they may take the form of humans as well. Examples of trickster tales include Thomas King's *A Coyote Columbus Story,* Ashley F. Bryan's *The Dancing Granny* and Ishmael Reed's *The Last Days of Louisiana Red.*

Trimeter: See *Meter*

Triple Rhyme: See *Rhyme*

Trochee: See *Foot*

U

Understatement: See *Irony*

Unities: Strict rules of dramatic structure, formulated by Italian and French critics of the Renaissance and based loosely on the principles of drama discussed by Aristotle in his *Poetics.* Foremost among these rules were the three unities of action, time, and place that compelled a dramatist to: (1) construct a single plot with a beginning, middle, and end that details the causal relationships of action and character; (2) restrict the action to the events of a single day; and (3) limit the scene to a single place or city. The unities were observed faithfully by continental European writers until the Romantic Age, but they were never regularly observed in English drama. Modern dramatists are typically more concerned with a unity of impression or emotional effect than with any of the classical unities. The unities are observed in Pierre Corneille's tragedy *Polyeuctes* and Jean-Baptiste Racine's *Phedre.* Also known as Three Unities.

Urban Realism: A branch of realist writing that attempts to accurately reflect the often harsh facts of modern urban existence. Some works by Stephen Crane, Theodore Dreiser, Charles Dickens, Fyodor Dostoyevsky, Emile Zola, Abraham Cahan, and Henry Fuller feature urban realism. Modern examples include Claude Brown's *Manchild in the Promised Land* and Ron Milner's *What the Wine Sellers Buy.*

Utopia: A fictional perfect place, such as "paradise" or "heaven." Early literary utopias were included in Plato's *Republic* and Sir Thomas More's *Utopia,* while more modern utopias can be found in Samuel Butler's *Erewhon,* Theodor Herzka's *A Visit to Freeland,* and H. G. Wells' *A Modern Utopia.*

Utopian: See *Utopia*

Utopianism: See *Utopia*

V

Verisimilitude: Literally, the appearance of truth. In literary criticism, the term refers to aspects of a work of literature that seem true to the reader. Verisimilitude is achieved in the work of Honore de Balzac, Gustave Flaubert, and Henry James, among other late nineteenth-century realist writers.

Vers de societe: See *Occasional Verse*

Vers libre: See *Free Verse*

Verse: A line of metered language, a line of a poem, or any work written in verse. The following line of verse is from the epic poem *Don Juan* by Lord Byron: "My way is to begin with the beginning."

Versification: The writing of verse. Versification may also refer to the meter, rhyme, and other mechanical components of a poem. Composition of a "Roses are red, violets are blue" poem to suit an occasion is a common form of versification practiced by students.

Victorian: Refers broadly to the reign of Queen Victoria of England (1837–1901) and to anything with qualities typical of that era. For example, the qualities of smug narrowmindedness, bourgeois materialism, faith in social progress, and priggish morality are often considered Victorian. This stereotype is contradicted by such dramatic intellectual developments as the theories of Charles Darwin, Karl Marx, and Sigmund Freud (which stirred strong debates in England) and the critical attitudes of serious Victorian writers like Charles Dickens and George Eliot. In literature, the Victorian Period was the great age of the English novel, and the latter part of the era saw the rise of movements such as decadence and symbolism. Works of Victorian literature include the poetry of Robert Browning and Alfred, Lord Tennyson, the criticism of Matthew Arnold and John Ruskin, and the novels of Emily Bronte, William Makepeace Thackeray, and Thomas Hardy. Also known as Victorian Age and Victorian Period.

Victorian Age: See *Victorian*

Victorian Period: See *Victorian*

W

Weltanschauung: A German term referring to a person's worldview or philosophy. Examples of *weltanschauung* include Thomas Hardy's view of the human being as the victim of fate, destiny, or impersonal forces and circumstances, and the disillusioned and laconic cynicism expressed by such poets of the 1930s as W. H. Auden, Sir Stephen Spender, and Sir William Empson.

Weltschmerz: A German term meaning "world pain." It describes a sense of anguish about the nature of existence, usually associated with a melancholy, pessimistic attitude. *Weltschmerz* was expressed in England by George Gordon, Lord Byron in his *Manfred* and *Childe Harold's Pilgrimage,* in France by Viscount de Chateaubriand, Alfred de Vigny, and Alfred de Musset, in Russia by Aleksandr Pushkin and Mikhail Lermontov, in Poland by Juliusz Slowacki, and in America by Nathaniel Hawthorne.

Z

Zarzuela: A type of Spanish operetta. Writers of *zarzuelas* include Lope de Vega and Pedro Calderon.

Zeitgeist: A German term meaning "spirit of the time." It refers to the moral and intellectual trends of a given era. Examples of *zeitgeist* include the preoccupation with the more morbid aspects of dying and death in some Jacobean literature, especially in the works of dramatists Cyril Tourneur and John Webster, and the decadence of the French Symbolists.

Cumulative Author/Title Index

C

D

E

F

G

H

I

T

U

V

W

X

Y

Z

Cumulative Nationality/Ethnicity Index

Argentinian

Asian American

Austrian

Bohemian (Czechoslovakian)

Canadian

Chilean

Chinese

Cuban

Cuban American

Czechoslovakian

Dutch

English

French

German

Greek

Hispanic

Indochinese

Irish

Italian

Subject/Theme Index

*Boldface denotes discussion in *Themes* section.